Prospect Theory

Prospect Theory: For Risk and Ambiguity provides the first comprehensive and accessible textbook treatment of the way decisions are made both when we have the statistical probabilities associated with uncertain future events (risk) and when we lack them (ambiguity). The book presents models, primarily prospect theory, that are both tractable and psychologically realistic. A method of presentation is chosen that makes the empirical meaning of each theoretical model completely transparent.

Prospect theory has many applications in a wide variety of disciplines. The material in the book has been carefully organized so as to allow readers to select pathways relevant to their own interests. With numerous exercises and worked examples, the book is ideally suited to the needs of students taking courses in decision theory in economics, mathematics, finance, psychology, management science, health, computer science, Bayesian statistics, and engineering.

A companion website with exercises, additional assignments, and solutions is available at www.cambridge.org/wakker.

PETER P. WAKKER is Professor at the Econometric Institute, Erasmus University. He has worked in departments of mathematics, statistics, psychology, business, medicine, and economics in the Netherlands and in the USA, and has published in leading journals in all of these fields. He serves on the editorial boards of several major journals, including *Journal of Behavioral Decision Making*, *Journal of Mathematical Psychology*, *Journal of Risk and Uncertainty*, *Management Science*, *Medical Decision Making*, and *Theory and Decision*.

Prospect Theory
For Risk and Ambiguity

Peter P. Wakker

CAMBRIDGE
UNIVERSITY PRESS

CAMBRIDGE
UNIVERSITY PRESS

University Printing House, Cambridge CB2 8BS, United Kingdom

Cambridge University Press is part of the University of Cambridge.

It furthers the University's mission by disseminating knowledge in the pursuit of education, learning and research at the highest international levels of excellence.

www.cambridge.org
Information on this title: www.cambridge.org/9780521748681

First published 2010
3rd printing 2011

A catalogue record for this publication is available from the British Library

Library of Congress Cataloguing in Publication data
Wakker, Peter P.
Prospect theory : for risk and ambiguity / Peter P. Wakker.
        p. cm.
    ISBN 978-0-521-76501-5 (Hardback) – ISBN 978-0-521-74868-1 (Pbk.)
    1. Decision making.   2. Risk.   3. Uncertainty.   4. Probabilities.
    I. Title. HD30.23.W34 2010 338.5–dc22

                                                    2010008581

ISBN 978-0-521-76501-5 Hardback
ISBN 978-0-521-74868-1 Paperback

Contents

Preface

This book is the culmination of 14 years of teaching. In the 15th year, when for the first time I did not feel like rereading or rewriting, the time had come to publish it. The book received helpful comments from Han Bleichrodt, Arie de Wild, Itzhak Gilboa, Glenn Harrison, Amit Kothiyal, Gijs van de Kuilen, Georg Weizsäcker, and many students during the past 14 years. Thorough comments from Rich Gonzalez and Vitalie Spinu are especially acknowledged. I am most indebted to Stefan Trautmann for the numerous improvements he suggested. This book has also benefited from many inspiring discussions with Craig Fox, with whom I share the privilege of having collaborated with Amos Tversky on uncertainty during the last years of his life.

Introduction

This book has been written and organized especially for readers who do not want to read all of its contents, but want to skip parts and select the material of their own interest. This has been achieved by an organization of exercises explained later, and by an Appendix K that describes the interdependencies between sections. Because of this organization, this book can be used by readers with different backgrounds.

We will examine theories of individual decision making under uncertainty. Many of our decisions are made without complete information about all relevant aspects. This happens for instance if we want to gamble on a horse race and have to decide which horse to bet on, or if we are in a casino and have to decide how to play roulette, if at all. Then we are uncertain about which horse will win or how the roulette wheel will be spun. More serious examples include investments, insurance, the uncertain results of medical treatments, and the next move of your opponent in a conflict. In financial crises, catastrophes can result from the irrational attitudes of individuals and institutions towards risks and uncertainties.

Two central theories in this book are expected utility theory and prospect theory. For all theories considered, we will present ways to empirically test their validity and their properties. In many applications we require more than just qualitative information. We may want to know exactly that spending 1 percent more on a new medicine will generate a 3 percent increase in quality of life for the patient group affected, rather than just knowing that spending more money improves the quality of life. Similarly, we may want to know that a person is willing to pay a maximum of $350 extra tax so as to avoid a 1:100 risk of losing savings to the value of $30,000 in case a bank goes bankrupt. Hence, for all the theories presented in this book, methods will be provided for obtaining precise quantitative measurements concerning those theories and their parameters. Thus precise quantitative predictions can be made. The possibility of obtaining tractable quantitative measurements was a selection criterion for the theories presented in this book.

Typical for the analyses in this book is the interaction between, on the one hand, theoretical and algebraic tools, and, on the other hand:

- prescriptive considerations as relevant for consultancies, policy decisions, and your own decision making;
- descriptive considerations as relevant in psychology and other empirical disciplines.

Prospect theory

Until the end of the 1970s, irrational behavior was believed to be chaotic and unsuited for modeling. The normative expected utility model was taken to be the best approximation of descriptive behavior (Arrow 1951a p. 406; Tversky & Kahneman 1981 opening sentence). Kahneman & Tversky's (1979) prospect theory provided a major breakaway. It was the first descriptive theory that explicitly incorporated irrational behavior in an empirically realistic manner (Kahneman 2003 p. 1456), while at the same time being systematic and tractable. It was the first rational theory of irrational behavior, so to say.

Tversky & Kahneman (1992) introduced an improved version of prospect theory. First, they used Quiggin's (1982) rank dependence to correct a theoretical problem in probability weighting. Second, and more importantly, they extended the theory from risk (known probabilities) to uncertainty and ambiguity (unknown probabilities), using Schmeidler's (1989) rank dependence. In this manner, for the first time a theory has resulted that combines empirical realism with theoretical soundness and tractability. Prospect theory comprises the happy marriage between the empirical insights of Kahneman & Tversky (1979) and the theoretical insights of Gilboa (1987) and Schmeidler (1989).

At this moment of writing, 30 years after its invention, prospect theory is still the only theory that can deliver the full spectrum of what is required for decision under uncertainty, with a natural integration of risk and ambiguity. Therefore, a textbook on the theory is useful. The main purpose of this book is to make this theory accessible to a wide audience by presenting it in a manner as tractable as possible.

Behavioral foundations

Behavioral foundations will play a central role in this book. For a particular decision model, a behavioral foundation gives a list of conditions, stated directly in terms of observable preferences, that hold if and only if the decision model holds. Preference foundations translate the meaning of quantitative decision models and their subjective parameters ("theoretical constructs"), such as subjective probabilities or utilities, into observables. Descriptively, they show how to verify or falsify decision models. Normatively, they provide the terms to justify or criticize models. When de Finetti (1931a), von Neumann & Morgenstern (1944), and Savage (1954) provided behavioral foundations for expected utility, this gave a big boost to the popularity of this theory in many fields. Those fields include economics and game theory (Mas-Colell, Whinston, & Green 1995), management science under the name decision analysis

(Keeney & Raiffa 1976), medicine (Weinstein *et al.* 1980) where utilities are often referred to as QALYs, and statistics (reviving the Bayesian approach; DeGroot 1970). Behavioral foundations ensure the intrinsic soundness of a decision model, preventing historical accidents such as happened for what is known as the separate-probability-transformation model (details in Chapter 5).

Homeomorphic versus paramorphic modeling

A model is *paramorphic* if it describes the empirical phenomena of interest correctly, but the processes underlying the empirical phenomena are not matched by processes in the model (Harré 1970). For example, as emphasized by Milton Friedman (1953; see Bardsley *et al.* 2010 Box 2.4), market models can make correct predictions even if their assumptions about consumers do not match actual consumers' behavior. A model is *homeomorphic* if not only its empirical phenomena match reality, but also its underlying processes do so. We will seek homeomorphic models of decision making. Not only do the decisions predicted by the model match the decisions observed, but also we want the theoretical parameters in the model to have plausible psychological interpretations.

Friedman's arguments in favor of paramorphic models are legitimate if all that is desired is to explain and predict a prespecified and limited domain of phenomena. It is, however, usually desirable if concepts are broadly applicable, also for future and as yet unforeseen developments in research. Homeomorphic models are best suited for this purpose. In recent years, economics has been opening up to introspective and neuro-imaging data. It is to be expected that the concepts of prospect theory, in view of their sound psychological basis, will be well suited for such future developments and for connections with other domains of research. Behavioral foundations with plausible preference conditions support the homeomorphism of a model.

Intended audience

No particular mathematical background knowledge is required, besides a basic knowledge of probability theory and calculus. A willingness to work with formal models and to follow abstract trains of thought is needed for this book though. The measurement methods and behavioral foundations presented in this book will be as simple and transparent as possible, so as to be accessible to as many readers as possible.

Mathematically sophisticated readers may be interested in this book, and will perhaps be surprised by it, from a didactic perspective. For example, Gilboa's (1987) and Schmeidler's (1989) rank-dependent utility theory, and Tversky & Kahneman's (1992) new prospect theory have often been considered to be complex, with presentations based on a comonotonicity concept. These theories can, however, be presented and derived in an elementary manner if we use ranks instead of comonotonicity, as will be done in this book.

Decisions under uncertainty are relevant in many fields, including finance, economics, psychology, management science, medicine, computer science, Bayesian statistics, and engineering. Readers from any of these fields can rest assured that no advanced concepts will appear from any of the other fields because the author does not have a bachelor's degree in any of the fields mentioned.

Attractive feature of decision theory

An attractive feature of decision theory is that the reader can always imagine that he or she is the decision maker. For each preference condition presented in the text, you can ask yourself whether you would want to satisfy this condition in your own decisions. It is easiest to read this book with this question in mind. Hence, the decision maker and the readers will usually be referred to as "you."

Structure

The material in this book has been structured so as to be accessible to readers with different backgrounds, levels, and interests. Many results that will be relevant to some readers but not to all have been stated in exercises, whose elaborations are in Appendix J. This structure gives different readers the chance to skip and select different parts. Italicized superscripts a, b, c indicate which exercises are suited for which readers. The superscript a refers to exercises that are easiest, and the superscript c refers to exercises that are most difficult and that will be of interest only to the most theoretically oriented readers. Many readers, especially empirically oriented readers who are not used to working with formal models, will want to skip almost all exercises. Typically, psychology students interested in formal models will be a-students who will study the empirical parts of this book; mathematical students are c-students who are required to study the theoretical parts; and economics students are somewhere in between, so that they are usually b students.

The best way to completely master the material in this book – if there are no time restrictions – is to stop reading after every exercise and then first do that exercise. Readers who are satisfied with a less thorough and time-consuming study can use the exercises flexibly. *Sometimes an exercise contains results that are needed to understand the rest of the text. This is indicated by an exclamation! as superscript. Then every reader, even those not doing the exercise, should read its results.*

Exercises are interspersed throughout the text, and are located where they are most relevant. Some sections conclude with assignments. These are further exercises that serve to grade students and/or to practice. Their results play no role in the theory development in the main text, and no elaborations of assignments are given in this book. On the author's homepage, further exercises and assignments are provided. This serves teachers who wish to have more exercises without solutions available to the students. Teachers can obtain solutions to assignments from the publisher. Proofs of theorems are collected in appendices at the end of chapters.

For the use of this book, with comprehensive theoretical discussions and comprehensive discussions of empirical implications, Appendix K is instrumental. It illustrates how sections depend on preceding sections. By using this appendix, you need not read the book from start to finish. In a backward approach, you pick out any topic of interest, and then use Appendix K to see which preceding material you need to read for it. In a forward approach, you skip whatever you do not like. If needed later after all, then Appendix K will show you so. If you are interested in only part of the book, this organization allows you to use the book efficiently. In particular, teachers can easily select the material targeted at the interests of specific students.

If you want to know the definition of prospect theory for unknown probabilities in §12.1, then you can select the texts depicted in Figure K.1 in Appendix K. The sections listed there comprise about 46 pages to be read. If you are not interested in the tradeoff technique of §4.1 and §4.5, then you can skip all of Chapter 4 except for §4.2 and §4.9, and then skip §§6.5, 9.4, 10.5, and 12.3. If you are interested only in decision under risk, then you can learn about the definition of prospect theory in §9.2, using the same method and the same figure, skipping virtually all sections on decision under uncertainty, and reading approximately 34 pages. If you want to learn about a pragmatic index of ambiguity aversion under prospect theory, then you can similarly use Figure K.2. If you want to understand as quickly as possible how the popular value at risk (VaR) for measuring the reliability of banks is a special case of prospect theory and rank dependence (Exercise 6.4.4), then you can find the shortest path: §§6.4, 6.3, 6.1, 3.2, 2.5, 2.4, 2.2, 2.1, 1.3, 1.2, 1.1.

For 10 meetings of three hours each, a typical timetable may be: *meeting 1*: §1.1–§1.8; *meeting 2*: §2.1–§2.9; *meeting 3*: §3.1–§3.6, §4.1; *meeting 4*: §4.2–§4.7, §4.9.1, §4.11, §4.12; *meeting 5*: §5.1–§5.7, §6.1, §6.3–§6.5; *meeting 6*: §7.1–§7.4, §7.6–§7.11; *meeting 7*: §8.1–§8.5, §9.1–§9.5; *meeting 8*: §10.1–§10.6, §10.7.1, §10.8; *meeting 9*: §11.1, §11.4–§11.8; and *meeting 10*: §12.1–§12.3, §12.7. I have used this book in teaching advanced master's students in economics who had digested large parts of Mas-Colell, Whinston, & Green (1995). I would then cover the material allocated to the first four meetings above in about two meetings, after which I would follow the above timetable. The total workload of this selection for students is about 120 hours of full-time work.

A nice way to teach only part of this book is by restricting all models only to binary (two-outcome) prospects. This domain is rich enough to measure and define all components of risk attitude, utility, probability- or event-weighting, and loss aversion. Rank dependence and prospect theory are considerably simplified on this domain. This is how I taught this course to business students. They are particularly interested in prescriptive applications of decision theory.

Preview

The book consists of three parts. Part I deals with the classical expected utility theory, and Parts II and III consider deviations. In Part I, §1.1 and §1.2 present the basics of decision under uncertainty. The rest of Chapter 1 presents the famous bookmaking condition of de Finetti, developed in the 1930s to justify the use of subjective probabilities for one-shot events. This condition is equivalent to the no-arbitrage condition in finance, which implies that market prices of financial derivatives have to be based on what are called as-if risk neutral evaluations. That is, these conditions imply expected utility when probabilities are unknown but utility is known (linear). Chapter 2 deals with expected utility when probabilities are known ("decision under risk") but utilities are unknown. There are so many applications of this long-existing theory that they are presented separately in Chapter 3. Chapter 4 turns to the more complex topic of expected utility when both probabilities and utilities are unknown, using tradeoffs between outcomes as a tool to measure utility differences. It ends with some empirical violations of expected utility, preparing for the parts to follow.

Part II deals with deviations from expected utility for decision under risk, where probabilities are known. We present rank-dependent utility, which generalizes expected utility by adding a new dimension of risk attitude: probabilistic sensitivity – i.e., the nonlinear ways in which people may process probabilities. This dimension is descriptively as relevant for risk attitudes as the nonlinear ways in which people process outcomes (utility), and had been sorely missing in the models used before. In 1982 John Quiggin introduced a correct theoretical manner of modeling such nonlinear processing, the rank-dependent formula. It was only then that a serious descriptive analysis of risk attitudes could begin.

Chapter 5 presents mathematical and psychological arguments to show that the rank-dependent model naturally captures probabilistic sensitivity. Chapter 6 defines the theory formally, and shows how it can be used to tractably capture prevalent phenomena regarding risk attitude. We use ranks, introduced by Abdellaoui & Wakker (2005), as a tool to measure probability weight differences. We can then define ranked probabilities, which are the analogs in the probability dimension of the tradeoffs in the outcome dimension used in Chapter 4. Ranked probabilities facilitate the analyses of the rank-dependent model and are more tractable than the comonotonicity concepts that have been used in the literature. Chapter 7 presents empirical findings and special cases of rank dependence.

In Chapters 8 and 9 we turn to prospect theory. In 1992, Tversky and Kahneman incorporated Quiggin's idea of rank dependence to solve a theoretical problem of their original prospect theory of 1979. It led to the present version of prospect theory, also called cumulative prospect theory. To prepare for prospect theory, Chapter 8 introduces another generalization of expected utility beyond rank dependence: reference dependence. Outcomes are reinterpreted as changes with respect to a reference point (often the status quo). With reference dependence introduced, all ingredients are now available to define and analyze prospect theory for risk (Chapter 9).

Part III concerns decision under uncertainty, where probabilities need not be known. Ambiguity attitudes, which deviate from expected utility in fundamental ways and may not even admit the existence of (subjective) probabilities, are analyzed. Chapter 10 starts by extending Quiggin's definition of rank dependence from risk to the more subtle context of uncertainty, for which Schmeidler (1989, first version

1982) conceived it independently. Chapter 11 presents the main novelties of uncertainty, namely source dependence, which includes ambiguity aversion. We show how rank dependence can be used to analyze uncertainty, and to provide tractable measures of ambiguity aversion and sensitivity to ambiguity. These measures encompass the currently popular α-maxmin model.

Chapter 12 presents the most important model of this book, namely prospect theory for uncertainty. This model entails a common generalization of all the models presented up till then. Relative to Chapters 10 and 11, it allows ambiguity attitudes for losses to be different than for gains. This generalization is desirable because empirical studies have shown that such differences are pronounced. Prospect theory is the first theory for decision under uncertainty that is both theoretically sound and empirically realistic. It means that only since 1992 do we have a satisfactory theory that can deliver the full spectrum of what is needed for decision under risk and uncertainty. Chapter 13 concludes the main text.

Appendices A–K complete the book. I will only discuss a few here. §A.1 in Appendix A contains a general methodological discussion of models being imperfect with inconsistencies in data, and of the nonparametric measurements that are central to this book. Appendix B presents some general issues of the revealed-preference paradigm. Appendix F shows that the influential Fehr–Schmidt model for welfare evaluations is a special case of rank dependent utility, and Appendix J contains the elaborations of the exercises in the book.

Our five-step presentation of decision models

We usually present decision theories in five steps that serve to make the empirical meaning of the theories tangible for the readers. The first step is, simply, to define the decision model. We specify the subjective parameters of the model and give a formula describing how these parameters imply preferences. In expected utility with given probabilities (risk), the subjective parameter is utility. In prospect theory for risk, the subjective parameters are utility, probability weighting, and loss aversion. In the second step, it is demonstrated how decisions can be derived from the model using simple numerical exercises.

Although we do not endorse Lord Kelvin's maxim "science is measurement" as a universal principle, measurement is central to this book. Thus, the third step in our analysis presents what is called the elicitation method. It demonstrates how the subjective parameters of a decision theory can be measured from observed preferences in as simple and direct a way as possible. The third step reverses the second step. Now, preferences are not derived from the subjective parameters but the subjective parameters are derived from preferences.

To illustrate the third step for readers who know the expected utility model, assume expected utility with utility U for given probabilities. Assume a scaling U($0) = 0 and U($100) = 1 (such scaling is always possible as we will see later). Then, for any $α between $0 and $100, an indifference between receiving $α for sure or receiving

$100 with probability p and receiving $0 with probability $1-p$ immediately implies $U(\$\alpha) = p$, as we will see later. In this manner we can relate utility to observed choice in a direct and simple manner. Using such observations, we always obtain the right utility function whatever this function is. For instance, we need not assume that utility belongs to a particular family such as the family of power functions ("CRRA"; $U(\alpha) = \alpha^\theta$ for some power θ). In descriptive applications we can use such measurements of utility to make predictions about future preferences. In prescriptive applications, simple indifferences as just described can be used to determine preferences in real and complex situations.

A necessary condition for a model to hold is that different ways to measure its subjective parameters should not run into contradictions. This leads to the fourth step in our analysis of decision models: we define preference conditions to preclude such contradictions. These preference conditions then turn out to be not only necessary, but also sufficient, for the decision model considered to hold. That is, they provide behavioral foundations of the models, presented in the fifth step. This means that the behavioral foundations in this book will all be closely related to direct empirical measurements of the subjective parameters of models. The preference conditions are thus easily observable and testable.[1] They all involve a limited number of tractable choices. Comment 2.6.4 will describe the five steps for the expected utility model in Chapter 2. I first developed these five steps when I taught prospect theory to a selected group of high school students (in 30 hours), where this approach worked well. I have maintained it ever since.

After having thus introduced decision models, we discuss their empirical properties, and give suggestions for applications to various fields. I hope that this book will enhance further applications, to be developed by readers specialized in such fields.

---

[1] Gilboa (2009 end of Ch. 8) pointed out that, conversely, simple preference axioms (= conditions) can be used to obtain simple elicitation methods: "Yet, the language of the axioms, which is concrete and observable, and the quest for simple axioms often facilitate the elicitation/calibration problem significantly."

Part I

Expected utility

1 The general model of decision under uncertainty and no-arbitrage (expected utility with known utilities and unknown probabilities)

1.1 Basic definitions

This section introduces the general notation and terminology for decision under uncertainty.

Examples of decision making under uncertainty

Example 1.1.1 [Vendor]. Imagine that you are a street vendor. You have to decide which merchandise to take along with you tomorrow. Merchandise can be ice cream, hot dogs, newspapers, magazines, and so on. The net profits resulting from the merchandise depend on the weather tomorrow, and can be negative because goods not sold tomorrow are lost. Although weather conditions constitute a continuum of possibilities, we assume for simplicity that we need to distinguish only between three eventualities: either there will be no rain (s_1), or there will be some rain (s_2), or it will rain all day (s_3). You do not know for sure whether s_1, s_2, or s_3 will occur. Table 1.1.1 presents, in dollar units, the profits that can result from your decision depending on the weather tomorrow.

Table 1.1.1. *Net profits obtained from merchandise, depending on the weather*

	no rain (s_1)	*some rain* (s_2)	*all rain* (s_3)
x ("ice cream")	400	100	−400
y ("hot dogs")	−400	100	400
0 ("neither")	0	0	0
x + y ("both")	0	200	0

We assume, for simplicity, that the supply of ice cream does not affect the profits obtained from hot dogs, and vice versa, in the lowest row "both." □

Example 1.1.2 [Finance]. Imagine that you want to speculate on the copper price next month. You can buy a financial portfolio, denoted x and costing 30K (K = $1000), that yields 80K in the event E_1 of the copper price (per pound) exceeding \$2.53 next month, and nothing otherwise. Such portfolios can be replicated by proper combinations of options and other financial instruments (Hull 2005 end of §10.4). All payments take place next month, so that we can ignore discounting. The net profits are shown in Table 1.1.2. You can also buy a portfolio y at the same price of 30K, yielding 80K in the event E_3 of the copper price falling below \$2.47 and nothing otherwise. E_2 denotes the residual event of a copper price being between \$2.47 and \$2.53. You can also buy both portfolios, or buy neither.

Table 1.1.2. *Net profits depending on the copper price*

	price $\geq$ 2.53 (E_1)	2.53 > *price* $\geq$ 2.47 (E_2)	2.47 > *price* (E_3)
x	50K	−30K	−30K
y	−30K	−30K	50K
0 ("neither")	0	0	0
x + y ("both")	20K	−60K	20K

□

Example 1.1.3 [Elections]. You have to decide which investment to choose in a foreign country. There will be elections in this foreign country, and exactly one of the participating candidates will win. s_j designates the eventuality of the jth candidate winning. The net profits of an investment depend on which candidate will win. □

Example 1.1.4 [Horse race]. You are at a horse race, and have to decide which gamble to play. Exactly one horse will win. s_j designates the eventuality of horse j winning. Not gambling is one of the "gambles" available to you, yielding outcome 0 whichever horse will win. □

Example 1.1.5 [Medical example]. You are a doctor and have to decide on the treatment of a patient. The patient has exactly one of a number of potential diseases, and it is uncertain which one it is. The outcome of the treatment – i.e., the health state resulting for the patient – depends on the treatment chosen and on the disease of the patient. □

Example 1.1.6 [Agriculture]. You are a farmer and have to decide which crops to grow. The resulting profits will depend on the crops chosen and on the weather conditions during the coming year, which are uncertain. □

Many other didactical examples are in Lavalle (1978 §1.5) and throughout Clemen (1991).

The basic concepts of uncertainty. We will model uncertainty through a *state space* S. One state $s \in S$ is true and the other states are not true. It is uncertain which state is the true one. The decision maker does not have any influence on which state is true (for details, see §1.7). In Example 1.1.1 (vendor), the uncertainty concerns the weather, and the state space S is $\{s_1, s_2, s_3\}$. In Example 1.1.2 (finance) the uncertainty concerns the copper price next month. We take the nonnegative real axis as state space, so that $S = [0, \infty)$ and S is infinite. In Example 1.1.4, the uncertainty concerns which horse will win and S is the set of participating horses. Every horse corresponds to the state that this horse will win the race. States are also called *states of nature*. Although the terms states and states of nature may not be the most natural ones, they are generally used in decision theory and we will use them too.

Subsets of the state space are called *events*. In Example 1.1.2, the subset $[0, 2.47)$ of S concerns the event of the copper price falling below $2.47; i.e., it is event E_3. If, in Example 1.1.4, horses s_1, s_3, s_6 are French horses, and the others are not, then the event "A French horse will win" is described by the subset $\{s_1, s_3, s_6\}$ of S. An event is *true* if it contains the true state. Event $\{s_1, s_3, s_6\}$ is true if the true state is s_1, s_3, or s_6, that is, if a French horse wins. For event E, E^c denotes the *complementary event* $S - E$ of all states $s \in S$ not contained in E; it is the negation of E.

The *outcome set* is $\mathbb{R}$, with real numbers designating amounts of money. Apart from a few exceptions specified later, this outcome set is assumed throughout this book. Thus, we mostly deal with financial risks. Outcomes are usually denoted by Greek letters α, β, γ, δ, or by Roman letters with subscripts such as x_1. In this book, subscripts virtually always refer to events, and superscripts are used for all other indexing purposes. Superscripts thus usually do not refer to power-taking. We use the term increasing in the same, weak, sense as nondecreasing: A function $U: \mathbb{R} \to \mathbb{R}$ is *increasing*, or *nondecreasing*, if $\alpha > \beta$ implies $U(\alpha) \geq U(\beta)$. It is *strictly increasing* if $\alpha > \beta$ implies $U(\alpha) > U(\beta)$. *Decreasing, nonincreasing*, and *strictly decreasing* are defined similarly.

Prospects designate state-contingent outcomes. They are courses of action, the outcome of which depends on which state of nature is the true one. Formally, *prospects* map states to the reals, describing the resulting outcome for every state if that state is the true state. They are random variables, but possibly without probabilities specified. We assume throughout that prospects take only finitely many values. In the vendor Example 1.1.1, prospects describe the net profits (which can be negative in the case of a loss, such as for unsold ice cream that will be lost) conditional on each weather condition. Prospect x assigns $x(s_1) = 400$ to s_1, $x(s_2) = 100$ to s_2, and $x(s_3) = -400$ to s_3. In the finance Example 1.1.2, prospects describe the net profits conditional on the copper price next month.

Notation for prospects. Prospects x are often denoted as $(E_1:x_1, \ldots, E_n:x_n)$, yielding x_1 under event E_1 (i.e. for each state $s \in E_1$), $\ldots$, and x_n under event E_n. In the finance Example 1.1.2, x can be written as $(E_1:50K, E_2:-30K, E_3:-30K)$. In the vendor Example 1.1.1, x can be written as $(s_1:400, s_2:100, s_3:-400)$. For $x + y$ in Example 1.1.1 we can write $E_1 = \{s_1, s_3\}$, $E_2 = s_2$, and then we have $x + y = (E_1:0, E_2:200)$. We often suppress brackets, colons, and commas, if no confusion will arise. We may thus write $E_1x_1 \cdots E_nx_n$ or E_1x_1, E_2x_2, E_3x_3.

If there are only two outcomes and events, such as in $(E:\alpha, E^c:\beta)$, then we often suppress the second event, and write $\alpha_E\beta$. For example, for $x + y$ in the vendor Example 1.1.1 we may write $0_{E_1}200$ rather than $(E_1:0, E_2:200)$. In the finance

Example 1.1.2, for x + y we may write $-60K_{E_2}20K$. In the agriculture Example 1.1.6, $-2000_{E_1}2000 = (E_1:-2000, E_1{}^c:2000)$ may refer to the growing of a crop that will die, bringing a net loss of 2000, if the minimum temperature is below 32 °F (E_1), and that will survive otherwise, bringing a net profit of 2000 ($E_2 = E_1{}^c$). Because it is uncertain which state is true, it is uncertain what the outcome of a chosen prospect will be, and the decisions indeed have to be made under uncertainty.

The prospects $A\alpha,B\alpha,C\beta$ and $(A \cup B)\alpha,C\beta$ assign the same outcome to each state of nature, so that they refer to the same map from S to $\mathbb{R}$. Given that prospects are defined to be such maps, $A\alpha,B\alpha,C\beta$ and $(A \cup B)\alpha,C\beta$ are identical *by definition*. For different formal definitions where different ways of notation ("framing") can matter, see Birnbaum (2008a) and Luce (1990, 2000).

Consider, in the vendor Example 1.1.1, the prospect (s_1:100, s_2:100, s_3:100). It yields outcome 100 for sure, irrespective of the weather conditions. Such prospects, yielding the same outcome for each state, are called *constant* prospects. For a constant prospect there is no uncertainty about the outcome, and we often denote the prospect simply as that outcome. For example, we write 100 instead of (s_1:100, s_2:100, s_3:100). In the finance Example 1.1.2, the prospect denoted 0 is constant, yielding 0 profit whatever the copper price.

For a given prospect denoted $E_1x_1\cdots E_nx_n$, the events E_j are called the *outcome events*. These are the payoff-relevant events. It is implicitly assumed for each prospect that the outcome events are exhaustive and mutually exclusive. That is, they partition the state space S. Exactly one of them is true (contains the true state) and the others are not true. If the partition ($E_1,. . .,E_n$) is understood, we sometimes suppress the events and write, briefly, ($x_1,. . .,x_n$). Such partitions will be central to this book, and the state space S will usually be in the background. We sometimes use the longer term *event-contingent prospect* instead of prospect, to distinguish the general prospects defined here from their subclass called (probability-contingent) prospects that will be defined in later chapters.

The domain of preference. We assume throughout that all maps from S to $\mathbb{R}$ taking finitely many values are prospects, and are available in the domain of preference.

Preferences and evaluations. The *preference relation* of the *decision maker*, usually assumed to be you, over the prospects is denoted by $\succcurlyeq$, a curved version of the greater-equal sign $\geq$. $x \succcurlyeq y$ means that you prefer x to y and are willing to choose x from {x,y}. We thus interpret preference as nothing other than binary choice. Multiple choice can be derived from binary choice by assuming that from the multiple available prospects a prospect is chosen that is best according to binary preference (Appendix B). We use the following notation for preferences.

strict preference: $x \succ y$ if $x \succcurlyeq y$ and not $y \succcurlyeq x$;
equivalence/indifference: $x \sim y$ if $x \succcurlyeq y$ and $y \succcurlyeq x$;
reversed preference: $x \preccurlyeq y$ if $y \succcurlyeq x$;
strict reversed preference: $x \prec y$ if $y \succ x$.

Hence, if you prefer x to y ($x \succcurlyeq y$) and are willing to choose x from {x,y}, then either you consider x to be equally preferable to y ($x \sim y$) and you would also be willing to choose y, or you consider x to be strictly preferable $(x \succ y)$ and you are not willing to choose y.

A *certainty equivalent (CE)* of a prospect x is an outcome α such that $\alpha \sim x$ where, as often, the symbol α also designates a constant prospect. If you just received x, its CE will be the minimum price at which you are willing to sell x. A function V *represents* $\succcurlyeq$ if V evaluates prospects in agreement with preference. That is, V assigns to each prospect a real number that indicates the value of the prospect in the sense of the following logical equivalence: $[x \succcurlyeq y \Leftrightarrow V(x) \geq V(y)]$. That is, $x \succcurlyeq y$ if and only if $V(x) \geq V(y)$. We then also say that $\succcurlyeq$ *maximizes* V. Examples of representing functions are the expected value function examined later in this chapter, and the expected utility function examined in Chapter 2. The following two exercises serve to clarify the basic model of decision under uncertainty.

Exercise 1.1.1.[a] Assume that S = {Bill, Jane, Kate, no-one}, describing who will first enter your office before lunch, if anyone does. In deviation from the default assumption in this book, do not assume that the outcome space is $\mathbb{R}$, but assume that it contains only two elements, α (apple) and n (nothing), designating what you will receive for food before lunch.

(a) Describe formally the events A: a man will enter first; B: no woman will enter first; C: someone will enter; D: a woman will enter first; E: someone whose name contains an "a" will enter first.
(b) Use the formal prospect-notation of this section to denote the following prospects:
    x. You receive an apple if and only if no man enters;
    y. You receive an apple if and only if Kate enters.
    z. You receive nothing if and only if a woman or no-one enters.
(c) How many prospects do there exist?
(d) How many constant prospects do there exist? Write them using the notation of this section. □

Exercise 1.1.2.[b] Assume that probabilities are given in Example 1.1.4, with $P(s_1) = \frac{1}{2}$, $P(s_2) = \frac{1}{4}$, and $P(s_3) = \frac{1}{4}$. Two events A and B are *(stochastically) independent* if $P(A \cap B) = P(A) \times P(B)$. Are s_1 and s_2 independent? □

1.2 Basic properties of preferences

Whereas no theoretical result in this book can be understood completely without having studied this section, this section may still be skipped by readers with a minimal theoretical interest. If a representing function exists, then $\succcurlyeq$ is a *weak order*; i.e., $\succcurlyeq$ is *transitive* (if $x \succcurlyeq y$ and $y \succcurlyeq z$ then $x \succcurlyeq z$) and *complete* (for all x, y, $x \succcurlyeq y$ or $y \succcurlyeq x$, where possibly both preferences hold). Weak ordering entails a ranking of prospects with ties permitted. A violation of transitivity suggests a violation of a conservation-of-preference principle. With $x \prec z$, $z \preccurlyeq y$, and $y \preccurlyeq x$, we could create positive preference value through each replacement $[x \rightarrow z]$, $[z \rightarrow y]$, $[y \rightarrow x]$, yet ending up in a final position that has not been improved relative to the initial position. Bear in mind in the following exercise that an exclamation mark indicates that it is useful for all readers to read the results of the exercise.

Exercise 1.2.1.[!a] Show that $\succcurlyeq$ is a weak order if a representing function V exists. □

Exercise 1.2.2.[!a] Show that, if V represents $\succcurlyeq$, then:

(a) $[x \succ y \Leftrightarrow V(x) > V(y)]$.
(b) $[x \sim y \Leftrightarrow V(x) = V(y)]$. □

Here are further properties of preference relations $\succcurlyeq$ that will usually, although not always, be satisfied in what follows.

Nontriviality: $x \succ y$ for some prospects x,y.
Reflexivity: For all x, $x \sim x$.
Monotonicity: if $x(s) \geq y(s)$ for all states s, then $x \succcurlyeq y$, and, if $x(s) > y(s)$ for all states s, then $x \succ y$.

It is plausible that your preference relation – say, over bets on a horse race – satisfies all these conditions. The conditions in the following exercise are also natural.

Exercise 1.2.3.[!c] Assume that $\succcurlyeq$ is a weak order. Show that:

(a) $\succcurlyeq$ and $\sim$ are reflexive.
(b) $\succ$ is transitive.
(c) For no x and y we have $x \succ y$ and $y \succ x$ ($\succ$ is *asymmetric*).
(d) For no x and y we have $x \succcurlyeq y$ and $y \succ x$.
(e) If $x \succcurlyeq y$ and $y \succ z$ then $x \succ z$.
(f) If $x \succ y$ and $y \succcurlyeq z$ then $x \succ z$.
(g) If $x \succcurlyeq y$, $y \succcurlyeq f$, $f \succcurlyeq g$, then $x \succcurlyeq g$.
(h) $\sim$ is an *equivalence relation*; i.e., $\sim$ is reflexive, transitive, and *symmetric* ($x \sim y$ then $y \sim x$).
(i) If $y \sim x$ then y is *substitutable* for x in every preference; i.e., $[x \succcurlyeq f \Leftrightarrow y \succcurlyeq f]$, $[x \preccurlyeq f \Leftrightarrow y \preccurlyeq f]$, $[x \succ f \Leftrightarrow y \succ f]$, $[x \prec f \Leftrightarrow y \prec f]$, and $[x \sim f \Leftrightarrow y \sim f]$.
(j) $x \succ y \Leftrightarrow$ (not $y \succcurlyeq x$). □

The result of the following exercise is often useful. It implies that we may assume in many situations that all prospects considered refer to the same partition $E_1, \ldots, E_n$.

Exercise 1.2.4[b] [Partition flexibility].

(a) Consider two prospects $x = A_1 a_1 \cdots A_k a_k$ and $y = B_1 b_1 \cdots B_\ell b_\ell$. Show that there exists one partition $E_1, \ldots, E_n$ such that $x = E_1 x_1 \cdots E_n x_n$ and $y = E_1 y_1 \cdots E_n y_n$ for properly chosen $x_1, \ldots, x_n, y_1, \ldots, y_n$, with $n = k\ell$. Note that, if A_i is logically incompatible with B_j, then an event E_k referring to their intersection will be the empty set, referring to the vacuous, impossible, event. It is permitted that some events E_k are empty.

(b) Explain in spoken words, without writing, that for every finite set of prospects there exists one partition $E_1, \ldots, E_n$ such that all prospects considered are of the form $E_1 x_1 \cdots E_n x_n$. $\square$

Exercise 1.2.5.[b]

(a) Assume monotonicity and weak ordering. Show that $[\alpha \succcurlyeq \beta \Leftrightarrow \alpha \geq \beta]$.
(b) Assume monotonicity, weak ordering, and assume that for each prospect x a certainty equivalent $CE(x)$ exists. Show that CE represents $\succcurlyeq$. $\square$

To avoid trivialities, we assume *nondegeneracy*: $\gamma_E \gamma \succ \gamma_E \beta \succ \beta_E \beta$ for some event E and outcomes γ, β. For example, assume $100_{\text{no rain}} 100 \succ 100_{\text{no rain}} 0 \succ 0_{\text{no rain}} 0$ in the vendor Example 1.1.1. The last, second, preference shows that the event of no rain can affect preference and should be reckoned with, and the first preference shows the same for the complementary event. Nondegeneracy ensures that there is real uncertainty and that you do not know the true state of nature for sure, because you apparently reckon with the possibility of E containing the true state but also with the possibility of E^c containing the true state. We summarize the assumptions made.

Structural Assumption 1.2.1 [Decision under uncertainty]. S is a, finite or infinite, state space, and $\mathbb{R}$ is the outcome set. Prospects map states to outcomes, taking only finitely many values. The domain of preference is the set of all prospects, i.e., of all such maps. $\succcurlyeq$ is a preference relation on the set of prospects. Nondegeneracy holds. $\square$

Assignment 1.2.6.[b] Show that, under weak ordering: If $x \succcurlyeq y$, $y \succcurlyeq f$, $f \succcurlyeq g$, $g \succ h$, then $x \succ h$. $\square$

1.3   Expected value

One plausible way to make decisions under uncertainty is by choosing probabilities, sometimes called subjective, for the uncertain events, and then maximizing expected value with respect to those probabilities. *Probabilities* P satisfy, besides the obvious $P(S) = 1$ and $P(\emptyset) = 0$, *additivity*: $P(A \cup B) = P(A) + P(B)$ for all disjoint (empty intersection; incompatible) events A and B.

Definition 1.3.1. Expected value (EV) holds if there exist (subjective) probabilities P such that preferences maximize the *expected value (EV)* of prospects defined by

$$E_1 x_1 \cdots E_n x_n \mapsto P(E_1) x_1 + \cdots + P(E_n) x_n. \square$$

Under EV, the (subjective) probabilities are the subjective parameters that characterize the decision maker. The following exercise shows how to derive decisions from the EV model. Its elaboration is immediately given in the main text.

Exercise 1.3.1.[a] Consider the vendor Example 1.1.1. Assume EV with P(no rain) = 0.40, P(some rain) = 0.30, and P(all rain) = 0.30. Calculate the EV of the four prospects in Table 1.1.1, and determine which prospect is chosen. $\square$

In Exercise 1.3.1:

$EV(x) = 0.40 \times 400 + 0.30 \times 100 + 0.30 \times (-400) = 70$;

$EV(y) = 0.40 \times (-400) + 0.30 \times 100 + 0.30 \times 400 = -10$;

$EV(0) = 0$;

$EV(x+y) = 0.30 \times 200 = 60$.

Hence x has the highest EV and is chosen.

Exercise 1.3.2.[a] Consider the vendor Example 1.1.1. Assume EV with $P(s_1) = \frac{1}{2}$, $P(s_2) = \frac{1}{4}$, and $P(s_3) = \frac{1}{4}$. What is the preference between $x = 300_{s_1}0$ and $y = 200_{s_3}100$? $\square$

In the literature, the term subjective expected value has often been used to stress that the probabilities need not have an objective basis but may be subjective. Market probabilities in finance are an example of subjective probabilities. Throughout this book we will treat objective probabilities (risk) not as a different case, but as a subcase, of subjective probabilities (uncertainty). It is, therefore, convenient to use the same terms for risk and for uncertainty whenever possible, which is why we usually suppress "subjective."

EV can be used to derive preferences as we just saw. We now discuss the *elicitation method*, which consists of reversing the direction of derivation. For example, if from $EV(x) > EV(y)$ we can derive $x \succ y$, then from an observation $y \succcurlyeq x$ we can derive $EV(y) \geq EV(x)$. In general, from observed preferences we can derive properties of decision models. Such reversed moves, where empirical observations are used to derive implications for a theoretical model, are indispensable for the operationalization of every empirical field. Thus, the derivation of utility from preference has a long tradition in economics (Stigler 1950). De Finetti (1931a) and Ramsey (1931) provided remarkable early examples in decision theory. They showed how the subtle concept of subjective probability can be derived from observed preferences. Another remarkable example is Samuelson (1938) for another context (Appendix B)[1]. The reversed move described in this paper played an important role in the ordinal revolution in economics (Lewin 1996). William James (1884, p. 190) wrote, on a similar reversed move for the study of emotions: "that the more rational statement is that we feel sorry because we cry, angry because we strike, afraid because we tremble, and not that we cry, strike, or tremble, because we are sorry, angry, or fearful."

Exercise 1.3.3.[a] Assume, in Example 1.1.1, that we observe $400_{s_1}0 \succ 400_{s_3}0$. Show that, under EV, $P(s_1) > P(s_3)$. $\square$

In a descriptive context, if we know that EV holds but we do not know the subjective probabilities of a decision maker, then we can derive those from observed preferences. This is illustrated by the following exercise, which is particularly useful. If you have no clue how to resolve it, then you probably have not yet fully internalized the conceptual meaning of decision models. Then a rereading of some of the preceding text is useful – rather than reading the solution to the exercise, which is given in the text immediately following the exercise.

---

[1] Because of the difference in context, we cannot use Samuelson's term "revealed preference" for the elicitation method.

Exercise 1.3.4.[a] Assume that you want to find out, in Example 1.1.1, what the probabilities $P(s_1)$, $P(s_2)$, and $P(s_3)$, denoted p_1, p_2, p_3, are of the street vendor. However, the only thing that you can observe about the street vendor is his preferences between prospects. That is, for each pair of prospects x, y, you know which of the two the street vendor prefers and, for instance, for each prospect you know the certainty equivalent. This holds for all prospects, that is, for all mappings from the states to the reals and not just for those considered in Example 1.1.1. You know that the street vendor maximizes expected value. How can you find out the street vendor's probabilities p_1, p_2, p_3? In other words, how can you elicit these probabilities from the street vendor's preferences? (What is the easiest way you can think of?) □

If expected value holds, then the probabilities can easily be elicited from preferences as follows. For an event E, find the number $0 \leq p \leq 1$ such that

$$p \sim 1_E 0. \tag{1.3.1}$$

Then

$$p = P(E) \times 1 + (1 - P(E)) \times 0 = P(E). \tag{1.3.2}$$

Eq. (1.3.1) shows that p can be interpreted as an index of your willingness to bet on event E. The equations give a direct link between subjective probabilities and preferences. Probabilities inferred from choice this way can be used to predict future decisions.

Exercise 1.3.5.[a] Assume EV in the vendor Example 1.1.1 with $100_{s_1}0 \sim 50$ and $100_{s_2}0 \sim 25$. What are $P(s_1)$, $P(s_2)$, $P(s_3)$, and what is $CE(100_{s_3}0)$? What is the preference between $100_{s_2}0$ and $100_{s_3}0$? □

In a general normative context on decision under uncertainty, if we have made up our mind on a number of preferences (such as the first two in Exercise 1.3.5), then these can be used to determine probabilities from which subsequently other preferences can be derived. Such types of inferences are typical of decision theory as presented in this book.

1.4 Data fitting for expected value

This section gives numerical examples and exercises to illustrate how EV can be used to describe and predict preferences. It can be skipped by readers not interested in data fitting (as can be inferred from the figures in Appendix K). Interested readers have to read §A.2 in Appendix A. Throughout this section we assume the vendor Example 1.1.1. The perspective will be descriptive. We assume that the street vendor is someone else and you are observing and predicting the street vendor's choices without a commitment to whether or not these choices are rational.

Assumption 1.4.1. Three states of nature (events) s_1, s_2, and s_3 are given. These events are suppressed in the notation of prospects, as in (x_1,x_2,x_3). EV holds with, possibly unknown, probabilities $P(s_1) = p_1$, $P(s_2) = p_2$, and $P(s_3) = p_3$. □

The solution to the following exercise is immediately given in the ensuing example.

Exercise 1.4.1[a] [Deterministic nonparametric measurement]. We observe the following indifferences: $(4,0,0) \sim 2$, $(0,3,0) \sim 1$, and $(3,0,3) \sim 2$.

(a) Show that EV can accommodate these observations, and determine the probabilities of the three events.
(b) Predict the CEs of the prospects $(6,6,12)$ and $(16,0,0)$, and predict the preference between these prospects, assuming EV. □

Example 1.4.2 [Elaboration of Exercise 1.4.1]. Assume the indifferences of Exercise 1.4.1. We consider the first two and apply EV calculation. $4p_1 = 2$ implies $p_1 = \frac{1}{2}$ and $3p_2 = 1$ implies $p_2 = \frac{1}{3}$. Then p_3 must be $1 - \frac{1}{2} - \frac{1}{3} = \frac{1}{6}$. The third indifference is consistent with these results with, indeed, $(\frac{1}{2}) \times 3 + (\frac{1}{6}) \times 3 = 2$. We then have $EV(6, 6, 12) = \frac{6}{2} + \frac{6}{3} + \frac{12}{6} = 7$ and, hence, $CE(6, 6, 12) = 7$. $EV(16, 0, 0) = \frac{16}{2} = 8$ and, hence, $CE(16,0,0) = 8$. The resulting preference is $(6,6,12) \prec (16,0,0)$. □

The probabilities in Example 1.4.2 could be obtained particularly easily because the data came in a form similar to Eq. (1.3.1). In general, the derivation of subjective parameters such as probabilities from data may be less easy and usually it requires resolving linear equations if indifferences are given or it requires solving linear inequalities if preferences are given. For example, indifferences $(4,12,6) \sim 7$ and $(4,6,6) \sim (8,3,0)$ can be seen to imply $p_1 = \frac{1}{2}$, $p_2 = \frac{1}{3}$, and $p_3 = \frac{1}{6}$, as in Example 1.4.2, but the derivation is less easy.[2] In this book we will strive for measurements, and preference conditions derived from those, that are directly targeted towards the parameters of interest, as in Example 1.4.2. That is, the data have been devised such that the subjective parameters, such as subjective probabilities, can be derived from the data as easily as possible. Thus, the subjective parameters are linked to empirical choices in a clear and transparent manner.

In the following example EV does not hold exactly, but is used to approximate observed preferences as closely as possible.

Example 1.4.3 [Measurement with errors and fitting]. We observe the following indifferences: $(4,0,0) \sim 2$, $(0,3,0) \sim 1$, and $(3,0,3) \sim 1.5$. EV fails as readily follows from Example 1.4.2: The first two indifferences imply $p_1 = \frac{1}{2}$ and $p_2 = \frac{1}{3}$, so that $p_3 = \frac{1}{6}$, but then $CE(3,0,3)$ should be 2 and not 1.5 as it is here. We may nevertheless use EV to approximate the data. Then either we assume that the observed data contain errors, or we are satisfied with an approximate model. We may find the best-fitting probabilities as follows, using a special case of a general distance measure presented in §A.2.

We consider each possible probability vector (p_1,p_2,p_3) of the form $(i/100, j/100, (100-i-j)/100)$, with i and j integers. For each we consider by how far the CEs of the

---

[2] The equations implied are $4p_1 + 12p_2 + 6(1-p_1-p_2) = 7$ and $4p_1 + 6p_2 + 6(1-p_1-p_2) = 8p_1 + 3p_2$. These have the solution mentioned.

three prospects predicted by the probability vectors are off from the observed CEs. For instance, for the first prospect the predicted CE is $4p_1$, so that the probability vector is off by $|4p_1 - 2|$, with squared distance $(4p_1 - 2)^2$. We similarly take the squared distances for the other two prospects, take the average of these three squared distances, and then take its square root. It leads to the following distance formula:

$$\sqrt{\frac{(4p_1 - 2)^2 + (3p_2 - 1)^2 + (1.5 - 3p_1 - 3p_3)^2}{3}}.$$

The distance has money as its unit and can be interpreted as the amount by which the model is off in dollars. By calculations for various combinations of probabilities using a computer[3] it can be verified that the probabilities $p_1 = 0.50$, $p_2 = 0.42$, and $p_3 = 0.08$ best fit the data. They give certainty equivalents $CE(4,0,0) = 2$, $CE(0,3,0) = 1.26$, and $CE(3,0,3) = 1.74$, with distance

$$\sqrt{\frac{(2 - 2)^2 + (1.26 - 1)^2 + (1.74 - 1.5)^2}{3}} = 0.20.$$

To predict the preference between $(6,6,12)$ and $(16,0,0)$, we find that the CEs for these prospects are 6.48 and 8, respectively, so that the predicted preference is $(6,6,12) \prec (16,0,0)$. $\square$

Exercise 1.4.2[a] [Deterministic nonparametric measurement]. Assume that we observe the following indifferences: $(8,0,0) \sim 2$, $(8,8,0) \sim 4$, and $(0,4,4) \sim 3$.

(a) Show that EV can accommodate these observations, and determine the probabilities of the three events.
(b) Determine the CEs for the prospects $(6,6,12)$ and $(32,0,0)$, and the preference between these prospects. $\square$

Exercise 1.4.3[b] [Measurement with errors and fitting]. We observe the following indifferences: $(8,0,0) \sim 2$, $(8,8,0) \sim 4$, and $(0,4,4) \sim 2$.

(a) Show that EV cannot accommodate these observations.
(b) Take a distance measure similar to Example 1.4.3, which now amounts to

$$\sqrt{\frac{(8p_1 - 2)^2 + (8p_1 + 8p_2 - 4)^2 + (4p_2 + 4p_3 - 2)^2}{3}}.$$

For each of the following three probability vectors (p_1,p_2,p_3) determine their distance from the data,[4] and determine which of them fits the data best: $(0.25, 0.25, 0.50)$, $(0.28, 0.22, 0.50)$, and $(0.24, 0.24, 0.52)$.

---

[3] In this case, an exact analytical method using first-order optimality conditions can easily be obtained. In many later exercises, no analytical solution can be obtained and numerical analyses using the computer have to be used.
[4] We equate a probability tuple with its corresponding EV model in what follows.

(c) Which probability vector (i/100, j/100, (100−i−j)/100) fits the data best? What is its distance? Predict the CE's of (8,0,8) and (24,0,0), and the preference between these prospects. □

Assignment 1.4.4ª [Measurement with errors and fitting]. We observe the following indifferences: (10,0,0) ∼ 1, (0,10,0) ∼ 2, and (10,10,0) ∼ 3.

(a) Show that EV can accommodate these observations, and determine the probabilities of the three events.
(b) Predict the CE's of (7,7,0) and (0,0,3), and the preference between these prospects. □

Assignment 1.4.5ª [Measurement with errors and fitting]. We observe the following indifferences: (10,0,0) ∼ 1, (0,10,0) ∼ 2, and (10,10,0) ∼ 4.

(a) Show that EV cannot accommodate these observations.
(b) Take a distance measure similar to Example 1.4.3, which now amounts to

$$\sqrt{\frac{(10p_1 - 1)^2 + (10p_2 - 2)^2 + (10p_1 + 10p_2 - 4)^2}{3}}.$$

Determine the distance for each of the following three probability vectors, and determine which of them fits the data best: (0.10, 0.20, 0.70), (0.12, 0.22, 0.66), and (0.08, 0.18, 0.74).
(c) Which probability vector (i/100, j/100, (100−i−j)/100) best fits the data? What is its distance? Predict the CE's of (4,0,4) and (24,0,0), and the preference between these prospects. □

1.5   The bookmaking argument of de Finetti, or the no-arbitrage condition from finance

Whereas the preceding section primarily concerned descriptive applications of expected value, using it to explain and predict observed data, the analysis in the next two sections primarily concerns prescriptive and normative applications. In Example 1.1.1, imagine that you are the street vendor and want to make decisions as wisely as possible. Alternatively, the street vendor could be someone else, to whom you want to give the best advice.

In Eqs. (1.3.1) and (1.3.2) we demonstrated how subjective probabilities are directly related to preferences. A behavioral foundation of expected value can be obtained by imposing consistency on such measurements. This is the topic of Assignment 1.6.9. We will use a somewhat different method in this section and the next one to obtain a behavioral foundation.

In finance, arbitrage means that you can combine a number of portfolios in such a way that you always (in every state of the world) make a profit. In such a case, you can make money from the market without contributing anything, which you will of course do as much as possible. In practice, arbitrage opportunities disappear within fractions of seconds because they are immediately exploited by the largest and quickest market participants, i.e. investment banks that use automated computer programs. A fundamental result in finance is that no-arbitrage implies an as-if risk neutral (= EV) evaluation of financial assets. This result will be proved in the next section. The same result was discovered before by de Finetti (1931a) for individual choice, where arbitrage is called a Dutch book.

De Finetti's bookmaking result has been fundamental in decision theory because it provided the basis for subjective probability and Bayesian statistics. De Finetti (1931a) formulated his idea as a game between a bookmaker and a bettor where it was in the interest of the bookmaker to report true subjective probabilities. This was probably the first incentive-compatible mechanism presented in the literature, preceding the economics Nobel prize winner Hurwicz (1972).

In finance, the market sets prices for all financial portfolios and they can be bought and sold in any desired quantity at that price. We assume throughout that there are no transaction costs. To apply our techniques of individual choice to the market, we model the market as one decision maker. The price of a portfolio (= prospect) is interpreted as its certainty equivalent. Preferences between portfolios are represented by the certainty equivalents. The ease with which we can restate the fundamental no-arbitrage theorem from finance as a result from decision theory illustrates the flexibility of the decision-theory model (summarized in Structural Assumption 1.2.1).

Prospects can be added, as for instance in the last row of the tables in Examples 1.1.1 (vendor) and 1.1.2 (finance) for prospects x, y. The prospect $x + y$ assigns $x(s) + y(s)$ to each state s. The following condition is central to this and the following section.

Definition 1.5.1. Additivity holds if:

$[x \succcurlyeq y \Rightarrow x + z \succcurlyeq y + z]$ for all prospects x,y,z. □

That is, improving an ingredient in a sum improves the sum. The condition is self-evident in finance, where, if buying x is more expensive than buying y, then buying both x and z is obviously more expensive than buying both y and z. Additivity is illustrated in Tables 1.5.1–1.5.4.

In Table 1.5.1, prospect z is constant, and its outcome does not depend on the weather tomorrow. In Table 1.5.2, the outcome of prospects z similarly does not depend on the copper price. The prospects z added in the following examples are not constant. They correlate with the other prospects.

In Table 1.5.3, we can obtain $x + z$ from supplying both ice cream and magazines under the assumption that the profits made from selling magazines are independent of the supply of ice cream, and vice versa. We can obtain $y + z$ from offering both hot dogs and magazines under similar independencies.

Additivity is reasonable for moderate amounts of money. The extra receipt of z on your bank account does not change your situation much if z's outcomes are moderate. It will, accordingly, not affect your preference between x and y. Only if the amounts

Table 1.5.1

		no rain	some rain	all rain			no rain	some rain	all rain
If	x	400	100	−400	⩾	y	−400	100	400
	z	500	500	500		z	500	500	500
then	x + z	900	600	100	⩾	y + z	100	600	900

Notes: x: ice cream.
y: hot dogs.
z: message from the tax authorities that you receive a tax credit of $500.

Table 1.5.2

		E_1	E_2	E_3			E_1	E_2	E_3
If	x	50K	−30K	−30K	⩾	y	−30K	−30K	50K
	z	30K	30K	30K		z	30K	30K	30K
then	x + z	80K	0	0	⩾	y + z	0	0	80K

Note: z: message from the tax authorities that you receive a tax credit of 30K.

Table 1.5.3

		no rain	some rain	all rain			no rain	some rain	all rain
If	x	400	100	−400	⩾	y	−400	100	400
	z	150	100	50		z	150	100	50
then	x + z	550	200	−350	⩾	y + z	−250	200	450

Notes: x: ice cream.
y: hot dogs.
z: magazines.

in z are so large that they significantly affect your life and, thus, significantly affect the value of extra money for you, can the receipt of z matter for the choice between x and y.[5] The following example illustrates this point.

Example 1.5.2. Look at the finance Example 1.1.2 where you consider x and y. Now assume, however, that you wrote options before that together yield the benefits described by z in Table 1.5.4.

   Here z provides leverage for the payments of x and a hedge for those of y. Without z available you would prefer x to y. Assume that losses not exceeding 40K can be handled with no problem, but larger losses lead to liquidity problems. A loss of 70K even leads to bankruptcy. Then x + z in Table 1.5.4 is too risky, implying x + z ≺ y + z. This preference together with x ⩾ y fails additivity. The loss of 40K at event

---

[5] If you know the concept of utility: It only happens if outcomes are so large that utility significantly deviates from linearity. This typically concerns outcomes exceeding a two-months salary. In a later chapter on expected utility we will show that a Dutch book and arbitrage are possible as soon as there is risk aversion (Assignment 3.3.6).

Table 1.5.4

		E_1	E_2	E_3			E_1	E_2	E_3
If	x	50K	−30K	−30K	$\succcurlyeq$	y	−30K	−30K	50K
	z	40K	0	−40K		z	40K	0	−40K
then?	x + z	90K	−30K	−70K	$\succcurlyeq$?	y + z	10K	−30K	10K

E_3 generated by z has changed your situation and the value of money. You cannot afford losses from there on. □

The example demonstrated that large amounts of money at stake can affect your way of living and, hence, additivity need not be reasonable then (Arrow 1951a p. 431). It would be interesting to restrict the following analysis to a restricted domain of moderate amounts, where additivity is plausible. In the practice of finance, for instance, upper bounds are placed on the volume of assets that can be traded, and arbitrage opportunities can freely be searched only for limited financial transactions. For simplicity of analysis, we will examine the condition with the whole real line $\mathbb{R}$ as outcome set in what follows. Note how we use superscripts rather than subscripts to index prospects because subscripts refer to events.

Exercise 1.5.1.[b] Assume that $\succcurlyeq$ is transitive and additive. Prove:

(a) [Improving one prospect in a sum of prospects improves the whole sum]. If $\mathbf{x^i} \succcurlyeq \mathbf{y^i}$
then $y^1 + \cdots + y^{i-1} + \mathbf{x^i} + y^{i+1} + \cdots + y^n \succcurlyeq y^1 + \cdots + y^{i-1} + \mathbf{y^i} + y^{i+1} + \cdots + y^n$.

(b) [Improving several prospects in a sum of prospects improves the whole sum].
If $x^i \succcurlyeq y^i$ for all i then $x^1 + \cdots + x^m \succcurlyeq y^1 + \cdots + y^m$. Table 1.5.5 illustrates this result for m = 2.

Table 1.5.5

		no rain	some rain	all rain			no rain	some rain	all rain
If	x^1	400	100	−400	$\succcurlyeq$	y^1	−400	100	400
and	x^2	200	100	0	$\succcurlyeq$	y^2	50	100	150
then	$x^1 + x^2$	600	200	−400	$\succcurlyeq$	$y^1 + y^2$	−350	200	550

Notes: x^1: ice cream.
y^1: hot dogs.
x^2: newspapers.
y^2: umbrellas.

□

We next introduce Dutch books, also called arbitrage. Using Exercise 1.5.1, it can be shown that, if a Dutch book exists, then the conditions just introduced (transitivity, additivity, monotonicity) cannot all hold true. You will be asked to show this in Exercise 1.5.2. Dutch books thus entail a particular way to violate the conditions introduced before.

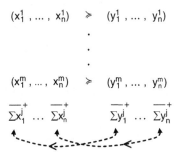

Figure 1.5.1 Arbitrage (a Dutch book).

Definition 1.5.3. Arbitrage, or a *Dutch book*, consists of preferences $x^j \succcurlyeq y^j$, $j = 1, \ldots$, m such that the preferred prospects x^j, when combined, always (for each state s) yield less than the nonpreferred prospects y^j. That is, $\sum_{j=1}^{m} x^j(s) < \sum_{j=1}^{m} y^j(s)$ for all $s \in S$. (See Figure 1.5.1.) □

The x's are individually judged preferable but jointly they turn out to be impoverishing under all states. We say that *arbitrage* is possible if arbitrage – or a Dutch book – exists; that is, there exist x^j's and y^j's as in Definition 1.5.3. Appendix 1.10 discusses mathematical differences between Definition 1.5.3 and the versions commonly presented in the literature. In particular, our definition does not involve scalar multiplication, so that a weaker preference condition and more general theorems will result. By Exercise 1.2.4b (partition flexibility), we may assume that all prospects refer to the same partition $(E_1, \ldots, E_n)$, which we suppress.

In financial markets, arbitrage cannot exist for an extended period. Assume it would, as in Figure 1.5.1. Then you obtain a sure and effortless profit by buying all y's and selling all x's. To see this point, first note that each x^j is more expensive than y^j, so that more is paid to you than you pay to others for the trades made. In addition, you receive an amount $(y_i^1 + \cdots + y_i^m) - (x_i^1 + \cdots + x_i^m)$ for the event E_i that will be true, and this amount is positive for all i. Thus the trading of prices to pay and receive has brought you a positive gain, and the portfolio you bought, being a Dutch book, also brings you a positive gain (no matter which state is true). You have indeed extracted a sure profit from the market while rendering no service in return, and you will continue repeating this transaction as long as the market allows it. Markets in such positions should quickly change or they will break down.

For individual choice, a Dutch book in your preference system suggests an irrationality on your part: You would prefer to replace y^j by x^j for all j, but all together these replacements simply make you worse off no matter which state is the true one. Dutch books can be interpreted as violations of a conservation-of-preference principle: The preferences suggest that there is more total goodness comprised in the x-outcomes to the left, but the column-inequalities suggest the opposite, with more total goodness comprised in the y-outcomes to the right.

A Dutch book can be justified if there are interactions between outcomes. I explain the point briefly for interested readers in the rest of this paragraph. First, there may be interactions between outcomes "in the horizontal direction" when aggregating the outcomes of a prospect into an overall preference value of the prospect. For example, with $n = 3$, an outcome $M = \$1$ million (instead of 0) contingent on event E_3 may add more preference value when the outcomes under events E_1 and E_2 are also both M, such as in $(E_1:M,E_2:M,E_3:M)$ versus $(E_1:M,E_2:M,E_3:0)$, than when they are \$5 million and 0, such as in $(E_1:5M,E_2:0,E_3:M)$ versus $(E_1:5M,E_2:0,E_3:0)$. In the former case the outcome is exactly what is required to bring certainty.[6] Second, there may be interaction between outcomes in the vertical direction when adding them. Possibly an extra outcome M adds more goodness when added to an outcome \$0 than when added to an outcome \$4M.[7] The following exercises concern the logical relations between Dutch books and preference conditions introduced before.

Exercise 1.5.2.[b] Show that transitivity, monotonicity, and additivity preclude the existence of a Dutch book. □

Exercise 1.5.3. Suppose that $\succcurlyeq$ is a weak order, that for each prospect a certainty equivalent exists, and that no Dutch book can be made. Derive the following claims (a and b together entail monotonicity).

(a)[a] If $x(s) > y(s)$ for all states s, then $x \succ y$;
(b)[c] If $x(s) \geq y(s)$ for all states s, then $x \succcurlyeq y$;
(c)[c] Additivity holds. □

1.6 A behavioral foundation of subjective probabilities and expected value using no-arbitrage and no-book

If you consider additivity to be an appropriate rationality requirement for your decisions then, given that transitivity and monotonicity are natural too and given the result of Exercise 1.5.2, you will not want to have a Dutch book in your preference system. It leads to the following theorem. Equivalence of statements in the theorem means that one statement holds if and only if the other does. That is, it refers to logical equivalence. Throughout this book, proofs are in appendices at the end of chapters. The following theorem is thus proved in Appendix 1.11.

Theorem 1.6.1 [De Finetti; no-arbitrage]. Under Structural Assumption 1.2.1 (decision under uncertainty), the following three statements are equivalent.

(i) Expected value holds.
(ii) The preference relation $\succcurlyeq$ is a weak order, for each prospect there exists a certainty equivalent, and no arbitrage (Dutch book) is possible.

---

[6] In the terminology of §4.8, the sure-thing principle, designating separability between disjoint events, will be violated then.
[7] In the terminology of Chapter 2, the utility of money then will be nonlinear. Exercise 3.3.2 will elaborate on this point.

(iii) The preference relation $\succcurlyeq$ is a weak order, for each prospect there exists a certainty equivalent, and additivity and monotonicity are satisfied. $\square$

Statement (i) claims existence of subjective probabilities such that expectation with respect to these can be taken to accommodate preference. At this stage, it may be conjectured that many different probability measures could serve this purpose. This is not so and the probabilities are unique, as stated next.

Observation 1.6.1' [Uniqueness result for Theorem 1.6.1]. In (i) of Theorem 1.6.1, the probabilities are uniquely determined. $\square$

   Under statement (i), certainty equivalents and expected values are the same. In finance, Theorem 1.6.1 implies that market trades are as-if risk neutral. For individual choice theory it implies that, if the preference conditions in (ii) and (iii) are considered desirable, then uncertainties have to be expressed in terms of subjective probabilities. A detailed discussion of behavioral foundations such as Theorem 1.6.1 is in §1.8. The rest of this section presents examples and exercises.

Example 1.6.2. Consider Table 1.6.1. The three events "no rain," "some rain," and "all rain" refer to tomorrow's weather. Assume that a person uses the following decision strategy: when choosing between two prospects, prefer the prospect that yields a positive gain for most of the three events. It turns out that this person cannot be described by expected value maximization because a Dutch book can be made against him. Table 1.6.1 shows how a Dutch book can be made.

Table 1.6.1

	no rain	some rain	all rain			no rain	some rain	all rain
x^1	0	100	100	$\succcurlyeq$	y^1	300	0	0
x^2	100	0	100	$\succcurlyeq$	y^2	0	300	0
x^3	100	100	0	$\succcurlyeq$	y^3	0	0	300
$x^1 + x^2 + x^3$	200	200	200		$y^1 + y^2 + y^3$	300	300	300

$\square$

   In the vendor Example 1.1.1 and its subsequent discussions we modeled the three weather conditions as states of nature. It is usually not necessary to specify the states of nature. Thus, in Example 1.6.2, we need only specify that the three weather conditions concern events. We demonstrated that the combination of y's yielded more for each of the three events considered. It then automatically follows that the combination of y's yields more for every state of nature even if we did not specify those states of nature. The state space S will usually play such a hidden role, implicit and in the background, in this book. We will mostly specify events without specifying states of nature in this book.

Exercise 1.6.1.[b] Consider the vendor Example 1.1.1. Assume that a person uses a maxmin decision strategy, valuing prospects by their worst outcome. Construct a Dutch book against this person. Here and later, you can use any prospect you like, and are not confined to those in Table 1.1.1. $\square$

Exercise 1.6.2.[b] Consider Example 1.1.1. Assume that a person uses a maximax decision strategy, valuing prospects by their best outcome ("I choose the prospect for which I can gain most"). Construct a Dutch book against this person. □

Ad hoc threshold criteria such as those in the following exercise are popular in practical policy decisions and, for instance, in grading in teaching. They entail noncompensatory heuristics; i.e., heuristics avoiding weighting pros against cons, making them simple to implement but often leading to irrational decisions. Empirical studies into such heuristics include Brandstätter, Gigerenzer, & Hertwig (2006), Birnbaum (2008b), and Glöckner & Betsch (2008). Swait (2001) provides a model intermediate between compensatory and noncompensatory evaluations.

Exercise 1.6.3[b] [Ad hoc threshold criteria]. Consider Example 1.1.1. Assume that a person maximizes EV with respect to the probabilities $P(s_1) = P(s_2) = P(s_3) = \frac{1}{3}$, but adds an extra safety requirement: at most one of the possible outcomes may be negative. In other words, EV is modified in the following sense: if prospect x has two or more negative outcomes and prospect y has at most one, then y is preferred to x regardless of their EVs. For example, $100_{s_1}(-1) \prec (-1)_{s_1}1$. Construct a Dutch book. □

Exercise 1.6.4.[b] Show that Statement (i) in Theorem 1.6.1 implies Statements (iii) and (ii) (deriving (iii) is easiest). □

The following exercise presents a highly appealing method for measuring subjective probabilities, using what are known as proper scoring rules. An explanation is given in the elaboration of the exercise.

Exercise 1.6.5[c] [Proper scoring rules].

(a) Assume that you satisfy the conditions of Theorem 1.6.1, and that P denotes your probabilities. You have to choose a number r between 0 and 1 now, called your reported probability of E (rain tomorrow). Tomorrow you will receive the prospect $(1-(1-r)^2)_E(1-r^2)$. Which number r do you choose (to be expressed in terms of P(E))?
(b) Same question, only now you receive the prospect $ln(r)_E ln(1-r)$ (so that you will lose money). □

The following exercise considers deviations from EV (EV is "risk neutrality"), with risk aversion specified in part (a) and risk seeking specified in part (b). Any such deviation directly implies arbitrage.

Exercise 1.6.6.[b] Assume that a coin will be tossed, giving heads (H) or tails (T). Assume weak ordering, with $\alpha_H\beta \sim \beta_H\alpha$ for all outcomes α, β. This symmetry condition can be interpreted as H and T having probability ½.

(a) Assume risk aversion in the sense that there exist $\gamma > \beta$ such that $CE = CE(\gamma_H\beta) < (\beta+\gamma)/2$. Show that arbitrage is possible.
(b) Assume risk seeking in the sense that there exist $\gamma > \beta$ such that $CE = CE(\gamma_H\beta) > (\beta+\gamma)/2$. Show that arbitrage is possible. □

Because the result of the following exercise is conceptually important, the elaboration is immediately given in the main text. It shows that, if nonarbitrage and the other conditions in Theorem 1.6.1 are necessary conditions for rational choice, they surely are not sufficient.

Exercise 1.6.7.$^{!a}$ Assume a symmetric six-sided die with E_j the event of j coming up. Paul and everybody agree that each E_j has an objective probability of 1/6 of coming up. Paul maximizes EV as in Theorem 1.6.1, but his subjective probabilities, denoted Q here, differ from the objective ones denoted P. He has $Q(E_1) = \frac{1}{2}$, $Q(E_2) = \cdots = Q(E_6) = 1/10$ and is willing to take any bet favorable according to his judgment, such as $100_{E_1}(-99)$. Can you make a book against Paul?

Elaboration. Paul maximizes EV with respect to Q so that, by Theorem 1.6.1, no book can be made against Paul. Nevertheless, his behavior does not seem to be wise. Behavior that is not vulnerable to arbitrage can still be silly by, for instance, using silly probabilities. In the literature, overly strict interpretations of what is called the coherence viewpoint have sometimes been advanced (de Finetti 1931b; properly discussed by Tversky & Kahneman 1981 p. 458; for recent references, see Olsson 2005, and Hammond 2006). These interpretations claim that preferential consistency conditions are not only necessary, but also sufficient, for rational behavior (see Appendix B.1). □

The following assignment presents a generalized way of measuring subjective probabilities, and gives a behavioral foundation to EV through the requirement that these measurements do not run into contradictions. Such behavioral foundations, using requirements of consistency of measurement of subjective parameters, are central to the rest of this book.

For the following assignment, as for all exercises unless explicitly stated otherwise, you can use all theorems, exercises, and results that preceded it. In particular, you can use the equivalences established in Theorem 1.6.1.

Assignment 1.6.8.^{a} Show that the following statement is equivalent to each statement in Theorem 1.6.1: Monotonicity holds, for each prospect a CE exists that represents preference, and the CE function is additive $(CE(x + y) = CE(x) + CE(y))$. □

Assignment 1.6.9.^{c} As demonstrated in Eqs. (1.3.1) and (1.3.2), an equivalence

$$p \sim 1_{E_1} 0 \tag{1.6.1}$$

implies $P(E_1) = p$. A drawback of this particular measurement is that a riskless amount is compared to an uncertain prospect, and it is well known that such choices are prone to many biases. Hence an alternative measurement, through

$$E_1(x_1 + \alpha), E_2 x_2, \ldots, E_n x_n \sim E_1(x_1 + p\alpha), \ldots, E_n(x_n + p\alpha), \quad (\alpha \neq 0) \tag{1.6.2}$$

and also implying $P(E_1) = p$ under EV, can be useful. For EV to hold, measurements of Eqs. (1.6.1) and (1.6.2) should not lead to contradictions and should give the same p value. Hence, a necessary preference condition for EV is the following implication:

$$[\text{Eq. (1.6.1)} \Rightarrow \text{Eq. (1.6.2)}] \text{ for all } E_1, \ldots, E_n, x_1, \ldots, x_n, \text{ and } \alpha \neq 0. \qquad (1.6.3)$$

Equation (1.6.2) enables us to avoid riskless outcomes when measuring subjective probabilities. Equation (1.6.3) is a weakened version of additivity, restricting the implication $x \succcurlyeq y \Rightarrow x + z \succcurlyeq y + z$ to indifference ($\sim$) and imposing it only for x and y as in Eqs. (1.6.1) and (1.6.2).

Assume weak ordering, monotonicity, and the existence of a CE for every prospect. Show that Eq. (1.6.3) holds if and only if EV holds. If you do not see how to do this, you can find a hint in the footnote.[8] □

Assignment 1.6.10[a] [Tversky & Kahneman 1981 p. 454, with underlying events added]. Consider an event E with known probability ¼. Its complement has probability ¾. In an experiment of Tversky & Kahneman (1981), a majority of subjects expressed the following preferences:

$$240_E 240 \succcurlyeq 1000_E 0$$
$$0_E - 1000 \succcurlyeq -750_E - 750.$$

Show that these preferences entail arbitrage. Tversky & Kahneman (1981) offered both choices simultaneously to their subjects, so that the arbitrage effectively took place and a straight violation of monotonicity resulted. It makes it extra remarkable that these majority preferences were still found. □

Assignment 1.6.11[b] [The put-call parity in finance]. In deviation from the conventions in the rest of this book, we consider prospects with infinitely many outcomes in this assignment. Similar to Example 1.1.2 (finance), we assume that the state space S is $[0,\infty)$, describing the copper price per pound next month. We consider three prospects, $x(s) = s \times 10K - 25K$, $y(s) = \max\{x(s), 0\}$, and $z(s) = \min\{0, x(s)\}$, depicted in the figure. We assume zero discounting.

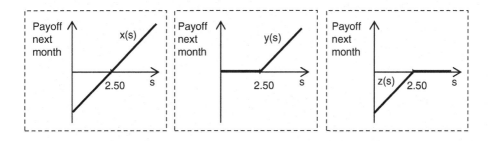

---

[8] It can be seen that in the proof of Theorem 1.6.1 we never need more than this weak version of additivity. Figure 1.11.1 only needs x and y as in Eqs. (1.6.1) and (1.6.2) and Lemmas 1.11.1 and 1.11.2 can also be restricted to such cases, where further only indifferences are involved. Thus, additivity in Statement (iii) of Theorem 1.6.1 can be weakened to Eq. (1.6.3).

In finance, x(s) designates a forward contract committing you to buy 10,000 pounds of copper at ("strike") price \$2.50 a pound next month; i.e., it requires a payment of 25K for something worth $s \times 10K$. The payoff next month is, therefore, $(s \times 10K) - 25K$. y(s) designates a (European) call option where you have the right, at your discretion, to buy 10,000 pounds of copper for a (strike) price of \$2.50 a pound next month. Its payoff next month will be 0 if the market copper price s will be below \$2.50, and it will be $s-\$2.50$ per pound if s will exceed \$2.50. z(s), finally, designates a short position in a (European) put option. This means that another agent has the right, at his discretion, to sell 10,000 pounds of copper for a (strike) price of \$2.50 a pound to you next month, and will do so only if the market prices will be below \$2.50.

Assume that the market prices of x, y, and z today are X, Y, and Z, respectively. Show that no-arbitrage implies the following equality, not by using de Finetti's Theorem 1.6.1, but by directly constructing arbitrage from violations of the equality.

$$X = Y + Z \ [\textit{The put-call parity}] \tag{1.6.4}$$

□

Assignment 1.6.12[a] [Race track betting]. In the 1986 Kentucky derby, a horse ("Ferdinand") paid \$8.40 per \$1 at a bookmaker ("Hollywood Park") in California, and \$18.70 at a bookmaker ("Aqueduct") in New York (Thaler & Ziemba 1988 p. 167). Let E be the event of the horse winning. Assume that you can buy or sell as many gambles on the horse as you like. That is, you can receive or give away, at your discretion, the prospects $7.40_{E_1}(-1.00)$ and $17.70_{E_1}(-1.00)$ as well as multiples of these. Demonstrate that there is a possibility for arbitrage. □

The most important condition in de Finetti's bookmaking argument is the additivity condition. Yet de Finetti mostly stressed monotonicity. The following assignment shows how violations of additivity can be presented as violations of monotonicity.

Assignment 1.6.13[c] [Turning violations of additivity into a book]. Assume that there exists an m and $x^1,\dots,x^m, y^1,\dots,y^m$ such that $x^1 \succcurlyeq y^1,\dots,x^m \succcurlyeq y^m$, and $x^1 + \cdots + x^m \prec y^1 + \cdots + y^m$. By Exercise 1.5.1b, this entails a violation of additivity. It, in itself, is no book however because the sum of y^i's need not dominate the sum of x^i's in every state. Show that a book can nevertheless be made. You may assume the following continuity in this assignment: If $x \succ y$, then for some small positive ϵ, $x \succ y + \epsilon$. □

1.7   Discussion of Structural Assumption 1.2.1 (Decision under uncertainty)

Throughout, we require that the decision maker does not have any influence on the truth of the events (Drèze 1987 §1.2.1; Machina 1987 p. 148). Gilboa (2009 §2.6) wrote: "The distinction between the acts, over which the decision maker has control, and states, over which she hasn't, is one of the pillars of rational choice. Many mistakes in everyday life have to do with an inappropriate distinction between acts and states." In the elections Example 1.1.3, you have no right to vote. In the finance

Example 1.1.2, you are a price taker (economic term for a consumer who cannot influence prices). In the vendor Example 1.1.1, you are not a rainmaker who can generate rain tomorrow and can, thus, make state of nature s_3 come true.

The absence of influence on the truth of events implies, in particular, that there is no moral hazard. Moral hazard originated from insurance, where it designates an increase in the risk of loss or damage caused by becoming more careless when insured. It is nowadays used as a general term to refer to situations where the likelihood of uncertain events can be influenced. The techniques of this book cannot be applied directly to such cases. However, they can be applied after a proper remodeling of the state space, incorporating all relevant influences you have in the prospects to be chosen and specifying as states and events the uncertainties completely outside your control. Such remodelings are useful in making essential aspects of the situation explicit.

In many practical situations, obtaining a strict separation between what is completely under your control (which prospect is chosen from those available) and what is completely outside of your control (states, events) is nontrivial. If you are a student taking an exam, then you have partial influence on the grade you will get, and states of nature and events cannot directly refer to your future grade. It is then not easy to specify what exactly your own influence is and what the uncertainties are outside your influence. Your grade does become an event outside of your control, and amenable to probability theory, if you condition on your influence and, for instance, assume that you will make the maximal effort, or a regular effort. The strict "Cartesian" separation of what is under your influence and what is outside your influence is the key in Savage's (1954) model, as it is in the many studies, including this book, that build on Savage's model. To understand the limitations of this model, it is instructive to study alternative models, such as Jeffrey's (1965) thought-provoking one, or Lewis' (1987) caused decision theory. In the brilliant early contribution by Ramsey (1931), no separation as just described was made in any clear manner. (Arrow 1951a, p. 424 described Ramsey's contribution as "none too clear.") Discussions of the limitations include Ahn (2008), Drèze (1987 §1.2), Fishburn (1970 p. 161, §12.1; p. 166, §12.2; p. 168, end of §12.2), Gilboa (2009 Ch. 11), Jeffrey (1965), Karni (2006), Krantz *et al.* (1971 §8.2.1), Kreps (1988 pp. 35–38), Luce (2000 §1.1.6.1), and Nau (2001).

In our structural assumption, states and outcomes are taken as primitives and prospects are constructed from these, mapping states to outcomes. Consequently, the prospect set is larger than the state space or the outcome space. In applications, some prospects, states – or events – and outcomes will be naturally given, and others are defined in terms of these. We may, for instance, sometimes take a state and a prospect and define as outcome whatever results if that state obtains and that prospect is chosen. Or we can easily specify the conceivable prospects and the conceivable outcomes, but not the states of nature. Then we may define a state by specifying for each prospect which outcome will result (Gilboa 2009 §11.1.2). Savage's assumption that consequences are portable across states need not hold in the latter approaches.

In all aforementioned constructions, the resulting model will contain some artificially constructed objects that do not match conceivable real objects. There is no clear recipe for the best way to model an actual decision situation, and modeling is an art that has to be learned in practice. Works besides the aforementioned references that have challenged Savage's way of modeling include Green & Osband (1991) and Krantz *et al.* (1971 §9.6.3).

Exercise 1.7.1.[b] Suppose that you have to decide whether or not to smoke for the rest of your life. You construct the model in Table 1.7.1.

Table 1.7.1

	lung cancer	no lung cancer
smoke	pleasant life, then disease	pleasant life, healthy
don't smoke	unpleasant life, then disease	unpleasant life, healthy

Outcomes are assumed monetary in the main text with a few exceptions that are noted explicitly. This example concerns such an exception. You decide from this model that smoking gives a superior outcome for every state of nature, so that by monotonicity you would decide that smoking is to be preferred to not smoking. Obviously, something is wrong with this model. Can you point out what? □

1.8   The general nature and usefulness of behavioral foundations

This section elaborates on the discussion of behavioral foundations in the introduction to this book. Related discussions are in Gilboa, Postlewaite, & Schmeidler (2008 pp. 177–178) and Gilboa (2009 §8.4). Behavioral foundations are mathematical results, stating a logical equivalence between a list of preference conditions and a decision model. They show that the subjective parameters in the decision model (subjective probabilities in Theorem 1.6.1) are the relevant parameters for determining decisions. They change the status of such subjective parameters from being ad hoc into being scientifically well founded.

Historical examples. Already in the 1930s, there had been many discussions of the plausibility and implausibility of the concept of subjective probabilities, often based on philosophical arguments. This topic was central in the debates on Bayesian versus frequentist statistics. De Finetti (1931a), Ramsey (1931), and Savage bypassed such philosophical debates and instead showed that subjective probabilities must exist by giving them behavioral foundations.

For models that did not receive preference foundations, this absence is usually considered a drawback, and the unfortunate history of the separate-probability-transformation model serves as a warning (details in Chapter 5). The well-known Analytical Hierarchy Process, Saaty's (1980) popular and pragmatic technique for multiattribute decisions, has often been criticized for such an absence

(Smith & von Winterfeldt 2004). Birnbaum's (2008a) models that fitted data better than prospect theory in several experiments, also lack a preference foundation and have not been widely used in theoretical works. The same holds for Busemeyer's decision field theory (Busemeyer & Diederich 2002). Although the multiple priors model had been available since Wald (1950) and Hurwicz (1951), it only became popular when Gilboa & Schmeidler (1989) provided a preference foundation for the case of linear utility.

Convincing people of the prescriptive appropriateness of a model. When teaching, I use the following thought experiment to explain the usefulness of behavioral foundations. Imagine that someone, a decision analyst, out of the blue advises you to make your decisions under uncertainty in agreement with EV. That is, you should choose probabilities (the Ps in the EV maximization of Theorem 1.6.1, which can be subjective), then take the probability-weighted average of the outcomes as evaluation of each prospect, and then, finally, choose from all available prospects the one with the highest value calculated in this manner. Such is the advice.

As it stands, the advice would be ad hoc and unconvincing. Why would you express uncertainties in terms of probabilities, and why would you carry out the calculations as recommended? Why not take squares or exponents of probabilities, and why sum the products of probabilities and outcomes? An additional problem is that it is not very clear from the advice of the decision analyst *how* the probabilities should be chosen. The probabilities seem to come like manna from heaven. The advice, if presented in the ad hoc manner as just described, would be unconvincing.

Imagine now that the decision analyst apologizes for having given you such unconvincing advice, and then changes the topic of conversation. He recommends that your preferences satisfy completeness and transitivity, and you, being a rational person, agree. You also agree that the existence of a certainty equivalent for each prospect is reasonable. Then, the decision analyst explains to you what a Dutch book is. You do not want your preference system to contain a Dutch book.

Then, however, a surprise will be awaiting you. The decision analyst says, triumphantly, that he **has** convinced you of his first claim (EV maximization) after all, and comes up with Theorem 1.6.1. This theorem proves that, by accepting some seemingly natural conditions on your preferences, your behavior can be described, like it or not, as in Statement (i). In particular, there are probabilities representing your uncertainties. You behave in accordance with Statement (i), consciously or subconsciously.

This thought experiment shows how behavioral foundations can convince people to use particular quantitative models of decision making. The models in themselves are not directly meaningful[9] in an empirical sense. It is not clear why Statement (i) of Theorem 1.6.1 in isolation without further justification would lead to wise behavior. Statement (ii) shows why it can do so. Statement (ii) is stated directly in terms of preference conditions, which makes it directly empirically meaningful. In finance,

---

[9] Formalizations of empirical meaningfulness are in Narens (2002) and Pfanzagl (1968 Ch. 2).

"risk neutral" evaluations as in Statement (i) are similarly justified by the absence of arbitrage as in Statement (ii).

Criticizing a model. In general, a behavioral foundation gives necessary and sufficient behavioral conditions – conditions stated directly in terms of your preferences – for a general kind of quantitative model. In the preceding discussion, the behavioral foundation was used to convince a person that a model is appropriate by arguing that the preference conditions are appropriate. Behavioral foundations can equally well be used to criticize models. Maybe you felt that the method of Statement (i) appeared to be sensible at first sight, but then you decided that the existence of Dutch books is sometimes appropriate still. Theorem 1.6.1 would then convince you that the EV model of statement (i) there, with probabilities, is not appropriate after all. Similarly, Allais' (1953a) famous criticism of expected utility (presented in §4.12) was targeted on the independence condition, the most critical condition in behavioral foundations of expected utility.

Descriptive use in the experimental heaven. In teaching, I refer to the "experimental heaven" for explaining the descriptive use of behavioral foundations. There are unbounded measurement facilities in the sense that we can observe all, infinitely many, preferences, and we can analyze them all. Further, there are no measurement errors so that all preferences are observed exactly and we can use a deterministic model. A descriptive model can then readily be verified or falsified using the conditions in a behavioral foundation. In reality, of course, only a limited number of observations can be made, and we must reckon with measurement errors so that we have to use statistical tools.

Identifying relevant parameters. Example 3.7.1 will illustrate another use of behavioral foundations, through an example with chronic health states (Q,T), designating T years of life in health state Q followed by immediate death. It may not be very clear, a priori, what kind of model should be used to evaluate chronic health states, and which concepts are relevant. A behavioral foundation (Observation 3.7.2) will show how plausible preference conditions imply that we should use a multiplicative model defined by $U(Q,T) = V(Q)W(T)$. Here V measures quality of life and W measures the value of life years (incorporating discounting). This model is the famous QALY model, used throughout the health domain. In this way, behavioral foundations help to identify the relevant parameters and to measure value in situations where it is not clear, a priori, how to do so.

Gentlemanly distant? The aforementioned reasons for developing behavioral foundations do not specify whether the preference conditions in a behavioral foundation should be close in nature to the corresponding preference functional, or whether it is preferable that they are, or at first seem to be, of a different nature. In mathematics, it is usually considered desirable that conditions that are logically equivalent to some hypothesis are "gentlemanly distant" from this hypothesis, because otherwise the logical equivalence is too trivial and unsurprising and does not give many new insights. For these reasons it may be preferred that preference conditions do not resemble the corresponding functional very closely.

There are reasons that make a close resemblance between preference conditions and the corresponding functional desirable after all. The preference conditions then better clarify the empirical meaning of the preference functional, and better show the empirical meaning of parameters in the functional. Indeed, the technique for obtaining behavioral foundations used in this book, deriving them from the exclusion of contradictions in empirical measurements, will mostly lead to preference conditions that are close to the corresponding functionals. They thus help to illustrate that the functionals are homeomorphic to the decision process (see Introduction). For example, the additivity preference condition in Theorem 1.6.1 is close to the additive probabilities and expectations used in the representing functional, and in that sense the theorem may not be very surprising. I think that, in return, this additivity preference condition better captures the empirical meaning of subjective probabilities than any other condition that I can think of, implying that choices can be isolated from many aspects of the context. The purpose of preference foundations is to identify empirical content, and not to be mathematically complex. The simpler the better. I hope that the mathematically sophisticated readers are willing to accept, in return, the drawback (from their perspective) that the mathematics in this book is simpler than in most other studies on behavioral foundations.

De Finetti's electrifying writing. When I, as a mathematics student in 1978, expressed amazement about the claim made by my statistics teacher – a frequentist as I now know – that the probability of life on Mars could not be defined, and that it was even treated differently than the probability of a random repeatable event such as related to coin tosses, he referred me to Bruno de Finetti's work. ("There is a crazy Italian who thinks such things" were his exact words.) De Finetti's (1972) first chapter, written in a thought-provoking manner, opened up to me the technique of behavioral foundations, and the possibility of defining something as seemingly intangible as one's subjective degree of belief, in a tangible manner. De Finetti showed how we can read the minds (beliefs, i.e. subjective probabilities) of people. I felt electrified by his ideas, and decided that I wanted to work on them. I hope that the readers will also sense some of the magic of these ideas.

Appendix 1.9   Natural, technical, and intuitive preference conditions, and the problematic completeness condition

Natural and technical preference conditions. Some natural preference conditions – transitivity and monotonicity – are assumed throughout this book. In addition to those natural preference conditions, the behavioral foundations in this book adopt some technical richness assumptions, entailing that the set of prospects constitutes a continuum. By adding continuity assumptions, we can then carry out measurements to any desired degree of precision. Continuity was incorporated in this chapter by the assumption that a certainty equivalent exists for each prospect. We have assumed throughout that the outcome set is a continuum. In Chapter 2 this assumption could be dropped – although we will maintain it – because we will have a continuum of probabilities there.

Three problems for completeness. Throughout, we have assumed completeness of preference. One reason that has often been advanced in the literature for violating completeness concerns indeterminacy of preference: agents cannot make up their minds in a decision situation they face and are undecided which of two prospects to choose (Bewley 1986; Eliaz & Ok 2006; Gilboa, Postlewaite, & Schmeidler 2008 pp. 179–180; Levi 1980; Mandler 2005; Walley 1991). We will assume throughout that an agent simply has to choose one prospect in every decision situation faced (Gilboa 2009 §6.1). A prospect "doing nothing," if available, is simply a choice option available in the set to be chosen from. In this sense, our completeness assumption can be taken as one more natural preference condition of the same kind as transitivity and monotonicity.

A second argument against completeness concerns the unrealistic nature of some prospects in our models. We assume that all assignments of outcomes to events are available in the preference domain. However, some of these assignments may be too artificial to even be conceivable. In a famous discussion, Savage gave the example of "being hung so long as it be done without damage to my health or reputation" (Drèze 1987 p. 78, Appendix 2.A; discussed by Gilboa 2009, §12.2.2). Assuming preferences over such prospects is indeed problematic. Even if two prospects are both conceivable, a choice situation where both are available may still be inconceivable. For example, a choice between fries with curry sauce to be served and consumed immediately, or foie gras to be served and consumed immediately, may not be realistic if these dishes are only served at places far apart.

A third argument against completeness concerns the richness of the models assumed, that constitute continuums, with choices between all prospect pairs assumed observable. We will never observe infinitely many data, let alone continuums (Davidson & Suppes 1956). Here completeness is an idealization that we make to facilitate our analyses. Although it has sometimes been suggested that completeness and continuity for a continuum-domain are innocuous assumptions (Arrow 1971 p. 48; Drèze 1987 p. 12), several authors have pointed out that these assumptions do add empirical (behavioral) implications to other assumptions. It is, unfortunately, usually unclear what exactly those added implications are (Ghirardato & Marinacci 2001b; Krantz *et al.* 1971 §9.1; Pfanzagl 1968 §6.6; Schmeidler 1971; Suppes 1974 §2; Wakker 1988).[10]

Behavioral conditions. Besides the natural and technical assumptions made throughout, behavioral foundations use preference conditions typical of the model considered, such as the bookmaking argument or additivity in this chapter. Such a condition will, for example, be independence – or its modified version called SG

---

[10] In Savage's model, the second and third argument are aggravated because he assumed that the state space specify all uncertainties relevant to the decisions. This assumption has caused many misunderstandings, and we will not follow it. We will only consider what Savage (1954) informally called small worlds.

consistency – for the von Neumann–Morgenstern expected utility model studied in Ch. 2. Such conditions are referred to as the intuitive conditions, and they are the focus of attention in the analysis of a theory. The natural and behavioral conditions are usually necessary for the basic decision model that interests us in the sense that they are implied by that model.

General discussion and necessity and sufficiency of conditions. We would hope to find natural and behavioral conditions that are necessary and sufficient for the decision model of interest, at least for finite models. Unfortunately this task is, usually, too difficult (so-called first-order logic axioms cannot do it: Suppes 1974 p. 164). We, therefore, usually add the technical richness conditions, which simplify our task. Whereas the natural and intuitive conditions in isolation are only necessary for the decision model of interest (this necessity is usually easy to prove), together with the technical conditions they become necessary and sufficient (which is usually hard to prove).

I consider the second problem of completeness (the unrealistic nature of some prospects), aggravated by the richness of the model assumed through the technical conditions, to be the weakest point of the revealed-preference paradigm and of the theoretical results of this book. The third problem of completeness (we can only make finitely many observations) is also troublesome. These two problems make it desirable to develop results for incomplete preferences defined on finite domains. Obtaining such results is, in my opinion, the major challenge for the theory of behavioral foundations to date. It can, however, be extremely difficult (see Shapiro, 1979 for subjective expected utility), which is why this book focuses on conventional models with completeness on continuums of preference domains. For other discussions of the different kinds of preference conditions, see Suppes (1974 §2), Krantz *et al.* (1971 §1.4 and §9.1), and Pfanzagl (1968 §6.6).

Appendix 1.10   The relation of Theorem 1.6.1 to the literature

In finance, de Finetti's Theorem 1.6.1 implies that market trades can be analyzed as-if risk neutral. For individual choice, Theorem 1.6.1 has presented de Finetti's book idea as a coherence condition. De Finetti formulated his idea differently. He considered a game context, where the decision maker (you) has to play a role similar to the market in finance. That is, you have to make all your preferences public, for example by making all your certainty equivalents public. An opponent can take you up on any of your preferences $x^j \succcurlyeq y^j$, $j = 1, \ldots, n$, and ask you to exchange y^j for x^j with him for each j, which means that you give him $(y^1 - x^1) + \cdots + (y^n - x^n)$. Then your opponent, even if absolutely ignorant about the states of nature, can make a sure profit from you (arbitrage) whenever a Dutch book exists in your preferences, that is, whenever you do not go by subjective probabilities and expected value.

De Finetti thus formulated the bookmaking argument as a game with an opponent where the mechanism has been devised such that out of self-interest it is best to reveal private information about subjective probabilities. De Finetti's formulation is more vivid than ours. In his formulation you will surely lose money to a cunning opponent the moment your preference system contains a Dutch book. It is, however, less clean because it is distorted by dynamic and game-theoretic complications. These are most problematic if your opponent has information about the states of nature that you do not have. Then your opponent can make money from you whatever you do, and the bookmaking game is a lost game anyway. It then seems to be immaterial whether or not your preference system contains a Dutch book, and the book-thought-experiment is not very interesting. Finally, de Finetti used the terms fair price or prevision rather than our term certainty equivalent.

In finance, it is often assumed that no person can be better informed than the market, or can only be so for a short time period (the efficient market hypothesis). The moment someone knows that a stock is underpriced, this person starts buying the stock and its price will move up until it has reached its proper level. In this way, the market automatically aggregates all information possessed by its players into the market prices, as if driven by an invisible hand.

To articulate more clearly the individual coherence interpretation of Theorem 1.6.1, imagine that you are alone in a hotel room some evening. Tomorrow you can choose one prospect from a pair of available prospects, being the one you prefer most, but you do not know which pair of prospects it will be. You do know that the payments will be moderate. You know your entire preference system over all prospect pairs, having the unbounded calculation power to know all these infinitely many preferences. If you know that your preference system contains a Dutch book, should you consider this to be irrational and should you change it? De Finetti's formulation does not apply here because there is no other person involved who could benefit from your preferences in some sense.

Another reason why de Finetti's thought experiment does not apply is that only one of your preferences will be realized, rather than several preferences as in de Finetti's formulation.[11] The latter reason also implies that no law of large numbers applies. The coherence principles can still convince you to change your preferences. If $x \succ y$, but after addition of z we have $x + z \preccurlyeq y + z$ whereas you think that z is too moderate to change your preference between x and y, then this can convince you that at least one of the two preferences does not give what best serves your interests, and that these preferences should be reconsidered. You thus satisfy additivity and behave as-if maximizing EV using subjective probabilities despite the fact that you face a one-shot individual decision.

In finance, and also in de Finetti's work, not only addition, but also scalar multiplication is considered in the constructions of arbitrage. Trades $\lambda_1(x^1 - y^1) + \cdots + \lambda_n(x^n - y^n)$ are allowed in the arbitrage Definition 1.5.3, where the λ_j's are nonnegative

---

[11] Appendix B will explain that repeated choice is not an explicit part of the revealed-preference paradigm, and §B.3 will discuss the (absence of) repetition for expected value maximization. This point is central to Cubitt & Sugden's (2001) discussion of bookmaking arguments.

real numbers at the discretion of your opponent (or an agent in the market).[12] Theorem 1.6.1 generalizes these results by showing that scalar multiplication need not be invoked, and that it is implied by the other conditions. This generalization was introduced by Diecidue & Wakker (2002). I find the mere summation of prospects and preferences more satisfactory for individual choice than scalar multiplications, because the former can directly be interpreted in terms of a joint receipt of prospects.

De Finetti also showed how the requirement of completeness of preference over all prospects can be restricted, in mathematical terms, to the linear space spanned by your expressed preferences (de Finetti 1974 Ch. 3). In finance, attention is also often restricted to incomplete markets with only particular stocks and their riskless hedges. Then an as-if risk neutral evaluation is obtained only for these, and risk aversion for other portfolios is not excluded. We shall not elaborate on these points.

Appendix 1.11   Proof of Theorem 1.6.1 and Observation 1.6.1′

Hopefully the proof presented here will be appealing to the readers. I invested much time into getting the most appealing proof of de Finetti's theorem, in particular through Figure 1.11.1. It was de Finetti's theorem that brought me into this field. The uniqueness in Observation 1.6.1′ follows from the indifference $1_E0 \sim P(E)$, plus the uniqueness of $P(E)$ in view of the implied monotonicity. From now on, we focus on Theorem 1.6.1.

Exercise 1.5.2 has demonstrated that transitivity, monotonicity, and additivity preclude the existence of a Dutch book. That is, (iii) in the theorem implies (ii). By Exercise 1.5.3, the absence of Dutch books together with weak ordering and the existence of CEs implies additivity and monotonicity; i.e., (ii) in the theorem implies (iii). Hence, it suffices to derive equivalence of (i) and (iii). Exercise 1.6.4 demonstrated that (i) implies (iii) (and also (ii)).

In the rest of the proof, we assume (iii) and derive (i). Figure 1.11.1 shows the main steps in the proof. By Exercise 1.2.5b, CE represents preference, which we will use many times. The following lemma considers combinations of prospects.

Lemma 1.11.1 [Combining prospects]. CE is additive; i.e., $CE(f + g) = CE(f) + CE(g)$.

Proof. $f \sim CE(f)$ and $g \sim CE(g) \Rightarrow f + g \sim CE(f) + CE(g)$, by Exercise 1.5.1b with $m = 2$, and applied both with $\succcurlyeq$ for $\sim$ and with $\preccurlyeq$ for $\sim$. Hence $CE(f + g)$, the constant amount equivalent to $f + g$, must be $CE(f) + CE(g)$. □

An alternative way to prove Lemma 1.11.1, and lemmas to follow, is by setting up arbitrage against any violation. Additivity is also known as Cauchy's functional

---

[12] de Finetti mostly considered the special case where y^j is the certainty equivalent of x^j so that the preferences are indifferences and the λ_j's can be any real number (de Finetti 1974). Further, he sometimes (e.g. de Finetti 1931a) restricted attention to the case where the x^j's are indicator functions of events so that the certainty equivalents y^j reflect subjective probabilities. In the presence of other conditions such as monotonicity and the linear combinations considered, these restricted conditions do still imply EV and the conditions described in the text.

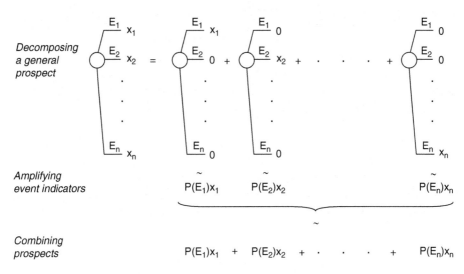

Decomposing a general prospect

Amplifying event indicators

Combining prospects

Figure 1.11.1 Deriving expected value.

equation. It is well known that under weak additional assumptions (e.g. monotonicity suffices) additivity implies that CE must be linear (Aczél 1966 Theorem 2.1.1.1). The remainder of this proof establishes this result in our context. We call prospects of the form 1_E0 *event indicators.*

We define $P(E) = CE(1_E0)$ for all events E. That is, $P(E)$ is the CE of the event indicator of E. P is a probability measure because

- $P(S) = CE(S{:}1) = 1$;
- $P(\emptyset) = CE(S{:}0) = 0$;
- $0 \leq P(E)$ (by monotonicity);
- For disjoint A,B, $P(A \cup B) = CE(1_{A \cup B}0) =$ (by additivity of CE; that is, by Lemma 1.11.1) $CE(1_A0) + CE(1_B0) = P(A) + P(B)$.

Lemma 1.11.2 [Amplifying event indicators]. $CE(\lambda_E0) = P(E)\lambda$ for all E and λ.

proof.
CASE 1   [$\lambda = 0$]. Follows immediately.
CASE 2   [$\lambda = k$ for a natural number k]. By repeated application of Lemma 1.11.1, CE $(k_E0) = CE(1_E0 + \cdots + 1_E0) = CE(1_E0) + \cdots + CE(1_E0) = P(E)k$ for all natural numbers k.
CASE 3   [λ is positive and rational; i.e., $\lambda = m/k$ for natural numbers k and m]. $CE(m/k_E0) = P(E)m\frac{1}{k}$ because (by Case 2) $P(E)m = CE(m_E0) = CE(m/k_E0 + \cdots + m/k_E0)$ (k terms) $= CE(m/k_E0) + \cdots + CE(m/k_E0) = kCE(m/k_E0)$.
CASE 4   [λ is negative and rational]. Follows from the result for all positive rational λ and the equality $CE(-f) = -CE(f)$ for all prospects f. The latter equality follows because $0 = CE(f - f) = CE(f) + CE(-f)$.

CASE 5   [Nonrational λ]. The derivation for this case does not need continuity, and mainly uses monotonicity. $P(E)$ can be zero or positive in what follows. By monotonicity, for all rational ℓ ("low") and h ("high"), $\ell_E 0 \preccurlyeq \lambda_E 0 \preccurlyeq h_E 0$ whenever $\ell < \lambda < h$. Hence, $P(E)\ell = CE(\ell_E 0) \leq CE(\lambda_E 0) \leq CE(h_E 0) = P(E)h$. $P(E)\lambda$ is the only real number $CE(\lambda_E 0)$ that satisfies these inequalities for all $\ell < \lambda < h$. □

Figure 1.11.1 demonstrates, for a general prospect $E_1 x_1 \ldots E_n x_n$ (depicted left in the figure), that its CE is its expected value $P(E_1)x_1 + \cdots + P(E_n)x_n$, so that the latter formula represents preference. This completes the proof of Theorem 1.6.1.

We obtain the following corollary, a result that is usually added as an assumption in analyses of arbitrage in finance, as it was in de Finetti's analyses. We have demonstrated that it follows from the other assumptions.

Corollary 1.11.3 [Amplifying general prospects]. $CE(\lambda f) = \lambda CE(f)$. □

2 Expected utility with known probabilities – "risk" – and unknown utilities

The important financial decisions in our life concern large stakes, and then the maximization of expected value may not be reasonable. Most of our decisions concern nonquantitative outcomes such as health states. Then expected value cannot be used because it cannot even be defined. For these reasons, a more general theory is warranted. We now turn to such a theory – expected utility. For simplicity, we consider only the case where probabilities are known in this chapter. This case is called decision under risk. The general case of both unknown probabilities and unknown utility is more complex, and will be dealt with in later chapters. Whereas Chapter 1 showed how to read the minds (beliefs, i.e. subjective probabilities) of people, this chapter will show how to read their hearts (happiness, i.e. utility).

2.1 Decision under risk as a special case of decision under uncertainty

Probabilities can be (un)known to many degrees, all covered by the general term uncertainty. Decision under risk is the special, limiting case where probabilities are objectively given, known, and commonly agreed upon. Risk is often treated separately from uncertainty in the literature. It is more efficient, and conceptually more appropriate, to treat risk as a special case of uncertainty. I will discuss this point in some detail in this and the following sections. This point will be especially important in the study of ambiguity in Part III. Machina (2004) provided a formal model supporting this point.

Throughout this chapter and in fact throughout this whole book, Structural Assumption 1.2.1 (decision under uncertainty) is maintained. Assumptions will be added. All results from uncertainty can immediately be applied to risk, and results from risk can often be extended to uncertainty. I commonly advise students to work on uncertainty rather than on risk as much as possible, because the numerical probability scale often confounds rather than simplifies what is essential. This point also explains the zigzag structure of Part I of this book. The first big chunk upcoming, Chapters 2 and 3, concerns decision under risk, and the second big chunk, Chapter 4, concerns decision under uncertainty. We nevertheless started in Chapter 1 with decision under uncertainty and not with decision under risk. I did so to encourage the readers, from the beginning, to think of decision under risk as being embedded in decision under uncertainty, and never to have thought of decision under risk in isolation.

We begin with an introductory example that can be skipped by theoretically oriented ("c") readers.

Example 2.1.1 [Vendor with probabilities given]. Assume Example 1.1.1. Assume that, in addition, there is extensive statistical data available about the weather. One out of four times there will be no rain, one out of four times it will be all rain, and half the times there is some rain. This data is objective and agreed upon by everyone. Writing P for objective probability, we have $P(s_1) = P(s_3) = ¼$ and $P(s_2) = ½$.

Prospect x (taking ice cream) generates (¼: 400, ½: 100, ¼: −400), meaning that it yields 400 with probability ¼, 100 with probability ½, and −400 with probability ¼. Similarly, y generates (¼:−400, ½: 100, ¼: 400), 0 generates (1:0) (also denoted as just 0), and x + y generates (½:200, ½:0). Note that y generates the same probability distribution over outcomes as x does, assigning the same probability to each outcome. In decision under risk we assume that the *preference value* of a prospect (i.e., its indifference class) is determined entirely by the probability distribution it generates over the outcomes. Then x and y have the same preference value and are equivalent. For determining preference it then suffices to know the probability distribution generated over the outcomes by a prospect. Hence we often give only that probability distribution. Then x and y are both described by (¼: 400, ½: 100, ¼: −400) and they are equated.

The assumption x ∼ y can be violated if utility (defined later) is state dependent. Then the goodness or badness of gaining or losing 400 depends on the weather conditions. We will assume that there is no such dependence. □

For decision under risk, we assume that an objective probability P is given on S, assigning to each event E its probability P(E). Then, with p_j denoting $P(E_j)$, each prospect $(E_1:x_1,\ldots,E_n:x_n)$ generates a probability distribution $(p_1:x_1,\ldots,p_n:x_n)$ over the outcomes, assigning probability p_j to each outcome x_j. Probability distributions over outcomes taking only finitely many values are called *probability-contingent prospects*. We now define decision under risk.

Assumption 2.1.2 [*Decision under risk*]. Structural Assumption 1.2.1 (decision under uncertainty) holds. In addition, an objective probability measure P is given on the state space S, assigning to each event E its probability P(E). Different event-contingent prospects that generate the same probability-contingent prospect are preferentially equivalent. □

Because of Assumption 2.1.2, it suffices to describe only the generated probability-contingent prospect for determining the preference value of a prospect, without specifying the underlying event-contingent prospect. This will be the approach of the next section.

Example 2.1.3 [Decision under risk violated]. Assume a small urn with 20 balls numbered 1 to 20, and a large urn with 200 balls numbered 1 to 200, where from each a random ball will be drawn and its number inspected. Many subjects prefer gambling on numbers 1–10 from the large urn – for, let us say, \$100 – to gambling on number 1 from the small urn ("I have more chances"), even though both event-contingent prospects generate the same probability-contingent prospect (1/20:100, 19/20:0) (Kirkpatrick & Epstein 1992). This implies an empirical violation of Assumption 2.1.2. □

Exercise 2.1.1.[a] Reconsider Exercise 1.6.7, with Paul and everyone agreeing that the $P(E_j)$'s $= \frac{1}{6}$ are objective probabilities. Does Assumption 2.1.2 hold for Paul? □

The most commonly used measure on the real axis assigns to each interval $[\alpha,\beta]$ its length $\beta - \alpha$, and to disjoint unions of intervals the sum of their separate lengths. It is called the *Lebesgue measure*, often denoted λ, and we will use it sometimes. On the unit interval $[0,1)$ it is a probability measure.

Exercise 2.1.2.[a] Assume weak ordering, and Assumption 2.1.2.

(a) Assume that $S = [0,1)$ and that the probability measure P on S is the Lebesgue measure. Let x be the event-contingent prospect $([0,\frac{1}{3}):3, [\frac{1}{3},\frac{2}{3}):8, [\frac{2}{3},1):2)$. What probability-contingent prospect is generated by x? Let y be the event-contingent prospect $([0,\frac{1}{3}):3, [\frac{1}{3},\frac{2}{3}):4, [\frac{2}{3},1):5)$. What probability-contingent prospect is generated by y? Assume that $y \succcurlyeq x$. Let f be the event-contingent prospect $([0,\frac{1}{3}):8, [\frac{1}{3},\frac{2}{3}):2, [\frac{2}{3},1):3)$. Let g be the event-contingent prospect $([0,\frac{1}{3}):5, [\frac{1}{3},\frac{2}{3}):4, [\frac{2}{3},1):3)$. What is the preference between f and g?
(b) Consider the probability-contingent prospect $(\frac{3}{4}:8,\frac{1}{4}:2)$. Define two different event-contingent prospects that generate it. □

Example 2.1.4 [Regret (Bardsley *et al.* 2010 Box 3.5)]. Violations of Assumption 2.1.2 may arise because of regret, where you may care about correlations between outcomes (Bell 1982). Assume that $S = [0,1)$ is endowed with the Lebesgue measure as objective probability P, reflecting a random choice of a number from $[0,1)$. Consider a preference

$$([0, \tfrac{1}{6}) : 10, [\tfrac{1}{6}, \tfrac{2}{6}) : 20, \ [\tfrac{2}{6}, \tfrac{3}{6}) : 30, [\tfrac{3}{6}, \tfrac{4}{6}) : 40, [\tfrac{4}{6}, \tfrac{5}{6}) : 50, [\tfrac{5}{6}, 1) : 60) \prec$$

$$([0, \tfrac{1}{6}) : 60, [\tfrac{1}{6}, \tfrac{2}{6}) : 10, \ [\tfrac{2}{6}, \tfrac{3}{6}) : 20, [\tfrac{3}{6}, \tfrac{4}{6}) : 30, [\tfrac{4}{6}, \tfrac{5}{6}) : 40, [\tfrac{5}{6}, 1) : 50).$$

Fishburn (1988 p. 273) and Loomes & Sugden (1982 Table 6) argued that this preference can be rational because the regret for an upper choice under the event of $s<\frac{1}{6}$ will be very big, whereas there is only low regret for the lower prospect under all other events. However, the two event-contingent prospects generate the same probability-contingent prospect, assigning probability $\frac{1}{6}$ to each outcome. Hence they must be equivalent under the assumption of decision under risk, and the preference violates decision under risk. As the aforementioned references show, regret leads to violations of transitivity. We will throughout assume Assumption 2.1.2 of decision under risk, and will not consider regret or violations of transitivity. □

2.2 Decision under risk: basic concepts

In decision under risk, as in decision under uncertainty, the *outcome set* is $\mathbb{R}$, with real numbers designating money. As defined in the preceding section, *probability-contingent prospects*, or, briefly, *prospects*, are probability distributions over $\mathbb{R}$ that take only finitely many values.[1] The generic notation for a prospect is $(p_1:x_1, \ldots, p_n: x_n)$, yielding outcome x_j with probability p_j for each j. Here n is a natural number that can be different for different prospects. Again, we often drop brackets, commas, and colons, writing $p_1x_1\ldots p_nx_n$ if no confusion with multiplication is likely to arise; another notation is p_1x_1,p_2x_2,p_3x_3. If there are only two outcomes and probabilities, then we often suppress the second probability and write $x_{1_{p_1}} x_2$ instead of $(p_1:x_1, p_2: x_2)$, and $\alpha_p\beta$ instead of $(p:\alpha, 1-p:\beta)$. For a given prospect, the probabilities p_j are the *outcome probabilities*. It is implicitly understood that outcome probabilities are nonnegative and sum to 1. A prospect x, being a probability distribution over the reals, assigns to each interval in the reals the probability that the outcome of the prospect will fall into that interval. The *preference relation* over prospects is again denoted by $\succcurlyeq$.

The figure illustrates the prospect $(\frac{3}{6}:20, \frac{1}{6}:14, \frac{2}{6}:12)$. The circle at the beginning is a *chance node*. *Branches* lead to the outcomes. The corresponding probabilities have been indicated.

The next figure illustrates the riskless prospect $(1:10)$. In general, a *riskless*, or *degenerate*, prospect yields one fixed outcome with probability 1. It is identified with the outcome. For instance, the outcome 10 is identified with the depicted riskless prospect.

The following assumption is commonly made for decision under risk, and we make it too. It requires that the underlying state space that generates the randomness is sufficiently rich to generate all probabilities. In particular, S is infinite.

Assumption 2.2.1 [Richness for decision under risk]. Every probability distribution over the outcomes that takes only finitely many values is available in the preference domain. □

---

[1] Formally: There is a finite set of outcomes that has probability 1.

Although probabilities are unknown in most practical decision situations, cases of known probabilities are still important. In such cases decision theory can be applied especially fruitfully, in particular if several persons are involved so that agreement and clear communication about probabilities are desirable. Decisions under risk can also serve as a useful benchmark for general decisions under uncertainty, for example when defining attitudes towards ambiguity, as will be explained later.

2.3   Decision under risk as a special case of decision under uncertainty; continued

This is one of several sections in this book that can be skipped without loss of continuity. Such possibilities can be inferred from Appendix K. Hence, in similar cases in future sections this point will not be mentioned again.

It is useful to keep in mind that decision under risk is a special case of decision under uncertainty with the underlying state space suppressed for the sake of convenience. The state space describes the physical process that generates the randomness underlying the probabilities. The following example shows that for decision under risk without a state space specified, a state space (we will construct $S = [0,1)$) can always be defined to serve as underlying state space after all, with respect to which Structural Assumption 1.2.1 (decision under uncertainty) is satisfied.

Example 2.3.1. We assume decision under uncertainty with the unit interval $[0,1)$ as (infinite) state space S, as in Example 2.1.4. In what follows, it will be notationally convenient to have S and other events left-closed and right-open (so that disjoint unions generate same kinds of events). We imagine that an arbitrary number will be drawn from S, and the true state s is the number that will be drawn. Event $[\frac{3}{6}, \frac{4}{6})$, for instance, refers to the event that the number drawn will weakly exceed $\frac{3}{6}$ but will be strictly below $\frac{4}{6}$. An example of an event-contingent prospect is $([0, \frac{3}{6}) : 20, [\frac{3}{6}, \frac{4}{6}) : 14, [\frac{4}{6}, 1) : 12)$, yielding outcome 20 if the number s drawn is less than $\frac{3}{6}$, yielding outcome 14 if $\frac{3}{6} \leq s < \frac{4}{6}$, and yielding outcome 12 if $\frac{4}{6} \leq s < 1$. We will henceforth use event-contingent prospects – random variables – defined on intervals, such as $x = ([0,q_1):x_1, [q_1,q_2):x_2, \ldots, [q_{n-1},1):x_n)$, yielding x_j if $q_{j-1} \leq s < q_j$, for $0 = q_0 < q_1 < \cdots < q_n = 1$.

We use the Lebesgue measure λ defined in §2.1 as probability measure on $S = [0,1)$. Writing $p_j = q_j - q_{j-1}$, the prospect x yields outcome x_1 with probability $p_1,\ldots$, and outcome x_n with probability p_n. It constitutes a probability distribution $p_1x_1\ldots p_nx_n$ over the reals, with the p_j's the outcome probabilities. In other words, it generates a probability-contingent prospect. The event-contingent prospect $([0, \frac{3}{6}) : 20, [\frac{3}{6}, \frac{4}{6}) : 14, [\frac{4}{6}, 1) : 12)$, for example, generates the depicted probability-contingent prospect $(\frac{3}{6} : 20, \frac{1}{6} : 14, \frac{2}{6} : 12)$. The event-contingent prospects $([0, \frac{1}{3}) : 30, [\frac{1}{3}, \frac{2}{3}) : 20, [\frac{2}{3}, 1) : 10)$ and $([0, \frac{1}{3}) : 20, [\frac{1}{3}, \frac{2}{3}) : 10, [\frac{2}{3}, 1) : 30)$ both yield the outcomes 10, 20, or 30, each with probability $\frac{1}{3}$, so

that both generate the probability-contingent prospect $(\frac{1}{3} : 10, \frac{1}{3} : 20, \frac{1}{3} : 30)$.
We assume Assumption 2.1.2. Assumptions 1.2.1 and 2.2.1 are also satisfied. □

The following example illustrates a case where both subjective and objective
probabilities are given, and where they must agree. For simplicity, we assume
expected value in the example. That the result holds in almost complete generality,
also if expected value is not assumed, is shown after.

Example 2.3.2 [Objective and subjective probabilities agree under expected value
maximization]. Assume Example 2.1.1. Further assume that decision under risk holds,
and that the conditions of de Finetti's Theorem 1.6.1 also hold. Then preferences
maximize expected value with respect to a subjective probability measure Q that in
principle might be different from P. We show

$$Q = P. \tag{2.3.1}$$

Explanation. The prospects $(s_1:0, s_2:100, s_3:0)$ and $(s_1:100, s_2:0, s_3:100)$ generate
the same objective probability distribution over outcomes, namely $100_{\frac{1}{2}}0$. Hence,
they are equivalent by the assumption of decision under risk. This implies that their
subjective expected values, $Q(s_2)100$ and $(Q(s_1) + Q(s_3))100$, must be the same.
Hence, $Q(s_2) = (Q(s_1) + Q(s_3)) = \frac{1}{2}$. The prospects $(s_1:100, s_2:0, s_3:0)$ and $(s_1:0, s_2:0,$
$s_3:100)$ also generate the same objective probability distribution over outcomes,
namely $(\frac{1}{4}:100, \frac{3}{4}:0)$, and are therefore also equivalent by the assumption of decision
under risk. Then $Q(s_1)100 = Q(s_3)100$, and $Q(s_1) = Q(s_3)$ follows. Because these
subjective probabilities sum to $\frac{1}{2}$, each must be $\frac{1}{4}$. We conclude that Eq. (2.3.1)
holds. Hence, preferences maximize objective expected value in this example. □

The following exercise shows that, under mild assumptions, subjective probabilities must agree with objective probabilities, also if expected value maximization does
not hold. This result will hold for all models considered later in this book. The result
implies that the (subjective) probability models developed by de Finetti (1931a),
Savage (1954), and others do not *deviate* from objective probability models, but
generalize them by also incorporating situations in which no objective probabilities
are given. There have been some misunderstandings about this issue, primarily in
the psychological literature. It was sometimes believed, erroneously, that the
("subjective") expected utility models of Savage (1954) and others were developed
to allow subjective probabilities to deviate from objective probabilities (Edwards
1954 pp. 396–397, corrected in Edwards 1962 p. 115; Lopes 1987 p. 258). In modern
papers, the term subjective probability is still sometimes used in this unfortunate
sense. This misunderstanding may have contributed to the unfortunate separation
between risk and uncertainty in some parts of the literature. Mosteller & Nogee (1951
p. 398 and footnote 16) presented a clear and correct discussion.

Exercise 2.3.1[b] [Subjective probabilities must agree with objective probabilities
under stochastic dominance]. Assume that S = [0,1) with P the Lebesgue measure
$(P([a,b)) = b - a)$, and assume weak ordering. Define $E_j = [\frac{j-1}{6}, \frac{j}{6})$. Consider
event-contingent prospects of the form $E_1x_1. . .E_6x_6$, assigning x_j to all states s in

the interval $[\frac{j-1}{6}, \frac{j}{6})$. Assume (deviating from Exercise 1.6.7) that decision under risk holds in two ways at the same time for the preference relation $\succcurlyeq$: it holds with respect to the objective probability measure P, but also with respect to a, possibly different, subjective probability measure Q. Note that this concerns one and the same preference relation, for which both of these assumptions hold at the same time.

Regarding P, the value of a prospect depends only on the probability distribution generated over outcomes through P. For example, the event-contingent prospect $100_{E_1}0$, yielding 100 if the true state is below $\frac{1}{6}$ and yielding zero otherwise, is equivalent to the event-contingent prospect $100_{E_6}0$, yielding 100 if the true state is at least $\frac{5}{6}$ and yielding 0 otherwise. We further assume a strict stochastic dominance condition with respect to Q: $100_A0 \succ 100_B0$ whenever $Q(A) > Q(B)$. This condition holds, for instance, under EV maximization. Write $q_j = Q(E_j)$. Show that $q_1 = \cdots = q_6 = \frac{1}{6}$.

Comment.[!] For any event E with objective probability $P(E) = \frac{1}{6}$ we can construct a 6-fold partition of S with E one of the elements and all elements of the partition having P-value $\frac{1}{6}$. It follows in the same way as in Exercise 2.3.1 that these events have Q-value $\frac{1}{6}$, too. We can in the same way show that all events with objective probability $1/m$ must also have subjective probability $1/m$. By taking unions we see that all events with objective rational probabilities j/m have the same subjective probabilities j/m. It then readily follows (bounding between rational-probability sub- and supersets) that irrational (in the mathematical sense of being no fraction of integers) objective probabilities must also be identical to subjective probabilities. Hence, for rich event spaces, subjective probabilities must indeed agree with objective probabilities.

Further Comment. I briefly discuss situations in which the result of this exercise can be violated. One assumption underlying our analysis is typical of decision theory and is made throughout this book: All prospects are conceivable and the preference relation is complete over all these conceivable prospects. De Finetti, more generally, proved his bookmaking theorem (Theorem 1.6.1) on any linear subspace of prospects. Such cases are important in finance. Financial markets are often incomplete, i.e. it cannot be assumed that all conceivable prospects are available. For example, a prospect 100_E0 with E the event that the economy goes down dramatically and every one is losing is not plausible. It may then happen that the result of this exercise does not hold, and risk neutral market ("subjective") probabilities can deviate from objective statistical probabilities. The deviation may be generated by risk aversion and state dependence of utility (see Example 2.1.1; it will be defined formally later) for instance, with different marginal utilities for different events. This point is central to many works (Kadane & Winkler 1988; Karni 1996; Nau 2003 opening paragraph). The discrepancy between market probabilities and objective probabilities can be used to estimate risk aversion (Bliss & Panigirtzoglou 2004).[2] □

---

[2] Pfanzagl (1968 Theorem 12.6.17) presented further results on the equality of objective and subjective probabilities.

Assignment 2.3.2.[b] Assume weak ordering, monotonicity, and Assumption 2.1.2 (decision under risk). Assume S = [0,1), with the probability measure P on S the Lebesgue measure. Let x be the event-contingent prospect ([0,⅓):1, [⅓,⅔):2, [⅔,1):3), and let y be the event-contingent prospect ([0,⅓):3, [⅓,⅔):4, [⅔,1):2). Show that y ≻ x. □

2.4   Choices under risk and decision trees

Fig. 2.4.1a shows two prospects, the upper one yielding $80 with probability 0.5 and $60 with probability 0.5, and the lower one yielding $95 with probability 0.5 and $70 with probability 0.5. The figure displays a choice situation in which you have to choose between the upper and the lower prospect. The square is a *decision node*; that is, it indicates a situation in which you must choose. Such figures are read from left to right. For instance, Fig. a illustrates a situation where first you arrive at the square node and have to choose if you prefer up or down. If you choose up, you end up in the circle designating the prospect 80½60. If you choose down, you receive 95½70. Fig. b again starts with a decision node where you are to decide which way to go, up or down. Then chance nodes result where chance decides where to go. In Fig. b you have to choose between two prospects each yielding $40 or $20, yielding the higher outcome with probability 0.7 (after up in the decision node) or with probability 0.6 (after down in the decision node).

Exercise 2.4.1.[a] Determine in each of the eight situations depicted in Figure 2.4.1 whether you prefer the upper or the lower prospect. Keep your answers for later use. □

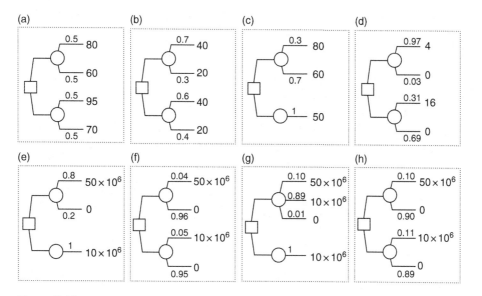

Figure 2.4.1

The choice situations in (a), (b), and (c) were trivial. The lower prospect in (a) results from the upper one by replacing the outcome 80 by the outcome 95 and the outcome 60 by the outcome 70. In other words, the lower prospect simply gives better outcomes. It is therefore obvious that the lower prospect is preferable. In (b), the upper prospect results from the lower one by shifting 0.1 probability mass from the bad outcome 20 to the good outcome 40, which again is a definite improvement. In (c), the lower prospect results from the upper one by replacing both outcomes by the worse outcome 50 (or, by shifting all probability mass from the outcomes 80 and 60 to the worse outcome 50) and, hence, it is obvious that the upper prospect is preferable.

If you are indifferent, in Fig. 2.4.1e, between the upper and the lower prospect, then your certainty equivalent for the upper prospect is 10×10^6. It implies that you would equally well like to receive 10×10^6 for sure as 50×10^6 with probability 0.8 (and nothing with probability 0.2).

Exercise 2.4.2.[a] Substitute your own certainty equivalent for both prospects depicted in Figure 2.4.2.

(a)   (b)

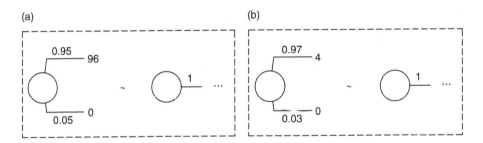

Figure 2.4.2

☐

Further discussion of the choices is postponed until §2.8, although it can be understood at this stage so that interested readers can read §2.8 immediately.

Finally, we define risk aversion and risk seeking. Although these concepts will be analyzed only in later chapters, they are defined here to stress their theory-free status. They concern phenomena regarding preferences without any theory assumed. Unfortunately, risk aversion is often confused with concave utility (concepts defined later) in the economic literature. As always in this book, preference without qualification refers to weak preference and not to strict preference.

Definition 2.4.1.

- *Risk aversion* holds if every prospect is less preferred than its expected value.
- *Risk seeking* holds if every prospect is preferred to its expected value.
- *Risk neutrality* holds if every prospect is indifferent to its expected value. ☐

Risk aversion implies, for example, $50 \succcurlyeq 100_{1/2}0$, and risk seeking implies $50 \preccurlyeq 100_{1/2}0$. Risk neutrality means that both risk aversion and risk seeking hold, and it is just another name for expected value maximization. Then $50 \sim 100_{1/2}0$. It was used in Chapter 1.

2.5 Expected utility and utility measurement

De Finetti's Theorem 1.6.1 gave a behavioral foundation for expected value maximization for decision under uncertainty. The result can be applied to decision under risk as well. Exercise 2.3.1 and its comment showed that objective and subjective probabilities usually agree. Hence, Theorem 1.6.1, when stated for decision under risk, can serve as a behavioral foundation for expected value maximization.

For expected value maximization under risk there are no free subjective parameters in the model. Preferences are uniquely determined and all expected value maximizers behave the same way. With probabilities and outcomes given, we can immediately calculate expected value. The expected value criterion is thus directly observable by itself and does not need a behavioral foundation. It is its own, trivial, behavioral foundation so to speak. In terms of expected utility for uncertainty defined later, expected value for decision under risk concerns the special case where both probabilities and utilities are known, so that nothing about decision attitude remains to be discovered.

Table 1.5.4 of finance with bankruptcy at $-70K$ illustrated a case where outcomes were so large that violations of expected value were plausible. The rest of this chapter examines this case for decision under risk. Henceforth, probabilities are known but now utilities will be unknown. The following illustration of a violation of expected value is not very realistic and has a didactical confound (the complexities of infinity). To my surprise, experience has shown that it still works well didactically because students like it. The example is historically important because it led Bernoulli (1738) to develop expected utility. We will return to the example with Bernoulli's explanation later.

Example 2.5.1 [St. Petersburg paradox]. Consider the following game. A fair coin will be flipped until the first heads shows up. If heads shows up at the kth flip, then you receive $\$2^k$. Thus, immediate heads gives only $2, and after each tails the amount doubles. After 19 tails you are sure to be a millionaire. Think for yourself how much it would be worth to you to play this game. The expected value of the game is

$$\tfrac{1}{2} \times 2 + \tfrac{1}{4} \times 4 + \tfrac{1}{8} \times 8 + \tfrac{1}{16} \times 16 + \cdots = 1 + 1 + 1 + 1 + \cdots = \infty.$$

Thus if you maximize expected value, then this game is worth more to you than any amount of money. In reality, people pay considerably less to participate in the game, something like $5 (as Bernoulli wrote based on casual observations), showing that expected value does not hold empirically when large amounts are involved. □

In Chapter 1 we first introduced a number of plausible preference conditions. We then came to the, possibly surprising, conclusion that a specific preference model was implied, namely EV. §1.8 further discussed general features of such behavioral foundations. We could present all behavioral foundations in the same spirit, especially those with a normative status. For brevity's sake, we will not do so. We follow a different system henceforth, as stated in the Introduction. It is shorter and can be applied both normatively and descriptively, and is as follows. First an empirical measurement of the subjective parameters is described that relates them directly to preferences. Next, consistency of measurement gives a behavioral foundation.

We summarize the structural assumption needed for the following analysis. It is implied by Assumptions 1.2.1 (decision under uncertainty), 2.1.2 (decision under risk), and 2.2.1 (richness), as can be seen.

Structural Assumption 2.5.2 [Decision under risk and richness]. $\succcurlyeq$ is a preference relation over the set of all (probability-contingent) prospects, i.e., over all finite probability distributions over the outcome set $\mathbb{R}$. □

Definition 2.5.3. Under Structural Assumption 2.5.2, *expected utility (EU)* holds if there exists a strictly increasing function U, the *utility (function)*, from the outcome set to $\mathbb{R}$, such that the evaluation depicted in Figure 2.5.1 represents preferences. □

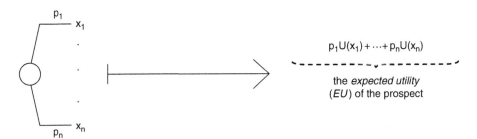

Figure 2.5.1

Under EU, the utility function is the subjective parameter characterizing the decision maker. The following exercise shows how to derive decisions from the EU model. Its elaboration is immediately given in the main text.

Exercise 2.5.1.[a] Assume EU with $U(0) = 0$, $U(100) = 1$, $U(81) = 0.9$. Determine the preference between $100_{0.9}0$ and $100_{0.1}81$. □

In Exercise 2.5.1
$EU(100_{0.9}0) = 0.90 \times U(100) + 0.10 \times U(0) = 0.90$;
$EU(100_{0.1}81) = 0.10 \times U(100) + 0.90 \times U(81) = 0.10 + 0.81 = 0.91$.
Hence $100_{0.1}81$ has the higher EU and is preferred.

Exercise 2.5.2.[a] Assume EU with $U(\alpha) = \sqrt{\alpha}$. Determine the preference between $49_{0.9}16$ and $81_{0.7}16$. □

Example 2.5.4 [St. Petersburg paradox explained using EU]. Consider Example 2.5.1. Bernoulli argued that expected utility with a logarithmic utility function is plausible. Then the expected utility of the game is

$$\sum_{j=1}^{\infty} 2^{-j} ln(2^j) = \sum_{j=1}^{\infty} j \, 2^{-j} ln(2) = 2ln(2) = ln(4).^3$$

Hence the certainty equivalent is $4, fitting Bernoulli's empirical claims well. □
    As in §1.3, we can use the elicitation method, and derive properties of utility from observed choices. Part (a) of the following exercise, and what follows, illustrate this point. The exercise illustrates the applicability of expected utility, with some choices used to assess the model and this assessment subsequently used to predict new choices. Its elaboration is given immediately following the exercise.

Exercise 2.5.3.[a] Assume that you observe some preferences of an agent. You know that the agent satisfies EU, and can set $U(0) = 0$ and $U(100) = 1$.

(a) Assume that $50 \sim 100_{0.58}0$ for the agent. What is $U(50)$?
(b) Under the indifference in part (a), you can predict the agent's preference
    between (0.40:100, 0.20:50, 0.40:0) and (0.33:100, 0.33:50, 0.34:0). What is it?

Elaboration.

(a) Because of the equivalence, $U(50) = EU(100_{0.58}0) = 0.58 \times 1 + 0.42 \times 0 = 0.58$.
(b) $EU(0.40{:}100, 0.20{:}50, 0.40{:}0) = 0.40 \times 1 + 0.20 \times 0.58 + 0.40 \times 0 =$
    $0.40 + 0.116 + 0 = 0.516$.

   $EU(0.33{:}100, 0.33{:}50, 0.34{:}0) = 0.33 \times 1 + 0.33 \times 0.58 + 0.34 \times 0 = 0.33 +$
   $0.191 + 0 = 0.521$.

   The latter prospect has the higher EU and is preferred. □

Exercise 2.5.4.[a] Assume EU with $U(0) = 0$ and $U(100) = 1$.

(a) Assume that $60 \sim 100_{0.70}0$ for the agent. What is $U(60)$?
(b) Under the indifference in part (a), what is the preference between $60_{0.70}0$
    and $100_{0.49}0$? □

The best way to learn about the general way to measure utility is to invent it by yourself. You can do so in the following exercise. Its elaboration is given next in the main text.

Exercise 2.5.5.[a] Assume EU with $U(0) = 0$ and $U(100) = 1$. What kind of preferences should you observe to find out what $U(30)$ and $U(70)$ are? □

---

[3] Second"=": $\sum_{j=1}^{\infty} j2^{-j} = \sum_{j=1}^{\infty} 2^{-j} + \sum_{j=1}^{\infty}(j-1)2^{-j} = 1 + \frac{1}{2}\sum_{j=2}^{\infty}(j-1)2^{-(j-1)} = 1 + \frac{1}{2}\sum_{j=1}^{\infty} j2^{-j}$.
Then $\sum_{j=1}^{\infty} j2^{-j} = 2$.

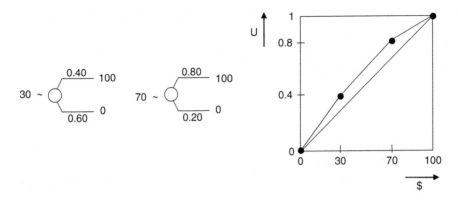

Figure 2.5.2 Two indifferences and the resulting U curve.

Measuring utility. To analyze risky decisions, we want to measure utility U. Figure 2.5.2 shows an example. Assume EU with the normalization U(0) = 0 and U(100) = 1.

The first indifference implies

$$U(30) = 0.40 \times U(100) + 0.60 \times U(0) = 0.40.$$

The second indifference implies

$$U(70) = 0.80 \times U(100) + 0.20 \times U(0) = 0.80.$$

The graph in Figure 2.5.2 then results from linear interpolation.

In general, assume two fixed outcomes M > m, and assume that we have normalized U(m) = 0 and U(M) = 1. (In Figure 2.5.2, m = 0 and M = 100.) We will see later (Exercise 2.6.4) that we may always assume such normalized utility values. For each outcome α such that M ≥ α ≥ m, we can elicit the *standard-gamble (SG) probability* with respect to m and M, being the probability p such that the equivalence in Figure 2.5.3 holds. Applying EU gives

$$U(\alpha) = pU(M) + (1 - p)U(m) = p \; [\textit{the SG Eq.}] \tag{2.5.1}$$

In other words, U(α) is simply the SG probability p. Exercises 2.5.3a and 2.5.4a illustrated this procedure.

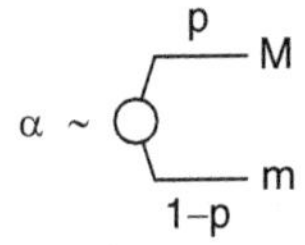

Figure 2.5.3 The SG probability p of α.

The SG method directly relates utility to decisions, in a very simple manner. The method shows how to make exchanges between outcomes and probability. This way outcomes and probabilities become commensurable. Through a SG consistency condition defined later, this commensurability will capture the essence of EU. Surveys of utility measurement under EU are in Farquhar (1984) and Seidl & Traub (1999).

Assignment 2.5.6.[c] This assignment does not concern binary choice, as does most of this book, but it concerns choosing from a continuum of prospects.

(a) Assume that you can invest an amount β at your discretion in a stock that with ½ probability yields a return of 2.5β and, thus, a profit of 1.5β. There is a probability ½ of ruin, in which case you lose your investment β. You maximize EU, with utility function $U(\alpha) = 1 - e^{-\alpha}$. How much do you invest? What are the resulting EU and CE?
(b) The same question, but now $U(\alpha) = 1 - e^{-\theta\alpha}$ for a general $\theta > 0$. (Hint: substitute $\theta\alpha$ for α in part (a)). □

2.6 Consistency of measurement and a behavioral foundation of expected utility

We assume in this chapter, as we do throughout this book, that the outcome set is $\mathbb{R}$. It can be seen, though, that the behavioral foundation of expected utility presented in Theorem 2.6.3, and the analysis of this whole chapter, hold for general outcome sets, and that we never need the outcome set to be $\mathbb{R}$. The only change required for general outcomes is that inequalities between outcomes such as $M > m$ be replaced by preferences between outcomes such as $M \succ m$.

A necessary condition for EU to hold, and for the measurement of utility to work well, is that a probability p to solve the indifference in Figure 2.5.3 exists for all $M > \alpha > m$. This requirement is called *standard-gamble (SG) solvability*. It is the only continuity-like condition needed in the analysis to follow. It entails that the probability scale is at least as refined as the outcome scale. Solvability conditions are less restrictive and better capture the empirical meaning of a model than continuity (which essentially needs connectedness of the reals in preference foundations; Luce *et al.* 1990 p. 49 l. 10; Wakker 1988).

Another immediate implication of EU, based on utility being strictly increasing, is as follows.

Standard-gamble (SG) dominance. For all outcomes M > m and probabilities p > q:

Moving positive probability mass from an outcome to a strictly better outcome entails a strict improvement. The condition is a weak version of stochastic dominance (defined later).

Exercise 2.6.1.[a] Assume EU. Verify, for general U(M) > U(m), that $p = (U(\alpha) - U(m))/(U(M) - U(m))$ in Figure 2.5.3. □

Exercise 2.6.2.[b] Show that SG dominance holds under EU. In other words, assume a preference relation over prospects that can be represented by EU. Show that the preference relation satisfies SG dominance. □

Exercise 2.6.3.[b] Assume weak ordering, SG dominance, and SG solvability. Show, for M > m, that for the SG probability p in Figure 2.5.3:

(a) p is uniquely determined.
(b) If $\alpha \sim m$, then p = 0.
(c) If $\alpha \sim M$, then p = 1.
(d) If $m < \alpha < M$, then $0 < p < 1$. □

The following exercise deals with an important property of the utility function in expected utility. If you have no clue how to resolve the exercise, then a comment similar to the one preceding Exercise 1.3.4 applies. You probably have not yet fully internalized the conceptual meaning of decision models. A rethinking of Definition 2.5.3 and Exercise 2.5.3, and a rereading of some of the preceding text, may then be useful. Alchian (1953) gives a didactic and detailed account of the empirical meaning of utility and of the following exercise.

Exercise 2.6.4[a] [Free level and unit of U]. Show that, if EU holds with a utility function U – i.e., the expectations of U as in Figure 2.5.1 represent preferences – then so does EU with utility function $U^* = \tau + \sigma U$, where $\tau \in \mathbb{R}$ and $\sigma > 0$. □

Exercise 2.6.4 shows that we can normalize the utility scale as we like, and choose where U will be 0 and 1.

Exercise 2.6.5.[c] Assume EU. Show that U is continuous if and only if there exists a certainty equivalent for each prospect. □

The implications of EU just described are relatively uncontroversial. We now turn to the most interesting, and most controversial, implication – the well-known independence condition. We consider here a version called standard gamble consistency, which states the condition in terms of consistency of utility measurement. Most normative discussions of EU concern the independence condition. Empirical tests of EU and its alternatives usually examine how independence is violated, and most nonexpected utility models weaken independence in specific ways. Such alternative models will be presented later.

In a perfect world where EU would hold perfectly well, the utility measurement through the SG probability in Figure 2.5.3 would provide exact measurements of U that would give perfect predictions. Unfortunately, there usually are measurement errors and biases, and models do not hold perfectly well. McCord & de Neufville (1986) criticized the SG method for being particularly prone to empirical biases. The main reason is that this method involves a riskless outcome α, and such outcomes are often evaluated in deviating manners, generating violations of EU. It may, therefore, be safer to avoid their use. McCord & de Neufville, and several other authors (Carthy *et al.* 1999 §2; Davidson, Suppes, & Siegel 1957; Officer & Halter 1968 p. 259), recommended embedding SG indifferences as in Figure 2.5.3 into more complex risky choice prospects. To prepare for this embedding, we discuss the (probabilistic) mixing of prospects such as $x_\lambda y$, clarified in the next example.

Example 2.6.1 [Probabilistic mixing of prospects]. Consider the left-hand two-stage prospect in Figure 2.6.1. In the first chance node there is a ½ probability of going up and a ½ probability of going down. If up, the prospect $200_{1/3}0$ results. These ⅓ and ⅔ probabilities are conditional probabilities, being conditional on the event of going up. The other probabilities are similar. The probability of receiving \$200 is, therefore, $\frac{1}{2} \times \frac{1}{3} = \frac{1}{6}$, the probability of \$100 is also ⅙, and the probability of 0 is $\frac{1}{2} \times \frac{2}{3} + \frac{1}{2} \times \frac{2}{3} = \frac{2}{3}$. That is, the probability distribution is the same as in the right-hand prospect.

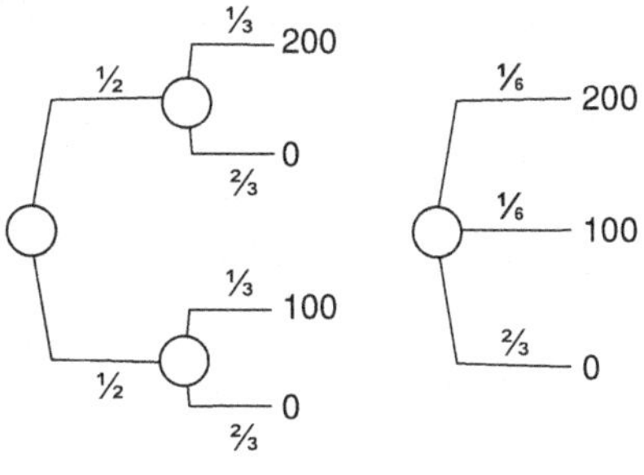

Figure 2.6.1

□

Definition 2.6.2. For general prospects x, y, and $0 \leq \lambda \leq 1$, the mixture depicted in Fig. 2.6.2a, also denoted $x_\lambda y$, is the prospect that assigns, to each outcome α, λ times the probability of α under x plus $1-\lambda$ times the probability of α under y. It is called a (*probabilistic*) *mixture* of x and y. □

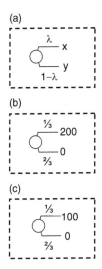

Figure 2.6.2

In Figure 2.6.1, x was the prospect in Fig. 2.6.2b, y was the one in Fig. 2.6.2c, and λ was ½. The mixture $x_\lambda y$ can be thought of as resulting from a two-stage procedure, where in the first stage prospect x results with probability λ and prospect y with probability 1−λ, and in the second stage the prospect resulting from the first stage (x or y, as the case may be) is played out.[4] Figure 2.6.3 shows another example.

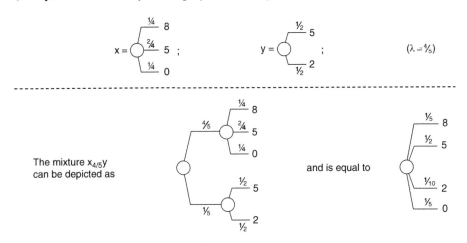

Figure 2.6.3

---

[4] This footnote is meant to be read only by specialists in decision theory. It concerns the reduction of compound lotteries (= prospects) assumption. If mixtures of prospects are interpreted as physically resulting from a two-stage procedure, with physical time proceeding, then the *reduction of compound prospects assumption* is used, which entails that probabilities of subsequent chance nodes are multiplied. In our analysis, the only objects considered are one-stage prospects. Two-stage illustrations are only a didactic device for depicting one-stage prospects.

I next discuss linearity of EU in probabilities. Because this property is important for understanding EU, I shall explain it in some detail. We first consider this property for general integrals. If with probability ½ you receive a prospect with expected return $100, and with probability ½ you receive a prospect with expected return $200, then your expected return is ½ × 100 + ½ × 200 = 150. If you receive a medical treatment where:

- with probability ¼ people live for another 40 years on average,
- with probability ¾ people live for another 4 years on average,

then on average you live for another ¼ × 40 + ¾ × 4 = 10 + 3 = 13 years.

In general, if prospect x has an expectation (of money, life duration, or whatever) EV(x) and prospect y has an expectation EV(y), then receiving x with probability λ and y with probability $1-\lambda$ has expectation λEV(x) + $(1-\lambda)$EV(y). This means that expectation is linear with respect to probabilistic mixing. The result holds in particular for EU, that is, not only if the expectation concerns money or life years, but also if the expectation concerns utility. If x has expected utility EU(x), and y has expected utility EU(y), then receiving x with probability λ and y with probability $1-\lambda$ has expected utility λEU(x) + $(1-\lambda)$EU(y).

Exercise 2.6.6.[a] Show that EU is *linear in probability*; i.e., EU($x_\lambda y$) = λEU(x) + $(1-\lambda)$EU(y). □

We now return to the idea of McCord & de Neufville (1986). They proposed to consider equivalences such as in Figure 2.6.4, rather than the SG equivalences of Figure 2.5.3. They called the resulting measurement method the lottery-equivalent method. Basically, the same indifference is elicited as in Figure 2.5.3, but now α and the equivalent SG-prospect have been mixed with another "common" prospect C. This way they avoid the use of riskless prospects.

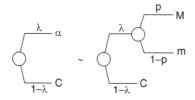

Figure 2.6.4 The lottery-equivalent method of McCord & de Neufville (1986) ($\lambda > 0$).

Because of the linearity in probability of EU (Exercise 2.6.6), the EU of the left prospect in the figure is λU(α) + $(1-\lambda)$EU(C), and of the right prospect it is λ(pU(M) + $(1-p)$U(m)) + $(1-\lambda)$EU(C). The equality of these expected utilities implies the same equality U(α) = pU(M) + $(1-p)$U(m) = p as resulting from the SG equivalence of the preceding section (the SG Eq. (2.5.1)).[5]

---

[5] Cancel the common term $(1-\lambda)$EU(C), divide by the positive λ, and set again U(m) = 0 and U(M) = 1.

In a perfect world where EU would hold perfectly well, there would be no inconsistencies in observations. Then it would not matter if we use Figure 2.5.3 or Figure 2.6.4 to measure p, and p should be the same in both figures. This identity requirement is called standard-gamble (SG) consistency. Then the indifference in Figure 2.5.3 should always imply the indifference in Figure 2.6.4. This implication is stated formally in Figure 2.6.5.

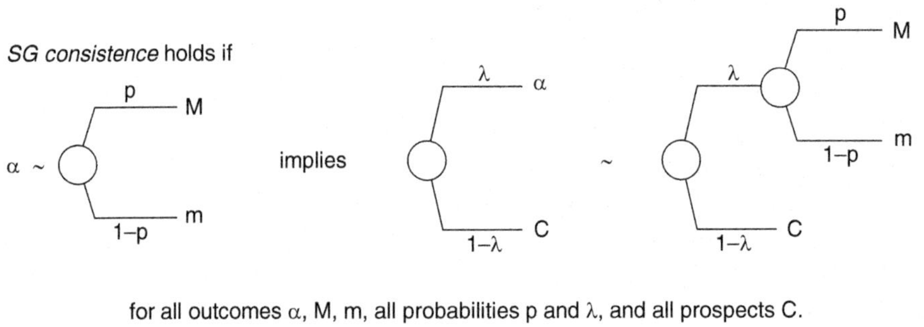

SG consistence holds if

for all outcomes α, M, m, all probabilities p and λ, and all prospects C.

Figure 2.6.5

The condition has normative appeal. If the left indifference in Figure 2.6.5 – i.e., the indifference in Figure 2.5.3 – holds, then in the right indifference (Figure 2.6.4) you receive the same C for both prospects if going down $(1-\lambda)$, and equivalent things if going up (λ), so that you are equally well off in either case. Hence, the two compound prospects seem to be equally attractive to you. The following theorem shows that SG consistency, a weak version of the well-known independence condition (see next section) together with some natural conditions, is not only necessary, but also sufficient, for EU. Von Neumann & Morgenstern (1947) presented a first version of this theorem, but their result was incomplete. Several authors have subsequently contributed to variations of the result (Fishburn 1970 p. 103). The following theorem is yet another variation.

Theorem 2.6.3 [EU for risk]. Under Structural Assumption 2.5.2 (decision under risk and richness), the following two statements are equivalent.

(i) Expected utility holds.
(ii) $\succcurlyeq$ satisfies:
   • weak ordering;
   • SG solvability;
   • SG dominance;
   • SG consistency. □

We saw, in Exercise 2.6.4, that the utility U can be replaced by any $U^* = \tau + \sigma U$ for real τ and positive σ. Here σ is the *unit parameter* because it determines the unit of measurement and τ is the *level parameter* because it affects absolute levels of utility. It turns out that no other utility functions are possible than the ones just described.

In general, a function in a particular model is *unique up to unit and level* if it can be replaced by another function if and only if the other function differs by unit and level. We also call such functions *interval scales*. The term cardinal has also been used to refer to this mathematical property, but this term has many interpretational connotations. We therefore will not use it.

Observation 2.6.3′ [Uniqueness result for Theorem 2.6.3]. In EU, utility is unique up to level and unit. □

Comment 2.6.4 [Organization of measurements and behavioral foundations; the five-step presentation]. The line of presentation leading to Theorem 2.6.3 is typical of the presentation of decision models throughout this book. It involved the following five steps: (1) The model, EU, was defined in Definition 2.5.3, with utility as subjective parameter; (2) Exercises 2.5.1 and 2.5.2 showed how to derive decisions from the model's parameters; (3) Exercises 2.3–2.5 and Eq. (2.5.1) presented the elicitation method for deriving the model's parameters from decisions; (4) §2.6 presented consistency conditions for measurements; (5) the consistency conditions for measurements gave a behavioral foundation in Theorem 2.6.3. □

Comment 2.6.5 [Variance of utility]. It may be surprising that only the probability-weighted average of utility plays a role under EU, and no other aspects of the utility distribution. Receiving a utility of 0.6 for sure is equated with receiving utility 1 with probability 0.6 and utility 0 with probability 0.4. It may seem that the risk and, for instance, the variance of the utility received should also be relevant and that they are inappropriately ignored here (Gandjour 2008 p. 1210; Rode *et al.* 1999 p. 271). The key to understanding why this is not so, and to understanding the essence of utility, lies in the SG Figure 2.5.3. Because utility is measured in this way, essentially in terms of probabilities, it becomes commensurable with probability and risk. The critical condition of EU, SG consistency, implies that the exchange rate between value and risk as measured in the SG equivalence is universally valid, also within complex decision trees. In this manner, all of probability and risk that is relevant for the preference value of prospects is captured by utility and its average. □

2.7   Independence and other preference conditions for expected utility

In the literature, many variations have been used of the preference conditions presented in the preceding section. Somewhat stronger (more restrictive) than SG consistency is the *substitution principle*:

$$x \sim y \text{ implies } \quad \underset{1-\lambda}{\overset{\lambda}{\underset{}{}}} \begin{matrix} x \\ c \end{matrix} \sim \underset{1-\lambda}{\overset{\lambda}{\underset{}{}}} \begin{matrix} y \\ c \end{matrix} .$$

It entails that replacing a prospect in a mixture by another equally good prospect does not affect the preference value of the mixture. SG consistency concerned the special case where x was a sure outcome and y a two-outcome prospect. Yet stronger is the *independence condition*, a condition most often used in the literature for behavioral foundations of EU:

$$x \succcurlyeq y \text{ implies} \quad \bigcirc \!\!\begin{array}{l} \overline{}^{\lambda}\!\!-x \\ \underline{}_{1-\lambda}\,C \end{array} \succcurlyeq \bigcirc \!\!\begin{array}{l} \overline{}^{\lambda}\!\!-y \\ \underline{}_{1-\lambda}\,C \end{array} \;.$$

It entails that improving a prospect in a mixture improves the mixture. Substitution follows by first applying independence with $x \succcurlyeq y$ and then with $x \preccurlyeq y$. A violation of independence suggests a violation of a conservation-of-preference principle, alluded to before when discussing Dutch books. Although I will not try to formalize this general idea, the following reasoning may be suggestive: If the preference between the mixtures were reversed so that replacing x by y in the mixture would lead to a strictly preferred prospect, then we would have created positive preference value by keeping C fixed and worsening x. It signals that there must be some positive interaction between C and y (or negative between C and x). Given that in no possible physical world C and x, or C and y, can coexist (you never receive both C and x, or both C and y), the interaction must be purely psychological, occurring only in the mind of the decision maker. The decision maker is, magically, creating value out of nothing but own imagination.

Independence, and its weakenings presented here, may seem to be completely self-evident at first sight, and I also think they *are* normatively compelling. However, these conditions have many implications, and many people, upon examining the implications, come to reject independence as a universal normative principle. As the psychologist Duncan Luce once put it (Luce 2000 §2.4.2), "Although this line of rational argument seems fairly compelling in the abstract, it loses its force in some concrete situations." We will return to criticisms of independence in later sections.

Because SG consistency is weaker than independence, the implication of (ii) ⇒ (i) in Theorem 2.6.3 (EU for risk) with SG consistency is a stronger result than it would be if independence were to replace SG consistency. The result with independence follows as an immediate corollary of the result with SG consistency and this does not hold the other way around. In this sense, SG consistency is a more useful preference condition.

In many applications, the implication (i) ⇒ (ii) in Theorem 2.6.3 is useful. Strong preference conditions may be interesting in such applications. For example, if we want to falsify EU empirically, then it will be easier to obtain violations of independence than of SG consistency. Because independence is stronger than SG consistency, violations of the former are easier to detect than violations of the latter. For example, if there are no indifferences in our data then SG consistency cannot be falsified in any direct manner, but independence can be. This will happen, for instance, when we discuss the Allais paradox in §4.12. This paradox directly falsifies independence, showing that EU is violated, but it does not directly falsify SG consistency. Hence, it is useful to know various preference conditions for decision theories, and not only the weakest ones that give the most general behavioral foundations.

In the presence of the other conditions for EU, SG dominance implies a very natural condition, usually considered a hallmark of rationality, namely *(first-order) stochastic dominance*: shifting probability mass from an outcome to a preferred outcome should lead to a preferred prospect. In other words, the more money the better. This preference condition extends SG dominance to general prospects with possibly more than two outcomes, using weak (unqualified) rather than strict preference. As will be explained later, the condition defined here is equivalent to other formulations used in the literature, stated in terms of distribution functions or improvements of outcomes.

Exercise 2.7.1.[!a] Show that EU implies stochastic dominance. □

Exercise 2.7.2.[b] Use Exercise 2.6.6 to show that EU implies independence. □
The following variation of independence is similar to Savage's (1954) sure-thing principle, requiring that preference be independent of common outcomes, and defined later for uncertainty (Eq. (4.8.1)). We call it the *sure-thing principle for risk*, and it is defined in Figure 2.7.1. It can be seen that independence and this condition are, in general, logically independent. In the presence of natural conditions plus a probabilistic continuity condition they become equivalent. Hence, the sure-thing principle for risk could also be used to obtain a preference foundation for EU. We do not elaborate on this point.

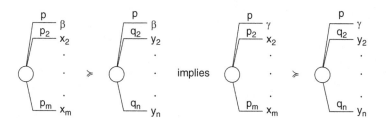

Figure 2.7.1 The sure-thing principle for risk.

Exercise 2.7.3.[!a] Show that EU implies the sure-thing principle for risk. □

2.8   Basic choice inconsistencies

The following exercise will be discussed immediately in the text that follows.

Exercise 2.8.1.[a] Substitute your own certainty equivalent for both prospects depicted in Figure 2.8.1.

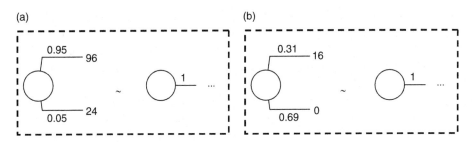

Figure 2.8.1

☐

Violations of EU will be discussed in later chapters, and the choices in Figure 2.4.1 will then play a role. This section only discusses some violations of general choice principles, revealed by the choices in Figures 2.4.1, 2.4.2, and 2.8.1. The choice in Fig. 2.4.1d can be related to Figs. 2.4.2b and 2.8.1b, where the two prospects reappear. It is natural that the prospect that you preferred in Fig. 2.4.1d had the highest certainty equivalent. If this is not the case for you, then a violation of stochastic dominance or transitivity can be derived from your choices. Empirically, a majority of subjects exhibit such a violation. That is, they choose the upper prospect in Fig. 2.4.1d but assign a lower CE to it in Fig. 2.4.2b relative to Fig. 2.8.1b. These violations are known as preference reversals (Bardsley *et al.* 2010 Box 3.4).

The certainty equivalents in Figs. 2.4.2a and Fig. 2.8.1a can also be related to each other. The prospect in Fig. 2.8.1a dominates the one in Fig. 2.4.2a because the 0 outcome has been replaced by the better outcome 24. Hence, the prospect in Fig. 2.8.1a should be preferred to the one in Fig. 2.4.2a. It should, therefore, have a higher certainty equivalent. If your certainty equivalent in Fig. 2.8.1a was lower than in Fig. 2.4.2a, then a violation of stochastic dominance or transitivity can be derived from your choices. Empirically, a majority of subjects exhibit such a violation. (You were exposed to about the most tricky stimuli that this field has developed.) This choice anomaly was first discovered by Birnbaum *et al.* (1992). Their explanation is that zero outcomes generate special biases, with people sometimes overweighting their role but on other occasions, such as here, improperly ignoring them.

Empirical findings such as those just discussed are notorious because they reveal many violations of rationality requirements, such as transitivity or stochastic dominance. The prevalence of such anomalies has led some authors to conclude that studying individual preference is a hopeless task because, as they argue, such anomalies clearly show that we are not measuring "true values" in any sense, and we are only measuring random choices. Such views are captured in pessimistic versions of the constructive view of preference, discussed by Slovic (1995). There remain, fortunately, enough regularities in data to make the empirical study of decision theory worthwhile. In addition, for many decisions, individual preferences and utilities are the crucial and decisive factors. We then have to measure them as well as we can, no matter what the difficulties are. Optimistic versions of the constructive view of preference argue that we, decision analysts, aware of the deficiencies of our measurement instruments, should work and interact more with clients, "not as archae-ologists, carefully uncovering what is there, but as architects, working to build a defensible expression of value" (Gregory, Lichtenstein, & Slovic 1993 p. 179). Using interactive sessions we can get more out of fewer subjects.

Whereas it is common jargon in the field to refer to choice anomalies as irration-alities and biases on the part of the decision makers, it may be argued that these anomalies are a problem of our measurement instruments rather than of the decision makers. The purported biases and irrationalities are usually discovered in experimental measurements of preference values. Such measurements, especially if based on hypothetical choice – as done in Figures 2.4.1, 2.4.2, and 2.8.1 – are hard to relate to for subjects. When answering the questions concerning these figures, you may have felt that your answers were at least in part random. Thus our measurement instruments, even if the best conceivable, do not perfectly tap into the value systems of subjects. In measurements of preference and value it is, therefore, desirable to clarify the nature of stimuli to subjects as much as possible, and to use real incentives in descriptive studies whenever possible.

For prescriptive purposes, a big value of decision theory lies in uncovering anomalies such as those just described. Such anomalies do exist in individual choices and indeed cannot reflect true values. By revealing such anomalies, decision theory can show people that in some situations they are not following their true value system, and that they can and should improve their decisions in such situations. In other words, in such situations decision theory can bring new insights and improve deci-sions. It can do this by using simple consistency checks, without any need to know the exact true values of a client. As pointed out by Raiffa (1961), it is not problematic but, rather, essential for prescriptive applications of decision theory that violations of the rational models exist in natural behavior.

Appendix 2.9   Proof of Theorem 2.6.3 and Observation 2.6.3′

The proof of Theorem 2.6.3 is simple. It makes a crucial achievement of EU transparent, namely that EU provides commensurability between outcomes and probability. SG measurements settle the exchange rate between outcomes and prob-abilities, and this exchange rate should subsequently apply to all situations. This is the idea underlying the proof.

It was explained in the main text that the preference conditions are necessary for EU. We, henceforth, assume the preference conditions and derive EU. Take two outcomes $M > m$. Define $U(m) = 0$ and $U(M) = 1$ for now. For each $m < \alpha < M$ define $U(\alpha)$ as the SG probability of α (Figure 2.5.3), which can be done because of SG solvability. Consider a prospect with all outcomes between m and M. Figure 2.9.1 is explained next.

The first equivalence follows from SG consistency, by replacing the riskless prospect x_j by its equivalent standard gamble. The second equivalence follows the same way, by repeated application. The equality is by multiplication of probabilities. Every prospect is thus equivalent to the prospect that with a probability equal to the EU of the original prospect yields outcome M, and outcome m otherwise. By SG

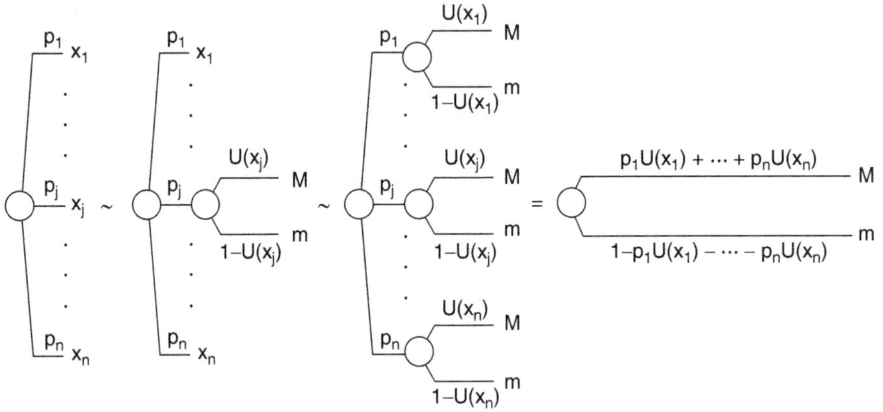

Figure 2.9.1

dominance, the latter prospects, having only m and M as outcomes, are ordered by their EU. By transitivity, so are all prospects with outcomes between m and M. We have proved that EU holds on the domain of those prospects.

For the uniqueness result in Observation 2.6.3′ applied to the domain of all prospects with outcomes between m and M, we can freely choose unit and level of U by Exercise 2.6.4. This is the only freedom we have. For any alternative U^*, we can substitute $U^*(m) = \tau$ and $U^*(M) = \sigma + \tau$ for any real τ and $\sigma > 0$, after which U^* is uniquely determined from SG equivalences as $\tau + \sigma U$ for the utility U with $U(m) = 0$ and $U(M) = 1$.

We can carry out the above reasoning for any m < M, thus obtaining EU on every bounded part of our domain and, finally, obtain EU on the whole domain by routine extensions. For the extensions of the domain (reducing m and enlarging M) it is easiest to rescale all newly defined models such that utility is 0 at the original m we started with and it is 1 at the original M we started with. Then these models all coincide on common domains by the uniqueness result just established, and they are genuine extensions of each other. Observation 2.6.3′ thus holds on the domain limited by any m and M and, consequently, on the whole domain.

By SG dominance with p = 1 and q = 0, $\alpha > \beta$ implies $\alpha \succ \beta$. This implies that U increases strictly. The proof is now complete.

The proof presented here adapts some appealing substitution-based proofs in the literature (Arrow 1951a pp. 424–425; Luce & Raiffa 1957 pp. 27–28) to our preference conditions. I constructed the proof of the bookmaking theorem in Appendix 1.11 by using the proof of this appendix and then applying a duality between states and outcomes (Abdellaoui & Wakker 2005 end of §1). Figure 1.11.1 is the analog of Figure 2.9.1. In the former figure we replaced every event E by its certainty equivalent P(E) and then used linearity in outcomes. In the latter figure we replaced every outcome by its standard-gamble probability (of getting M versus m) and then used linearity in probability. □

3 Applications of expected utility for risk

Given the many applications of expected utility for decision under risk, we dedicate a separate chapter to this topic. *Throughout this chapter we make the following assumption, often without further mention.* It implies Structural Assumption 2.5.2 (decision under risk and richness), adding the assumption of EU.

Structural Assumption 3.0.1 [Decision under risk and EU]. $\succcurlyeq$ is a preference relation over the set of all (probability-contingent) prospects, which is the set of all finite probability distributions over the outcome set $\mathbb{R}$. Expected utility holds with a utility function U that is continuous and strictly increasing. $\square$

The assumption that all finite probability distributions are available in the preference domain entails, in fact, a strong richness restriction, similar to our assumption that all real-valued outcomes are available in the domain. The assumption is, however, commonly made in the literature on decision under risk and it facilitates the analysis, which is why we use it too.

3.1 An application from the health domain: decision tree analysis

My experience with applications of decision theory mostly come from the medical domain. Although discussions of medical examples can at times be depressing, dealing with human suffering, the medical domain is one of the most important fields of application for decision theory. Hence, I present a medical application. We consider a simplified decision analysis for patients with laryngeal cancer in stage T3 (a particular medical state of the cancer with no metastases; McNeil *et al.* 1981). In this subsection, as an exception, outcomes are nonmonetary. We, accordingly, drop the assumptions that U be continuous or strictly increasing.

The choice between surgery and radiotherapy is difficult for stage T3, and there are no clear medical indications favoring one treatment over the other. The advantage of surgery is that there is a smaller chance of recurrence, so that the patient has a better chance of survival. The disadvantage is, however, that the voice is lost and the patient will have to live with artificial speech. The best treatment decision crucially depends on the individual subjective preferences of the patient. For a teacher, the loss of the voice may be a serious loss and the teacher may, therefore, prefer radiotherapy. A piano player may prefer surgery. At any rate, it is not possible to prescribe a general treatment that would be optimal for all patients. It is essential for the best treatment to consider the subjective value system of the patient. Inputs from the patient should play an explicit role in the decision process. Giving formal status to patient inputs is an important contribution of decision theory to the health domain.

Up until the early 1980s, no technique was available in the medical domain to incorporate subjective individual preferences of patients in a systematic way. An often-used criterion was the five-year survival rate, describing how many patients were still alive five years after treatment. A breakthrough was achieved when McNeil *et al.* (1978, 1981) demonstrated how the techniques of decision theory can be used for medical decisions. It led to a revolution in the medical domain, where quality of life and inputs from the patient became generally recognized as essential components of optimal treatments.

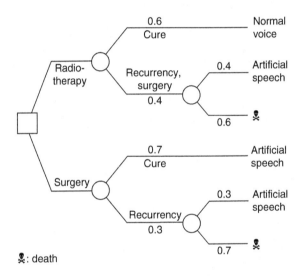

Figure 3.1.1 Choice between radiotherapy or surgery for a patient with larynx-cancer (stage T3).

Figure 3.1.1 depicts the risks and the events of the situation considered here. In an EU analysis, we should not only determine the probabilities of risks, but also the utilities of outcomes. In the health domain, the probabilities are usually provided by epidemiologists, based on large studies of the literature and of medical data. The probabilities in Figure 3.1.1 have been obtained in this manner. We will not discuss them further. To determine the utilities of the patient, the standard gamble (SG) method can be used. The best outcome in the analysis, normal voice, is assigned utility 1 and the worst outcome, death, is assigned utility 0.

Next the SG probability p of life with artificial speech with respect to normal voice and death is determined (Figure 3.1.2, which is the analog of the SG Figure 2.5.3). Needless to say that such measurements need extensive psychological preparations,

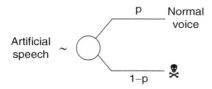

Figure 3.1.2 The SG question: For which p is the gamble equivalent to the certain outcome?

and that the relevant questions can be answered meaningfully only by some of the patients. The utility of artificial speech is equal to p (the SG Eq. (2.5.1)). These utilities are substituted in Figure 3.1.1 and the treatment with the highest EU is preferred. For example, if Figure 3.1.2 reveals that U(artificial speech) is 0.9, then EU(radiotherapy) $= 0.6 \times 1 + 0.16 \times 0.9 + 0.24 \times 0 = 0.744$ and EU(surgery) $= 0.7 \times 0.9 + 0.09 \times 0.9 + 0.21 \times 0 = 0.711$. Consequently, radiotherapy has the highest EU and is recommended.

This method for applying EU is commonly used in the health domain. With the probability estimates provided by epidemiologists, utilities of patients are elicited using simple SG questions, or alternative methods for measuring quality of life. Advanced computer programs for analyzing complex decision trees have been developed (such as Arborist from Texas Instruments, or TreeAge Pro; see www. treeage.com/resources/academic.html). Such EU analyses are used for individual decision situations but also at the level of policy making and as part of large cost–benefit analyses (Drummond *et al.* 1987; Gold *et al.* 1996; Sox *et al.* 1986; Weinstein *et al.* 1980).

Exercise 3.1.1.[b] Determine the switching utility β for artificial speech, in Figure 3.1.1. That is, determine the utility of artificial speech that makes the two treatments equivalent. If the utility of artificial speech is higher than the switching utility then surgery is optimal, and if the utility of artificial speech is lower then radiotherapy is optimal. □

3.2 Risk aversion

Henceforth, outcomes are monetary again. We consider the classical account of insurance in terms of EU theory.

We will analyze risk aversion (Definition 2.4.1) under EU in this chapter using Figure 3.2.1. Risk aversion will then amount to concave utility. For other models considered later the implications will be different, and need not imply concave utility. For instance, Example 6.3.1 will give risk aversion with a strictly convex utility function under the rank-dependent generalization of EU. For now, however, we restrict attention to EU where the classical conclusion of concave utility will follow. Note that the x-axis of the figure represents money. For instance, $p\alpha + (1-p)\beta$ on the x-axis designates a monetary amount, and not a prospect.

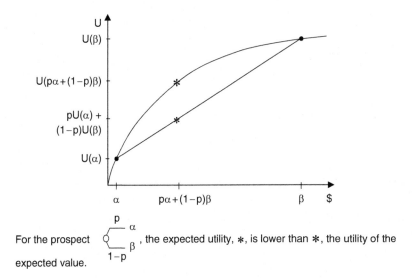

For the prospect, the expected utility, ∗, is lower than ∗, the utility of the expected value.

Figure 3.2.1 Risk aversion.

It is the expected value of the corresponding prospect. Because of linearity of the diagonal drawn, the height indicated by the small asterisk ∗ at outcome $p\alpha + (1-p)\beta$ (this outcome is the $p/1-p$ mixture of outcomes α and β) is the $p/1-p$ mixture of the heights. Hence it is $pU(\alpha) + (1-p)U(\beta)$, which is the EU of the prospect $\alpha_p\beta$.

The properties of utility that correspond to risk aversion, risk neutrality, and risk seeking are (see Figure 3.2.2):

concavity: $U(\lambda\alpha + (1-\lambda)\beta) \geq \lambda U(\alpha) + (1-\lambda)U(\beta)$ for all $0 < \lambda < 1$ and α, β; (3.2.1)

linearity[1]: $U(\lambda\alpha + (1-\lambda)\beta) = \lambda U(\alpha) + (1-\lambda)U(\beta)$ for all $0 < \lambda < 1$ and α, β; (3.2.2)

convexity: $U(\lambda\alpha + (1-\lambda)\beta) \leq \lambda U(\alpha) + (1-\lambda)U(\beta)$ for all $0 < \lambda < 1$ and α, β. (3.2.3)

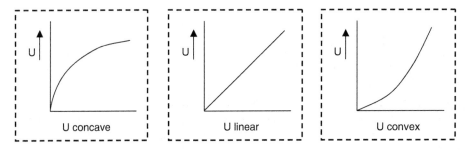

Figure 3.2.2 Concavity, linearity, and convexity.

---

[1] A comment for mathematical readers: As commonly done in empirical fields, linear is used in the same sense as affine and does not require $U(0) = 0$. Because utility is unique up to unit and level, $U(0) = 0$ can always be obtained.

Theorem 3.2.1. Under Structural Assumption 3.0.1 (decision under risk and EU):

(a) [Risk aversion $\Leftrightarrow$ U is concave];
(b) [Risk neutrality $\Leftrightarrow$ U is linear];
(c) [Risk seeking $\Leftrightarrow$ U is convex]. $\square$

Exercise 3.2.1.

(a)[b] Show that risk aversion holds when restricted to prospects with no more than one or two outcomes if and only if U is concave.
(b)[c] Prove Theorem 3.2.1 in general (for all prospects). $\square$

The result in part (a) of the theorem is central to EU theory. It was first obtained, for two-outcome prospects, by Marshall (1890 Footnote IX in Mathematical Appendix). Concave utility corresponds to *diminishing marginal utility*, which is a natural assumption: "all these successive units have for their possessor an intensity of utility decreasing from the first unit which responds to the most urgent need to the last, after which satiety sets in" (Walras 1896 p. 98). For a prospect, the *risk premium* is the difference between the expected value of the prospect and its certainty equivalent.

Example 3.2.2. Consider the prospect $80_{\frac{1}{2}}(-20)$ and assume $U(\alpha) = 1 - \exp(-\theta\alpha)$ with $\theta = 0.005$. U is a concave function. The expectation of the prospect is 30. Straightforward calculations (Exercise 3.2.2) demonstrate that its certainty equivalent is 23.81, which is less than the expectation in agreement with risk aversion. The risk premium is $30 - 23.81 = 6.19$. $\square$

Exercise 3.2.2.[a] Verify the calculations in Example 3.2.2. $\square$

Exercise 3.2.3.[b]

(a) Indicate on the x-axis of Figure 3.2.1 where the certainty equivalent of the prospect lies. Which distance in the figure corresponds to the risk premium?
(b) Show that the risk premium is nonnegative for all prospects if and only if risk aversion holds. $\square$

The risk premium is important for insurance. Assume that during the next year you are bearing a risk – e.g., burglary in your house – that is, a probability distribution over negative outcomes. Assume that the expected value is −$100. If you are risk averse, your certainty equivalent will be lower; say, −$120. This means that you are willing to pay an insurance premium of up to −$120 to insure against burglary. Because the insurance company has many clients, offering such an insurance will cost the insurance company on average −$100 per client (by the law of large numbers that some of the readers may know from probability theory courses). Hence, it can make up to $20 by offering you (and people like you) insurance against burglary. The risk premium describes the exact profit margins for insurance, and is the basis of insurance.

3.3   Applications of risk aversion

Exercise 3.3.1.[a] Consider bike insurance. Assume that for the relevant amounts of money, which are moderate, your utility is linear. Does EU recommend insuring your bike? □

Exercise 3.3.2.[b] You play in the final of the TV game show "Deal or No Deal." There are 26 numbered suitcases. There are also 26 predetermined and known prizes between \$0.05 and \$5 $\times 10^6$. Each suitcase contains one prize, but it is unknown which suitcase contains which prize.[2] You randomly selected one of 26 numbered suitcases, namely no. 13. All suitcases not selected by you except one, no. 7, have been opened after that, and only the prizes \$0.05 and \$2.5 $\times 10^6$ are left. One of these two prizes is, therefore, contained in your suitcase no. 13, and the other is in suitcase no. 7. As part of the TV game, a bank that does not know more about the content of the suitcases than you do, offers you $\$10^6$ for your suitcase. What do you prefer, keeping your suitcase or accepting the bank offer? And what would your hypothetical preference be between suitcase no. 7 and the bank offer? Most people will prefer the sure prize $\$10^6$ in each case. Show that a Dutch book can be made against these preferences (EV is violated). Show that EU can accommodate such preferences. □

The following exercise concerns an important skill: developing a decision tree to model a decision situation.

Exercise 3.3.3[c] (from Bierman & Fernandez, 1995 Exercises 10.5 and 10.6). An executive at a publishing house has just been given two stock options as a bonus. Each option gives the executive the right (but not the obligation) to purchase one share of the publishing company's stock for \$50, as long as he does it before the closing of the stock market tomorrow afternoon. When the executive exercises either option, he must immediately sell the stock bought from the company at the market prize in effect at the time. An option can only be exercised once.

The stock's price today is \$55. The executive knows this price today before deciding what to do today. Hence, if he exercises either option today he is guaranteed a profit of \$5 per option exercised. The stock price tomorrow will either be \$45 or \$65 with equal probability. The executive will know the price tomorrow before deciding what to do that day. This means that if he waits until tomorrow and the stock price rises to \$65, he can exercise any remaining options for a profit of \$15 per option exercised. On the other hand, if the stock price falls to \$45, then exercising either option would result in a loss of \$5 per option exercised, which the executive obviously will not do, then preferring to let any option left expire unused.

Today the executive can: (1) exercise both options; (2) exercise one option today and wait until tomorrow to decide about the second one; or, (3) exercise neither

---

[2] This program is broadcasted in many countries in the world. The stakes mentioned are used in the Netherlands where the program was invented and first transmitted, and these stakes are the highest in the world.

option today and wait until tomorrow to decide what to do about both. Tomorrow the executive must either exercise any option(s) not already cashed in or let it (them) expire unused. Assume that there are no brokerage commissions or taxes. Draw a decision tree.

Suppose that the executive maximizes EU, with a utility function given by $U(0) = 0$, $U(5) = 10$, $U(10) = 18$, $U(15) = 25$, $U(20) = 31$, $U(25) = 36$, and $U(30) = 40$. What is the best decision for the executive? You may want to verify that you drew the right decision tree before doing the calculations. □

For prospect $(p_1:x_1,\ldots,p_n:x_n)$, an *elementary mean-preserving spread* replaces an outcome x_j and its probability p_j by two outcomes M, m with probabilities qp_j and $(1-q)p_j$ such that the expectation of the prospect is unaltered. That is, $x_j = qM + (1-q)m$. The resulting prospect is $(p_1:x_1,\ldots,p_{j-1}:x_{j-1},p_jq:M,p_j(1-q):m,p_{j+1}:x_{j+1}\ldots p_n:x_n)$. Figure 3.3.1 illustrates the case. A *mean-preserving spread* results from a finite number of replacements of this kind, in other words, from a finite number of elementary mean-preserving spreads.[3] The opposite of mean-preserving spread is called *mean-preserving contraction. Aversion to mean-preserving spreads* means that mean-preserving spreads are less preferred than the original prospect. It can be verified that every prospect is a mean-preserving spread of its expectation (elaboration of Exercise 3.2.1). Hence, aversion to mean-preserving spreads implies risk aversion. For general decision models, aversion to mean-preserving spreads, sometimes called strong risk aversion, is a more restrictive condition than risk aversion (sometimes called weak risk aversion), as we will see later. Under EU, however, and

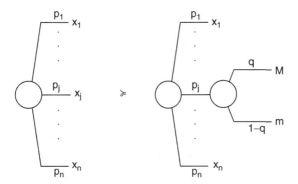

qM + (1−q)m = xj, so that the means
are the same.

Figure 3.3.1 Aversion to elementary mean-preserving spreads.

---

[3] For prospects with infinitely many outcomes, every outcome is replaced by a conditional distribution with the same expectation, which may require infinitely many elementary mean-preserving spreads and limit-taking. This book considers only finitely many outcomes.

its implication of independence, it is not difficult to infer from Figure 3.3.1 that risk aversion implies aversion to mean-preserving spreads (elaboration of Exercise 3.2.1).

Observation 3.3.1. Under EU, aversion to mean-preserving spreads is equivalent to risk aversion, which is equivalent to concavity of utility. □

A small variation of aversion to mean-preserving spreads is known as second-order stochastic dominance; it adds first-order stochastic dominance. Alternative equivalent definitions in terms of integrals have often been used (Bawa 1982). These conditions can be useful if we do not know the utility function precisely or have incomplete preferences. For example, if all we know about utility is that it is concave, then already we can conclude what the preference must be between a prospect and its mean-preserving spread. If we have incomplete preferences, and only prefer a prospect to another if it has higher EU for all concave utility functions, then we can still conclude that a prospect is preferred to any mean-preserving spread. See Bawa (1982) and Levy (1992) for early surveys. Baucells & Heukamp (2006) provided a recent application of such techniques to prospect theory. Using such techniques, Baucells & Shapley (2008) and Dubra, Maccheroni, & Ok (2004) independently and simultaneously found an appealing extension of Theorem 2.6.3 to incomplete preferences. Such extensions are important given that completeness is the most questionable condition in Theorem 2.6.3.

Assignment 3.3.4.[a] Assume that $U(\alpha) = 1 - \exp(-\alpha/100)$. What is the risk premium of $100_{1/2}0$? □

Assignment 3.3.5 [Risk aversion versus variance].[c] This assignment demonstrates that risk aversion need not always imply aversion to increased variance. Assume risk aversion (concave utility). Throughout, x and y are two prospects with the same expectation, where x has a larger variance.

(a) Assume $x = x_{1\,1/2}x_2$ and $y = y_{1\,1/2}y_2$ with $x_1 > x_2$ and $y_1 > y_2$. Show that $y \succcurlyeq x$. Hence, risk aversion does imply aversion to increased variance for two-outcome prospects.

(b) Consider three-outcome prospects $x = \frac{1}{3}x_1, \frac{1}{3}x_2, \frac{1}{3}x_3$ and $y = \frac{1}{3}y_1, \frac{1}{3}y_2, \frac{1}{3}y_3$. Give an example where U and x, y are such that $x \succ y$. That is, higher variance may be preferred despite risk aversion. □

Assignment 3.3.6.[c] This assignment demonstrates that risk aversion implies arbitrage. More generally, it shows that every deviation from risk neutrality implies arbitrage.

You may assume that risk neutrality for all 50–50 prospects implies complete risk neutrality.[4] Show that arbitrage is possible whenever there is no risk neutrality, for instance as soon as there is strict risk aversion. A difficulty in this assignment is that we have defined risk neutrality for decision under risk, and arbitrage has been

---

[4] This follows mainly from Theorem 1 of §2.1.4 of Aczél (1966), or from Hardy, Littlewood & Pòlya (1934 Theorems 111 and 86). Note that their term convex has the same meaning as the modern term midpoint-convex. The result follows first on the interior, then by continuity also for the boundary. This shows for instance that midpoint concavity implies concavity under continuity or monotonicity.

defined for decision under uncertainty. You, therefore, have to understand §2.1–2.3 to be able to do this assignment. □

3.4   Indexes of risk aversion

Consider two persons with preference relations $\succcurlyeq_1$ and $\succcurlyeq_2$, respectively, over prospects. Assume that they maximize EU with utilities U_1 and U_2. We say that $\succcurlyeq_2$ is *more risk averse* than $\succcurlyeq_1$ if

$[\alpha \sim_1 x \Rightarrow \alpha \succcurlyeq_2 x]$ for all prospects x and outcomes α.

In other words, whenever a riskless prospect α is equivalent to a risky prospect x for person 1, then person 2, being more risk averse, prefers the riskless prospect.

Theorem 3.4.1. Person 2 is more risk averse than person 1 if and only if $U_2(\cdot) = \varphi(U_1(\cdot))$ for a concave transformation φ. □

Theorem 3.4.1 is an almost trivial corollary of Theorem 3.2.1a, taking as unit of outcome not money, but utility of person 1, as will be elaborated in §3.9. If utility U is twice continuously differentiable then a well-known measure of concavity of utility is $-U''/U'$, the *Pratt–Arrow measure*. Because concavity of U corresponds with risk aversion under EU, the measure can also be taken as an index of risk aversion here.

Whereas risk aversion cannot be defined for general outcomes if expected value and the corresponding risk neutrality level cannot be defined, comparative risk aversion then still is meaningful (Yaari 1969). Theorem 3.4.1 holds with no alteration for general outcomes (Peters & Wakker 1987 Theorem 2). These observations suggest that comparative risk aversion is the more basic concept, with absolute risk aversion resulting from a choice of a risk neutrality level.

Exercise 3.4.1.[c] Assume that U_1 and U_2 are twice continuously differentiable with positive first derivative everywhere. Show that $\succcurlyeq_2$ is more risk averse than $\succcurlyeq_1$ if and only if $-U_2''/U_2' \geq -U_1''/U_1'$ everywhere. □

Exercise 3.4.1 illustrates that the Pratt–Arrow measure is indeed a useful index of risk aversion. Hence, it also is a useful index of concavity of utility. Sometimes the term *risk tolerance* is used to designate the reciprocal $-U'/U''$ of the Pratt–Arrow measure. The best interpretation of these concepts will be given later in Exercise 3.5.5b, where an empirical meaning will be given to them.

On the domain of positive outcomes $\alpha > 0$, an alternative popular measure of risk aversion, or concavity of utility, is $\alpha \times (-U''(\alpha)/U'(\alpha))$. It is sometimes called the *relative* (or *proportional*) *measure of risk aversion*. It is the most used measure of risk aversion in the expected utility literature today. The Pratt–Arrow measure is also called the *absolute measure of risk aversion*.

One of the main messages of this book is the following observation: Under models more general than EU, risk aversion is no longer equivalent to concave utility. It then depends on other factors besides utility. We will study those factors in later chapters. The Pratt–Arrow measure of utility then no longer is an index of risk aversion, but a measure of concavity of utility. Unfortunately, this observation concerns a widespread misunderstanding in the economic literature today. Although economists often assume that EU is violated descriptively, and assume more general models, they nevertheless continue to use the logical implications that they have learned only under EU and that need not hold for the more general models. They thus continue to use the term risk aversion to refer to concave utility, and indexes of concavity of utility are still called indexes of risk aversion, even though this terminology is clearly inappropriate when EU is abandoned. It is preferable in more general contexts to simply call concavity of utility what it is (concavity of utility) and not what it is not (risk aversion). Remember, therefore, that concavity of utility and the Pratt–Arrow index can be related to risk aversion *only if EU is assumed*. The latter assumption is made in this chapter.

An interesting case occurs when U_1 is the utility U of a person and U_2 the utility of that same person when richer by an amount $\varepsilon > 0$, that is, we compare $U_2(\alpha) = U(\alpha + \varepsilon)$ with $U(\alpha)$. If for all $\varepsilon > 0$, U_2 is less concave than U_1, then we say (assuming EU as throughout this chapter) that the person exhibits *decreasing risk aversion*. This holds if and only if $- U''/U'$ is decreasing. *Increasing risk aversion* refers to U_2 being more concave than U_1 for all $\varepsilon > 0$.

3.5   Parametric families of utility

Wakker (2008a) provides a more extensive didactic account of the material presented in this section.

Power utility. The most popular parametric family of utility is the *power family*, in economics often called the family of constant relative risk aversion (CRRA). With the parameter denoted θ, we define the family on $\mathbb{R}^+$.

For $\alpha > 0$:

for $\theta > 0$, $U(\alpha) = \alpha^\theta$;

for $\theta = 0$, $U(\alpha) = ln(\alpha)$;

for $\theta < 0$, $U(\alpha) = -\alpha^\theta$.   (3.5.1)

Multiplication by -1 for negative θ serves to have the function increasing. For $\theta > 0$ the function can also be defined at $\alpha = 0$, where it then is 0. For $\theta \leq 0$ the function is $-\infty$ at $\alpha = 0$. For $\theta = 1$ the function is linear, corresponding to expected value and risk neutrality. As Figure 3.5.1 will illustrate, θ is an anti-index of concavity. The smaller θ is, the more concave U is and the more risk aversion will be generated. In economics, the parameter $1-\theta$, called the (relative or proportional) index of risk aversion, is often used to describe the family. Under EU, the functions U are interval scales and we can replace them by any function $\tau + \sigma U$ for $\tau \in \mathbb{R}$ and $\sigma > 0$. We can thus define concisely:

For all $\theta \neq 0$, $U(\alpha) = \alpha^\theta/\theta$,   (3.5.2)

which amounts to the scaling $U'(1) = 1$.

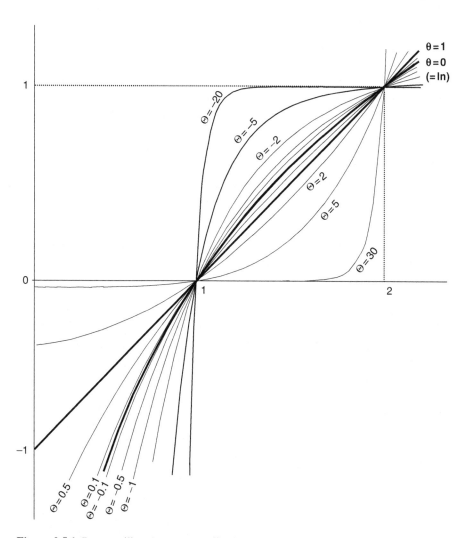

Figure 3.5.1 Power utility curves, normalized at 1 and 2.

The definition of the power family may seem to be ad hoc concerning the transition from $\theta > 0$ to $\theta < 0$, but Wakker (2008a) demonstrated that this transition is natural, and in fact is the only natural way to define the family. Figure 3.5.1 depicts some power functions normalized at $\alpha = 1$ and $\alpha = 2$. That is, they were obtained from a power function U using the normalization

$$\frac{U(\alpha) - U(1)}{U(2) - U(1)}.$$

Figure 3.5.1 illustrates that the transition from $\theta > 0$ to $\theta < 0$ is natural.

The following property, imposing invariance of preference under a change of unit of the outcomes, will characterize power utility for positive outcomes.

The preference between two prospects is not affected if all outcomes
of both prospects are multiplied by the same positive number $\lambda > 0$.   (3.5.3)

This condition is usually called constant relative risk aversion, whence power
utility is often called the CRRA family in the economic literature. Then the index
of relative risk aversion, defined as $-\alpha U''/U'$, and equal to $1-\theta$ and independent of α,
is commonly used as an index of risk aversion as explained in §3.4.1. We avoid this
terminology because under the nonexpected utility models studied later in this book,
risk aversion and risk attitudes can no longer be equated with utility curvature, but
depend also on other factors. Better terminologies would result with concavity of
utility instead of risk aversion, but we will not pursue this point, and will leave the
condition as a numbered equation.

Observation 3.5.1. Assume EU with continuous strictly increasing utility, restricted
to positive outcomes. Then utility is from the power family if and only if Eq. (3.5.3)
(invariance of preference under a change of unit) holds. □

Exercise 3.5.1.[a] Show that the condition in Eq. (3.5.3) is satisfied for power utility. □
    Assuming power utility, a choice between 100 for sure or $200_{\frac{1}{2}}50$ can serve as a
diagnostic for observing the sign of the power. For power 0 (logarithmic utility)
indifference results, with the risky prospect either yielding $ln(2)$ utility units more or
less than the sure prospect. There is more risk aversion and a negative power if the
sure 100 is preferred and more risk seeking with a positive power if the risky prospect
is preferred.
Exponential utility. Another popular family of utility is the *exponential family*, often
called the family of constant absolute risk aversion (CARA) in the economic literature, and defined on the entire outcome set $\mathbb{R}$:

for $\theta > 0$, $U(\alpha) = 1 - e^{-\theta\alpha}$;

for $\theta = 0$, $U(\alpha) = \alpha$;

for $\theta < 0$, $U(\alpha) = e^{-\theta\alpha} - 1$.   (3.5.4)

It is the power family applied to e^{α} rather than to α, and with $-\theta$ instead of θ. Hence,
the transition from $\theta > 0$ to $\theta < 0$ is, again, not ad hoc but natural. The parameter θ is
an index of concavity, with linear utility for $\theta = 0$, concave utility for $\theta > 0$, and
convex utility for $\theta < 0$. Again, the functions U are interval scales under EU and we
can replace them by any function $\tau + \sigma U$ for $\tau \in \mathbb{R}$ and $\sigma > 0$. We can thus define
concisely:

For all $\theta \neq 0$, $U(\alpha) = (1 - e^{-\theta\alpha})/\theta$,   (3.5.5)

which amounts to the scaling $U'(0) = 1$. This form, behaviorally equivalent to the
form in Eq. (3.5.4), has more convenient numerical and analytical properties, making
it useful for data fitting.

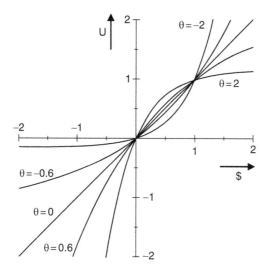

Figure 3.5.2 Exponential utility, normalized at 0 and 1.

The following property, imposing invariance of preference under a change of level of the outcomes, will characterize exponential utility:

> The preference between two prospects is not affected if all
> outcomes of both prospects are increased by the same term μ.   (3.5.6)

This condition is usually called constant absolute risk aversion, whence exponential utility is often called the CARA family in the economic literature. Similar objections apply to this terminology as to the CRRA terminology discussed before.

Exercise 3.5.2.[a] Assume exponential utility. Show that the index of absolute risk aversion, $-U''/U'$, is θ. It is independent of α. $\square$

Observation 3.5.2. Assume EU with continuous strictly increasing utility. Then utility is from the exponential family if and only if Eq. (3.5.6) (invariance of preference under a change of level of the outcomes) holds. $\square$

Exercise 3.5.3.[a] Show that Eq. (3.5.6) is satisfied for exponential utility. $\square$

Exercise 3.5.4.[b] This exercise illustrates Eqs. (3.5.3) and (3.5.6). Consider the prospects S ("safe") $= 30$ and R ("risky") $= 100_{1/2}0$. The criterion for being "close to" will be a distance less than 0.1. We write CE_1 for the certainty equivalent of $200_{1/2}0$ and CE_2 for the certainty equivalent of $200_{1/2}100$.

(a) Assume that $U(\alpha) = \alpha^\theta$ with $\theta > 0$. Determine the preference between the prospects for all $0 < j \le 100$ and $\theta = j/100$, and find an analytic expression for the θ that yields indifference between S and R. Give a three-digits approximation of the indifference-θ. Assuming this value of θ, give an analytic expression for CE_1 and CE_2, and give a three-digits approximation for each. Is CE_1 close to twice 30, or is it considerably larger or smaller? Is CE_2 close to $30 + 100$, or is it considerably larger or smaller?

(b) Assume that $U(\alpha) = 1 - e^{-\theta\alpha}$ with $\theta > 0$. You can spend some time trying to find an analytic solution for θ under indifference between S and R, but will not succeed. Let your computer determine the preference between the prospects for all $0 < j \le 100$ and $\theta = 0.001 + j/1000$. Give a three-digits approximation of the indifference-θ. Assuming this value of θ, give an analytic expression for CE_1 and CE_2, and give a three-digits approximation for each. Is CE_1 close to twice 30, or is it considerably larger or smaller? Is CE_2 close to $30 + 100$, or is it considerably larger or smaller? □

Empirical meaning of risk tolerance

Exercise 3.5.5.[c] Assume exponential utility with $\theta > 0$, and consider the following prospects, for various β.

(a) Express the optimal value of β numerically in terms of θ.
(b) Show that the prospect is indifferent to not gambling (receiving \$0 with probability 1) for $\beta \approx 0.96/\theta \approx 1/\theta$. □

Part (b) gives an easy way to measure the Pratt–Arrow index θ and its reciprocal, risk tolerance, empirically (assuming EU!):

Observation 3.5.3. If your risk tolerance is constant, then it is approximately the maximum stake for which you are willing to take a 50–50 gamble if in case of a loss, half of the loss gets reimbursed. □

   At the level of your risk tolerance, losses seem to weigh about twice as much as gains, with a gain $1/\theta$ offsetting a loss $-1/2\theta$. Later, when we introduce prospect theory, we will consider other interpretations of such factors ("loss aversion"). A convenient aspect of risk tolerance is that its unit is money, that is, your risk tolerance is simply a monetary amount. This makes it easy to conceptualize and to avoid confusion about its unit.

   The results of this section also hold for general intervals as domain. This follows from Lemma 1 in Miyamoto (1983), applied to $U(ln(\alpha))$ or $U(\alpha)$, respectively.

Observation 3.5.4. Observation 3.5.1 also holds if the domain of utility is an arbitrary subinterval of $\mathbb{R}^+$. Observation 3.5.2 also holds if the domain of utility is an arbitrary subinterval of $\mathbb{R}$. □

Empirical findings. The common finding of empirical measurements of utility under EU is: (a) Absolute risk aversion, measured by the Pratt–Arrow measure $-U''(\alpha)/U'(\alpha)$, decreases in wealth; (b) relative risk aversion, measured by the index $-\alpha U''(\alpha)/U'(\alpha)$ (only for $\alpha > 0$), increases in wealth.[5] A richer person will then choose larger absolute, but smaller proportional, risky investments. Utility should then be between exponential and power. It led Abdellaoui, Barrios, & Wakker (2007) to introduce a new parametric family of utility, called expo–power utility, which is between exponential and power utility.

The preceding empirical findings on utility fit well with the ratio–difference principle from psychology (Stevens & Davis 1938; Baron 1997). Here subjects, when carrying out quantitative tasks, as a heuristic either carry out additive operations or multiplicative operations. Then group averages give results between constant additive and constant multiplicative attitudes. Constant relative risk aversion was found by several studies.[6] Uncommon findings exist.[7]

3.6 Data fitting for expected utility under risk

This section gives numerical examples and exercises to illustrate how EU can be used to describe and predict preferences using data fitting techniques. We fit the data by minimizing the distance between predictions of a theory and observed data described in §A.2, and based on calculations by computer. We usually assume parametric families of utility.

Exercise 3.6.1[a] [Deterministic fit (no error and perfect fit)]. We observe the following indifferences: $0.01 \sim 1_{0.10}0$, $0.36 \sim 1_{0.60}0$, and $0.81 \sim 1_{0.90}0$.

(a) Show that EU can accommodate these observations. Set $U(0) = 0$ and $U(1) = 1$ and determine the utility of the outcomes 0.01, 0.36, and 0.81.
(b) Show that $CE(0.81_{2/3}0) = 0.36$.
(c) Assume that utility is a power function, that is, $U(\alpha) = \alpha^\theta$ for some $\theta > 0$. What is θ? Give the predicted CE's of $1_{0.80}0$ and $0.80_{0.70}0.25$, and the predicted preference between them. □

Exercise 3.6.2[b] [Measurement with errors and fitting]. Assume that we observe the three indifferences of Exercise 3.6.1, but in addition we observe a fourth indifference, $0.81_{2/3}0 \sim 0.40$. As part (b) of Exercise 3.6.1 showed, EU must be violated. Find the power $\theta = j/100 > 0$ (for an integer j) such that EU with power utility $U(\alpha) = \alpha^\theta$ best fits the data in the sense of §A.2. Give the distance. Predict the CE's of $1_{2/3}0$

---

[5] Arrow (1971 p. 96); Binswanger (1981); Campbell (1996); Fetherstonhaugh *et al.* (1997); Holt & Laury (2002); Kachelmeier & Shehata (1992); Meyer & Meyer (2005); Ogaki & Zhang (2001); Post *et al.* (2008); Yesuf & Bluffstone (2009).
[6] Brunnermeier & Nagel (2008); Friend & Blume (1975); Harrison, Lau, & Rutström (2007); Pälsson (1996); Rapoport (1984); Szpiro (1986).
[7] Blake (1996); Cohn *et al.* (1975 p. 606); Gollier (2001b p. 187) found decreasing RRA. Cohen & Einav (2007) found increasing ARA.

and $0.81_{\frac{2}{3}}0.20$, and the preference between these prospects. If you do not know how to proceed, read the footnote.[8] □

Exercise 3.6.3.[c] Consider the following seven choice pairs, where preferences have to be substituted for question marks:
$x^1 = 300_{0.50}0$? 20, $x^2 = 200_{0.50}0$? 100, $x^3 = 200_{0.01}0$? 10, $x^4 = 100_{0.05}0$? 14, $x^5 = 96_{0.50}0$? 39, $x^6 = 72_{0.95}0$? 55, $x^7 = 100_{0.95}0$? 78.

As an index of risk aversion we take the number of safe choices made. Assume that the median number of safe choices in our data set is 3. There is no analytic solution to the following problems. Obtain the results by trial and error, using your computer to calculate the result for many θ.

(a) Translate the finding of 3 safe choices into the relative risk aversion index often used in the economic literature. That is, assume EU with a power utility $U(\alpha) = \alpha^\theta$ and determine the powers θ that imply 3 safe choices. (The index of relative risk aversion is $1-\theta$.) Assume for simplicity that $\theta > 0$. You may assume, and your calculations will verify it, that the number of safe choices decreases in θ.

(b) Translate the finding of 3 safe choices into the absolute Pratt–Arrow risk aversion index. That is, assume EU with exponential utility $U(\alpha) = 1 - \exp(-\theta\alpha)$ and determine the values θ (the Pratt–Arrow index of risk aversion) that imply 3 safe choices. If you do not know how to proceed, suggestions are given in the footnote.[9] □

Exercise 3.6.4.[c] Consider the following certainty equivalent measurements for seven risky prospects x^j. $x^1 = 300_{0.50}0 \sim 112$, $x^2 = 200_{0.50}0 \sim 45$, $x^3 = 200_{0.01}0 \sim 6$, $x^4 = 100_{0.05}0 \sim 8$, $x^5 = 96_{0.50}0 \sim 23$, $x^6 = 72_{0.95}0 \sim 34$, and $x^7 = 100_{0.95}0 \sim 45$.

Under EU with utility to be specified, determine which model best fits the data, using the distance measure of §A.2.

(a) Assume exponential utility, that is, $U(\alpha) = 1 - \exp(-\theta\alpha)$ for all $\theta > 0$. Determine the optimal value of θ (= the Pratt–Arrow index of risk aversion) for all $\theta = j/1000$ for $0 < j \leq 100$. Report the optimal θ and the corresponding distance, and the distances for $\theta - 0.001$, $\theta - 0.002$, $\theta + 0.001$, and $\theta + 0.002$. If you do not know how to proceed, read the footnote.[10] Predict the CE's of $300_{\frac{2}{3}}250$ and $285_{\frac{2}{3}}276$, and the preference between these prospects.

---

[8] For a θ considered, first calculate EU of the prospects, then the predicted certainty equivalents $U^{-1}(EU)$ ($= EU^{1/\theta}$ for $\theta > 0$); and so on.

[9] First verify that $\theta = 0$ has only two safe choices and one indifference, so that it just fails to fit the data. Then verify that $\theta = -0.00001$ generates too much risk seeking because there are only two safe choices. You may assume that all $\theta < 0$ similarly generate too much risk seeking. Then calculate the EU differences for $\theta = 0$, $0.1, 0.01, 0.001, 0.005, 0.008$, and 0.009. On the basis of these calculations, find (up to a difference of 0.001) the largest $\theta > 0$ such that for larger θ there is too much risk aversion and there are more than three safe choices, but for θ between this upper bound and $\theta = 0$ there are exactly three safe choices. You may assume, and your calculations will verify it, that the number of safe choices increases in θ.

[10] For the θ considered, first calculate the EU of the prospects, then the predicted certainty equivalents $U^{-1}(EU)$ ($= -ln(1-EU)/\theta$ for $\theta > 0$), and then the squared distances; and so on.

(b) Assume power utility, $U(\alpha) = \alpha^\theta$. Determine the optimal value of θ over all $\theta = j/100$ for $j \geq 10$. Predict the CE's of $300_{2/3}250$ and $285_{2/3}276$, and the preference between these prospects.

(c) (This part is best answered after parts (a) and (b) have been done and their answers have been verified.) Which family fits better, the exponential family or the power family? Which preference between $300_{2/3}250$ and $285_{2/3}276$ would you recommend?

Additional Comment [Motivating distance measure chosen]: The distance measure refers to differences between certainty equivalents, designating amounts of money, for both parametric families. It, therefore, makes sense to compare them. Had we taken EU differences as distance measure, then these would not have been related very clearly to objects with a physical meaning, and they would have been more difficult to compare. For example, halving one utility function does not change any empirical implication, but would affect the EU distances and the comparisons between the different utility functions. □

Exercise 3.6.5.[b] The following eight indifferences are median observations from Tversky & Kahneman (1992):
GAINS: $150_{0.05}50 \sim 64$; $100_{0.50}0 \sim 36$; $100_{0.95}0.00 \sim 78$;
LOSSES: $0_{0.75}(-100) \sim -23.50$; $0_{0.50}(-50) \sim -21.00$; $0_{0.05}(-100) \sim -84$;
MIXED: $101_{0.50}(-50) \sim 0$; $50_{0.50}(-20) \sim 112_{0.50}(-50)$.
  We use these eight indifferences to assess the utility function of EU. We then use the assessed EU model to make a prediction.
  To avoid some analytical inconveniences of power utility at negative inputs and 0, we assume exponential utility: $U(\alpha) = 1 - \exp(-\theta\alpha)$. Find the $0.0000 < \theta = j \times 0.0001 < 0.0100$ that best fits the data. Give the distance according to §A.2. Predict $CE(-100_{0.05}(-200))$. □

Exercise 3.6.5'.[b] The median value of $CE(-100_{0.05}(-200))$ found by Tversky & Kahneman (1992) was -179. Determine by how far your prediction in Exercise 3.6.5 is off from the actually observed value. □

Assignment 3.6.6.[a] We observe the following indifferences: $10 \sim 120_{0.10}0$, $30 \sim 60_{0.60}0$, $81 \sim 100_{0.90}0$. Assume power utility, with $U(\alpha) = \alpha^\theta$ for $0 < \theta = j/100 < 2$. Which θ fits best? Predict the CE's of $100_{0.80}0$ and $80_{0.80}25$, and the preference between these prospects. □

3.7 Multiattribute utility

This section assumes, in deviation from most of this book, that outcomes need not be monetary.

Example 3.7.1. Consider a decision about a medical treatment where it is uncertain what the resulting health state will be, but it is understood that the health state can then be expected to be stable for the rest of one's life. (Q,T) refers to the *chronic health state* of living T years in health state Q and then dying. The set of outcomes is the product of a set of health states and a set of possible life durations where the latter contains 0 (and no negative numbers). We assume EU with U(Q,T) the utility of chronic health state (Q,T). We seek to simplify the task of determining U for each (Q,T), and formulate some plausible preference conditions.

For simplicity, we assume *monotonicity in life duration*, i.e. $(Q,T+\varepsilon) \succ (Q,T)$ for all $\varepsilon > 0$. This rules out negative and null health states such as death. The *zero-condition* requires that all (Q,0) are equivalent, which is a self-evident requirement. Assume further that we consider it reasonable that SG equivalences over life duration be independent of the health state assumed (Figure 3.7.1), a condition that we only need when one prospect outcome is immediate death. □

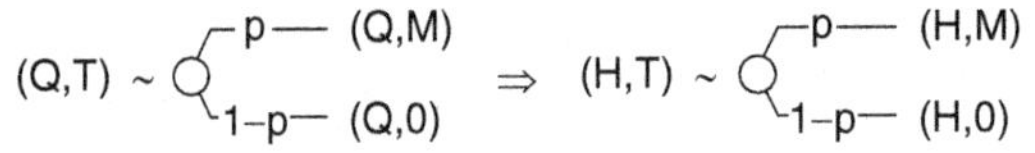

Figure 3.7.1 *SG invariance.*

Observation 3.7.2. The following two statements are equivalent.

(i)   Monotonicity in life duration, SG invariance, and the zero-condition hold;
(ii) U is *multiplicative*, i.e.

$$U(Q, T) = V(Q) \times W(T) \tag{3.7.1}$$

for some functions V and W with $W(0) = 0$, W strictly increasing in T, and $V(Q) > 0$ for all Q. □

Exercise 3.7.1.^{c} Prove Observation 3.7.2. This result was proved by Miyamoto *et al.* (1998 Theorem 3.1). □

V designates quality of life and W designates the value of life duration. W incorporates discounting. The model is the *generalized QALY* (quality of life) *model*. The *QALY model* concerns the special case of a linear W.

Eq. (3.7.1) greatly simplifies our task. We can separately determine quality of life (V) and the value of life years (W), and need not consider all combinations of quality of life and life duration separately. This example illustrates once more how behavioral foundations help to find the right model, identifying the parameters and concepts relevant for our decisions. As virtually all preference conditions in this book, SG invariance requires consistency between different measurements. □

In general multiattribute utility, the *outcome set*, denoted X, is a product set $X^1 \times \cdots \times X^m$. X^i may be a general set. Outcomes are denoted $\alpha = (\alpha^1, \ldots, \alpha^m)$, where α^i is the ith *attribute* (or coordinate) of α. The set X^i is the ith *attribute set* (or component). Here superscripts designate attributes and not powers. I use superscripts because subscripts refer to the different outcomes of a prospect. In Example 3.7.1, the first attribute concerns quality of life and the second concerns life duration. Another example results if outcomes designate cars, with m = 3, and with attribute 1 describing the maximum speed, attribute 2 describing the color, and attribute 3 describing the price, under the assumption that these are considered the only relevant properties of cars.

In applications, one should incorporate enough attributes to capture the essence of the decision problem, but so few that the model remains tractable. Similar points hold not only for the number of attributes to incorporate in multiattribute utility, but for modeling in general and, for instance, also for the number of states of nature to incorporate in the state space. Especially the art of keeping the model simple by leaving out many details but without losing the essence is crucial (von Winterfeldt 2007). Lancaster (1966) argued that objective attributes (such as speed of a car) are often better regrouped into more fundamental attributes (such as safety of a car). In what follows, we assume that the description of outcomes is complete: all relevant aspects of the car concern the aforementioned three aspects (attributes). More examples are in Appendix D.

This section considers the special case of multiattribute utility where: (a) Probability-contingent prospects – i.e. probability distributions – are given over the m-tuples; (b) these prospects are evaluated by EU, as assumed throughout this chapter. EU implies a linearity in probability that simplifies the analysis. This section briefly describes some of the main behavioral foundations. A detailed analysis is in Keeney & Raiffa (1976). Fishburn (1982) contains many advanced technical results. Recent applications include André (2009) and Yang (2008). A jth outcome x_j in a prospect $x = (p_1 : x_1,. . .,p_n : x_n)$ is $x_j = (x_j^1,. . .,x_j^m)$, with x_j^i the ith attribute of outcome x_j; see Figure 3.7.2. As throughout this book, x_j denotes the jth outcome of prospect x and α denotes a general outcome that is not related to a particular prospect.

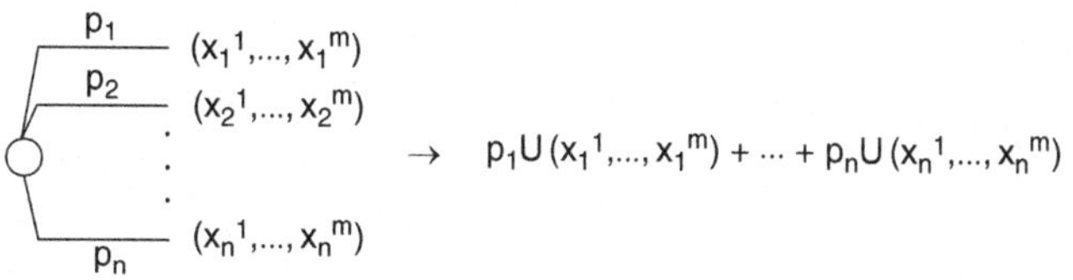

Figure 3.7.2 A prospect with multiattribute outcomes and its expected utility.

We examine how different attributes are aggregated into an overall evaluation. That is, we examine how an evaluation $U(\alpha^1,. . .,\alpha^m)$ of an outcome can be obtained as an aggregation of attribute utility functions $U^i(\alpha^i)$. Aggregation questions are central to many domains. Decision under uncertainty, the main topic of this book, can be considered a special case of aggregation, with states of nature as attributes. This will be central to §4.9.3.

A prospect $p_1x_1. . .p_nx_n$ over X generates a *marginal prospect* $p_1x_1^i. . .p_nx_n^i$ over the attribute set X^i. Figure 3.7.3 depicts an example that will now be explained. Consider, for m = 2, the prospect

$$(5\text{years, blind})_{1/2}(20\text{years, healthy}). \tag{3.7.2}$$

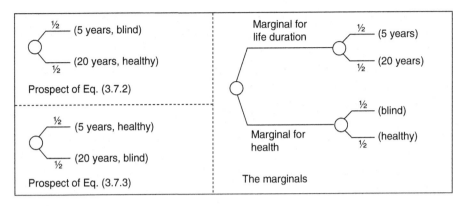

Figure 3.7.3 Two prospects with the same marginals.

Here outcomes are chronic health states (defined in Example 3.7.1). The first attribute of the chronic health state designates the duration and the second designates the health state. The prospect in Eq. (3.7.2) generates the marginal distribution 5years$_{1/2}$20years over life duration and the marginal distribution blind$_{1/2}$healthy over health states. Marginal distributions lose information about joint distributions, including correlations. For example,

$$(5\text{years, healthy})_{1/2}(20\text{years, blind}), \tag{3.7.3}$$

generates the same marginals as the prospect in Eq. (3.7.2).

Multiattribute risk aversion and additive decomposability. For attribute $\gamma^i \in X^i$ and outcome α, the outcome $\gamma^i \alpha$ denotes outcome α with attribute α^i replaced by γ^i. Assume that you own a prospect $\gamma^i \alpha_{1/2} \gamma^i \beta$. You then know for sure that the resulting ith attribute value will be γ^i. Assume that $\gamma^i \alpha \preccurlyeq \gamma^i \beta$. Imagine that you can choose to have γ^i improved into a preferred attribute level δ^i for either $\gamma^i \alpha$ or $\gamma^i \beta$ in the prospect. That is, you can choose between $\delta^i \alpha_{1/2} \gamma^i \beta$ and $\gamma^i \alpha_{1/2} \delta^i \beta$. *Multiattribute risk aversion* holds if you always prefer to have the attribute improved for the worst outcome; i.e., $\delta^i \alpha_{1/2} \gamma^i \beta \succcurlyeq \gamma^i \alpha_{1/2} \delta^i \beta$. *Multiattribute risk seeking* holds if the reversed preference always holds (de Finetti 1932; Payne, Laughhunn, & Crum 1984; Pliskin, Shepard, & Weinstein 1980 p. 210; Richard 1975).

Before reading the following text, you are invited to determine your preference between the chronic health states in Eqs. (3.7.2) and (3.7.3). For chronic health states multiattribute risk seeking is the common finding: Taking prospect (5years, blind)$_{1/2}$(20years, blind) as point of departure, people usually prefer the improvement in Eq. (3.7.2), with vision regained for the 20-year period, to the improvement in Eq. (3.7.3), with vision regained for the 5-year period. The intersection of multiattribute risk aversion and multiattribute risk seeking may be called *multiattribute risk neutrality*. It means that an improvement of an attribute is evaluated the same way independently of whatever the other attribute levels are, and it signals an absence of interactions between attributes. It can indeed be shown that multiattribute risk neutrality holds if and only if we have an additive decomposition:

$$U(\alpha^1, \ldots, \alpha^m) = U^1(\alpha^1) + \cdots + U^m(\alpha^m) \tag{3.7.4}$$

(Wakker, Stiggelbout, & Jansen 2004 Corollary 3.4(ii)). For such a decomposition there are, indeed, no interactions between the attributes. Fishburn (1965) proposed a stronger condition to characterize additive decomposability, which constitutes a classical result in multiattribute utility theory:

Theorem 3.7.3. The additive decomposition of Eq. (3.7.4) holds if and only if the preference value of a prospect depends only on the marginal prospects generated over the attributes ("marginal independence"). □

This result was alluded to by Arrow (1951a pp. 431–432). The condition in Theorem 3.7.3 implies that the prospects in Eqs. (3.7.2) and (3.7.3) are equivalent. Hence, it implies multiattribute risk neutrality. In the presence of EU as assumed here, it is equivalent to multiattribute risk neutrality.

Utility independence. Keeney & Raiffa (1976) considered many utility independence conditions, where some attributes of outcomes are kept fixed at a deterministic level, and then prospects over the remaining attributes are considered. *Strong utility independence* means the following: Imagine that for a subset I of {1,. . .,m}, we fix the attribute level of every attribute in I. Then the preferences over the remaining prospects should be independent of the particular levels at which we fixed the attributes from I. This condition should hold for every subset I. SG invariance in Example 3.7.1 is implied by strong utility independence. We next consider another example.

Example 3.7.4. Assume that m = 3, $X = \mathbb{R}^3$. We take I = {2,3}, fix the first attribute at the deterministic level 0, and observe $(0,6,7)_{\frac{1}{2}}(0,2,3) \sim (0,5,6)_{\frac{1}{2}}(0,3,4)$. Then, when fixing the first attribute at the deterministic level 1, strong utility independence implies $(1,6,7)_{\frac{1}{2}}(1,2,3) \sim (1,5,6)_{\frac{1}{2}}(1,3,4)$. □

Theorem 3.7.5. Strong utility independence holds if and only if either U is additively decomposable as in Eq. (3.7.4), or U is multiplicatively decomposable:

$$U(\alpha^1, \ldots, \alpha^m) = U^1(\alpha^1) \times \cdots \times U^m(\alpha^m) \tag{3.7.5}$$

where no U^i takes the value 0 or changes sign. □

A weak version of utility independence concerns the condition when only imposed on all sets I containing all but one of the attributes. This allows for multilinear representations with many kinds of interactions between the attributes. Torrance and his collaborators used this general model extensively in the health domain (Furlong *et al.* 2001; Torrance *et al.* 1995).

Guerrero & Herrero (2005) presented an appealing intermediate result. Attributes 1,. . .,n refer to time points and each set {j,. . .,n} of time points is utility independent from the past. A "semi-separable" utility

$$U(x_1, \ldots, x_n) = \sum_{j=1}^{n} \left(u_j(x_j) \prod_{i=1}^{j-1} c_i(x_i) \right)$$

results, as proved simply using their Eq. 1.

Homogeneous attribute sets (Anscombe & Aumann 1963; Harsanyi 1955). In the rest of this section we consider the special case where $X^1 = \cdots = X^m$. Then we can equate these sets with a set $C = X^1 = \cdots = X^m$, called the set of *prizes*. Anscombe & Aumann (1963) considered this case, and added a monotonicity condition. I will now explain their condition in the terminology of this section.[11] Assume, similarly as in the utility independence conditions of Keeney & Raiffa (1976), that all but the ith attribute are kept fixed at a deterministic level, and prospects over the remaining attribute i are considered. It results in a preference relation over prospects over C that, in general, will depend on i and on the fixed deterministic levels of the other attributes. Under the additive decomposition $U^1(\alpha^1) + \cdots + U^m(\alpha^m)$ of Eq. (3.7.4), the resulting preferences then maximize EU with U^i as utility function. *A&A monotonicity* requires that all resulting preference relations over prospects over C that are not degenerate (one equivalence class; e.g., in Eq. (3.7.4) if U^i is constant) are the same; see their Assumption 1 ("monotonicity in the prizes"). So, they are not only independent of the levels at which the other attributes are kept fixed (as implied by Eq. (3.7.4)), but also of the particular attribute i chosen. This condition together with Fishburn's (1965) marginal independence condition (Theorem 3.7.3) characterizes a representation

$$U(\alpha^1, \ldots, \alpha^m) = q^1 u(\alpha^1) + \cdots + q^m u(\alpha^m) \qquad (3.7.6)$$

for a function u and nonnegative q^i that sum to 1. The proof is so simple that we give it here in the main text.

Theorem 3.7.6 [Anscombe & Aumann]. Assume $X^1 = \cdots = X^m = C$. Then the additive decomposition of Eq. (3.7.6) holds if and only if the preference value of a prospect depends only on the marginal prospects generated over the attributes and A&A monotonicity holds.

Proof. Necessity of the conditions follows from substitution. Hence we assume the preference conditions and discuss their implications. By Theorem 3.7.3 we obtain the representation $U(\alpha^1, \ldots, \alpha^m) = U^1(\alpha^1) + \cdots + U^m(\alpha^m)$ (Eq. (3.7.4)). By A&A monotonicity and the uniqueness result in Observation 2.6.3′ (EU for risk), all nonconstant U^i are the same up to level and unit. We can give them all the same level so that they are proportional, and by normalization can scale them as in Eq. (3.7.6). □

Anscombe & Aumann interpreted $(\alpha^1, \ldots, \alpha^m)$ as a gamble on a horse race, where m horses participate, exactly one will win, and α^i is the prize won if horse i wins. That is,

---

[11] An equivalent account from a different perspective will be given in a footnote in Example 4.9.7.

they interpreted multiattribute outcomes as event-contingent prospects, and q^i as the (subjective) probability of horse i winning the race. As overall representation of prospects we get

$$\left(\left(p_1 : \left(x_1^{\,1}, \ldots, x_1^{\,m}\right), \ldots, p_n : \left(x_n^{\,1}, \ldots, x_n^{\,m}\right)\right)\right) \mapsto \sum\nolimits_{j=1}^{n} p_j\left(\sum\nolimits_{i=1}^{m} q^i u\!\left(x_j^{\,i}\right)\right). \quad (3.7.7)$$

The representation in Eqs. (3.7.6) and (3.7.7) were also characterized by Harsanyi (1955), who interpreted $(\alpha^1, \ldots, \alpha^m)$ as a welfare allocation of good α^i for individual i in a society, $i = 1, \ldots, m$. That is, attributes reflect individuals. Harsanyi, in fact, considered more general outcome sets X that need not be full product sets $X^1 \times \cdots \times X^m$, but can be almost any subset. Hence, he did not need to specify the decomposition of X. Instead, he took a general set X of social states, where for social state x we can interpret α^i to designate what this state means for individual i. Harsanyi needed only minimal richness assumptions in his proof, such as the requirement that for each individual i a social state is available yielding utility 1 for i and utility 0 for all other individuals.

3.8 Taxation and welfare theory with cardinal utility

Another, controversial, application of EU concerns the allocation of resources over different individuals, such as in welfare theory and taxation. The most natural approach is to maximize the average or, equivalently, the total utility of the group, that is, the sum of individual utilities (utilitarianism). This approach is, however, not well defined if utility is ordinal (determined only up to a strictly increasing transformation). At the beginning of this century, economists came to assume that utility was ordinal and, therefore, refrained from utilitarianism. A famous result is the voting paradox of Arrow (1951b), which attempted to derive group behavior in a strictly ordinal spirit and then ran into a paradox. Some authors have argued, and I agree with them, that Arrow's negative finding shows that an ordinal approach to welfare theory does not lead to satisfactory results (Edwards 1954 p. 390; Keeney & Raiffa 1976 §10.2.1).

When von Neumann & Morgenstern (1944, 1947) presented their EU theory, with a utility unique up to level and unit ("cardinal"), the interest in the maximization of sums of individual utilities was revived. A famous result based on such a maximization is Harsanyi (1955), discussed in the preceding section. Such applications of cardinal utility for risk to welfare evaluation are, however, controversial. Many economists have argued that a cardinal utility index derived from risk behavior need not be the relevant cardinal index for welfare theory. Arguments to nevertheless identify these two indexes are in Wakker (1994). Blaug (1962) and Stigler (1950) presented the history of cardinal utility up to the middle of the preceding century. Abdellaoui, Barrios, & Wakker (2007 §3) updated this history.

Young (1990) considered tax rates in various countries under the equal-sacrifice principle, entailing that every individual should sacrifice the same amount of utility to tax. Under logarithmic utility this principle implies, for instance, proportional tax, where every individual should pay the same percentage of wealth. Young estimated the utility function that best explains tax rates imposed in various countries and, then, explicitly related this to utility functions estimated from decision under risk. He thus deliberately related utility derived under risk to ("riskless") utility used in welfare evaluations.

3.9   Proofs for Chapter 3

Proof of Observation 3.3.1. First assume risk aversion. Then, in Figure 3.3.1, x_j is preferred to the prospect $qM(1-q)m$. By independence, the left prospect is preferred to the right. This implies aversion to elementary mean-preserving spreads. By transitivity, aversion to mean-preserving spreads follows.

Conversely, assume aversion to mean-preserving spreads, and consider a prospect $p_1x_1\ldots p_nx_n$ with expectation μ. The rest of this proof will demonstrate that the prospect is a mean-preserving spread of μ, by reducing the prospect to μ through a number of reversed mean-preserving spreads. Then, because of aversion to mean-preserving spreads, $\mu \succcurlyeq p_1x_1\ldots p_nx_n$ and we are done. We may assume that all p_j's are positive.

Assume that there is an outcome that is different from μ. Let j be such that $p_j|x_j-\mu| > 0$ (the change in expected value when moving all probability mass from x_j to μ) is minimal; say, $x_j > \mu$. There must exist an $x_i < \mu$. Move the p_j-probability mass from x_j to μ, reducing expectation. Also move $p_j(x_j-\mu)/(\mu-x_i)$ probability mass from x_i to μ, after which the expectation becomes μ again. This can be done because $p_i \geq p_j(x_j-\mu)/(\mu-x_i)$ by the definition of j. What has resulted is the prospect that assigns probability 0 to x_j, probability $p_i - p_j(x_j-\mu)/(\mu-x_i)$ to x_i, extra probability $p_j + p_j(x_j-\mu)/(\mu-x_i)$ to outcome μ, and other than that has the same probabilities as the original prospect. The original prospect is an elementary mean-preserving spread of the newly constructed prospect. The newly constructed prospect has one outcome more that is equal to μ than the original prospect did.

We continue the process. After at most $n-1$ steps it stops because no outcome different from μ can be left. Each prospect along the way was an elementary mean-preserving spread of the one to be constructed next, and was less preferred. The original prospect is a mean-preserving spread of μ and μ is preferred: risk aversion. □

Proof of Theorem 3.4.1. This result follows from Theorem 3.2.1a by expressing all payments in terms of utilities of person 1. In terms of these payments, person 1 is risk neutral and orders prospects by the expectation of these units. Person 2 being more risk averse than person 1 means precisely that, in terms of U_1 units, person 2 prefers every prospect less than its expected value. That is, if payment is in U_1 units, then person 2 is risk averse. The latter holds if and only if U_2 is concave in U_1 units. This is what should be proved. □

Proof of Observation 3.5.1. This result was demonstrated by Keeney & Raiffa (1976 §4.10). That power utility (Eq. (3.5.3)) implies was also established in Exercise 3.5.1. □

Proof of Observation 3.5.2. This result was first presented and proved by Pfanzagl (1959). It can also be derived from Observation 3.5.1 through the substitution exp(α). Elaboration is omitted. The result is discussed by Keeney & Raiffa (1976 §4.8), but without a complete proof. Conversely, Observation 3.5.1 can be derived from Observation 3.5.2 through the substitution *ln*(α). Hence, Pfanzagl (1959) was the first to obtain these results. □

Proof of Theorem 3.7.3. See Fishburn (1965), or Keeney & Raiffa (1976 Theorem 6.4), or Wakker, Jansen, & Stiggelbout (2004 following Corollary 3.4). □

Proof of Theorem 3.7.5. See Keeney & Raiffa (1976 §5.4.3 and §6.3, "Remark Before Proof"). □

Proof of Theorem 3.7.6. See Anscombe & Aumann (1963). □

4 Expected utility with unknown probabilities and unknown utilities

In this chapter we return to general decision under uncertainty, with event-contingent prospects. As in Chapter 1, we assume that prospects map events to outcomes, as in $E_1x_1 \cdots E_nx_n$. Superscripts should again be distinguished from powers. EU is linear in probability and utility and, hence, if one of these is known – as was the case in the preceding chapters – then EU analyses are relatively easy. They can then exploit the linearity with respect to the addition of outcome utilities or with respect to the mixing of probabilities. Then the modeling of preferences amounts to solving linear (in) equalities. It was, accordingly, not very difficult to measure probabilities in Chapter 1 and to derive the behavioral foundation there, or to measure utility in Chapter 2 and to derive the behavioral foundation there.

In this chapter, we assume that neither probabilities nor utilities are known. In such cases, results are more difficult to obtain because we can no longer use linear analysis, and we have to solve nonlinear (in)equalities. We now face different parameters and these parameters can interact. This will be the case in all models studied in the rest of this book. This chapter introduces a tradeoff tool for analyzing such cases. This tool was recommended by Pfanzagl (1968 Remark 9.4.5). Roughly speaking, it represents the influence that you have in a decision situation given a move of nature.

4.1 Fifteen preference questions

Answering the following questions by yourself will take about half an hour without you knowing at this stage what the questions will serve for. They are presented here, prior to explanations of the theories involved, because it is best to answer them according to your own subjective preference, without concerns about theories. We will use your answers later for measuring your utility and other concepts under various theories, and for preference foundations of those theories. Appendix K shows which parts of this book are based on this section (§§4.3, 4.4, 4.5, 4.6, 4.7, 4.8.2, 4.10, 4.11, 6.5, 9.4, 10.5, 12.3). The closer your answers are to your true preferences, the better the concepts calculated later will fit with you and the more interesting they are. There are no right or wrong answers to the questions, and they only and exclusively concern your subjective tastes. If you like to use calculations to determine your answers then you can do so, but it is not necessary. Calculations are relevant only to the extent that you feel that they support your subjective preferences.

An additional benefit of working on the following questions is that the structures of these questions will serve the development of concepts introduced later. If you plan to study the many analyses in this book of the following figures in detail, then you may make copies so as to have them easily available. If you prefer not to invest much time at this stage but still want to read sections based on this one, then you can proceed as follows: Skip the questions but, whenever data is needed, take the preferences of some subject described later – say, subject 5 in Table 4.3.1 – as default data.

Fig. 4.1.1a illustrates the first question. $1000 is the intended unit of payment, but you may take in mind any other unit if you wish. Imagine that there will be elections in a foreign country with two candidates participating, of whom exactly one will win. The party of candidate 1, or $cand_1$ as we will write more compactly (with $cand_2$ similar), mostly won in the past, but this time around their campaign went badly. You have to decide on an investment in this country, the profits of which depend on which candidate will win. You have to make your decision now as is, without further information.

When the outcome written on the dotted lines in Fig. 4.1.1a is, say, 11, then virtually everyone will prefer the right prospect in the figure, and when that outcome is 200 then virtually everyone will prefer the left prospect. That is, for low outcomes on the dotted line, the right prospect is preferred, and for high ones the left is preferred. In between the high and low outcomes there will be a switching value, where your preference changes from left to right, and where you have no clear preference. Call this value α^1. If you have no clear preference for a whole region of outcomes, then the midpoint of that "region of indecisiveness" is taken as the best guess for the switching value α^1.

The measurement is chained, which means that an answer given to one question, such as α^1 in Fig. a, is an input to the next question. The next question is in Fig. 4.1.1b, and the right prospect there has α^1 as a possible outcome. You are again invited to determine the switching value on the dotted line, which is called α^2. Obviously, $\alpha^2 > \alpha^1$. Similarly, Figs. c and d elicit α^3 and α^4. Now please fill out the figure.

Figure 4.1.2 shows the following four preference questions. In Fig. 4.1.2a, the answer α^1 given in Fig. 4.1.1a again serves as an input. Before asking the preference question, we first determine another input of the stimuli, namely the outcome g of the left prospect. For outcome g, choose a round number of approximately $1.5 \times \alpha^4$. For the preference question, then determine the outcome $G > g$ to be inserted on the dotted line such that the two prospects are indifferent. Because this experiment is chained, a misunderstanding in an early question can bias all subsequent data. For example, if you by accident took $g = 1.5 \times \alpha^1$ as opposed to $g = 1.5 \times \alpha^4$, then much will go wrong in measurements and analyses presented later in this book.

(a)

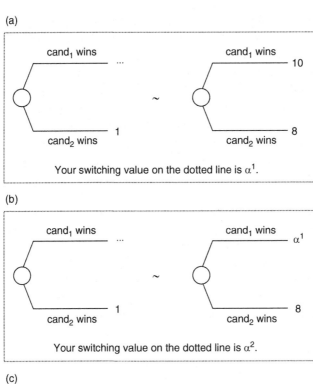

(b)

(c)

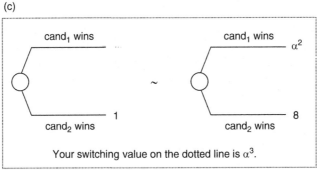

(d)

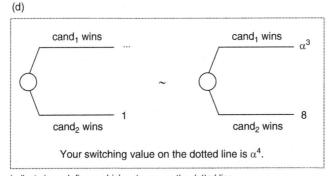

Indicate in each figure which outcome on the dotted line ...
makes the two prospects indifferent (the switching value).

Figure 4.1.1 [*TO upwards*] Eliciting $\alpha^1 \dots \alpha^4$ for unknown probabilities.

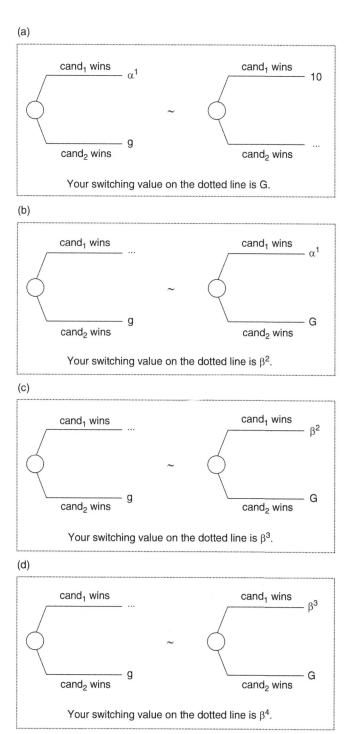

(a)

cand$_1$ wins α^1 cand$_1$ wins   10

$\sim$

cand$_2$ wins   g   cand$_2$ wins   ...

Your switching value on the dotted line is G.

(b)

cand$_1$ wins   ...   cand$_1$ wins α^1

$\sim$

cand$_2$ wins   g   cand$_2$ wins   G

Your switching value on the dotted line is β^2.

(c)

cand$_1$ wins   ...   cand$_1$ wins β^2

$\sim$

cand$_2$ wins   g   cand$_2$ wins   G

Your switching value on the dotted line is β^3.

(d)

cand$_1$ wins   ...   cand$_1$ wins β^3

$\sim$

cand$_2$ wins   g   cand$_2$ wins   G

Your switching value on the dotted line is β^4.

Indicate in each figure which outcome on the dotted line ···
makes the two prospects indifferent (the switching value).

Figure 4.1.2 [*2nd TO upwards*] Eliciting β^2, β^3, β^4.

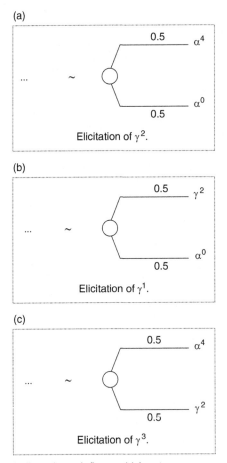

(a)

0.5 α^4

...   ~ $\sim$

0.5 α^0

Elicitation of γ^2.

(b)

0.5 γ^2

...   ~

0.5 α^0

Elicitation of γ^1.

(c)

0.5 α^4

...   ~

0.5 γ^2

Elicitation of γ^3.

Indicate in each figure which outcome
on the dotted line ..., if received with
certainty, is indifferent to the prospect.

Figure 4.1.3 [CEs] Eliciting $\gamma^2, \gamma^1, \gamma^3$.

In Figs. 4.1.2b−4.1.2d, we always insert the values g and G just obtained. In Fig.
4.1.2b, determine the outcome β^2 that makes the two prospects equivalent for you,
and then determine β^3 and β^4 likewise.

Figure 4.1.3 shows the next triple of preference questions. They concern probability-contingent prospects with given probabilities. The α's are similar to those in
Figure 4.1.1, with $\alpha^0 = 10$. We elicit γ^2 before γ^1, in Fig. a. You are asked to give
your certainty equivalents of the three prospects.

The questions in Figure 4.1.4 are structured the same way as the preceding
questions. Now the values elicited decrease. In Fig. a you determine a switching
value $\delta^3 < \alpha^4$, in Fig. b you determine a switching value $\delta^2 < \delta^3$; and so on.

Figure 4.1.5 shows the final triple of preference questions. They again concern
probability-contingent prospects with given probabilities. You are asked to indicate

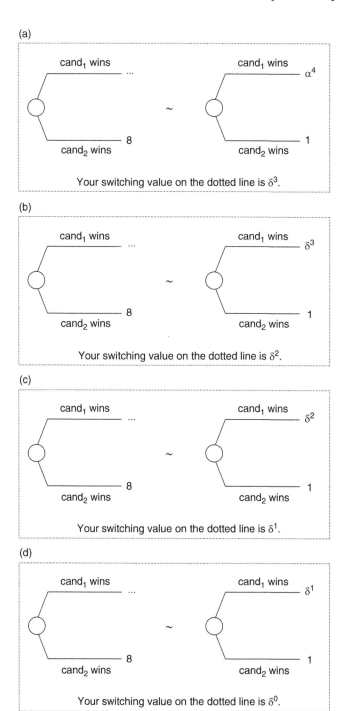

Indicate in each figure which outcome on the dotted
line ... makes the two prospects indifferent (the
switching value).

Figure 4.1.4 [*TO downwards*] Eliciting $\delta^3 \dots \delta^0$.

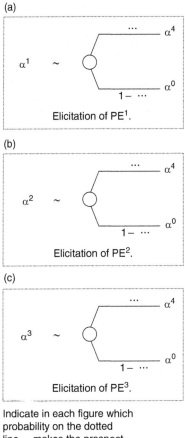

(a)

Elicitation of PE^1.

(b)

Elicitation of PE^2.

(c)

Elicitation of PE^3.

Indicate in each figure which probability on the dotted line ... makes the prospect indifferent to receiving the sure amount to the left.

Figure 4.1.5 *[PEs]* Eliciting PE^1, PE^2, PE^3.

which probabilities in the risky prospects generate indifference. Hence this method is often called the *probability equivalent method*. The abbreviation PE in the figure refers to this name.

We will analyze your answers assuming EU in this chapter.

4.2   (Subjective) expected utility

This section gives elementary definitions for expected utility.

Definition 4.2.1. Under Structural Assumption 1.2.1 (decision under uncertainty), *expected utility* *(EU)* holds if there exist a probability measure P and a strictly increasing *utility (function)* U : ℝ → ℝ, such that

$$E_1 x_1 \cdots E_n x_n \mapsto \sum_{j=1}^{n} P(E_j) U(x_j), \tag{4.2.1}$$

the *EU* of the prospect, represents preference. □

In this model, the probability measure P and the utility function U are the subjective parameters that characterize the decision maker. The following exercise shows how to derive decisions from the EU model. Its elaboration is immediately given in the main text.

Exercise 4.2.1.[a] Consider the vendor Example 1.1.1. Assume EU with $P(s_1) = \frac{1}{4}$, $P(s_2) = \frac{1}{2}$, $P(s_3) = \frac{1}{4}$, $U(400) = 1$, $U(200) = 0.7$, $U(100) = 0.5$, $U(0) = 0$, and $U(-400) = -2$. Calculate the EUs of the four prospects in Table 1.1.1, and determine which prospect is chosen. □

In Exercise 4.2.1:

$$EU(x) = \frac{1}{4} \times 1 + \frac{1}{2} \times 1/2 + \frac{1}{4} \times (-2) = 0;$$

$$EU(y) = \frac{1}{4} \times (-2) + \frac{1}{2} \times 1/2 + \frac{1}{4} \times 1 = 0.$$

$$EU(0) = 0;$$

$$EU(x + y) = \frac{1}{2} \times 0.7 = 0.35.$$

Hence $x + y$ has the highest EU and is chosen.

Exercise 4.2.2.[a] Consider the vendor Example 1.1.1 again. Assume EU with $P(s_1) = \frac{1}{2}$, $P(s_2) = \frac{1}{3}$, $P(s_3) = \frac{1}{6}$, $U(400) = 1$, $U(200) = 0.7$, $U(100) = 0.5$, $U(0) = 0$, and $U(-400) = -2$. Calculate the EUs of the four prospects in Table 1.1.1, and determine which one is chosen. □

We next turn to the elicitation method for deriving theoretical constructs from observed choice. From now on this will be more complex than in the preceding chapters because all models in the rest of this book will involve at least two unknown functions, making it harder to identify each separately. In the model considered here, EU, the task is relatively easy because of additivity of probability. The elaboration of the following exercise is immediately given in the text.

Exercise 4.2.3.[a] Consider a partition $\{E_1, E_2, E_3\}$. Assume EU with the normalized $U(0) = 0$ and $U(100) = 1$, and assume $25_{E_1}0 \sim 25_{E_2}0 \sim 25_{E_3}0$ and $25 \sim 100_{E_1}0$. What are $P(E_1)$, $P(E_2)$, $P(E_3)$, and $U(25)$? □

In Exercise 4.2.3, the first two indifferences imply

$$P(E_1)U(25) = P(E_2)U(25) = P(E_3)U(25),$$

so that all three events have the same probability. These sum to 1 and must be $\frac{1}{3}$ each. Then $25 \sim 100_{E_1}0$ implies $U(25) = P(E_1)U(100) = \frac{1}{3}$. Hence, if we find equally likely events, then we can easily infer their probabilities and also measure utility. This was the basic idea of Davidson & Suppes (1956), Ramsey (1931), and Savage (1954).

Exercise 4.2.4.[a] Consider a partition $\{E_1, E_2, E_3\}$. Assume EU with the normalized $U(0) = 0$ and $U(100) = 1$, and assume $25_{E_1 \cup E_2} 0 \sim 25_{E_3} 0, 25_{E_1} 0 \sim 25_{E_2} 0$, and $15 \sim 100_{E_1} 0$. What are $P(E_1)$, $P(E_2)$, $P(E_3)$, and $U(15)$? □

The probabilities in EU for uncertainty are sometimes called *subjective*. They need not be given beforehand and need not be based on objective grounds, although they may be (Exercise 2.3.1). They may describe subjective opinions of a person and may vary across different persons. In this respect they have the same status as utilities. Subjective probabilities appeared before in Chapter 1, where U was linear and expected value was maximized. In the literature, the term subjective expected utility, abbreviated SEU, is sometimes used instead of EU. As explained before, we will use the same terminology for risk and uncertainty whenever possible, so that we use the term EU for both contexts.[1]

The elicitation method worked out easily in the preceding two exercises, readily giving both probabilities and utilities. This was, however, due to luck because we had convenient equally probable events that made life easy. Such events are often not available in our observations, and there then is no very easy way to measure probabilities and utilities. Using the richness of outcomes as assumed throughout this book, the next section will present a way of measuring utilities and then probabilities that does work in general. Before turning to that, the rest of this section presents some preparatory results for EU.

Exercise 4.2.5.[!a] Assume EU. Show that the following two claims hold. Together they amount to monotonicity as defined in Chapter 1. Assume that $f = E_1 x_1 \ldots E_n x_n$ and $g = E_1 y_1 \ldots E_n y_n$. By Exercise 1.2.4 (partition flexibility), we may assume the same partition for both prospects.

(a) Show that, if $f(s) \geq g(s)$ for all s, then $f \succcurlyeq g$ (weak monotonicity).
(b) Show that, if $f(s) > g(s)$ for all s, then $f \succ g$ (strict monotonicity). □

We use the notation

$$\alpha_E x \tag{4.2.2}$$

to refer to the prospect yielding α under event E, and yielding the outcomes of x off E. With $x = (E_1:10, E_2:12, E_3:8)$, for example, we have $15_{E_1} x = (E_1:15, E_2:12, E_3:8)$ and $13_{E_3} x = (E_1:10, E_2:12, E_3:13)$. A special case of this notation, $\alpha_E \beta$, when x is the constant prospect β, was used before. The notation $\alpha_E x$ is most convenient if E is an outcome event of x, and we will usually restrict attention to such cases. For $x = E_1 x_1 \cdots E_n x_n$ and a general event E,

---

[1] Several authors have used the term decision under risk whenever decisions are based on probabilities, be they objective as in Chapter 3 or subjective as considered here. Thus, they argued that Savage's (1954) preference foundation of expected utility showed that decision under uncertainty can always be reduced to decision under risk. We will not follow this terminology but will use the term decision under risk exclusively for cases where the probabilities are objective and can be used as empirical primitives. Decisions based on nonobjective probabilities belong to decision under uncertainty and not to decision under risk in this book.

$$EU(\alpha_E x) = P(E)U(\alpha) + \sum_{j=1}^{n} P(E_j - E)U(x_j),$$

where E_j-E denotes set-difference, which means that E_j-E contains the states contained in E_j but not those in E.

An event E is *null* if $\alpha_E x \sim \beta_E x$ for all prospects x and outcomes α and β, and *nonnull* otherwise. Outcomes of null events can be ignored for determining the preference value of a prospect. Null events are considered to be impossible. To avoid triviality, we assume that there is a partition with two nonnull events, as in Structural Assumption 1.2.1 (decision under uncertainty).

Exercise 4.2.6.[a] Assume Structural Assumption 1.2.1 (decision under uncertainty) and assume EU. Show that an event E is null if and only if $P(E) = 0$. □

The uniqueness of utility is the same for uncertainty as it was for risk, as partly illustrated by the following exercise. We will later see that probability is uniquely determined.

Exercise 4.2.7.[a] Show that, if EU holds with a utility function U, then it also holds with utility function $U^* = \tau + \sigma U$, where $\tau \in \mathbb{R}$ and $\sigma > 0$. □

The rest of this section can be skipped by readers with little theoretical interest. $\succcurlyeq$ is *continuous* if, for every partition $(E_1,\ldots,E_n)$ of S, the preference relation restricted to prospects $(x_1,\ldots,x_n)$ with outcome events $E_1,\ldots,E_n$ satisfies the usual Euclidean continuity condition: the sets $\{(x_1,\ldots,x_n): (x_1,\ldots,x_n) \succcurlyeq (y_1,\ldots,y_n)\}$ and $\{(x_1,\ldots,x_n): (x_1,\ldots,x_n) \preccurlyeq (y_1,\ldots,y_n)\}$ are closed subsets of $\mathbb{R}^n$ for each $(y_1,\ldots,y_n)$. Wakker (1993a) demonstrated that this finite-dimensional continuity condition suffices for obtaining the traditional behavioral foundations.

The implication of the following assignment can be reversed under nondegeneracy, so that U is continuous if and only if preference is (Wakker 1988).

Assignment 4.2.8.[b] Assume EU. Show that $\succcurlyeq$ is continuous if U is. □

4.3 Measuring utility and testing EU for §4.1

This section analyzes the choices in §4.1 in terms of EU. Relative to Chapter 2, an extra difficulty is that the probabilities need not be known. $Cand_1$ abbreviates candidate1, and $cand_2$ is similar.

Exercise 4.3.1.[a] Consider Figure 4.1.1 (TO upwards; do not consider the other figures). Assume that both candidates have a nonzero probability of winning. Show that, under EU (with $\alpha^0 = 10$, p_1 for the (subjective) probability of $cand_1$ winning, and $p_2 = 1 - p_1$):

$$U(\alpha^4) - U(\alpha^3) = U(\alpha^3) - U(\alpha^2) = U(\alpha^2) - U(\alpha^1) = U(\alpha^1) - U(\alpha^0). \quad (4.3.1)$$

First derive the last equality using only Figs. 4.1.1a and b. □

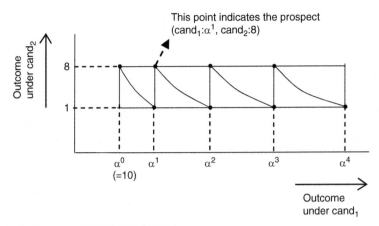

Curves designate indifference.

Figure 4.3.1 Your indifferences in Figure 4.1.1.

The exercise has shown that $\alpha^0,\ldots,\alpha^4$ are equally spaced in utility units. I am making this claim about your utility without knowing your (subjective) probability of cand$_1$ winning. Under EU, your probability will obviously affect which outcomes $\alpha^1,\ldots,\alpha^4$ you chose, but it apparently does not affect the correctness of the claim in the exercise. Whatever your α's are, they are equally spaced in utility units. The pattern of Figure 4.3.1 clarifies why the term sawtooth method has sometimes been used for related measurement methods (Fishburn 1967 p. 450; Louviere, Hensher, & Swait 2000).

If we normalize $U(\alpha^0) = 0$ and $U(\alpha^4) = 1$, which can always be done (Exercise 4.2.7), then the four equally big steps $U(\alpha^j) - U(\alpha^{j-1})$, jointly bridging a distance 1, must each be ¼, and we can draw a graph of utility as in Figure 4.3.2. The figure shows that the measurement of the α^j's can be interpreted as the measurement of inverses of utility, with $\alpha^j = U^{-1}(j/4)$ for all j.

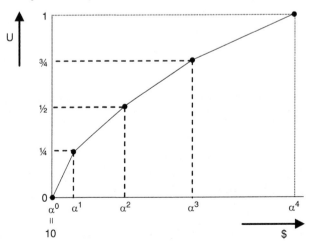

Figure 4.3.2 Utility graph derived from Figure 4.1.1.

Using refined versions of the measurement now explained, taking the "gauge" outcomes (8 and 1 in Figures 4.1.1 and 4.3.1) closer to each other, taking the starting value α^0 lower if desired, and measuring more than four steps, we can measure utility to any desired degree of precision and extent. Next, with utility available, we can measure subjective probabilities using the same techniques as in Chapter 1, where in fact we assumed utility available (it being equal to money there). For example, for each pair of disjoint events we can measure the exchange rate of utility units between them, giving the proportion of their probabilities. And for each event we can measure how much utility for sure is equivalent to receiving one utility unit conditional on the event and zero utility units otherwise, after which the equivalent utility for sure is the probability of the event. Thus we can, in principle, completely measure subjective probabilities and utilities in full generality, be it that it takes more work than we needed in preceding chapters. We now turn to consistency checks of the measurements.

Utility measurements similar to those inferred from Figure 4.1.1 can be derived for the questions in Figure 4.1.2 (2nd TO upwards). Figures 4.1.1 and 4.1.2 together provide a consistency test of EU, as part (b) of the following exercise demonstrates.

Exercise 4.3.2.[a] Assume EU for Figures 4.1.1 and 4.1.2, with nonzero probabilities of winning for both candidates.

(a) Show that $U(\beta^4) - U(\beta^3) = U(\beta^3) - U(\beta^2) = U(\beta^2) - U(\alpha^1) = U(\alpha^1) - U(\alpha^0)$.
(b) Show that $\beta^j = \alpha^j$ for all j. $\square$

As the exercise shows, Figures 4.1.1 and 4.1.2 provide two different ways of measuring the same values $\alpha^j = \beta^j$ under EU. If the equalities do not hold then either EU must be abandoned or the answers must be reconsidered, possibly using an error theory. Figure 4.1.3 (CEs) also provides a consistency test of EU when combined with Figure 4.1.1:

Exercise 4.3.3.[a] Assume EU for Figures 4.1.1 and 4.1.3, with nonzero probabilities of winning for both candidates. Show that $\gamma^j = \alpha^j$ for all j. $\square$

If consistency checks reveal systematic inconsistencies, then for descriptive purposes nonexpected utility models can be developed to accommodate these inconsistencies.

Figures 4.1.1 and 4.1.4 together test elementary properties of EU, as we will see next. These elementary properties also hold true for the nonexpected utility models introduced later, so that violations of EU found through Figures 4.1.1 and 4.1.4 cannot be accommodated by those models.

Exercise 4.3.4.[a] Do not assume EU (deviating from the title of this section). Assume only weak ordering of your preference relation. Further assume *strong monotonicity*, which means that any prospect becomes strictly better as soon as one of its outcomes is strictly improved. Under EU, not assumed here, the latter assumption would amount to all outcome events being nonnull. Show that $\delta^j = \alpha^j$ for all j in Figures 4.1.1 and 4.1.4. □

Exercise 4.3.5.[a] Assume EU for Figure 4.1.5. Throughout we normalize $U(\alpha^0) = 0$ and $U(\alpha^4) = 1$. Assume the data of Figure 4.1.1, and the implications of EU there. Do not consider your own answers PE^j in Figure 4.1.5. Instead, consider the answers PE^j that EU predicts given $U(\alpha^j) = j/4$ for all j. Show that EU predicts $PE^j = j/4$ for all j. In other words, your answers in Figures 4.1.1 and 4.1.5 violate EU unless $PE^j = j/4$ for all j. □

Exercises 4.3.1–4.3.5 have demonstrated that, if EU holds deterministically, then all elicited values in Figures 4.1.1–4.1.4 should agree ($\alpha^j = \beta^j = \gamma^j = \delta^j$ for all j), and $PE^j = j/4$ for all j. You can verify whether your answers satisfy these equalities. A statistical analysis of these choice questions will be given later, based on the answers given by five students in individual interviews done in 1996. Table 4.3.1 contains their answers.

Table 4.3.1. *Data of five subjects*

	Subject 1	Subject 2	Subject 3	Subject 4	Subject 5
α^0	10	10	10	10	10
α^1	20	17	28	25	17
α^2	42	27	50	50	32
α^3	55	42.5	80	85	47
α^4	67	60	115	140	62.5
α^0	10	10	10	10	10
α^1	20	17	28	25	17
β^2	40	27	56	50	27.5
β^3	57	40	105	85	41
β^4	70	52	160	130	55
α^0	10	10	10	10	10
γ^1	18	18	25	18	13.5
γ^2	30	32	45	35	20
γ^3	48	40	75	65	30
α^4	67	60	115	140	62.5
δ^0	20	15	22	40	13
δ^1	30	23	35	50	22
δ^2	40	32	55	70	35
δ^3	50	45	80	100	47
α^4	67	60	115	140	62.5
PE^1	0.35	0.25	0.625	0.30	0.25
PE^2	0.50	0.50	0.75	0.70	0.75
PE^3	0.80	0.75	0.85	0.90	0.90
g	120	200	200	200	100
G	135	255	350	270	122

The subjects in the experiment violate deterministic EU in many ways. Even, virtually all equalities implied by EU are violated. For example, $\alpha^4 = \beta^4$ is violated for every subject, and so is the equality $\alpha^j = \gamma^j$ for every subject and every j. Also $\delta^0 = \alpha^0$ is violated for every subject. These violations may of course result from randomness in the answers rather than from a genuine violation of EU. A statistical analysis will be given later. A first inspection of the data suggests that the differences between the β's and the α's are not systematic, that the γ's are mostly below the α's, that the δ's mostly exceed the α's, and that the PE^j's exceed j/4.

If our sole purpose is to measure the utility function of a person, then it is usually easier to use events with known probabilities as in Figures 4.1.3 and 4.1.5 than events with unknown probabilities as in the other figures. The main reason for the use of unknown probabilities here is that this case best prepares for theories developed later.

Assignment 4.3.6.^{a} Assume EU with a positive probability of cand$_2$ winning. Show that $U(G) - U(g) = U(8) - U(1)$. □

4.4 A decision process

This section presents an interpretation of some indifferences in §4.1, and for the tradeoff tool used in most of this book. Parts of this section closely follow Köbberling & Wakker (2004).

The decision process for making the decisions in the experiment of §4.1 that best fits with the theories to be derived, and that matches the algebraic derivations of the exercises in §4.3, is as follows. We focus on the indifferences of Figs. 4.1.1a and 4.1.1d (TO upwards), writing E for the event of cand$_1$ winning:

$$\alpha^1{}_E 1 \sim \alpha^0{}_E 8 \text{ and}$$

$$\alpha^4{}_E 1 \sim \alpha^3{}_E 8.$$

In both indifferences, the lower branches in Figs. 4.1.1a and 4.1.1d provide an argument in favor of the right prospect, because then 8 is received instead of 1, conditional on E^c (cand$_2$ wins). For now, $8 \ominus 1$ is a linguistic abbreviation of "receiving outcome 8 instead of outcome 1." It reflects the influence, i.e. the preference value created by the decision maker's choice for the right prospect, if E^c is true. Thus, the mathematical notation reflects a component in the decision making process, in agreement with the homeomorphic approach of this book.[2]

In both indifferences, the upper branches provide an argument in favor of the left prospect, corresponding to $\alpha^1 \ominus \alpha^0$ (receiving outcome α^1 instead of outcome α^0) in Fig. 4.1.1a and to $\alpha^4 \ominus \alpha^3$ (receiving outcome α^4 instead of outcome α^3) in Fig. 4.1.1d, both contingent on E. Obviously, the strength of the argument in favor of the right prospect provided by $8 \ominus 1$ depends not only on how much better it is to receive

---

[2] The notation $\ominus$ was suggested to me by Duncan Luce, as an analog of his joint receipt symbol $\oplus$.

8 instead of 1, but also on event E^c, in particular its perceived likelihood. (The likelihood of) E is similarly relevant to the weight of the arguments provided by $\alpha^1 \ominus \alpha^0$ and $\alpha^4 \ominus \alpha^3$. At any rate, the indifference of Fig. 4.1.1a suggests the following interpretation:

$\alpha^1 \ominus \alpha^0$ contingent on E exactly offsets $8 \ominus 1$ contingent on E^c.

The indifference in Fig. 4.1.1d is interpreted similarly:

$\alpha^4 \ominus \alpha^3$ contingent on E exactly offsets $8 \ominus 1$ contingent on E^c.

These two interpretations together suggest that $\alpha^4 \ominus \alpha^3$ can do the exact same thing as $\alpha^1 \ominus \alpha^0$, i.e. offset $8 \ominus 1$ contingent on event E^c while itself being contingent on event E. We interpret this as $\alpha^1 \ominus \alpha^0$ being an equally good improvement as $\alpha^4 \ominus \alpha^3$, and use the notation

$$\alpha^1 \ominus \alpha^0 \sim^t \alpha^4 \ominus \alpha^3 \tag{4.4.1}$$

as a linguistic abbreviation of this interpretation. The superscript t abbreviates trade-off. The relation will be formalized in §4.5.

$8 \ominus 1$ contingent on event E^c served as a gauge to establish Eq. (4.4.1). We will investigate the pros and cons of the interpretation given here in what follows, and see under which conditions it does or does not make sense. The interpretation given here appeals to a rational way of making decisions: by weighing arguments pro and con, while discouraging noncompensatory heuristics such as just going for certainty.

4.5   General utility measurement and the tradeoff notation

This section formalizes the concepts discussed so far for general prospects, and introduces a general tradeoff notation used in several parts of the book. The relationships $\sim^t$ of Eq. (4.4.1) can be derived from other prospects than those just discussed. Figure 4.5.1 illustrates the following analysis. Consider general multiple-outcome prospects x, y, and consider the following two indifferences:

$$\alpha_E x \sim \beta_E y \tag{4.5.1}$$

and

$$\gamma_E x \sim \delta_E y. \tag{4.5.2}$$

Definition 4.5.1. We write

$$\alpha \ominus \beta \sim^t \gamma \ominus \delta \tag{4.5.3}$$

whenever we can find prospects x,y and a nonnull event E such that the indifferences in Eqs. (4.5.1) and (4.5.2) hold. The $\sim^t$ relation is called *t-indifference* (abbreviating tradeoff indifference), or just *indifference* if it is clear from the context that tradeoffs are involved. □

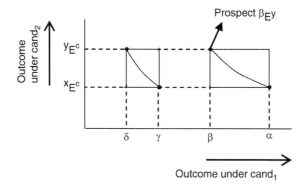

Curves designate indifference. α instead of β
apparently offsets y_{E^c} instead of x_{E^c}, and so
does γ instead of δ.

Figure 4.5.1 $\alpha \ominus \beta \sim^t \gamma \ominus \delta$.

The t-indifferences formalize the reasoning that was discussed in §4.4.[3] In Eqs. (4.5.1) and (4.5.2), $\alpha \ominus \beta$ and $\gamma \ominus \delta$, contingent on event E, offset the same gauge (receiving the x outcomes instead of the y outcomes) contingent on not-E. This suggests again that $\alpha \ominus \beta$ and $\gamma \ominus \delta$ are equally good improvements. The gauge now considered is more complex than gauges we saw in preceding sections. Now we allow that various outcomes and events are involved, but this does not alter the reasoning. In the notation of Eq. (4.5.3), we seem to be forgetting about E, x, and y. The extent to which such forgetting is justified, and entails separability-like assumptions, will appear from Theorem 4.6.4. An early version of the t-indifference relation $\sim^t$ can be recognized in Pfanzagl (1968 Definition 8.6.8).

Exercise 4.5.1.[!a] Verify that $\alpha^j \ominus \alpha^{j-1} \sim^t \alpha^i \ominus \alpha^{i-1}$ for all i,j in Figure 4.1.1 (TO upwards; no elaboration provided). □

Example 4.5.2 [A subject's choices from Table 4.3.1]. The events E (cand$_1$ wins) and E^c (cand$_2$ wins) will be suppressed. The responses of subject 4 in Table 4.3.1 for Figs. 4.1.1a and 4.1.1d show that

$$(1, \mathbf{25}) \sim (8, \mathbf{10}) \text{ and}$$
$$(1, \mathbf{140}) \sim (8, \mathbf{85}),$$

implying

$$25 \ominus 10 \sim^t 140 \ominus 85.$$

---

[3] For example, the two indifferences in Figs. 4.1.1a and 4.1.1d are a special case of those in Eqs. (4.5.1) and (4.5.2): $E_1 = E$, $E_2 = E^c$, $\alpha = \alpha^4$, $\beta = \alpha^3$, $\gamma = \alpha^1$, $\delta = \alpha^0$; because the values of x and y under E are immaterial, we can define x as a sure gain of 1 and y as a sure gain of 8.

For this subject, receiving 25 instead of 10 was apparently an equally good tradeoff as receiving 140 instead of 85. □

The t-indifference relation satisfies natural symmetry conditions, with the following four relationships being equivalent:

$$\alpha \ominus \beta \sim^t \gamma \ominus \delta; \ \gamma \ominus \delta \sim^t \alpha \ominus \beta; \ \beta \ominus \alpha \sim^t \delta \ominus \gamma; \ \delta \ominus \gamma \sim^t \beta \ominus \alpha. \tag{4.5.4}$$

That each one of these relationships implies all others follows mainly from symmetry of the $\sim$ relation between prospects. Equation (4.5.4) does not need any assumption about the preference relation $\succcurlyeq$, not even weak ordering, so that it holds true for all preference relations.

Exercise 4.5.2.[a] Show that Eq. (4.5.4) holds. □
We also have the natural

$$\alpha \ominus \alpha \sim^t \beta \ominus \beta. \tag{4.5.5}$$

This follows under weak ordering from any $\alpha_E x \sim \alpha_E x$ and $\beta_E x \sim \beta_E x$ for any nonnull event E. The following exercise demonstrates that t-indifference elicits equalities of utility differences, generalizing the results of Exercise 4.3.1 (regarding α's in Figure 4.1.1) and several exercises that followed.

Exercise 4.5.3.[a] Show that, under EU,

$$\alpha \ominus \beta \sim^t \gamma \ominus \delta \Rightarrow U(\alpha) - U(\beta) = U(\gamma) - U(\delta). \tag{4.5.6}$$

□

Formally, we call the method of measuring utility using t-indifferences the *tradeoff method*. It was used for instance in the "tradeoff" figures 4.1.1, 4.1.2, and 4.1.4, and gave the graph of the utility function in Figure 4.3.2.

4.6   A behavioral foundation of expected utility

This section considers cross-checks and inconsistencies in the utility measurements described in the preceding section. It will lead to a behavioral foundation of EU for uncertainty. Thus, we now cover the joint roles of probability and utility. The first to obtain such a result was Savage (1954), building on an earlier result by Ramsey (1931). Theorem 4.6.4 will, therefore, be an alternative to Savage's (1954) behavioral foundation of EU. Whereas Savage required an infinite state space, Theorem 4.6.4 will allow for finite state spaces. In return, Theorem 4.6.4 requires infinitely many outcomes whereas Savage's model could also handle cases of finitely many outcomes.

For general preferences (not necessarily representable by EU) it is possible that simultaneously $\alpha \ominus \beta \sim^t \gamma \ominus \delta$ and $\alpha' \ominus \beta \sim^t \gamma \ominus \delta$ for $\alpha' \neq \alpha$.[4] Then there exist prospects

---

[4] In general, if strict monotonicity – as assumed in our main results – does not hold and/or if outcomes are not monetary, then we replace $\alpha' \neq \alpha$ by $\alpha' \not\sim \alpha$.

x, y and a nonnull event E such that $\alpha_E x \sim \beta_E y$ and $\gamma_E x \sim \delta_E y$, but there exist other prospects f, g, and a nonnull event F, such that $\alpha'_F f \sim \beta_F g$ and $\gamma_F f \sim \delta_F g$. We give an example.

Example 4.6.1. This example is a continuation of Example 4.5.2. Figs. 4.1.2d and 4.1.2a imply for subject 4 (inferring from Table 4.3.1 that $g = 200$, $G = 270$, and so on) that

$$(200, \mathbf{130}) \sim (270, \mathbf{85}) \text{ and}$$
$$(200, \mathbf{25}) \sim (270, \mathbf{10}),$$

implying $130 \ominus 85 \sim^t 25 \ominus 10$.

Thus, receiving [*130* instead of 85] is an equally good tradeoff as receiving [*25* instead of 10]. However, Example 4.5.2 suggested, differently, that receiving [*140* instead of 85] is an equally good tradeoff as receiving [*25* instead of 10]. [*140* instead of 85] should be a better tradeoff than [*130* instead of 85]. Hence, both being equally good as the same third tradeoff suggests an inconsistency for $\sim^t$ of subject 4. □

If a phenomenon as in Examples 4.5.2 and 4.6.1 occurs, then the t-indifferences $\sim^t$ suggest that there are inconsistencies. The interpretation of $\alpha \ominus \beta \sim^t \gamma \ominus \delta$ indicating that "receiving α instead of β is as good a tradeoff as receiving γ instead of δ" then is not appealing, because $\alpha' \ominus \beta \sim^t \gamma \ominus \delta$ suggests differently. Tradeoff consistency holds if an inconsistency as just described never occurs. That is, if $\alpha \ominus \beta \sim^t \gamma \ominus \delta$ and $\alpha' > \alpha$ then $\alpha' \ominus \beta \sim^t \gamma \ominus \delta$ cannot hold.[5] Because of the symmetry of the outcomes in the $\sim^t$ relation (Eq. (4.5.4)), similar observations hold for β, γ, and δ as they do for α. We thus obtain the following condition.

Definition 4.6.2. Tradeoff consistency holds if improving an outcome in any t-indifference breaks that indifference. □

Tradeoff consistency is again reminiscent of a conservation of preference principle that we alluded to in preceding chapters. The following sentence, while not formalizing the idea, may suggest such an intuition:

Given event E, $\alpha \ominus \beta$ reflects your influence when choosing $\alpha_E x$ instead of $\beta_E y$ (choosing the left prospect in Eq. (4.5.1)), and the indifference $\alpha \ominus \beta \sim^t \gamma \ominus \delta$ (as in Eq. (4.5.3)) suggests that this influence $\alpha \ominus \beta$ creates as much preference value as the influence $\gamma \ominus \delta$ does.

Tradeoff consistency is more complex than de Finetti's additivity or SG consistency, and refers only to very basic cases of observed influences, with the creation of preference value out of nothing to be avoided there. We have to restrict ourselves to those basic cases now because there are no directly observable linear scales of utility or probability available. Appendix 4.14 elaborates on this point. The following observation is an immediate corollary of Exercise 4.5.3 and utility being strictly increasing.

---

[5] For general nonmonetary outcomes, $\alpha' \succ \alpha$ would be taken instead of $\alpha' > \alpha$.

Observation 4.6.3. EU implies tradeoff consistency. □

We are ready for the main theorem of this section, a behavioral foundation of EU. As it turns out, tradeoff consistency is not only necessary, but also sufficient, to ensure that EU holds in the presence of some natural conditions. That is, it provides a critical test of EU.

Theorem 4.6.4 [Uncertainty-EU]. Under Structural Assumption 1.2.1 (decision under uncertainty), the following two statements are equivalent.

(i)   Expected utility holds with continuous strictly increasing utility.
(ii) $\succcurlyeq$ satisfies:
  • weak ordering;
  • monotonicity;
  • continuity;
  • tradeoff consistency. □

Observation 4.6.4' [Uniqueness result for Theorem 4.6.4]. In (i) of Theorem 4.6.4, the probabilities are uniquely determined, and utility is unique up to unit and level. □

If tradeoff measurements reveal systematic inconsistencies, then we know that we have to turn to theories more general than EU, and to modifications of the t-indifference. As we will see in Parts II and III, we then have to modify the t-indifference relation by forgetting less about x,y, and E than we did in Eq. (4.5.3).

Assignment 4.6.1.[a] Check out where your own answers in Figures 4.1.1 and 4.1.2 violate tradeoff consistency. □

Assignment 4.6.2.[c] Assume $S = \{s_1, s_2\}$, where we suppress the states in the notation (x_1, x_2) for prospects. $P(s_1) = P(s_2) = \frac{1}{2}$. Assume that EU holds with "state-dependent" utility and $U_1(\alpha) = \alpha$, $U_2(\alpha) = e^\alpha$, so that a prospect (x_1, x_2) is evaluated by $(x_1 + e^{x_2})/2$. Show that tradeoff consistency is violated. If you have no clue how to proceed, there is a hint in the footnote.[6] □

4.7   Further discussion of Theorem 4.6.4 (Uncertainty-EU)

It may be surprising that the absence of inconsistencies in utility measurement implies not only the existence of a consistent index of utility, but also of probability. Apparently, no separate consistency requirement needs to be imposed on measurements of probabilities. Probability and utility are so closely linked together, indeed, that any deviation in the probability dimension would automatically generate inconsistencies in our measurements of utility (cf. Pfanzagl 1959 p. 287, 6th para). There

---

[6] Utility differences are ordered differently for state s_1 than for state s_2. Hence, violations of tradeoff consistency will readily follow if one t-indifference is derived for state s_1 and another one for state s_2.

will be examples in Parts II and III where violations of additivity of probability generate violations of tradeoff consistency. A dual approach, where avoidance of inconsistency in the probability dimension instead of in the outcome dimension is also enough to give EU (implying consistency in the outcome dimension after all), is in Abdellaoui & Wakker (2005 Theorem 5.3).

Besides tradeoff consistency, transitivity is also a natural condition for t-indifference. It turns out that such transitivity can be violated by general preferences over prospects, just as tradeoff consistency can be. Köbberling & Wakker (2004) demonstrated that, in Theorem 4.6.4, tradeoff consistency (d) is equivalent to transitivity of t-indifference. That is, transitivity of $\sim^t$ could also have been used as behavioral foundation for EU rather than tradeoff consistency. Although transitivity of $\sim^t$ provides an appealing alternative to tradeoff consistency, we will not pursue this point in this book. The reason is that transitivity of $\sim^t$ cannot be adapted to the nonexpected utility theories in later chapters as easily as tradeoff consistency can be.

Whenever derived concepts such as $\sim^t$ are used in behavioral foundations, it should be verified that the preference conditions are easily observable, and can be restated directly in terms of empirical primitives. Those primitives are the domain of stimuli (the prospects) and the preferences in the revealed-preference approach of this book. Conditions in terms of t-indifference can, indeed, be restated directly in terms of the preference relation by substituting the definition of $\sim^t$: Tradeoff consistency holds if and only if

$$
\left.
\begin{pmatrix}
\alpha_E x & \sim & \beta_E y & \& & \alpha'_F f & \sim & \beta_F g & \& \\
\gamma_E x & \sim & \delta_E y & \& & \gamma_F f & \sim & \delta_F g &
\end{pmatrix}
\right\} \tag{4.7.1}
$$
$$
\Rightarrow \alpha' = \alpha
$$

for all $\alpha, \beta, \gamma, \delta, \alpha'$, nonnull events E,F, and prospects x,y,f,g. Verification is left to the readers. §4.1 further illustrated that tradeoff consistency has a clear empirical meaning. Pfanzagl (1968) pleaded for the use of tradeoffs, which he called distances. His Remark 9.4.5 ends with: "We are of the opinion that the indirect way over distances makes the whole approach more intuitive."

As decision under risk is a special case of decision under uncertainty, we can also use the tradeoff method to measure utility for decision under risk. Because a notation for uncertainty that we used in Eqs. (4.5.1) and (4.5.2) is not available for risk, we first illustrate those equations using Fig. 4.7.1a. For that figure we can give an analog for risk, in Fig. 4.7.1b.

Exercise 4.7.1.[a] Show that, under EU for risk, we have $U(\alpha) - U(\beta) = U(\gamma) - U(\delta)$ in Fig. 4.7.1b. □

If EU holds for risk then we can use the SG Eq. (2.5.1) to measure utility, which is easier than the tradeoff method. The tradeoff method can, however, be easily

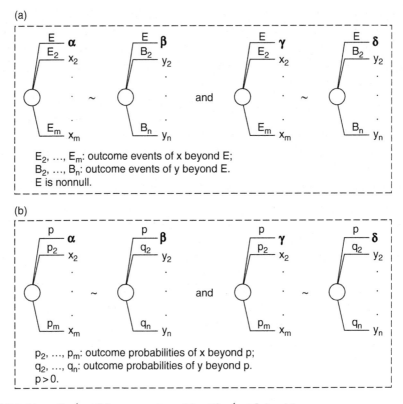

Figure 4.7.1 (a) $\alpha \bigcirc \beta \sim^t \gamma \ominus \delta$ for uncertainty. (b) $\alpha \ominus \beta \sim^t \gamma \ominus \delta$ for risk.

extended to nonexpected utility models introduced later, unlike the SG method. Hence, we will use the tradeoff method also for decision under risk in the chapters to follow.

4.8   Further implications of expected utility

4.8.1   *Savage's sure-thing principle*

The most important implication of EU is Savage's (1954) sure-thing principle.[7] It can be identified with a condition called separability in consumer theory, which concerns preferences over commodity bundles. This condition requires that the preferences over particular ("separable") groups of commodities be independent of the level of the other commodities. The sure-thing principle requires that preferences between prospects be independent of the level of common outcomes.

---

[7] Savage used the term in a broader sense, but it is used nowadays in the restrictive sense discussed next.

Definition 4.8.1. The *sure-thing principle* holds if:

$$\alpha_E x \succcurlyeq \alpha_E y$$
$$\Leftrightarrow \qquad\qquad\qquad (4.8.1)$$
$$\beta_E x \succcurlyeq \beta_E y$$

for all α, β, x, y, E. □

Consider the first preference $\alpha_E x \succcurlyeq \alpha_E y$. Under event E it is immaterial which prospect is chosen, because the two prospects yield the same outcome α there. The sure-thing principle requires that event E then play no role in the choice. The same reasoning can be applied to the preference $\beta_E x \succcurlyeq \beta_E y$, and if event E is ignored there too, then the two choices concern the same options. Hence, the two choices should be the same.

Exercise 4.8.1.[a] Show that EU implies the sure-thing principle. □

Besides the sure-thing principle, Savage used another implication of EU, his preference condition P4, which refers to preferences $1_A 0 \succcurlyeq 1_B 0$. Such a preference for betting on A rather than on B suggests that A is considered more likely than B and, under EU, implies $P(A) \geq P(B)$. If the state space is rich then we can use such measurements to elicit probability. For instance, if $E_i \sim E_j$ for all i,j of a partition $(E_1, \ldots, E_n)$, then these events must all have the same probability, which must be $1/n$. Event $E_1 \cup \cdots \cup E_m$ then has probability m/n. In this manner we can elicit all probabilities that are rational numbers, and approximate probabilities that are not rational numbers.

A contradiction in Savage's likelihood measurements, and a falsification of EU, would result if we observed $1_A 0 \succcurlyeq 1_B 0$ and then $M_A m \prec M_B m$ for some other outcomes $M > m$. Savage's preference condition P4 excludes such inconsistencies of measurements. For rich state spaces, Savage's sure-thing principle and his condition P4, in combination with some common and some technical conditions, provide a behavioral foundation of EU different from the one given here. This book follows an alternative route, with rich outcome spaces rather than rich state spaces.

4.8.2   *Utility analysis based on t-indifferences*

Exercise 4.8.2.[c] Assume continuity, EU, and nondegeneracy. Derive the following strengthening of Exercise 4.5.3:

$$\alpha \ominus \beta \sim^t \gamma \ominus \delta \Leftrightarrow U(\alpha) - U(\beta) = U(\gamma) - U(\delta). \ \square$$

Under the conditions of the exercise, t-indifferences can elicit all equalities of utility differences. It can be seen, but will not be explained here, that such equalities capture all relevant information about utility, given that utility is increasing and unique up to level and unit. The t-indifference relation is particularly convenient for examining properties of utility that can be expressed directly in terms of orderings of utility differences. To prepare for what comes, we state concavity using only midpoints

(Hardy, Littlewood, & Pòlya 1934 Observation 88)[8]. This midpoint analysis was introduced by Baillon, Driesen, & Wakker (2009). As throughout this book, we avoid the use of derivatives and use discrete differences instead, because the latter are more closely related to observable choice.

Observation 4.8.2. The continuous function U is concave if and only if, for all α, β, γ:

$$U(\alpha) - U(\beta) = U(\beta) - U(\gamma) \Rightarrow \beta \leq (\alpha + \gamma)/2. \ \square$$

The results in Eqs. (4.8.2)–(4.8.5) follow immediately from Exercise 4.8.2 and Observation 4.8.2. They illustrate how t-indifference facilitates the analysis of utility. Under the conditions of Theorem 4.6.4 (uncertainty-EU):

$$\text{U is concave} \quad \Leftrightarrow \quad [\alpha \ominus \beta \sim^t \beta \ominus \gamma \Rightarrow \beta \leq (\alpha + \gamma)/2]. \tag{4.8.2}$$

The condition does indeed reflect diminishing marginal utility, with U increasing more over the left half of the interval $[\alpha, \gamma]$ than over the right half. For known probabilities, concave utility can alternatively be inferred from risk aversion, but for unknown probabilities such an inference is not so easily observable (Exercise 4.8.4). Then t-indifferences provide a better tool to test for concave utility.

Under the conditions of Theorem 4.6.4 we also have:

$$\text{U is convex} \Leftrightarrow [\alpha \ominus \beta \sim^t \beta \ominus \gamma \Rightarrow \beta \geq (\alpha + \gamma)/2] \tag{4.8.3}$$

and

$$\text{U is linear}^9 \Leftrightarrow [\alpha \ominus \beta \sim^t \beta \ominus \gamma \Rightarrow \beta = (\alpha + \gamma)/2]. \tag{4.8.4}$$

It can be seen that a person exhibits decreasing risk aversion in the sense of §3.4 if and only if the following implication holds:

$$[\varepsilon > 0, U(\alpha) - U(\beta) = U(\beta) - U(\gamma) \text{ and}$$
$$U(\alpha + \varepsilon) - U(\beta' + \varepsilon) = U(\beta' + \varepsilon) - U(\gamma + \varepsilon)] \Rightarrow \beta' \geq \beta. \tag{4.8.5}$$

This condition holds if and only if the following preference condition holds:

$$[\varepsilon > 0, \alpha \ominus \beta \sim^t \beta \ominus \gamma \text{ and } (\alpha + \varepsilon) \ominus (\beta' + \varepsilon) \sim^t (\beta' + \varepsilon) \ominus (\gamma + \varepsilon)] \Rightarrow \beta' \geq \beta. \tag{4.8.6}$$

Exercise 4.8.3.[b] Show for the α^j in Figure 4.1.1 (TO upwards) that, under EU:

- If U is concave then $\alpha^j - \alpha^{j-1}$ increases in j.
- If U is linear then $\alpha^j - \alpha^{j-1}$ is the same for all j.
- If U is convex then $\alpha^j - \alpha^{j-1}$ decreases in j. $\square$

The following exercise is conceptually important because it illustrates an important observability requirement for preference conditions, explained in its elaboration.

---

[8] These authors used the term concave for what we call midpoint-concave.
[9] For mathematical readers, recall that linear is used here in the same sense as affine, and it does not require that U(0) be 0.

Exercise 4.8.4.^{lb} It can be shown that, under the assumptions of Theorem 4.6.4, U is concave if and only if $E_1x_1 \cdots E_nx_n \preccurlyeq \sum_{j=1}^n P(E_j)x_j$. That is, every prospect is less preferred than its expected value. This result is, of course, similar to Theorem 3.2.1a. The mathematical proof is more difficult because, in this case, not all probability distributions need to be available, but only those that can be generated by the state space and the latter may, for instance, be finite. This exercise does not concern the proof, but the interpretation. The result of Theorem 3.2.1 is useful for decision under risk and can be used in experimental tests. The result just mentioned is less useful. Do you know why? How about the condition in Eq. (4.8.2)? □

4.8.3 *Debreu's additive decomposability and state-dependent utility*

An important tool in a formal proof of Theorem 4.6.4, and underlying most of the theorems in this book, is a famous result by Debreu (1960). An appealing version appeared before in Fleming (1952). Because the result is important on its own, we give it here.

Theorem 4.8.3. Assume Structural Assumption 1.2.1 (decision under uncertainty), and let there be a partition $\{E_1,E_2,E_3\}$ with all three events nonnull. Then the following two statements are equivalent.

(i)   There exists a continuous function V_E for each event E that is constant if E is null and strictly increasing if E is nonnull, such that

$$E_1x_1 \cdots E_nx_n \mapsto V_{E_1}(x_1) + \cdots + V_{E_n}(x_n) \tag{4.8.7}$$

represents preference.

(ii) $\succcurlyeq$ satisfies:
  • weak ordering;
  • monotonicity;
  • continuity;
  • the sure-thing principle. □

The main step in the proofs of behavioral foundations based on tradeoff consistency is that tradeoff consistency implies the sure-thing principle, so that we can use Theorem 4.8.3. This implication is the topic of the following exercise.

Exercise 4.8.5.^{c} Assume weak ordering, monotonicity, and continuity. Show that tradeoff consistency implies the sure-thing principle, and do this in three parts. For the first part tradeoff consistency is not needed, but for the last two parts it is.

(1)[10]   Show that weak ordering, monotonicity, and continuity imply
    restricted solvability:
    if $\alpha_Ex \succ y \succ \gamma_Ex$ then there exists β such that $\beta_Ex \sim y$.

---

[10] The result of part (1) can be assumed without proof by readers with little mathematical background who nevertheless want to do parts (2) and (3).

(2)   Show that $\alpha_{EX} \sim \alpha_{EY}$ and $\beta_{EX} \prec \beta_{EY}$ cannot occur simultaneously.

(3)   Show that $\alpha_{EX} \succ \alpha_{EY}$ and $\beta_{EX} \prec \beta_{EY}$ cannot occur simultaneously. □

In some contexts it is desirable to allow the utility of an outcome to depend on the event under which the outcome is obtained (Drèze 1987 §2.1.3, 2.8; Karni 1993, 1996; Mongin 1998; Nau 1995, 2003; Schervish, Seidenfeld, & Kadane 1990; Skiadas 1997, 1998). This can occur, for instance, in health insurance. If E specifies the event of a bad disease for the decision maker, then the value of money under E is usually different from the value under E^c. Such phenomena lead to state-dependent expected utility

$$E_1 x_1 \ldots E_n x_n \mapsto P(E_1)U(x_1, E_1) + \cdots + P(E_n)U(x_n, E_n). \tag{4.8.8}$$

In this model, without information other than the preferences assumed here, it is impossible to empirically separate the factors P and U. For instance, preferences are not affected if we multiply $P(E_1)$ by any $\lambda > 0$, divide $U(x_1, E_1)$ by λ, and then renormalize probability. Thus, nonzero odds $P(E_1)/P(E_2)$ can be changed into any other nonzero odds, and nonzero probabilities are undetermined. We can only observe the composite functions $V_j = P(E_j)U(x_j, E_j)$ without knowing $P(E_j)$ and the state-dependent $U(x_j, E_j)$, so that state-dependent expected utility of Eq. (4.8.8) is data-equivalent to Eq. (4.8.7) (Kreps 1988 Eqs. (4.4) and (7.13)). Extra information can lead to an identification of probability and utility after all. For details see Drèze (1987 Ch. 2), Grant & Karni (2005), Luce & Krantz (1971), Karni (1993), and Rubin (1987).

Part (a) of the following assignment follows up on the sure-thing principle. It considers the case where it is immaterial which prospect is chosen (in the sense of yielding the same outcome) for more than one event, and shows that any number of such events can be ignored when choosing. Hence their complements are all separable. In the terminology of consumer demand theory the sure-thing principle thus means that all events are separable.

Assignment 4.8.6.[a] Suppress the partition $(E_1, \ldots, E_n)$, and assume the sure-thing principle. Show that

$$(c_1, c_2, c_3, x_4, \ldots, x_n) \succcurlyeq (c_1, c_2, c_3, y_4, \ldots, y_n) \Leftrightarrow$$
$$(d_1, d_2, d_3, x_4, \ldots, x_n) \succcurlyeq (d_1, d_2, d_3, y_4, \ldots, y_n). \quad □$$

4.9   A hybrid case: subjective probabilities and utilities when also objective probabilities are given

Measurements and behavioral foundations of subjective probabilities can be greatly facilitated if, besides events with unknown probabilities, also events with known probabilities are available. The unknown probabilities can then readily be calibrated using the known ones. We, in fact, already considered a case with both objective and subjective probabilities in §4.1, where Figure 4.1.3 dealt with known probabilities whereas the other figures had unknown probabilities. We now first present a general ("single-stage") approach, and then a two-stage approach by Anscombe & Aumann (1963).

4.9.1   A general ("single-stage") approach

As usual in this book, we first describe ways to measure the subjective parameters of our model. Those subjective parameters are, first, the subjective probabilities, the main focus of this section, and, second, the utilities of the outcomes. We assume that the latter have been obtained using the techniques of Chapter 2, which can be used here because we assume objective probabilities to be available. The behavioral foundations in the following subsection will then follow from requirements that the measurements of subjective probabilities do not run into contradictions. This approach will lead to the simplest behavioral foundation of EU with subjective probabilities that I am aware of.

The following assumption combines Structural Assumption 2.5.2 (decision under risk and richness) with Structural Assumption 1.2.1 (decision under uncertainty).

Structural Assumption 4.9.1 [*Uncertainty plus EU-for-risk*]. Structural Assumption 1.2.1 (decision under uncertainty) holds. In addition, for some of the events, called *probabilized events* with generic symbol R, a probability P(R) is given. If, for a prospect $R_1x_1...R_nx_n$, all outcome events are probabilized with $P(R_j) = p_j$, then this prospect generates the probability distribution $p_1x_1...p_nx_n$, a probability-contingent prospect, over the outcomes. Event-contingent prospects that generate the same probability-contingent prospect are equivalent, and are equated with that probability-contingent prospect. Preferences over probability-contingent prospects maximize EU.[11] □

Machina (2004) showed that probabilized events can be identified under fairly general circumstances under Structural Assumption 1.2.1. For example, if the uncertainty concerns the temperature at some remote place about which we know very little and have no statistics, then it still is plausible that the event of a 10th digit of temperature equal to 3 has objective probability 0.10.

Throughout, the letter R refers to probabilized events, and the letter E refers to general events that may but need not be probabilized. The following concept is useful for measuring the subjective probability of an event E: Whenever a number q exists such that

$$1_E0 \sim 1_q0 \tag{4.9.1}$$

we call q the *matching probability* of E. The additivity condition defined later will imply that a matching probability exists for each event. Figure 4.9.1 shows an

---

[11] This book assumes that U is strictly increasing under EU. The only implication needed in this section is that there are two outcomes – say, 1 and 0 – that have different utility.

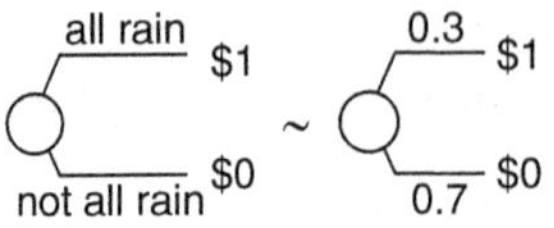

Figure 4.9.1 Matching probability of all rain (tomorrow) is 0.3.

example. The measurement method for matching probabilities is similar to the SG measurement of utility (Figure 2.5.3).

If EU holds for probability-contingent prospects, then the matching probability is unique. Obviously, matching probabilities of probabilized events then are identical to their probabilities. The following result immediately follows from substitution, and is left to the readers.

Observation 4.9.2. If EU holds for all prospects, then matching probabilities agree with subjective probabilities for all events. □

Thus, in the hybrid model we can measure subjective probabilities of events very easily using their matching probabilities. A particularly clarifying and didactical illustration of the use of matching probabilities, as of expected utility and the measurements of its subjective parameters in general, is in Winkler (1972, Example in §5.10, continued in §6.4 and §6.5).

Exercise 4.9.1.[a] Consider the vendor Example 1.1.1.

(a) Assume that $100_{\text{all rain}}0 \sim 100_{1/4}0$. What is the matching probability of all rain?
(b) Assume that $100_{\text{some rain}}0 \sim 100_{1/4}0$. What is the matching probability of some rain?
(c) Assume that parts (a) and (b) hold. Further, $100_{\text{no rain}}0 \sim 100_{1/3}0$. Do you think that EU can hold? □

4.9.2 A behavioral foundation for the single-stage approach

We will use the terminology of Sarin & Wakker (1997). The first preference condition requires that a direct probability measurement of the union of two events be consistent with the separate measurements.

For all disjoint events E_1, E_2 there exist matching probabilities q_1, q_2 that further satisfy

$$1_{E_1 \cup E_2}0 \sim 1_{q_1+q_2}0 \quad (additivity; \text{ see Figure 4.9.2}). \tag{4.9.2}$$

The second preference condition concerns a more complex, but also more comprehensive, way to measure subjective probabilities, and to carry out cross checks. We now do not just match probabilities of single events, but of whole partitions of the state space.

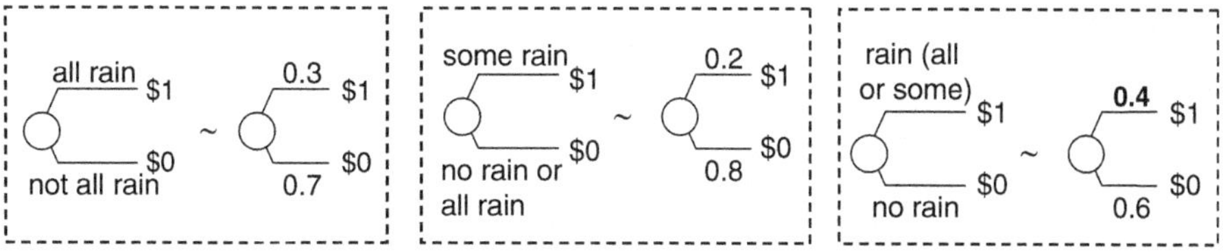

For additivity to hold, the bold probability 0.4 should have been 0.3 + 0.2 = 0.5.

Figure 4.9.2 Violation of additivity (Raiffa 1968 §4; Jaffray & Philippe 1977 p. 165).

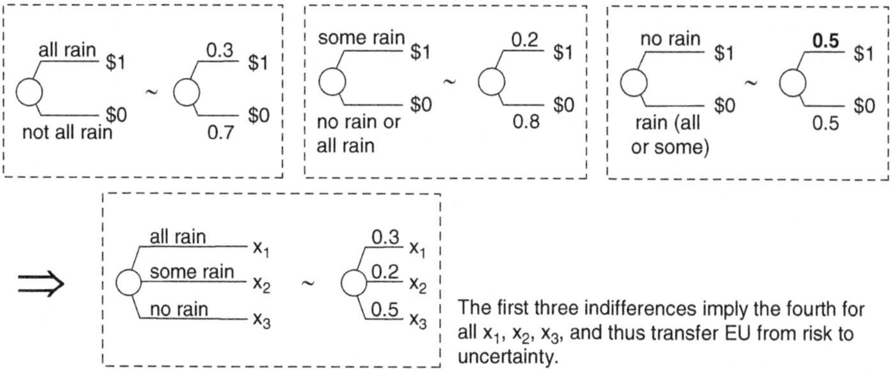

The first three indifferences imply the fourth for all x_1, x_2, x_3, and thus transfer EU from risk to uncertainty.

Figure 4.9.3 Probabilistic matching.

Definition 4.9.3 (see Figure 4.9.3). *Probabilistic matching* holds if, for each partition $E_1, \ldots, E_n$, the indifference

$$E_1 x_1 \ldots E_n x_n \sim q_1 x_1 \ldots q_n x_n \qquad (4.9.3)$$

holds for all outcomes x_j whenever each q_j is the matching probability of event E_j. □

Thus, elicitations of probabilities from complex prospects as in Eq. (4.9.3) should be consistent with the simple measurements based on matching probabilities. I give an example with some useful properties. Under EU, two indifferences

$$(E^1 : 7, E^2 : 6, E^3 : 5, \mathbf{E^4 : 0}) \sim (q_1 : 7, q_2 : 6, q_3 : 5, \mathbf{q_4 : 0}) \text{ and}$$
$$(E^1 : 7, E^2 : 6, E^3 : 5, \mathbf{E^4 : 1}) \sim (q_1 : 7, q_2 : 6, q_3 : 5, \mathbf{q_4 : 1}) \qquad (4.9.4)$$

imply $P(E^4) = q_4$, because only then the left EU increase $P(E^4)(U(1) - U(0))$ and the right EU increase $q_4(U(1) - U(0))$ are equal. This measurement method is central to Abdellaoui & Wakker (2005).

Theorem 4.9.4.[12] Under Structural Assumption 4.9.1 (Uncertainty plus EU-for-risk), the following two statements are equivalent.

---

[12] Based on a suggestion by Pavlo Blavatskyy, the monotonicity condition 3.3 used by Sarin & Wakker (1997) can and has been dropped.

(i)   EU holds.
(ii) $\succcurlyeq$ satisfies:
  • weak ordering;
  • additivity;
  • probabilistic matching. □

Theorem 4.9.4 assumes EU for probability-contingent prospects and, therefore, does not comprise a complete behavioral foundation. Such a complete behavioral foundation can be obtained by replacing the assumption of EU for probabilistic events by preference conditions as, for instance, in Theorem 2.6.3 (EU for risk).

Summarizing the steps in Theorem 4.9.4: (a) We obtain EU for the probabilized events; (b) we obtain matching probabilities for all events; (c) additivity of matching probabilities follows from the additivity preference condition; (d) the EU representation for probabilized events extends to all events and all prospects by the probabilistic matching condition. Each of these steps is elementary and, hence, Theorem 4.9.4 is elementary too. The pros and cons of preference foundations as elementary, and close to the functional in question, as Theorem 4.9.4 were discussed in §1.8. We next consider a generalization.

Observation 4.9.5. Theorem 4.9.4 remains valid if we replace the outcome set $\mathbb{R}$ by any general outcome set that contains at least two nonequivalent outcomes. □

Matching probabilities were commonly used in the early decision analysis literature of the 1970s in informal derivations of EU and in applications (Lavalle 1978 §3.6; Raiffa 1968; Winkler 1972 p. 272). They were also mentioned by Arrow (1951a, Footnote 4). I am not aware of a formal statement of a behavioral foundation such as in Theorem 4.9.4 in this literature. Probably the result was known (LaValle 1978 Ch. 3 comes close) but was considered too elementary to state. Because of its importance, Sarin & Wakker (1997 Theorem 3.8) nevertheless wrote it down.

4.9.3   *The multi-stage approach of Anscombe & Aumann (1963)*

This subsection presents Anscombe & Aumann's (1963) model. Relative to the preceding analysis, we add the assumption that the state space has a two-stage decomposition. We will not use Anscombe & Aumann's model in the rest of this book but, because of its popularity, present it nevertheless.

Two versions of the Anscombe & Aumann model. Before considering the version of the model that is most popular today, we consider an equivalent version based on the multiattribute utility models of §3.7.

Example 4.9.6 [Roulette–horse]. Assume a two-stage decomposition where the state space S is a product space $\mathcal{R} \times \mathcal{H}$. As in Anscombe & Aumann (1963), we assume that the uncertainty of $\mathcal{H} = \{h^1, \ldots, h^m\}$ concerns which of m horses $h^1, \ldots, h^m$ participating in a horse race will win. (Event h^j of horse j winning will correspond to the subset of S, or event, $\mathcal{R} \times h^j$.) For events concerning $\mathcal{H}$ no probabilities need

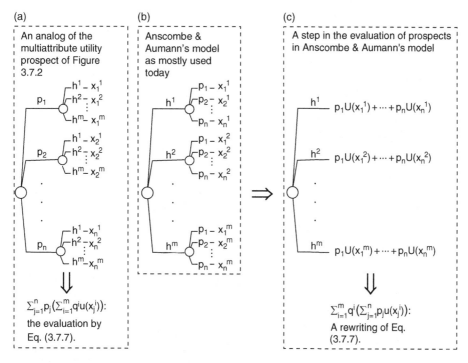

Figure 4.9.4 Different presentations and evaluations of multi-stage prospects.

to be given. Events of $\mathcal{R}$ are generated by means of an objective chance mechanism; say, a roulette wheel. For all events concerning $\mathcal{R}$ probabilities are given. The symbol $\mathcal{R}$ refers to roulette wheel or risk, and $\mathcal{H}$ refers to horse. The set $\mathcal{R}$ serves as an auxiliary tool, and the uncertainty concerning $\mathcal{H}$ is what really interests us. In the first stage the uncertainty concerning $\mathcal{R}$ is resolved, and in the second stage the uncertainty concerning the horse race $\mathcal{H}$ is resolved. Fig. 4.9.4a depicts a typical prospect. We denote the first-stage events by their probabilities.

For each prospect, conditional on the resolution of the first-stage uncertainty an $\mathcal{H}$-event-contingent prospect results with outcomes depending on $\mathcal{H}$. For example, conditional on the p_1 probability event in Fig. 4.9.4a, the prospect $(h^1{:}x_1^1,\ldots,h^m{:}x_1^m)$ results. Hence, we are dealing with probability distributions over event-contingent prospects, where the outcome-relevant events for the latter refer to $\mathcal{H}$. This example concerns a special case of multiattribute utility theory with attributes referring to states of nature, and with Fig. 4.9.4a an illustration alternative to Figure 3.7.2. □

Formally, Anscombe & Aumann's (1963) behavioral foundation of EU was presented in Theorem 3.7.6 (where EU for probability-contingent prospects was assumed as throughout Chapter 3), with an interpretation added following the theorem. We discuss an alternative way of modeling in the next example.

Example 4.9.7 [Horse–roulette]. Assume Example 4.9.6. One preference condition in Anscombe & Aumann's (1963) Theorem 3.7.6 requires that preference depend only on the marginal distributions (probability-contingent prospects) over outcomes generated for each element of $\mathcal{H}$. Those marginal distributions for the prospect of Fig. 4.9.4a are depicted in Fig. 4.9.4b, with for instance $(p_1{:}x_1{}^1,\ldots, p_n{:}x_n{}^1)$ generated under h^1. (Marginal distributions were also depicted in Figure 3.7.3.) It then suffices for the preference value of the prospect in Fig. 4.9.4a to give only the generated marginal distributions, as is done in Fig. 4.9.4b. In particular, all information about correlations between the marginal distributions is irrelevant. In general we can then describe prospects as functions that assign to each horse a probability distribution over outcomes, as in Fig. 4.9.4b.[13] The preference value of a prospect is determined entirely by the EU value of the generated marginal distributions, which is the EU value obtained conditionally on each h^j, similar to Fig. 4.9.4c.[14] □

The Anscombe & Aumann model is commonly used today as in Example 4.9.7 and in Figs. 4.9.4b and 4.9.4c (Fishburn 1970). Relative to Example 4.9.6 and Fig. 4.9.4a, the model is restrictive in the sense that it does not allow considerations of correlations between outcomes conditional on different horses. Mark Machina once, jokingly, called Example 4.9.6 the Aumann–Anscombe model, to indicate its reversal relative to Example 4.9.7.

Anscombe & Aumann (1963) originally used a three-stage model with probabilized uncertainty both before and after $\mathcal{H}$. Their Assumption 2 ("reversal of order in compound lotteries") allows the reduction of their three-stage model to Example 4.9.7. It is the analog of Fishburn's (1965) assumption that only the generated marginal distributions matter. The full richness of the three stages was used by Drèze (1961, 1987 Ch. 2) and Seo (2009).

The model of Example 4.9.7 is easier to analyze than that of Example 4.9.6. Its main advantage is that it can easily be combined with nonexpected utility models for prospects contingent on $\mathcal{H}$, which will be the topic of later chapters. We can then maintain expected utility for the given probabilities of $\mathcal{R}$. Whereas we then abandon the evaluation of Eq. (3.7.7) at the bottom of Fig. 4.9.4a, we still use the presentation of the prospect in the middle of Fig. 4.9.4c with EU at the terminal nodes. In a mathematical sense, the linearity of the EU functional in terms of probabilistic mixing then greatly facilitates mathematical analyses. A drawback is that the probabilistic mixture of prospects now is to be defined per stage h^j which is less convincing conceptually than probabilistic mixtures in Fig. 4.9.4a.

An analogous model in experimental economics. More or less independently, the special case of Anscombe & Aumann's model in Example 4.9.7 with only two prizes has been proposed in experimental economics as a way to generate linear utility. Denote the two prizes as $\gamma \succ \beta$; we normalize $U(\gamma) = 1$ and $U(\beta) = 0$. Then marginal distributions are of the form $\gamma_p\beta$ with EU value p. Let us equate marginal distributions

---

[13] For any such map we can arrange the same probabilities $p_1,\ldots,p_n$ for every horse by splitting probabilities, similarly as in Exercise 1.2.4 (partition flexibility), so that Fig. 4.9.4b is generic.

[14] The conditions of Theorem 3.7.3 imply EU representations conditional on every state h^j, through utility functions U^j that may depend on j. A&A monotonicity implies that U^j can be taken independently of j, as in Fig. 4.9.4c.

$\gamma_p\beta$ with the probability p of receiving the best outcome γ. Then paying a prize p under horse h_i generates utility p under that horse. In other words, paying in terms of the probability of the best outcome generates linear utility and expected value maximization. This approach was proposed independently by Allen (1987), Berg *et al.* (1986), Roth & Malouf (1979), and Smith (1961 §13, p. 13), with a closely related idea in Castagnoli & Li Calzi (2005). For this idea to work empirically, it is crucial that EU is satisfied empirically for known probabilities, and that the multi-stage model is not too complex for subjects. Selten, Sadrieh, & Abbink (1999) tested the model empirically and found that it performed poorly, generating more deviation from expected value than with payments in money. Hence, the Anscombe & Aumann approach has lost popularity in experimental economics. In later chapters we will introduce probability weighting, which will explain the strong deviations from expected value found here.

4.9.4 *Comparing the Anscombe & Aumann model with the single-stage approach*
In both Examples 4.9.6 (roulette–horse) and 4.9.7 (horse–roulette) the Structural Assumption 4.9.1 is satisfied, so that the general approach of the single-stage approach can be used. The probabilized events are the ones referring to $\mathcal{R}$. Figures 4.9.5 and 4.9.6 depict a way in which a prospect $(p_1:x_1,\ldots,p_n:x_n)$ can result for Examples 4.9.6 and 4.9.7. The outcomes depend on the probabilities p_j but not on which horse will win the race.

To apply the techniques of the general (single-stage) model, note that an indifference $1_{h_1}0 \sim 1_{p^1}0$ gives a matching probability p^1 for h^1. Indifferences $1_{h_j}0 \sim 1_{p^j}0$ ($j = 1, \ldots, n$) generate the EU representation $\sum_{j=1}^{n} p^j U(x^j)$ for the horse-contingent prospect $(h^1:x^1,\ldots,h^n:x^n)$. Hence, also if the two-stage model is available, we can get by with the single-stage approach and we simply need not use any two-stage stimuli.

We next consider an example where the event space is not a product set, so that the two-stage approach of Anscombe & Aumann cannot be used, but the general single-stage approach still can be.

Example 4.9.8 [Binumbered balls]. An urn contains 100 balls with a black and red number written on each. Each number between 1 and 100 appears exactly once as a black number. For each ball with a black number of 50 or less, the red number is identical to the black number. For each ball with a black number of 51 or more, we know that the red number is also between 51 and 100, but we do not know what it is. Some numbers between 51 and 100 may not appear as red numbers, whereas others may appear several times as a red number. We do not know about the correlation between the black and red numbers exceeding 50.

One ball will be drawn randomly from the urn, and its two numbers will be inspected. The state space S is $\{1,\ldots,50\} \cup (\{51,\ldots,100\} \times \{51,\ldots,100\})$, where $j \leq 50$ concerns a ball with black and red number j, and (i,j) for i and j exceeding 51 indicates a ball with black number i and red number j. Although we know that

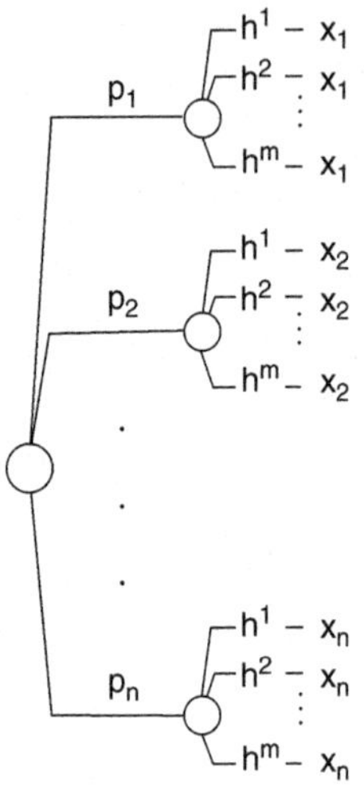

Figure 4.9.5 $(p_1:x_1, \ldots, p_nx_n)$ in the roulette–horse Example 4.9.6.

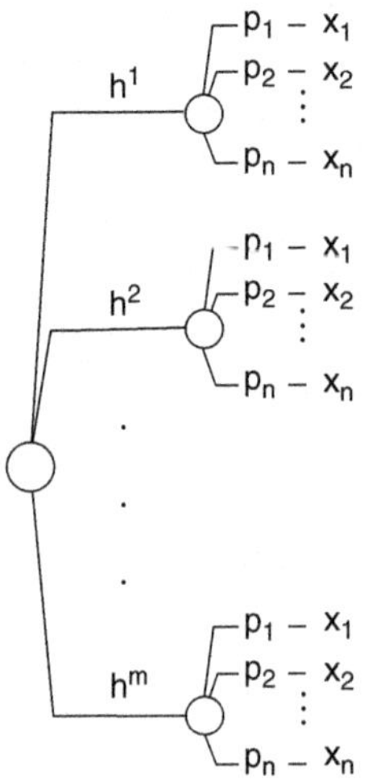

Figure 4.9.6 $(p_1:x_1, \ldots, p_nx_n)$ in the horse–roulette Example 4.9.7.

many such combinations (i.,j) are not contained in the urn, we do not know which, and any of them is possible. □

Another drawback of Anscombe & Aumann's multistage approach is that it requires a commitment to backward induction for solving dynamic decisions. This commitment is not needed in Theorem 4.9.4. Backward induction, while uncontroversial for classical expected utility, is highly controversial for the nonexpected utility models considered in later chapters (see Appendix C). Machina (1989), for example, strongly argued against backward induction for nonexpected utility. Hence the single-stage approach will become even more preferable for nonexpected utility. To summarize, the single-stage approach, as customary in the decision analysis literature of the 1970s, is simpler, more general, and avoids a commitment to questionable dynamic decision principles.

Some authors have argued that adding auxiliary objective probabilities, as done in this section, is generally unobjectionable (Drèze 1987 Ch. 2). Others have argued, in agreement with this author's opinion, that such auxiliary structure may sometimes be more cumbersome than helpful, adding an additional layer of richness (Suppes 1974 pp. 162–163). Hence, the techniques of this section should be used with caution.

4.10   Data fitting for expected utility under uncertainty

§4.3 has demonstrated that the measurements in §4.1 allow for a nonparametric measurement of utility. We can nevertheless also use parametric fitting if we want, of course.[15] It is the topic of this section, most of which is presented in exercises. In this section, italicized superscripts indicate powers. Nonitalicized superscripts as in $\alpha^0,\ldots,\mathrm{PE}^4$ do not concern powers but are just indexes. They always concern the integers $0,\ldots,4$. We will sometimes, but not always, assume in this section:

Assumption 4.10.1 [50–50]. Both candidates in §4.1 win with probability ½, and Structural Assumption 2.5.2 (decision under risk) holds. □

Under this assumption, the data fitting here is similar to that in §3.6 for decision under risk.

Exercise 4.10.1.[b] For the elections example of §4.1, Paul maximizes EU. Assumption 4.10.1 holds. What answers does Paul give in Figures 4.1.1–4.1.5 in the following two cases?

(a) $U(\alpha) = \sqrt{\alpha}$;
(b) $U(\alpha) = 1 - \exp(-0.03\alpha)$. □

Throughout the rest of this section we assume:

Assumption 4.10.2 [Power-EU subj.5]. We consider the data of subject 5 in Table 4.3.1. EU holds with power utility $U(\alpha) = \alpha^\theta$. □

Answers to the following exercises, given in Appendix J, are sometimes discussed in the main text.

---

[15] *Nonparametric* measurement means that we do not reduce the dimensionality of our subjective parameters, and exactly accommodate the data with no need to optimize a nonperfect fit. *Parametric fitting* means that we reduce the dimensionality of our subjective parameters, such as by assuming that utility is of the power family, and that we then search for the "parameter" (say the power) that gives the best fit with the data. The term parametric does not refer to general subjective parameters such as subjective probability or utility, but to the parameter(s) used to reduce the dimensionality, such as the power for power utility. These terminological conventions are so common that we cannot avoid this ambiguous use of the term parameter.

Exercise 4.10.2^b [Basic analysis of TO data]. Assume $0 < \theta = j/100 < 2$. We only use the equal-spacedness in utility units of $(\alpha^0, \alpha^1, \alpha^2, \alpha^3, \alpha^4)$, of $(\alpha^0, \alpha^1, \beta^2, \beta^3, \beta^4)$, and of $(\delta^0, \delta^1, \delta^2, \delta^3, \alpha^4)$ in this exercise, referring to Figures 4.1.1, 4.1.2, and 4.1.4. We will later see that this part of the data gives the most reliable account of the utility function of the subject. We test a midpoint property as follows.

(a) Consider $\alpha^0, \alpha^1, \alpha^2, \alpha^3, \alpha^4$, for EU with utility function U. Take $1 \leq i \leq 3$. The "theoretical" midpoint between α^{i-1} and α^{i+1} (in utility units) is the value α^{i*} such that

$$\alpha^{i*} = U^{-1}((U(\alpha^{i-1}) + U(\alpha^{i+1}))/2). \tag{4.10.1}$$

For the distance of EU from the data we take the square root of the average squared distances between the observed midpoints α^i and the theoretically predicted α^{i*}:

$$\sqrt{\frac{\sum_{i=1}^{3}(\alpha^i - \alpha^{i*})^2}{3}}. \tag{4.10.2}$$

This value indicates again by how much money the theoretical model is off.[16] Find the power θ that best fits $\alpha^0, \alpha^1, \alpha^2, \alpha^3, \alpha^4$ in the sense of minimizing Eq. (4.10.2). Determine by how far the model is off, and predict $CE(80_{\frac{1}{2}}40)$.

(b) Analyze the quintuple $\alpha^0, \alpha^1, \beta^2, \beta^3, \beta^4$ in the same way.

(c) Analyze the quintuple $\delta^0, \delta^1, \delta^2, \delta^3, \alpha^4$ in the same way. □

A crucial component of EU, the subjective probability of cand$_1$ – assumed to be ½ in Assumption 4.10.1 but not here – was not mentioned in Exercise 4.10.2 because it played no role there. This probability will play a role later on. The answers to Exercise 4.10.2 in Appendix J show that the values of θ obtained in the different parts do not differ by much. The different observations thus seem to refer to a common characteristic.

Exercise 4.10.3^b [CE data]. Analyze the indifferences of Figure 4.1.3, under Assumption 4.10.2 (power-EU subj.5), using the distance measure in §A.2. The indifferences exhibit much risk aversion and, hence, utility will have to be very concave to fit the data. It can be seen that the positive part of the power family as considered before $(U(\alpha) = \alpha^\theta$ for $\theta > 0)$ does not fit the data well, with a distance always exceeding 4.18. We have to consider negative powers. Wakker (2008a) explained the role of positive and negative powers in the power family of utility, with negative powers generating more concavity than positive powers. You may just assume that you have to use a negative power, as follows: Define $U(\alpha) = -\alpha^\theta$ for $0 > \theta = -j/100 > -2$, find the negative θ that best fits the data, and predict $CE(80_{\frac{1}{2}}40)$. □

---

[16] Although conceptually different, the calculations with this distance measure are the same as if we observed indifferences $\alpha^i \sim \alpha^{i+1}{}_{\frac{1}{2}}\alpha^{i-1}$ for decision under risk, used EU to fit such data, and used the distance measure of §A.2. Hence, the analysis here does not require the development of new calculation tools or software, which is why it was chosen.

The answers to Exercise 4.10.3 in Appendix J show that the CE data suggest utility curvature – which can be equated with risk attitude under EU and only under EU – that largely deviates from what was found in Exercise 4.10.2, with considerably lower CEs predicted. Whereas EU would imply that the power in Exercise 4.10.3 should be the same as the powers found in Exercise 4.10.2, the resulting power is very different. The CE questions seem to measure a different characteristic than the TO questions in a way suggesting inconsistent utility. In other words, they suggest a violation of EU.

Exercise 4.10.4[b] [PE data]. Analyze the indifferences of Figure 4.1.5, assuming Assumption 4.10.2 and the distance measure of §A.2. Similar to Exercise 4.10.3, we consider negative powers and define $U(\alpha) = -\alpha^\theta$ for $0 > \theta = -j/100 > -2$. Find the negative θ that best fits the data, and predict CE($80_{1/2}40$). □

In our analysis of the TO results in Exercise 4.10.2 we only used the indifferences between the right- and left-hand prospects "indirectly," to show that the numbers elicited were equally spaced in utility units. From there on we only used the latter inference. We did not use the aforementioned indifferences directly and, thus, part of the data was not used. We will give theoretical arguments later. In brief, the indifferences themselves are strongly distorted by violations of EU, unlike the indirect inferences that we used. At this stage, we provide numerical results to illustrate this point. We will now fit EU directly to the aforementioned indifferences, to find that the fit is, indeed, not very good. Subject 5's subjective probability of cand$_1$ now plays a role. We first assume that it is ½.

Exercise 4.10.5[b] [Equivalences in TO data]. Make Assumptions 4.10.1 (50–50) and 4.10.2 (power-EU subj.5) with $0 < \theta = j/100 < 2$. Use the distance measure of §A.2. Find the power θ that best fits the indifferences, determine by how far the model is off, and predict CE($80_{\text{cand}_1}40$) for:

(a) The indifferences in Figure 4.1.1.
(b) The indifferences in Figure 4.1.2.
(c) The indifferences in Figure 4.1.4.
(d) All indifferences in parts (a)–(c) jointly. □

As the elaborations in Appendix J will show, the powers and CEs in Exercise 4.10.5 exhibit more volatility between the different parts than what we found in Exercise 4.10.2, suggesting that they are less reliable. We next investigate the role of subjective probabilities, dropping the 50–50 Assumption 4.10.1.

Exercise 4.10.6.[b] Consider the same data as in Part (d) of Exercise 4.10.5, that is, consider all indifferences in Figures 4.1.1, 4.1.2, and 4.1.4. Assumption 4.10.2 holds.

(a) Assume $\theta = 0.65$. Investigate which subjective probability $p = P(\text{cand}_1) = j/100$ of subject 5 best fits the data and determine the distance to the data. Predict CE($80_{\text{cand}_1}40$).
(b) Now we consider the general case, with $0 < \theta = i/100 < 2$, and $p = P(\text{cand}_1) = 0 < j/100 < 1$. Find the combination of θ and p that best fits the data and determine the distance. Predict CE($80_{\text{cand}_1}40$). □

The elaborations of Exercise 4.10.6 will show that the subjective probability of $cand_1$ that optimally fits the data is close to ½ for subject 5. The deviation from ½ does improve the fit relative to Exercise 4.10.5d.

In Exercise 4.10.6b we, for the first time, considered parametric fitting with more than one parameter involved. A danger with such multi-parameter fittings on general data sets is that the parameters can interact, depending on the numerical structure (Harrison 2006 p. 61; Loomes, Moffat, & Sugden 2002). For example, it is possible that subject 5 used $P(cand_1) = p = 0.50$ when answering, but that the slightly higher $p = 0.54$ in combination with the utility parameter just works better to numerically fit the risk aversion of this subject. The utility method presented in the preceding sections entails a way to maximally separate utility from subjective probability. Indeed, when, in Exercise 4.10.7, we incorporate more indifferences than those targeted towards utility as in Exercise 4.10.6, the interaction will become stronger. The problem of separating parameters will be more difficult in theories presented later, where there are more subjective parameters than under EU. Throughout this book we will seek measurements of preferences that best identify the parameters of various theories and that separate them as much as possible.

Exercise 4.10.7.[b] Now take as data all 18 indifferences given by subject 5 in Figures 4.1.1–4.1.5. Assumption 4.10.2 holds.

(a) Make Assumption 4.10.1 (50–50). Find the power $\theta = j/100$ between 0.01 and 2 that best fits the data, determine the distance, and predict $CE(80_{cand_1} 40)$.
(b) Find the subjective probability $P(cand_1) = i/100$ for $0 \leq i \leq 100$ and the power $\theta = j/100$ between 0.01 and 2 that best fit the data, determine the distance, and predict $CE(80_{cand_1} 40)$. □

Exercise 4.10.8.[b] This exercise uses the answers to Exercises 4.10.2 and 4.10.6 in Appendix J. Imagine that you have to decide whether subject 5 receives $100_{1/2}0$ or 31.50, and it is important for you to choose what is most preferable for subject 5. Assumption 4.10.2 holds.

(a) Exercise 4.10.2 suggests that $\theta \leq 0.56$. Which choice is suggested?
(b) Which choice is suggested by Exercise 4.10.6b?
(c) Which choice is better according to you, the one in part (a) or the one in part (b)? There is no clear-cut answer to this question, and you are invited to speculate. □

Assignment 4.10.9.[c] Assumption 4.10.2 holds with $\theta > 0$. We will find the θ that best fits the data of subject 2 in Table 4.3.1 regarding the choices in Figure 4.1.1, with $\alpha^0 = 10$, $\alpha^1 = 17$, $\alpha^2 = 27$, $\alpha^3 = 42.5$, $\alpha^4 = 60$. The only information we use is that the α^j's are equally spaced in utility units, as in Exercise 4.10.2a. We now use a different way to analyze the data. We assume α^0 and α^4 given, and calculate which $\tilde{\alpha}^1, \tilde{\alpha}^2, \tilde{\alpha}^3$ are such that $\alpha^0, \tilde{\alpha}^1, \tilde{\alpha}^2, \tilde{\alpha}^3, \alpha^4$ are equally spaced in utility units. Find the value $\theta = j/100$ that minimizes the distance of §A.2 (and Eq. (4.10.2)); i.e.,

$$\sqrt{\frac{(\alpha^1 - \tilde{\alpha}^1)^2 + (\alpha^2 - \tilde{\alpha}^2)^2 + (\alpha^3 - \tilde{\alpha}^3)^2}{3}}.$$

If you do not know what to do, there is a hint in the footnote.[17] □

4.11   A statistical analysis of the experiment of §4.1, revealing violations of expected utility

This book has mostly been normatively oriented so far, with the exception of some data fitting exercises, and we have focused on EU. In Parts II and III, we will turn to descriptive questions and derive models for empirically observed decision making. We will then study models that deviate from EU. The next two sections provide a transition. We examine the experimental results of §4.1 statistically, using an experiment done with five students, whose raw data are in Table 4.3.1.

Table 4.11.1 gives descriptive statistics. Table 4.11.2 tests whether values x^j are identical to other values as EU would predict, and whether the PE^j's satisfy EU's predictions. All tests in Table 4.11.2 – except against the β^j's, whose results were nonsignificant by any standard – were one-tailed t-tests, with predictions $\gamma^j < \alpha^j$ (the "certainty effect"), $\delta^j > \alpha^j$ (framing and loss aversion[18]), and $PE^j > j/4$ (the certainty effect and some framing effects; Bleichrodt 2002). The following pattern emerges from these data.

(1) [Tradeoff consistency verified]. The two different utility elicitations based on $\alpha^1,\ldots,\alpha^4$ and $\beta^1,\ldots,\beta^4$ should, by tradeoff consistency and EU, yield identical values (Exercise 4.3.2b). This seems to hold true and the direct test of tradeoff consistency does not reveal violations.

(2) [The certainty effect]. The elicitations through $\alpha^1,\ldots,\alpha^3$ and $\gamma^1,\ldots,\gamma^3$ should yield identical results under EU (Exercise 4.3.3), and the PE^j elicitations should also be consistent. However, the γ^j's were significantly lower and the PE^j's for $j=2,3$ were significantly higher. This may be caused by the *certainty effect*, entailing that riskless outcomes – such as involved in the elicitation of γ^1, γ^2, γ^3 and PE^1, PE^2, PE^3 – are overvalued in a way that EU cannot capture. Consequently, subjects were satisfied with smaller certain amounts γ^j and required larger probabilities PE^j.

(3) [Elementary principles violated]. The elicitations through $\alpha^0,\ldots,\alpha^3$ and $\delta^0,\ldots,\delta^3$ should also yield identical results, merely by weak ordering and strong monotonicity. However, we find significant differences. A framing effect can explain

---

[17] If you normalize U to be 0 at α^0 and 1 at α^4, then $\tilde{\alpha}^j = U^{-1}(j/4)$. In general, we have $U(\tilde{\alpha}^j) = U(\alpha^0) + j(U(\alpha^4) - U(\alpha^0))/4$, so that $\tilde{\alpha}^j = U^{-1}((U(\alpha^0) + j(U(\alpha^4) - U(\alpha^0))/4)$ for each j.

[18] Framing means that different, logically equivalent, ways to formulate a decision problem can influence decisions. A famous example is the Asian disease problem of Tversky & Kahneman (1981), where an equivalent framing in terms of gains or losses matters. A similar phenomenon plays a role in the comparison of the X^j's and the x^j's. Loss aversion means that losses are weighted more heavily than gains in decisions, and will be examined in detail later.

Table 4.11.1. *Descriptive statistics*

Variable	Mean	Standard Dev.	Min	Max	Label
α^0	10	0.0	10	10	starting value
α^1	21.4	4.9	17	28	1st value of 1st TO measurement (Fig 4.1.1a)
α^2	40.2	10.4	27	50	2nd value of 1st TO measurement (Fig 4.1.1b)
α^3	61.9	19.4	42.5	85	3rd value of 1st TO measurement (Fig 4.1.1c)
α^4	88.9	36.4	60	140	4th value of 1st TO measurement (Fig 4.1.1d)
β^2	40.1	13.0	27	56	2nd value of 2nd TO measurement (Fig 4.1.2b)
β^3	65.6	28.6	40	105	3rd value of 2nd TO measurement (Fig 4.1.2c)
β^4	93.4	48.8	52	160	4th value of 2nd TO measurement (Fig 4.1.2d)
γ^1	18.5	4.1	13.5	25	1st value of CE measurement (Fig 4.1.3b)
γ^2	32.4	9.0	20	45	2nd value of CE measurement (Fig 4.1.3a)
γ^3	51.6	18.3	30	75	3rd value of CE measurement (Fig 4.1.3c)
δ^0	22.0	10.7	13	40	1st value of reversed TO measurement (Fig 4.1.4d)
δ^1	32.0	11.4	22	50	2nd value of reversed TO measurement (Fig 4.1.4c)
δ^2	46.4	15.9	32	70	3rd value of reversed TO measurement (Fig 4.1.4b)
δ^3	64.4	24.4	45	100	4th value of reversed TO measurement (Fig 4.1.4a)
PE^1	0.40	0.15	0.25	0.63	1st value of probability equivalent (Fig. 4.1.5a)
PE^2	0.67	0.17	0.50	0.90	2nd value of probability equivalent (Fig. 4.1.5b)
PE^3	0.84	0.07	0.75	0.90	3rd value of probability equivalent (Fig. 4.1.5c)

Table 4.11.2. *Statistical tests of equalities*

	β^0	β^1	β^2	β^3	β^4	α^0	γ^1	γ^2	γ^3	α^4	δ^0	δ^1	δ^2	δ^3	α^4	PE^1	PE^2	PE^3
α^0	=					=					*							
α^1		=					*					*				ns		
α^2			ns					*					ms		*			
α^3				ns					*					ns				*
α^4					ns					=					=			

Notes: empty: no test done; =: identity by definition; ns: nonsignificant at level 0.10, with no direction specified; ms: marginally significant (at level 0.10); *: significant (at level 0.05).

this finding. When determining the α's people usually think in terms of gains ("how much more do I want so as to"); when determining the δ's they usually think in terms of losses ("how much less do I want so as to").[19] It is known that such strategically irrelevant differences in framing affect human choices in ways in which they should not by rationality standards (Tversky & Kahneman 1981).

Our findings are consistent with common findings in the literature: There are systematic violations of EU. The rest of this book will deal with nonexpected

---

[19] The data analyzed here were obtained in individual interviews where I formulated each question in Figure 4.1.2 as "how much do you want to give up relative to ... so as to".

utility models, i.e. models alternative to EU. We will maintain the elementary conditions of transitivity, completeness, monotonicity, and stochastic dominance. The sophisticated conditions for EU, SG consistency – or the independence condition – for decision under risk, and tradeoff consistency for decision under uncertainty will be relaxed.

The models presented in Parts II and III will accommodate the violation of EU in the second finding (the certainty effect). They will not accommodate the violation in the third finding concerning elementary principles. Thus, although we are making progress, we are not doing a complete job. Individual decision under risk is notorious for the large amount of noise in the data, and the many phenomena that cannot yet be explained. In view of the importance of assessing individual values, we continue to search for the best results available even though they are imperfect. While the model most central to what follows, prospect theory, is probably the best descriptive theory for individual choice under risk presently available, numerous violations of this theory have nevertheless been reported in the literature. Tversky & Kahneman (1992) wrote about this point:

Theories of choice are at best approximate and incomplete. One reason for this pessimistic assessment is that choice is a constructive and contingent process. When faced with a complex problem, people employ a variety of heuristic procedures in order to simplify the representation and the evaluation of prospects. These procedures include computational shortcuts and editing operations, such as eliminating common components and discarding nonessential differences (Tversky, 1969). The heuristics of choices do not readily lend themselves to formal analysis because their application depends on the formulation of the problem, the method of elicitation, and the context of choice. (p. 317)

4.12   The Allais paradox: a well-known violation of expected utility

In §4.11 we found some empirical violations of EU. Much empirical evidence against EU has been obtained (Starmer 2000). Post *et al.* (2008) found such evidence in choices with real incentives of hundreds of thousands of dollars. The best known violation is the Allais paradox (Allais 1953a). A famous conference near Paris in 1952, where Savage (1953) first presented his famous EU model published in full in 1954, was also attended by the French economist and later Nobel prize winner Maurice Allais, also known for his work in physics criticizing Einstein's relativity theory (Aujard 2001). He presented Savage with choices similar to those in Figs. 2.4.1e, f, g, and h. Savage chose as the majority does: the sure prospect of 10×10^6 if available (in Figs. e and g), and risky if there was no sure prospect (as in Figs. f and h). The following exercise demonstrates that these choices violate EU.

Exercise 4.12.1. Consider Figure 2.4.1.

(a)[/a] Show that your choices in Figs. 2.4.1e and f should be identical (i.e. both up or both down) under EU for risk. Which preference condition of EU under risk is tested here?

(b)[a] Show that under EU, your choices in Fig. 2.4.1g and h should be identical (i.e. both up or both down).

(c)[b] Show that the majority preferences in Figs. 2.4.1g and h violate the sure-thing principle for risk. □

One common reason for the switches of preference between Fig. 2.4.1e versus f (sometimes called the common ratio effect), and Fig. 2.4.1g versus h (sometimes called the common consequence effect), is that in e and g people have a special preference for the certainty of 10×10^6, whereas in f and h they perceive the probabilities as similar and, therefore, go for the higher amount. Another common reason is that in Figs. e and g, after a risky choice and then outcome 0, it would be clear that a sure 10×10^6 had been foregone because of the decision taken, which may generate strong regret. Because people anticipate this regret they go for certainty. In Figs. 2.4.1f and h effects of regret would not be so clear. These two reasons contribute to the certainty effect, entailing more preference for certainty than EU can explain.

Contrary to what has often been thought, the Allais paradox is relevant to uncertainty as much as it is to risk. This was pointed out in the impressive paper by MacCrimmon & Larsson (1979 pp. 364–365), and in Tversky & Kahneman (1992), Wu & Gonzalez (1999), and others. To see this point, first consider the version of the Allais paradox for risk in Figure 4.12.1, with majority preferences indicated, and with K denoting $1000.

The preferences entail a violation of EU. After dropping the italicized common terms 0.87U(0) and 0.87U(25K), we obtain the same expected-utility inequality for

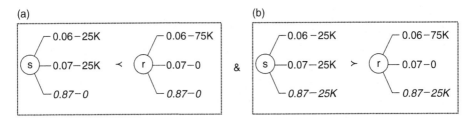

Figure 4.12.1 An example of the Allais paradox for risk.

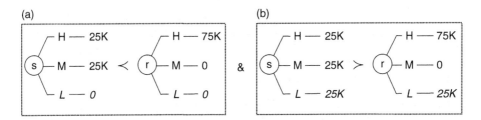

Figure 4.12.2 The certainty effect (Allais paradox) for uncertainty.

Fig. 4.12.1a and Fig. 4.12.1b. Hence, either both preferences should be for the left safety or both preferences should be for the right riskiness. They cannot change as in Figure 4.12.1.

We now turn to uncertainty. Figure 4.12.2 presents an empirical demonstration by Tversky & Kahneman (1992 §1.5). The analogy with Figure 4.12.1 should be apparent. The authors conducted the following within-subjects experiment. Let d denote the difference between the closing value of the Dow Jones index on the day of the experiment and on the day after divided by 100. We consider the events H(igh): $d > 35$, M(iddle): $35 \geq d \geq 30$, L(ow): $30 > d$. The total Dow Jones value at the time of the experiment was about 3000. Of 156 money managers during a workshop, 77% preferred the risky prospect r in Fig. 4.12.2a, but 68% preferred the safe prospect s in Fig. 4.12.2b. This majority preference violates EU, similarly as under risk: After dropping the italicized common terms $P(L)U(0)$ and $P(L)U(25K)$ (P denotes probability), we obtain the same expected utility inequality for Fig. 4.12.2a and Fig. 4.12.2b. Hence, either both preferences should be for the left safety, or both preferences should be for the right riskiness, and they cannot change as in Figure 4.12.2. This reasoning holds regardless of the values of the probabilities $P(H)$, $P(M)$, and $P(L)$. In the following parts of this book we will accommodate empirical violations of EU such as the Allais paradox.

Appendix 4.13   Experimental economics' real-incentive principle and the tradeoff method

The early studies on choice anomalies often used experiments that were not very carefully designed, and they overemphasized the importance of choice irrationalities and their implications for economic models. A reaction came from Gigerenzer (1991, 2008) who demonstrated that, in many experiments with careful explanations, subjects are less prone to irrationalities. Another reaction came from experimental economists, who also stressed the importance of careful experimental procedures. Besides arguing against deception, where subjects are not instructed truthfully, they strongly emphasized the desirability of using real incentives in incentive-compatible manners. Then selfish subjects who are interested only in making as much money as possible will answer truthfully, and this is a way to instruct and motivate subjects (Smith 1982; Harrison & Rutström 2008). These inputs led to great improvements of the experimental procedures used today. For a balanced account of the material discussed here, see Bardsley *et al.* (2010, Ch. 6).

Experimental economists have sometimes overemphasized their antithesis, leading some to completely eschew hypothetical choice. Thus, the literature based on hypothetical choice is often ignored by experimental economists. For example, in an experimental measurement of risk attitude under expected utility that was impressively well designed, Holt & Laury (2002) did not cite the extensive preceding literature. This literature includes surveys by Farquhar (1984), Seidl & Traub

(1999), and Starmer (2000), and an exemplary implementation of choice lists (see below) with real incentives by Cohen, Jaffray, & Said (1987, Figures 1, 2). The latter authors warned against using expected utility (used by Holt & Laury) to analyze these data in view of its descriptive problems (pp. 10–11). Tversky & Kahneman (1992), also not cited by Holt & Laury (2002), can be considered the generalization of Holt & Laury (2002) from expected utility to prospect theory, using the choice list to obtain indifferences as did Holt & Laury. The only difference is, indeed, that Tversky & Kahneman (1992) did not use real incentives, whereas Holt & Laury were ingeniously innovative in observing two within-subject choices, both incentivized, but yet without any income effect.

Real incentives should be used whenever possible, but in some circumstances there is no alternative to hypothetical choice. Examples are large-stake decisions such as life-and-death decisions often considered in the health domain (§3.1), or the measurement of utility of money. The latter is mostly interesting for stakes too large to implement for real – unless there are lucky exceptional circumstances such as in Post *et al.* (2008). In prescriptive applications of decision theory, hypothetical choice is an essential tool (§3.1; Gold *et al.* 1996; Keeney & Raiffa 1976; McNeil *et al.* 1978, 1981 p. 1398; von Winterfeldt 2007). Savage (1954), providing not only the most impressive behavioral foundation in the literature but also illuminating discussions of methodology, wrote:

> If the state of mind in question is not capable of manifesting itself in some sort of extraverbal behavior, it is extraneous to our main interest. ... There is a mode of interrogation intermediate between what I have called the behavioral and the direct. One can, namely, ask the person, not how he feels, but what he would do in such and such a situation. ... in the theory's more important normative interpretation ... the intermediate mode seems to me to be just the right one. (§3.1)

Thus, not only did Savage fully endorse the revealed-preference principles, but also did he recognize hypothetical choice as a central tool for normative applications.

In marketing, hypothetical (called "stated") and real (called "revealed preference" there) choices are often combined so as to take the best of both ("data fusion"; Mark & Swait 2004). Blackburn, Harrison, & Rutström (1994) and Blumenschein (2008 *et al.*) showed that hypothetical choices can serve to predict real choices. Camerer & Hogarth (1999) and Hertwig & Ortmann (2001) reviewed empirical studies into differences between real and hypothetical choice.

In individual choice experiments, researchers almost exclusively use the *random incentive system* (Harrison, Lau, & Rutström 2007; Holt & Laury 2002; Myagkov & Plott 1997) to implement real incentives. The subject makes a number of choices in the experiment, one of which is randomly selected at the end of the experiment and played for real. Under some assumptions verified by Starmer & Sugden (1991) and Lee (2008), the random incentive system is incentive compatible so that selfish subjects will answer truthfully in every experimental question.

The tradeoff method is based on measurements of indifferences. Indifferences can be measured in an incentive-compatible manner using the Becker–DeGroot–Marschak method (see Becker, de Groot, & Marschak 1964), or using the choice list method. For the latter, we present a number of versions of Fig. 4.1.1a (TO upwards), first with a low value substituted for α^1, next with higher values instead, each time asking to choose between the two prospects. The midpoint between the two values where preference is switched is then taken as an estimate of the indifference value α^1. The binary choices used can be incentivized using the random incentive system. For a detailed study and discussion of the literature, see Andersen *et al.* (2006).

The tradeoff method is chained, which means that an answer resulting from a first question is used as input in a second question. If subjects understand this procedure, then in a naïve experimental implementation of real incentives a subject may have an interest in not revealing the true indifference value α^1 in Fig. 4.1.1a but rather a value α^1 as high as possible. Thus, the subject is faced with prospects as favorable as possible in the next question in Fig. 4.1.1b. We call such behavior strategic. Harrison (1986) and Harrison & Rutström (2008) called attention to the problem of strategic behavior for chained experiments. One pragmatic solution is to present choices in such a manner that subjects will not be aware of the possibility of strategic behavior. This approach was taken by van de Kuilen & Wakker (2009), who interviewed subjects after the experiment and found that no subject had been aware of the possibility of strategic behavior. I next present two ways to implement the tradeoff method in an incentive-compatible manner, each assuming that indifferences have been implemented in one of the ways just described (Bardsley *et al.* 2010 Box 6.1).

The first way is based on an idea of Bardsley (2000), originally developed so as to "deceive subjects without deceiving them." He interspersed non-chained filler questions with the experimental questions. At the end of the experiment, the choice played for real is one randomly chosen from the filler questions. Subjects do not know which questions are fillers and which are parts of chaining, and it is in their interest to answer every question truthfully.

The second incentive-compatible way is based on an idea by Johnson (2008). I describe it briefly, in the context of binary choices between event-contingent prospects. Prior to the experiment, a predetermined set of pairs of prospects has been composed, each pair enclosed in an opaque envelope. At the beginning of the experiment, the subject randomly selects one of these envelopes, containing the pair of prospects to be chosen from for real at the end of the experiment. The subject is informed about some characteristics of the set of predetermined pairs, such as their average gain and possibly their maximal and minimal outcomes, but does not know any more about the pairs contained in the predetermined set. Neither does the subject know which pair is contained in the opaque envelope selected.

During the experiment, the subject will make hypothetical choices between pairs of prospects, possibly involving chaining. The subject knows that there is an overlap between the predetermined set of prospect pairs and the pairs presented in the experiment, but does not know what this overlap is. Finally, when the subject has made all experimental choices, the opaque envelope will be opened and the choice pair contained will be inspected. If it happened to occur in the experiment, the choice announced in the experiment will be implemented. If it did not, the subject can choose from the two prospects in the opened envelope on the spot.

In Johnson's approach, it is completely obvious to the subjects that their choices during the experiment cannot influence which choice pair will be the pair to be really chosen from, because the latter has been determined prior to the experiment. If a subject in each experimental choice truthfully reveals real preference, then the subject can be sure to receive the most preferred prospect in the choice played for real at the end, whether this choice appeared in the experiment or not. As soon as the subject in some experimental choice does not reveal preference truthfully, the subject risks not receiving the most preferred prospect from the opaque envelope selected for real if this turns out to be the experimental choice with the untruthful revelation. Hence, it is in the subject's best interest to truthfully reveal preference during the experiment. Johnson's idea entails a general solution to the incentive-compatibility problem of chained experiments put forward by Harrison (1986).

Summarizing then, real incentives are highly desirable for descriptive purposes and should be used whenever possible. Descriptive studies exist, however, where the implementation of real incentives is not possible, so that hypothetical choice then should be used nevertheless. Hypothetical choice is also useful in normative applications.

Appendix 4.14 Tradeoff consistency as a generalization of de Finetti's bookmaking

In the early 1980s I developed a first version of tradeoff consistency as a generalization of de Finetti's bookmaking argument, so as to allow for nonlinear utility, and later leading to Wakker (1984). I knew additive representations of Debreu (1960), but was unaware of the closely related standard sequence invariance condition in Krantz *et al.* (1971 §6.11.2). I explain next how tradeoff consistency naturally results as a generalization of de Finetti's bookmaking.

Additivity, the basis of bookmaking, entails that a preference $x \succcurlyeq y$ is not affected if we add another prospect z:

$$x \succcurlyeq y \Rightarrow x + z \succcurlyeq y + z. \tag{4.14.1}$$

It can be seen that it suffices, in the presence of monotonicity, to impose this condition only for indifferences, and for simplicity of presentation I consider only indifferences henceforth:

$$x \sim y \Rightarrow x + z \sim y + z. \tag{4.14.2}$$

A seemingly weaker but equivalent statement is that indifference is not affected if we add an amount ($\gamma - \alpha = \delta - \beta$ below) to only one event and require

$$\alpha_E x \sim \beta_E y \Rightarrow \gamma_E x \sim \delta_E y \quad \text{whenever } \alpha - \beta = \gamma - \delta. \tag{4.14.3}$$

That is, we require Eq. (4.14.2) only for prospects z of the form $(\gamma - \alpha)_E 0$ (which is $(\delta - \beta)_E 0$). Equation (4.14.3) implies Eq. (4.14.2) for general $z = E_1 z_1 \cdots E_n z_n$ by repeated application: First we add $z_{1_{E_1}} 0$ (in the role of $(\gamma - \alpha)_E 0$), then we add $z_{2_{E_2}} 0, \dots$, and, finally, we add $z_{n_{E_n}} 0$, each time leaving indifference unaffected, and ending up with having added z while leaving indifference unaffected. Hence, Eqs. (4.14.2) and (4.14.3) are equivalent.

The natural analog of Eq. (4.14.3) for EU is:

$$\alpha_E x \sim \beta_E y \Rightarrow \gamma_E x \sim \delta_E y \quad \text{whenever } U(\alpha) - U(\beta) = U(\gamma) - U(\delta). \tag{4.14.4}$$

The difficulty with this condition is that the equality $U(\alpha) - U(\beta) = U(\gamma) - U(\delta)$ is not directly observable, because utility is not. We have to find a way to derive this equality of utility difference from preference. The way to do so is readily inferred from Eq. (4.14.4) using the usual reversal move of the elicitation method. That is, we conjecture the equality

$$U(\alpha) - U(\beta) = U(\gamma) - U(\delta) \quad \text{whenever } \alpha_E x \sim \beta_E y \text{ and } \gamma_E x \sim \delta_E y. \tag{4.14.5}$$

We then use two indifferences as in Eq. (4.14.5) to elicit the equality of utility difference, after which we can predict the implication of Eq. (4.14.4) for two other indifferences with different events E and different prospects x, y but of the same configuration. This leads to tradeoff consistency as in Eq. (4.7.1). The reasoning just given shows how tradeoff consistency is a natural generalization of de Finetti's additivity when the linearity of the utility scale is no longer available.

In Eq. (4.14.5) we could, for theoretical purposes, equally well have chosen the tradeoffs $\alpha \ominus \gamma$ and $\beta \ominus \delta$ instead of $\alpha \ominus \beta$ and $\gamma \ominus \delta$. $\alpha \ominus \gamma$ and $\beta \ominus \delta$ are also equally spaced in utility units and they are easier to understand at first. We rather chose the tradeoffs $\alpha \ominus \beta$ and $\gamma \ominus \delta$ because they can better serve as a basis for decision theory. They reflect arguments in favor of the left choice and play a role in the actual decision making process, and in the mind of the decision maker. They reflect the influence of the decision maker when choosing left conditional on event E. $\alpha \ominus \gamma$ and $\beta \ominus \delta$ do not reflect something actually going on in the decision making process. One of the insights of the marginal revolution, initiated by Jevons (1871), Menger (1871), and Walras (1874), is that not utility in any absolute sense but, rather, differences of utility, are basic in decision making. They reflect the influences of the decision maker. Thus, tradeoff consistency can be interpreted as a simple conservation principle concerning the influences of the decision maker. These considerations suggest again that $\alpha \ominus \beta$ can serve well as a basis of decision theory.

Appendix 4.15   Proofs for Chapter 4

Proof of Theorem 4.6.4 and Observation 4.6.4'. See Köbberling & Wakker (2003 Corollary 10) for finite state spaces, with the extension to infinite state spaces in our Appendix G. A sketch of the proof is as follows.

Assuming EU, we saw before that monotonicity holds (Exercise 4.2.5) and that continuity of preference is implied by continuity of utility (Assignment 4.2.8).

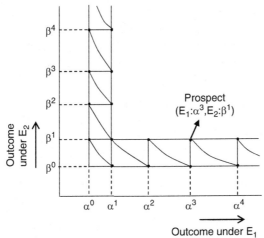

Curves designate indifference.

Figure 4.15.1 Illustration of standard sequences.

Weak ordering and tradeoff consistency were established before. We have shown that (i) implies (ii). We assume henceforth that (ii) holds, and derive (i) for an illustrative case.

We keep a partition $\{E_1,E_2\}$ fixed and suppress it, writing prospects as (x_1,x_2) and so on. For simplicity, we assume strong monotonicity (both events are nonnull). Figure 4.15.1 illustrates the following construction. We take a small outcome $\alpha^0 = \beta^0$ and a somewhat larger outcome α^1, and define $\beta^1 > \beta^0$ by

$$(\alpha^1, \beta^0) \sim (\alpha^0, \beta^1). \tag{4.15.1}$$

For small enough $\beta^0 \ (= \alpha^0)$ and α^1 such a β^1 exists. For as many i as possible (this may be infinitely many), we define α^{i+1} by

$$(\alpha^{i+1}, \beta^0) \sim (\alpha^i, \beta^1). \tag{4.15.2}$$

For as many j as possible (this may again be infinitely many), we, likewise, define β^{j+1} by

$$(\alpha^1, \beta^j) \sim (\alpha^0, \beta^{j+1}). \tag{4.15.3}$$

We used β^1 and β^0 as gauge outcomes to define what was called a standard sequence α^0, α^1, α^2 ..., and we used α^1 and α^0 as gauge outcomes to define a standard sequence β^0, β^1, β^2 ... We have $\alpha^{i+1} \ominus \alpha^i \sim^t \alpha^1 \ominus \alpha^0$ and $\beta^{j+1} \ominus \beta^j \sim^t \beta^1 \ominus \beta^0$ for all i,j. In terms of the EU model yet to be derived, both sequences will be equally spaced in utility units, where the ratio of their step sizes will reflect the probability ratio.

Because, for each i, $\alpha^{i+1} \ominus \alpha^i \sim^t \alpha^1 \ominus \alpha^0$ and $(\alpha^1, \beta^j) \sim (\alpha^0, \beta^{j+1})$, tradeoff consistency implies $(\alpha^{i+1}, \beta^j) \sim (\alpha^i, \beta^{j+1})$ for each j. That is, for a prospect, decreasing one superscript by 1 and increasing the other by 1 does not affect the preference value. By repeated application, decreasing one superscript by an arbitrary number and increasing the other by the same number does not affect the preference value. If we define $V_1(\alpha^i) = i$ and $V_2(\beta^j) = j$, then $V_1(\alpha^i) + V_2(\beta^j)$ represents preference over all (α^i, β^j), and the α's and β's are in this sense perfectly exchangeable units. All that remains to be done is to determine probabilities $P(E_1)$ and $P(E_2)$ and utility U such that $V_1 = P(E_1)U$ and $V_2 = P(E_2)U$.

The following reasoning shows how tradeoff consistency not only ensures consistency of utility, but also of the utility-exchange rate between different events, i.e., of probabilities. If $\alpha^1 > \beta^1$ then, under EU (yet to be derived), it will follow that $P(E_1) < P(E_2)$. In general, the exchange rate between the α's and β's determines the probabilities. We will complete the proof for one illustrative case, namely the case where $\alpha^1 = \beta^3$. This suggests that event E_1 is 3 times less probable than event E_2, so that the odds are 1:3, and $P(E_1) = ¼$ and $P(E_2) = ¾$ under EU. We have to ensure that the 1:3 exchange rate applies consistently to other parts of the standard sequences, and not only to the beginning.

From $(\alpha^0, \beta^6) \sim (\alpha^3, \beta^3)$ and $(\alpha^0, \beta^3) \sim (\alpha^3, \beta^0)$ we conclude that $\beta^6 \ominus \beta^3 \sim^t \beta^3 \ominus \beta^0$ or, substituting $\alpha^1 = \beta^3$ and $\alpha^0 = \beta^0$, $\beta^6 \ominus \alpha^1 \sim^t \alpha^1 \ominus \alpha^0$. Because also $\alpha^2 \ominus \alpha^1 \sim^t \alpha^1 \ominus \alpha^0$, tradeoff consistency implies $\beta^6 = \alpha^2$. By a similar reasoning we can show that $\beta^9 = \alpha^3$, and that $\beta^{3i} = \alpha^i$ for all i. Indeed, three β steps equal one α step everywhere. It follows that $V_1(\alpha^i) = i = V_1(\beta^{3i}) = V_2(\beta^{3i})/3$, so that $V_1 = V_2/3$. Thus, preferences over (α^i, β^j) are represented by $V_1(\alpha^i) + V_2(\beta^j) = V_2(\alpha^i)/3 + V_2(\beta^j)$. This is $P(E_1)U(\alpha^i) + P(E_2)U(\beta^j)$ with $P(E_1) = ¼$, $P(E_2) = ¾$, and $U = 4/3 \times V_2$.

We have established EU on the set (α^i, β^j). By taking $\alpha^0 = \beta^0$ sufficiently small, and α^1 sufficiently close to α^0, we obtain EU on an arbitrarily dense and wide subset of prospects. By continuity it can be extended to all prospects.

A similar reasoning can be applied to other exchange rates between E_1 and E_2. For general partitions $(E_1, \ldots, E_n)$ we can similarly establish tradeoffs between every pair of events and, thus, we can capture the whole preference relation. Monotonicity implies that the utility function is strictly increasing. Continuity of utility follows from continuity of preference (Wakker 1988), but the derivation of this implication is not very elementary. This completes the proof. $\square$

We discuss some conditions in the literature related to tradeoff consistency. Bouyssou & Pirlot (2003 Table 1 on p. 683; 2004) showed that tradeoff consistency can be reinterpreted as a weak separability condition – a kind of monotonicity – for tradeoffs $\alpha \ominus \beta$ in binary preferences. Tradeoff consistency is similar to the standard sequence invariance condition of Krantz et al. (1971 §6.11.2; see also Figure 1 in their §1.3.2). A standard sequence is a sequence of outcomes contingent on a particular event that are equally spaced in utility units and that have been measured while using two outcome levels on another event as "gauge outcomes." An example is provided by the sequence $\alpha^0, \alpha^1, \ldots$ in Eq. (4.15.2). Measuring utility using standard sequences was proposed before by Fishburn (1967 p. 450; the sawtooth method). Such techniques have often been used in marketing (see Interpretation D.4 in Appendix D).

Our analysis extended this technique by considering component weights (probabilities under EU) that drop from the equations.

Proof of Observation 4.8.2. It is straightforward to show that concavity of U implies the implication in the observation. (If U is differentiable this follows because U' is decreasing.) Hence, we assume the implication in the observation and derive concavity of U. Take any $\mu > \sigma$ in the domain of U. By continuity, there is a ν between these which is the utility midpoint of μ and σ. From the implication in the observation (set $\mu = \alpha$, $\nu = \beta$, $\sigma = \gamma$) it follows that $\nu \leq (\mu+\sigma)/2$. Hence, U satisfies $(U(\mu) + U(\sigma))/2 \leq U((\mu+\sigma)/2)$, a condition known as midpoint concavity. For a continuous U, this implies concavity (Wakker 1989a, Lemma A1.1). □

Proof of Theorem 4.8.3. The proof for finite state spaces is in Debreu (1960; supplemented by Chateauneuf & Wakker 1993) and Wakker (1989a, Theorem III.4.1). The extension as given here follows from the technique presented in Appendix G. □

Proof of Theorem 4.9.4 And Observation 4.9.5. In this proof, the additivity condition comprises a solvability or richness assumption because it requires the existence of probabilities of a particular kind. [(i) $\Rightarrow$ (ii)] is obvious. We, therefore, assume Statement (ii) and derive EU. For the general outcome space of Observation 4.9.5, take two outcomes $\gamma \succ \beta$. All claims in the main text remain true if we replace outcome 1 by γ and outcome 0 by β.

Consider a prospect $(E_1:x_1,\ldots,E_n:x_n)$. The main work will be to show that the matching probabilities $p_1,\ldots, p_n$ sum to 1. Once this is done, probabilistic matching and weak ordering immediately imply that EU gives the preference value of the prospect. In the rest of this proof we show that the matching probabilities sum to 1.

By additivity, there exist matching probabilities p_1,p_2 for E_1,E_2, with $1 \geq p_1+p_2$ the matching probability of $E_1 \cup E_2$. This demonstrates that matching probabilities are additive. Assume, by induction, that we have obtained matching probabilities $p_1,\cdots,p_i$ for events $E_1,\ldots,E_i$ such that $E_1 \cup \cdots \cup E_i$ has matching probability $p_1 + \cdots + p_i \leq 1$, for $i < n$. Taking $E_1 \cup \cdots \cup E_i$ and E_{i+1} as two disjoint events with matching probabilities $p_1 + \cdots + p_i$ and p_{i+1}, additivity implies that $E_1 \cup \cdots \cup E_i \cup E_{i+1}$ has matching probability $p_1 + \cdots + p_i + p_{i+1}$. It implies in particular that the latter probability does not exceed 1. We, finally, obtain all matching probabilities $p_1,\ldots,p_n$ where these sum to 1 or less. $1 = (E_1 \cup \cdots \cup E_n:1) \sim 1_{p_1+\ldots+p_n}0$ and EU for probability-contingent prospects implies that $p_1 + \cdots + p_n = 1$ must hold. □

Part II

Nonexpected utility for risk

Preference foundations of expected utility, supporting the rationality of this theory, became widely known in the 1960s. They gave a big boost to the popularity of expected utility in many fields. Clarifying illustrations of early applications include Keeney & Raiffa (1976 Chs. 7 and 8), McNeil *et al.* (1978, 1981), Weinstein *et al.* (1980 Ch. 9), and Winkler (1972 §5.10). After a first, optimistic, period it gradually became understood that there are systematic empirical deviations, and that applications will have to be more complex than first meets the eye. Kahneman & Tversky's (1979) prospect theory was the major paper to disseminate this insight, and to initiate new and more refined nonexpected utility models. In the same way as Bernoulli's (1738) expected utility entailed a departure from objectivity, prospect theory entailed a departure from rationality. Another influential paper to initiate new models was Machina (1982) who, however, argued for a rational status of those new models. Parts II and III of this book are dedicated to descriptive nonexpected utility theories that may depart from rationality.

5 Heuristic arguments for probabilistic sensitivity and rank dependence

This chapter presents the intuition and psychological background of rank-dependent utility. There will be no formal definitions, and the chapter can be skipped if you are only interested in formal theory. After Preston & Baratta (1948) it took 30 years before Quiggin discovered a proper way to transform probabilities, being through rank dependence. After Keynes (1921) and Knight (1921), it even took over 60 years before David Schmeidler discovered a proper way to model uncertainty (the topic of later chapters), through rank dependence. This history shows the depth of the rank-dependent idea, which is why we dedicate this chapter to developing the underlying intuition.

§5.1 presents the important intuition of probabilistic sensitivity, which is an essential component, in addition to utility curvature, to obtain empirically realistic models of risk attitudes. Probabilistic sensitivity underlies all nonexpected utility (nonEU) theories. The question is how to develop a sound decision model that incorporates this component. The rest of the chapter argues that rank-dependent utility can serve as a natural model to obtain such a sound theory. The arguments are based on psychological interpretations and heuristic graphs. These suggest, first, that the rank-dependent formula is natural from a mathematical perspective. They also suggest that the rank-dependent formula matches psychological processes of decision making, in agreement with the homeomorphic approach taken in this book. Heuristic ideas as presented in this chapter may have led John Quiggin and David Schmeidler to invent the rank-dependent model.

5.1 Probabilistic sensitivity versus outcome sensitivity for single-nonzero-outcome-prospects

Consider SG probability measurements with amounts between $0 and $100. Assume that we observe the five indifferences displayed in Figs. 5.1.1(a)–(e). The amounts $0 and $100 are called the *extreme amounts*. The data reveal considerable deviations from expected value maximization and linearity: There is pronounced risk aversion.

Figure 5.1.2 summarizes the data in two equivalent ways. In Fig. a, the money amounts between the extremes are on the x-axis, and the corresponding SG

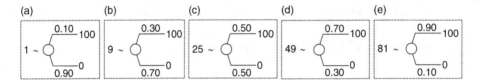

Figure 5.1.1 Five SG observations.

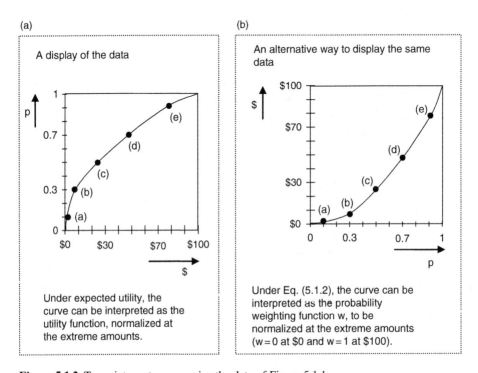

Figure 5.1.2 Two pictures to summarize the data of Figure 5.1.1.

probabilities are on the y-axis. Fig. b also shows the data, but has the axes interchanged. In other words, it results from Fig. a by rotating left and flipping horizontally. We first focus on Fig. a. The figure can be taken as merely an objective display of data, without any interpretation added or theory assumed.

Turning to a theory now, EU assumes a linear processing of probabilities. The deviation from linearity in the data must then be ascribed to a nonlinear processing in the outcome dimension, modeled by nonlinear utility. With the normalization of $U(0) = 0$ and $U(100) = 1$ at the extreme amounts, Fig. 5.1.1a implies $U(1) = 0.10U(100) + 0.90U(0) = 0.10$, Fig. 5.1.1b implies $U(9) = 0.30U(100) + 0.70U(0) = 0.30$, and so on. In general, for a pair p, x with $100_p0 \sim x$ we have $U(x) = p$ (as in the SG Eq. (2.5.1)). In this manner, Fig. 5.1.2a shows the graph of the utility function, normalized at the extreme amounts. The figure suggests, for instance, that the marginal utility of money is diminishing, with the extra utility generated by the first dollar considerably larger than the extra utility generated by an extra dollar added to $99.

Theorem 3.2.1a presented one of the most famous results of classical EU: risk aversion – each prospect less preferred than its expectation – holds if and only if utility is concave. I expect that most people, when they first learned about the characterization of risk aversion through concave utility, were amazed. Utility seems to describe sensitivity to money, and this seems to be a concept different than attitude to risk. How can your feelings about money determine your risk attitude? What about your utility and behavior for other quantitative outcomes, such as amounts of wine, life duration, or hours of listening to music? And what about your behavior for nonquantitative outcomes such as health states? Shouldn't risk attitude have something to do with feelings about probabilities? Utility curvature does not seem to capture risk attitude in a homeomorphic manner.

It was primarily psychologists who, since the 1950s, and based on intuitions as just described, objected to the modeling of risk attitude through the utility of money. For example, Lopes (1987) wrote: "Risk attitude is more than the psychophysics of money" (p. 283). Psychophysics is the field of psychology that examines sensations generated by physical stimuli. Utility can be taken as the scale that describes the sensations generated by receiving money. It was also primarily this intuition that led David Schmeidler to invent his rank-dependent model.[1] An additional argument against EU concerns the considerable risk aversion that is found empirically for small amounts of money, because it is not plausible that the marginal utility of money changes as much over small amounts as is required to explain such risk aversion.

In general, economists have not been very concerned about criticisms based on introspection rather than on revealed preference. Since economists are trained to express everything in terms of money, the assertion that "risk aversion means concave utility of money" does not set alarm bells ringing for them. Hence, until the beginning of the 1980s, models deviating from EU were considered primarily in the psychological literature (Edwards 1954).

In general, the perception of money will be approximately linear for moderate amounts of money, unlike in Fig. 5.1.2a. Psychologists have suggested that risk attitude will have more to do with how people feel about probability than with how they feel about money. The deviation from linearity in the data is then better explained by a nonlinear evaluation or perception in the probability dimension. In a prospect $100_{0.90}0$, 90% of the *probability mass* does not carry 90% of the *value* of certainty, as EU has it, but it carries less value. If EU describes deviations from a linear evaluation

$$\alpha_p 0 \mapsto p\alpha$$

by transforming the outcome α nonlinearly in

$$\alpha_p 0 \mapsto pU(\alpha), \tag{5.1.1}$$

---

[1] Personal communication.

wouldn't it then be more natural to instead transform the probability nonlinearly, as in

$$\alpha_p 0 \mapsto w(p)\alpha. \tag{5.1.2}$$

so the argument goes. Here w is a nonlinear probability weighting function.

Under Eq. (5.1.2), the equivalence in Fig. 5.1.1a implies $w(0.10) \times 100 = 1$, so that $w(0.10) = 1/100$. Similarly, Fig. b gives $w(0.30) = 9/100$; and so on. In general, for a pair p,x with $100_p 0 \sim x$ we have $w(p)100 = x$ so that $w(p) = x/100$. In this manner, Fig. 5.1.2b can be interpreted as the nonnormalized graph of the probability weighting function w. The graph of w results after normalization of $w = 1$ at the extreme amount $x = 100$ (with $w = 0$ at the extreme amount $x = 0$). The figure suggests, for instance, that the weight $w(0.90)$ – the perception of a 90/100 probability – is less than a 90% share of certainty.

In the earliest experimental study of risky choice that I am aware of, by the psychologists Preston & Baratta (1948), the authors assumed that deviations from expected value result from a nonlinear perception of probability, as in Eq. (5.1.2), rather than from a nonlinear perception of the utility of outcomes. In the decades that followed, when EU governed the field, these authors were criticized for having assumed linear utility and their work was ignored. According to modern views, however, the original method of Preston & Baratta may have been more natural for descriptive purposes than EU. For small amounts of money, Eq. (5.1.2) (Fig. 5.1.2b) represents a plausible model. For such amounts, EU ascribes the empirically found nonlinearities (risk aversion) to the wrong axis in Fig. 5.1.2a.

For large amounts, a combination of Eqs. (5.1.1) and (5.1.2) is plausible, as in

$$\alpha_p 0 \mapsto w(p)U(\alpha). \tag{5.1.3}$$

Then both sensitivity to outcomes and sensitivity to probabilities generate deviations from risk neutrality.

An answer (without elaboration) to the following exercise will immediately be given in the main text, so that if you want to do the exercise then you should do it before reading on.

Exercise 5.1.1.[b] Assume that we measure, for each $0 < \alpha < 100$, the SG probability p of α with respect to the extreme amounts 0, 100. That is, p is such that $\alpha \sim 100_p 0$. Assume that we find $p = \sqrt{\alpha/100}$ for each α. In other words, $\alpha = 100p^2$ for each p.

(a) Assume EU. Give a formula in terms of α for the utility function $U(\alpha)$.
(b) Assume Eq. (5.1.2).[2] Give a formula in terms of p for the weighting function $w(p)$. □

Exercise 5.1.1 and its elaboration show that the data in Figures 5.1.1 and 5.1.2 can be accommodated by EU with $U(\alpha) = \sqrt{\alpha}$ (or any renormalization), but also by

---

[2] Hence, utility is linear. It will not matter for the result of this part if we normalize utility to be 1 at 100, using the formula $\alpha_p 0 \mapsto w(p)(\alpha/100)$, as we often do in SG measurements, or if we leave utility nonnormalized as in Eq. (5.1.2).

Eq. (5.1.2) with $w(p) = p^2$. Thus EU with square root utility accommodates the same data as Eq. (5.1.2) with a square weighting function. The two models are called *data equivalent* on the domain considered (equivalences $\alpha \sim 100_p0$), which means that they are two different ways of accommodating the same phenomena.

If probability weighting had nothing more to offer than to provide a model that is data-equivalent to EU and that maybe provides more plausible explanations, then there would be only limited interest in probability weighting. It would then accommodate all the same phenomena and would give the same empirical predictions as EU, and we might as well stick with the theory we already know. In more general domains with multi-outcome prospects, however, probability weighting will not just be data-equivalent to EU, but will lead to essentially different models and predictions. This will be the topic of the following sections.

We mention two examples here, in addition to many to come later, where probability weighting gives different predictions than utility curvature. Köbberling & Peters (2003) theoretically examined bargaining games where increased risk aversion in terms of utility curvature leads to less favorable outcomes, but increased risk aversion in terms of probability weighting leads to more favorable outcomes. Onay & Öncüler (2007) developed stimuli with risk and time involved, where probabilistic and outcome-based risk aversion led to opposite predictions. The predictions based on probabilistic risk aversion were confirmed in an experiment.

5.2 Probabilistic sensitivity for multi-outcome prospects, and the old way of transforming probabilities

For the sake of later arguments, Figure 5.2.1 shows the expected value of a prospect $p_1x_1 \ldots p_nx_n$. We have ranked the outcomes such that $x_1 > \cdots > x_n$. For now, the ranking only serves convenience. Later, when we consider rank-dependent models, rankings will be essential.

We next depict expected value in an alternative manner. The area of Figure 5.2.1, obviously, does not change if the figure is rotated left (Fig. 5.2.2a) and next flipped horizontally (Fig. 5.2.2b). Fig. 5.2.2b shows the graph of the *decumulative distribution* function G of the prospect, which assigns to each outcome α the probability $G(\alpha)$ that the prospect yields more than α. The function G is dual to the regular ("cumulative") *distribution functions* commonly used in probability theory and statistics, which assign to each number the probability of that number or less. In our analyses it will be more convenient to use decumulative distribution functions. The probabilities $G(\alpha)$ will be called ranks or, informally, good-news probabilities, later on. Because the graph in Fig. 5.2.2b is of the decumulative distribution function G, it follows that the expectation can be calculated as the integral of that function G.

EU, introduced to model deviations from linearity – linearity means expected value – is illustrated in Figure 5.2.3. Relative to Figure 5.2.1, heights of columns, i.e., distances from points all the way down to the x-axis, have been U-transformed. We will assume $U(0) = 0$ in all figures in this chapter.

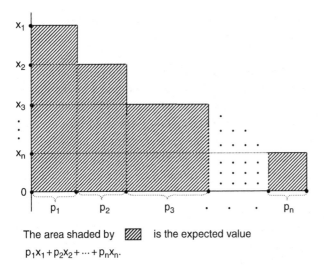

The area shaded by ▨ is the expected value
$p_1x_1 + p_2x_2 + \cdots + p_nx_n.$

Figure 5.2.1 Expected value.

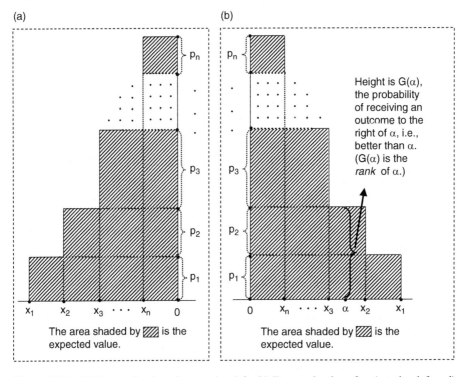

(a)

(b)

Height is $G(\alpha)$,
the probability
of receiving an
outcome to the
right of α, i.e.,
better than α.
($G(\alpha)$ is the
rank of α.)

The area shaded by ▨ is the
expected value.

The area shaded by ▨ is the
expected value.

Figure 5.2.2 (a) Expected value after rotating left. (b) Expected value after (rotating left and) flipping horizontally.

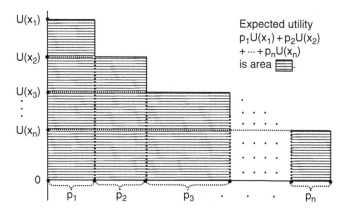

To calculate expected utility, the distance from x_j ("all the way") down to the x-axis has been transformed into the distance $U(x_j)$, for all j.

Figure 5.2.3 Expected utility.

EU describes deviations from linearity in $\sum_{j=1}^{n} p_j x_j$ by transforming the outcomes x_j nonlinearly – pulling the graph of Figure 5.2.1 in the y-axis direction; i.e., in the outcome direction.

In the psychological approach to transforming probabilities, the following formula was originally taken to be the natural extension of Eq. (5.1.2) $(w(p)\alpha)$ to multi-outcome prospects:

$$\sum_{j=1}^{n} w(p_j) x_j \text{ [Old weighting].} \tag{5.2.1}$$

In this dual approach, the area is deformed in the probability direction rather than in the outcome direction. As a convention, the equation assumes that $x_i \neq x_j$ if $i \neq j$; i.e., all identical outcomes have been collapsed. It is natural that w is increasing, with $w(0) = 0$ and $w(1) = 1$, as in Figure 5.2.4 for example.

Figure 5.2.5 illustrates Eq. (5.2.1). Such models of probability transformations have been considered in the psychological literature since the 1950s, such as in several papers by Ward Edwards and in Preston & Baratta (1948). Unfortunately, the model of Eq. (5.2.1) was often called subjective EU, the same name as used for Savage's (1954) model, although it is very different from Savage's model (Exercise 2.3.1).

The psychological works were mostly based on direct intuition, and have been criticized by economists who adhere to revealed preference. Although the theory of transformed probability in Eq. (5.2.1) was a standard part of psychological theory, routinely showing up in textbooks, it never had much impact and it has never been used widely. This holds even though its basic intuition, that nonlinear attitudes towards probability should be considered, is important. We will next see why Eq. (5.2.1) did not lead to fruitful applications.

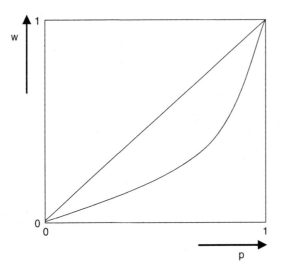

Figure 5.2.4 A probability weighting function.

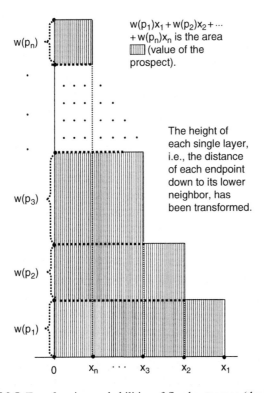

Figure 5.2.5 Transforming probabilities of fixed outcomes (the "old" model).

5.3 A violation of stochastic dominance

At the end of the 1970s, there was renewed interest in nonlinear probabilities, generated by Handa (1977) and, primarily, Kahneman & Tversky (1979), two papers that appeared in leading economic journals. This exposure to a mathematically sophisticated audience immediately led to the discovery that, apparently, had remained unnoticed in the psychological literature up to that point. In reaction to its publication of Handa (1977), the *Journal of Political Economy* received several letters pointing out a fundamental theoretical problem in Eq. (5.2.1) (old weighting): it violates stochastic dominance. They published Fishburn's (1978) letter. Among the letters not published – and not mentioned – was one by a then unknown Australian undergraduate honours student, John Quiggin. His letter initiated the development of one of the major ideas in decision under risk of the last decades. We will now illustrate the violation of stochastic dominance.

If w is linear and $w(p) = p$ for all p, then the theory is not new and nothing new will happen. We, therefore, assume that $w(p) \neq p$ for at least one p. Then w is nonlinear. It is well known, and will be assumed without proof (for a proof see Aczél, 1966, the Cauchy equation), that there must then be probabilities p_1 and p_2 with

$$w(p_1 + p_2) \neq w(p_1) + w(p_2). \tag{5.3.1}$$

We show that anomalies result from this inequality. First consider the case

$$w(p_1 + p_2) > w(p_1) + w(p_2). \tag{5.3.2}$$

We discuss the reversed inequality later. Violations of stochastic dominance can be detected by inspecting what happens to Eq. (5.2.1) and the evaluation of the prospect in Figure 5.2.5 if x_1 is gradually reduced. This is illustrated in Figure 5.3.1. Fig. a illustrates a small reduction of x_1. Nothing special happens. Some area has been lost, indicated at the right-hand end of the figure. Hence, the evaluation of the prospect has decreased somewhat. No heights of layers changed. In Fig. b, x_1 has decreased more, and it approximates x_2. More area has been lost, and the value of the prospect has decreased even further. Still no heights of columns have changed.

In Fig. c, x_1 has been decreased a little further, such that it hits x_2. Before inspecting the figure in detail, we first note that x_1 and x_2 are now one and the same outcome. Its probability of occurring is $p_1 + p_2$. The layers of x_1 and x_2 should now be lumped together and be treated as one layer. We should now transform the probability $p_1 + p_2$ into its w value $w(p_1 + p_2)$, which replaces the two parts $w(p_1)$ and $w(p_2)$.

We assumed that $w(p_1 + p_2) > w(p_1) + w(p_2)$ (Eq. (5.3.2)). Thus, a sudden explosion of new area occurs at the bottom of the figure, shaded darker. The area has been added below, moving the origin down, for easy comparison. The height of the dark layer is $w(p_1 + p_2) - w(p_1) - w(p_2)$.

The sudden explosion of area by an infinitesimal change in x_1 from Fig. b to Fig. c entails a violation of continuity, which is undesirable. More serious is a second problem, being that the explosion entails a violation of stochastic dominance. Lowering an outcome has raised the valuation. This is very undesirable.

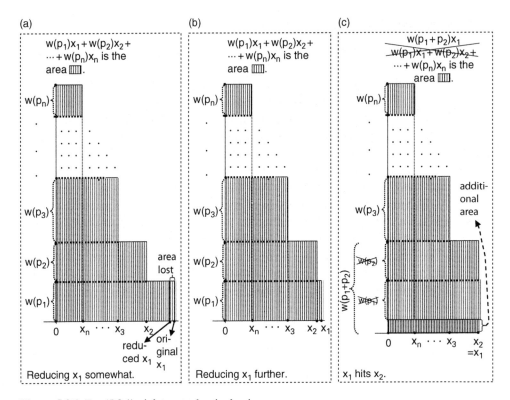

Figure 5.3.1 Eq. (5.2.1) violates stochastic dominance.

For the case

$$w(p_1 + p_2) < w(p_1) + w(p_2),$$

similar violations of stochastic dominance and continuity arise. In this case we gradually increase x_2 up towards x_1. At the moment when x_2 hits x_1, a sudden implosion of area occurs. Improving an outcome then has led to a smaller area and a lower evaluation of the prospect, again violating stochastic dominance.

Even though violations of stochastic dominance have been found empirically (Birnbaum *et al.* 1992; Tversky & Kahneman 1986 p. S263, problem 7), they are usually not of the kind just exhibited. They depend crucially on psychological details of framing. Imposing such violations systematically as through Eq. (5.2.1) (old weighting), without any reference to framing effects, is undesirable (Machina 1982 p. 292; see Starmer 1999 for opposite viewpoints).

The more general formula

$$\sum_{j=1}^{n} w(p_j)U(x_j), \tag{5.3.3}$$

allowing nonlinear utility, is similarly unsound. As soon as w is not the identity function, there are cases where increasing the utility of outcomes leads to a lower evaluation of the prospect in the exact same way as the increase of outcomes just analyzed did.

Summarizing then, there are good intuitive reasons for considering transformations of probability, put forward by psychologists. It is not clear at this point, though, what a sensible decision model based on transformed probability could be. The seemingly most natural decision model, and one popular in the psychological literature up to 1980, has turned out to be unsound. We need a model that incorporates sensitivity to probability and uncertainty through nonlinear probability weighting, but that avoids the theoretical anomalies of Eq. (5.2.1). This was the state of decision theory at the beginning of the 1980s, when John Quiggin and, independently, David Schmeidler, invented the rank-dependent model that will solve the problems sketched here, and that will be presented in the next sections.

5.4   Rank-dependent utility: discovering the formula using psychological intuition

I will first argue that good-news probabilities, or ranks as they will be called formally, are sometimes more relevant to decisions than the probabilities of fixed outcomes. If you own a prospect then the information that the prospect yields more than 40 is good news. For example, imagine that you own the prospect that pays you according to the number of a card, randomly drawn from a pack of 100 numbered cards, according to Table 5.4.1. If the number is between 1 and 20 then you receive $80, and so on.

Table 5.4.1

# card:	1−20	21−40	41−60	61−80	81−100
$-gain:	80	60	40	20	0

This event-contingent prospect corresponds to the following probability-contingent prospect.

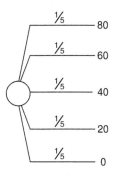

If you receive the information that the prospect yields more than 20, then this is good news. The probability of receiving more than 20, 3/5, is a good-news probability. This term obviously does not refer to the probability 3/5 in isolation, but depends on the particular prospect faced and on the underlying event of the number of the card drawn being below 61.

Definition 5.4.1. For prospect y and outcome α, the *rank* – or, informally, the *good-news probability* – describes the probability of y yielding an outcome ranked strictly better than α. □

Thus, ranks are numbers between 0 and 1 in this book and not integers. The following example suggests that in some respects ranks may be more relevant to decision making than the probability or event of receipt of a separate outcome.

Example 5.4.2 [Relevance of ranks for decisions]. Consider again the depicted prospect. Imagine that you receive the information that the prospect will be changed, if you agree, as follows:

Proposed Change 1. The separate-outcome probability P(receiving $40) is increased by changing the outcome at one card.

You are asked if you want this change to take place. Your first reaction will be that the information is incomplete. Will the outcome changed be a worse outcome, 0 or 20, in which case you like the change, or will it be a better outcome, 60 or 80, in which case you do not like the change? In short, this information about an increase of a separate-outcome probability does not help much in our decision making.

In the following thought experiment, consider again the depicted prospect. Imagine that you receive the information that the prospect will be changed, if you agree, as follows:

Proposed Change 2. The rank P (receiving more than $20) is increased by changing the outcome at one card.

You are asked if you want this change to take place. It entails that either outcome 0 or outcome 20 will be changed into outcome 40, 60, or 80, at one card. Without knowing more than just this, you can conclude that this increase of one rank is favorable and that you will accept the change. This information about an increase of a rank does help you to decide. □

Example 5.4.2 suggests that, for evaluating prospects, ranks are sometimes more relevant than probabilities of separate outcomes. Increasing a rank of α is surely favorable, whereas increasing a probability of receiving α can be either favorable or unfavorable.

The relevance of ranks can be further illustrated by the stochastic dominance condition. A first prospect *stochastically dominates* a second one if the first prospect can be obtained from the second by some shifts of probability mass from worse to better outcomes. For example, the lower prospect in Fig. 2.4.1a., $95_{0.5}70$, stochastically dominates the upper one, $80_{0.5}60$, with 0.5 probability mass shifted from 80 to 95 and 0.5 probability mass shifted from 60 to 70. The upper prospect in Fig. 2.4.1b, $40_{0.7}20$, stochastically dominates the lower one, $40_{0.6}20$, because a 0.1 probability mass was shifted from the 20 to the 40 outcome. By the stochastic dominance *preference* condition defined in §2.7, the dominating prospect then is to be preferred to the dominated one. The following exercise shows that stochastic dominance can naturally be expressed in terms of ranks, amounting to all ranks (good-news probabilities) being at least as good.

Exercise 5.4.1. We have:
prospect x stochastically dominates prospect y

$$\Leftrightarrow$$

for all outcomes α the rank of receiving more than α is at least as large under x as it is under y.[3]

(a)[b] Show that the upper statement implies the lower one.
(b)[c] Show that the lower statement implies the upper one. □

Figure 5.4.1 (similar to Keeney & Raiffa 1976 Figure 4.2), illustrates the case for continuous distributions. It may not be very clear from Fig. a which prospect is to be preferred. In Fig. b, for every outcome the rank (the probability of getting something better than that outcome) under x exceeds that under y, so that x stochastically dominates y and is to be preferred.

Comment [Early references on ranks]. In many theories, ranks play a special role. An example is the range-frequency theory of Parducci (1965, 1995). Imagine that we

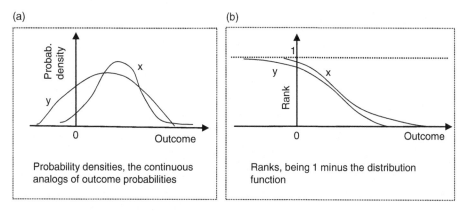

(a)

Probability densities, the continuous analogs of outcome probabilities

(b)

Ranks, being 1 minus the distribution function

Fig. b displays the same prospects as Fig. a, but now in terms of ranks, i.e., the probability of receiving a strictly better outcome, which is 1 minus the usual distribution function.

Figure 5.4.1 The usefulness of ranks.

---

[3] When we compare the ranks of different outcomes of the same prospect, as done in many places in this book, then low ranks indicate good outcomes. When we compare the ranks of the same outcome for different prospects, then high ranks indicate good prospects.

observe n real-valued stimuli $x_1 > \ldots > x_n$. Then, according to this theory, our perception of x_i is a combination of its rank $(i-1)/n$ and its absolute position $(x_i-x_n)/(x_1-x_n)$. This idea led Birnbaum (1972, 1973, 1974) to introduce his configural weighting theory, first for general psychological perceptions, then for decision under risk (Birnbaum *et al.* 1992). Many studies have shown that for the happiness derived from income, the rank in society, i.e., the percentage of people who are richer, is important (Clark, Frijters, & Shields 2008; Easterling 1995; van Praag & Ferrer-i-Carbonell 2004). Similarly, rank dependence is widely used for welfare evaluations (Ebert 1988, 2004; Weymark 1981 Theorem 3; see also Appendix F). For applications in finance, see Tsanakas (2008) and its references. When evaluating streams of income, the ranking pattern of this stream is important (Barsky *et al.* 1997 p. 567; Constantinides 1990; Frank 1989; Gilboa 1989a; Hsee & Abelson 1991; Loewenstein & Prelec 1991; Loewenstein & Sicherman 1991). When evaluating episodes (periods in our life), besides the last experience, the best and worst experience play a special role (Kahneman 1994; Kahneman & Krueger 2006). □

The preceding observations have suggested informally that ranks may be useful for the evaluation of prospects. It may, accordingly, be interesting to apply probability-transformations not to separate-outcome-probabilities, but to ranks. This is how we will generalize EU. To develop a theory as suggested, consider the following prospect.

The EU formula is:

$$\tfrac{1}{6} \times U(80) + \tfrac{1}{2} \times U(30) + \tfrac{1}{3} \times U(20).$$

Modifying this formula was an easy task for the theory that transformed separate-outcome probabilities because those probabilities, $\tfrac{1}{6}$, $\tfrac{1}{2}$, and $\tfrac{1}{3}$, were already standing there, ready to be transformed, so to speak. They then led to the formula

$$w(\tfrac{1}{6}) \times U(80) + w(\tfrac{1}{2}) \times U(30) + w(\tfrac{1}{3}) \times U(20),$$

which, as explained before, is not sound.

Our plan is to transform ranks, one way or the other. Ranks are $\tfrac{1}{6}$ (probability of more than 30), and $\tfrac{1}{6} + \tfrac{1}{2} = \tfrac{2}{3}$ (probability of more than 20), besides the trivial ranks 0 (probability of more than 80) and 1 (probability of more than, say, 0). We rewrite the EU formula in the following way:

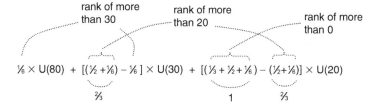

$\frac{1}{6} \times U(80) + [(\frac{1}{2} + \frac{1}{6}) - \frac{1}{6}] \times U(30) + [(\frac{1}{3} + \frac{1}{2} + \frac{1}{6}) - (\frac{1}{2} + \frac{1}{6})] \times U(20)$

The roundabout rewriting shows:

Under EU, the weight[4] of a utility is the difference between two *ranks*.   (5.4.1)

We rewrite the EU formula as

$$\frac{1}{6} \times U(80) + [\quad \frac{2}{3} \quad - \quad \frac{1}{6}] \times U(30) + [\quad 1 - \quad \frac{2}{3}] \times U(20). (5.4.2)$$

You are invited to invent the formula of the new theory by yourself at this stage, before reading on. In other words, please now invent the variation of the EU formula in which ranks are transformed by the w transformation function. Putting the point yet another way, please now make the same invention as Quiggin (1982) did. This invention is the topic of the next exercise. The answer is given in the footnote and is discussed in the subsequent text.

Exercise 5.4.2.[a] Invent the formula of the new theory by yourself, by modifying Eq. (5.4.2). The answer is in the footnote.[5] □

Exercise 5.4.3.[a] Calculate the value of the prospect under the theory just derived (rank-dependent utility) for $U(\alpha) = \alpha$ and $w(p) = \sqrt{p}$. The answer is in the footnote.[6] □

We next consider the formula for a general prospect

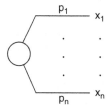

To obtain ranks, which of course is our plan again, it is convenient to have $x_1 > \cdots > x_n$. We then call the outcomes *completely ranked*. We assume complete ranking in

---

[4] Weight is the number by which utility will be multiplied.

[5] Answer: $w(\frac{1}{6}) \times U(80) + [w(\frac{2}{3}) - w(\frac{1}{6})] \times U(30) + [w(1) - w(\frac{2}{3})] \times U(20)$. We can, of course, substitute 1 for $w(1)$.

[6] $w(\frac{1}{6}) \times 0.408$, $w(\frac{2}{3}) = 0.816$. The value of the prospect is $0.408 \times 80 + (0.816-0.408) \times 30 + (1-0.816) \times 20 = 0.408 \times 80 + 0.408 \times 30 + 0.184 \times 20 = 48.6$.

the rest of this chapter. In other cases the outcomes are reordered. We have collapsed equal outcomes so that all remaining outcomes are different. This requirement will be relaxed later. The EU of the prospect is:

$$\sum_{j=1}^{n} p_j U(x_j).$$

We again rewrite it as

rank of x_{j+1} rank of x_j (0 for $j = 1$)

$$\sum_{j=1}^{n} [(p_j + \cdots + p_1) - (p_{j-1} + \cdots + p_1)]U(x_j).$$

Thus, in general, the weight assigned to $U(x_j)$ by EU is the difference between two ranks as in Eq. (5.4.1). EU, written in an equivalent but more evocative format, is:

$$\sum_{j=1}^{n} [\ (p_j + \cdots + p_1) \ - \ (p_{j-1} + \cdots + p_1) \ ]U(x_j). \tag{5.4.3}$$

You are invited to invent the formula of the new theory by yourself. The footnote of the next exercise gives the answer.

Exercise 5.4.4.[a] Invent the formula of the new theory by yourself, by modifying Eq. (5.4.3). The answer is in the footnote.[7] □
The formula just derived (in the footnote), is rank-dependent utility (RDU), modifying Eq. (5.4.1).

> *Under RDU, the weight of a utility is the difference between two*
> transformed ranks   (5.4.4)

The first rank transformed is the probability of receiving the outcome with the utility considered or any better outcome; the second rank transformed is the probability of receiving any better outcome. This weight is called a *decision weight*. It is the marginal contribution, measured in w-units, of the outcome probability to the total probability of receiving better outcomes. The function w is often called a *probability weighting function* rather than a probability transformation function.

It is useful to keep in mind from the very beginning that the probability weighting function does not transform just any probabilities without any interpretation added, but that it transforms ranks, i.e., good-news probabilities. We will later consider loss-ranks, referring to events and probabilities of receiving any

---

[7] Answer: $\sum_{j=1}^{n} [w(p_j + \cdots + p_1) - w(p_{j-1} + \cdots + p_1)]U(x_j)$. For $j = 1$, the term is $w(p_1)U(x_1)$.

outcome worse than a particular given outcome. Confusion can arise here if it is not kept in mind which kind of probabilities a weighting function is supposed to be applied to.

The idea of probability transformation alone is not enough to obtain a new decision theory because it is not clear how to evaluate multi-outcome prospects. Neither is rank dependence alone without probability transformation enough to obtain a new decision theory, as this only yields an alternative way of stating a known theory; cf. Fig. 5.2.2b. By taking the two ideas together we get a new decision theory. One of the first to propose the idea of nonlinear probability was Shackle (1949a, b). He, however, did not succeed in developing a useful method for evaluating prospects and, hence, no useful theory resulted.

This section has presented a heuristic way in which a psychological reasoning can lead to the discovery of the new theory: It makes sense to transform probabilities; then, it makes more sense to transform ranks than to transform fixed-outcome probabilities; the result, then, is the new formula. Many questions can be raised at this stage. Is the formula, besides being psychologically plausible, also plausible in the sense of exhibiting plausible mathematical properties? The next section will give a partial answer to the latter question, by showing that the formula is a natural analog of regular integration. We will later give a complete answer to the mathematical naturalness of the formula by providing a behavioral foundation. Another question to be addressed is whether the new formula performs well in an empirical sense. This question will be discussed in later chapters. We will first present a heuristic way in which a mathematician might discover the new theory.

5.5   Rank-dependent utility: discovering the formula using mathematical intuition

This section demonstrates that the rank-dependent transformation of probabilities, rather than Eq. (5.2.1) (old weighting), is the natural dual of expected utility's transformation of outcomes. To make this duality transparent, we first restrict attention to the special case of rank dependence when there is no utility transformation; i.e., we assume linear utility. Then rank-dependent utility is dual to EU, as we will see, in agreement with Yaari (1987). To facilitate the comparison of some figures, they have been reproduced in Figure 5.5.1.

Reconsider Figure 5.2.3 (= Fig. 5.5.1a; EU) and Figure 5.2.5 (= Fig. 5.5.1b; old probabilistic sensitivity and old weighting). Upon closer inspection, old weighting is not a true dual to EU. In EU, distances from endpoints of columns all the way down to the x-axis are transformed, whereas in old weighting distances from endpoints of columns to their lower neighbor endpoint are transformed. We obtain a true dual to EU if we, also when transforming probabilities, transform distances from endpoints of columns all the way down to the x-axis. This dual result is shown in the right part of Fig. 5.5.1c with some details added in Figure 5.5.2.

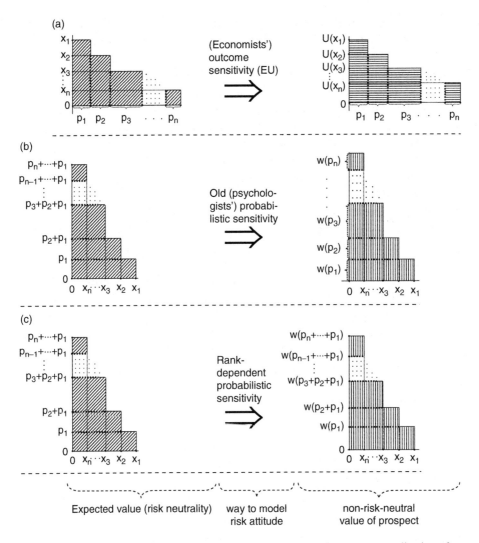

Figure 5.5.1 Combination of preceding figures, with rank dependence as an application of an economic technique to a psychological dimension.

The area in Figure 5.5.2 is

$$w(p_1)x_1 +$$

$$(w(p_2 + p_1) - w(p_1))x_2 +$$

$$\cdots +$$

$$(w(p_n + \cdots + p_1) - w(p_{n-1} + \cdots + p_1))x_n,$$

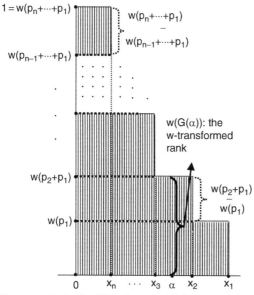

The area shaded by ⬚ is the value of the prospect.
Distances of endpoints of layers ("all the way") down to
the x-axis are transformed, similar to Figure 5.2.3. The
endpoint of the last layer now remains at a distance of 1
from the x-axis, reflecting normalization of the bounded
probability scale.

Figure 5.5.2 Rank-dependent utility with linear utility.

which is rank-dependent utility with linear utility as we saw before. It is the integral
of the transformed decumulative probability distribution G. In other words, it is the
expectation of the prospect with ranks $w(G(\alpha))$ rather than $G(\alpha)$.

Figure 5.2.2 illustrates that ranks are the analogs of outcomes, and probabilities are
the analogs of differences of outcomes rather than of outcomes. The decision weight
of an outcome is the marginal weight contribution of its outcome-probability to its
rank, and is therefore a *difference* between two weights of ranks.

We conclude that the psychologists' idea from the 1950s of transforming probabilities was a good idea. But it should have been applied to the right probabilities. Not to
those of fixed outcomes, but to good-news probabilities, that is, to ranks.

We obtain the general rank-dependent utility theory if we allow utility to be
nonlinear. Then transformations in both the outcome- and the probability-direction
are considered. Figures 5.5.3 and 5.5.4 illustrate the general formula.

This section has presented a heuristic way in which a mathematician may discover the
new theory. If we want to do in the probability dimension what expected utility does in
the outcome dimension, in a truly dual manner, then rank dependence is the way to go.

The history of probability weighting resembles the history of utility. Until approximately 1870, economists did not know well how to use the tool of utility, primarily

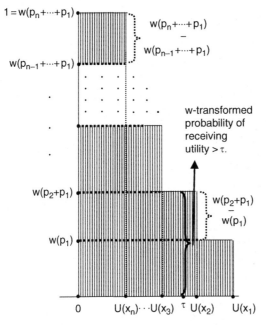

For points on the y-axis (endpoints of layers), their
distances down to the x-axis are transformed using w.
For points on the x-axis (endpoints of columns), their
distances leftwards to the y-axis are transformed using U.

Figure 5.5.3 Rank-dependent utility with general utility.

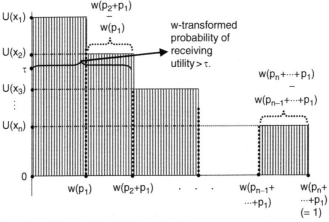

Relative to Figure 5.5.3, this figure has been
rotated left and flipped horizontally.

Figure 5.5.4 Another illustration of general rank-dependent utility.

because of the water–diamond paradox: people pay more for a diamond than for a month's water consumption, which suggests that the utility of the diamond is bigger. However, people need the water to survive and not the diamond, which suggests that the utility of water is bigger. A major step forward was made by what is called the marginal revolution (Jevons 1871; Menger 1871; Walras 1874). These authors showed that differences of utility, rather than absolute levels of utility, are basic for decisions. With this insight the water–diamond paradox could be resolved: the paradox disappears if we specify the counterfactual event of what happens if a commodity is *not* received, in particular whether or not water if not received can be replaced by other water.

Only with the insight from the marginal revolution could utility become a useful tool, with utility differences and their infinitesimals, marginal utility, central rather than utility in any absolute sense. Similarly, the probability dimension could only become a fruitful tool for analyzing attitudes towards risk when, in the terminology of this book, Quiggin (1982) and Schmeidler (1989, first version 1982) put marginal weights of ranks central.

5.6 Calculating rank-dependent utility

This section uses the definition of RDU given in Exercise 5.4.4. The characteristic feature of rank-dependent theories is that the weight of an outcome depends not only on its probability of occurring, but also on its rank. Therefore, it is convenient to rank outcomes, in other words, to order them from good to bad when calculating RDU. Consider the following, left, prospect. The outcomes have not been written in a ranked manner. It is convenient to first rewrite the prospect with the outcomes ranked as on the right.

The RDU value of the prospect is

$$w(\tfrac{3}{8})U(70) + [w(\tfrac{1}{2} + \tfrac{3}{8}) - w(\tfrac{3}{8})]U(30) + [1 - w(\tfrac{1}{2} + \tfrac{3}{8})]U(20).$$

In general, an easy way to reproduce the general RDU formula is as follows.
STEP 1. Completely rank the outcomes from best to worst.
STEP 2. Write the EU formula.
STEP 3. Rewrite the probabilities in the EU formula as differences of ranks.
STEP 4. Transform those ranks by means of the w function.
A procedure for calculating the RDU value of a prospect is as follows:
STEP 1. Completely rank outcomes from best to worst.
STEP 2. For each outcome, calculate the rank r.

STEP 3. For all ranks, calculate their w value.

STEP 4. For each outcome α, calculate the marginal w contribution of its outcome probability p to its rank; i.e., calculate $w(p + r) - w(r)$. Note that $w(p + r)$ is the rank of the outcome in the prospect next-worse to α.

STEP 5. Determine the utility of each outcome.

STEP 6. Multiply the utility of each outcome by its decision weight and sum the results.

We analyze an example by means of the procedure, where trivial ranks 0 or 1 can be added if desired.

Example 5.6.1. Consider the following prospect. We calculate its RDU value, assuming that $w(p) = p^2$ and $U(\alpha) = \alpha$.

```
        0.3
    ┌───────── 50
    │
    │   0.2
  ◯─┼───────── 80
    │
    │   0.5
    └───────── 10
```

STEP 1:   We completely rank the outcomes. This gives:

```
        0.2
    ┌───────── 80
    │
    │   0.3
  ◯─┼───────── 50
    │
    │   0.5
    └───────── 10
```

STEP 2:

- The rank of 80 is 0.
- The rank of 50 is 0.2.
- The rank of 10 is $0.3 + 0.2 = 0.5$.

STEP 3:

- $w(0) = 0$.
- $w(0.2) = 0.04$.
- $w(0.5) = 0.25$

STEP 4:

- The decision weight of 80 is $w(0.2) - w(0) = 0.04 - 0 = 0.04$.
- The decision weight of 50 is $w(0.5) - w(0.2) = 0.25 - 0.04 = 0.21$.
- The decision weight of 10 is $w(1) - w(0.5) = 1 - 0.25 = 0.75$.

STEP 5:

- $U(80) = 80.$
- $U(50) = 50.$
- $U(10) = 10.$

STEP 6:

$$w(0.2)U(80) + [w(0.5) - w(0.2)]U(50) + [1 - w(0.5)]U(10)$$

$$= 0.04 \times 80 + 0.21 \times 50 + 0.75 \times 10 = 21.2.$$

The RDU value is 21.2. □

Exercise 5.6.1.[a] Calculate the RDU values of the following prospects. Assume that $w(p) = p^2$ and $U(\alpha) = 10\sqrt{\alpha}$.

(a)   (b)

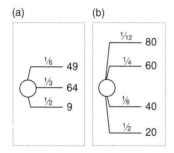

□

The RDU value of a prospect x in itself does not contain much information because this value depends on the level and unit of utility chosen. It is more interesting to report the certainty equivalent CE(x), satisfying $U(CE(x)) = RDU(x)$, so that

$$CE(x) = U^{-1}(RDU(x)). \tag{5.6.1}$$

Exercise 5.6.2.[a] Consider the following prospect.

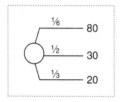

Take $U(\alpha) = \alpha$ and $w(p) = p^2$. What is the certainty equivalent of the prospect under RDU? □

Assignment 5.6.3.[a] Calculate the RDU value of the depicted prospect, and its certainty equivalent. Assume that $w(p) = p^2$ and $U(\alpha) = 10\sqrt{\alpha}$.

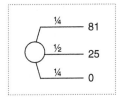

☐

5.7   Conclusion

This chapter has presented intuitive arguments of a psychological and of a mathematical nature supporting the rank-dependent model. The following chapters will analyze the model formally and empirically.

6 Probabilistic sensitivity and rank dependence analyzed

This chapter presents the theoretical definition of rank-dependent utility from scratch. It then shows how rank-dependence can be used to model risk attitudes.

6.1 Ranks, ranked probabilities, and rank-dependent utility defined

For rank-dependent theories, the main topic of the remainder of this book, a convention regarding summation is useful. Consider, for a sequence of numbers $x_1, x_2, \ldots,$ the summation $\sum_{j=1}^{0} x_j$, that is, a sum of zero terms. Because adding zero terms is the same as adding the term 0 (if you can follow what I am saying), it is natural to define:

$$\sum_{j=1}^{0} x_j = 0. \tag{6.1.1}$$

Hence,

$$\text{for } j = 1 : p_1 + \cdots + p_{j-1} = 0 \tag{6.1.2}$$

irrespective of the numbers $p_1, p_2, \ldots$

A *probability weighting function* is a function w: $[0,1] \rightarrow [0,1]$ that increases strictly and satisfies $w(0) = 0$ and $w(1) = 1$. We do not require continuity because discontinuities at 0 and 1 are empirically interesting.

We restrict attention to one fixed prospect for a while. Assume that we have determined a complete ranking of its outcomes. For simplicity of notation, assume that this ranking corresponds with the indexing. That is,

$$x_1 \geq \cdots \geq x_n \text{ for prospect } p_1 x_1 \ldots p_n x_n. \tag{6.1.3}$$

In the preceding chapter we only considered the case of strict inequalities in Eq. (6.1.3). Then all the same outcomes had been taken together and were denoted as one outcome. Such a notation is referred to as the *collapsed* form. For example, the collapsed form of ($\frac{1}{6}$:9, $\frac{1}{3}$:9, $\frac{1}{2}$:3) is $9_{\frac{1}{2}}3$. In general, it will be more convenient to work with weak inequalities so that $x_i = x_{i+1}$ is allowed for some i, and this we do henceforth. We now have the liberty to denote the same prospect in different manners.

For each i in Eq. (6.1.3) we define the *rank* of p_i as $p_{i-1} + \cdots + p_1$. We also call it the rank of x_i.[1] It is the probability of receiving an outcome that is ranked better. Ranks depend on the whole prospect and on its notation in Eq. (6.1.3). This dependence will not cause logical problems (Appendix 6.7). The present definition generalizes ranks of the preceding chapter to the noncollapsed form.

In preparation of the definition of rank-dependent utility, we define the decision weight of an outcome x_i. It depends on two probabilities, namely its outcome probability p_i and its rank $r_i = p_{i-1} + \cdots + p_1$. Formally, a *ranked probability*, denoted $p^{\backslash r}$, is a pair p,r with p an outcome probability and r a rank; hence, $p \geq 0$, $r \geq 0$, and $p + r \leq 1$. We often drop $\backslash$ and write p^r, if no confusion with exponents is likely to arise. We denote the *decision weight* of a ranked probability p^r as $\pi(p^r)$. It is defined as

$$\pi(p^r) = w(p + r) - w(r); \tag{6.1.4}$$

– see Figure 6.1.1. In the preceding chapter we sometimes described decision weights as differences of weights of two ranks. Indeed, not only r is a rank (of an outcome considered), but also $p + r$ is, being the rank of the next-best ranked outcome. The best way to memorize decision weights is by interpreting Eq. (6.1.4) as follows:

decision weight = marginal w-contribution of outcome probability to rank.

Definition 6.1.1. Under Structural Assumption 2.5.2 (decision under risk and richness), *rank-dependent utility (RDU)* holds if there exist a continuous strictly increasing *utility function* U: $\mathbb{R} \rightarrow \mathbb{R}$ and a *(probability) weighting function* w

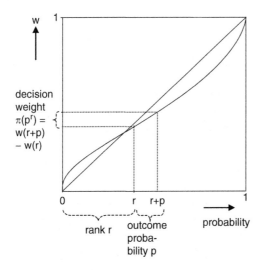

Figure 6.1.1 Decision weight of ranked probability p^r as marginal w-contribution.

---

[1] To distinguish this concept of rank from (event-)ranks defined later for decision under uncertainty, we also use the term *probability-rank*.

such that each prospect $p_1x_1 \cdots p_nx_n$ with a complete ranking $x_1 \geq \cdots \geq x_n$ is evaluated by

$$\sum\nolimits_{j=1}^{n} \pi_j U(x_j) = \sum\nolimits_{j=1}^{n} \pi(p_j^{p_{j-1}+\cdots+p_1})U(x_j)$$
$$= \sum\nolimits_{j=1}^{n} (w(p_j + \cdots + p_1) - w(p_{j-1} + \cdots + p_1))U(x_j),$$

the *RDU* of the prospect.[2] □

Appendix 6.7 will demonstrate that different ways of denoting the same prospect always lead to the same RDU value, as they should. In RDU, the utility function U and the weighting function w are the subjective parameters that characterize the decision maker. Expected utility is the special case where w is the identity, so that $\sum_{j=1}^{n} p_j U(x_j)$ is the value of the prospect. Exercises to calculate RDU values and derive preferences from those values were presented in the preceding chapter. The elicitation method, deriving the theoretical concepts from observed preferences, is more difficult now than it was for the expected utility models because now we deal with nonlinearity both in outcomes and in probabilities. The experiment of §4.1 can still serve this purpose. We will elaborate on this later.

Consistent with linguistic conventions, for within-prospect comparisons of outcomes, ranks that are low numbers correspond to good, favorable, or high outcomes, with $r = 0$ the rank of the best outcome (x_1 in Eq. (6.1.3)). Ranks that are high numbers correspond to bad, unfavorable, outcomes. To avoid confusion with other conventions that assign high numbers to good outcomes (as with utilities), we will call ranks good, bad, best, worst, and we will avoid using the adjectives high, low, ... Rank 0 is the *best rank*, being the rank of the best outcome of the prospect considered. For outcome probability p the rank $1-p$ is the *worst rank* possible, where this then concerns the worst outcome of the prospect considered. For outcome probability p, a rank r worse than (so larger than) $1-p$ cannot be because then p and r would sum to more than 1. The best and worst ranks are the ones used most frequently, and we introduce a special notation for them.

Notation 6.1.2. The best rank (0) is also denoted by the superscript b, and the worst rank ($1 - p$ for probability p) by the superscript w. That is, $p^b = p^0$ and $p^w = p^{1-p}$. □

The letter w is also used to denote the weighting function, but this will not raise confusion. We use π as a generic symbol for decision weight, and often do not express all variables that it depends on in notation. We may, for instance, denote the decision weight $\pi(p_j^{p_{j-1}+\cdots+p_1})$ as π_j or $\pi(p_j)$ or $\pi(x_j)$, if no misunderstanding can arise. Such abbreviated notation cannot always be used. For example, if the prospect considered is $100_{1/2}10$, then we should specify for a probability ½ whether it refers to the best outcome 100 or to the worst outcome 10. Then the concise notation $\pi(½)$ is ambiguous and should be avoided. We may then write $\pi(½^b)$, for instance.[3]

---

[2] Remember that $p_{j-1} + \cdots + p_1 = 0$ for $j = 1$ (Eq. (6.1.2)) so that $\pi_1 = w(p_1) - w(0) = w(p_1)$.

[3] In some situations we may then use more detailed notation such as $\pi(½, 100)$, specifying both the probability and the outcome. Such cases are rare and will not arise in this book.

6.2   Ranks, ranked probabilities, and rank-dependent utility discussed

Decision weights can be compared to marginal utility. To determine the marginal utility of ε – the extra utility of receiving ε *extra* – we have to know the amount β to which ε is added. This is similar to the dependence of decision weights on ranks. To determine the decision weight of outcome probability p, we have to know the rank r to which the probability p is added. In preceding chapters we often used tradeoffs $(\beta+\varepsilon)\ominus\beta$, i.e., pairs of outcomes, to analyze outcome sensitivity. Although we have preferred to use the somewhat different notation p^r for ranked probabilities, ranked probabilities can be seen to be dual to the tradeoffs for outcomes. The discovery of rank dependence by Quiggin and Schmeidler is thus dual to the marginal revolution of utility in economics (see §5.5). In the same way as the latter was needed to capture outcome sensitivity, the former is needed to capture probabilistic sensitivity.

Outcome probabilities under EU can be considered the special case of ranked probabilities where the rank is immaterial and, hence, it has been suppressed. Many results under EU readily extend to RDU with outcome probabilities replaced by ranked probabilities, as we will see later.

Theories should not be too general, and for instance should not give up too much of EU, because it would then become impossible to derive useful predictions. We will see that RDU preserves many useful features of EU. A disadvantage of RDU having more parameters than EU is, of course, that it is more difficult to estimate those parameters from data. In this respect it is harder to derive predictions. The following sections will demonstrate how rank dependence can be used to model risk attitudes in a psychologically plausible manner. It will generate useful empirical predictions.

6.3   Where rank-dependent utility deviates from expected utility: optimism and pessimism

We use the informal term *probabilistic risk attitude* to refer to the effect of probability weighting on risk attitudes. This section presents optimism and pessimism, new phenomena that can be accommodated by probability weighting and rank dependence whereas this was not possible under EU. This section and the one following it will demonstrate how the weighting function impacts risk attitude. We will see how to "read" the graph of the weighting functions. The inputs of w are ranks rather than outcome probabilities. The decision weight of an outcome, being determined by w differences, will be affected by the steepness of w around its rank rather than by the absolute level of w there.

Consider the four prospects in Figure 6.3.1, and the decision weight of the outcome 80 in each of them. Assume the convex probability weighting function $w(p) = p^2$, which gets steeper as p increases (Fig. 6.3.2a). As we move to the right, outcome 80 gets weighted more heavily because its rank becomes worse (i.e., larger) and, for the particular w chosen here, marginal probability weighting increases as ranks get worse. Note that the outcome-probability of 80 remained fixed throughout.

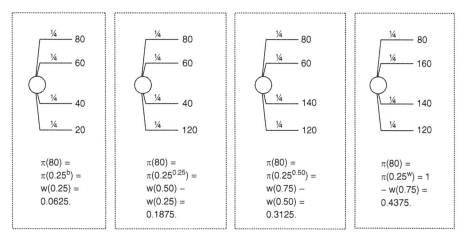

Figure 6.3.1 Rank dependence of decision weight for $w(p) = p^2$.

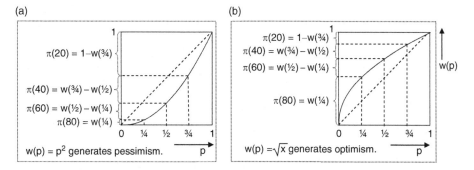

Figure 6.3.2 Decision weights $\pi(\alpha)$ of outcomes α from graphs of weighting functions.

We next consider the decision weights of the four outcomes in the left prospect in Figure 6.3.1 ((¼:80, ¼:60, ¼:40, ¼:20)). To focus on the role of rank-dependent probability weighting, we assume linear utility $U(\alpha) = \alpha/100$. Figure 6.3.2 shows two weighting functions, the convex $w(p) = p^2$ (Fig. a) and the concave $w(p) = \sqrt{p}$ (Fig. b), and illustrates the decision weights of the outcomes of the prospect. For completeness, Table 6.3.1 gives the numerical calculations of RDU and of the certainty equivalents of the prospect, using the superscript \r to indicate the rank r. (We mostly use superscripts without the \ symbol to indicate ranks.)

Ranks of favorable outcomes are smaller (= better) than those of unfavorable outcomes. Therefore, the slope of the left part of w, for small (good) ranks is relevant for the good outcomes. The slope of the right part of w, for large (bad) ranks, is relevant for the bad outcomes. The graph in Fig. 6.3.2a, for $w(p) = p^2$, is shallow to the left, with small w-differences and, hence, low decision weights for favorable outcomes. The graph is steep to the right, yielding high decision weights for unfavorable outcomes. This w reflects a pessimistic attitude. A low certainty equivalent and

Table 6.3.1. *Calculations for ($\frac{1}{4}$:80, $\frac{1}{4}$:60, $\frac{1}{4}$:40, $\frac{1}{4}$:20) with w from Fig. 6.3.2a or Fig. 6.3.2b*

Fig. a	Fig. b
$\pi(80) = \pi(\frac{1}{4}^b) = w(\frac{1}{4}) = 0.0625.$	$\pi(80) = \pi(\frac{1}{4}^b) = w(\frac{1}{4}) = 0.50.$
$\pi(60) = \pi(\frac{1}{4}\backslash^{\frac{1}{4}}) = w(\frac{1}{2}) - w(\frac{1}{4})$ $= 0.25 - 0.063 = 0.1875.$	$\pi(60) = \pi(\frac{1}{4}\backslash^{\frac{1}{4}}) = w(\frac{1}{2}) - w(\frac{1}{4}) = 0.707 - 0.50 = 0.207.$
$\pi(40) = \pi(\frac{1}{4}\backslash^{\frac{1}{2}}) = w(\frac{3}{4}) - w(\frac{1}{2})$ $= 0.563 - 0.25 = 0.3125.$	$\pi(40) = \pi(\frac{1}{4}\backslash^{\frac{1}{2}}) = w(\frac{3}{4}) - w(\frac{1}{2}) = 0.866 - 0.707 = 0.159.$
$\pi(20) = \pi(\frac{1}{4}^w) = w(1) - w(\frac{3}{4})$ $= 1 - 0.563 = 0.4375.$	$\pi(20) = \pi(\frac{1}{4}^w) = w(1) - w(\frac{3}{4}) = 1 - 0.866 = 0.134.$
RDU $= 0.0625 \times 0.80 + 0.1875$ $\times 0.60 + 0.3125 \times 0.40$ $+ 0.4375 \times 0.20 = 0.375.$ The certainty equivalent is $U^{-1}(0.375) = 37.5.$	RDU $= 0.5 \times 0.80 + 0.207 \times 0.60 + 0.159 \times 0.40 + 0.134$ $\times 0.20 = 0.6146.$ The certainty equivalent is $U^{-1}(0.6146) = 61.46.$

considerable risk aversion result. Indeed, the CE of 37.5 is way below the expectation of 50, even though U is linear. In Figure 6.3.1 this w also generated higher decision weights of outcome 80 as the rank of 80 became worse. Obviously, a low w-graph corresponds with small slopes to the left and large slopes to the right:

A low w-graph enhances pessimism and risk aversion.

Fig. 6.3.2b generates effects opposite to Fig. 6.3.2a:

A high w-graph enhances optimism and risk seeking.

The illustrations show how RDU generalizes EU. Extra weight can be given to unfavorable outcomes, indicating pessimism/risk aversion, or to favorable outcomes, indicating optimism/risk seeking. Formally:
Pessimism holds if worsening the rank increases the decision weight; i.e.,

$$\pi(p^{r'}) \geq \pi(p^r) \text{ whenever } r' \geq r \,(\pi(p^r) \text{ increases in } r) \tag{6.3.1}$$

(bigger decision weights for worse ranks).
Optimism holds if improving the rank increases the decision weight; i.e.,

$$\pi(p^{r'}) \geq \pi(p^r) \text{ whenever } r' \leq r \,(\pi(p^r) \text{ decreases in } r) \tag{6.3.2}$$

(bigger decision weights for better ranks).
   It is easy to see that pessimism is equivalent to convexity of the weighting function. One of the many ways to define convexity of w is by the following logical equivalence:

w is convex $\Leftrightarrow$

$$w(p + r') - w(r') \geq w(p + r) - w(r) \text{ whenever } r' \geq r \geq 0. \tag{6.3.3}$$

Under differentiability, the condition is equivalent to w' being increasing or $w'' \geq 0$. Equation (6.3.3) follows immediately from Eq. (6.3.1) by substituting the definition of decision weights. Similarly, optimism is equivalent to concavity of w, which can be defined as follows.

w is concave $\Leftrightarrow$

$$w(p + r') - w(r') \leq w(p + r) - w(r) \text{ whenever } r' \geq r \geq 0. \tag{6.3.4}$$

The definitions just given can also be seen to be equivalent to the definitions of convexity and concavity given in Eqs. (3.2.1) and (3.2.3). Pessimism implies that the worst-ranked outcome is overweighted most, as in the certainty effect and in the Allais paradox.[4] This is discussed in more detail later.

The implications of probability weighting for risk attitude can be compared to those of utility. Concave utility curves enhance risk aversion. Similarly, *convex* weighting curves enhance pessimism and risk aversion. The similarity between concave utility and convex probability weighting was suggested by Figure 5.1.2. Convex utility curves enhance risk seeking and so do *concave* weighting curves.

Under RDU, the degree of risk aversion depends on both utility and probability weighting. For example, a risk averse person can have strictly convex utility if probability weighting generates sufficient risk aversion ("pessimism"). In an empirical study, Abdellaoui, Bleichrodt, & L'Haridon (2008) found convex utility together with risk aversion for losses.

Example 6.3.1 [Risk aversion with strictly convex utility]. Assume RDU with $U(\alpha) = \alpha^2$ and $w(p) = p^2$. Then utility is strictly convex. Yet risk aversion can be seen to hold (Corollary 2 of Chateauneuf & Cohen, 1994; not explained here). $\square$

Exercise 6.3.1.[a] Assume RDU with $U(\alpha) = \alpha^2$ and $w(p) = p^2$. What is the certainty equivalent of $100_{0.5}20$? Is it consistent with risk aversion or with risk seeking? $\square$

In many applications of risk theory today, risk attitudes are still analyzed in terms of EU and utility curvature (Holt & Laury 2002). Example 6.3.1 and Exercise 6.3.1 illustrate that such approaches can run into problems. Many other illustrations will follow later. I end with one further illustration. Consider the measurements in §4.1 for decision under risk with the 50–50 Assumption 4.10.1 added. These measurements can capture the entire utility function and, hence, according to EU, they capture the entire risk attitude. However, the only probability ever considered is ½! It is counterintuitive that we could capture the entire risk attitude, which should primarily concern probabilities, without even looking at those probabilities (apart from $p = ½$), and by instead inspecting the outcomes in great detail. Probability weighting, as for instance in Fig. 6.3.2a makes more sense. We inspect the entire probability interval on the x-axis, and see how each outcome probability is transformed into a decision weight on the y-axis by the curve of w. In Fig. 6.3.2a, well-ranked outcome probabilities are

---

[4] The certainty effect as in the Allais paradox can also be modeled by likelihood insensitivity, defined later.

contracted because w is shallow to the left, and badly ranked outcome probabilities are enlarged because w is steep to the right. This figure captures the intuition of risk aversion in a more natural manner than EU does.

We end this section with an obvious difference between RDU and EU: the measurement of utility. For example, with $U(0) = 0$ and $U(100) = 1$, a SG indifference $70 \sim 100_{0.80}0$ as in Figures 2.5.2 (and 2.5.3) no longer implies $U(70) = 0.80$. Now we can only conclude $U(70) = w(0.80)$, which does not help much if we do not know the subjective w function. The measurement of utility is more complex under RDU than under EU because there is an extra unknown: probability weighting w. Section 6.5 will demonstrate that we can still measure utility fairly easily under RDU by using the tradeoff method.

6.4   Further deviations of rank-dependent utility from expected utility

6.4.1   The certainty effect

Historically, the primary reason to develop nonEU theories was to accommodate the Allais paradox. We first discuss the case for the version in Figure 4.12.1, reproduced here.

(a)

(b)

Unlike EU, rank dependence can readily accommodate the reversal of preference, as we will explain next. It is a useful exercise to find out on your own how this can be done. Then do so before reading on because the explanation is given next.

The 0.06 branch has the best rank in both choice situations in the figure and contributes the same RDU difference $\pi(0.06^b)(U(75K) - U(25K))$ in favor of the right prospect in both situations. The italicized 0.87 branch yields the same RDU difference $0 = \pi(U(0) - U(0)) = \pi'(U(25K) - U(25K))$ in both choice situations, despite its different rank and different decision weight in the two situations. The preference change must, therefore, be generated by a change regarding the 0.07 branch. In the left situation it has rank 0.06, and decision weight $\pi(0.07^{0.06})$, generating an RDU difference $\pi(0.07^{0.06})(U(25K) - U(0))$ in favor of the left prospect. This difference is not big enough to yield a "safe" s-choice (the left prospect, indicated by s); i.e.,

$$\pi(0.07^{0.06})(U(25K) - U(0)) > \pi(0.06^b)(U(75K) - U(25K)).$$

In the right choice situation the 0.07 branch has the worst rank (namely 0.93) and decision weight $\pi(0.07^w)$, generating an RDU difference $\pi(0.07^w)(U(25K) - U(0))$ in favor of the choice s. Now the difference is big enough to yield a left s-choice; i.e.,

$$\pi(0.07^w)(U(25K) - U(0)) > \pi(0.06^b)(U(75K) - U(25K)).$$

The change in preference can be accommodated by

$$\pi(0.07^w) > \pi(0.07^{0.06});$$

i.e., by letting w be steeper on [0.93,1] than on [0.06, 0.13]. For instance, we can take $U(\alpha) = \alpha$ for all α, $w(p) = p/10$ on [0,0.93] so that $w(0.93) = 0.093$, and let w be linear on [0.93,1].

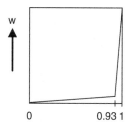

Then, indeed, w is considerably steeper on [0.93, 1] than on [0.06, 0.13]. We have $\pi(0.07^w) = w(1) - w(0.93) = 1 - 0.093 = 0.907$, which considerably exceeds all other decision weights, and all inequalities are satisfied. The w function constructed exhibits pessimism as in Fig. 6.3.2a, with an overweighting at bad (high) ranks and, thus, for unfavorable outcomes. This effect contributes to the certainty effect, with risky prospects evaluated low relative to sure outcomes. Under RDU the certainty effect is thus usually equated with steepness of the weighting function at $p = 1$. Note how this analysis of the Allais paradox was facilitated by the flexibility regarding the ranking of identical outcomes, discussed in detail in Appendix 6.7. Thus, we could always use the same ranking for two prospects within one choice situation.

Exercise 6.4.1.[a] Reconsider Figure 2.4.1 and Exercise 4.12.1.

(a) As explained in the text preceding Exercise 4.12.1, the majority of subjects prefer down in Fig. 2.4.1e and up in Fig. 2.4.1f. Show that such choices can be accommodated by RDU, even with linear utility.

(b) The majority of subjects prefer down in Fig. 2.4.1g and up in Fig. 2.4.1h. Show that such choices can be accommodated by RDU, even with linear utility.

This exercise shows that RDU has the logical possibility to accommodate phenomena that EU cannot. Empirical plausibility will be considered later. □

RDU for risk being general enough to accommodate the Allais paradox by itself need not be a big achievement, because any theory sufficiently general can accommodate any phenomenon. Hence we use the term "accommodate" rather than the term "explain" (this point is further discussed in the conclusion in Example B.2 in Appendix B). For RDU to provide new explanations, more is needed. This is the topic of the present and the following chapters.

Another violation of EU that we saw before and that can be accommodated by rank dependence, concerns point (2) in §4.11 (regarding the certainty effect). We found there that EU's predictions, that the values γ^j in the SG questions should be equal to the values α^j in the tradeoff questions (Exercise 4.3.3), and that the PE^j's should be equal to j/4 (Exercise 4.3.5), were violated because of a certainty effect. We will next analyze these exercises for risk.

Exercise 6.4.2.[a] Make Assumption 4.10.1 (50–50 in §4.1). We will later see that $U(\alpha^j) = j/4$ still holds for all j (Observation 6.5.1), and you may assume this result in this exercise. Reconsider Exercise 4.3.3, but now assume RDU instead of EU. Verify that γ^2 can now be different from α^2. Possible differences between γ^1 and α^1 and between γ^3 and α^3 follow similarly and need not be verified. Specify enough of U, w, $\alpha^0,\ldots,\alpha^4$, γ^1, γ^2, γ^3 to imply that γ^2 and α^2 are different. □

We will also see later that RDU can accommodate differences $PE^j \neq j/4$.

6.4.2   Further discussion of rank dependence

Figure 6.4.1a depicts how the decision weight of outcome probability 0.01 depends on its rank r, for $w(p) = p^2$ as in Fig. 6.3.2a. It illustrates the pessimism of Eq. (6.3.1). Fig. 6.4.1b depicts the dependency for $w(p) = \sqrt{p}$, illustrating optimism. The decision weights $w(p+r) - w(r)$ are close to p times the derivative $w'(r)$. Thus, the graph

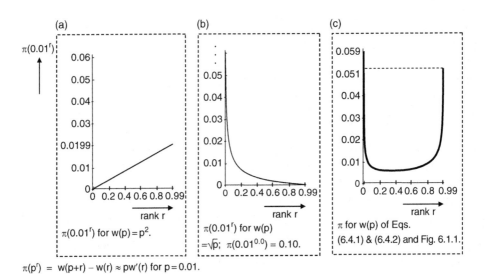

$\pi(p^r) = w(p+r) - w(r) \approx pw'(r)$ for p = 0.01.

Figure 6.4.1 Dependence of decision weight on rank.

in Fig. 6.4.1a is close to $0.01 \times 2r$, and the graph in Fig. 6.4.1b is close to $0.01 \times \frac{1}{2\sqrt{r}}$. Fig. 6.4.1c depicts the related graph for Figure 6.1.1. The latter figure showed the graph of Prelec's (1998) *compound invariance* family

$$w(p) = \left(exp(-(-ln(p))^a)\right)^b \qquad (6.4.1)$$

with

$$a = 0.65 \text{ and } b = 1.0467. \qquad (6.4.2)$$

Prelec's family will be discussed in more detail later.

Under RDU with $U(\alpha) = \alpha$, $w(p)$ is the RDU value of the prospect 1_p0. The decision weight $\pi(p^r)$ is the RDU increase of the prospect $(r{:}\gamma, p{:}\beta, 1-r-p{:}\alpha)$ with $\gamma > \beta > \alpha$ if we increase β by 1, assuming that its rank is not affected ($\gamma > \beta + 1$). It is also the derivative of $RDU(r{:}\gamma, p{:}\beta, 1-r-p{:}\alpha)$ with respect to β.

In human behavior, optimistic and pessimistic attitudes of paying special attention to favorable or unfavorable outcomes, which deviates from EU, are commonly observed (van Osch & Stiggelbout 2008; Savage 1954 end of Ch. 4; Sherrick *et al.* 2000; Showers 1992). Rank dependence is a realistic psychological phenomenon (Birnbaum 1974; Brown *et al.* 2008; Diecidue & Wakker 2001; Lopes 1984, 1987; Weber 1994). It can be caused by an irrational belief that unfavorable events tend to happen more often, leading to an unrealistic overweighting of unfavorable likelihoods (Murphy's law). If rank dependence is taken to be normative, then a pessimistic attitude can result from consciously and deliberately paying more attention to unfavorable outcomes in decisions without overestimating their likelihood (Ellsberg 1961 p. 667; Fellner 1961 p. 681; Greenspan 2004 p. 37; Lopes & Oden 1999 p. 310; Weber 1994 p. 236). Such procedures are common in finance, where risk analyses often focus on the worst outcomes (Roy's 1952 "safety first," or the "value at risk", Hull 2005). An extreme example concerns worst-case scenarios and minimax optimizations.

Similarly, people can overweight favorable outcomes. Considerably more than 50 percent of all car drivers assume that they belong to the best 50 percent of car drivers (called unrealistic optimism or overconfidence; Guppy 1992; Hoelzl & Rustichini 2005; van den Steen 2004; Wenglert & Rosen 2000). It has often been observed that people report probabilities not so as to describe their state of belief, but so as to justify decisions taken by overweighting the positive outcomes of their decisions (DeKay, Patiño-Echeverri, & Fischbeck 2009). In an impressive contribution, Drèze (1961, 1987 Ch. 2) demonstrated how moral hazard, where a decision maker can influence outcomes, can lead to higher probabilities of outcomes depending on their favorability as regards other outcomes.

Further generalizations of EU can obviously be considered. Under RDU, if an outcome is improved, then its decision weight remains unaltered until the moment the rank changes. Then the decision weight suddenly and drastically changes in a noncontinuous manner. Gradual changes of decision weights as distances between outcomes change, also with ranks invariant, may be more natural (Starmer 2000 p. 348). A theory of this kind, preferably not more general or intractable than RDU, will be desirable, but remains to be discovered. Tversky & Kahneman (1992) wrote, on this point, where "cumulative functional" refers to prospect theory which is from the rank-dependent family:

Despite its greater generality, the cumulative functional is unlikely to be accurate in detail. We suspect that decision weights may be sensitive to the formulation of the prospects, as well as to the number, the spacing and the level of outcomes. In particular, there is some evidence to suggest that the curvature of the weighting function is more pronounced when the outcomes are widely spaced (Camerer 1992). The present theory can be generalized to accommodate such effects but it is questionable whether the gain in descriptive validity, achieved by giving up the separability of values and weights, would justify the loss of predictive power and the cost of increased complexity. (p. 317)

Exercise 6.4.3.[a] Consider the prospect

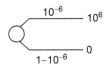

(a) Determine the certainty equivalent for you. That is, how much money for sure is equivalent to this prospect for you in your subjective perception?
(b) The majority of subjects have a certainty equivalent CE exceeding 1, so that they prefer the prospect to receiving 1 for sure. Can this preference be explained by EU with concave or linear utility?
(c) Can the majority choice be explained by RDU with linear utility?
(d) Can the majority choice be explained by RDU with strictly concave utility ($U'' < 0$ everywhere)? □

Let us return to the health example in §3.1. Consider the SG utility elicitation as in Figure 3.1.2. Assume that we have observed a probability p from a subject, and want to derive the utility of artificial speech. We used EU calculations to conclude from Figure 3.1.2 that U(artificial voice) $= p$. However, according to the present state of the art, the average subject evaluates the prospect by $w(p)U(\text{normal voice}) + (1-w(p))U(\text{death}) = w(p)$ where the commonly found shapes of w will be discussed later. Hence, it seems appropriate to correct utility measurement for probability transformation and to conclude that U(artificial speech) $= w(p)$. Because $w(p)$ is mostly below p, EU in general overestimates the probability weights (by assuming $w(p)=p$). This leads to utility values for artificial speech – as well as for other health states – that are too high. RDU can improve utility measurement for the health domain over the measurement methods that are most common to date, and that are based on EU (Bleichrodt, Pinto, & Wakker 2001).

Exercise 6.4.4[b] [Value at risk as a special case of RDU]. Assume that prospects are evaluated by their 99% *value at risk* (*VaR*), which is the outcome (if existing and unique) such that the probability at a worse outcome is 1%. In general, it is the supremum of the outcomes for which the probability of an equal or worse outcome is 1% or less. Show that this evaluation is a special case of RDU, where w is, however, allowed to be increasing in a nonstrict sense (if p > q then w(p) ≥ w(q) and not necessarily w(p) > w(q)). For further relations between rank-dependent utility and measures of risk, see Denuit *et al.* (2006). The 99% VaR for 10-day periods is commonly used to determine how much capital banks are required to hold for credit risks (Hull 2005 Business snapshot 18.1). Rostek (2010) provided a general behavioral foundation of VaR for a subjective probability measure. □

6.5 What rank-dependent utility shares with expected utility

The preceding sections demonstrated how the general RDU can accommodate some empirical findings that EU cannot accommodate. A theory should, however, not be too general, and should also impose restrictions on preferences. This section illustrates some restrictions that RDU imposes. These are restrictions of EU that continue to hold under RDU.

6.5.1 *Measuring utility under rank-dependent utility*

Because RDU is more complex than EU, it will be harder to measure its parameters (Suppes & Winet 1955 2nd para; Tversky & Kahneman 1992 p. 311 2nd para). The early methods used in the literature to measure weighting functions and utilities were based on complex simultaneous parametric fittings of data. We will see that utility measurements can be obtained fairly easily using modified t-indifferences. We will let outcomes relate not just to the same events or probabilities but also to the same ranked probabilities (or ranked events), as will be explained next.

A result of EU that is maintained is in Exercise 4.3.1, concerning the equal-spacedness of the α^j's in utility units. This result later led to an empirical prediction under EU (Exercise 4.3.2b; $\beta^j = \alpha^j$) that we will reconsider. We make the 50–50 Assumption 4.10.1 (both candidates win with probability ½) throughout this section. It is a useful exercise to analyze Exercise 4.3.1 for RDU on your own. Then do not read on, because this analysis is given next. Consider Figure 4.1.1 (TO upwards), but now assume RDU.

The equivalence in Fig. 4.1.1a implies

$$\pi(\tfrac{1}{2}^b)U(\alpha^1) + \pi(\tfrac{1}{2}^w)U(1) = \pi(\tfrac{1}{2}^b)U(\alpha^0) + \pi(\tfrac{1}{2}^w)U(8)$$

or

$$\pi(\tfrac{1}{2}^b)(U(\alpha^1) - U(\alpha^0)) = \pi(\tfrac{1}{2}^w)(U(8) - U(1)).$$

Similarly, the other three equivalences in the figure imply

$$\pi(\tfrac{1}{2}^b)(U(\alpha^2) - U(\alpha^1)) = \pi(\tfrac{1}{2}^w)(U(8) - U(1)),$$

$$\pi(\tfrac{1}{2}^b)(U(\alpha^3) - U(\alpha^2)) = \pi(\tfrac{1}{2}^w)(U(8) - U(1)),$$

$$\pi(\tfrac{1}{2}^b)(U(\alpha^4) - U(\alpha^3)) = \pi(\tfrac{1}{2}^w)(U(8) - U(1)).$$

We see that the right-hand sides are all the same and, hence, the left-hand sides must be the same too. Because w increases strictly we have $\pi(\tfrac{1}{2}^b) > 0$ and this factor can be dropped from the equalities, leading to

$$U(\alpha^4) - U(\alpha^3) = U(\alpha^3) - U(\alpha^2) = U(\alpha^2) - U(\alpha^1) = U(\alpha^1) - U(\alpha^0).$$

The $\alpha^0, \ldots, \alpha^4$ are equally spaced in utility units. This conclusion was derived before under EU but, as we have just found, remains valid under RDU, with ranked probabilities in a role similar to probabilities under EU. The key in the derivation was that the same complete ranking of probabilities and, hence, the same decision weights were involved in the four equivalences. We conclude:

Observation 6.5.1. Under Assumption 4.10.1 (50–50), the questions of Figure 4.1.1 still measure utility and generate the utility function of Figure 4.3.2 under RDU because all α^j's are ranked better than the "gauge" outcomes 8 and 1. □

Bleichrodt & Pinto (2005) applied Observation 6.5.1 in the health domain to measure the utility of life duration. The following exercises re-analyze the other measurements of §4.1 from the perspective of RDU. Exercise 6.5.1 reconsiders an empirical prediction of EU that is maintained under RDU. It concerns equalities $(\alpha^j = \beta^j)$ of values elicited in a different manner.

Exercise 6.5.1.[a] Make Assumption 4.10.1 (50–50). Show that not only under EU, but also under RDU, the β's in Figure 4.3.2 are equally spaced in utility units and must equal the α's in Figure 4.1.1 (cf. Exercises 4.3.2a and b) under the assumption that $\beta^4 \leq g < G$. The necessity of the latter assumption will be demonstrated later (Example 6.5.7). □

In the following exercise you are asked to inspect the role of the γ's, and summarize the results of the last exercises.

Exercise 6.5.2.[a] Make Assumption 4.10.1. Reconsider the conclusions of the statistical analysis in §4.11. To what extent does RDU improve upon EU? □

In Figure 6.5.1, and several similar figures to follow, outcomes have not necessarily been denoted in a ranked manner. For example, α may be ranked somewhere in the middle between $x_2, \ldots, x_m$ in the left prospect in Figure 6.5.1.

Utility can be measured under RDU much as it could be under EU. The only complication is that we have to ensure that not only the same outcome probabilities are used throughout the measurement but, more restrictively, the same ranked probabilities. The general pattern is as follows.

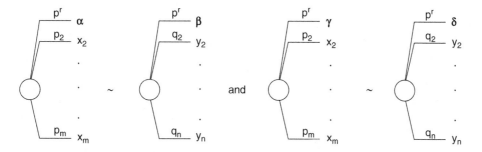

We have p>0. The superscript r indicates the rank of p,
which is the same for all prospects.

Figure 6.5.1 $\alpha \ominus \beta \sim_c^t \gamma \ominus \delta$ for risk.

Notation 6.5.2. We write $\alpha \ominus \beta \sim_c^t \gamma \ominus \delta$ if the indifferences in Figure 6.5.1 hold for some outcome probability p > 0 and rank r (and m, n, p_2, ...,p_m, x_2, ...,x_m, q_2, ...,q_n, y_2, ...,y_n). $\square$

Figure 6.5.1 adapts Fig. 4.7.1b to the case of rank dependence. The subscript c in the notation $\sim_c^t$ indicates that a Common rank was maintained in the measurement. Because the proof of the following observation is useful for understanding the analysis of this section, it is given in the main text.

Observation 6.5.3. Under RDU,

$$\alpha \ominus \beta \sim_c^t \gamma \ominus \delta \Rightarrow U(\alpha) - U(\beta) = U(\gamma) - U(\delta).$$

Proof of Observation 6.5.3. We may drop zero probabilities. That is, we may assume that for all i and j, $p_i > 0$ and $q_j > 0$. The following derivation is the same as that for EU in Exercise 2.7.3. We assume here that the same decision weights π_i can be used for the first and third prospect with outcomes x_i in Figure 6.5.1, and also the same decision weights π_j' can be used for the second and fourth prospect with outcomes y^j. We justify this assumption later in this proof, and suppress several ranks for now. The first indifference in Figure 6.5.1 implies

$$\pi(p^r)U(\alpha) + \sum\nolimits_{i=2}^{m} \pi_i U(x_i) = \pi(p^r)U(\beta) + \sum\nolimits_{j=2}^{n} \pi_j' U(y_j),$$

and the second indifference implies

$$\pi(p^r)U(\gamma) + \sum\nolimits_{i=2}^{m} \pi_i U(x_i) = \pi(p^r)U(\delta) + \sum\nolimits_{j=2}^{n} \pi_j' U(y_j).$$

We have

$$\pi(p^r)U(\alpha) - \pi(p^r)U(\beta) = \sum\nolimits_{j=2}^{n} \pi_j' U(y_j) - \sum\nolimits_{i=2}^{m} \pi_i U(x_i)$$
$$= \pi(p^r)U(\gamma) - \pi(p^r)U(\delta).$$

Because w increases strictly, $\pi(p^r) > 0$, and $U(\alpha) - U(\beta) = U(\gamma) - U(\delta)$ follows.

We, finally, justify the assumption about decision weights used above in a technical lemma whose proof can be skipped by a-exercise readers. We will rank collapsed outcomes in the way most convenient to us.

Lemma 6.5.4. For the first and third prospect with the outcomes x_i in Figure 6.5.1, all ranks can be chosen the same and, hence, the same complete ranking of outcome probabilities can be chosen for both prospects. Similarly, for the second and fourth prospect with the outcomes y_j all ranks can be chosen the same.

Proof. We prove the lemma only for the first and third prospect. Because α and γ have the same rank r, there can be no x_i strictly between them. If x_i coincides with the worst of α and γ, then we rank it worse than α and γ. If x_i coincides with the best of α and γ, then we rank it better than α and γ. In this way, each x_i can be given the same rank and the same decision weight π_i for both prospects. *QED*
□

Observation 6.5.3 showed in a mathematical way that the $\sim_c^t$ relation measures equalities of utility differences. These algebraic considerations are matched by psychological considerations: The psychological effects of pessimistic or optimistic over- and underweighting are the same for all choices, similarly as the decision weights are the same in the equalities. Thus, no changes in these effects or weights distort the equalities of utility differences. When measuring utility, it is better to keep ranks constant. We thus avoid distorting effects because of the psychologically realistic dependence on ranks due to, for instance, pessimism. In this sense, the rank-dependent model is not just an as-if model, but it aims to be a process model, in keeping with the homeomorphic modeling that we strive after throughout this book.

The subscript c in $\sim_c^t$ can be taken as a quality mark. In the same way as wine that is preserved under a constant temperature can receive a special quality mark, to guarantee that changes in temperature did not spoil it, so too are the $\sim_c^t$ observations guaranteed to have been made with ranks kept constant, so that rank-dependence effects did not confound the utility measurements.

6.5.2   A behavioral foundation of rank-dependent utility

Rank-tradeoff consistency holds if the measurements do not run into contradictions. It is obviously a necessary condition for RDU.

Definition 6.5.5. Rank-tradeoff consistency holds if improving an outcome in any $\sim_c^t$ relationship breaks that relationship. □

As we will see next, and in line with earlier results in this book, the absence of contradictions in measurements as just described is not only necessary, but also sufficient for RDU to hold. We use one continuity condition. If you are not interested in theoretical details then you can skip this condition. $\succcurlyeq$ is *continuous* if, for every probability vector $(p_1,...,p_n)$ with probabilities summing to 1, the preference relation restricted to prospects $(x_1,...,x_n)$ with the p_j's as outcome probabilities (not expressed in notation) satisfies the usual Euclidean continuity condition: $\{(x_1,\ldots,x_n): (x_1,\ldots,x_n) \succcurlyeq (y_1,\ldots,y_n)\}$ and $\{(x_1,\ldots,x_n): (x_1,\ldots,x_n) \preccurlyeq (y_1,\ldots,y_n)\}$ are closed subsets of $\mathbb{R}^n$ for each $(y_1,\ldots,y_n)$. By restricting the condition to fixed probability n-tuples, we avoid the ("topological") complications of infinite-dimensional continuity.

We use a stronger stochastic dominance condition than considered before, namely *strict stochastic dominance*: shifting positive probability mass from an outcome to a strictly preferred outcome leads to a strictly preferred prospect.

Theorem 6.5.6. Under Structural Assumption 2.5.2 (decision under risk and richness), the following two statements are equivalent.

(i) RDU holds.
(ii) $\succcurlyeq$ satisfies:
  • weak ordering;
  • strict stochastic dominance;
  • continuity;
  • rank-tradeoff consistency. □

The theorem is proved in Appendix 10.14. For EU we saw that the absence of inconsistencies in utility measurement automatically implies a consistent index of probabilities. A similar observation holds here, where a consistent weighting function is automatically implied too. The following subsection gives a numerical illustration of the concepts of this and preceding sections.

6.5.3 An elaborated example

Example 6.5.7. We make Assumption 4.10.1 (50–50). To begin with, assume that we observed only the indifferences in Figure 6.5.2, and not those in Figure 6.5.3. Figure 6.5.2 is a special case of Figure 4.1.1, and we define $\alpha^0 \ldots \alpha^4$ as 10, 46.50, 109.75, 199.74, and 316.47. We have $\alpha^i \ominus \alpha^{i-1} \sim^t \alpha^1 \ominus \alpha^0$ for all i, and even $\alpha^i \ominus \alpha^{i-1} \sim^t_c \alpha^1 \ominus \alpha^0$ for all i. These data suggest that $U(\alpha) = \sqrt{\alpha}$ under RDU, because then the α^i's are indeed equally spaced in utility units.

Next assume that we obtain new information, being the indifferences in Figure 6.5.3. This figure is a special case of Figure 4.1.2. We did, however, not take g as recommended in §4.1 ($g > \alpha^4$), but we took $g = \alpha^2 = 109.75$. Define $G = 316.47$ ($= \alpha^4$) and $\beta^2 = 109.75$ ($= \alpha^2$), $\beta^3 = 316.47$ ($= \alpha^4$), and $\beta^4 = 1050.87$. The result of Exercise 4.3.2 remains valid: under EU the β's should be equally spaced in utility units and they should be equal to the α's. The latter, however, holds only for β^2 and not for β^3 and β^4; β^3 and β^4 strongly deviate from α^3 and α^4. Hence, EU is falsified. Tradeoff consistency fails because the indifferences in Fig. 6.5.2b and c imply **199.74** $\ominus$ 109.75 $\sim^t$ 109.75 $\ominus$ 46.50, but the indifferences in Fig. 6.5.3b and c imply **316.47** $\ominus$ 109.75 $\sim^t$ 109.75 $\ominus$ 46.50.

RDU is not violated by these observations. In Fig. 6.5.3c, the rank of the probability of $cand_1$, being the outcome probability of the β outcome, is different for the left prospect where it is best than for the right prospect where it is worst.

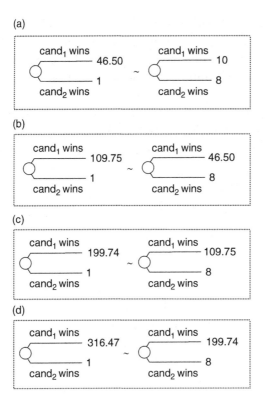

Figure 6.5.2 Four indifferences.

Hence, we do **not** have **316.47** $\ominus$ 109.75 $\sim_c^t$ 109.75 $\ominus$ 46.50. From an algebraic perspective, the decision weight of the probability of $cand_1$ is different for the left prospect in Fig. 6.5.3c where it is $\pi(\frac{1}{2}^b)$ than for the right one where it is $\pi(\frac{1}{2}^w)$. Under RDU, the β outcomes are not equally spaced in utility units. As regards Exercise 6.5.1, the requirement of $g > \beta^4$ in that exercise is not satisfied, which explains why the conclusion of that exercise fails here. $\square$

In keeping with the homeomorphic principles of this book, the algebraic arguments of Example 6.5.7, based on RDU, are matched by psychological arguments. In Figs. 6.5.3a and b and for the right prospect in Fig. 6.5.3c, $cand_1$ delivers the worst outcome. For the left prospect in Fig. 6.5.3c and for the prospects in Fig. 6.5.3d the candidate delivers the best outcome. This change can be expected to generate different psychological perceptions that will distort the utility measurement. A pessimist will pay more attention to $cand_1$ when delivering the worst outcome than when delivering the best outcome. $Cand_1$ is then "underweighted" for both prospects in Fig. 6.5.3d and for the left prospect in Fig. 6.5.3c, leading to overly large outcomes β^3 and β^4 to generate the required indifferences. The psychological effects of pessimism were not kept constant in Figure 6.5.3, and distorted the utility measurement there. The latter is, accordingly, not of good quality.

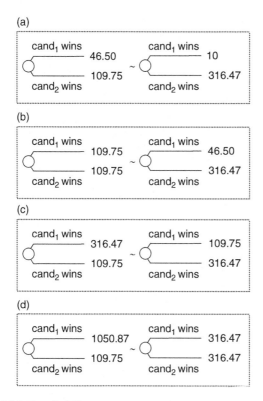

Figure 6.5.3 Four indifferences.

Exercise 6.5.3.[b] Specify an RDU model that accommodates all indifferences in Figures 6.5.2 and 6.5.3. In particular, determine w(½). □

Exercise 6.5.4.[b] Assume RDU, and assume that you observed indifferences $\alpha^j{}_{1/2}0 \sim \alpha^{j-1}{}_{1/2}1$ for j = 1, ..., 50, with $\alpha^0 = 4$. You define $\beta^0 = \alpha^0 = 4$, $\beta^1 = \alpha^1$, and $g = \alpha^1$. Then you elicit G such that $(\alpha^1 =) \alpha^1{}_{1/2}g \sim \alpha^0{}_{1/2}G$, and you find that $G = \alpha^4$. Finally, you elicit β^2, β^3, β^4 such that $\beta^j{}_{1/2}g \sim \beta^{j-1}{}_{1/2}G$ for j from 2 to 4. It trivially follows that $\beta^2 = \alpha^4$. Although now 50 α's have been observed, let us nevertheless normalize $U(\alpha^0) = 0$ and $U(\alpha^4) = 1$. What can you say about β^3 and β^4? If you cannot find the solution, there is a hint in the footnote.[5] □

Assignment 6.5.5. Make Assumption 4.10.1 (50–50).

(a)[b] Show that, under RDU, the claim of Assignment 4.3.6 need not hold, even if $\beta^4 \leq g < G$. If you do not see how to solve this problem, then read the hint in the footnote.[6]

(b)[a] Show that, under RDU, the results of Assignment 4.10.9 still hold. □

---

[5] The α's are equally spaced in utility units. We can set $U(\alpha^j) = j/4$ as we did before, where now the α^j's will have utility exceeding 1 for j > 4. From the elicitation of G you can derive w(½). From this, you can derive the remaining β's.

[6] Take any w(½) ≠ ½, and substitute RDU in Figs. 4.1.1a and 4.1.2a.

6.5.4   Abdellaoui's method of measuring probability weighting

The following exercise presents an appealing result: Figure 4.1.5 (PEs) provides measurements of the probability weighting w.

Exercise 6.5.6.[a] Make Assumption 4.10.1. We have $U(\alpha^j) = j/4$ by Observation 6.5.1. Extend Exercise 4.3.5 to RDU by showing that, under RDU, $PE^j \neq j/4$ can be. Show that, in fact, $w(PE^j) = j/4$ for all j. □

Because of its empirical importance, we display the result obtained in Exercise 6.5.6.

Observation 6.5.8. Under RDU, $w(PE^j) = j/4$ for all j. □

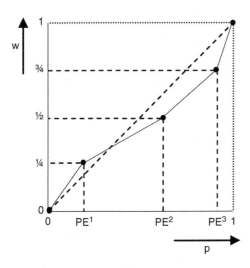

Figure 6.5.4 Probability weighting graph derived from Figures 4.1.1 and 4.1.5.

Figure 6.5.4 shows that the PE^j's are measurements of the w-inverses of j/4. Thus, the experiment in §4.1 actually provided an easy way to measure not only utilities, but also probability weighting and, thus, all subjective parameters of RDU. Abdellaoui (2000) introduced this method.

6.5.5   Further implications of rank-dependent utility

Figure 6.5.5 shows how the sure-thing principle for risk can be adapted to RDU, simply by replacing probabilities by ranked probabilities. Note that the probability p should have the same rank (r) for all four prospects. This defines the *rank-sure-thing principle for risk*.

Exercise 6.5.7.[b] Show that RDU implies the rank-sure-thing principle for risk. □

Exercise 6.5.8.[a] Reconsider the majority choices in Figs. 2.4.1g and h. We saw in Exercise 4.12.1c that these choices violate the sure-thing principle for risk, so that EU cannot hold. Explain directly that the rank-sure-thing principle is not violated, by verifying that the rank of the common-outcome probability is not constant. □

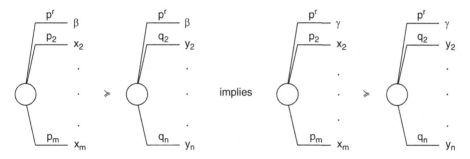

Figure 6.5.5 The rank-sure-thing principle for risk.

Exercise 6.5.1 demonstrated that Figures 4.1.1 and 4.1.2 contain not only a test of tradeoff consistency, but also of rank-tradeoff consistency. Observation 6.5.3 showed that by means of $\sim^t_c$ relations we can analyze utility under RDU. We can characterize and test concave, linear, or convex utility similarly as this was done under EU in §4.8.2, where the results hold true irrespective of probability weighting.[7] These results are unlike the classical EU result of risk aversion corresponding to concave utility. This latter one-to-one correspondence can be distorted by probability weighting and it no longer holds true under RDU (Example 6.3.1).

The following exercise shows how an experimenter can erroneously think that utility is concave if EU is erroneously assumed, whereas in reality RDU holds. It then shows how the experimenter can observe a violation of tradeoff consistency, signaling the failure of EU. The experimenter then has to reconsider the analysis, and has to use a different model. Wakker (2003) similarly showed that a utility analysis in Levy & Levy (2002) could be corrected by incorporating probability weighting.

Exercise 6.5.9.[b] Make Assumption 4.10.1 (50–50). Assume that an agent maximizes RDU with linear utility, and with $w(\frac{1}{2}) = 7/20$. An experimenter, erroneously, thinks that the agent maximizes EU. Consider the experiment of §4.1. In Figure 4.1.1, the agent answers $\alpha^1 = 23$, $\alpha^2 = 36$, $\alpha^3 = 49$, $\alpha^4 = 62$, as follows from applying RDU. The linear utility function over the interval $[\alpha^0, \alpha^4] = [10, 62]$ that results from the tradeoff method in Figure 4.3.2 is correct, as we have seen before. The experimenter will, however, conclude that the utility difference $U(8) - U(1)$ must be the same as $U(\alpha^1) - U(\alpha^0) = U(23) - U(10)$, as would be implied by EU in Fig. 4.1.1a, but is not correct under RDU as assumed by us. The experimenter incorrectly concludes that the marginal utility on the small interval $[1,8]$

---

[7] It can indeed be proved that U is concave under RDU if and only if Eq. (4.8.2) holds with $\sim^t_c$ rather than $\sim^t$, with similar results holding for convexity and linearity. The proof of this result is more difficult under RDU because an analog of Exercise 4.8.2 does not hold under RDU. The result is first derived locally and, next, globally, similar to Wakker (1994). No elaboration is provided here.

exceeds that on the larger interval [10, 23]. He incorrectly concludes that utility is concave and nonlinear around 9.

Assume that the experimenter also elicits α^5 such that $\alpha^5{}_{cand_1} 1 \sim \alpha^4{}_{cand_1} 8$. Fortunately, the experimenter is wise enough to do a cross check. For this purpose he turns to Figure 4.1.2 where he, however, skips Fig. a and immediately turns to Figs. b-d, taking $g = \alpha^4$ and $G = \alpha^5$.

(a) What answers β^2, β^3, β^4 will the experimenter expect?
(b) What answers β^2, β^3, β^4 will the agent give?
(c) Without verifying, the experimenter, erroneously, thinks that $\alpha^0{}_{cand_1}\alpha^5 \sim \alpha^1{}_{cand_1}\alpha^4$ in Fig. 4.1.2a. Explain that the experimenter can derive a violation of tradeoff consistency from this erroneous assumption and the answers actually given (assuming deterministic choice).

The experimenter could, alternatively, falsify EU directly by testing Fig. 4.1.2a, to find that his $g = \alpha^4$ and $G = \alpha^5$ give no indifference there. At any rate, the experimenter may conclude at this stage that, under RDU instead of EU, the $\alpha^0,\ldots,\alpha^4$ are still equally spaced in utility units, as are the α^1, β^2, β^3, β^4, but the utility differences between the β's and also between 1 and 8 are different from the utility differences between the α^j's. □

Exercise 6.5.9 further illustrates that analyses of risk attitude in terms of EU can run into problems, a point illustrated before by Example 6.3.1, that can be amended by the greater generality of RDU. It is conceivable that the greater generality of RDU can sometimes lead to extra problems. If EU holds but the data also contain noise, then models with more parameters will merely pick up noise through those extra parameters. They then seemingly fit the data better, but actually perform *worse* for predicting future data. The extra parameters will also distort the estimations of the original and empirically valid parameters, such as the utility function in EU. Such problems are especially prone to arise for parametric fittings that use models with many parameters for data not especially designed to avoid interactions between the different parameters. Such a phenomenon was found by Hey, Lotito, & Maffioletti (2008) and Mangelsdorff & Weber (1994) for uncertainty, the topic of Chapter 10. Hey & Orme (1994) also suggested that EU with noise describes the data better than some nonexpected utility models do.

Appendix 6.6   Yet further deviations of rank-dependent utility from expected utility

Chateauneuf (1999) introduced an interesting weakening of rank-tradeoff consistency. He only considered cases where particular outcome events are nested. The resulting condition is a direct weakening of the independence condition of §2.7, which makes it particularly appealing. Abdellaoui (2002) presented a generalization of Theorem 2.6.3 (EU for risk) to rank dependence that, unlike our Theorem 6.5.6, does not need continuity of utility.

Whereas additivity of probability is given up for the weighting function, it is in a particular way maintained for decision weights, if all decision weights are related to the same complete ranking of outcomes. The following exercise clarifies this point.

Exercise 6.6.1 [Additivity of decision weights].

(a)$^{!a}$ Show that $\pi((p_1+p_2)^b) = \pi(p_1{}^b) + \pi(p_2{}^{p_1})$. Note that all decision weights relate to a prospect $p_1x_1,p_2x_2,\ldots,p_nx_n$ with a complete ranking $x_1 \geq x_2 \geq \cdots \geq x_n$.

(b)^b Show that $\pi((p_1+p_2)^r) = \pi(p_1{}^r) + \pi(p_2{}^{p_1+r})$. Note that all decision weights relate to a prospect $rx_0,p_1x_1,p_2x_2,\ldots,p_nx_n$ with a complete ranking
$x_0 \geq x_1 \geq x_2 \geq \cdots \geq x_n.$ $\square$

Theorem 4.6.4 showed, for the general context of uncertainty, that, given some natural conditions, EU holds if and only if tradeoff consistency holds. Risk is a special case of uncertainty and, hence, a violation of EU under risk should also imply a violation of tradeoff consistency. For RDU with nonlinear w, we should be able to find such violations, comprising yet another difference between EU and RDU. They were indeed found in Exercise 6.5.9.

The following example illustrates "first-order risk aversion," a phenomenon that RDU can accommodate but EU cannot (Segal & Spivak 1990). It implies that there is a bid-ask spread of prices of an asset, i.e., a range of prices for which people neither buy nor sell the asset.

Example 6.6.1 [First-order risk aversion generated by rank dependence]. Consider an asset $x = (p_1:x_1,\ldots,p_n:x_n)$ at price ε per unit ($\varepsilon < 0$ means you are rewarded by the positive amount $-\varepsilon$ if you take a unit of this asset). You buy μ units ($\mu < 0$ means you sell). The resulting prospect is

$$(p{:}\mu(x_1 - \varepsilon), \cdots, p_n{:}\mu(x_n - \varepsilon)).$$

We assume throughout that μ is close to zero, $U(0) = 0$, and $U'(0) > 0$, so that first-order Taylor expansions can be used at 0.

(a) Assume EU. The EU of the resulting prospect is

$$\sum\nolimits_{j=1}^n p_jU(\mu x_j - \mu\varepsilon) \approx \sum\nolimits_{j=1}^n p_jU'(0)\mu(x_j - \varepsilon) = \mu U'(0)\left(\sum\nolimits_{j=1}^n p_jx_j - \varepsilon\right).$$

As demonstrated by Arrow & Lind (1970) (explained in Gollier 2001a, §21.4.2), there is no bid-ask spread. That is, if the price ε is less than the expectation $\sum_{j=1}^n p_jx_j$, so that $\sum_{j=1}^n p_jx_j - \varepsilon > 0$, then you will buy at least a small amount of the asset and $\mu > 0$. If the price ε exceeds the expectation, so that $\sum_{j=1}^n p_jx_j - \varepsilon > 0$, then you will sell at least a small amount of the asset, and $\mu < 0$. Only if ε is the exact expectation of the prospect, may it happen that you stay put and neither buy nor sell. An interpretation is that in a first-order approximation, EU is locally risk neutral, so that "first-order risk aversion" is not possible under EU.

(b) Now assume RDU with $w(0.50) = 0.42$, μ close to 0, and concave utility. We only consider the simple case of an asset $x = x_{1_{0.50}}x_2$ with $x_1 > x_2$. The resulting prospect is

$$\mu(x_1 - \varepsilon)_{0.50}\mu(x_2 - \varepsilon).$$

The RDU of the resulting prospect if you buy ($\mu > 0$) is

$$0.42 \times U(\mu x_1 - \mu\varepsilon) + 0.58 \times U(\mu x_2 - \mu\varepsilon) \approx 0.42\mu U'(0)(x_1 - \varepsilon)$$
$$+0.58\mu U'(0)(x_2 - \varepsilon) = \mu U'(0)(0.42x_1 + 0.58x_2 - \varepsilon),$$

which is as-if EU for $\mu(x_1-\varepsilon)_{0.42}\mu(x_2-\varepsilon)$. Hence, you will only buy a quantity $\mu > 0$ if $\varepsilon < 0.42x_1 + 0.58x_2$. That is, the price must be considerably below the expectation of $\mu(x_1)_{0.50}\mu(x_2)$ for you to buy.

If you sell ($\mu < 0$, so that $\mu x_1 - \mu\varepsilon < \mu x_2 - \mu\varepsilon$), then the RDU of the resulting prospect is

$$0.42 \times U(\mu x_2 - \mu\varepsilon) + 0.58 \times U(\mu x_1 - \mu\varepsilon) \approx 0.42\mu U'(0)(x_2 - \varepsilon)$$
$$+0.58\mu U'(0)(x_1 - \varepsilon) = \mu U'(0)(0.42x_2 + 0.58x_1 - \varepsilon),$$

which is as-if EU for $\mu(x_1-\varepsilon)_{0.58}\mu(x_2-\varepsilon)$. You will only sell a quantity ($\mu < 0$) if $\varepsilon > 0.58x_1 + 0.42x_2$. That is, the price must exceed the expectation of $\mu(x_1)_{0.50}\mu(x_2)$ considerably for you to sell. There is a domain of prices ε, namely the interval $[0.42x_1 + 0.58x_2, 0.58x_1 + 0.42x_2]$ for which you neither buy nor sell. In this manner, RDU can explain bid-ask spreads, generating an inertia where people neither buy nor sell assets but stay put in their status quo. RDU can exhibit substantial risk aversion in a local sense. An interpretation is that RDU can exhibit first-order risk aversion. We will later see that loss aversion provides an alternative explanation (Example 9.3.2). □

The following exercise considers probabilistic mixing, with some superscripts indicating difficulty within subparts. Condition (4) provides the simplest preference condition characterizing convex weighting functions known to me.

Exercise 6.6.2. Assume RDU. In this exercise, mixing applies to probabilities, as defined in §2.6.

(a) For the following statements, derive the implications $(1) \Rightarrow (2)^c$, $(2) \Rightarrow (3)^b$, and $(3) \Rightarrow (4)^b$.
  (1) w is convex;
  (2) the RDU functional is *convex with respect to probabilistic mixing*; i.e., $RDU(x_\lambda y) \leq \lambda RDU(x) + (1-\lambda)RDU(y)$;
  (3) the RDU functional is quasi-convex with respect to probabilistic mixing; i.e., if $RDU(x) \geq RDU(y)$, then for all $0 < \lambda < 1$, $RDU(x) \geq RDU(x_\lambda y)$;
  (4) $\succcurlyeq$ is convex with respect to probabilistic mixing; i.e., $x \succcurlyeq y \Rightarrow x \succcurlyeq x_\lambda y$ for all $0 < \lambda < 1$.
(b)^{c8} Do the reverse implications hold if w is continuous? □

---

[8] This part is for volunteers, and no elaboration is provided in the appendix. The implications $[(4) \Rightarrow (3)]$ and $[(2) \Rightarrow (1)]$ are not difficult to prove. I expect that $[(3) \Rightarrow (2)]$ is too hard to be proved right or wrong by any of the readers. The answer is available "somewhere" in this book, but I will give you a chance to work on this question independently now.

Under some differentiability assumptions, Chew, Karni, & Safra (1987) demonstrated that aversion to mean-preserving spreads holds under RDU if and only if U is concave and w is convex. Chateauneuf & Tallon (2002) provided an appealing alternative characterization of these conditions, which they further generalized to uncertainty (see Theorem 10.9.2). Because risk aversion can be combined with strictly convex utility (Example 6.3.1), it also follows that aversion to mean-preserving spreads is a more restrictive condition than risk aversion under RDU. Ryan (2006) gave further results. Extensions to prospect theory are in Schmidt & Zank (2008).

Exercise 6.6.3^c (parts a–c are based on Young, 1990). The tax authorities adhere to the equal sacrifice principle of John Stuart Mill: All people should lose the same amount of utility when paying tax. Assume homogeneous citizens, all with the same utility function U of total wealth I. The total population in the country consists of 1001 persons, of whom 1 is rich, with total wealth I = \$1,000,000, and 1000 are poor, each with total wealth I = \$1000. The authorities need \$500,000.

(a) Show that, if $U(\alpha) = ln(\alpha)$, then the tax rate should be flat, and for some $0 < \tau < 1$, every citizen should pay a τ-part of their wealth. How much tax will the rich citizen pay, and how much will the poor citizens pay?

(b) Now assume that the tax authorities do not know the utility function U (applied to total wealth). They assume that U is from the power family, defined in §3.5, with power θ. They will take the median function as representative of all society. The only information they have is that the median certainty equivalent CE of $30000_{\frac{1}{2}}930$ is 4000 (outcomes refer to total wealth). They assume EU. Use your computer to determine which of the following powers θ of the utility function best fits the data (in predicting the closest CE): $\theta = 1$; $\theta = 0$; $\theta = -1$; $\theta = -2$; $\theta = -0.1$, $\theta = -0.5$, $\theta = -0.188$, and verify that $\theta = -0.188$ does so best. If you do not know which formulas to use, then, and only then, read the hints in the footnote.[9]

(c) Take the best parameter $\theta = -0.188$ found in part (b). If the poor people each pay tax amount t, then the rich person must pay tax $500000 - 1000t$. Calculate the utility loss for the rich and the utility losses for the poor for the following taxes: $t = 250$, $t = 200$, $t = 100$, $t = 150$, $t = 125$, $t = 120$. Which tax best fits Mill's equal sacrifice principle, so that it will be imposed? How much tax does the rich person then have to pay?

(d) Assume data and power utility U as before. Now, however, the tax authorities discovered that people do not behave according to EU, so that not all of their risk aversion reflects the utility of money. Instead, the median citizen satisfies RDU, with $w(\frac{1}{2}) = 0.42$. Use your computer again to determine which of the following powers θ of the utility function best fits the data: $\theta = 1$; $\theta = 0$; $\theta = -1$; $\theta = -2$; $\theta = -0.1$, $\theta = -0.5$, $\theta = -0.188$.

---

[9] Calculate the EU of the prospect as $EU = \frac{1}{2} \times U(30000) + \frac{1}{2} \times U(930)$. Then determine the CE as the inverse utility of EU; i.e., $U^{-1}(EU)$. For $\theta = 0$, $U^{-1}(EU) = \exp(EU)$. For $\theta < 0$ and $EU < 0$, $U^{-1}(EU) = (-EU)^{1/\theta}$. Then inspect which CE is closest to 4000.

(e) How much tax will the authorities impose on the citizens under the
assumptions of part (d)? Without necessarily giving away the plot of this part,
let me point out that you are lucky if the answer to part (d) happens to be
$\theta = 0$, because then you already answered this question in part (a).

(f) Will the rich person lobby for RDU or for EU? □

Appendix 6.7   Ranking identical outcomes and collapsing outcomes

A point of concern may be raised regarding the definition of RDU and, in fact, also
regarding the definition of EU. The value of a prospect should not depend on the
particular notation of the prospect chosen. The EU and RDU formulas should, for
example, give the same result when applied to $(\frac{1}{6}:9, \frac{1}{3}:9, \frac{1}{2}:3)$ as to $9_{\frac{1}{2}}3$, because
these different notations refer to the same prospect. It is well known that such a
consistency holds for the EU formula, with

$$(\tfrac{1}{6}:9, \tfrac{1}{3}:9, \tfrac{1}{2}:3) \rightarrow \tfrac{1}{6} \times U(9) + \tfrac{1}{3} \times U(9) + \tfrac{1}{2} \times U(3)$$

and

$$9_{\frac{1}{2}}3 \rightarrow \tfrac{1}{2} \times U(9) + \tfrac{1}{2} \times U(3)$$

indeed being the same. A similar consistency holds for the RDU formula. Here
$$(\tfrac{1}{6}:9, \tfrac{1}{3}:9, \tfrac{1}{2}:3) \rightarrow w(\tfrac{1}{6}) \times U(9) + (w(\tfrac{1}{2}) - w(\tfrac{1}{6})) \times U(9) + (1 - w(\tfrac{1}{2})) \times U(3)$$
and

$$9_{\frac{1}{2}}3 \rightarrow w(\tfrac{1}{2}) \times U(9) + (1 - w(\tfrac{1}{2})) \times U(3)$$

are also the same because terms with $w(1/6)U(9)$ cancel.

The consistency just established holds in general. Every different way to denote
a prospect leads to the same RDU value, in agreement with the RDU value of its
collapsed form. In particular, if we have the liberty to rank two identical outcomes as
we like, then for the RDU value of the prospect it will be immaterial how we rank
them. We state the result formally, and then give its proof.

Observation 6.7.1 [Collapsing]. If, for a prospect $p_1x_1 \ldots p_nx_n$, we have $x_i = x_j$ for
$i \neq j$, then it is immaterial for the RDU value whether we collapse the outcomes.
Consequently, it is also immaterial for the RDU value how we rank x_i and x_j
(i.e. which complete ranking we choose).

Proof of Observation 6.7.1. To verify Observation 6.7.1 in general, assume that
$x_i = x_{i+1}$ in a prospect $p_1x_1, \ldots, p_{i-1}x_{i-1}, p_ix_i, p_{i+1}x_{i+1}, p_{i+2}x_{i+2}, \ldots, p_nx_n$ with the
ranking $x_1 \geq \ldots \geq x_n$. We collapse these two outcomes; i.e., we rewrite the prospect
as $p_1x_1, \ldots, p_{i-1}x_{i-1}, (p_i + p_{i+1})x_i, p_{i+2}x_{i+2}, \ldots, p_nx_n$. The total joint decision weight of
$U(x_i) = U(x_{i+1})$ in the former notation is

$$w(p_i + \cdots + p_1) - w(p_{i-1} + \cdots + p_1) + w(p_{i+1} + \cdots + p_1) - w(p_i + \cdots + p_1).$$

Cancelling the terms $w(p_i + \cdots + p_1) - w(p_{i-1} + \cdots + p_1)$, we obtain $w(p_{i+1} + \cdots + p_1) - w(p_{i-1} + \cdots + p_1)$, which is exactly the decision weight of $U(x_i)$ with the two outcomes collapsed. We can, therefore, collapse outcomes as we like without affecting the RDU value. In particular, we can use the "completely" collapsed form. This point also shows that we can always reverse the ranking of $x_i = x_{i+1}$, as in $p_1x_1,\ldots,p_{i-1}x_{i-1}, \mathbf{p_{i+1}x_{i+1}, p_ix_i, p_{i+2}x_{i+2}},\ldots,p_nx_n$, because this will yield the same collapsed form. When ranking outcomes to obtain a complete ranking, we are free to choose whichever ranking we want for identical outcomes. □

Strictly speaking, the logical status of ranks is more complex than is captured by our notation, because ranks depend on the complete ranking chosen. In a complete formalization of ranks, 2n-tuples $(p_1,x_1,\ldots,p_n,x_n)$ should be taken as the formal primitive rather than probability distributions over prizes. A preference condition should then be added that different 2n-tuples that refer to the same probability distribution over outcomes are equivalent. Had this book been written merely for a mathematical audience, I would have taken this approach. For general readers the simpler approach taken, while not fully formalized, is more convenient. The notation of prospects chosen and the definition of ranks will always be clear.

The logical complications regarding ranks could be avoided by restricting attention to collapsed forms. Our approach with complete flexibility regarding the notation of prospects and the rankings chosen, is so very convenient in many analyses that we chose it nevertheless.

The following exercise shows that, under mild assumptions, decision weights must necessarily be derived from a weighting function as in RDU. That is, it is not easy to develop a weighting theory other than rank-dependent. The elaboration of the exercise will also illustrate the role of collapsing outcomes – also called coalescing in the literature – in developing well-defined functionals. It can, for instance, be seen that many functionals proposed by Allais (1953a) as deviations from EU in fact reduce to EU by the collapsing of outcomes. The "mild assumptions" and the resulting model in the following exercise include as special cases old weighting (Eq. (5.2.1)), Birnbaum's (2008a) RAM and TAX models, and Viscusi's (1989) prospective reference theory, when combined with an elementary "coalescing" condition[10] assumed throughout this book. The exercise, therefore, shows that such models can deviate from rank dependence only by violating elementary rationality conditions (coalescing and stochastic dominance).

Exercise 6.7.1^c [Quiggin's (1982) analysis]. Assume that $\succcurlyeq$ is represented by a functional V from prospects to the reals. V is defined as follows for each prospect.

(a) There exists a strictly increasing utility function U, and there exists a function π that assigns to each probability n-tuple $(p_1,\ldots,p_n)$ a decision-weight n-tuple

---

[10] That is, each notation of a prospect has the same evaluation as its collapsed form. We, thus, apply the formulas of these theories only to collapsed forms.

$(\pi_1^n(p_1,\ldots,p_n),\ldots,\pi_n^n(p_1,\ldots,p_n))$, where decision weight $\pi_j^n(p_1,\ldots,p_n) > 0$ whenever $p_j > 0$ and decision weights sum to 1.

(b) Completely rank the outcomes of the prospect, and write the prospect as $p_1x_1 \cdots p_nx_n$ with $x_1 \geq \cdots \geq x_n$.

(c) The V-value of the prospect is $\sum_{j=1}^n \pi_j^n(p_1,\ldots,p_n)U(x_j)$.

In this approach, π_j^n can depend on the entire completely ranked probability n-tuple $(p_1,\ldots,p_n)$, but it does not depend on the outcomes $(x_1,\ldots,x_n)$ other than through the ranking of the probabilities that they generate. RDU is the special case of such a functional for which a strictly increasing function w exists such that $\pi_j^n(p_1,\ldots,p_n) = w(p_j + \cdots + p_1) - w(p_{j-1} + \cdots + p_1)$. The functional V will have to satisfy the same requirements regarding the collapsing of outcomes as discussed in this section for RDU. That is, the V value should be independent of whether or not we collapse outcomes. It should assign the same value to $(\frac{1}{3}{:}5, \frac{1}{3}{:}5, \frac{1}{3}{:}4)$ as to $5_{\frac{2}{3}}4$.

Show that V must be an RDU functional. In other words, RDU is the only case of such a functional that satisfies the required property for collapsing outcomes.

It can be seen that a restriction of the functional to noncollapsed outcomes does not lead to more general cases. By continuity and monotonicity the functional then still must correspond to a functional as analyzed in this exercise. As an historical note, Quiggin (1982) first gave a behavioral foundation for the functional V, by means of preference conditions not given here. He then used continuity and stochastic dominance to show that V is an RDU functional. As demonstrated in this exercise and its elaboration, continuity is not needed if we exploit the collapsing of outcomes. It can be seen that the collapsing of outcomes implicitly played a role in Quiggin's proof. □

Psychologically, it can matter in which way prospects appear to us. The psychologists Birnbaum (2008a) and Luce (1991, 2000) developed theories that allow for such differences. Then not prospects, but framings of prospects, are the objects of choice. We will restrict attention to theories about choices between prospects, and assume that the particular framing of prospects is immaterial.

The flexibility of rank-dependent utility where we can denote prospects with outcomes collapsed or not constitutes another difference with the original separate-outcome probability transformation theories (Eqs. (5.2.1) and (5.3.3)). For these theories, it was essential how we denote prospects, and the convention had to be introduced of using only the collapsed form (Fishburn 1978; Kahneman & Tversky, 1979 "combination" on p. 274, and p. 283 line −4). Thus, discontinuities result, which could have served as another signal that the separate-probability transformation formula is not sound. In summary then, we have the convenience of choosing a complete ranking as we like under rank-dependent utility, and we can be reassured that no problems will arise.

Assignment 6.7.2.[b] Consider the prospect $x = (0.1{:}25, 0.2{:}16, 0.3{:}16, 0.4{:}9)$. That is, it is $p_1x_1\ldots p_nx_n$ with $n = 4$, shown in Fig. a.

Assume RDU with probability weighting function $w(p) = p^2$ and utility function $U(x) = \sqrt{x}$.

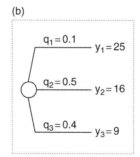

(a) Take the complete ranking $x_1 \geq x_2 \geq x_3 \geq x_4$. Calculate the decision weights $\pi_1, \pi_2, \pi_3, \pi_4$. Calculate the RDU value and the certainty equivalent of the prospect.

(b) Take the complete ranking $x_1 \geq x_3 \geq x_2 \geq x_4$. Calculate the decision weights $\pi'_1, \pi'_3, \pi'_2, \pi'_4$. Calculate the RDU value and the certainty equivalent of the prospect.

(c) Collapse the outcomes x_2 and x_3 so that the prospect is denoted $(0.1{:}25, 0.5{:}16, 0.4{:}9)$ (Fig. b). Calculate the decision weights $\lambda_1, \lambda_2, \lambda_3$. Calculate the RDU value and the certainty equivalent of the prospect. $\square$

Appendix 6.8   An interpretation of rank-dependent utility using the derivative of w

This book avoids the use of differential calculus because conditions on derivates are not easily translated into observable conditions on discrete choice. It is, nevertheless, instructive to interpret rank-dependent utility in such terms, and such an interpretation is briefly presented in this appendix. The discussion is analogous to §6.3, but is now couched in terms of derivatives ("infinitesimals") whereas §6.3 used discrete differences.

As explained before, a major achievement of EU was that it made utility and probability commensurable. SG consistency postulated that the exchange rate between utility and probability be universally valid, and that the exchange rate apply within every subpart of every prospect. Consistent with the interpretation of decision weights as marginal w contribution, the derivative w' of w at the rank intervenes in the exchange rate between probability and utility under RDU. This will be explained next, using differential analyses for continuous distributions.

In Figure 5.2.3, the area, EU, is

$$\int_0^1 U(t)dt. \tag{6.8.1}$$

In Figure 5.5.4, the area, RDU, is

$$\int_0^1 w'(t)U(t)dt, \tag{6.8.2}$$

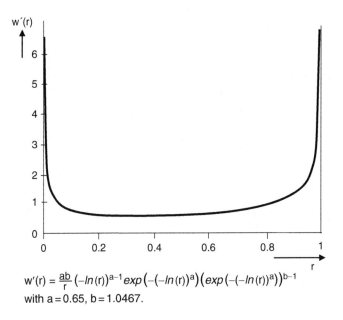

$$w'(r) = \frac{ab}{r} \left(-\ln(r)\right)^{a-1} exp\left(-(-\ln(r))^a\right) \left(exp\left(-(-\ln(r))^a\right)\right)^{b-1}$$
with $a = 0.65$, $b = 1.0467$.

Figure 6.8.1 The derivative of the weighting function.

which follows from substituting $w(p_i + \cdots + p_1) - w(p_{i-1} + \cdots + p_1) = \int_{p_{i-1}+\cdots+p_1}^{p_i+\cdots+p_1} w'(t)dt$.
We compare Eq. (6.8.2) to Eq. (6.8.1). Each t can be interpreted as a rank, describing the probability of receiving an outcome to the left (ranked better). Relative to Eq. (6.8.1), in the RDU formula of Eq. (6.8.2), the weighting of utilities is adjusted by the derivative w' at the rank.

The observation just made provides the easiest way to "read" graphs of weighting functions such as in Figure 6.1.1. The x-axis refers to ranks and not to outcome probabilities. It is the derivative w' at the rank, i.e., the steepness of w there, that describes how much the outcome with that rank is over- or underweighted, in other words, how much the exchange rate between probability and utility has to be adjusted. The shape in Figure 6.1.1 is often described as "overestimation of small probabilities and underestimation of large probabilities." A better description under RDU is that outcomes and probabilities at good and bad ranks are overweighted – because the function is steep there – with the outcomes and probabilities at intermediate ranks underweighted.

Figure 6.8.1 depicts the derivative of Prelec's weighting function (Figure 6.1.1 and Eqs. (6.4.1) and (6.4.2)), with limits ∞ at $p=0$ and $p=1$. The graph clearly shows that good and bad outcomes are overweighted, and that intermediate outcomes are underweighted. It is virtually identical to Fig. 6.4.1c (multiplied by 100).

Under rank dependence, pessimism concerns the overweighting of bad outcomes, and means that decision weights $\pi(p^r)$ become larger as their rank becomes worse. In other words, they are increasing in r, reflecting an increasing derivative and convexity. Figures 6.1.1 and 6.8.1 exhibit an *extremity orientedness*, with best and worst outcomes overweighted. Such phenomena will be the topic of the next chapter.

To relate the derivates of this appendix to the discrete differences in §6.3, note that, as is well known, the difference $w(r+p) - w(r)$ is the integral of w' over the interval $[r, r+p]$. That is to say, it is $\int_r^{r+p} w'(t)dt$. Thus $\frac{w(r+p)-w(r)}{p}$, the factor by which the probability $p = (r+p) - r$ has to be adjusted before calculating expectation, is $\int_r^{r+p} w'(t)dt/p$, which is the average of w' over the (rank-)interval $[r, r+p]$. This explains once more why the graphs in Figure 6.4.1 are virtually indistinguishable from derivatives of w (times p). Figure 6.4.1 does not exhibit divergence all the way to ∞ at the extremes though.

Observation 6.8.1. The decision weight $\pi(p^r)$ results from multiplying the outcome probability p by an adjustment factor that is the average slope of w over the interval $[r, r+p]$. For a small outcome probability p this slope is approximately $w'(r)$. $\square$

Appendix 6.9: RDU for continuous distributions and figures for negative outcomes

Figures 6.9.1 and 6.9.2 adapt Figures 5.5.3 and 5.5.4 to the case of negative utilities. They prepare for an alternative way of writing RDU. In addition, they prepare for prospect theory defined later. The expression for RDU in Eq. (6.9.1) has often been used in the literature. Its main advantage is that it can readily be applied to prospects with infinitely many outcomes. The formula will not be used in this book. Prospects with infinitely many outcomes are important in finance, for instance, where stock prices are often assumed to be lognormally distributed. For a probability distribution x over $\mathbb{R}$, the RDU value of the prospect x can be written as follows:

$$RDU(x) = \int_{\mathbb{R}^+} w(G_{x,U}(t))dt - \int_{\mathbb{R}^-} [1 - w(G_{x,U}(t))]dt, \qquad (6.9.1)$$

where $G_{x,U}$ is the decumulative distribution function for the U values generated by the probability distribution x. That is, $G_{x,U}(t)$ is the probability that x yields an outcome with utility more than t. It is $1 - F^*_{x,U}(t)$ with F^* the regular distribution function of $U(\alpha)$. The demonstration that the integral definition of RDU in Eq. (6.9.1) is identical to Definition 6.1.1 is left as Exercise 6.9.1.

In steps, the RDU value of a continuous distribution over outcomes can be calculated as follows. Assume that F denotes the distribution function of the distribution, assigning to each real number t the probability at t or less.

STEP 1. Consider the decumulative distribution $1 - F$ of outcomes, assigning to each outcome its rank.

STEP 2. Consider the decumulative distribution function for utilities instead of outcomes, namely $(1 - F) \circ U^{-1}$ (denoted $G_{x,U}$ in Eq. (6.9.1)).

STEP 3. Transform the function using the probability weighting w, into $w((1-F) \circ U^{-1})$.

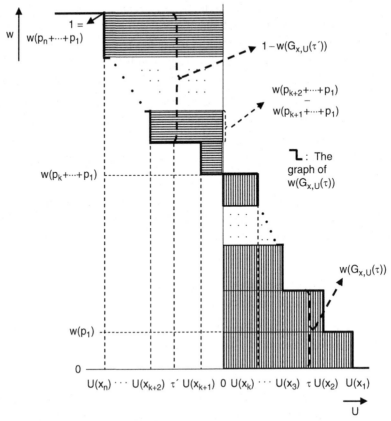

The prospect is $p_1x_1 \cdots p_nx_n$, with $U(x1) \geq \cdots \geq U(x_k) \geq 0 \geq U(x_{k+1}) \geq \cdots \geq U(x_n)$. $w(G_{x,U}(\tau))$ is the w-transform of the probability of receiving utility $> \tau$. The figure illustrates Eq. (6.9.1). For $\tau > 0$ the integrand is $w(G_{x,U}(\tau))$, and for $\tau' < 0$ it is the negative of $1 - w(G_{x,U}(\tau))$. RDU is the area ▓ minus the area ▤ .

Figure 6.9.1 RDU of a prospect with positive and negative utilities.

STEP 4. Calculate the expectation of the decumulative distribution function obtained. (It corresponds to the distribution function $1 - w((1-F) \circ U^{-1})$.)

An alternative way to write the integral of Eq. (6.9.1) is as follows. Remember that x is a probability distribution so that $x(U(\alpha) > t)$, for example, is the probability at an outcome α with utility exceeding τ.

$$RDU(x) = \int_{\mathbb{R}^+} w(x(U(\alpha) > t))dt - \int_{\mathbb{R}^-} [1 - w(x(U(\alpha) > t))] \, dt. \qquad (6.9.2)$$

Here $(U(\alpha) > t)$ can be rewritten as $(U^{-1}(t,\infty))$. We can replace $(U(\alpha) > t)$ by $(U(\alpha) \geq t)$ because this changes the integrand at no more than countably many points, which does not affect the integral. Similarly, we can replace the function $G_{x,U}(t)$ in Eq. (6.9.1)

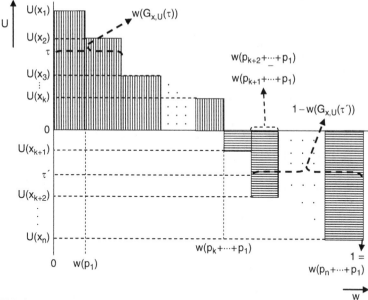

This figure has resulted from Figure 6.9.1 by rotating left and flipping horizontally.

Figure 6.9.2 An illustration alternative to Figure 6.9.1.

by the function $G^*_{x,U}(t)$, giving the probability that x yields an outcome with utility more than *or equal to* t.

If f is the density function of F, then EU (w linear) can be calculated as

$$\int_{\mathbb{R}} U(\alpha)f(\alpha)d\alpha \tag{6.9.3}$$

and RDU can be calculated as

$$\int_{\mathbb{R}} U(\alpha)w'(1-F(\alpha))\,f(\alpha)d\alpha. \tag{6.9.4}$$

The negative part in Eq. (6.9.1) can be recognized in Figure 6.9.1 as follows. The negative area to be subtracted in the figure, when taken as the area below the line with ordinate (i.e. the coordinate on the "y-axis") equal to 1 (so, the line at the level of $w(p_n + \cdots + p_1)$, which is 1), is readily seen to be the integral of $1 - w(G_{x,U}(t))$ over the negative utility axis, as in Eq. (6.9.1). It suggests that $1 - w(G_{x,U}(t))$ plays a role for losses similar to $w(G_{x,U}(t))$'s role for gains. Thus, the negative parts of Eq. (6.9.1) and Figure 6.9.1 provide a first signal in this book of the following point: When using ranks (probabilities of receiving something better) for gains, it may be more natural to use their duals (probabilities of receiving something worse) for losses. This point suggests a symmetry about zero. The dual ranks, called loss-ranks, will be defined formally for prospect theory (§7.6).

Exercise 6.9.1.^{c}

(a) Verify, for a prospect x that with probability 1 yields outcomes with positive utility, that $\int_{\mathbb{R}^-}[w(G_{x,U}(t)) - 1]dt = 0$.

(b) Verify that the integral definition of RDU in Eq. (6.9.1) agrees with the definition of RDU in Definition 6.1.1 for a prospect x that with probability 1 yields outcomes with positive utility.

(c) Verify that the integral definition of RDU in Eq. (6.9.1) agrees with the definition of RDU in Definition 6.1.1 for a general prospect x that can yield negative utilities. □

7 Applications and extensions of rank dependence

In the preceding chapter we saw how rank dependence can be used to model pessimism and optimism. Another important component of probability weighting, orthogonal to the optimism–pessimism component, and cognitive rather than motivational, concerns likelihood sensitivity. This component is introduced informally in the following section, and is presented formally in §7.7. Several other extensions and applications of rank dependence are given.

7.1 Likelihood insensitivity and pessimism as two components of probabilistic risk attitudes

Figures 7.1.1–3 illustrate how two kinds of deviations from additive probabilities combine to create the probability weighting functions commonly found. Fig. 7.1.1a depicts traditional EU with probabilities weighted linearly; i.e., $w(p) = p$. Fig. 1b depicts pessimism as discussed in the preceding chapter.

Fig. 2a shows another psychological phenomenon. It reflects "diminishing sensitivity" for probabilities, which we will call likelihood insensitivity. Relative to EU, the weighting function is too shallow in the middle region, and too steep near both endpoints. An extreme case is shown in Fig. 3a. Here w is extremely steep at 0 and 1, and completely shallow in the middle. Such behavior is typically found if people distinguish only between "sure to happen," "sure not to happen," and "don't know." An example of such a crude distinction is in Shackle (1949b p. 8). The expression 50–50 is commonly used to express such crude perceptions of uncertainty. "Either it happens or it won't; you can't say more about it." is another way of expressing such beliefs. No distinction is made between different levels of likelihood.[1]

Fig. 2a displays an intermediate case between the complete absence of discrimination of Fig. 3a and the perfect discrimination of Fig. 1a. People do distinguish different levels of likelihood in the middle, but fail to do so sufficiently (Loewenstein *et al.* 2001 p. 276). Accordingly, they are overly sensitive to the changes from

---

[1] Piaget & Inhelder (1951), in an analysis of the development of probabilistic thinking in children, found that children at the age of 4 or 5 (their starting level "IA") perceive probability as in Fig. 3a.

impossible to possible and from possible to certain. The regressive shape in Fig. 2a, with weights correlating imperfectly with probabilities, and with as much overweighting of good as of bad outcomes, suggests that perceptual and cognitive limitations, prior to any consideration of value, underlie this effect. People do not deviate from EU only because of extra pessimism as in Fig. 1b, but also because they do not adequately understand probability, as in Fig. 2a.

The two factors in Figs. 1b and 2a have similar implications (underweighting and risk aversion) for prospects x_p0 with a large probability p of a gain x, but they have opposite effects for prospects x_p0 with a small probability p of a gain x. In the latter case, pessimism still generates risk aversion but likelihood insensitivity generates risk seeking. The prevailing experimental finding is a combination of pessimism and likelihood insensitivity, shown in Fig. 2b, with small probabilities overweighted.[2] Evidence against likelihood insensitivity has also been found,[3] and there have been several discussions of the psychological interpretation of the two factors.[4]

The function in Fig. 2b first is steep exceeding the diagonal, which suggests optimism and risk seeking (discussed for the concave weighting function in Fig. 6.3.2b). It next intersects the diagonal at approximately $1/3$. Finally, in the major part of the domain, it is below the diagonal, becoming steep again near 1, which suggests pessimism and risk aversion there. w($1/2$) is approximately 0.42. For this

---

[2] Abdellaoui (2000); Abdellaoui, Bleichrodt, & L'Haridon (2008); Abdellaoui, Vossmann, & Weber (2005); Ali (1977); Allais (1988); Attneave (1959); Beach & Phillips (1967); Bernasconi (1994); Birnbaum *et al.* (1992); Bleichrodt, Doctor, & Stolk (2005; for welfare evaluations); Bleichrodt & Pinto (2000); Bleichrodt, van Rijn, & Johannesson (1999); Booij, van de Kuilen, & van Praag (2010); Brandstätter, Kühberger, & Schneider (2002); Bruhin, Fehr-Duda, & Epper (2010); Camerer (2007); Camerer & Ho (1994); Cohen & Jaffray (1988); Einhorn & Hogarth (1985, 1986); Etchart (2004); Fehr-Duda, de Gennaro, & Schubert (2006); Fox, Rogers, & Tversky (1996); Fox & Tversky (1995); Fox & Tversky (1998); Gayer (2010); Gonzalez & Wu (1999); Griffith (1949); Hogarth & Einhorn (1990); Hogarth & Kunreuther (1985); Kachelmeier & Shehata (1992); Hogarth & Kunreuther (1989 Table 2, Figure 2, Tables 4 and 5); Kahneman & Tversky (1979); Kilka & Weber (2001); Krzysztofowicz (1994 §5.2); Lattimore, Baker, & Witte (1992); Loehman (1998 p. 295); Lopes (1995 p. 207); Luce & Suppes (1965 §4.3, review); McGlothlin (1956); Preston & Baratta (1948); Reyna & Brainerd (1995); Rosett (1965, 1971); Sprowls (1953); Stalmeier & Bezembinder (1999); Tversky & Fox (1995); Tversky & Kahneman (1992); Viscusi & Evans (2006); Wu & Gonzalez (1996); Wu & Gonzalez (1998); Yaari (1965 end of Section IV). In a neurostudy, Berns *et al.* (2008) measured neurobiological probability response ratios derived from experiences without decisions involved, and found that they predicted choice-based observations of likelihood insensitive probability weighting well. Overweighting of extreme outcomes because of insensitivity is also central to intertemporal preference for the evaluation of episodes (Kahneman 1994; Kahneman & Krueger 2006).

[3] Barron & Erev (2003); Birnbaum (2008a, pp. 484–486); Bleichrodt (2001); Goeree, Holt, & Palfrey (2002, 2003); Henrich & Mcelreat (2002); Humphrey & Verschoor (2004); Jullien & Salanié (2000); Loomes (1991); Luce (1996); Mosteller & Nogee (1951); van de Kuilen & Wakker (2009). Stott (2006) found almost no probability weighting. Phenomena for very small probabilities are sometimes irregular, where people may ignore rather than overweight small probabilities (Kunreuther & Pauly 2003; Schmidt & Zimper 2007). Hence, Kahneman & Tversky (1979) did not commit themselves to any curve very close to 0 and 1. The prevailing finding is, however, the overweighting of small probabilities, and Tversky & Kahneman (1992) incorporated this phenomenon. Bearden, Wallsten, & Fox (2007) suggested that empirical findings of likelihood insensitivity may be driven by noise.

[4] Einhorn & Hogarth (1985); Gayer (2010); Hogarth & Einhorn (1990); Lopes (1987); Tversky & Fox (1995); Tversky & Wakker (1995); Weber (1994). The discussion in Gonzalez & Wu (1999) is particularly instructive. Kunreuther, Novemsky, & Kahneman (2001) and Reyna & Brainerd (1995) provided evidence supporting the cognitive interpretation of the inverse-S phenomenon.

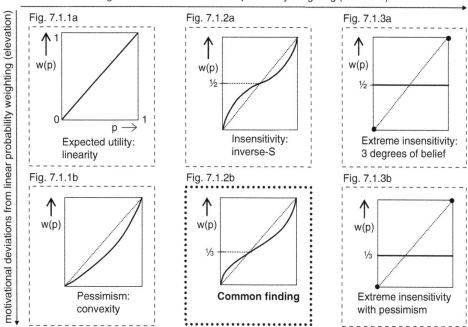

Cognitive deviations from linear probability weighting (curvature)

motivational deviations from linear probability weighting (elevation)

Fig. 7.1.1a
Expected utility: linearity

Fig. 7.1.2a
Insensitivity: inverse-S

Fig. 7.1.3a
Extreme insensitivity: 3 degrees of belief

Fig. 7.1.1b
Pessimism: convexity

Fig. 7.1.2b
Common finding

Fig. 7.1.3b
Extreme insensitivity with pessimism

weighting function, the best-ranked outcomes receive relatively high decision weights and the worst-ranked outcomes even more. The moderate intermediate outcomes receive low decision weights. Apparently, people pay (too) much attention to extreme and exceptional outcomes. This weighting function suggests that people are mostly risk averse, but not always, which deviates from the often-suggested universal risk aversion. Most authors in the theoretical economic literature on RDU assume universal pessimism, with weighting functions that underweight all probabilities, such as in Fig. 1b. Empirical investigations, starting with Preston & Baratta (1948), have mostly found inverse S-shapes as in Fig. 2b.

Public lotteries constitute a classical example of risk seeking for long-shot prospects. Such risk seeking is also found in the health domain, where patients with bad prospects often prefer very risky treatments with only a very small probability of success mostly because this offers hope. In Exercise 6.4.3, people perceive of the probability 10^{-6} as a possibility of gaining 10^6, and are not sufficiently aware of how small this probability is, which is why they give too much weight to it. They understand better how large the outcome $\$10^6$ is than how small the probability 10^{-6} is.

The steepness of w at 1 implies a strong overweighting of the worst outcome – the minimal outcome level that one is sure to obtain from a prospect. This phenomenon, discussed informally several times before in this book, is called the *certainty effect*. The steepness of w at 0 implies an overweighting of the best outcome of the prospect. This phenomenon is called the *possibility effect*. It is worthy of note that the

coexistence of gambling and insurance[5], a classical paradox in the economic literature, can be explained by RDU. Even more than that, the same basic property
underlies both gambling and insurance: the overweighting of extreme-outcome probabilities, being the small probability of winning a big prize under gambling (possibility effect) and the small probability of a catastrophe under insurance (certainty
effect); see Kahneman & Tversky (1979 p. 286), and Assignment 7.2.4.

A tongue-in-cheek Bayesian evolutionary interpretation of Figures 7.1.1–7.1.3
could be as follows. Figure 7.1.3 shows the behavior of primitive organs that can
distinguish between certain and uncertain, but cannot distinguish between different
levels of uncertainty. Accordingly, they cannot respond differently to different situations of uncertainty. Mankind has made progress and has reached Fig. 7.1.2b.
Fig. 7.1.1a is a next step still ahead of us, with Bayesians outnumbering the rest of
mankind more and more in future generations.

7.2   Parametric forms of weighting functions

Tversky & Kahneman (1992) proposed the following parametric family of weighting
functions:

$$w(p) = \frac{p^c}{(p^c + (1-p)^c)^{1/c}} \qquad (7.2.1)$$

for $c \geq 0.28$; for smaller c the functions are not strictly increasing. Tversky &
Kahneman (1992) estimated

$$c = 0.61 \qquad (7.2.2)$$

as a value that best fits prevailing data. Fig. 7.1.2b showed this function. Figure 7.2.1
depicts some more cases. It shows that $c = 1$ gives EU with a linear w. Decreasing c at
the same time generates a more pronounced inverse-S shape and more pessimism.
The overweighting of probabilities near 0 is probably too strong for this family. For c
exceeding 1 we obtain S-shapes.

Exercise 7.2.1.[b] Consider the parametric family of Tversky and Kahneman
(Eq. (7.2.1)) with $c = 0.5$; i.e.,

$$w(p) = \frac{\sqrt{p}}{\left(\sqrt{p} + \sqrt{1-p}\right)^2}.$$

Assume that $U(\alpha) = \alpha/100$.

---

[5] This is economic jargon for the phenomenon that people at the same time take insurance exhibiting risk
  aversion, and buy public lotteries exhibiting risk seeking. Under expected utility, the former suggests concave
  utility and the latter suggests convex utility. Hence the paradox.

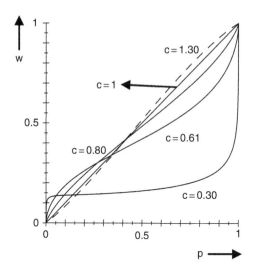

Figure 7.2.1 Tversky & Kahneman's (1992) family (Eq. (7.2.1)).

(a) Verify that $w(0) = 0$ and $w(1) = 1$.
(b) Calculate (computer/pocket calculator!) $w(1/5)$ and $w(4/5)$.
(c) What are the decision weights of outcome 70, of outcome 50, and of outcome 30, for the RDU-value calculation of the prospect (1/5:70, 3/5:50, 1/5:30)?
(d) Calculate the RDU value of the prospect in (c) and its certainty-equivalent. □

Prelec (1998) proposed the compound invariance family $(exp(-(-ln(p))^a))^b$ (Eq. (6.4.1)) with a and b as parameters (Figure 7.2.2). Ongoing empirical research suggests that $a = 0.65$ and $b = 1.0467$ (as in Eq. (6.4.2)), giving an intersection with the diagonal at 0.32, are good parameter choices for gains. Then the graph is almost identical to the one in Fig. 7.1.2b. A distinguishing feature of Prelec's proposal is that it is well-suited for very small and very large probabilities (satisfying a property called subproportionality by Kahneman & Tversky, 1979). Another advantage is that this family is analytically more tractable than the family of Tversky & Kahneman (1992). Further, the family has a behavioral foundation (Prelec 1998). Prelec's main condition in this behavioral foundation requires the implication (with superscript m designating a power.)

$$[\gamma_p 0 \sim \beta_q 0, \ \gamma_r 0 \sim \beta_s 0, \ \text{and} \ \gamma'_{p^m} 0 \sim \beta'_{q^m} 0] \Rightarrow \gamma'_{r^m} 0 \sim \beta'_{s^m} 0 \tag{7.2.3}$$

for all integers m (*compound invariance*). Prelec paid special attention to the subfamily for $b = 1$, but larger values of b seem to fit data better.

Another useful two-parameter family (that can be seen to be linear in log-odds) was first proposed by Goldstein & Einhorn (1987 Eqs. 22−24). It was introduced independently by Lattimore, Baker, & Witte (1992), and Ostaszewski, Green, & Myerson

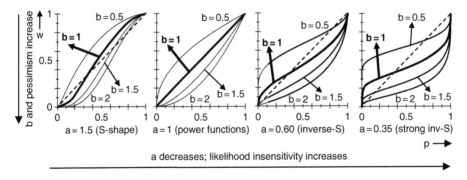

Figure 7.2.2 Prelec's compound invariance family (Eq. (6.4.1)).

(1998) who obtained it by applying a hyperbolic function – often used in intertemporal choice – to the odds ratio $p/(1-p)$. See Figure 7.2.3.

$$w(p) = \frac{bp^a}{bp^a + (1-p)^a}.$$ (7.2.4)

Parameter $a > 0$ affects likelihood insensitivity (curvature) similarly as in Prelec's family, and b now is an anti-index of pessimism. The choices $a = 0.69$ and $b = 0.77$ fit commonly found data well. Bruhin, Fehr-Duda, & Epper (2010) used this family and found that, relative to Swiss students, Chinese students are more likelihood insensitive (a bigger) and more optimistic (b smaller). Diecidue, Schmidt, & Zank (2009) gave an efficient and appealing preference foundation of RDU with: (a) Power w; (b) exponential w; (c) inverse-S w that is a concave power function cp^a up to a reflection point t, and a convex dual-power function $1-d(1-p)^b$ thereafter.

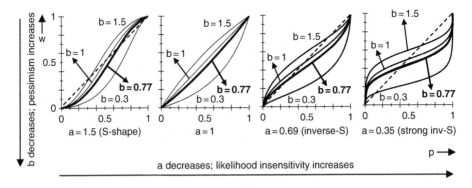

Figure 7.2.3 The family of Eq. (7.2.4).

Because the main deviations from EU occur at the boundaries $p = 0$ and $p = 1$, the following, simple, *neo-additive* family is particularly useful.

$$w(0) = 0; w(1) = 1; \ 0<p<1 : w(p) = b + ap; a \geq 0, b \geq 0, a + b \leq 1. \quad (7.2.5)$$

For the opposite of inverse-S shapes, which could be called S-shapes, neo-additive functions can be used with b < 0 and a + b > 1, in which case w is to be truncated at the values 0 and 1 and can be taken constant near p = 0 and p = 1. For strict pessimism, b < 0 is useful. For simplicity, we focus on the most common case, Eq. (7.2.5), in what follows. In the regression literature, the symbols a and b are often interchanged, but we will use the notation closest to Prelec's parameters. For later use we display an interpretation of the parameters that can readily be inferred from the figure, with (2b+a)/2 a linear transform of b − (1 − a − b):

a is an index of likelihood sensitivity ("curvature," or "inverse-S shape")[6];
(2b + a)/2 is an index of optimism (elevation).   (7.2.6)

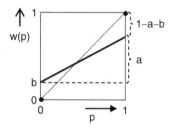

Figure 7.2.4 The neo-additive family.

We have

$$RDU(p_1x_1 \cdots p_nx_n) = b \times \max\{U(x_j) : p_j > 0\} + a \times EU(x)$$
$$+ (1 - a - b) \times \min\{U(x_j) : p_j > 0.\} \qquad (7.2.7)$$

The neo-additive function entails an overweighting of the best and worst outcomes, and compliance with EU otherwise. The latter compliance entails, in terms of preferences, that EU holds on subsets of prospects that all yield the same best positive-probability outcome and also all yield the same worst positive-probability outcome. When comparing such prospects, the max- and min-terms in Eq. (7.2.7) cancel.

Several papers have argued for the importance of the neo-additive family (Bell 1985; Birnbaum & Stegner 1981 Eq. 3; Chateauneuf, Eichberger, & Grant 2007; Cohen 1992; Gilboa 1988; Loomes, Moffat, & Sugden 2002; Teitelbaum 2007). The discontinuities at the extremes can, however, cause analytical problems, and the commitment to EU in the middle region can be restrictive because some deviations from EU have still been found in the middle region (Harless & Camerer 1994 p. 1281; Wu & Gonzalez 1996). Therefore, different families are useful. Nevertheless, the neo-additive functions are among the most promising candidates regarding the

---

[6] Thus a is an anti-index of likelihood insensitivity. The latter corresponds positively with curvature and inverse-S.

optimal tradeoff of parsimony and fit. A special advantage of this family, because of which I will use it later, is that the interpretation of its parameters is clearer and more convincing than with other families. Finding the best-fitting neo-additive weighting function for a given set of weighting-function values amounts to finding the optimal linear regression over the interval (0,1) (with the endpoints 0 and 1 excluded), so that existing software can readily be used.

Exercise 7.2.2.[b]

(a) Assume that you have decided that it is wise to pay additional attention to the worst outcomes because you think that they should be more important for your decisions than the other outcomes. You want to assign decision weight ½ to the ⅓ probability mass allocated to the worst outcomes (that is, to the left tail of the probability distribution of the prospect), decision weight ⅓ to the ⅓ probability mass allocated to the middle outcomes, and to the ⅓ probability mass allocated to the best outcomes (the right tail) you want to assign the remaining decision weight, being $1-½-⅓ = ⅙$. Draw a graph of a weighting function that generates such a decision weight allocation. Draw it by hand; it need not be very precise.

(b) Assume that you have decided that it is wise to pay additional attention to bad outcomes, but also to good outcomes. You want to assign decision weight ⅓ to the ¼ probability mass allocated to the worst outcomes, decision weight ⅓ to the ¼ probability mass allocated to the best outcomes, and the remaining ⅓ decision weight to the probability mass ½ allocated to the middle outcomes. Draw a graph of a weighting function that generates such a decision weight allocation. Again, draw it by hand. □

Example 7.2.1. We consider the risk premium of the prospect $80_½-20$. Assume RDU with $U(\alpha) = 1 - \exp(-\theta\alpha)$ and $w(p) = \frac{p^c}{(p^c+(1-p)^c)^{1/c}}$ (as in Eq. (7.2.1)) for $\theta = 0.005$ and $c = 0.61$. Exercise 3.5.5 gave an interpretation of θ. The expected value of the prospect is 30. Straightforward calculations (Exercise 7.2.3) demonstrate that the certainty equivalent is 16.19. The risk premium is $30 - 16.19 = 13.81$. This risk premium is generated by utility and probability weighting. Table 7.2.1 shows the risk premia for some related models. The nonlinear components of the models have been written between brackets. The third row gives the risk premium if there is no probability weighting (w linear, $c = 1$), a case considered before in Example 3.2.2. The fourth row gives the risk premium if there is no utility curvature (linear utility, which is parametrized by $\theta = 0$; see §3.5). The results suggest that the overall risk premium of 13.81 has been generated more by probability weighting than by utility curvature. □

Exercise 7.2.3.[a] Verify the calculations of Example 7.2.1. □

The following assignment demonstrates how the estimations of Tversky & Kahneman (1992) predict the coexistence of gambling and insurance.

Table 7.2.1

Model	θ (for U)	c (for w)	risk premium
EV	0 (linear)	1	0
EU (U)	0.005	1	6.19
RDU (w)	0 (linear)	0.61	7.94
RDU (U, w)	0.005	0.61	13.81

Assignment 7.2.4.[b] Assume w as in Eqs. (7.2.1) and (7.2.2) and $U(\alpha) = \alpha^{0.88}$, which are the probability weighting function and utility function estimated by Tversky & Kahneman (1992). Assume that the agent, who cares only about the total monetary value of all his assets, owns a house worth $100,000, and $4 in cash, totalling a value of $100,004. There is a 0.00001 probability that the house will burn down and will be completely lost during the next year. An insurance company charges $2 for insurance of the house. At the same time, there is a public lottery costing $2, which with probability 0.00001 yields a prize of $100,000 and nothing otherwise. For simplicity, assume that the probability of both the house burning down and the lottery being won is 0. The agent can choose between four things to do, with the resulting prospect indicated.

- buy insurance and lottery: $200{,}000_{0.00001}100{,}000$;
- buy insurance but not lottery: 100,002 for sure;
- buy lottery but not insurance: (0.00001: 200,002, 0.00001: 2, 0.99998: 100,002);
- do not buy anything: $4_{0.00001}100{,}004$.

What will the agent do? □

7.3 Data fitting for rank-dependent utility under risk

This section adapts the fitting results of §4.10, which assumed EU, to RDU. Again, italicized superscripts indicate powers and nonitalicized powers as in $\alpha^0,\ldots,PE^4$ are superscripts. As throughout this chapter, we assume decision under risk, with probabilities given for all events.

Exercise 7.3.1.[b] We consider again the eight indifferences from Tversky & Kahneman (1992) of Exercise 3.6.5. We assume RDU with U from the same family as in Exercise 3.6.5 (i.e. $U(\alpha) = 1 - \exp(-\theta\alpha)$), and with w(p) as in Eq. (7.2.1). Find the $0.0000 < \theta = i \times 0.0001 < 0.0100$ and $0.30 \leq c = j \times 0.01 \leq 1.50$ (for integers i and j) that best fit the data, give the distance according to the distance measure of §A.2, and predict $CE(-100_{0.05}(-200))$. □

Exercise 7.3.1'.[b] The median value of $CE(-100_{0.05}(-200))$ that was empirically observed by Tversky & Kahneman (1992) was -179. Determine by how far your prediction in Exercise 7.3.1 is off from the actually observed value. □

Exercise 7.3.2.[b] Consider the eight indifferences from Tversky & Kahneman (1992) of Exercise 3.6.5. We assume RDU with U from the same family as in Exercise 3.6.5 (i.e. $U(\alpha) = 1 - \exp(-\theta\alpha)$), and with neo-additive $w(p) = b + ap$ (Eq. (7.2.5)). Find the $0.0050 < \theta = i \times 0.00001 < 0.0150$, $0.00 \leq b = j \times 0.01 < 1.00$ and $0 < a = k \times 0.01 \leq 1 - b$ (for integers i, j, k) that best fit the data, give the distance according to the distance measure of §A.2, and predict $CE(-100_{0.05}(-200))$. □

Exercise 7.3.2.'[b] The median value of $CE(-100_{0.05}(-200))$ that was empirically observed by Tversky & Kahneman (1992) was -179. Determine by how far your prediction in Exercise 7.3.2 is off. □

Relative to the EU analysis in Exercise 3.6.5, probability weighting is capturing part of the risk aversion so that utility now is less concave. As the elaborations in Appendix J show, the fit (distance to the data) has been improved, but not by very much. The pattern for losses seems to be very different from the pattern for gains, so that it should come as no surprise that RDU does not fit the data very well. A different treatment of gains and losses is desirable, and this will be the topic of later chapters. $CE(-100_{0.05}(-200))$ has improved relative to Exercise 3.6.5 (see elaborations) but, again, not by very much.

We assume throughout the rest of this section without further mention:

Assumption 7.3.1. Assumption 4.10.1 (50–50) holds. RDU holds with power utility $U(\alpha) = \alpha^\theta$ and $w(p)$ as in Eq. (7.2.1). □

Exercise 7.3.3.[b] Assume that $c = 0.61$ and $\theta = 0.88$, as in Tversky & Kahneman (1992). Which answers $\alpha^1, \ldots, PE^3$ are given in Figures 4.1.1–4.1.5? (For Figure 4.1.5 I do not know an analytical solution and had my computer search numerically, with trial and error, for the answers.) □

Because the results of several of the following exercises are discussed in the text, the answers are immediately given following the exercises. The results of Exercise 4.10.2 (basic analysis of TO data, with α's equally spaced in utility units) are as relevant to RDU as they are to EU (Observation 6.5.1), so that they can be copied into this section without any modification.

Exercise 7.3.4[b] [CE data]. Analyze the indifferences of subject 5 of Figure 4.1.3 using the distance measure of §A.2. This time the weighting function captures so much of the risk aversion that utility can be more natural, and no negative powers have to be considered. Hence, find the $0.28 \leq c = j/100 \leq 2$ and the $0 < \theta = i/100 < 2$ that optimally fit the data, give the distance, and predict $CE(80_{1/2}40)$. □

Exercise 7.3.5[b] [PE data]. Analyze the indifferences of subject 5 in Figure 4.1.5 using the distance measure of §A.2. Here we still need utility with a negative power. Find the $0.28 \leq c = j/100 \leq 2$ and the $0 > \theta = i/100 > -1$ that optimally fit the data, give the distance, and predict $CE(80_{1/2}40)$. □

As the elaborations in Appendix J show, under EU, the powers of utility derived from the CE questions (Exercise 4.10.3) and the PE questions (Exercise 4.10.4) deviate dramatically from those derived from the TO questions (Exercise 4.10.2). Under RDU, Exercises 7.3.4 and 7.3.5 replace Exercises 4.10.3 and 4.10.4, and now the discrepancy has been reduced. Nevertheless, a large discrepancy remains, suggesting that the data also contain deviations from RDU.

We next reconsider the analysis of the TO questions in Figure 4.1.1, 4.1.2, 4.1.4 using the part of the data regarding the indifferences, which involve the right-hand prospects.

Exercise 7.3.6[b] [Equivalences in TO data]. Consider again the choices of subject 5 in Table 4.3.1. Use the distance measure from §A.2. Find the parameters θ and c that best fit the indifferences, determine by how far the model is off, and predict $CE(80_{1/2}40)$ for:

(a) The indifferences in Figure 4.1.1.
(b) The indifferences in Figure 4.1.2.
(c) The indifferences in Figure 4.1.4.
(d) All indifferences in Parts (a)–(c) jointly. □

The answers to parts (a), (b), and (c) will show that, in each single figure with TO questions, RDU brings virtually no improvement over EU for this subject. Because Figures 4.1.1, 4.1.2, and 4.1.4 generate different powers under EU, so that EU does not fit these data jointly very well, it can be expected that RDU can bring some improvement when the three figures are considered jointly. The answer to part (d) confirms this expectation.

Exercise 7.3.7[b] [Equivalences in TO data]. Redo Exercise 7.3.6, but now as an exception in this section, do not assume the 50–50 Assumption 4.10.1. Instead, assume that $P(cand_1) = 0.541$, which was the best-fitting subjective probability in §4.10. Then, using the distance measure from §A.2, find the parameters θ and c that best fit the indifferences, determine by how far the model is off, and predict $CE(80_{0.541}40)$ for:

(a) The indifferences in Figure 4.1.1.
(b) The indifferences in Figure 4.1.2.
(c) The indifferences in Figure 4.1.4.
(d) All indifferences in Parts (a)–(c) jointly. □

There is considerable variation in the results of Exercises 7.3.6 and 7.3.7. Thus, adding the equivalences with right-hand prospects primarily seems to enlarge noise, as it did under EU in §4.10.

Exercise 7.3.8[b] Make Assumption 4.10.1, and consider all 18 indifferences given by subject 5 in Figures 4.1.1–4.1.5. Using the distance measure from §A.2, find the parameters θ and c that best fit the indifferences, determine by how far the model is off, and predict $CE(80_{1/2}40)$. □

In Exercise 7.3.8, when fitting all data of subject 5, utility curvature is moderate, and most of the deviation from risk neutrality is captured by probability weighting. The fit is better than when using only utility curvature as in Exercise 4.10.7a.

Exercise 7.3.9. This exercise illustrates Eqs. (3.5.3) and (3.5.6) for RDU, for which theory they can be seen to hold as they do under EU. Consider the prospects S ("safe") $= 30$ and R ("risky") $= 100_{\sqrt[3]{2}}0$. The criterion for being "close to" will be that the distance is less than 0.1. We write CE_1 for the certainty equivalent of $200_{\sqrt[3]{2}}0$ and CE_2 for the certainty equivalent of $200_{\sqrt[3]{2}}100$. Assume RDU with $w(p) = p^2$.

(a)[b] Assume that $U(\alpha) = \alpha^\theta$ with $\theta > 0$. Determine the preference between the prospects for all $0 < j \leq 100$ and $\theta = j/100$, and find an analytic expression for the θ that yields indifference between S and R. Give a three-digits approximation of the indifference-θ. Give an analytic expression for CE_1 and CE_2, and give a three-digits approximation for each. Is CE_1 close to twice 30, or is it considerably larger or smaller? Is CE_2 close to $30 + 100$, or is it considerably larger or smaller?

(b)[b] Assume that $U(\alpha) = 1 - e^{-\theta\alpha}$ with $\theta > 0$. You can spend some time trying to find an analytic solution for θ under indifference between S and R, but will not succeed. Let your computer determine the preference between the prospects for all $0 < j \leq 100$ and $\theta = 0.001 + j/1000$. Give a three-digits approximation of the indifference-θ. Give an analytic expression for CE_1 and CE_2, and give three-digits approximations for each. Is CE_1 close to twice 30, or is it considerably larger or smaller? Is CE_2 close to $30 + 100$, or is it considerably larger or smaller? □

7.4   Direct ways to test convexity, concavity, and likelihood insensitivity using violations of the sure-thing principle

In EU, the subjective parameter determining risk attitude was the utility function, and we examined how to measure and test it. We then extended these results to RDU. The empirical findings regarding nonlinear decision weights obtained in the literature so far, and reported in the preceding sections, were mostly based on parametric fittings of w and U simultaneously. It is obviously of interest to directly measure nonlinear decision weights under RDU, and test their properties. Such direct measurements serve the purpose of this book of relating properties of subjective parameters to preferences as directly and elementarily as possible. Given the novelty of rank-dependent utility, not many results of this kind have been available in the literature yet. This section presents some. The results presented here do not require the measurement of utility, and accordingly are not affected by errors in utility measurement. Thus probability weighting is isolated as an independent component.

The following result provides the easiest way to test for concavity and convexity of probability weighting known to me. Its proof is not elementary.

Theorem 7.4.1. Assume Structural Assumption 2.5.2 (decision under risk and richness) and RDU with a continuous weighting function w. Then w is convex if and only if preferences satisfy the following (quasi)convexity condition: If $x \succcurlyeq y$ then $x \succcurlyeq x_\lambda y$ for all $0 \leq \lambda \leq 1$. (Here the mixing is probabilistic.) w is concave if and only if preferences satisfy the following (quasi)concavity condition: If $x \succcurlyeq y$ then $x_\lambda y \succcurlyeq y$ for all $0 \leq \lambda \leq 1$. $\square$

The following example is useful for developing an intuition of the effects of rank dependence. It also shows how empirical tests of the sure-thing principle in the literature give information about the way in which decision weights depend on ranks.

Example 7.4.2 [Violations of the sure-thing principle as a test of properties of rank dependence; Birnbaum 2008a pp. 484–486; Wu & Gonzalez 1996]. Consider a left prospect $\ell = (q{:}c, p_2{:}\boldsymbol{\delta}, p_3{:}\alpha)$ and a right prospect $r = (q{:}c, p_2{:}\gamma, p_3{:} \boldsymbol{\beta})$, depicted in Figure 7.4.1, and originating from the unpublished Chew & MacCrimmon (1979). Here c denotes a common outcome and $\boldsymbol{\delta} > \gamma > \boldsymbol{\beta} > \alpha$. The ranking of c is discussed later. Both for the pair α, $\boldsymbol{\beta}$ and for the pair γ, $\boldsymbol{\delta}$, the better of the two outcomes has been printed in bold. Thus, each branch in Figure 7.4.1 provides an argument for going in the bold direction: The p_2 branches suggest going for the left prospect ℓ, and the p_3 branches suggest going for the right prospect r.

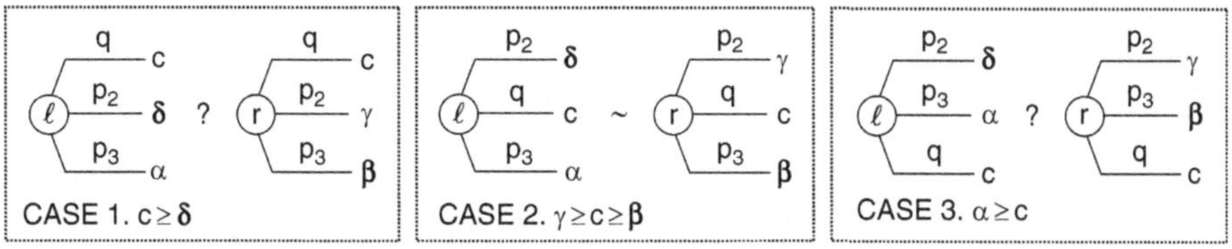

Figure 7.4.1 Testing the sure-thing principle.

Under EU, changes in c do not affect the preference. Under RDU they can, and they give information about properties of w. We consider three exclusive (but not exhaustive) cases (as in Figure 7.4.1), and list some logical equivalences for each.

CASE 1 $[c \geq \boldsymbol{\delta}]$. Then

$$\ell \quad \succ \quad r \quad \Leftrightarrow \quad \pi\big(p_2{}^q\big)(U(\boldsymbol{\delta}) - U(\gamma)) > \pi\big(p_3{}^w\big)(U(\boldsymbol{\beta}) - U(\alpha));$$

$$\text{''} \quad \sim \quad \text{''} \quad \Leftrightarrow \quad \text{''} \qquad \text{''} \qquad = \qquad \text{''} \qquad \text{''},$$

$$\text{''} \quad \prec \quad \text{''} \quad \Leftrightarrow \quad \text{''} \qquad \text{''} \qquad < \qquad \text{''} \qquad \text{''}.$$

CASE 2 $[\gamma \geq c \geq \boldsymbol{\beta}]$. Then

$$\ell \quad \succ \quad r \quad \Leftrightarrow \quad \pi\big(p_2{}^b\big)(U(\boldsymbol{\delta}) - U(\gamma)) > \pi\big(p_3{}^w\big)(U(\boldsymbol{\beta}) - U(\alpha));$$

$$\text{''} \quad \sim \quad \text{''} \quad \Leftrightarrow \quad \text{''} \qquad \text{''} \qquad = \qquad \text{''} \qquad \text{''},$$

$$\text{''} \quad \prec \quad \text{''} \quad \Leftrightarrow \quad \text{''} \qquad \text{''} \qquad < \qquad \text{''} \qquad \text{''}.$$

CASE 3 $[\alpha \geq c]$. Then

$$\ell \quad \succ \quad r \quad \Leftrightarrow \quad \pi\big(p_2{}^b\big)(U(\boldsymbol{\delta}) - U(\gamma)) > \pi\big(p_3{}^{p_2}\big)(U(\boldsymbol{\beta}) - U(\alpha));$$

$$\text{''} \quad \sim \quad \text{''} \quad \Leftrightarrow \quad \text{''} \qquad \text{''} \qquad = \qquad \text{''} \qquad \text{''},$$

$$\text{''} \quad \prec \quad \text{''} \quad \Leftrightarrow \quad \text{''} \qquad \text{''} \qquad < \qquad \text{''} \qquad \text{''}.$$

Assume that we take α, β, γ, and δ such that indifference results in Case 2; see Figure 7.4.1. In Case 2 both decision weights in the inequalities have an extreme rank. It is a useful exercise to figure out by yourself which preferences are implied in Cases 1 and 3 by convexity of the weighting function and which are implied by concavity. Answers are immediately given in the text that follows. Although we did not yet define likelihood insensitivity formally, with its interpretation of extremity-orientedness you can already see what its predictions must be in Figure 7.4.1.

In Case 1, the larger $\pi(p_2^q)$ is, the larger the difference $\pi(p_2^q)(U(\delta) - U(\gamma))$ is, and the more preference there is for the prospect ℓ. Given the indifference in Case 2, the preference for ℓ over r in Case 1 corresponds exactly to the ordering of $\pi(p_2^q)$ relative to $\pi(p_2^b)$. That is, it corresponds with the properties of the preference relation added between brackets in what follows.

CASE 1 $[c \geq \delta]$. Then

$$\ell \quad \succ \quad r \quad \Leftrightarrow \quad \pi(p_2^q) > \pi(p_2^b) \qquad \text{(pessimism)};$$

$$'' \quad \sim \quad '' \quad \Leftrightarrow \quad '' \quad = \quad '' \qquad \text{(EU)};$$

$$'' \quad \prec \quad '' \quad \Leftrightarrow \quad '' \quad < \quad '' \qquad \text{(optimism and likelihood ins.)}.$$

Thus, we can directly reveal from the preferences in Cases 1 and 2 how the decision weight of p_2 is affected by a change in rank from b $(= 0)$, the rank in Case 2, to q, the rank in Case 1.

In Case 3, the larger $\pi(p_3^{p_2})$ is, the larger the difference $\pi(p_3^{p_2})(U(\beta) - U(\alpha))$ is and, hence, the *weaker* the preference for ℓ is. Given the indifference in Case 2, the preference for ℓ over r in Case 3 is inversely related to the ordering of $\pi(p_3^{p_2})$ and $\pi(p_3^w)$.

CASE 3 $[\alpha \geq c]$. Then

$$\ell \quad \succ \quad r \quad \Leftrightarrow \quad \pi(p_3^{p_2}) < \pi(p_3^w) \qquad \text{(Pessimism and likelihood ins.)};$$

$$'' \quad \sim \quad '' \quad \Leftrightarrow \quad '' \quad = \quad '' \qquad \text{(EU)};$$

$$'' \quad \prec \quad '' \quad \Leftrightarrow \quad '' \quad > \quad '' \qquad \text{(optimism)}.$$

The design of Figure 7.4.1 has been tested in numerous papers, often with the purpose of testing theories other than RDU, such as weighted utility in Chew & Waller (1986). All of their findings, and virtually all empirical tests of the sure-thing principle, entail a test of the properties of rank dependence in the way just explained. Wakker (2001) gives a survey of such studies, and theoretical results based on this design. □

The following exercise shows that "local" properties of w can be verified by restricting attention to small outcome probabilities p and letting the rank r range over the [0,1] interval. Examples of such local properties are convexity and concavity: these properties can be defined as positivity or negativity of the second derivative $w(r)''$ for all r, and can be verified by inspecting small intervals $[r-\epsilon, r + \epsilon]$ for all r. In this sense these properties are local.

Exercise 7.4.1.[b] Assume RDU. For each $i = 1, \ldots, 98$, we write $r_i = i/100$. For each i we assume $9 \geq \alpha_i \geq 4$ such that

$$(r_i : 9, \ 0.01 : \alpha_i, \ (1 - r_i - 0.02) : 2, \ 0.01 : \mathbf{0}) \sim$$

$$(r_i : 9, \ 0.01 : \mathbf{4}, \ (1 - r_i - 0.02) : 2, \ 0.01 : \mathbf{1}).$$

Show that:

- If r_i is in a region where w is concave then α_i increases in i there. More specifically, if w is concave on $[r_i, r_i + 0.02]$ then $\alpha_{i+1} \geq \alpha_i$.
- If r_i is in a region where w is convex then α_i decreases in i there. More specifically, if w is convex on $[r_i, r_i + 0.02]$ then $\alpha_{i+1} \leq \alpha_i$. □

The following exercise presents a paradox put forward by Cox *et al.* (2007). (It is an analog for probability weighting of Rabin's well-known paradox for utility presented later, in Example 8.6.1). A list of choices that each by themselves seem to reflect weak risk aversion, together imply extreme risk aversion in the sense that $w(\frac{1}{2}) < 0.01$. We conclude that the individual choices by themselves do reflect extreme risk aversion after all. Such lists of choices differing only by common outcomes are called preference ladders by Wu & Gonzalez (1996).

Exercise 7.4.2.[c] Assume RDU. For each $i = 0, \ldots, 98$, we write $r_i = i/100$. Assume that a subject exhibits risk averse preferences as follows:

$$(r_i : 6, \ 0.01 : \mathbf{6}, \ 0.01 : \mathbf{0}, \ (1 - r_i - 0.02) : 0) \prec$$

$$(r_i : 6, \ 0.01 : \mathbf{2}, \ 0.01 : \mathbf{2}, \ (1 - r_i - 0.02) : 0)$$

and that, with $U(0) = 0$, $U(6)/U(2) > 2.1$. Show that $w(0.5) < 0.01$. □

7.5 An alternative direct way to directly investigate properties of nonlinear decision weights

The results and exercises of the preceding section were all based on tests of the sure-thing principle, with common outcomes replaced by other common outcomes. I briefly present another technique for directly testing qualitative properties of w, which is based on richness in the probability dimension. It will not be used in this book because we focus on richness in the outcome dimension. The alternative technique can be seen to be dual to the tradeoff utility measurement of Chapter 4, operating in the probability dimension in the same way as the tradeoff utility measurement operates in the outcome dimension (Abdellaoui & Wakker 2005 end of §1).

Example 7.5.1. Consider Figure 7.5.1. The question mark designates a preference yet to be determined, and we have $\gamma > \beta$. The probability p has rank r in both the first and the third prospect, and the probability q has rank r' in both the second and the fourth prospect. Determining your preference at the question mark amounts to

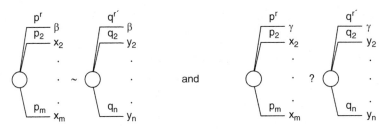

Figure 7.5.1 The superscript r indicates the rank of p, and is the same in the first and third prospect. The superscript r′ indicates the rank of q, and is the same in the second and fourth prospect.

determining whether, starting from the equivalence class of the two left prospects, you prefer an improvement of β into γ for the ranked probability p^r, or for the ranked probability $q^{r'}$. This will be determined by which decision weight is larger, $\pi(p^r)$ or $\pi(q^{r'})$ (using Lemma 6.5.4 to ensure same ranks). The only change regarding the RDU values of the prospects is that the third prospect yields $\pi(p^r)(U(\gamma) - U(\beta))$ more than the first, and the fourth yields $\pi(q^{r'})(U(\gamma) - U(\beta))$ more than the second. The preference between the third and fourth prospect, consequently, is in agreement with the ordering of $\pi(p^r)$ and $\pi(q^{r'})$, with the left prospect preferred if and only if $\pi(p^r) \geq \pi(q^{r'})$. The configuration of the figure thus gives a direct way to compare decision weights of different ranked probabilities, independently of utility.

We can use comparisons as just described for quantitative measurements. For example, if we find that $\pi(p_j^{p_{j-1}\,|\,\cdots+p_1})$ is the same for all j, for $p_1 + \cdots + p_n = 1$, then we can conclude that these decision weights are all 1/n. Then, for instance, $w(p_1 + \cdots + p_j) = j/n$ for all j. We can use the configuration in Figure 7.5.1 to test how decision weights depend on ranks and test for optimism, pessimism, and likelihood insensitivity. A full analysis of the empirical and theoretical implications of this technique is in Abdellaoui & Wakker (2005). They demonstrated that this method for measuring decision weights is dual to the measurement of utility using the t-indifference relation of Chapter 4.

You may have noticed the similarity between Figure 7.5.1 and Figure 6.5.1. It can be seen that Figure 7.5.1 does indeed do in the probability dimension what the $\sim^t$ and $\sim_c^t$ relations (depicted in Figure 6.5.1) do in the outcome dimension. This duality is similar to the duality between utility and rank-dependent probability weighting exploited in §5.5. We will not elaborate on this point. □

Assignment 7.5.1.[b] Assume RDU with $\gamma > \beta > 0$ and $\gamma \ominus \beta \sim_c^t \beta \ominus 0$, so that $U(\gamma) - U(\beta) = U(\beta) - U(0)$. Assume $U(0) = 0$. Write $r = (i-1)/100$ for some i. Consider indifferences of the form

$$(r : \gamma, \mathbf{p} : \gamma, (1 - r - p) : 0) \sim$$
$$(r : \gamma, \mathbf{1/100} : \boldsymbol{\beta}, \ \mathbf{1/100} : \boldsymbol{\beta}, \ (1 - r - 2/100) : 0)$$

Show that $p \leq 1/100$ for regions $(r, r + 2/100)$ where w is concave and $1/100 \leq p \leq 2/100$ for regions $(r, r + 2/100)$ where w is convex. Here p is an outcome probability and r is a rank. By varying the values $r = i/100$ we can investigate concavity and convexity of w throughout its domain [0,1]. □

7.6 Bad-news probabilities or loss-ranks

This section describes a duality in RDU that has confused many people when first studying this theory. The topic of this section can be skipped for a first study of RDU, but will be essential when we introduce prospect theory in later chapters. The confusion can arise if people take the probability weighting function w in isolation, without sufficient awareness that w should only weigh ranks (good-news probabilities) and not other kinds of probabilities or events. The point discussed here is conceptually important because it cautions against naïve interpretations of nonadditive measures as indexes of belief.

Imagine that someone criticizes rank-dependent utility theory as developed here, arguing that not good-news events, ranks, should be central, as they were in our analysis, but rather bad-news events should be. For an outcome we should determine not the probability r of getting something ranked better, but the probability ℓ of getting something ranked worse; ℓ is called the *loss-rank*. We then consider *loss-ranked probabilities* $p_{\setminus\ell}$, or, briefly, p_ℓ. Loss-ranks are denoted as subscripts, and not as superscripts (as are gain-ranks). We should transform those loss-ranks ℓ nonlinearly using a function denoted, say, z. The decision weight of an outcome should be the marginal contribution of its outcome probability to its loss-rank; i.e.,

$$\pi(p_\ell) = z(p + \ell) - z(\ell).$$

This argument leads to the evaluation of prospects $p_1 x_1 \cdots p_n x_n$, with $x_1 \geq \cdots \geq x_n$, by

$$\sum_{j=1}^{n} \pi_j U(x_j) = \sum_{j=1}^{n} \pi(p_{j_{p_{j+1}+\cdots+p_n}}) U(x_j) =$$
$$\sum_{j=1}^{n} (z(p_j + \cdots + p_n) - z(p_{j+1} + \cdots + p_n)) U(x_j). \qquad (7.6.1)$$

Some authors considered Eq. (7.6.1) under the assumption that z be the same as w in Definition 6.1.1 (RDU). To ensure that both equations generate the same ordering of prospects, it can then be demonstrated that w must be *symmetric*; i.e., $w(p) = 1 - w(1-p)$ (Gilboa 1989b; Nehring 1994; Sarin & Wakker 1997). The result was sometimes interpreted to be a paradox because a symmetry restriction for w is undesirable.

How can we respond to the aforementioned criticism and resolve the paradox? In agreement with this criticism, there seems to be no prior reason to privilege good-news probabilities over their bad-news counterparts, and ranks over loss-ranks. In Example 5.4.2, an increase of the rank of receiving more than 20 is the same as a decrease of the loss-rank of receiving less than 40, and loss-ranks just as well give useful information leading to clear decisions. In Exercise 5.4.1, it can also be shown that one prospect stochastically dominates another if and only if all its loss-ranks are smaller or equal. Hence, why not transform loss-ranks instead of ranks?

The key to the resolution of the paradox is what we alluded to before, being that one had better not think of the probability weighting function w in isolation. It is better to always keep in mind to what kind of events and probabilities w is to be applied. w is a rank-transformation function and it is applied to ranks, i.e., to good-news events/ probabilities. It is not applied to probabilities of the receipt of separate outcomes, as we explained before. Neither should it be applied to bad-news events or loss-ranks, the concepts considered by our critic. Similarly, one should not discuss ranks in isolation, as did the critic, without considering the probability weighting function to be used for them.

The next step in the resolution of the paradox is the demonstration that one can equally well consider loss-ranks as ranks. Then one should, however, not use our rank-weighting function[7] w, but another weighting function z, one for loss-ranks. We can call z the *loss-rank weighting function*, and w can also be called the *gain-rank weighting function*. The approach of the critic in Eq. (7.6.1), and RDU in Definition 6.1.1, then become identical, simply by defining the loss-rank weighting function as the *dual* of w:

$$z(p) = 1 - w(1 - p); \text{i.e. } w(p) = 1 - z(1 - p). \tag{7.6.2}$$

We next explain that Eq. (7.6.1) with z designating loss-ranks is indeed equivalent to Definition 6.1.1 with w for gain-ranks, so that z is indeed the appropriate loss-rank weighting function. Figure 7.6.1 illustrates that w and z are two sides of the same coin.

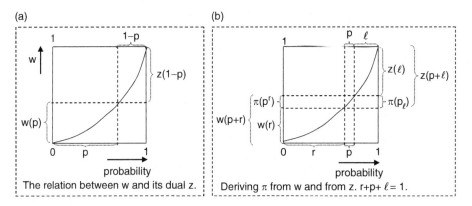

(a)

(b)

The relation between w and its dual z.   Deriving π from w and from z. $r+p+\ell = 1$.

Figure 7.6.1 w, z, and π.

For a prospect with outcome α and outcome probability p, we have for rank r and loss-rank ℓ,

$$\ell = 1 - p - r \text{ and } r = 1 - p - \ell. \tag{7.6.3}$$

Thus, the rank of p uniquely determines the loss-rank and vice versa, with p and its two ranks always summing to 1. The two ranks essentially comprise the same

---

[7] Had the, more appropriate, term rank-weighting function become the convention in decision theory rather than the term probability weighting function, our critic would not have had an opening to begin with.

information. Sometimes we use the term *gain-rank* rather than rank, to stress its difference from loss-rank.[8] Figure 7.6.1 now illustrates the following result.

Observation 7.6.1. Under Eq. (7.6.2), p's decision weight, $\pi(p)$, is $\pi(p^r)$, i.e., p's marginal w-contribution to p's gain-rank r, which is $\pi(p_\ell)$, i.e., p's marginal z-contribution to p's loss-rank ℓ. □

We can equally well take ranked probabilities and their w-decision weights, or loss-ranked probabilities and their z-decision weights, yielding identical decision theories. Which approach is taken is merely a matter of convenience, and not of substance, and all findings from one approach can be translated into findings from the other approach. For example, convex probability weighting of gain-ranks is equivalent to concave probability weighting of loss-ranks. Thus, we can now reassure the critic: It is immaterial which of the two approaches is taken, because they are completely equivalent.

Conclusion 7.6.2. When using a weighting function, always keep in mind the kind of events and probabilities that it should be applied to. We will use the weighting function w to be applied to ranks (good-news events and probabilities). We could equally well have used the loss-rank weighting function z defined in Eq. (7.6.2), then keeping in mind that this function is to be applied to loss-ranks. □

The early papers on rank dependence for risk mostly used loss-ranks, because those are used in definitions of distribution functions in probability theory and statistics (Chew, Karni, & Safra 1987).[9] Nowadays, however, gain-ranks are commonly used in rank-dependent theories for risk. Then w(p) is the value of receiving a utility unit with probability p and utility 0 otherwise. The convenience of this result is considered to be more important than the use of distribution functions. In rank dependence for uncertainty, the topic of later chapters, gain-ranks have been used from the beginning. Consistency between uncertainty and risk is another important reason for using gain ranks rather than loss ranks for risk.

Obviously, convexity of the loss-rank weighting function is to be equated with concavity of our gain-rank weighting function, and so on. For example, the underweighting of large loss-ranks ("probabilities") found in Loomes, Moffat, & Sugden (2002), a recent exception still using the loss-rank weighting function, should be equated with the overweighting of small gain-ranks ("probabilities") of our gain-rank weighting function. Fortunately, the field has converged almost universally to the conventions that we will also use.

The equivalence of gain and loss ranks was obtained within the revealed-preference paradigm followed in this book, where the only empirical inputs are observed preferences. The situation can change, and the good- or bad-news approaches need no longer be equivalent, if empirical inputs other than observed decisions are considered and are related to probability weighting. For example, imagine that

---

[8] ℓ can refer to loss or low. Later we will often use the symbol g rather than the symbol r for gain-ranks, with g referring to gain or good.

[9] For perfect agreement, the loss rank of an outcome can include the outcome probability.

neuroeconomic measurements[10] reveal cognitive patterns close to gain-rank weighting functions w and not close to loss-rank weighting functions z. Then we might prefer to use gain-ranks rather than loss-ranks.[11] In this book we will, however, restrict attention to revealed preference, in which case gain-rank and loss-rank probability weightings are data equivalent.

Any interpretation of w as reflecting belief or probability (mis)perception is to be left to speculations beyond revealed preference. Such speculations are important because proper future relations with concepts from other domains such as artificial intelligence, cognitive psychology, or neuroscience are important for the future of decision theory. Within the domain of revealed preference, however, any interpretation that assigns a privileged status, such as being an index of belief or being an index in updating, to one of w or z rather than to the other, is unfounded.

The negative parts of the integral definition of RDU in Eq. (6.9.1) and Figures 6.9.1 and 6.9.2 suggested that it may be more natural to use gain-ranks for gains and loss-ranks for losses. We will adopt this convention in prospect theory, where the distinction between gains and losses is substantial. Then the weight of outcome probability p for losses will be the value of receiving minus one utility unit with probability p and utility 0 otherwise, which will be convenient.

We end with a *notation*. As for gain-ranks, best and worst loss-ranks are indicated by letters b and w, which are now subscripts. p_w now denotes p_0 because 0 is the worst loss-rank possible (concerns the worst outcome of the prospect considered), and $p_b = p_{1-p}$ (concerns the best outcome of the prospect considered).

7.7 A formal definition of likelihood insensitivity (inverse-S)

There have been many discussions and empirical analyses of the inverse-S shape, being the empirically prevailing shape of probability weighting. However, no accessible formal definition has been provided in the literature yet. This absence has hampered the theoretical development of the concept. This section will give a formal definition, more accessible than definitions given before. The formal term will be likelihood insensitivity. I first illustrate the concept without using symbols, in Figure 7.7.1. The definition consists of three steps.

(1) Specify an insensitivity region in the middle where w is to be shallow.
(2) Decision weights at extremes dominate those in the middle.
(3) Impose no comparisons between the extreme regions.

The likelihood insensitivity concept is best remembered using, first, the insensitivity region and, then, using Steps 1–3. Figure 7.7.1′ adds symbols to Figure 7.7.1 that will

---

[10] Ramsey (1931, p. 161) suggested the term psychogalvanometer for such instruments.
[11] Camerer (2007 p. C34) suggested that neurostudies support the general pattern of likelihood insensitivity in Figures 7.1.2 and 7.1.3.

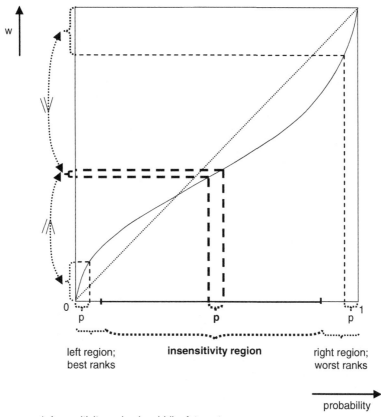

1. Insensitivity region is middle, fat, part.
2. Middle weight (solid left fat brace) is small.
3. Left lower dashed brace is not compared
   to left upper dashed brace.

Figure 7.7.1 Likelihood insensitivity (inverse-S).

be used in the formal definition. The notation and terminology regarding b_{rb} ("best-rank boundary") and w_{rb} ("worst-rank boundary") will be explained later.

Definition 7.7.1. w exhibits (*likelihood*) *insensitivity* with *insensitivity region* $[b_{rb}, w_{rb}]$ if we have

$$\pi(p^b) \geq \pi(p^r) \text{ on the left and middle region (i.e. on}^{12} [0, w_{rb}]) \qquad (7.7.1)$$

(left extreme dominates left and middle region)
and

$$\pi(p^w) \geq \pi(p^r) \text{ on the right and middle region (i.e. on}^{13} [b_{rb}, 1]) \qquad (7.7.2)$$

(right extreme dominates right and middle region). □

---

[12] The domain restriction is described as an inequality in Eq. (7.7.3).
[13] The domain restriction is described as an inequality in Eq. (7.7.4).

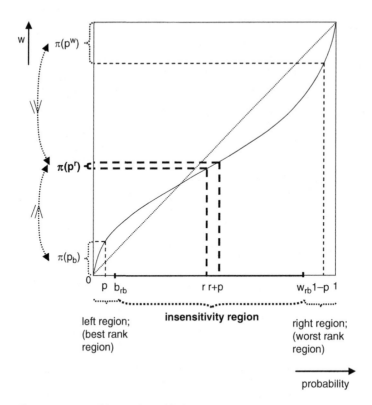

Figure 7.7.1′ Figure 7.7.1 with notation added.

The two inequalities in the definition reflect step 2, and the restrictions to regions reflect step 3. For example, to prevent weights from the left extreme to be compared to any weight at the right extreme (from $[w_{rb},1]$), Eq. (7.7.1) imposes the inequality only on the restriction of w to the left and middle region ($[0,w_{rb}]$, excluding the right region $[w_{rb},1]$). It only considers the case where all relevant probabilities (inputs of w) are contained in the left and middle region ($[0,w_{rb}]$). Those relevant probabilities are p and 0 for $\pi(p^b) = w(p) - w(0)$, and p + r and r for $\pi(p^r) = w(p + r) - w(r)$. It, obviously, suffices here that the largest of these probabilities, p + r, be contained in the left or middle region:

$$p + r \leq w_{rb}. \tag{7.7.3}$$

The particular w-function in Figure 7.7.1 has w steeper at rank r close to 1 than at r = 0, so that the inequality $\pi(p^b) \geq \pi(p^r)$ of Eq. (7.7.1) indeed cannot be imposed for ranks r from the right region ($[w_{rb},1]$), for this particular weighting function. This illustrates the necessity to restrict Eq. (7.7.1) to $[0,w_{rb}]$.

Similarly, the subdomain taken in Eq. (7.7.2) implies the inequality only for the right and middle region ($[b_{rb},1]$, excluding the left region $[0,b_{rb}]$). It concerns the case where all relevant probabilities (inputs of w) are contained in the right or middle region ($[b_{rb},1]$). Those relevant probabilities are 1 and $1-p$ for $\pi(p^w) = w(1) - w(1-p)$, and $p + r$ and r for $\pi(p^r) = w(p + r) - w(r)$. It, obviously, suffices here that the lowest of these probabilities, r, is in the right or middle region:

$$r \geq b_{rb}. \tag{7.7.4}$$

For the particular weighting function in Figure 7.7.1, Eq. (7.7.2) does hold on the whole domain $[0,1]$, so that the restriction to the right and middle region ($[b_{rb},1]$) was not necessary for this particular case. In general, however, we do not commit ourselves here to any inequalities outside the right and middle region. Expressed directly in terms of the weighting function w, the inequalities are as follows:

$$w(p) \geq w(p + r) - w(r) \text{ if } p + r \leq w_{rb}; \tag{7.7.5}$$

$$1 - w(1 - p) \geq w(p + r) - w(r) \text{ if } r \geq b_{rb}. \tag{7.7.6}$$

That the conditions for best and worst ranks are symmetric can be seen by considering loss-ranks in Eqs. (7.7.1), (7.7.3), and (7.7.5). For example, $p + r$ in Eq. (7.7.3) is a loss-rank in the same way as r in Eq. (7.7.4) is a gain-rank. We do not elaborate on this symmetry. I give some more terms that may be convenient. They need not be memorized for understanding the following text.

Definition 7.7.2. The interval to the left of the insensitivity region, i.e., $[0,b_{rb}]$, is the *best-rank region*. The interval to the right, $[w_{rb},1]$, is the *worst-rank region*. b_{rb} is the *best-rank boundary* and w_{rb} is the *worst-rank boundary*.[14] Eq. (7.7.1) reflects *best-rank overweighting* (on $[0,w_{rb}]$), and Eq. (7.7.2) reflects *worst-rank overweighting* (on $[b_{rb},1]$). □

Best-rank overweighting has sometimes been called subadditivity, or lower subadditivity (Tversky & Wakker 1995), and worst-rank overweighting has sometimes been called upper subadditivity (Tversky & Wakker 1995).

Unlike convexity and concavity, likelihood insensitivity is not a local property. That is, its verification for small outcome probabilities p need not imply the condition for large outcome probabilities p. We also have to verify the condition for large outcome probabilities p. Figure 7.7.2 depicts the condition for an outcome probability p larger than the one in Figure 7.7.1.

Exercise 7.7.1.[c] Reconsider Example 7.4.2 and the predictions for Figure 7.4.1. Formally derive the predictions of likelihood insensitivity there, where you need only predict weak inequalities and not the strict inequalities as claimed in §7.4. In doing so, specify for which insensitivity regions your reasoning works. That is, specify the required inequalities relating w_{rb} to p_3 and b_{rb} to p_2. □

---

[14] They were called boundary constants by Tversky & Wakker (1995).

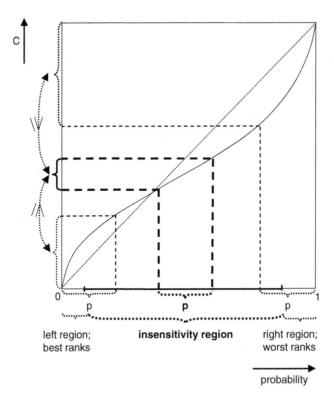

Figure 7.7.2 Likelihood insensitivity (inverse-S) for a large outcome probability p.

7.8 The choice of insensitivity region

We next discuss the choice of the insensitivity region, in other words, the choice of b_{rb} and w_{rb}.

Exercise 7.8.1.[a] Assume EU ($w(p) = p$ for all p). Show that likelihood insensitivity holds with the maximal insensitivity region [0,1]. (No elaboration given.) □

The following observation is stated formally and proved in the exercise that follows.

Observation 7.8.1. The larger the insensitivity region is, the more restrictive likelihood insensitivity is. □

Exercise 7.8.2.[b] Assume that w satisfies likelihood insensitivity with insensitivity region $[b_{rb}, w_{rb}]$, and assume that $[a_{rb}, a_{rw}] \subset [b_{rb}, w_{rb}]$; in other words, $b_{rb} \leq a_{rb} \leq a_{rw} \leq w_{rb}$. Show that w satisfies likelihood insensitivity with insensitivity region $[a_{rb}, a_{rw}]$. □

The following exercise shows that neo-additive weighting functions have close-to-maximal insensitivity regions.

Exercise 7.8.3.[b] Assume that w is neo-additive (Eq. (7.2.5)). Show that w satisfies likelihood insensitivity with insensitivity region $[b_{rb}, w_{rb}]$ for each $0 < b_{rb} < w_{rb} < 1$. □

As demonstrated in Exercise 7.8.3, the neo-additive weighting functions in Figs. 7.1.3a and b depicted extreme cases. Any subinterval $[b_{rb}, w_{rb}]$ of (0,1) can be chosen as insensitivity region. In practice, [0.05, 0.95] is a good choice of the insensitivity region. Empirically, the conditions are usually satisfied for larger regions, with for instance [0.00, 0.963] the largest possible indifference region for the function advanced by Tversky & Kahneman (1992) (Eqs. (7.2.1) and (7.2.2)), as a mathematical analysis can show. For most of the desirable empirical implications, smaller regions suffice. Therefore, the theory is not very sensitive to the particular insensitivity region chosen. We will thus not incorporate the insensitivity region in pragmatic measures of likelihood sensitivity developed later.

In practice, worst-rank overweighting is usually stronger than best-rank over-weighting, and b_{rb} can usually be taken to be 0. Then by Eq. (7.7.2), w's jump from $p = 1$ to $p = \frac{1}{2}$ exceeds that from $p = \frac{1}{2}$ to $p = 0$, so that the w-graph intersects the diagonal of the identity function below $\frac{1}{2}$ and we have $w(\frac{1}{2}) \leq \frac{1}{2}$.

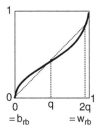

Figure 7.8.1 Finding b_{rb} and w_{rb}.

Figure 7.8.1 illustrates an easy graphical way of finding the maximal value of w_{rb} for such functions that works in virtually all practical cases. The value q is taken such that, with the diagonal line as in the figure, $\pi(q^q) = \pi(q^b)$; i.e., $w(2q) = 2w(q)$. If we substitute $p = r = q$ in Eq. (7.7.1), then the inequality holds weakly; i.e., it is an equality. For a larger probability $t > q$, $\pi(t^t) > \pi(t^b)$, and, with $p = r = t$, Eq. (7.7.1) is violated. As numerical analyses of many parametric functions have demonstrated, $w(2q) = 2w(q)$ usually implies that we can take $w_{rb} = 2q$. Then w_{rb} can, obviously, also be any smaller value.

7.9 Discussion of likelihood insensitivity

Likelihood insensitivity reflects diminishing sensitivity for a scale bounded from two sides. This concept originated from inspection of empirical data as in Fig. 7.1.2b. It suggests a new psychological concept (the cognitive likelihood insensitivity), and new mathematical tools have to be developed to analyze this phenomenon. These tools are different from the well-known tools of convex analyses that can be used to study the motivational (value-based) pessimism-component in Fig. 7.1.1b. The first formal definitions of likelihood insensitivity were given by Tversky & Wakker (1995). They were tested by Tversky & Fox (1995) and Wu & Gonzalez (1999 p. 155), under the name of bounded subadditivity. Tversky & Wakker (1995) and Tversky & Fox (1995) also formalized and tested qualitative comparisons of insensitivity. Quantitative measures are proposed in the next section.

Likelihood insensitivity can be related to regression to the mean. It is not a statistical artifact resulting from data analysis with noise, though, but it is a psychological phenomenon, describing how people perceive and weigh probabilities in decisions. In weighting probabilities, a regression to the mean takes place, with people failing to discriminate sufficiently between intermediate probabilities and taking them all too much as the same ("50–50," "don't know"). The parameters a and b of neo-additive weighting functions (Figure 7.2.4) that determine the degree of likelihood insensitivity can be compared to the intercept and slope in linear regressions. They reflect how responsive an agent's perception of likelihood is to probability. Tversky & Wakker (1995 p. 1266) suggested, tongue-in-cheek, that this responsiveness provide a good measure of rationality.

An important point underlying the inverse-S shape is that, in the process of decision making, probabilities are ingredients for determining decisions by the decision maker, and not the other way around. For further discussion of the role of dependent and independent variables, and the particular noise in their relationship when generating inverse-S shapes, see Erev, Wallsten, & Budescu (1994) and Brenner (2000). The latter also discussed the overconfidence found in calibrations of subjective probabilities.

Whereas people will mostly be little sensitive to probability – Carthy et al. (1999 p. 188) inferred this from tape recordings – there may be special circumstances in which people become oversensitive to probability. Then the opposite of likelihood insensitivity results, with low probabilities underweighted and high probabilities overweighted. Experiments by Hertwig et al. (2003), elaborated on and extended in several other papers, found such phenomena. One interpretation of their findings is that their setup makes people overly sensitive to probabilities and uncertainty, and undersensitive to the outcomes.

In general, probability weighting is a less stable component than outcome utility. According to many, including the author, probability weighting is irrational and will be reduced with proper learning and incentives (van de Kuilen 2009). Its shape is, then, influenced by details of perception, and concerns a volatile phenomenon. Therefore, findings on probability weighting cannot be expected to be as stable as findings on utility curvature.

Ebert & Prelec (2007) systematically analyzed the effects of insensitivity for time duration (for intertemporal choice, see Interpretation D.3 in Appendix D). Many studies have found that people are very insensitive to time duration (Ainslie 2001; Ebert & Prelec 2007; Kahneman 1994; Zauberman, Bettman, & Malkoc 2005). They seem to be more so than to probability. A difference between probability and time is that the probability scale is bounded from two sides, whereas the time scale for future decisions is commonly taken to be bounded from one side (the present) only.

7.10   Indexes of pessimism and likelihood insensitivity

The following indexes of pessimism for probability weighting may be plausible at first sight. We may consider the difference $p - w(p)$ for some p, say $p = \frac{1}{2}$, or its average over some p's. Alternatively, we can find the power c such that $w(p) = p^c$ best fits the data and take c as pessimism index, similar to the CRRA measure $1 - \theta$ of risk aversion for power utility $U(\alpha) = \alpha^\theta$ (§3.5). Indeed, early studies of probability weighting usually considered power weighting functions (Hey & Orme 1994; Harless & Camerer 1994).

A drawback of the measures just proposed is that the degree of pessimism in these ways will depend much on the probabilities considered. For small probabilities at high gains, for instance, people often exhibit optimism rather than pessimism. This dependence comes as no surprise in view of the prominence of likelihood insensitivity. Better estimations will result if we distinguish pessimism and likelihood insensitivity, and provide an index of both. Then the estimation of pessimism reckons with likelihood sensitivity.

One way to obtain indexes of pessimism and likelihood sensitivity is to fit a probability weighting function from Prelec's compound invariance family $((exp(-(-ln(p))^a))^b)$ or from Goldstein & Einhorn's (1987) family $(bp^a/(bp^a + (1-p)^a))$, and in either case take parameter a as an index of likelihood insensitivity and parameter b as an index of pessimism. Based on a suggestion by Craig Fox (1995 personal communication), I will rather use neo-additive weighting functions

$$w(p) = b + ap \text{ for } 0<p<1 \tag{7.10.1}$$

(see Eq. (7.2.5)) to obtain the parameter a as an index of likelihood sensitivity and $(2b + a)/2$ as an index of optimism. I use the neo-additive family primarily because its parameters are best suited for the interpretations and concepts of interest here, irrespective of whether they best fit the data.

Example 7.10.1 [Deterministic indexes of pessimism and likelihood insensitivity assuming linear utility]. Assume that we measure

$$CE(100_{0.9}0) = 77; CE(100_{0.1}0) = 13.$$

We assume $U(\alpha) = \alpha$. The CEs give

$$(b + a \times 0.90) \times 100 = 77 \text{ and } (b + a \times 0.10) \times 100 = 13.$$

The difference gives $(a \times 0.80) \times 100 = 64$ so that $a = 0.80$, implying $b = 0.05$. We have optimism index $(2b + a)/2 = 0.45$ and likelihood sensitivity index $a = 0.80$. □

We next consider an example with a richer data set, where we also allow utility curvature.

Example 7.10.2 [Estimation of pessimism and likelihood insensitivity]. Say we observe the CEs in Table 7.10.1.

Table 7.10.1. *CEs*

prospect	$100_{1/2}0$	$100_{1/2}50$	$100_{0.1}0$	$100_{0.1}50$	$100_{0.9}0$	$100_{0.9}50$
CE	40	70	15	60	68	85

Assuming power utility $U(\alpha) = \alpha^{\theta}$ and neo-additive probability weighting, the best fit is obtained for $\theta = 0.89$, a $= 0.65$, and b $= 0.12$, with distance[15] \$0.88. We obtain likelihood sensitivity a $= 0.65$ and optimism index $(2b+a)/2 = 0.45$. □

By filtering out the cognitive likelihood sensitivity component, we obtain better indexes of the motivational optimism and pessimism. The indexes proposed here can, for instance, be used in between-person regressions to investigate which factors affect pessimism and insensitivity. They can also be used for within-person comparisons at different time points (Epstein 2008 §5.3; Wu 1999) or for between-person comparisons.

Exercise 7.10.1[b] [Deterministic indexes of pessimism and likelihood insensitivity assuming linear utility]. Redo the analysis of Example 7.10.1, but instead assume observations

$$CE(100_{0.1}0) = 17; \quad CE(100_{0.9}0) = 75.$$

Exercise 7.10.2[b] [Estimation of pessimism and likelihood insensitivity]. Redo the analysis of Example 7.10.2, but now with the following observed CEs. □

Table 7.10.2. *CEs*

prospect	$100_{1/2}0$	$100_{1/2}50$	$100_{0.1}0$	$100_{0.1}50$	$100_{0.9}0$	$100_{0.9}50$
CE	34	69	08	56	63	83

□

7.11 Binary rank-dependent utility

In between the restricted domain of prospects with only one nonzero outcome considered in §5.1 and the general domain of all finitely valued prospects considered in subsequent sections, there is a useful intermediate domain: the domain of all *binary* (= two-outcome) *prospects* $\alpha_p\beta$. This domain includes all degenerate prospects (p $= 0$ or p $= 1$). *Binary rank-dependent utility*[16] holds if RDU holds on the domain of all binary prospects. That is:

For $\alpha \geq \beta$, $\alpha_p\beta$ is evaluated by $w(p)U(\alpha) + (1 - w(p))U(\beta)$. (7.11.1)

---

[15] The theoretically predicted CEs are given by $100_{1/2}0 \sim 40.26$; $100_{1/2}50 \sim 71.78$; $100_{0.1}0 \sim 15.02$; $100_{0.1}50 \sim 58.95$; $100_{0.9}0 \sim 67.52$; $100_{0.9}50 \sim 84.87$.

[16] This term was used by Luce (1991; 2000). Ghirardato and Marinacci (2001a) used the term biseparable utility and Miyamoto (1988) used the term generic utility.

The set of binary prospects is rich enough to identify utility U and probability weighting w. The measurement of utility in §4.1, adapted to RDU in §6.5.1 with a measurement of w included in Observation 6.5.8, indeed did only use binary prospects (Abdellaoui 2000; Bleichrodt & Pinto 2000). We need only observe binary prospects to uniquely determine the complete risk attitude, and all preferences between all prospects, under RDU. An advantage of binary prospects is that they are easier to process for subjects in experiments than multi-outcome prospects are, and this will reduce biases.

Binary RDU had been known long before Quiggin (1982) extended the theory to general prospects.[17] Indeed, the main novelty of Quiggin's idea shows up only for three or more outcomes. For binary prospects, probabilities only have best or worst ranks and the theory is relatively simple. A useful feature of the restricted domain of binary prospects is that most of the other nonexpected utility theories are still in agreement with RDU there. They only deviate for three or more outcomes. Hence, the results derived for binary prospects, including the utility measurement of §4.1, are relevant for all those theories. Although those other theories have not been defined at this stage, we state the result. Original prospect theory will be defined in §9.8.[18]

Observation 7.11.1. For binary prospects, the following theories are of the form in Eq. (7.11.1): (a) Birnbaum's (2008a) RAM and TAX models; (b) Gul's (1991) disappointment aversion theory; (c) Kahneman & Tversky's (1979) original prospect theory when restricted to gains or to losses; Viscusi's (1989) prospective reference theory. □

Appendix 7.12   Alternative definition of likelihood insensitivity: first concave and then convex

Inverse-S shapes have sometimes been formalized as *cavexity*, i.e., concavity of w up to some probability t, the inflection point, followed by convexity. In terms of marginal decision weights $\pi(p^r)$ for small p, these then decrease in r from $r = 0$ to $r = t$, and increase from there on. Typically, t is approximately 0.3.

There are some drawbacks to the cavexity concept. First, it does not control the level of w(t), even though this level is crucial for the global shape of w and for the risk attitudes implied. Figure 7.12.1 illustrates this point. All functions are concave on [0,t] and convex on [t,1]. The highest curve, in Fig. a, is steeper in the middle of the

---

[17] Allais (1953b, Eq. 19.1 on p. 50 in the English translation of 1979); Birnbaum, Parducci, & Gifford (1971) for 50–50 prospects; Edwards (1954 p. 398 and Figure 3); Goldstein & Einhorn (1987 Eq. 1); Pfanzagl (1959 p. 287 under symmetry of w). Kahneman & Tversky invented it independently around 1977–1978 (Kahneman, email of January 22, 2008), after the first unpublished version of their prospect theory (Kahneman & Tversky 1975), so as to reduce violations of stochastic dominance, and it was used by Kahneman & Tversky (1979).

[18] Gul (1991 p. 677) indicated that his disappointment aversion theory is a special case of RDU for binary prospects; this observation was used by Abdellaoui & Bleichrodt (2007). For Birnbaum's and Viscusi's theories, the derivation is straightforward; Birnbaum (2008a p. 487) indicated the agreement with PT for binary prospects.

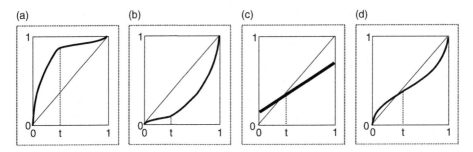

Figure 7.12.1 Cavex functions with different levels of inflection points.

region, to the left of t, than near 1, contrary to empirical findings. The lowest curve, in Fig. b, is steeper in the middle of the region, to the right of t, than near 0, again contrary to empirical findings. The level of w(t) – determining the average derivative of w on [0,t] and on [t,1] – is more important for the empirically implied optimism or pessimism than the local property of w being concave or convex there.

The aforementioned problem can be avoided by requiring that the inflection point be at the diagonal. There remain, however, some other drawbacks discussed next.

A second drawback of the cavexity definition is that it treats all probabilities in [0,t] alike without expressing that there is much curvature near 0 and little near other probabilities, with similar dual problems on [t,1]. Likelihood insensitivity mostly concerns the big jumps at 0 and 1. The definition of likelihood insensitivity (inverse S) chosen by Tversky & Fox (1995), Tversky & Wakker (1995), and presented in this book, focuses on the jumps at the extremes. It does not impose a particular commitment on curvature in the middle region because not much curvature is expected to be found there. The definition seeks to stay close to the shape of neo-additive weighting functions (Figure 7.2.4).[19]

A third difficulty concerns the focus on the inflection point t in the definition of cavexity. For empirical purposes, the exact location of t is not important or critical. There commonly is a large middle region where w is close to linear, and it does not matter much if the function is slightly convex or slightly concave there. The inflection point can equally well be 0.2 as 0.7, and minor perturbations of w may greatly affect the exact location of t. Yet, logically, the location of t crucially matters under cavexity because different locations give contradictory requirements on the domain in between. For t = 0.2 and t = 0.7, the definition of cavexity imposes opposite requirements on the domain [0.2, 0.7] in between. For likelihood insensitivity we also have to specify different regions, where the exact location does not matter very much. Here different specifications of insensitivity regions do not lead to mutually

---

[19] It also stays close to the curve of probability weighting in Figure 4 in Kahneman & Tversky (1979). The primary phenomenon exhibited in the latter figure concerns, indeed, the jumps at 0 and 1. Many authors interpreted this curve to primarily reflect convexity in the middle region. This convexity is, however, weak and the curve can be described as close to linear. Convexity in the middle region was not important to the authors who drew the curve by hand (Tversky, personal communication).

contradictory requirements, but only to more or less restrictive requirements (Exercise 7.8.2). This state of affairs combines better with the empirical status of the inflection point.

Appendix 7.13   Proofs for Chapter 7

Proof of Theorem 7.4.1. See Wakker (1994 Theorem 25e,f). □

8 Where prospect theory deviates from rank-dependent utility and expected utility: reference dependence versus asset integration

Prospect theory, defined in the next chapter, adds a new component to classical theories, namely reference dependence, which is the topic of this chapter. This component is of a different nature than concepts we have defined so far. It depends on aspects of framing and entails, I think, a bigger deviation from rationality than probability weighting. It is so volatile that it is hard to model theoretically (Fatas, Neugebauer, & Tamborero 2007; Kühberger, Schulte-Mecklenbeck, & Perner 1999), and much of the handling of reference dependence takes place in the modeling stage preceding the quantitative analyses presented in this book. Hence, up till now hardly any theory has been developed for reference dependence. Nevertheless, this deviation is of major empirical importance. I think that more than half of the risk aversion empirically observed has nothing to do with utility curvature or with probability weighting. Instead, it is generated by loss aversion, the main empirical phenomenon regarding reference dependence. Hence, this chapter will discuss reference dependence, even though, unlike the remainder of this book, it will have little theory and few quantitative assessments, and there will be almost no exercises either.

Before we can discuss reference dependence, two subtle points have to be clarified that have raised much confusion in the literature. First, inconsistencies that can arise between asset integration and isolation for moderate stakes (§8.1) will not be due to inappropriateness of either principle. Rather, they result from another cause: overly strong deviations from risk neutrality for moderate stakes (§8.2). Second, the essence of reference dependence is not that outcomes are modeled as changes with respect to some reference point. This way of modeling outcomes has been common throughout history, with "initial wealth" usually not expressed in the outcomes. This way of modeling is, therefore, not novel (§8.3 and §8.4, formalized in §8.9).[1] It is only after we have articulated these points that we can explain the novelty of reference dependence, being that the reference point can change during the analysis (§8.5, 8.9). And it

---

[1] Early and clear discussions are in Edwards (1954 p. 400), Edwards (1962 p. 116), and Pfanzagl (1959) who distinguished between money in front of the subject and money in the pocket of the subject.

is only then that the relationship with total wealth is broken. A careful discussion of this point in Kahneman & Tversky (1979), and misunderstandings about this point, are presented in §8.5 and §8.6. We will henceforth use the common term *final wealth* rather than *total wealth*.

8.1 A choice paradox

Consider the choice situations in Figs. 8.1.1a and b; do not yet consider Fig. 8.1.1c. Determine your preference in both situations.

The majority of subjects have a clear preference for the upper branch in Fig. 8.1.1a, exhibiting risk aversion. In Fig. 8.1.1b, the majority have a clear preference for the lower branch, exhibiting risk seeking, which deviates from the economic assumption of universal risk aversion. The choice in Fig. b seems to violate the predictions of the common RDU model, where w(½), the decision weight of the highest outcome 0 of the prospect, is supposed to be underweighted. Such underweighting will enhance risk aversion, in contrast to the risk seeking found in Fig. 8.1.1b. Figs. a and b suggest that people behave differently towards losses than towards gains.

The finding in Fig. 8.1.1b could be accommodated by RDU, by assuming that utility for losses is very convex. With w(½) = 0.42 and U(0) = 0, an inequality U(−50) < 0.58U(−100) could accommodate the preference. Although utility for losses may indeed be convex as we will see later, the strong degree of convexity implied here is not plausible. Something else must be going on, requiring a departure from RDU. As we will see later (§8.5), a fundamental departure from all classical decision models underlies the observed choices.

Now consider Fig. 8.1.1c, where a choice must be made between the same two loss-prospects as in Fig. b, but the news has just been received that a tax refund of $100 has been added to your bank account. How would you choose between the two loss-prospects after receipt of this news? In the mental accounting that many people

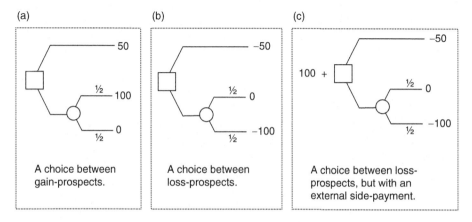

(a)   (b)   (c)

A choice between   A choice between   A choice between loss-
gain-prospects.   loss-prospects.   prospects, but with an
                                                    external side-payment.

Figure 8.1.1

adopt (Thaler 1985), the tax refund will be separated from a present prospect choice (*isolation*; Read, Loewenstein, & Rabin, 1999, use the term narrow bracketing). The choice in Fig. c will be the same as in Fig. b, exhibiting risk seeking again. If, however, you let your choice depend on your final wealth (*asset integration*), which seems to be normatively warranted, then you will integrate the outcomes in Fig. c. Such integration leads to the same choice as in Fig. a, and most subjects will then be risk averse. An inconsistency has resulted.

8.2   A discussion and the real culprit of the paradox

It has traditionally been accepted in economics that the choice of the utility function is a subjective choice to be made by the agent. As soon as some elementary requirements – e.g., monotonicity and, possibly, concavity – are satisfied, the choice of utility cannot be considered irrational, no matter what utility is (Gilboa, Postlewaite, & Schmeidler 2008 p. 181). It is usually not considered to be irrational if utility is extremely concave, for instance. Similarly, degrees of risk aversion are commonly considered subjective characteristics of agents that cannot be criticized for being irrational, even if they are extreme. With this understanding, the paradox just obtained presents a true dilemma, as we will see. The recommendations of asset integration and isolation then are mutually incompatible, and one of these has to give. Which one do you think it should be at this point?

The rational status of asset integration seems, and indeed should be beyond doubt, so that the choices in Figs. a and c should be the same. Then, the isolation of the prospect choice from the extra $100 in Fig. c seems to be the major culprit underlying the inconsistency revealed.

The conclusion just arrived at is at variance with a recommendation from Chapter 1 – additivity in §1.5. It was recommended there that choices be unaffected by small side payments for outcomes as modest as considered here ("additivity"). Then isolation is justified, and the prospect choice in Fig. c can be separated from the extra $100, implying the same choice in Figs. b and c. Indeed, we do commonly isolate our everyday decisions. None of us are aware of the exact variation of the wealth of our assets during the last 24 hours, and we are not able to integrate all of our assets even if we want to. Bounded rationality prevents us from doing so. We lack the calculation power to continuously keep track of all of our assets. For this reason, inconsistencies cannot be avoided.

There is, however, more to the paradox than bounded rationality. In normative discussions in this book, we ignore bounded rationality, and assume unlimited calculation capacities. Then asset integration is appropriate, which restores the paradox.

I believe that neither asset integration nor isolation should be abandoned. It then follows that the choices should be the same in Figs. a, b, and c! The real culprit of the inconsistency lies in the risk attitudes exhibited. There is too much risk aversion in Fig. a, and too much risk seeking in Fig. b. Risk neutrality for small stakes, or very weak risk aversion, is to be recommended (Burks *et al.* 2009; Kahneman & Lovallo

1993). Thus, I do not think that utility should be accepted whatever it is. It can be recommended that utility for small stakes should be approximately linear. And, thus, the "understanding" described in the first paragraph of this section should be abandoned. For a contrary view, see Arkes (1991 p. 495).

For readers who really do not want to be risk neutral for the moderate stakes considered, and who maintain a clear preference for risk aversion in Fig. a and for risk seeking in Fig. b, isolation and additivity should be abandoned. Then risk aversion will result in Fig. c as it does in Fig. a. Isolation and additivity do indeed amount to risk neutrality, with linear utility, as we saw in Chapter 1. They must necessarily be violated under risk aversion and risk seeking.

The paradox in Figure 8.1.1 is subtle. It is only if two, often debated, principles are both accepted (asset integration + isolation) that the paradox arises. The major culprit is, however, neither of the two often debated principles, but instead it is a third one, one that has not been debated much. The major culprit is the assumption that any utility function, no matter how nonlinear, is acceptable as soon as it satisfies some minimal requirements such as monotonicity. An illuminating exposition of this point is in Tversky & Kahneman (1981). The following finding (similar to Assignment 1.6.10, and verified with real incentives) is, I think, one of the most impressive paradoxes in the literature.

Example 8.2.1. (Tversky & Kahneman 1981 Problem 3). Subjects had to jointly make the following two choices:
$240_{1/4}240$ versus $1000_{1/4}0$
$0_{1/4}-1000$ versus $-750_{1/4}-750$.
The majority of subjects (73%) chose both left prospects, resulting in $240_{1/4}-760$. Choosing both right prospects leads to the superior, stochastically dominating, $250_{1/4}-750$. The majority choice was clearly irrational. The cause is a combination of much deviation from risk neutrality and absence of asset integration. Given the moderate amounts, the latter absence is reasonable according to Chapter 1, and the real culprit is the deviation from risk neutrality. □

The same insight as above is central to Benartzi & Thaler (1995). The combination of myopic accounting and asset integration play their part in generating the equity premium puzzle, but it is extreme loss aversion (defined later) that is the real culprit. An example similar to Figure 8.1.1 is in Raiffa (1968 §4.9) who, however, does not explicitly discuss isolation and asset integration. Before turning to the major deviations from classical theories that result from modeling the phenomena just discussed, we discuss another point: the difference between initial wealth and reference points.

8.3 Deviations from a fixed reference point ("initial wealth") as nothing but an alternative way of modeling final wealth, and of incorporating some empirical improvements

The example in the preceding section illustrated that people often process outcomes not in terms of final wealth, but by taking a reference point, usually their status quo, and by processing outcomes as deviations from the reference point. We discussed the example from a normative perspective. Reference dependence is, however, empirically prevailing, so that we now turn to modeling it for descriptive purposes. Before getting to this modeling, in §8.5, we need some preparation.

Bipolar perceptions of continua as in the preceding section, with a neutrality point chosen and the two relative sides of the scale perceived as qualitatively different categories, have been observed in many psychological domains (Nowlis & Nowlis 1956; Peeters & Czapinski 1990; Russell & Carroll 1999; Schimmack 2001). If we experience warmth, then there is a distinctive neutrality point: "neither hot nor cold." The other perceptions are perceived relative to that. In color vision, white is perceived as neutral. As in other domains, the corresponding physical level is adapted to circumstances, so that our perception focuses on contrasts ("neutrality adaptation"; Hurvich & Jameson 1951; see also Hevell & Kingdom 2008 and Grabisch & Labreuche 2008 §3). Based on a large-scale study, Nichol & Epstein (2008) argued for a separate treatment of gains and losses for health outcomes. Tom *et al.* (2007) provided neural data, and Hardisty & Weber (2009) provided intertemporal data.

In all choices considered so far in this book, we did not express outcomes in terms of the total assets of subjects. This would require an assessment of the total value of the subjects' bank accounts and other wealth (their status quo), and a description of outcomes as the sum of the total wealth plus what was added during the analysis. Rather, we expressed outcomes as the extra money that subjects received in addition to their status quo. We will call this status quo the *initial wealth*, denoted I. The same procedure has been used throughout history in virtually all experiments and analyses of EU and of other models in the literature, to the best of my knowledge. Because in all these cases the initial wealth – the total wealth of the subject except the outcomes (additional payments) – is fixed, there is a unique relation between the outcomes and the final wealth of the subjects. Hence, we say that payments are in terms of final wealth, even though the latter was never specified. For the same reason, classical EU is said to concern final wealth.

In Figure 8.1.1 something else happened, because the point of comparison was not kept fixed during the analysis, but varied between different choices. Subjects process outcome -100 in Fig. 8.1.1c the same way as in Fig. 8.1.1b, even though its final wealth is different (100 higher) in Fig. 8.1.1c. The point of comparison in Fig. 8.1.1c is different (100 higher). Such potentially variable points of comparison will be called reference points in later sections. In this section and the next, we focus on one fixed reference point, the initial wealth. The theory presented in the next section will be used in analyses of prospect theory presented later.

8.4 Loss aversion defined

The main empirical phenomenon concerning the distinction between gains and losses is loss aversion. It implies that people are more sensitive to losses than to gains. If a person gains 10 on the first two days, and loses 10 on the third day, then the total unhappiness felt because of the one loss may exceed the total happiness felt because of the two gains. "Losses loom larger than gains" (Kahneman & Tversky, 1979). The phenomenon can be modeled by a regular *basic utility function* u and a *loss aversion parameter* $\lambda > 0$, with $u(0) = 0$, and the utility function U of the form

$$U(\alpha) = u(\alpha) \text{ for } \alpha \geq 0$$

$$U(\alpha) = \lambda u(\alpha) \text{ for } \alpha < 0. \tag{8.4.1}$$

The idea behind this definition is that u captures the intrinsic value of outcomes and satisfies usual regularity conditions such as being smooth and differentiable at $\alpha = 0$, and λ is a factor separate from u. To distinguish U from u, we sometimes call U the *overall utility*. The unqualified term utility will continue to refer to U. We use the following scaling conventions for u and λ, which are plausible if u is differentiable at 0 and is approximately linear on the small interval $[-1,1]$. These points are discussed further in §8.8.

$$u(1) = 1, \ u(-1) = -1, \ U(1) = 1, \ \text{so that } \lambda = -U(-1). \tag{8.4.2}$$

This scaling convention was adopted implicitly by Tversky & Kahneman (1992), who chose $u(\alpha) = \alpha^\theta$ for gains and $u(\alpha) = -(-\alpha)^{\theta'}$ for $\alpha < 0$, with a θ' that possibly differs from θ. These scaling choices amount to the convention of $u(1) = 1$ and $u(-1) = -1$, as in Eq. (8.4.2). We will see in §9.6 that the power family, although often used, has some analytical problems and should be used with caution when analyzing loss aversion.

Loss aversion holds if $\lambda > 1$, so that losses are overweighted relative to gains. The opposite, $\lambda < 1$, will not often be found. Whereas loss aversion suggests avoidance of losses with little attention for gains, $\lambda < 1$ suggests a seeking for gains with little attention for losses. Hence $\lambda < 1$ is called *gain seeking*. With the plausible convention of u being differentiable at zero, loss aversion generates nondifferentiability of U at zero (Figure 8.4.1), and the kink is a measure of loss aversion. Mathematically, loss aversion can be interpreted as extreme, "infinite," concavity of U at $\alpha = 0$. The earliest reference to such a shape of utility that I am aware of is Robertson (1915 p. 135).

Commonly, λ is interpreted to reflect utility, where for $\lambda = 2$, for instance, the pain of losses is felt twice as much as the joy of gains. One may also interpret λ as concerning decision weights. Then the pain of losses is felt just as much as the pleasure of gains, but still losses are taken as twice as important for decisions as gains. The latter overweighting can be deliberate, if a decision maker thinks that more attention should be paid to losses than to gains, or perceptual, with losses simply drawing more attention (Peeters & Czapinski 1990 p. 46 top). The latter paper discussed the psychological backgrounds of the different interpretations in detail.

Kahneman and Tversky and many others working on prospect theory used the term value function instead of utility function. They did so to stress that outcomes are changes with respect to a given point. This given point is initial wealth in this section.

(a)   (b)

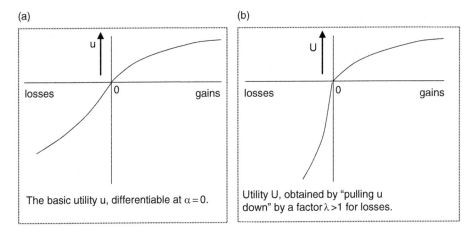

The basic utility u, differentiable at $\alpha = 0$.   Utility U, obtained by "pulling u down" by a factor $\lambda > 1$ for losses.

Figure 8.4.1 Loss aversion.

It can be a more general reference point in the following sections. This book continues to call U a utility function.

All topics discussed in this section, with initial wealth as one fixed reference point, concern traditional approaches. Although these topics will generate some descriptive improvements, they cannot explain the choice anomaly of Figure 8.1.1. This anomaly entails a major breakaway from traditional theories, discussed in the next section. A phenomenon that can be explained by loss aversion as modeled at this stage will be presented in Example 9.3.2.

8.5 Deviations from a variable reference point as a major breakaway from final-wealth models

The stimuli that generate a neutral experience may be different in different contexts. For the perception of warmth, a common demonstration involves two pails of warm water, one warmer than the other. A subject who immerses one hand in one of these pails and another hand in the other pail will eventually report that both hands feel alike, neither hot nor cold. Although the objective temperature is different, the neutral experience itself is nevertheless similar for the two different hands.

In decision under risk, the neutral reference point may similarly be related to different final-wealth positions in different choice situations. We will use the term *reference point* rather than initial wealth to refer to such points of comparison that can vary during the analysis. The phenomenon occurs in Figs. 8.1.1b and c. The extra $100 in Fig. c is not integrated with the payments of the prospect, leading to Fig. a. Rather, it is integrated with the reference point, leading to a prospect choice as in Fig. b, but with a different reference point. In such a case, an outcome such as -100 is not uniquely related to a final wealth position, but is related to a different final wealth position in Fig. b than in Fig. c.

It is only if reference points vary that the modeling of outcomes as changes with respect to a reference point really deviates from the modeling of outcomes as (referring to) final wealth. Such deviations entail major irrationalities, such as different choices in Figs. 8.1.1a and c, but are empirically realistic and constitute a primary cause for descriptive violations of classical decision models.

Example 8.5.1. Kahneman & Tversky (1979) tested the following two problems, where I use their numbering of the problems but our notation.

Problem 11: In addition to whatever you own, you have been given 1,000. You are now asked to choose between $1000_{1/2}0$ and 500.

Problem 12: In addition to whatever you own, you have been given 2,000. You are now asked to choose between $-1000_{1/2}0$ and -500.

They found an 84 percent majority choice for certainty in Problem 11, and a 69 percent majority choice against certainty in Problem 12. □

In the preceding example, Kahneman & Tversky carefully chose a framing that generated a different reference point in their subjects' perception, whereas in terms of final wealth the two problems are identical. Had the subjects gone by final wealth, we would have found the same result with either preference *for* certainty in both problems, or preference *against* certainty in both problems. The difference found must have been caused by the different reference points. It was only from that that the authors concluded: "the carriers of value or utility are changes of wealth, *rather than final asset positions*" (p. 273) [italics added here]. Although most readers have focused on the first part of this sentence, this part does not convey the main novelty. Changes of wealth have been used in decision models throughout history. The novelty is in the second part of the sentence, explicitly breaking the relationship with final wealth. A more detailed discussion of changes of reference points is in Kahneman & Tversky (1979 pp. 286 ff.).

In the absence of a theory of reference points[2], hypotheses about their location have to be based on pragmatic heuristics in applications. The perception of reference points by subjects will be based on volatile aspects of framing (Tversky & Kahneman 1981 p. 456), which will not be easy to model. Theoretical models work best for phenomena that do not deviate very much from rational behavior, which may explain why it is hard to develop a theory for reference points, and why we should sometimes accept using the concept in a pragmatic way without a well-developed theory available. Theoretical analyses, including the analysis of prospect theory presented in later

---

[2] Köszegi & Rabin (2006) proposed a theory of reference points. These are not exogenous and prior to choice as assumed here, but depend on deliberate choice by the decision maker. They may result as a solution from sophisticated optimization procedures. Introspective utility, not based on revealed preference, is assumed available. In our approach, the only deliberate choice ("influence") of the decision maker concerns the prospect chosen. Utility functions, reference points, and other subjective parameters of decision models are not chosen, but are theoretical constructs that serve as inputs (or outputs as per the elicitation method) to describe choice. To double your utility you should not multiply your utility function by 2, or overweight your gain probabilities by 2 (Brunnermeier & Parker 2005), but you should obtain a prospect twice as good.

chapters, usually assume that a reference point has already been determined, take it as given and fixed, and start only from there. Thus, Figure 8.1.1, and Figure 12.5.1 presented later, are the only examples in this theoretical book of the important phenomenon of varying reference points, with some more discussions in §8.6 and §8.7.

Despite the atheoretical status of reference points, they are still incorporated in prospect theory and in this book because reference dependence, in combination with loss aversion, is one of the most pronounced empirical phenomena in decision under risk and uncertainty. Descriptive applications have to reckon with it, as well as is possible. How important it is to recognize the role of reference dependence, even if no formal theory of it yet exists, is illustrated in the following section.

8.6   Rabin's paradox

The example of this section illustrates the devastating implications of ignoring reference dependence, and of mismodeling the risk aversion driven by reference dependence through other factors.

Example 8.6.1 [Rabin's (2000) paradox]. The preference in Figure 8.6.1 requires a moderate degree of risk aversion, which is satisfied by most people. Observations usually find stronger risk aversion than the risk aversion needed for the displayed preference.

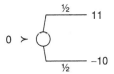

Figure 8.6.1 Rabin's preference.

Because such preferences are observed from various people at various wealth levels (Barberis, Huang, & Thaler 2006), it is plausible to assume that a single individual will exhibit this preference not only at the present wealth level w, but also at many other wealth levels w + m.

Preferences as just described can easily be accommodated by reference-dependent models. Let us for simplicity ignore probability weighting and assume that all probabilities are weighted linearly. We assume that the individual maximizes EU, with the modification however that outcomes are perceived as changes with respect to a reference point for which the status quo is taken, and which varies. Then the observed preference may imply no more than that for each reference point $I + m$ the utility function U_{I+m} of this person satisfies

$$U_{I+m}(11) - U_{I+m}(0) < U_{I+m}(0) - U_{I+m}(-10);$$

i.e., there is moderate concavity on the interval $[-10,11]$ for all functions U_{I+m}. Nothing more needs to be implied.

Now assume, however, that a researcher does not recognize the role of reference dependence, and analyzes the preferences in the classical way. He assumes the classical EU model with outcomes uniquely related to final wealth, as in §8.3. One reference outcome I is chosen for the sake of convenient modeling, but it is kept fixed throughout the analysis, so that a unique correspondence of every outcome α to total final wealth $I + \alpha$ is maintained. The preferences now imply

$$U_I(m + 11) - U_I(m) < U_I(m) - U_I(m - 10)$$

for many m. The value m now is not incorporated into the reference level, but into the outcomes. This seemingly minor change in book keeping has drastic empirical implications. The last inequality can be rewritten as

$$\frac{U_I(m + 11) - U_I(m)}{11} < \frac{10}{11} \times \frac{U_I(m) - U_I(m - 10)}{10}.$$

These preferences, therefore, imply that on each interval $[m-10, m + 11]$ of length 21, the average derivative of U_I over the right part of the interval $[m, m + 11]$, being $\frac{U_I(m+11)-U_I(m)}{11}$, is at most 10/11 times the average derivative $\frac{U_I(m)-U_I(m-10)}{10}$ of U_I over the left part $[m-10, m]$. For concave utility with U_I' decreasing, so that U_I' at the left end of each interval exceeds the average U_I' over that interval, and U_I' at the right end of each interval is less than the average U_I' over that interval, it implies $U_I'(m + 11) \leq \frac{10}{11} U_I'(m - 10)$.

Such a fast decline of marginal utility, dropping by a factor of at least 10/11 over each distance of 21, does not make sense. If you received \$1000 extra, the marginal utility of an extra dollar, and the resulting extra happiness and purchasing power, would be worth less than $(10/11)^{1000/21} = 0.012$ times its present value. If you received \$10,000 more, the marginal utility of an extra dollar would be less than $(0.012)^{10} \approx 10^{-18}$ times what it is now. These implications are absurd.

It can also be seen that the fast decline of marginal utility implies that utility is bounded above and that you would refuse a prospect $M_{1/2}(-100)$ no matter how large M is, even if M is trillion dollars, if the preference in the figure were to hold for all levels $w + m$. Such an extreme implication of EU in terms of final wealth is, again, absurd. □

Example 8.6.1 clearly illustrates the descriptive failure of classical EU, and the inadequacy of utility curvature to model the common empirical findings on risk aversion. By ignoring the prevalent reference dependence and loss aversion, EU has to "mismodel" risk aversion by concavity of utility, leading to absurd implications (Just & Peterson 2003; Johansson-Stenman 2010). Rabin (2000) pointed out that the phenomena described in his paper are best explained by loss aversion (pp. 1288–1289), which incorporates reference dependence. Although there can be other theoretical explanations for his paradox (Exercise 8.6.1), it is primarily loss aversion that drives it. Rabin's paradox demonstrates that, even if reference dependence is hard to model, we cannot escape from reckoning with it as well as we can in descriptive theories of risk and uncertainty. With this understanding, an observed indifference $(100_{\frac{1}{2}}-50 \sim 0)$ no more suggests a risk tolerance of \$100 (Observation 3.5.3), but rather linear basic utility with a loss aversion factor 2. A similar point may underlie the following citation from management science (Winkler 1991):

M.B.A. students studying decision analysis are often quite surprised at how risk averse their assessed utility functions are and at how much they must give up in expected value to accommodate their assessed risk attitudes. This realization often leads them to move towards less risk averse positions . . . (p. 295)

We have discussed the implications of reference dependence and loss aversion, and the unwarranted implications of ignoring reference dependence, in the context of EU. Ignoring these phenomena has similar implications for other models, such as for RDU. If RDU does not incorporate loss aversion, it will "mismodel" the risk aversion generated by loss aversion through both probability weighting and utility. This point suggests that not only is utility less concave than traditionally thought, but probability weighting is also less convex than traditionally thought. The shapes in Figures 7.1.1–7.1.3 will be higher than sometimes thought. Example 9.3.2 will demonstrate how first-order risk aversion, bid-ask spreads, and inertia (Example 6.6.1; Brunnermeier & Nagel 2008) – phenomena that are often ascribed to pessimistic probability weighting – may be generated by loss aversion.

In experimental economics, subjects are often paid repeatedly during an experiment, but each separate payment is analyzed as if de novo and without integration of the other payments received before, or after, during the experiment. Such analyses take outcomes as changes with respect to a reference point, which is taken to be the status quo of that moment, at each choice, and which changes during the experiment. Outcomes are not stated in terms of final wealth. The expression "utility of income" is then sometimes used to designate reference dependence. That is, experimental economics and prospect theory have converged on this point.

Exercise 8.6.1.[a] Assume the preference of Figure 8.6.1, and assume RDU with linear utility. What can you say about $w(\frac{1}{2})$? Show that $m \succ (m+11)_{\frac{1}{2}}(m-10)$ for all real m. In other words, the preference holds at all levels of wealth. □

Discussions of Rabin's paradox in the literature. Many economists first learned about reference dependence through Rabin's example. In view of the subtle nature of reference dependence (which is best understood by considering changing reference points, for which hardly any theory exists today), confusions arose and defensive reactions resulted. Palacios-Huerta & Serrano (2006) and Watt (2002), for example, cited studies that, *under the assumption of EU*, provided estimations of power utility irreconcilable with the preference of Figure 8.6.1 for various levels of wealth. Their evidence only adds to Rabin's observation that his assumed preference in Figure 8.6.1 cannot be reconciled with expected utility for any reasonable utility function. Whereas Rabin concluded from this irreconcilability that there are problems with EU, Palacios-Huerta & Serrano (2006) and Watt (2002) did not consider this direction of reasoning. Instead, they concluded that the preference in Figure 8.6.1 cannot be plausible after all.

Several other authors argued that Rabin's paradox does not require abandoning EU because all that is needed is to use utility of income as they called it (Cox & Sadiraj 2006; Watt 2002; Rubinstein 2006; Samuelson 2005 pp. 88–91). As just explained, the latter is a popular term for reference dependence in experimental economics (pointed out by Harrison, Lau, & Rutström 2007 Appendix). Except for the last reference, the authors of the aforementioned papers did not realize that they were arguing for the same explanation as Rabin (2000 pp. 1288–1289, where loss aversion entails reference dependence). These authors further did not realize how fundamental a breakaway reference dependence is from EU. Whereas traditional EU is, in my opinion, the hallmark of rationality, any deviation from final wealth due to reference dependence is utterly irrational. Rubinstein (2006) developed a paradox for time preference similar to Rabin's, apparently trying to suggest that Rabin's paradox would be a routine idea.

Whereas Rabin showed that EU plus *plausible* assumptions has implausible implications, which then turns against EU, several other authors showed that RDU plus *implausible* assumptions has implausible implications. They then, incorrectly, turned such observations against RDU. Neilson (2001), for example, assumed $0 \succ 125_p(-100)$ at every level of wealth for p such that $w(p) = \frac{1}{2}$. However, this p is small, which makes the assumption implausible. Safra & Segal (2008) assumed that the preference in Figure 8.6.1 holds when combined with a wide range of "background" risky prospects. This assumption is also empirically implausible. For example, the background risk can concern many independent replicas of the prospect in Figure 8.6.1. Then repeated application of the assumption together with transitivity implies rejecting many repetitions of the prospect, which violates the law of large numbers. This case also makes LeRoy's (2003) criticism of Rabin's paradox implausible.

8.7 Future directions for theories of reference dependence

Markowitz (1952) was among the first to propose reference dependence of outcomes. He pointed out that there was no theory of the location of the reference points, and considered this to be a weak point of his theory (p. 157). Unfortunately, the theoretical status of reference points has not improved much since then. A full-blown theory would specify how reference points are chosen, and let choices depend not only on the prospects available, but also on the reference point. A theoretical study considering the latter dependence, i.e., with preferences, utility, and probability weighting depending on reference points, is Schmidt (2003). If too much liberty is left concerning the choice of reference points, then the theory becomes too general and is almost impossible to refute empirically. It does not then yield valuable predictions.

The following example shows that the classical expected-utility equivalence of risk aversion and concave utility need no longer hold if reference points can be variable, even if there is no probability weighting. The example illustrates a new aspect of reference dependence.

Example 8.7.1 [Under reference-dependent utility, risk aversion need not imply concave utility]. It is not implausible that decision makers, when choosing between a sure outcome and a prospect, take the sure outcome as their reference point (Hershey & Schoemaker 1985; Johnson & Schkade 1989; Robinson, Loomes, & Jones-Lee 2001; van Osch & Stiggelbout 2008). Assume that, given each reference point, decision makers choose according to EU, with the utility of losses steeper than the utility of gains everywhere; i.e., $U'(\beta) \geq U'(\alpha)$ for all $\alpha > 0 > \beta$, consistent with loss aversion. Then it can be proved that every prospect is less preferred than its expected value, in other words, that risk aversion holds. However, utility need not be concave for gains and it need not be for losses either. □

For a given reference point ρ ("rho"), we cannot, for $\alpha \neq \rho$, observe choices between riskless prospects α and prospects in Example 8.7.1 because the reference point always has to be equal to the riskless prospect. Hence, the preference relation $\succcurlyeq_\rho$ indexed with the reference point does not satisfy completeness on the set of all prospects.

Completeness has been known to be problematic in traditional decision theories (Appendix 1.9). The requirement of availability of all preferences between all pairs of prospects is an idealization. If we add reference dependence, with a preference $\succcurlyeq_\rho$ for every ρ, then completeness of each of these preferences is an even stronger and less convincing idealization. It imposes such a formidable requirement on data to be collected that the model is very hard to manage. There have been some studies of incomplete preferences, such as preferences defined only on subdomains, but these theories are considerably more difficult than completeness-based theories. Reference dependence adds to the interest of developing such theories (Apesteguia & Ballester 2009; Bleichrodt 2007, 2009).

Schmidt's (2003) theory still assumed that every preference relation for every reference point satisfies completeness. The following chapter will present prospect theory for only one fixed reference point, and will also make the traditional assumption of completeness for simplicity of presentation. Generalizations are left to future work. Another direction for future research concerns multiattribute outcomes. Here reference points may be taken per attribute or holistically (Bleichrodt, Schmidt, & Zank 2009).

I end this section with an early appearance of loss aversion and reference dependence. These ideas have been alluded to in informal contexts by many people throughout history. Lapidus & Sigot (2000) described an interesting example from Bentham (1828–1843, [1782–1787]: 236), the founder of the utility concept, regarding optimal rewarding systems for workers. Bentham argued that a payment scheme with high salaries and fines for bad performance works better than low salaries and rewards for good performance, even if the two schemes are the same in terms of final wealth. He argued that in the former scheme the fines are perceived as losses, and that losses are felt more than equivalent gains: "It is by fear only and not by hope, that [a worker] is impelled to the discharge of his duty – by the fear of receiving less than he would otherwise receive, not by the hope of receiving more."

Appendix 8.8   Empirical meaningfulness problems of loss aversion

This appendix can be skipped if you are not interested in theoretical questions, although I recommend its reading if you are interested in empirical measurements of loss aversion. In the revealed-preference approach that we take in this book, three problems have to be solved before we can define loss aversion formally.

Problem 1 [A theoretically meaningful way to define loss aversion]. In RDU and prospect theory (defined later) we can reveal w and U from preferences. Given U, it is not immediately clear how U should be decomposed into λ and u. If we replace λ,u by λ^*,u* where $\lambda^* = 2\lambda$, u* = u for gains, and u* = u/2 for losses, then we obtain the same function U implying all the same preferences. Hence, the two decompositions are empirically indistinguishable. In the main text we chose a pragmatic but ad hoc solution based on differentiability of u at 0 and approximate linearity on $[-1,1]$, after which the decomposition became identifiable. Better and more convincing solutions are possible if we consider variable reference points (Köbberling & Wakker, in preparation), but we will not discuss this topic in this book. We restrict attention to one fixed reference point. □

Problem 2 [A pragmatic and empirically meaningful way to define loss aversion]. In practice, we cannot really infer derivatives of utility from discrete choices and, hence, we cannot really verify differentiability of u – or falsify differentiability of U – at 0. Therefore, although U can be derived from observable choice, such a derivation is more difficult to obtain for U's components u and λ. For most regular functions, the assumptions underlying the scaling convention in Eq. (8.4.2) are satisfied. Those assumptions are that u is differentiable and approximately linear on the small interval $[-1,1]$. Such an assumption of piecewise linearity of U with a kink at 0 was used for instance by Barberis, Huang, & Santos (2001 p. 17), Fehr & Schmidt (1999), Gächter, Herrmann, & Johnson (2007), and Rosenblatt-Wisch (2008). This approach is, obviously, even more satisfactory if linear utility can be assumed throughout, as in Schmidt & Zank (2007). Then we can directly compare basic-utility units between gains and losses at a cardinal level. □

Problem 3 [An empirically useful way to define loss aversion]. A point of concern for the definition of loss aversion used in this book (including Problem 2) is that it is determined by the local domain of outcomes close to the reference point 0. Prospects with such small stakes are not very interesting or important, and phenomena relating exclusively to them cannot be very important either. Another point of concern is that our definition essentially uses the linear structure of outcomes. If outcomes are qualitative, such as health states, and there is no direct way to relate outcomes more preferred than a reference point to outcomes less preferred than the reference point (to relate such monetary outcomes we used multiplication by -1), then the approach described above cannot be used.

We can give a more satisfactory meaning to λ if we can specify a function u on the whole outcome domain with, in particular, the exchange rate between positive and negative utilities u specified, and u also specified for outcomes remote from 0. Then λ determines the exchange rate between positive and negative utilities also for large outcomes, which makes it empirically significant.

Here again, more satisfactory definitions of λ are possible if variable reference points are considered (Köbberling & Wakker, in preparation). For now, we will however adhere to the pragmatic definition of λ as just proposed in Problem 2. □

The next observation considers rescalings of basic utility and loss aversion.

Observation 8.8.1[b] [Rescaling u and λ]. Assume Eq. (8.4.1) with U unique up to a unit,[3] meaning that U can be replaced by U* without affecting preference if and only if U* $= \lambda$U for a positive λ. Assume that we decide to rescale u* $=\sigma$u for gains and u* $= \tau$u for losses, for some $\sigma > 0$ and $\tau > 0$. Then, so as to represent the same preference relation as before the rescaling, we have to choose

$$\lambda^* = \sigma/\tau \times \lambda. \tag{8.8.1}$$

Proof. First assume that we rescale u** $=$u for gains and u** $= (\tau/\sigma)$u for losses. Then U** $=$U for gains. Because U is unique up to a unit, U** must also equal U for losses, that is, λ**u** $= \lambda$u must hold for losses. Hence we must rescale λ** $= \sigma/\tau \times \lambda$ so as to neutralize the rescaling of u for losses.

Next, u* concerns the rescaling resulting from multiplying u** by σ for both gains and losses. Then we can take λ* $= \lambda$**, resulting in a rescaling U* $= \sigma$U** for both gains and losses, which does not affect preference. □

Example 8.8.2. Consider the following definitions with U unique up to a unit.
  For $\alpha > 0$: $u(\alpha) = 1 - \exp(-0.0032\alpha)$;
  for $\alpha = 0$: $u(\alpha) = 0$;
  for $\alpha < 0$: $u(\alpha) = \exp(0.0061\alpha) - 1$;
  $\lambda = 0.94$.
At first sight it may seem that the loss aversion parameter deviates from the common empirical finding of $\lambda > 1$. This is not really so. λ depends crucially on the scaling of utility u, and this scaling has been done in an arbitrary manner above. If we rescale utility as recommended in Eq. (8.4.2), with $u(1) = 1$ and $u(-1) = -1$, then we obtain for u:

$$\text{for } \alpha > 0: \ u(\alpha) = \frac{1 - \exp(-0.0032\alpha)}{1 - \exp(-0.0032)};$$

$$\text{for } \alpha = 0: \ u(\alpha) = 0;$$

$$\text{for } \alpha < 0: \ u(\alpha) = -\frac{\exp(0.0061\alpha) - 1}{\exp(-0.0061) - 1}.$$

Now, by Eq. (8.8.1), $\lambda = 0.94 \times \frac{-(\exp(-0.0061)-1)}{1-\exp(-0.0032)} = 1.789$.

---

[3] Given $U(0) = 0$, this holds for all decision theories considered in this book.

This is a realistic assessment of parameters. Virtually the same assessment follows under the scaling recommended by Köbberling & Wakker (2005), i.e., Problem 1 above. The same assessment follows, in fact, for every scaling $u(\mu) = -u(-\mu)$ for $\mu > 0$ small. This claim will be elaborated on in Exercise 8.8.1. □

Exercise 8.8.1.[a] Let $\mu > 0$. Consider Example 8.8.2, but rescale basic utility u such that $u(\mu) = -u(-\mu) = 1$. (The first equality is crucial; setting it equal to 1 is immaterial and is only done for convenience.) Show that

$$\lambda = 0.94 \times \frac{1 - \exp(-0.0061\mu)}{1 - \exp(-0.0032\mu)}. \tag{8.8.2}$$

Calculate λ for $\mu = 2$ and $\mu = 0.01$. Also calculate λ if u is scaled as in Eq. 3.5.5 (which results as limit for μ tending to 0, so that derivatives at 0 decide). □

Appendix 8.9   A formal model of initial wealth and reference points

Because the notation for reference dependence introduced here will not be used in the rest of the book, it has been deferred to this appendix. We focus on the modeling of utility and outcomes in this appendix. *I* denotes initial wealth.

Reference Independence. In classical, reference-independent, models, outcome α generates final wealth $F = I + \alpha$. There exists a utility function U* of final wealth, and the utility function U we use is defined by $U(\alpha) = U*(I + \alpha)$. *I* need not be, and usually is not known. It suffices to know that *I* is fixed for claiming that utility depends (only) on final wealth.

	decomposition of final wealth F	interpretation	evaluation
	F	final wealth	U*(F)
classical model	*I* constant: innocuous rescaling of outcomes		
	$I + \alpha$	initial wealth + outcome	U(α)
reference dependence	**ρ variable: major breakaway from classical model**		
	$I + \rho + \alpha$	**initial wealth + reference point +** outcome	U(ρ,α)

Bold printing indicates a major breakaway from the classical model.

Figure 8.9.1 Decompositions of final wealth.

Reference dependence. The reference point, denoted ρ, is not chosen by the modeler for convenience of modeling, but it is chosen by the decision maker when deciding. The choice is psychologically driven. The major difference between I and ρ is that I is assumed fixed, whereas ρ varies during the analysis. There is not much of a rational basis for the choice of ρ. This choice is not based on sophisticated considerations such as complex resolutions of optimizations. Instead, it is determined by framing effects and usually is not done deliberately. For final wealth F we now have

$$F = \alpha + \rho + I. \tag{8.9.1}$$

In the paradox in Figure 8.1.1, most subjects take $\rho = 0$ in Figs. a and b, but $\rho = 100$ in Fig. c. They process the -50 in Fig. c the same way as the -50 in Fig. b, where it corresponds to a different level F of final wealth though. Figure 8.9.1 summarizes the analysis.

A common misunderstanding arises if authors, when discussing reference dependence in the context of Eq. (8.9.1), address the question of how preferences are affected if the reference point ρ is changed. To maintain Eq. (8.9.1), something else must then be changed in the equation as well. With it usually being understood that I is kept constant, it is often left ambiguous whether the change in ρ is to be accompanied with a change in F while keeping α constant, or with a change in α while keeping F constant (or yet with something else). One should clarify, when changing one of the variables in Eq. (8.9.1), which of the other variables is changed so as to maintain the equation.

9 Prospect theory for decision under risk

This chapter deals with prospect theory, which generalizes RDU by incorporating loss aversion. It thus integrates utility curvature, probabilistic sensitivity, and loss aversion, the three components of risk attitude.

9.1 A symmetry about 0 underlying prospect theory

It is plausible that utility has a kink at zero, and exhibits different properties for gains than for losses. Formally, for a fixed reference point these properties could also be modeled by rank-dependent utility, in the same way as §8.3 does not entail a real departure from final wealth models and expected utility. Prospect theory does generalize rank-dependent utility in one formal respect also for the case of one fixed reference point: It allows for different probability weighting for gains than for losses. Thus, risk attitudes can be different for losses than for gains in every respect.

It is plausible that sensitivity to outcomes and probabilities exhibits symmetries about the reference point. To illustrate this point, we first note that the utility difference $U(1020) - U(1010)$ is usually smaller than the utility difference $U(20) - U(10)$ because the former concerns outcomes farther remote from 0, leading to concave utility for gains. A symmetric reasoning for losses suggests that the utility difference $U(-1010) - U(-1020)$ will be perceived as smaller than the utility difference $U(-10) - U(-20)$. For the former difference, the losses are so big that 10 more does not matter much. This argument suggests convex rather than concave utility for losses, in agreement with many empirical findings (§9.5).

A similar symmetry can be expected for probabilistic sensitivity. For gains, comparisons to the reference point concern comparisons downward, and (gain-) ranks describe the probability of outcomes more remote from the reference point. For losses, comparisons to the reference point concern comparisons upward, and now loss-ranks describe the probability of outcomes more remote from the reference point. It seems plausible that properties such as the overweighting or underweighting of ranked probabilities in the case of gains are matched, in the case of losses, by similar phenomena for loss-ranked probabilities rather than for gain-ranked probabilities. Hence, it is also more natural to combine a convention using gain-ranked probabilities for gains with a similar convention using loss-ranked probabilities for losses. This will be the approach adopted by prospect theory and it will indeed lead to natural implications. The psychological argument just advanced is homeomorphic to the mathematical suggestion resulting from the integral definition of RDU in Eq. (6.9.1) and Figures 6.9.1 and 6.9.2, where also from a mathematical perspective loss-ranks for losses are the natural analogs of gain-ranks for gains. A similar kind of reflection is effective for utility and for probability weighting.

To further illustrate the symmetry about zero, reconsider the risk seeking commonly found in Fig. 8.1.1b. It is plausible that utility is close to linear for outcomes as moderate as in Figure 8.1.1. The risk seeking in Fig. 8.1.1b can then be explained by an underweighting of the probability ½ of the extreme outcome -100, in the same way as the risk aversion in Fig. 8.1.1a can be explained by an underweighting of the probability ½ of the extreme outcome $+100$.

9.2   The definition of prospect theory

As explained before, we assume one fixed reference outcome in prospect theory, which we take to be 0 and usually assume to be the status quo. An outcome of 10 means that you receive \$10 in addition to your reference point. Positive outcomes (0 not included) are *gains* and negative outcomes (again, 0 not included) are *losses*.

Prospect theory (PT), in its updated version as introduced by Tversky & Kahneman (1992), generalizes rank-dependent utility by incorporating reference dependence and loss aversion. Similarly as Schmeidler invented his functional without knowing Choquet's (1953–1954) preceding work, Tversky and Kahneman invented their functional without knowing Šipoš' (1979) preceding work. Tversky and Kahneman did know Quiggin's and Schmeidler's works based on Choquet integrals. Functionals similar to PT were introduced independently in decision theory by Luce & Fishburn (1991) and Starmer & Sugden (1989 Appendix).

For PT, there are two weighting functions, w^+ for gains and w^- for losses. w^+ relates to gain-ranked probabilities, as did w under RDU; w^- relates to loss-ranked probabilities. Because of symmetry about the reference point, we expect the functions w^+ and w^- to exhibit similar empirical properties. We now consider prospects

$$p_1x_1 \cdots p_nx_n \text{ with } x_1 \geq \cdots \geq x_k \geq 0 \geq x_{k+1} \geq \cdots \geq x_n. \qquad (9.2.1)$$

That is, we specify a complete ranking of the outcomes not only with respect to each other, but also with respect to the reference point 0. Such a ranking is called a *complete sign-ranking*.

Under Eq. (9.2.1),

$$PT(x) = \sum_{j=1}^{n} \pi_j U(x_j), \qquad (9.2.2)$$

where the decision weights π_j are nonnegative and are defined next.

Definition 9.2.1. Under PT, an outcome α with outcome probability p, gain-rank[1] g, and loss-rank $\ell = 1-p-g$ has the following *decision weight*.

• $\alpha > 0$: $\pi = \pi(p^g) = w^+(p+g) - w^+(g)$.

• $\alpha = 0$: $U(\alpha) = 0$ and the decision weight is irrelevant[2]; we usually take it to be $\pi(p^g)$.

• $\alpha < 0$: $\pi = \pi(p_\ell) = w^-(p+\ell) - w^-(\ell)$. □

In §7.6, we discussed loss-ranks without assuming that the associated outcomes were necessarily losses. From now on, however, we will make the following assumption without further mention:

Assumption 9.2.2. (Gain-)ranked probabilities p^g are applied to gains, with the decision weight $\pi(p^g)$ derived from w^+. Loss-ranked probabilities p_ℓ are applied to losses, with the decision weight $\pi(p_\ell)$ derived from w^-. □

Thus, the decision weight of an outcome depends not only on its rank, but also on its sign. Hence, Luce & Fishburn (1991) used the term rank- and sign-dependent utility for our term prospect theory. We obtain

$$\text{for } i \leq k: \pi_i = \pi(p_i^{p_{i-1}+\cdots+p_1}) = w^+((p_i+\cdots+p_1)) - w^+((p_{i-1}+\cdots+p_1)); \quad (9.2.3)$$

$$\text{for } j > k: \pi_j = \pi(p_{j_{p_{j+1}+\cdots+p_n}}) = w^-((p_j+\cdots+p_n)) - w^-((p_{j+1}+\cdots+p_n)). \quad (9.2.4)$$

The following formula of PT writes ranks and the rank dependence of decision weights in full.

$$PT(x) = \sum_{i=1}^k \pi(p_i^{p_{i-1}+\cdots+p_1})U(x_i) + \sum_{j=k+1}^n \pi(p_{j_{p_{j+1}+\cdots+p_n}})U(x_j). \quad (9.2.5)$$

We summarize the definition of PT.

Definition 9.2.3. Under Structural Assumption 2.5.2 (decision under risk and richness), *prospect theory* (*PT*) holds if there exist a strictly increasing continuous *utility function* $U : R \to R$ with $U(0) = 0$, and two (*probability*) *weighting functions* w^+ and w^-, such that each prospect $p_1x_1 \cdots p_nx_n$ with *completely sign-ranked* outcomes $x_1 \geq \cdots \geq x_k \geq 0 \geq x_{k+1} \geq \cdots \geq x_n$ for some $0 \leq k \leq n$ is evaluated by

$$\sum_{j=1}^n \pi_j U(x_j) = \sum_{i=1}^k \pi(p_i^{p_{i-1}+\cdots+p_1})U(x_i) + \sum_{j=k+1}^n \pi(p_{j_{p_{j+1}}+\cdots+p_n})U(x_j)$$

$$= \sum_{i=1}^k (w^+(p_i+\cdots+p_1) - w^+(p_{i-1}+\cdots+p_1))U(x_i)$$

$$+ \sum_{j=k+1}^n (w^-(p_j+\cdots+p_n) - w^-(p_{j+1}+\cdots+p_n))U(x_j),$$

the *PT value* of the prospect. □

---

[1] As explained before, gain-rank is an alternative term for rank. We use the notation g rather than r for (gain-) rank here.

[2] It is psychologically plausible, indeed, that people focus on deviations from the status quo, so that weights for the status quo are irrelevant. Hence, the mathematical choice of $U(0) = 0$, implying irrelevance of such weights, is also psychologically natural, in agreement with the homeomorphic principle.

In prospect theory, the utility function U and the probability weighting functions w^+ and w^- are the subjective parameters that characterize the decision maker. Ways to calculate PT and to derive choices from the model are discussed in §9.3. The elicitation method for PT, deriving its theoretical concepts from observed preferences, is discussed in §9.4.

As explained before, we assume that U agrees with a function u for gains and is λ times a function u for losses, with λ the loss aversion parameter. Because the properties of U for losses can be completely different from its properties for gains, and also w^- can be different from w^+, prospect theory allows for entirely different risk attitudes for losses than for gains. Some studies have suggested that risk attitudes for losses can be different and to some extent unrelated to those for gains (Cohen, Jaffray & Said 1987; Laury & Holt 2008; Weller *et al.* 2007), so that a reflection effect – loss attitudes mirroring gain attitudes; Kahneman & Tversky (1979) – does not hold in a strict sense at the individual level.

The term prospect theory is often used to refer to the general functional as now defined, without any further properties assumed. Alternatively, however, the term is also often used to refer to the general functional joint with a number of prevalent empirical assumptions added. We will discuss those assumptions later.

9.3   Properties of the prospect theory formula, and calculations

It is often useful to take the PT functional as the sum of an RDU functional applied to gains, and another RDU functional applied to losses. In this way we can easily verify that PT satisfies stochastic dominance, as we will see later. For a prospect x, x^+ is defined by replacing all negative outcomes of x by zero, and x^- is defined by replacing all positive outcomes by zero.[3] See Figure 9.3.1. If $x = p_1x_1, \ldots,$ $p_kx_k, p_{k+1}x_{k+1}, \ldots, p_nx_n$ with $x_1 \geq \cdots \geq x_k \geq 0 \geq x_{k+1} \geq \cdots \geq x_n$, then $x^+ = p_1x_1, \ldots,$ $p_kx_k, p_{k+1}0, \ldots, p_n0$ and $x^- = p_10, \ldots, p_k0, p_{k+1}x_{k+1}, \ldots, p_nx_n$.

Exercise 9.3.1.[!a] Assume, as throughout this section, that $U(0) = 0$. Show that

$$RDU(x) = RDU(x^+) + RDU(x^-). \tag{9.3.1}$$

Does this equation also hold if $U(0) \neq 0$? □

Exercise 9.3.2.[!a] Show that

$$PT(x) = PT(x^+) + PT(x^-). \tag{9.3.2}$$

□

The decision weights in Eq. (9.2.3) plus those in Eq. (9.2.4) need not sum to 1, and this may seem to be disconcerting. It may seem that, consequently, violations of stochastic dominance will be generated as they were by the transformations of fixed-outcome

---

[3] Our notation for x^- deviates from a convention in mathematics, where x^- is taken as -1 times our x^-. In decision theory we often work with nonquantitative outcomes α for which $-\alpha$ would not be defined. Hence, the definition we use is more convenient for our purposes.

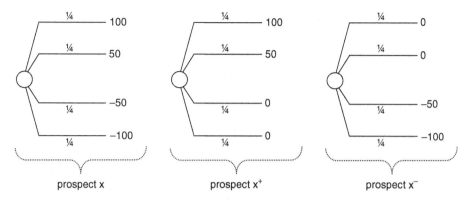

Figure 9.3.1 x^+ and x^-.

probabilities in Eq. (5.2.1) (old weighting), where weights also did not sum to 1. We will see that such problems do not arise, and that the PT formula does satisfy stochastic dominance (Observation 9.4.1). This is a surprising mathematical feature of this method of integration, first introduced by Šipoš (1979; see also Denneberg 1994 Ch. 7).

Exercise 9.3.3.[b] Demonstrate that the sum of the decision weights π_j in Eq. (9.2.3) plus those in Eq. (9.2.4) need not be 1. Give an example where they sum to more than 1, and an example where they sum to less than 1. □

PT(x) can be defined concisely as an RDU functional applied to the gains part x^+ plus another independently chosen RDU functional applied to the loss part x^-. The RDU weighting function for gains is w^+, and the RDU weighting function for losses is the dual of w^-.[4]

A procedure for calculating the PT value of a prospect is as follows:

STEP 1.   Completely rank outcomes from best to worst.
STEP 2.   Determine which outcomes are positive and which are negative.

Steps 1 and 2 together determine the complete sign-ranking.

STEP 3.   For each positive outcome, calculate the gain-rank g.
STEP 4.   For all resulting gain-ranks, calculate their w^+ value.
STEP 5.   For each positive outcome α, calculate the marginal w^+ contribution of its outcome probability p to its rank; i.e., calculate[5] $w^+(p+g) - w^+(g)$.

---

[4] From this perspective, we can assign decision weights in such a manner that they do always sum to the same total, this total being 2, as is explained next. First we consider x^+ with its decision weights generated by w^+, *where we also incorporate the decision weight assigned to the 0 outcome in x^+.* These decision weights always sum to 1, as is the case for RDU. We next consider x^- with its decision weights generated by the dual of w^-, where we also incorporate the decision weight assigned to the 0 outcome in x^-. These decision weights again always sum to 1. In this manner, the decision weights assigned to x^+ and x^- together always sum to a total of 2. If we always used decision weights in this manner, always adding to 2, and always incorporating the 0 outcome as described, then the convention of U(0) = 0 could be dropped. In this manner it can also be seen that PT does not violate stochastic dominance after all.

[5] p+g is the gain-rank of the gain in the prospect ranked worse than but next to α considered in Step 3.

Treat losses symmetrically; i.e.,

STEP 6.   For each negative outcome, calculate the loss-rank ℓ.

STEP 7.   For all resulting loss-ranks, calculate their w^- value.

STEP 8.   For each negative outcome β, calculate the marginal w^- contribution of its probability q to its loss-rank; i.e., calculate[6] $w^-(q + \ell) - w^-(\ell)$.

STEP 9.   Determine the utility of each outcome (taking $U = \lambda u$ for losses).

STEP 10.   Multiply the utility of each outcome by its decision weight.

STEP 11.   Sum the results of Step 10.

The most commonly used parametric specification of PT is described in the following example. The power functions used are not differentiable at 0 for the parameters commonly found. This leads to problems in the estimation of the loss aversion parameter λ. Hence, we caution against using Eqs. (9.3.5)–(9.3.7) below when estimating loss aversion from data. The problems are explained, with remedies suggested, in §9.6. Because the specification is so widely used we will also use it in several examples.

Example 9.3.1. Assume that PT (Definition 9.2.3) holds. Let w^+ and w^- be of the form in Eq. (7.2.1):

$$w^+(p) = \frac{p^c}{(p^c + (1-p)^c)^{1/c}}; \tag{9.3.3}$$

$$w^-(p) = \frac{p^d}{\left(p^d + (1-p)^d\right)^{1/d}}. \tag{9.3.4}$$

Let U be defined as follows:

$$\text{for } \alpha > 0 : U(\alpha) = \alpha^\theta; \tag{9.3.5}$$

$$\text{for } \alpha = 0 : U(\alpha) = 0; \tag{9.3.6}$$

$$\text{for } \alpha < 0 : U(\alpha) = -\lambda(-\alpha)^{\theta'}. \tag{9.3.7}$$

As regards utility, we use a power function $u(\alpha) = \alpha^\theta$ for basic utility for gains and a different power function $u(\alpha) = -(-\alpha)^{\theta'}$ for basic utility for losses, and λ is the loss aversion parameter. U is the overall utility. Tversky & Kahneman (1992) used this specification to fit data and found $c = 0.61$, $d = 0.69$, $\theta = \theta' = 0.88$, and $\lambda = 2.25$ as best fitting their data. □

---

[6] q+*l* is the loss-rank of the loss in the prospect ranked better than but next to β considered in Step 6.

Exercise 9.3.4.[a] Let U be as in Eqs. (9.3.5)–(9.3.7) with $\theta = \theta' = 0.5$ and $\lambda = 2$. Let $w^+(p) = p^2$, and $w^-(p) = p$. Determine the decision weights of each outcome, the PT value of the prospect x, and its certainty equivalent, for

(a) $x = (0.10{:}9, 0.40{:}4, 0.40{:}{-}4, 0.10{:}{-}9)$;
(b) $x = (0.10{:}36, 0.20{:}25, 0.30{:}{-}9, 0.40{:}{-}16)$. □

The following example shows how phenomena, ascribed to pessimistic probability weighting, may rather have been generated by loss aversion (Barberis, Huang, & Thaler 2006 footnote 1).

Example 9.3.2 [First-order risk aversion generated by loss aversion]. Reconsider Example 6.6.1b (first-order risk aversion generated by rank dependence), for an asset x_1, x_2 at price ε per unit. Loss aversion (instead of rank dependence) can also explain the bid-ask spread. To this effect, assume PT and no probability weighting, that is, $w^+(p) = w^-(p) = p$ for all p. Thus, rank dependence plays no role. Assume intrinsic utility u with $u'(0) > 0$, and loss aversion $\lambda > 1$. To avoid triviality, we consider only the case of $x_1 > \varepsilon > x_2$. Then, when buying μ units ($\mu > 0$), the PT value of the resulting prospect is

$$\tfrac{1}{2}u(\mu(x_1 - \varepsilon)) + \tfrac{1}{2}\lambda u(\mu(x_2 - \varepsilon)) \approx \tfrac{1}{2}u'(0)\mu((x_1 - \varepsilon) + \lambda(x_2 - \varepsilon)).$$

Buying is worthwhile only if $x_1 - \varepsilon + \lambda x_2 - \lambda \varepsilon \geq 0$, or $x_1 + \lambda x_2 \geq \varepsilon(1 + \lambda)$, that is,

$$\varepsilon \leq \frac{1}{1 + \lambda}x_1 + \frac{\lambda}{1 + \lambda}x_2 < \tfrac{1}{2}x_1 + \tfrac{1}{2}x_2.$$

Buying only takes place if the price is strictly below the expectation. When selling ($\mu < 0$) the PT value of the resulting prospect is

$$\tfrac{1}{2}\lambda u(\mu(x_1 - \varepsilon)) + \tfrac{1}{2}u(\mu(x_2 - \varepsilon)) \approx \tfrac{1}{2}u'(0)\mu(\lambda(x_1 - \varepsilon) + (x_2 - \varepsilon)).$$

Selling is worthwhile, in view of negativity of μ, only if

$$\lambda(x_1 - \varepsilon) + (x_2 - \varepsilon) \leq 0, \text{ or } \lambda x_1 + x_2 \leq (1 + \lambda)\varepsilon,$$

that is,

$$\varepsilon \geq \frac{\lambda}{1 + \lambda}x_1 + \frac{1}{1 + \lambda}x_2 > \tfrac{1}{2}x_1 + \tfrac{1}{2}x_2.$$

Selling only takes place if the price strictly exceeds the expectation. We obtain a price-interval of inertia for ε equal to

$$\left[\frac{1}{1 + \lambda}x_1 + \frac{\lambda}{1 + \lambda}x_2, \frac{\lambda}{1 + \lambda}x_1 + \frac{1}{1 + \lambda}x_2\right],$$

where the asset is neither bought nor sold and, again, a bid-ask spread has resulted. It resulted purely from loss aversion and not from rank dependence or probability weighting. □

Assignment 9.3.5.[a] Let U and w be as in Example 9.3.1. Determine the decision weights of each outcome, the PT value of the prospect x, and its certainty equivalent, for

(a) $x = (0.15:12, 0.35:7, 0.30:-2, 0.20:-5)$;
(b) $x = (0.70:36, 0.10:25, 0.10:-9, 0.10:-16)$. □

Example 9.3.3. We consider the risk premium of the prospect $80_{1/2}(-20)$. Assume PT with basic utility exponential (Eq. (3.5.4)) and $w^+(p) = w^-(p) = \frac{p^c}{(p^c+(1-p)^c)^{1/c}}$.

Assume that $\theta = 0.005$, $c = 0.61$, and $\lambda = 2.25$. U is the overall utility (Eq. (8.4.1)). The expected value of the prospect is 30. Calculations (Exercise 9.3.6) demonstrate that the certainty equivalent is 7.99. The risk premium is $30 - 7.99 = 22.01$.
This risk premium is generated by utility, probability weighting, and loss aversion. Table 9.3.1 shows the risk premia for some related models.

Table 9.3.1. *Risk premiums of $80_{1/2}(-20)$ for various models*

Model with nonlinear component(s) between brackets	θ (for U)	w reference dependent	c (for w, w^+, and w^-)	λ (loss aversion)	risk premium
EV	0	no	1	1	0
EU (U)	0.005	no	1	1	6.19
RDU (w)	0	no	0.61	1	7.94
RDU (U, w)	0.005	no	0.61	1	13.81
PT (λ)	0	yes	1	2.25	12.50
PT (U, λ)	0.005	yes	1	2.25	20.47
PT (w, λ)	0	yes	0.61	2.25	15.28
PT (U, w, λ)	0.005	yes	0.61	2.25	22.01

Note: For RDU, $w = w^+$, also for losses.

The first four rows also appeared in Table 7.2.1 and have no reference dependence. In other words, there is no loss aversion or gain seeking ($\lambda = 1$). Outcomes are weighted as for RDU (with $w = w^+$), with losses not weighted in a dual manner as under PT. For the remaining four rows, decision weights are determined as under PT, with the dual treatment for losses. For linear basic utility ($\theta = 0$), $U(\alpha) = \alpha$ for $\alpha \geq 0$ and $U(\alpha) = \lambda \alpha$ for $\alpha < 0$.

The results suggest that loss aversion contributes most to risk aversion. Probability weighting contributes much to risk aversion under RDU, and more so than utility does. Probability weighting contributes less to risk aversion under PT than under RDU, because under PT probability weighting exhibits a varied pattern where, for instance, for losses it can often generate risk seeking. □

Exercise 9.3.6.[b] Verify the calculations of Example 9.3.3. □

Exercise 9.3.7.[b] This exercise further illustrates the effect of different probability weighting under PT than under RDU, through the difference in parts (c) and (d). Under RDU with w as in Eq. (7.2.1) and $c = 0.61$, the lowest outcome, also if negative, is strongly overweighted generating considerable risk aversion. Under PT, the lowest outcome if negative and of moderate probability is not overweighted much because of probability weighting but rather because of loss aversion. Let w^+, w^-, and U be as in Eqs. (9.3.3)–(9.3.7), and w as in Eq. (7.2.1) (analogous to Eq. (9.3.3)). Consider the prospect

(0.01:80, 0.35:60, 0.35:30, 0.29:−30).

(a) Assume PT with the parameters as in Tversky & Kahneman (1992) (Example 9.3.1). Calculate the risk premium of the prospect.
(b) Assume EU. That is, probability weighting is linear ($c = 1$ for w^+ and w and $d = 1$ for w^-). Further, $\theta = \theta' = 0.88$ and $\lambda = 1$. Calculate the risk premium of the prospect.
(c) Assume RDU with linear utility. That is, $\theta = \theta' = 1$, $c = 0.61$ with one weighting function w, and $\lambda = 1$. Calculate the risk premium of the prospect.
(d) Assume PT with linear utility and no loss aversion. That is, $\theta = \theta' = 1$, and $\lambda = 1$. For comparison with part c, we take $c = d = 0.61$. Calculate the risk premium of the prospect.
(e) Assume PT with only loss aversion effective; i.e., $\theta = \theta' = 1$, $c = d = 1$, and $\lambda = 2.25$. Calculate the risk premium of the prospect. □

If two decision makers $\succcurlyeq_1$ and $\succcurlyeq_2$ have the same risk attitudes for gains and also for losses, so that their weighting functions and basic utility functions can be taken the same (implying that their overall utility functions also agree for gains), then their loss aversion can readily be compared. Take an indifference $x \sim_1 y$ between a mixed prospect x ($x^+ \succ 0 \succ x^-$) and a pure gain prospect y ($y^- = 0$). If $\succcurlyeq_2$ is strictly more loss averse than $\succcurlyeq_1$ so that $\lambda_2 > \lambda_1$, then $PT_2(y) = PT_1(y)$ (PT_i denotes the relevant PT functional), but $PT_2(x) < PT_1(x)$ ($= PT_1(y) = PT_2(y)$). Hence, $x \prec_2 y$. The certainty equivalent for the pure gain prospect x is the same for both decision makers, but for the mixed prospect it is smaller for the more loss averse decision maker. This is the basic idea of Köbberling & Wakker (2005).

The following exercise considers the same procedure as just discussed, but with a mixed and a pure loss prospect. At first acquaintance, the solution to the exercise (in Appendix J) may be paradoxical to some readers. It illustrates once more, in particular by the remark regarding certainty equivalents at the end, that loss aversion only concerns mixed prospects. Loss aversion does not affect preferences between pure gain prospects *nor preferences between pure loss prospects*. There have been many misunderstandings about the latter point, with some authors even erroneously using the term loss aversion to refer to risk seeking for losses.

Exercise 9.3.8.[b] Consider two decision makers $\succcurlyeq_1$ and $\succcurlyeq_2$ who both maximize PT. They have the same risk attitudes for gains, and also for losses, so that they have the same weighting functions $w_1^+ = w_2^+ = w^+$ and $w_1^- = w_2^- = w^-$, and the same basic utility function $u_1 = u_2 = u$. Only their loss aversion parameters differ, with $\lambda^2 > \lambda^1 > 1$, so that $\succcurlyeq_2$ is more loss averse than $\succcurlyeq_1$. Thus on $\mathbb{R}^+$ their overall utility is also the same, with $U_2 = U_1$ there. On $\mathbb{R}^-$ we have $\lambda_2 u_2 = U_2 < \lambda_1 u_1 = U_1 < 0$. Consider a mixed prospect x and a pure loss prospect y, with $x^+ \succ_i 0$, $y^+ = 0$, $x^- \prec_i 0$, and $y^- \prec_i 0$ for $i = 1,2$. Assume that $x \sim_1 y$; i.e. the less loss averse decision maker is indifferent. What is the preference of the more loss averse decision maker between the mixed x and the pure-loss y? □

Assignment 9.3.9.[b] Assume the specifications of Example 9.3.1, and w as in Eq. (7.2.1). Consider the prospect
(0.33:60, 0.33:30, 0:34:−30).

(a) Assume $\theta = \theta' = 0.88$, $c = d = 0.69$, and $\lambda = 2$. Calculate the risk premium of the prospect.
(b) Assume EU. That is, $\theta = \theta' = 0.88$, probability weighting is linear ($c = d = 1$) and $\lambda = 1$. Calculate the risk premium of the prospect.
(c) Assume RDU with linear utility. That is, $\theta = \theta' = 1$, $c = 0.69$ with one weighting function w, and $\lambda = 1$. Calculate the risk premium of the prospect.
(d) Assume PT with linear utility and no loss aversion. That is, $\theta = \theta' = 1$, $c = d = 0.69$, and $\lambda = 1$. Calculate the risk premium of the prospect.
(e) Assume PT with only loss aversion effective; i.e., $\theta = \theta' = 1$, $c = d = 1$, and $\lambda = 2$. Calculate the risk premium of the prospect. □

Assignment 9.3.10.[b] Formulate a condition on w^+ and w^- such that the PT functional is an RDU functional. □

Assignment 9.3.11.[a] We will calculate the risk premium of the prospect $80_{\frac{1}{2}}(-20)$. We consider PT with U as in Eqs. (9.3.5)–(9.3.7), and $w^+(p) = w^-(p) = p^c$, $\theta = \theta' = \frac{1}{2}$, $c = 2$, and $\lambda = 2.25$, as well as several variations of this model. Fill in the risk premiums in Table 9.3.2. Interpret the parameters as regards their effect on risk attitude.

Table 9.3.2.

Model with nonlinear component(s) between brackets	θ (for U)	w reference dependent	c (for w)	λ (loss aversion)	risk premium
EV	1	no	1	1	
EU (U)	0.5	no	1	1	
RDU (w)	1	no	2	1	
RDU (U, w)	0.5	no	2	1	
PT (λ)	1	yes	1	2.25	
PT (U, λ)	0.5	yes	1	2.25	
PT (w, λ)	1	yes	2	2.25	
PT (U, w, λ)	0.5	yes	2	2.25	

□

9.4 What prospect theory shares with rank-dependent utility and with expected utility, and one more reanalysis of the experiment of § 4.1

9.4.1 Monotonicity, stochastic dominance, and the sure-thing principle
If only gains are involved, then PT is the same as RDU with the weighting function $w = w^+$. Similarly, if only losses are involved, then PT is the same as RDU with the

weighting function $w(p) = 1 - w^-(1-p)$. Hence, much of PT is in agreement with earlier theories. We first show that monotonicity and stochastic dominance are satisfied under PT. These conditions were violated by the original version of PT of Kahneman & Tversky (1979), and getting these conditions satisfied in combination with reference dependence was the main mathematical, nontrivial, contribution of Tversky & Kahneman (1992) in addition to Schmeidler's (1989) RDU.

From Eq. (9.3.2) it can easily be seen that PT satisfies monotonicity and strict stochastic dominance. Because the proof of the following result may be instructive, it is given in the main text.

Observation 9.4.1. Under PT, replacing an outcome by a better outcome improves the prospect (monotonicity), and shifting probability mass from an outcome to a better outcome improves the prospect ((weak) stochastic dominance). The improvement is strict if the probability mass is positive and the better outcome is strictly better (strict stochastic dominance).

Proof. Assume that we improve an outcome in a prospect. We define three cases, and then discuss them.

CASE 1. We improve a gain into a better gain. This means improving an outcome in x^+ and leaving x^- unaffected.

CASE 2. We improve a loss into a better loss. This means improving an outcome in x^- and leaving x^+ unaffected.

CASE 3. We improve a strictly negative outcome into a strictly positive one. It means that for x^- the outcome is replaced by outcome 0, and for x^+ outcome 0 is replaced by a positive outcome. This means improving an outcome in x^- and also improving an outcome in x^+.

Because both PT when applied to x^+ and PT when applied to x^- are RDU functionals, $PT(x^+)$ increases in Case 1 whereas $PT(x^-)$ is unaffected, $PT(x^-)$ increases in Case 2 whereas $PT(x^+)$ is unaffected, and both $PT(x^+)$ and $PT(x^-)$ increase in Case 3. Hence, improving an outcome implies improving the PT value $PT(x) = PT(x^+) + PT(x^-)$ in all cases, and monotonicity holds. A similar reasoning applies to strict stochastic dominance, established in Theorem 6.5.6 for RDU. Further, note that shifting probability mass from an outcome to a better outcome can also be taken as replacing an outcome (conditional on the probability mass shifted) by a better outcome. □

Finally, we discuss the sure-thing principle for risk. Surprisingly, reference dependence does not affect this condition, as the following reasoning shows. Replacing a first common outcome by another second common outcome of a different sign can be done in two steps. First the first common outcome is replaced by 0, and next 0 is replaced by the second common outcome. In neither of the two replacements was an outcome replaced by an outcome of a different sign. Besides signs, also ranks remain unaffected in the two replacements if they did so in the original replacement. The elaboration of the following exercise completes the reasoning.

Exercise 9.4.1.[b] Show that PT implies the rank-sure-thing principle for risk (Figure 6.5.5). □

9.4.2   Measuring utility, event weighting, and loss aversion

We next turn to the measurement of utility, probability weighting, and loss aversion under PT.

Exercise 9.4.2.[a] Make Assumption 4.10.1 (50–50 for candidates). Show that, under PT (which implies strict stochastic dominance), the α^j's in Figure 4.1.1 are still equally spaced in utility units (Exercise 4.3.1 and Observation 6.5.1), and, if $\beta^4 \leq g$, so are the corresponding β values in Figure 4.1.2. Hence, the β's must still equal the α's (Exercise 4.3.2a, b, and Exercise 6.5.1; the answers to Assignment 6.5.5 also remain valid under PT). Also show that, for Figure 4.1.5, $w^+(PE^j) = j/4$ for all j (Observation 6.5.8 for w^+ instead of w). □

The preceding exercise shows that utility and probability weighting for gains can be measured under PT much as under EU and RDU, not only keeping track of ranks as we should do under RDU, but, in addition, also keeping track of the signs of the outcomes to ensure that they are all gains. If we want to maintain the scaling convention of $U(0) = 0$ under PT, then we will not rescale $U(\alpha^0) = 0$. To have $U(\alpha^0) = 0$, we can of course set up an alternative measurement where we start the a^j's with $\alpha^0 = 0$.

We can measure utility and probability weighting for losses similarly as we can for gains. We can define tradeoff indifferences $\alpha \ominus \beta \sim^t_{cs} \gamma \ominus \delta$ in this spirit, where the subscript c indicates that the rank was the same for each outcome, and the additional subscript s indicates that the sign profile was also kept constant. This relation formalizes the measurement of utility differences for gains and also for losses. The absence of inconsistencies in such measurements then provides a behavioral foundation of PT. Such results are in Chateauneuf & Wakker (1999). We will later, in Theorem 12.3.5, present such results for the more general context of uncertainty. The result for this section can be obtained by adding Structural Assumption 2.5.2 (decision under risk) to Theorem 12.3.5. For brevity's sake, we do not display these results here.

With utility and probability weighting measured for both gains and losses, it may seem that we are done and that we have measured all of PT. However, this is not so. The readers are invited to think through this point before reading on.

An empirical way to see that something is missing goes as follows. Measurements with only gains involved, and measurements with only losses involved can never give information about loss aversion, and the exchange rate between gain and loss utility units. To infer this exchange rate, we will surely have to consider mixed prospects (for confusions see Du & Budescu 2005 p. 1800, Gintis 2009 p. 25, Lopes & Oden 1999). Another, mathematical way to see this point, based on normalizations of utility, is as follows.

When we measure utility for gains and then, separately, for losses, then each of these two is determined only up to a unit (given $U(0) = 0$). Because these units are mutually independent given only pure-gain and pure-loss data, the exchange rate between gains and losses (related to λ in Eqs. (8.4.1) and (8.4.2)) cannot be determined yet. I discuss the point in more detail. We can use the liberty to choose the unit of U as we want and we can, for instance, set $U(1) = 1$. Then, however, U is uniquely determined (this is stated formally in Observation 12.3.5′). In particular, then $U(-1)$ is uniquely determined, and so is $\lambda = -U(-1)$. The latter now is not a scaling factor for us to choose, but it is an unknown to be inferred from data. The difficulty, so to say, that an extra measurement of the exchange rate λ between gain utilities and loss utilities is required is typical of PT. This difficulty can be taken as a virtue, because here again the theory is homeomorphic to the psychological reality. The exchange rate between gain and loss utilities is a special phenomenon with its own perceptions and effects, and it requires special attention. Theories, such as EU and RDU, that do not pay such special attention will run into problems, with extra inconsistencies when measuring utilities and decision weights for outcomes of different signs.

The following example gives a pragmatic way to approximate loss aversion, using mixed prospects. Any measurement of loss aversion has to consider mixed prospects, i.e., prospects with both gains and losses, because only for preferences with such prospects involved λ plays a role.

Example 9.4.2 [A pragmatic way to measure loss aversion]. A pragmatic estimate of loss aversion λ can be obtained as follows:

$$\text{If } \alpha_{1/2}(-1) \sim 0 \text{ then } \lambda = \alpha. \tag{9.4.1}$$

To clarify, we substitute PT:

$$w^+(\tfrac{1}{2})u(\alpha) + w^-(\tfrac{1}{2})\lambda u(-1) = 0.$$

Under the empirically plausible approximative assumption that $w^+(\tfrac{1}{2}) = w^-(\tfrac{1}{2})$ we get $u(\alpha) = -\lambda u(-1)$. Then, under the also empirically plausible approximative assumption that U is linear for small numbers close to 0, we get Eq. (9.4.1). □

The following exercise gives a general nonparametric way to measure λ and, hence, $U(-1)$, once u has been elicited. It is obviously more complex than Example 9.4.2. The importance of developing nonparametric measurements of loss aversion is underscored by §9.6. Abdellaoui, Bleichrodt, & Paraschiv (2007) introduced another method for measuring loss aversion in a nonparametric manner.

Exercise 9.4.3.[b] Scale utility as in Eq. (8.4.2). Take $\alpha > 0$ such that $1 \sim \alpha_{1/2} 0$, take $\beta > 0$ such that $\alpha_{1/2}(-\beta) \sim 0$, and take $\delta > 0$ such that $-\delta \sim 0_{1/2}(-\beta)$. Show that $\lambda = -1/u(-\delta)$. □

With the scaling $u(-1) = -1$ as in Eq. (8.4.2) (and $u(0) = 0$ as done throughout for PT), common measurement techniques of RDU, when applied to losses, can elicit a value $u(-\delta)$ for any loss $-\delta$. Exercise 9.4.3 shows that we can thus determine the loss aversion parameter λ given this u. Abdellaoui, Bleichrodt, & Paraschiv (2007), Booij & van de Kuilen (2009), and Schmidt & Traub (2002) used such a technique to measure loss aversion experimentally.

9.5   Empirical findings on prospect theory

This section presents results of empirical investigations. These have so far been based mostly on laboratory experiments with students. Gurevich, Kliger, & Levy (2009) and Heath, Huddart, & Lang (1999) confirmed these findings for US stock option data. Booij, van de Kuilen, & van Praag (2010) did so for a large representative sample from the Dutch population. Their Table 4.1 conveniently summarizes the results of parametric fittings in the literature.

In general, phenomena for gains are reflected for losses, but they are less pronounced there, and behavior for losses is closer to expected value maximization. This is enhanced by choices for losses being more difficult than choices for gains, so that they generate more noise and their patterns are less pronounced (Gonzalez *et al.* 2005; Lopes 1987). Cohen, Jaffray, & Said (1987, pp. 15–18) did find more likelihood sensitivity for losses though.

Fig. 7.1.2b showed the most commonly found weighting function for gains, corresponding to Eqs. (7.2.1) and (7.2.2). A similar form has been found for losses, but deviating less from linearity. In Tversky & Kahneman (1992), c = 0.69 gave the best approximation for losses. Note that, whereas $w(\frac{1}{2}) < \frac{1}{2}$ enhances risk aversion for gains, it enhances risk seeking for losses because of the dual way of integration. This illustrates how effects are mirrored about the reference point.

Fig. 8.4.1b shows the kind of utility function most commonly found. Descriptive utility is driven not only by the perception of purchasing power (diminishing marginal utility) but also by the perception of numbers and diminishing sensitivity (Köbberling, Schwieren, & Wakker 2007). These perceptions enhance concavity for gains and, indeed, utility for gains is commonly found to be concave. For losses the effects are opposite, with for example
$U(-110) - U(-120) > U(-10) - U(-20)$ according to purchasing power perception but
$U(-110) - U(-120) < U(-10) - U(-20)$ according to numerical perception.
The common finding so far has been that there is slightly more convex than concave utility for losses, but it is a close call (Köbberling, Schwieren, & Wakker's 2007 review in note 1; see also Winter & Parker 2007; Netzer 2009; Pietras *et al.* 2008). Utility of money becomes concave again near ruin (Kahneman & Tversky 1979 p. 279; Laughhunn, Payne, & Crum 1980; Libby & Fishburn 1977).

Probability weighting and utility curvature together imply the following four-fold pattern:

(a) risk aversion for moderate- and high-probability gains;
(b) risk seeking for moderate- and high-probability losses;
(c) risk seeking for small-probability gains;
(d) risk aversion for small-probability losses.

The most pronounced empirical finding is that utility is steeper for losses than for gains, reflecting loss aversion ($\lambda > 1$) (Abdellaoui, Bleichrodt, & L'Haridon 2008).

Nevertheless, it is volatile (Ert & Erev 2008; Plott & Zeiler 2005). The violations of asset integration entailed by reference dependence (the basis of loss aversion) are more irrational than for instance probability weighting. Accordingly, they will be even more sensitive to small details of framing, and will more quickly disappear under proper learning and incentives. Many empirical studies that made it likely for loss aversion to appear, found loss aversion parameters λ of approximately 2.25. An impressive study is Gächter, Herrmann, & Johnson (2007). Plott & Zeiler (2005), however, explicitly instructed the subjects about framing effects and loss aversion, after which the phenomenon virtually disappeared. Although their finding is not surprising in an empirical sense, it does convey a useful message to the field: loss aversion is volatile and depends much on framing, and $\lambda = 2.25$ cannot have the status of a universal constant. An appealing discussion of the (ir)rationality of loss aversion is in Huber, Ariely, & Fischer (2001), with an interesting separation of intrinsic utility and loss aversion.

The following exercise illustrates the extremity orientedness of PT, mostly driven by likelihood insensitivity.

Exercise 9.5.1.[a]

Table 9.5.1. *Prospects yielding outcome x_j with probability p_j*

	x_1	p_1	π_1	x_2	p_2	π_2	x_3	p_3	π_3	x_4	p_4	π_4	PT	CE	choice
$F_{1.I}$	−3000	0.50		4500	0.50		0	0	0	0	0	0			71%
$G_{1.I}$	−6000	0.25		3000	0.75		0	0	0	0	0	0			27%
F_2	−1600	0.25		−200	0.25		1200	0.25		1600	0.25				38%
G_2	−1000	0.25		−800	0.25		800	0.25		2000	0.25				62%
$F_{3.III}$	−1500	0.50		4500	0.50		0	0	0	0	0	0			76%
$G_{3.III}$	−3000	0.25		3000	0.75		0	0	0	0	0	0			23%

Note: The CE column (filling this in will be your task) should give the certainty equivalents according to prospect theory with the parameters estimated by Tversky & Kahneman (1992). Each π_j is the decision weight, according to prospect theory, of outcome x_j (also to be filled in by you). Bold underlining indicates the majority choice between the corresponding F and G prospects.

Levy & Levy (2002) considered prospect pairs F, G as in Table 9.5.1. In experiments, the underlined prospects printed in bold were chosen by the majority of subjects, with choice percentages given in the last column. For example, when facing a choice between $F_{1.I}$ and $G_{1.I}$, 71% chose $F_{1.I}$, 27% chose $G_{1.I}$ (2% undecided or invalid); and so on. Verify that prospect theory correctly predicts all majority choices. That is, take the model as in Example 9.3.1 with the parameters found by Tversky & Kahneman (1992). Calculate the decision weights of all outcomes, the PT value of each prospect, and its certainty equivalent. Fill in the open places in the table. Encircle the choices that prospect theory predicts. □

Exercise 9.5.2[b] [Data fitting for prospect theory]. We again consider the eight indifferences from Tversky & Kahneman (1992) of Exercise 3.6.5. We assume PT with $w^+(p) = w^-(p)$ as in Eq. (7.2.1). We write w for w^+ and w^- in the rest of this exercise. U is parametrized by θ, θ', and λ (yet to be explained). Find θ, θ', (specified in each part), $0.3 \leq c = j/100 \leq 1.5$, and $0 < \lambda = k/100 < 3$ that best fit the data, and give the distance measure of §A.2. Predict $CE(-100_{0.05}(-200))$. Throughout we rescale exponential utility as in Eq. (3.5.5). This rescaling is immaterial for parts (a)–(c), as for all exercises in this book up to now. We will see later (§9.6) that the rescaling is essential for part (d).

(a) Take U as in Exercises 3.6.5 and 7.3.1 but rescaled; i.e., $U(\alpha) = (1 - \exp(-\theta\alpha))/\theta$. Search for $0 < \theta = i/10000 < 0.01$, with i running from 1 to 100.

(b) We bring in loss aversion and define $U(\alpha) = (1 - \exp(-\theta\alpha))/\theta$ if $\alpha \geq 0$ and $U(\alpha) = \lambda(1 - \exp(-\theta\alpha))/\theta$ if $\alpha < 0$. Search for $0 < \theta = i/10000 < 0.01$, with i running from 1 to 100.

(c) $U(\alpha) = (1 - \exp(-\theta\alpha))/\theta$ if $\alpha \geq 0$ and $U(\alpha) = \lambda(1 - \exp(-\theta'\alpha))/\theta'$ if $\alpha < 0$ restricted to the case $\theta' = -\theta$. Search for $0 < \theta = i/10000 < 0.01$, with i running from 1 to 100.

(d) We now treat utility for gains and for losses as independent. We investigate in particular if utility for losses is convex or concave. Take $U(\alpha) = 1 - \exp(-\theta\alpha)$ if $\alpha \geq 0$ and $U(\alpha) = \lambda(\exp(-\theta'\alpha) - 1)$ if $\alpha < 0$, with now θ' independent of θ. Search for $0 < \theta = i/10000 < 0.0100$ and $-0.01 < \theta' = j/10000 < 0.0100$, with i running from 1 to 100 and j running from -100 to 100. Here four parameters must be fit to the data. The footnote gives suggestions for reducing calculation time.[7] □

Exercise 9.5.2′.[b] The median value of $CE(-100_{0.05}(-200))$ that was empirically observed by Tversky & Kahneman (1992) was -179. Determine by how far your prediction in Exercise 9.5.2 is off from the actually observed value in parts (a), (b), and (c) in Exercise 9.5.2. □

The elaborations in Appendix J will reveal the following points. In part (a), loss aversion λ played no role and the only difference with Exercise 7.3.1 was that we used the dual probability weighting for losses rather than the weighting of RDU. It led to an improved distance, showing that the dual weighting for losses of PT fits the data better than the weighting of RDU. For $CE(-100_{\frac{1}{2}}(-200))$ the prediction now is close to risk neutrality with slight risk seeking. In part (b) loss aversion is introduced. It further improves the fit. Utility now is close to risk neutrality, with a big risk tolerance, because most of the risk aversion is captured by loss aversion. CE $(-100_{\frac{1}{2}}(-200))$ now exhibits clear risk seeking.

Part (c) introduces a further change relative to RDU, by letting utility for losses be the reflection of utility for gains so that concave utility for gains is combined with convex utility for losses. This move again improves the fit, although not by very

---

[7] If necessary, you can reduce calculation time by first taking the step sizes between values considered 10 times larger and, thus, first finding a small range in which to search in more detail. Focusing on the role of θ' you can, next, consider only $0.6 \leq c = j/100 \leq 0.7$, $0.0050 < \theta = k/100 < 0.0060$, and $1.60 \leq \lambda \leq 1.7$.

much. It suggests that utility for losses is convex rather than concave although, again, not by very much. Because loss aversion, which concerns mixed prospects only, captures most of risk aversion, utility and probability weighting need no more "mismodel" this phenomenon as they did in classical EU and in RDU, and can show their true face. With loss aversion given its proper role, $CE(-100_{1/2}(-200))$ thus exhibits clear risk seeking, which is more in agreement with the data for losses in Exercise 3.6.5. The distance of the predicted $CE(-100_{1/2}(-200))$ to the observed CE also improves after each additional move, and in part (c) gets very close to 0. Part (d) confirms that a negative θ' and convex utility for losses, as in part (c), do indeed fit best. The fit of the data has improved slightly with respect to part (c). The prediction of $CE(-100_{1/2}-200)$ has become much worse. There can be two explanations for it. The first is that we use too many parameters to fit the data, so that the parameters pick up more noise than systematic effects. Statistics textbooks do indeed recommend using more than eight observations to fit four parameters. For didactical reasons I, nevertheless, used this simple data set. The second explanation is that the observed $CE(-100_{1/2}-200) = -179$ is not very representative.

9.6 Analytical problems of power utility for analyzing loss aversion

Power utility for gains and losses is defined as α^{θ} for $\alpha \geq 0$ and as $-(-\alpha)^{\theta'}$ for $\alpha < 0$, as in Example 9.3.1. In general, we consider a different power for losses than for gains. Power functions exhibit extreme and implausible behavior near $\alpha = 0$. For negative powers the function on $\mathbb{R}^+$ tends to $-\infty$ at 0. For positive powers the concave functions with power < 1 on $\mathbb{R}^+$ have their derivative tend to ∞ at 0. Such extreme behavior is unproblematic for studies where only large positive inputs remote from 0 play a role, as is often the case in finance and macro-economics. For the study of loss aversion, however, 0 is in the center of interest, and the extreme behavior is problematic.

9.6.1 The first problem: loss aversion depends on the monetary unit

We justified the choice of $u(1) = -u(-1)$ in our definition of loss aversion (Eq. (8.4.2)) by the assumption of differentiability and approximate linearity of u on $[-1,1]$. Had we chosen any other small numbers α to scale $u(\alpha) = -u(-\alpha)$, such as $\alpha = 0.01$ instead of $\alpha = 1$ (cents instead of dollars), then this would have given approximately the same results for differentiable utility u. Hence, it is immaterial which small number α we take to scale u. The aforementioned assumptions, while empirically plausible, do not hold for power utility. In particular, power functions cannot yield approximate linearity on $[-1,1]$ or on any other small interval around 0. Hence, for power utility there is no justification for scaling $u(1) = -u(-1)$ that I am aware of, and this scaling is arbitrary. Using other outcomes α and $-\alpha$ for the scaling, also if $\alpha > 0$ is very small, give drastically different results. We will even see that, irrespective of the data, we can obtain any loss aversion parameter $\lambda > 0$ by choosing

$\alpha > 0$ accordingly. I first state some preparatory algebraic equations, and then state the result. In words, the following lemma shows that, with power θ for gains and θ' for losses, a rescaling of the outcomes by a factor μ will change the gain-utility u by a factor μ^θ but the loss-utility u by a factor $\mu^{\theta'}$, so that (Eq. (8.8.1)) loss aversion λ is changed by a factor $\mu^\theta/\mu^{\theta'}$.

Lemma 9.6.1. Assume that PT holds with positive λ, θ, and θ', and

$$U(\alpha) = u(\alpha) = \alpha^\theta \text{ if } \alpha \geq 0 \text{ and} \tag{9.6.1}$$

$$U(\alpha) = \lambda u(\alpha) = -\lambda(-\alpha)^{\theta'} \text{ if } \alpha < 0. \tag{9.6.2}$$

Then

$$u(1) = -u(-1) \tag{9.6.3}$$

as in Eqs. (9.3.5)–(9.3.7). For any $\mu > 0$, PT also holds with

$$U^*(\alpha) = u^*(\alpha) = (\mu\alpha)^\theta \text{if } \alpha \geq 0 \text{ and} \tag{9.6.4}$$

$$U^*(\alpha) = \lambda^* u^*(\alpha) = -\lambda^*(-\mu\alpha)^{\theta'} \text{ if } \alpha < 0 \tag{9.6.5}$$

so that

$$u^*(1/\mu) = -u^*(-1/\mu), \tag{9.6.6}$$

where we set

$$\lambda^* = \lambda\mu^{\theta-\theta'}. \tag{9.6.7}$$

Proof. This can be derived from Eq. (8.8.1). We give an independent derivation here. By substitution, $U^*(\alpha) = \mu^\theta U(\alpha)$, a rescaling that does not affect preference[8]:
If $\alpha \geq 0$, then $U^*(\alpha) = \mu^\theta\alpha^\theta = \mu^\theta U(\alpha)$.
If $\alpha < 0$, then $U^*(\alpha) = -\lambda\mu^{\theta-\theta'}(-\mu\alpha)^{\theta'} = -\lambda\mu^\theta(-\alpha)^{\theta'} = \mu^\theta U(\alpha)$. □
   The following result is a corollary that follows because we can choose any $\mu > 0$ in Eq. (9.6.7).

Observation 9.6.2 [Complete dependence of loss aversion on the unit of money under power utility]. Assume that PT holds with utility and loss aversion as in Eqs. (9.6.1)–(9.6.3) and $\theta \neq \theta'$. Then, for any $\lambda^* > 0$, we can rescale the unit of money such that λ^* is the new loss aversion parameter. □
   The dependence in the observation is, obviously, undesirable.[9] We next give a numerical illustration.

---

[8] As is easy to see. Observation 12.3.5' will give a formal statement.
[9] It means that, at best, loss aversion can be defined relative to the unit of money α chosen to set $u(\alpha) = -u(-\alpha)$. Then loss aversion depends on the unit of money similarly as the Pratt–Arrow index of concavity of utility is defined only relative to the unit of money (Wakker 2008a). Only if $\theta = \theta'$ can loss aversion be a dimensionless quantity in the sense of Narens (2002).

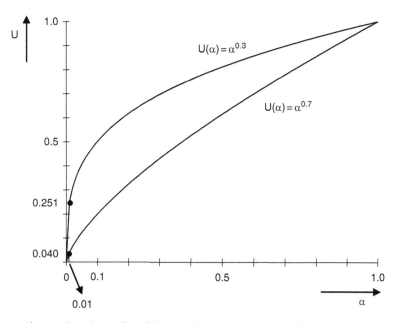

If we replace the scaling u(1) = −u(−1) = 1 by the scaling u(0.01) =
−u(−0.01), then we have to multiply the loss aversion parameter by
0.040/0.251; λ = 2.25 then turns into λ* = 0.36.

Figure 9.6.1 Dependence of loss aversion on scaling of money.

Example 9.6.3 [Dependence of loss aversion on unit of money]. See Figure 9.6.1.
Researcher1 expresses outcomes in dollars. From observed preferences between gain
prospects he derives $u(\alpha) = \alpha^{0.3}$ for $\alpha \geq 0$, and from observed preferences between
loss prospects he derives $u(\alpha) = -(-\alpha)^{0.7}$ for $\alpha < 0$. Empirical studies have indeed
suggested that utility for losses is closer to linear than utility for gains. Researcher1
accepts the scaling u(1) = −u(−1) and finds $\lambda = 2.25$.

Researcher2 observes the same data as researcher1 did, but thinks in terms of cents.
We will continue to express outcomes in terms of dollars. Where we write α reflecting
$\$\alpha$, researcher2 writes 100α reflecting 100α cents. From preferences between gain
prospects, researcher2 derives $u*(\alpha) = (100\alpha)^{0.3} = 100^{0.3}\alpha^{0.3} = 3.98u(\alpha)$ for $\alpha \geq 0$,
and from preferences between loss prospects he derives $u*(\alpha) = -(-100\alpha)^{0.7} =
-100^{0.7}(-\alpha)^{0.7} = 25.12u(\alpha)$ for $\alpha < 0$. For preferences between gain-prospects
and for preferences between loss-prospects the rescalings of utility are immaterial
and the implied preferences are unaffected. Researcher2, however, adopts the
scaling $u*(0.01) = -u*(-0.01)$ because the outcome $0.01 is his unit. Eq. (9.6.7)
shows that now[10] $\lambda* = 0.36$, which is roughly the reciprocal of λ. Whereas

---

[10] A numerical verification: by usual uniqueness results of U up to a positive scale (will be derived in
Observation 12.3.5′), we must have $U* = 100^{0.3}U$ for losses as it is for gains. Hence, for losses, we have
$\lambda*u* = 100^{0.3}\lambda u$ so that $\lambda* = \frac{100^{0.3}\lambda u}{u*} = \frac{100^{0.3}\lambda}{100^{0.7}} = 0.36$.

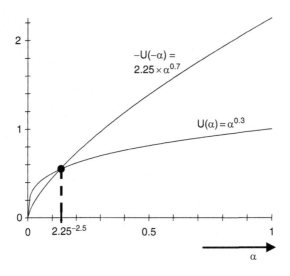

Figure 9.6.2 Anomaly for loss aversion.

researcher1 claims strong loss aversion, researcher2 claims the opposite, strong gain seeking.

Another researcher, researcher3, who adopts a scaling $u^{**}(100) = -u^{**}(-100)$ will, similarly, conclude that $\lambda^{**} = 14.20$, suggesting extreme loss aversion. A scaling $u(\alpha) = -u(-\alpha)$ for $\alpha > 0$ will give a λ arbitrarily close to 0 by taking $\alpha > 0$ sufficiently small, and λ arbitrarily large by taking α sufficiently large. □

Thus, there is no clear way to define loss aversion for power utility unless the powers for gains and losses agree. Tversky & Kahneman (1992) coincidentally found such an agreement.

9.6.2   The second problem: always $U(\alpha) > -U(-\alpha)$ for some outcome $\alpha > 0$

This subsection points out a problem with power utility put forward by Köbberling & Wakker (2003); see Figure 9.6.2. So as to avoid it, Harrison & Rutström (2008) and Post *et al.* (2008 footnote 6) restricted attention to the same power for gains as for losses. Tanaka, Camerer, & Nguyen (2010) did so too.

Consider, for $\alpha > 0$, $U(\alpha) = \alpha^{\theta}$ and, for $\alpha < 0$, $U(\alpha) = -\lambda(-\alpha)^{\theta'}$ with $\lambda > 0$. Whenever $\theta \neq \theta'$, the functions $U(\alpha) = \alpha^{\theta}$ for gains and U^* defined on gains by $U^*(\alpha) = -U(-\alpha) = \lambda\alpha^{\theta'}$ (the reflected U function for losses), intersect at $\alpha = \lambda^{1/(\theta - \theta')}$. Then one function dominates to the left, and the other dominates to the right, of the intersection point. Irrespective of the size of λ, there is always a part of the domain where $U(\alpha)$ dominates $-U(-\alpha)$. Thus, although it is empirically plausible that $-U(-\alpha) \geq U(\alpha)$ for all $\alpha > 0$, power utility cannot accommodate this phenomenon whenever the power for gains differs from that for losses. This second problem illustrates once more that power utility is not well suited for the study of loss aversion.

9.6.3 Ways to avoid the problems

A pragmatic variation of the power family, used by Vendrik & Woltjer (2007), can mitigate the problems. It is as follows:

$$U(\alpha) = u(\alpha) = (1 + \alpha)^\theta/\theta - 1/\theta \text{ for } \alpha > 0. \tag{9.6.8}$$

$$U(\alpha) = u(\alpha) = 0 \text{ for } \alpha = 0. \tag{9.6.9}$$

$$U(\alpha) = \lambda u(\alpha) = -\lambda(1 - \alpha)^{\theta'}/\theta' + \lambda/\theta' \text{ for } \alpha < 0. \tag{9.6.10}$$

(Logarithmic functions can be specified for $\theta = 0$.) For this family, u is differentiable at 0 with derivative 1. Hence, the conventions of $u(1) = -u(-1)$ or $u(\alpha) = -u(-\alpha)$ for any small α will give consistent estimations of λ, so that the first problem of §9.6.1 is avoided. At least for the empirically plausible case of $\theta \leq \theta'$, $\lambda \geq 1$ will imply[11] $(-U(-\alpha)) \geq U(\alpha)$ for all $\alpha > 0$ so that also the second anomaly is avoided.

Exponential utility can also solve the problems described in this section. Basic utility u should then be normalized to be differentiable at 0 also if the parameter for losses is different from the parameter for gains. This can be obtained by using the normalization of Eq. (3.5.5) both for gains and for losses, so that the derivative of u at $\alpha = 0$ is 1. De Giorgi & Hens (2006) gave further arguments in favor of prospect theory with piecewise exponential utility. In the same way as power utility is too steep for outcomes close to 0, exponential utility is too shallow for extreme positive outcomes – a phenomenon underlying Rabin's paradox in Example 8.6.1 – and too steep for extreme negative outcomes. This will also hamper estimations of loss aversion if extreme outcomes are involved.

Exercise 9.6.1.[b] Researcher1 expresses outcomes in dollars. From observed gain choices he derives $u(\alpha) = \alpha^{0.5}$ for $\alpha \geq 0$, and from observed loss choices he derives $u(\alpha) = -(-\alpha)^{0.88}$ for $\alpha < 0$. He accepts the scaling $u(1) = -u(-1)$ and finds $\lambda = 2.25$.

Researcher2 observes the same data as researcher1, but thinks in terms of cents. We will continue to express outcomes in terms of dollars. From gain choices researcher2 derives $u^*(\alpha) = (100\alpha)^{0.5} = 10u(\alpha)$ for $\alpha \geq 0$, and from loss choices he derives $u^*(\alpha) = -(-100\alpha)^{0.88} = 100^{0.88}u(\alpha)$ for $\alpha < 0$. Researcher2 accepts the scaling $u^*(0.01) = -u^*(-0.01)$. What is his estimate of loss aversion λ^*? □

Appendix 9.7 Some theoretical issues concerning prospect theory

We briefly discuss some theoretical aspects of prospect theory. For the PT formula, we choose a complete sign-ranking of the outcomes. As before (§6.7), we may have some freedom in the choice of this complete sign-ranking. If some outcomes of the prospect are 0 then we have some liberty in choosing k in Eq. (9.2.1). Again, as always, the definition of our functional is not affected by these choices, as it should be

---

[11] Any graphic program on your computer will convince you.

for the functional to be well defined. The particular choice of k is immaterial because $U(0) = 0$, so that the decision weight assigned to the 0 outcome does not matter.

The following integral definition of PT will not be used in this book, but is useful for prospects with infinitely many outcomes. We recall that a prospect x is a probability measure, so that for instance $x(U(\alpha) > t)$ denotes the probability that prospect x yields an outcome α with utility exceeding t.

$$PT(x) = \int_{\mathbb{R}^+} w^+(x(U(\alpha) > t))dt - \int_{\mathbb{R}^-} w^-(x(U(\alpha) < t))dt. \tag{9.7.1}$$

The derivation of this formula is identical to that of Eq. (6.9.1) in Exercise 6.9.1, with $w^-(p)$ substituted for $1 - w(1-p)$ for losses. The symmetry of the negative part relative to the positive part suggests that the formula is natural. This functional appeared in the appendix to Starmer & Sugden (1989) for the special case of $w^+ = w^-$.

For Eq. (9.7.1), as for the related Eq. (6.9.1), it is immaterial whether we use strict or weak inequalities in the integrand. This choice matters only for utility values t that have a positive probability of occurring, and there are at most countably many such utility values. The values of the integrand at countably many points do not affect the integral.

In steps, the PT value of a continuous distribution with distribution function F over outcomes can be calculated as follows.

STEP 1.   First, we take the positive part of the distribution denoted F^+, which entails that at all negative outcomes it is set equal to 0. F^+ we treat exactly as when calculating the RDU value of this continuous distribution, using the four steps in Appendix 6.9, with weighting function w^+.

STEP 2.   Next, we take the negative part of the distribution denoted F^-, which entails that at 0 and at all positive outcomes it is set equal to 1. We treat this negative part dually to the calculation of RDU, as follows.

STEP 3.   Consider the distribution function for utilities instead of outcomes $(F \circ U^{-1})$.

STEP 4.   Transform the function using the probability weighting w^-, into $w^-(F \circ U^{-1})$.

STEP 5.   Calculate the expectation of the distribution obtained.

STEP 6.   Add the result of Steps 1 and 5.

Assume that F is the regular distribution function of the prospect (G is the rank and $F = 1 - G$). Then Eq. (9.7.1) can be rewritten as

$$PT(x) = \int_{\mathbb{R}^+} w^+(G_{x,U}(t))dt - \int_{\mathbb{R}^-} w^-(F_{x,U}(t))dt. \tag{9.7.2}$$

If F has density function $f = F'$, then PT can be calculated as the following analog of RDU's Eq. (6.9.4):

$$\int_{\mathbb{R}^+} U(\alpha)w^{+\prime}(1 - F(\alpha))f(\alpha)d\alpha + \int_{\mathbb{R}^-} U(\alpha)w^{-\prime}(F(\alpha))f(\alpha)d\alpha. \tag{9.7.3}$$

Appendix 9.8   Original prospect theory of 1979

The first version of prospect theory, called *original prospect theory* (*OPT*) here, was published by Kahneman & Tversky (1979). We assume Structural Assumption 2.5.2 (decision under risk and richness) throughout. As does PT, OPT assigns a special role to a *reference outcome* 0. There exists a strictly increasing continuous *utility function* $U : \mathbb{R} \rightarrow \mathbb{R}$ with $U(0) = 0$ and a (*probability*) *weighting function* w. The same weighting function is used for gains and for losses. Kahneman & Tversky (1979) used the term value function for U, but we will maintain the term utility function. OPT deals with prospects with at most two nonzero outcomes; i.e., prospects of the form $p_1 x_1, p_2 x_2, p_3 0$. We will assume $x_1 > x_2$ with neither of these two outcomes equal to 0.[12] Prospects with only one nonzero outcome, or no zero outcome, are comprised by setting some of the p_j's equal to 0. A prospect is *strictly positive* if all its outcomes are gains ($p_3 = 0$ and $x_1 > x_2 > 0$), and it is *strictly negative* if all its outcomes are losses. A prospect is *regular* if it is neither strictly positive nor strictly negative. On the domain considered, a prospect is regular if and only if the product of all its possible outcomes is nonpositive. We have, for $x_1 > x_2$,

$$OPT(p_1 x_1, p_2 x_2, p_3 0) = w(p_1)U(x_1) + w(p_2)U(x_2)$$

if $p_1 x_1, p_2 x_2, p_3 0$ is regular

$\quad$ (either $p_3 > 0$; or $p_3 = 0, p_1 > 0, p_2 > 0$, and $x_1 > 0 > x_2$);   (9.8.1)

$$OPT(p_1 x_1, p_2 x_2, p_3 0) = U(x_2) + w(p_1)(U(x_1) - U(x_2))$$

if $p_1 x_1, p_2 x_2, p_3 0$ is strictly positive

$\quad$ ($p_3 = 0$ and $x_1 > x_2 > 0$);   (9.8.2)

$$OPT(p_1 x_1, p_2 x_2, p_3 0) = U(x_1) - w(p_2)(U(x_1) - U(x_2))$$

if $p_1 x_1, p_2 x_2, p_3 0$ is strictly negative

$\quad$ ($p_3 = 0$ and $x_2 < x_1 < 0$).   (9.8.3)

For prospects $\alpha_p 0$ with only one nonzero outcome α, these formulas give the evaluation $w(p)U(\alpha)$. For regular prospects, OPT amounts to the separate-outcome probability transformation theory (Eq. (5.3.3)). We summarize a number of cases where OPT agrees with rank dependence or PT. The cases all follow from substitution.

Observation 9.8.1.

OPT agrees with PT (with $w^+ = w^- = w$) on the domain of all:
− prospects with one or two outcomes;
− mixed three-outcome prospects (positive probability at gain and positive probability at loss).

---

[12] OPT has difficulties with the collapsing of outcomes and it therefore has to assume collapsed forms (all outcomes distinct).

This domain includes all strictly positive and all strictly negative prospects, and also all mixed prospects.

- OPT differs from PT only when prospects p_1x_1, p_2x_2, p_30 are considered for which no p_j is zero and the x_j's have the same sign.
- On the domain of prospects with one or two outcomes that are both nonnegative, OPT agrees with binary RDU.
- On the domain of prospects with one or two outcomes that are both nonpositive, OPT agrees with binary RDU with $1-w(1-p)$ instead of $w(p)$. □

Kahneman & Tversky (1979) explained the formula for strictly positive prospects using what they called an editing operation: The minimal outcome x_2 is taken as a kind of new reference point with utility $U(x_2)$, and the extra utility $U(x_1) - U(x_2)$ is added with weight $w(p_1)$. The negative formula is explained similarly. Thus they, partly, modified the separate-outcome probability transformation. They did so so as to mitigate undesirable implications explained later.

Kahneman & Tversky (1979 p. 288) wrote that the extension to more outcomes is straightforward. Their explanation of editing for strictly positive and strictly negative prospects suggests that they had the following formulas in mind:

For $p_1x_1 \cdots p_nx_n$ with $x_1 > \cdots > x_n$,

$$OPT(p_1x_1 \cdots p_nx_n) = w(p_1)U(x_1) + \cdots + w(p_n)U(x_n) \text{ (as Eq. (5.3.3))}$$

if $p_1x_1 \cdots p_nx_n$ is regular $(p_1 > 0, x_1 \geq 0, p_n > 0, x_n \leq 0)$;   (9.8.4)

$$OPT(p_1x_1 \cdots p_nx_n) = U(x_n) + w(p_1)(U(x_1) - U(x_n)) + \cdots +$$

$$w(p_{n-1})(U(x_{n-1}) - U(x_n))$$

if $p_1x_1 \cdots p_nx_n$ is strictly positive $(x_n > 0)$;   (9.8.5)

$$OPT(p_1x_1 \cdots p_nx_n) = U(x_1) - w(p_2)(U(x_1) - U(x_2)) - \cdots -$$

$$w(p_n)(U(x_1) - U(x_n))$$

if $p_1x_1 \cdots p_nx_n$ is strictly negative $(x_1 < 0)$.   (9.8.6)

This suggestion is supported by Kahneman & Tversky (1975 p. 18), where the authors applied the same generalization to many outcomes for their slightly different formulation of the theory.[13] I emphasize that Eqs. (9.8.4)–(9.8.6) are not OPT and that the latter concerns only prospects with at most two nonzero outcomes.

There have been many misunderstandings in the literature about OPT for strictly positive and strictly negative prospects with two nonzero outcomes. Some authors

---

[13] For strictly positive prospects, they did not take the minimal utility as point of departure, but the minimal outcome, subtracting this outcome from all other outcomes. For strictly negative prospects they subtract the maximal outcome from all other outcomes. In other words, they used utilities of differences rather than differences of utilities.

erroneously applied the separate-outcome probability transformation theory (Eq. (5.3.3); $w(p_j)U(x_j)$) to such prospects. Other authors deliberately used Eq. (5.3.3) as a variation of OPT because it is more tractable than OPT, using terms such as "separable prospect theory" (Camerer & Ho 1994 p. 185; Harrison & Rutström 2009 p. 140 and footnote 17) or "subjective expected utility theory" (Starmer & Sugden 1993), or "prospect theory without the editing operation" (Wu, Zhang, & Abdellaoui 2005). However, what prospect theory without editing should look like is merely speculation. Kahneman & Tversky (1979) deliberately did not go that way.

A drawback of the separable version is that it is highly implausible for nonmixed prospects with many outcomes. For many outcomes the probabilities of single outcomes are usually small. Then only the behavior of w close to 0, on some small interval $[0, \epsilon]$, matters, with the shape of w on $[\epsilon, 1]$ being irrelevant.[14] Close to 0 w usually overweights probabilities, so that the total decision weight will usually exceed 1. Then extreme violations of stochastic dominance result. The following example illustrates this point.

Example 9.8.2 [Separable prospect theory generates implausible violations of stochastic dominance]. Assume separable prospect theory ($w(p_j)U(x_j)$ as in Eq. (5.3.3)), with $w(p)$ and U as found by Tversky & Kahneman (1992; see Example 9.3.1). Consider ($1/4$:999, $1/4$:998, $1/4$:997, $1/4$:996). Its certainty equivalent is $U^{inv}(w(1/4)U(999) + w(1/4)U(998) + w(1/4)U(997) + w(1/4)U(996)) = 1184$. This value exceeds the maximum outcome of the prospect, entailing a clear violation of stochastic dominance. For ($1/12$: 999, $1/12$: 998, $1/12$: 997, $1/12$: 996, $1/12$:995, $1/12$:994, $1/12$:993, $1/12$:992, $1/12$:991, $1/12$:990, $1/12$:989, $1/12$:988) the certainty equivalent is 2238. It is more than twice the maximum outcome and entails an extreme violation of stochastic dominance.[15] □

Whether OPT or PT is a better descriptive theory for prospects with few outcomes is an open question (Gonzalez & Wu 2003; Starmer 2000; Wu, Zhang, & Abdellaoui 2005). One difficulty of OPT relates to the well-known problem that it violates stochastic dominance also for those prospects (Kahneman & Tversky 1979 pp. 283–284). This shows that OPT is not well suited for theoretical analyses.

Because the main reason for violations of stochastic dominance by Eq. (5.3.3) is that the weights do not sum to 1, authors continue to come up with the proposal to normalize the decision weights, leading to the formula

$$\frac{\sum_{j=1}^{n} w(p_j)U(x_j)}{\sum_{j=1}^{n} w(p_j)} \qquad (9.8.7)$$

---

[14] For plausible extensions of Eq. (5.3.3) to continuous distributions, the only aspect of w that matters is its derivative at 0 (Rieger & Wang 2008).

[15] Kahneman & Tversky (1979) assumed that violations of dominance will be overruled by editing in direct binary choice. However, the evaluations remain absurd when used for other purposes.

(Karmarkar 1978 p. 64). People usually conjecture, incorrectly, that this formula will not violate stochastic dominance. Unfortunately, also Tversky & Kahneman (1992 p. 299, l. -6) made this incorrect conjecture. Exercise 6.7.1 considered a wider class of transformation formulas and showed that the only model among them satisfying natural conditions, primarily stochastic dominance, is the rank-dependent function. To see why Eq. (9.8.7) violates stochastic dominance, consider $100_{0.1}0$ versus $(0.1{:}100, 0.01{:}0.90, 0.01{:}0.89, \ldots , 0.01{:}0.01)$, and assume $w(0.01) > 0.01$. For the second prospect the many small outcomes generate much decision weight, reducing the weight of outcome 100. Then the theoretical value of the second prospect is below that of the first. The second prospect, however, stochastically dominates the first, and stochastic dominance is violated. Birnbaum's (2008a) RAM and TAX models also use average decision weights, generalizing Eq. (9.8.7).

Summarizing, OPT is difficult to analyze for few outcomes because it uses different formulas for different prospects and is not readily extendable to many outcomes. The sometimes thought-to-be tractable and extendable version (separable weighting) does not stand scrutiny. Hence, OPT cannot be the basis of a plausible or tractable theory, which is why this book focuses on PT. The great contribution of OPT was that it was the first theory that combined indispensable psychological concepts for risk theories, being sensitivity to probability and loss aversion, into an accessible theory with empirical realism. The exact theory chosen was not sufficiently sound in the end. It needed the modification of Quiggin (1982) for risk and of Schmeidler (1989) for uncertainty to achieve a satisfactory status.

Part III

Nonexpected utility for uncertainty

Since Keynes (1921), Knight (1921), and Ellsberg (1961) it had been understood that we need a theory for decision under uncertainty when no probabilities are given. A first proposal came from de Finetti (1931a) and Ramsey (1931), and was later perfected by Savage (1954). These authors showed that, if no objective probabilities are given, then we have to provide subjective probabilities as well as we can, assuming some conditions. This led to expected utility for uncertainty, the topic of Chapter 4. Because we still had probabilities available, we could use many techniques from risk. No very new techniques had to be developed.

The results of de Finetti, Ramsey, and Savage were first challenged by Allais (1953a), who showed that people often do not maximize expected utility. Allais did not challenge the role of probabilities (the concern of Keynes and Knight), and assumed those given. A more serious challenge came from Ellsberg (1961). He provided a paradox where, again, the conditions of de Finetti *et al.* were violated. These violations were, however, more fundamental. They showed that under plausible circumstances no subjective probabilities can be provided in any manner. Thus Ellsberg put the question of Keynes and Knight back on the table: We need a new theory for decision under uncertainty, one that essentially extends beyond probabilistic reasoning. Yet, despite the importance of such a theory, for more than 60 years after Keynes (1921) and Knight (1921) no one had been able to invent it due to the subtle nature of uncertainty in the absence of probabilities. It was only in 1982 that David Schmeidler resolved this problem by inventing rank-dependent utility for uncertainty.

The main new phenomenon that makes uncertainty richer and more challenging than risk is source dependence. The term source refers to a mechanism that generates uncertainty. For example, one source of uncertainty may concern the performance of the Dow Jones index tomorrow and another source the performance of the Nikkei index tomorrow. Ellsberg's (1961) influential paradox provided the first well-known example of this phenomenon, with different sources generated by different urns from which balls are to be drawn. The general concept of a source was introduced in the early 1990s by Tversky. For different sources of uncertainty, a decision maker can exhibit different characteristics. Using Schmeidler's rank dependence this phenomenon can be modeled, so that, for instance, the classical Ellsberg paradox and the home bias, one of the great paradoxes in finance (French & Poterba 1991), can be accommodated.

Part III of the book continues to adopt Structural Assumption 1.2.1 (decision under uncertainty). The term *ambiguity attitude* is commonly used in the literature to designate differences between behavior under unknown probabilities and behavior under known probabilities (risk).[1] Comparisons between known and unknown probabilities, however, arise primarily in artificial experimental situations, and they rarely play a role in practice. More important for applications are comparisons between different sources that all have unknown probabilities. An example is the home bias. Hence, we will also consider general comparisons of the latter kind.

Events with known probabilities essentially comprise one source of uncertainty, which is why source dependence did not make an appearance in preceding chapters on decision under risk. Chapters on uncertainty so far assumed expected utility, in which case all events can also be treated as one source of uncertainty, so that source dependence did not make an appearance in those chapters either. Hence, it is only now that we can turn to this phenomenon. Despite the new aspects of uncertainty, several of its aspects and results are still similar to those for risk. They form the focus of Chapter 10. New phenomena, including source preference, will be in Chapter 11. For ambiguity, even more than for risk, the attitudes observed for losses are different than those observed for gains. Hence, the reference-dependent approach of prospect theory is desirable for ambiguity (Chapter 12).

---

[1] Budescu, Weinberg, & Wallsten (1988) argued, and I agree, that vagueness would be a better term than ambiguity. We will, however, follow the literature and use the term ambiguity.

10 Extending rank-dependent utility from risk to uncertainty

This chapter presents rank-dependent utility for uncertainty as a natural generalization of the same theory for risk. Much of the material in this chapter can be obtained from Chapters 7 and 8 (on rank dependence under risk) by using a word processor to search for "probability p" and by then replacing it with "event E" everywhere. Similarly, much of this chapter can be obtained from Chapter 4 (on EU under uncertainty) by searching for "outcome event E" and replacing it with "ranked event E^R," and "subjective probabilities of events" with "decision weights of ranked events." Most of this chapter should, accordingly, not be surprising. I hope that the readers will take this absence of a surprise as a surprise in a didactic sense. A good understanding of the material of §2.1–§2.3, relating risk to uncertainty, will facilitate the study of this chapter.

The literature on rank dependence for uncertainty has commonly used a "comonotonicity" concept that, however, is not very tractable for applications. Hence, our analysis will use ranks instead, in the same way as we did for risk. Comonotonicity is analyzed in Appendix 10.12.

10.1 Probabilistic sophistication

The assumption of expected utility maximization has traditionally been divided into two assumptions. The first one entails that all uncertainties can be quantified in terms of probabilities, so that event-contingent prospects can be replaced by probability-contingent prospects (Cohen, Jaffray, & Said 1987, Introduction; Savage 1954 Theorem 5.2.2). The second one entails that probability-contingent prospects are evaluated by an expectation of utility, i.e., by EU. *Probabilistic sophistication* maintains the first assumption but gives up the second. That is, it assumes that a probability measure P on S exists such that each event-contingent prospect is evaluated by the probability-contingent prospect generated over the outcomes. However, probability-contingent prospects need not be evaluated by expected utility. The decision maker may for instance use rank-dependent utility with transformed probabilities to evaluate probability-contingent prospects.

Several authors have used the term decision under risk for probabilistic sophistication, because Structural Assumption 2.5.2 (decision under risk and richness; richness is not essential in this discussion) then holds with respect to P (Epstein 1999; Stigler 1971). We will avoid such terminology, and will preserve the term decision under risk for situations where P is objectively available and can be used as directly observable input in measurements and preference conditions. The latter need not hold for probabilistic sophistication, where P can be subjective and may have to be elicited from preferences. Behavioral foundations for probabilistic sophistication are in Abdellaoui & Wakker (2005 Theorem 5.5), Chew & Sagi (2006), Epstein & LeBreton (1993), Machina & Schmeidler (1992), and Sarin & Wakker (2000). We will not study probabilistic sophistication for its own sake, but will consider it in the context of rank-dependent utility.

A first nonexpected utility model for decision under uncertainty results if we assume *RDU with probabilistic sophistication*: there exists a probability measure P on S, a probability weighting function w, and a utility function U, such that preferences maximize RDU with respect to P as in RDU's Definition 6.1.1. This model is one step more complex than RDU for risk because the probabilities P may be subjective. We will see that there is more to uncertainty than probabilistic sophistication. Uncertainty is richer, and more complex than the model just defined can capture, as the following examples will illustrate. Hence, we will have to develop more fundamental generalizations of the models we used for decision under risk.

Example 10.1.1 [Ellsberg's two-color paradox]. A known urn urn_k contains 50 red balls and 50 black balls, and an ambiguous ("unknown") urn urn_a contains 100 red and black balls in an unknown proportion. From each urn one ball will be drawn at random, and its color will be inspected. R_k denotes the event of a red ball drawn from the known urn, and the events B_k, R_a, and B_a are defined similarly. Gambling on an event means receiving $100 if the event obtains, and nil otherwise. People typically prefer gambling on a color from the known urn to gambling on a color from the unknown urn, as depicted in Figure 10.1.1 (Halevy 2007). These preferences are also found if people can themselves choose the color to gamble on after the composition of the urn has already been determined, so that there is no reason to suspect an unfavorable composition of the unknown urn.

Behavior as just described cannot be accommodated by probabilistic sophistication. In particular, it violates EU. The preference in Fig. a would imply $P(B_k) > P(B_a)$, and the one in Fig. b would imply $P(R_k) > P(R_a)$. This cannot be because $P(B_k)$ and $P(R_k)$ add up to 1 as do $P(B_a)$ and $P(R_a)$, and big numbers cannot add up to the same total as small numbers do. □

Example 10.1.2 [Home bias]. An American investor can choose between gaining an amount if the Dow Jones index goes up tomorrow, denoted DJ^+, or gaining that same amount if the Nikkei index goes up tomorrow (NK^+). He prefers the former (Fig. 10.1.2a). If the choice is between gaining if the Dow Jones index does not go up

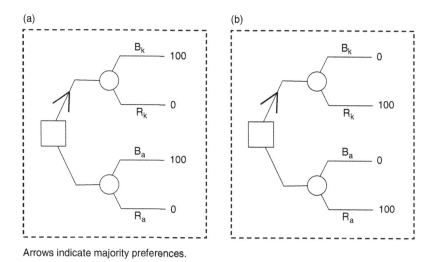

Arrows indicate majority preferences.

Figure 10.1.1 Ellsberg paradox.

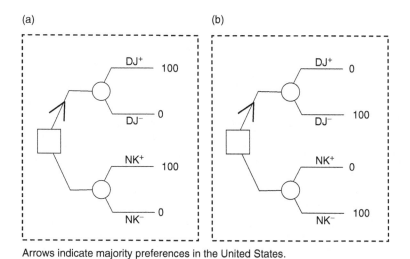

Arrows indicate majority preferences in the United States.

Figure 10.1.2 Home Bias.

tomorrow (DJ^-) or if the Nikkei index does not go up tomorrow (NK^-), the investor also prefers the former (Fig. 10.1.2b).

Again, this behavior cannot be accommodated by probabilistic sophistication, as follows similarly as in Example 10.1.1, with $P(DJ^+) > P(NK^+)$ and $P(DJ^-) > P(NK^-)$ leading to a contradiction. Whereas Example 10.1.1 involved some known probabilities, this example shows that probabilistic sophistication can also be violated in the absence of known probabilities, which is the more important practical case.[1] □

Because of the importance of the phenomena just illustrated, we have to develop a theory that generalizes decision under risk in more substantial ways than probabilistic sophistication can do. When presenting such a theory, RDU for uncertainty, we will first explain the similarities of this theory with RDU for risk despite the absence of probabilistic sophistication. Only later, in Chapter 11, will we turn to the phenomena for decision under uncertainty that are entirely new.

10.2   Rank-dependent utility defined for uncertainty and without probabilistic sophistication

To model the Ellsberg paradox, we will abandon probabilistic sophistication, and define RDU without it. As a preparation we will, however, first consider RDU with probabilistic sophistication. The probability measure is denoted P and the probability weighting function is denoted w. Consider an event-contingent prospect $E_1x_1...E_nx_n$ with a corresponding probability-contingent prospect $p_1x_1...p_nx_n$ ($p_j = P(E_j)$ for all j). Assume, as before, a complete ranking

$$x_1 \geq \cdots \geq x_n \text{ for prospect } E_1x_1 \ldots E_nx_n. \tag{10.2.1}$$

The weight of outcome x_j is

$$\pi(p_j^{p_{j-1}+\cdots+p_1}) = w(p_j + p_{j-1} + \cdots + p_1) - w(p_{j-1} + \cdots + p_1)$$

where E_j is the outcome event underlying p_j and $E_{j-1} \cup \cdots \cup E_1$ is the event underlying rank $p_{j-1} + \cdots + p_1$. Thus, for an outcome α of a prospect with probability p and rank r, the outcome event E has probability $P(E) = p$ and, further, the event R underlying rank r ($P(R) = r$) is disjoint from E.

We define the function W on events E by

$$E \mapsto W(E) = w(P(E));$$

i.e., W is the composition of w and P. The resulting decision weight under RDU is

$$\pi(p^r) = w(P(E \cup R)) - w(P(R)) = W(E \cup R) - W(R). \tag{10.2.2}$$

Because w can be nonlinear, W need not be additive and

$$W(A \cup B) \neq W(A) + W(B) \text{ with } A \cap B = \emptyset$$

---

[1] Readers who adhere to the efficient market hypothesis and who have extensive statistics available may believe that $P(DJ^+) = P(NK^+) = \frac{1}{2}$ in an objective manner. Then probabilities are not unknown. To generate a true case of unknown probability it may then be assumed that an exceptional event has just happened, leading to an unprecedented situation with different experts giving different probability estimates.

may occur.[2] Whereas the composition W is nonadditive, it does share some basic properties with probabilities:

$$W(\emptyset) = 0; \tag{10.2.3}$$

$$W(S) = 1 \text{ for the universal event S}; \tag{10.2.4}$$

If $A \supset B$ then $W(A) \geq W(B)$ (monotonicity with respect to set inclusion). (10.2.5)

We now drop the assumption of probabilistic sophistication. Rank-dependent utility has been extended to uncertainty, without probabilities for events, by also imposing Eqs. (10.2.3)–(10.2.5) on an event function W if no decomposition $W(\cdot) = w(P(\cdot))$ is possible.

Definition 10.2.1. W is an (*event*) *weighting function* if it maps events to [0,1] and it satisfies Eqs. (10.2.3)–(10.2.5). □

The term event weighting function distinguishes W from probability weighting functions. In agreement with our general approach of using the same terms for risk and uncertainty whenever possible, we will use the concise term weighting function in what follows, and no confusion will arise. Other terms used in the literature for a weighting function for uncertainty are capacity or nonadditive measure.

The subset of weighting functions W for which a decomposition $W(\cdot) = w(P(\cdot))$ exists so that probabilistic sophistication holds is a "thin" subset[3] of the set of all weighting functions. The existence of such P and w is therefore an exception, and violations of probabilistic sophistication will prevail. Further discussion and examples are in §10.3.

Analogously to ranked probabilities for decision under risk, we now consider ranked events. For a prospect we choose a complete ranking of outcomes as in Eq. (10.2.1) and then define the rank of each outcome, or of its associated outcome event, as the event of receiving an outcome ranked strictly better. Thus, $E_{j-1} \cup \cdots \cup E_1$ is the *rank*, or *gain-rank*, of x_j and E_j. In general, for an outcome event E and its rank R, E^R is the *ranked event* ($E \cap R = \emptyset$); we sometimes write G instead of R. To distinguish a rank R for decision under risk from (probability-)ranks, R can be called *event-rank*. No confusion will, however, arise from the concise term rank. For a weighting function W and a ranked event E^R, the *decision weight* $\pi(E^R)$ is defined as $W(E \cup R) - W(R)$. In the aforementioned prospect, x_j has decision weight $W(E_j \cup \cdots \cup E_1) - W(E_{j-1} \cup \cdots \cup E_1)$.

Definition 10.2.2. Under Structural Assumption 1.2.1 (decision under uncertainty), *rank-dependent utility* (*RDU*) holds if there exist a strictly increasing continuous

---

[2] A numerical example: Assume that the probabilities $P(A) \neq 0$ and $P(B) \neq 0$, and $w(p) = p^2$. Then $W(A \cup B) = w(P(A \cup B)) = w(P(A) + P(B)) = (P(A) + P(B))^2 \neq P(A)^2 + P(B)^2 = w(P(A)) + w(P(B)) = W(A) + W(B)$.

[3] We will not formalize this term; see Schmeidler (1989 Remark 4.2.2).

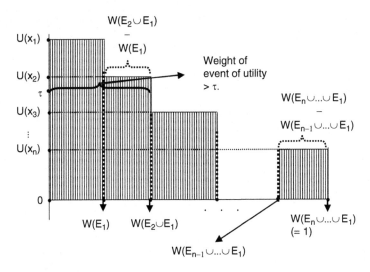

Figure 10.2.1 Rank-dependent utility for uncertainty. This figure extends Figure 5.5.4 to uncertainty.

utility function $U : \mathbb{R} \rightarrow \mathbb{R}$ and a weighting function W, such that each prospect $E_1 x_1 \ldots E_n x_n$ with a complete ranking $x_1 \geq \ldots \geq x_n$ is evaluated by

$$\sum_{j=1}^{n} \pi_j U(x_j) = \sum_{j=1}^{n} \pi(E_j^{E_{j-1}+\cdots+E_1}) U(x_j)$$
$$- \sum_{j=1}^{n} (W(E_j \cup \cdots \cup E_1) - W(E_{j-1} \cup \cdots \cup E_1)) U(x_j), \quad (10.2.6)$$

the *RDU* of the prospect (see Figure 10.2.1).[4] □

In RDU, the utility function U and the weighting function W are the subjective parameters that characterize the decision maker. The calculation of RDU for uncertainty is similar to that for risk, explained in §5.6, with W instead of w and with ranks R instead of r. The elaboration of the following exercise illustrates such calculations in detail, and the elaboration of Exercise 10.2.2 gives the calculations in a briefer and more tractable manner.

Exercise 10.2.1.[a] Assume that $S = \{s_1, s_2, s_3\}$, $U(\alpha) = \sqrt{\alpha}$, $W(s_1) = W(s_2) = W(s_3) = 0.4$, and $W(s_1, s_2) = W(s_1, s_3) = W(s_2, s_3) = 0.6$. Calculate the RDU value and the CE of the prospect $(s_1:1, s_2:0, s_3:9)$. □

Exercise 10.2.2.[a] Assume that $S = \{s_1, s_2, s_3\}$, $U(\alpha) = \alpha$, $W(s_1) = W(s_2) = W(s_3) = 0.4$, $W(s_1, s_2) = W(s_1, s_3) = 0.6$, and $W(s_2, s_3) = 0.7$. Calculate the RDU value and the CE of the prospect $(s_1:0, s_2:3, s_3:5)$. □

As regards the elicitation method of deriving theoretical concepts from observed preference, §10.5.2 will discuss the measurement of utility under RDU. Once utility

---

[4] As usual, for $j = 1$, $W(E_{j-1} \cup \cdots \cup E_1)$ is equal to $W(\emptyset) = 0$.

is known, the weighting function W can be elicited relatively easily. Before presenting an exercise, we give some preparatory notation. π is the generic symbol for *decision weight*. If no confusion can arise, we sometimes write π_j or $\pi(E_j)$ or $\pi(x_j)$ rather than $\pi(E_j^{Rj})$, and may call it the decision weight of event E_j or of outcome x_j. The decision weight of outcome x_j is the marginal W contribution of x_j's outcome event E_j to its rank. Again, an outcome α is ranked better as its rank R is smaller. The smallest rank $\emptyset$ is the *best rank*, and the largest rank E^c of an event E is the *worst rank*.

Notation 10.2.3. The best rank ($\emptyset$) is also denoted by the superscript b, and the worst rank (E^c for event E) is also denoted by the superscript w. That is, $E^b = E^\emptyset$ and $E^w = E^{E^c}$. $\square$

The following exercise shows that weighting functions and decision weights can easily be measured if utility is known, in which case we can express outcomes in terms of utility units. A special and easy case of known utility arises if utility may be assumed to be linear. This assumption is reasonable for moderate outcomes. Diecidue, Wakker, & Zeelenberg (2007) used it, and then used the method of the following exercise in an experiment. The solution to part (a) is given in the text that immediately follows.

Exercise 10.2.3. Assume that you want to find out, for a partition G,E,L of the state space S, what the decision weight $\pi(E^G)$ is of a person called Paul. You know that Paul maximizes RDU, with $U(\alpha) = \alpha$ for all α. However, the only thing that you can observe about Paul is his preferences and indifferences between prospects. In prospect notation, you can suppress the events E,G,L, and for instance write (x_1, x_2, x_3) instead of $(G:x_1, E:x_2, L:x_3)$.

(a)[b] Can you determine W(E) if you can observe no more than one
   certainty equivalent from Paul, where you can choose which it is?
(b)[b] Can you determine $\pi(E^G)$ if you can observe no more than two
   certainty equivalents from Paul, where you can choose which those are?
(c)[c] Can you indicate one observed indifference that suffices to determine
   $\pi(E^G)$? $\square$

We obtain the following analog of Eq. (1.3.1) (measuring P under expected value) under the assumption of linear utility. In the following equation, W(E) refers to the constant prospect giving outcome W(E) with certainty.

$$W(E) \sim 1_E 0. \tag{10.2.7}$$

Thus, W(E) can be interpreted as the willingness to bet on event E, an interpretation fitting well with the notation W. This equation comprises the solution to part (a) of Exercise 10.2.3: W(E) is obtained as the certainty equivalent of $1_E 0$.

As with decision under risk, there are several ways to denote a prospect but they all lead to the same RDU value (Appendix 10.11). With an EU model given, we know the decision weight of an outcome as soon as we know the corresponding outcome event E. In RDU we have to know two events, E and its rank R, leading to the ranked event E^R. The theory thus is more complex than EU, but not very much so.

Exercise 10.2.4.[a] Verify that the decision weights for a prospect x in Definition 10.2.2 are nonnegative and sum to 1. □

10.3 Rank-dependent utility and probabilistic sophistication once more

10.3.1 Ellsberg's violation of probabilistic sophistication

We have introduced RDU for uncertainty as a generalization of RDU with probabilistic sophistication. The question may be raised at this stage whether the theory introduced is really a generalization, or whether for every weighting function W satisfying Eqs. (10.2.3)–(10.2.5) there exist a probability measure P and a probability weighting function w such that $W = w(P(\cdot))$. Such w and P usually do not exist, and the theory is a genuine generalization that can, for instance, accommodate the Ellsberg paradox and the home bias, phenomena that violate probabilistic sophistication.

Example 10.3.1 [Ellsberg paradox and home bias accommodated]. We will discuss the Ellsberg paradox in detail. The home bias can be accommodated the same way. We can accommodate the Ellsberg paradox (Example 10.1.1) with general RDU simply by setting $W(B_k) = W(R_k) > W(B_a) = W(R_a)$.

Although the above reasoning has solved the question, for completeness we describe the whole decision model. For this whole decision model we must specify the weighting function for all combinations of resolutions of uncertainty. We define a state space $S = \{s_1,\ldots,s_4\}$ where each state describes the results of the drawings from the known and the unknown urn in Example 10.1.1. We define $s_1 = B_k B_a$, $s_2 = B_k R_a$, $s_3 = R_k B_a$, and $s_4 = R_k R_a$, with the obvious interpretations. Although the definition of W outside the events B_k, R_k, B_a, and R_a is immaterial for the explanation of the Ellsberg paradox, for completeness we give possible values.[5] Say, $W(s_1) = \cdots = W(s_4) = 1/6$, $W(s_1,s_2) = W(B_k) = W(R_k) = W(s_3,s_4) = 0.45$, $W(s_1,s_3) = W(B_a) = W(R_a) = W(s_2,s_4) = 0.35$, $W(s_2,s_3) = W(s_1,s_4) = 0.40$, $W(s_1,s_2,s_3) = W(s_1,s_2,s_4) = W(s_1,s_3,s_4) = W(s_2,s_3,s_4) = 4/6$. Obviously, $W(\emptyset) = 0$ and $W(s_1,\ldots,s_4) = 1$. This W function satisfies Eqs. (10.2.3)–(10.2.5).

We considered a case of moderate deviation from EU for known probability ($W(R_k) = W(B_k) = 0.45 < 0.50$), and a stronger deviation for unknown probability ($W(R_a) = W(B_a) = 0.35 < 0.50$). EU for known probability results if we have $W(B_k) = W(R_k) = 0.50$. □

---

[5] The requirement that all combinations of events have to be specified and that W has to be determined for all of them, even if irrelevant to the decision problem considered, entails a drawback of the classical decision model. In this regard the "experiments" of Luce (2000), and, as pointed out by Abdellaoui & Wakker (2005), the mosaics introduced by Kopylov (2007), are more convenient. Roughly, mosaics allow the consideration of different partitions of the universal event without requiring the presence of intersections of events belonging to different partitions. They seem to be better suited as a basis of decision theory in general than the commonly used algebras. This book will, however, focus on classical decision models and will use algebras.

W clearly was nonadditive in the preceding example with, for instance, $1 = W(S) = W(R_a,B_a) \neq W(R_a) + W(B_a) = 0.35 + 0.35 = 0.70$. RDU for uncertainty being general enough to accommodate the Ellsberg paradox and the home bias in itself entails not much of a success, because any theory general enough can accommodate any phenomenon. Hence we use the term "accommodate" rather than the term "explain" (this point will be discussed in more detail in the conclusion of Example B.2 in Appendix B). Special forms of RDU, providing useful insights and tractable tools for analyzing ambiguity and the home bias, will be introduced later.

10.3.2 Further observations

This subsection provides further background on probabilistic sophistication and RDU, and can be skipped by atheoretical readers.

Exercise 10.3.1.[c] Verify whether there exist a probability measure P on S and a function w such that $W(\cdot) = w(P(\cdot))$ in Exercises 10.2.1 and 10.2.2. □

For uncertainty, the term Choquet expected utility, introduced by Wakker (1990a), has been used in the literature instead of RDU. Because the theory for risk is simply the theory for uncertainty restricted to a particular subcase, we prefer to use the same terms for risk and for uncertainty, which is why we use the term RDU. If desirable, explanations can be added to distinguish the two contexts.

The following exercise shows that RDU for event-contingent prospects plus probabilistic sophistication implies that probability-contingent prospects must be evaluated by an RDU functional for risk, with $W(\cdot) = w(P(\cdot))$. Thus there is no other way to have probabilistic sophistication under RDU than the way considered before.

Exercise 10.3.2.[1b] [RDU for uncertainty plus probabilistic sophistication implies RDU for risk]. Assume RDU and probabilistic sophistication with respect to a probability measure P. Further, for each $p \in [0,1]$ there is an A with $P(A) = p$ (such a P is called surjective),[6] and strict stochastic dominance holds with respect to P. Show that there exists a strictly increasing function w such that $W(\cdot) = w(P(\cdot))$. That is, preferences over probability-contingent prospects must be governed by an RDU model. □

Assignment 10.3.3.[1b] Assume, in deviation from the rest of this section, Structural Assumption 2.5.2 (decision under risk and richness). Construct a state space S and whatever more is needed to make the situation of Exercise 10.3.2 arise with Structural Assumption 1.2.1 (decision under uncertainty) satisfied. Do so for a given general w and U. Bear in mind that Theorem 6.5.6 implies strict stochastic dominance. □

Whether or not a general weighting function $W(\cdot)$ can be decomposed as $w(P(\cdot))$, amounts to questions examined in qualitative probability theory (Chateauneuf 1996; Gilboa 1985). That is, it amounts to the existence of a probability measure P that orders events the same way as W does. Necessary and sufficient conditions are in

---

[6] This assumption is added only for simplicity.

Chateauneuf (1985), and a survey is in Fishburn (1986). In studies on coherent risk measures (Artzner *et al.* 1999), RDU with probabilistic sophistication has received much attention (Tsukahara 2009). Kusuoka (2001) is usually credited for having introduced our Assumption 2.1.2 (Decision under risk) in this domain under the name law invariance.

Interpretation of P under probabilistic sophistication. If no objective probability measure on the state space is given then, sometimes, and maybe by coincidence, there may exist a probability measure P on S and a function w such that probabilistic sophistication holds; i.e., $W(\cdot) = w(P(\cdot))$. At this stage, without further assumptions, P may be taken as a mathematical device without any particular empirical meaning.

Two generalizations of probabilistic sophistication. A joint generalization of probabilistic sophistication and RDU, called *weighting-function sophistication*, can be devised as follows. Recall that probabilistic sophistication generalizes EU by maintaining the assumption that the preference value of a prospect is entirely captured by the probability distribution generated over outcomes, but not requiring that this generated probability distribution be evaluated by an EU functional. Similarly, weighting-function sophistication generalizes RDU by maintaining the assumption that the preference value of a prospect is entirely captured by the weighting function generated over outcomes (defined in the natural way), but not requiring that this generated weighting function be evaluated by an RDU functional. Such an approach is desirable if we want to work with nonadditive measures of belief and wish to relate them to decision making, but do not want to commit ourselves to rank dependence. A concise behavioral foundation of weighting-function sophistication is in Sarin & Wakker (1994b).

Weighting functions over outcomes generated by event-contingent prospects can be used for another modification of RDU, *decision under nonadditive risk*. Remember that decision under risk considers objective probability distributions over outcomes without specifying an underlying state space. (Decision under risk can be considered a special case of decision under uncertainty by constructing an underlying state space after all, but such a construction is not needed for applications.) We can similarly work directly with weighting functions over outcomes without specifying an underlying state space (Jaffray 1989). Such weighting functions can be based on objective data, such as incomplete statistical data sets (Example 11.11.4), in ways that we will not elaborate on here. They may also have been derived endogenously from preferences, similar to subjective probabilities under probabilistic sophistication (where we can subsequently also focus on probability distributions generated over outcomes and suppress the state space).

10.4 Where rank-dependent utility under uncertainty deviates from expected utility in the same way as it did under risk

Even if, as is usually the case, RDU for uncertainty does not satisfy probabilistic sophistication so that there is no decomposition $W(\cdot) = w(P(\cdot))$, then still many properties of RDU are analogous to those under risk. This section discusses such properties. Some technical properties are deferred to §10.9.

10.4.1 Optimism and pessimism

For risk, we saw that RDU can explain many phenomena that EU cannot explain. For example, RDU can explain the Allais paradox in Exercise 6.4.1, and the discrepancies between the α^j's and the γ^j's in the experiment in §4.1. In this subsection we consider similar phenomena for uncertainty.

Exercise 10.4.1.[!a] Define an RDU model with linear utility that accommodates the preferences in Figure 4.12.2 (Allais paradox for uncertainty). If you do not see how to do this, then read the clue in the footnote.[7] □

Pessimism holds if worsening the rank increases the decision weight; i.e.

$$\pi(E^{R'}) \geq \pi(E^R) \text{ whenever } R' \supset R \ (\pi(E^R) \text{ increases in R}) \tag{10.4.1}$$

(bigger decision weights for worse ranks).

Optimism holds if improving the rank increases the decision weight; i.e.

$$\pi(E^{R'}) \geq \pi(E^R) \text{ whenever } R' \subset R(\pi(E^R) \text{ decreases in R}) \tag{10.4.2}$$

(bigger decision weights for better ranks).

Eq. (10.4.3) gives an equivalent definition of pessimism. Pessimism has often been called *convexity* in the literature, and we will also use that term on some occasions. The condition has also been called (strong) superadditivity, or 2-alternating, or supermodularity. Convex weighting functions have been used extensively in the literature. *Concavity* of W similarly refers to optimism.

Exercise 10.4.2.[!b] Show that pessimism is equivalent to the inequality

$$W(A \cup B) \geq W(A) + W(B) - W(A \cap B) \tag{10.4.3}$$

for all events A,B. Write $R' = R \cup C$ with $R \cap C = \emptyset$. □

Rewriting Eq. (10.4.1) as

$$W(E \cup R') - W(R') \geq W(E \cup R) - W(R)$$
$$\text{whenever } R' \supset R \text{ and } R' \cap E = \emptyset \tag{10.4.4}$$

we see that Eq. (10.4.1) is the natural analog of convexity of a real-valued function w as defined in Eq. (6.3.3).

Exercise 10.4.3.[b] Assume RDU with pessimism and consider an indifference

$$(E_1:11, E_2:9, E_3:6, E_4:1) \sim (E_1:12, E_2:8, E_3:6, E_4:1).$$

---

[7] Hint: Let W assign low values to all events except S, so that an outcome event always receives a high decision weight when ranked worst.

Show that an increase of the common outcome under event E_3 from 6 to 10 leads to the following preference:

$$(E_1:11, E_2:9, E_3:10, E_4:1) \succcurlyeq (E_1:12, E_2:8, E_3:10, E_4:1).$$

Do not reread Example 7.4.2, but think for yourself. If you need a hint, then read the footnote.[8] $\square$

10.4.2 Likelihood insensitivity (Inverse-S)

Empirical investigations have suggested that for uncertainty, even more than for risk, likelihood insensitivity is an important phenomenon. Although in general we cannot draw graphs for uncertainty because the x-axis refers to events and not to probabilities, the properties for uncertainty generalize those for risk in a natural manner. In what follows, the analog of the greater-than relation for probabilities will be a more-likely-than relation for events, derived from bets on events. *We write C $\succcurlyeq$ D if there exist outcomes $\gamma \succ \beta$ such that $\gamma_C\beta \succcurlyeq \gamma_D\beta$, and then call C (revealed) more likely than D.*[9]

Exercise 10.4.4.[la] Assume RDU. Show C $\succcurlyeq$ D $\Leftrightarrow$ W(C) $\geq$ W(D). $\square$

We write [A,B] for the set of events E with A $\preccurlyeq$ E $\preccurlyeq$ B. For example, [$\emptyset$,B] contains all events not more likely than B, and [A,S] contains all events not less likely than A.

The following conditions are natural extensions of the corresponding conditions for risk. The discussions given for risk are relevant here too, which is why the following presentation will be brief.

Definition 10.4.1. W exhibits (*likelihood*) *insensitivity* on *insensitivity region* [B_{rb},W_{rb}] if

$$\pi(E^b) \geq \pi(E^R) \text{ on}^{10} [\emptyset, W_{rb}] \tag{10.4.5}$$

and

$$\pi(E^w) \geq \pi(E^R) \text{ on}^{11} [B_{rb}, S]. \tag{10.4.6}$$

$\square$

The restriction to the subdomain [$\emptyset$,W_{rb}] in Eq. (10.4.5) ensures that the inequality is imposed only on the restriction of W to [$\emptyset$,W_{rb}], concerning the case where all relevant events (arguments of W) are contained in [$\emptyset$,W_{rb}]. Those relevant events are

---

[8] Show that E_2 has at least as much decision weight for the lower prospects as for the upper prospects. Note how its rank changes. The reasoning is similar to Example 7.4.2.

[9] We use the same symbol $\succcurlyeq$ for preferences over prospects, outcomes, and events. It is based on the interpretation of outcomes as constant prospects and of events as indicator-function prospects. The latter yield a predesigned good outcome (say, with utility 1) under the event considered and a predesigned bad outcome (say, with utility 0) under its complement. The prospect-interpretation of events is less common than that of outcomes, but is also natural. It was propagated by de Finetti (1974 §3.1.4).

[10] The domain restriction is described as an inequality in Eq. (10.4.7).

[11] The domain restriction is described as an inequality in Eq. (10.4.8).

E and $\emptyset$ for $\pi(E^b) = W(E) - W(\emptyset)$, and $E \cup R$ and R for $\pi(E^R) = W(E \cup R) - W(R)$. It, obviously, suffices here that the largest of these events, $E \cup R$, is less likely than W_{rb}:

$$E \cup R \preccurlyeq W_{rb}. \tag{10.4.7}$$

This restriction on the domain in Eq. (10.4.5) serves to avoid direct comparisons between $\pi(E^b)$ and weights $\pi(E^R)$ with rank R close to the worst rank.

Similarly, the subdomain in Eq. (10.4.6) imposes the inequality only on the restriction of W to the interval $[B_{rb},S]$, i.e., to the case where all relevant events (arguments of W) are contained in $[B_{rb},S]$. Those relevant events are S and $S-E$ for $\pi(E^w) = W(S) - W(S-E)$, and $E \cup R$ and R for $\pi(E^R) = W(E \cup R) - W(R)$. It, obviously, suffices here that the smallest of these events, R, exceeds B_{rb}:

$$R \succcurlyeq B_{rb}. \tag{10.4.8}$$

Exercise 10.4.5.[a] Assume that W satisfies likelihood insensitivity with insensitivity region $[B_{rb},W_{rb}]$, and assume that $[A_{rb},A_{rw}] \subset [B_{rb},W_{rb}]$; in other words, $B_{rb} \preccurlyeq A_{rb} \preccurlyeq A_{rw} \preccurlyeq W_{rb}$. Show that W satisfies likelihood insensitivity with insensitivity region $[A_{rb},A_{rw}]$. $\square$

I give some more terms that may be convenient but need not be memorized to understand the following text.

Definition 10.4.2. The interval to the left of the insensitivity region, i.e., $[\emptyset,B_{rb}]$, is the *best-rank region*. The interval to the right, $[W_{rb},S]$, is the *worst-rank region*. B_{rb} is the *best-rank boundary* and W_{rb} is the *worst-rank boundary*. Equation (10.4.5) reflects *best-rank overweighting* (on $[\emptyset,W_{rb}]$), and Eq. (10.4.6) reflects *worst-rank overweighting* (on $[B_{rb},S]$). $\square$

Likelihood insensitivity is a relatively new concept, introduced informally by Einhorn & Hogarth (1985) and advanced by Amos Tversky. It requires the development of new mathematical tools, new empirical tests, and new interpretations and concepts. This holds for decision under risk and even more for the richer domain of decision under uncertainty. The following extreme case of likelihood insensitivity is commonly observed in everyday life (Bruine de Bruin *et al.* 2005; Camerer 2007 p. C34). It distinguishes only between three levels of likelihood for an event.

- The event surely will happen;
- The event surely will not happen;

or

- Don't know ("50–50").

This extreme case of likelihood insensitivity is the analog under uncertainty of the step-weighting function in Figure 7.1.3, and is the topic of the following example.

Example 10.4.3. Assume that $W(E) = \alpha$ for some $0 \leq \alpha \leq 1$ and for all E different from $\emptyset$ and S. Then, for $x_1 \geq \cdots \geq x_n$, $RDU(E_1x_1 \ldots E_nx_n) = \alpha U(x_1) + (1-\alpha)U(x_n)$

as soon as E_1 and E_n are nonempty. This decision rule is known as the *α-Hurwicz criterion* (Arrow & Hurwicz 1972; Hurwicz 1951; Luce & Raiffa 1957) or as the *α-maxmin criterion*. Fig. 7.1.3b depicts the related case for risk with $α = ⅓$. (Some minor technical differences regarding null events are not elaborated on here.) □

Observation 10.9.3 will demonstrate that insensitivity for uncertainty is the natural generalization of insensitivity for risk. Empirical studies have shown that likelihood insensitivity is more pronounced for uncertainty than for risk. This was suggested by Fellner (1961 p. 684), and it was confirmed by Abdellaoui, Vossmann, & Weber (2005), Gayer (2010), Kahn & Sarin (1988 p. 270), Kahneman & Tversky (1975 p. 15 2nd para), Kahneman & Tversky (1979 p. 281 lines -6/-5 and p. 289 l. 5–6), Kilka & Weber (2001), and Weber (1994 pp. 237–238). It was central to Wakker (2004). The latter paper stated a preference condition that formalizes this phenomenon. This preference condition gives a behavioral foundation of a decomposition

$$W(E) = w(B(E)). \tag{10.4.9}$$

Here w is the probability weighting function for risk exhibiting insensitivity, and B exhibits additional insensitivity in a way that suggests that B may be a belief index. The decomposition in Eq. (10.4.9) had been used before under the name of two-stage model (Fox, Rogers, & Tversky 1996; Fox & Tversky 1998; Kahneman & Tversky 1975; Kilka & Weber 2001; Tversky & Fox 1995; Wu & Gonzalez 1999). These authors used this approach with B derived from introspective judgments of likelihood, and they investigated to what extent this model can accommodate preferences. Wakker's (2004) derivation was entirely based on revealed preference.

For unlikely events, likelihood insensitivity deviates from the commonly assumed universal pessimism and ambiguity aversion. Besides the references given before, the following references confirmed it: Chipman (1960), Curley & Yates (1989), Ellsberg (2001 p. 203 ll. 12–14; pp. 205–206) and Gärdenfors & Sahlin (1982). Mixed results are in Dolan & Jones (2004) and Sarin & Weber (1993).

10.4.3   *Direct ways to test convexity, concavity, and likelihood insensitivity using violations of the sure-thing principle*

The direct ways to test properties of decision weights using violations of the sure-thing principle, presented for risk in §7.4, readily extend to uncertainty. Hence they are presented briefly.

Example 10.4.4 [Violations of the sure-thing principle as a test of properties of rank dependence]. Figure 10.4.1 depicts prospects $\ell = (A:c; E_2:δ, E_3:α)$ and $r = (A:c; E_2:γ, E_3:β)$, with $δ > γ > β > α$. For the question marks, preferences are to be substituted. We consider three cases.

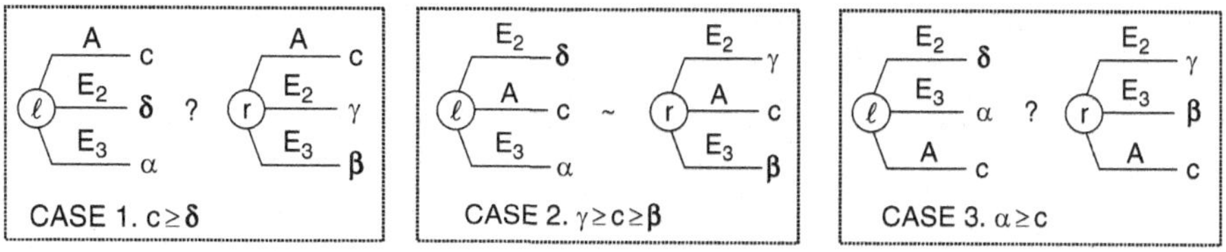

Figure 10.4.1 Testing the sure-thing principle.

CASE 1 [$c \geq \boldsymbol{\delta}$]. Then

$$\begin{array}{lllll} \ell & \succ & r & \Leftrightarrow & \pi(E_2^A)(U(\boldsymbol{\delta}) - U(\gamma)) > \pi(E_3^w)(U(\boldsymbol{\beta}) - U(\alpha)); \\ '' & \sim & '' & \Leftrightarrow & \quad '' \qquad\qquad '' \qquad = \qquad '' \qquad\qquad '', \\ '' & \prec & '' & \Leftrightarrow & \quad '' \qquad\qquad '' \qquad < \qquad '' \qquad\qquad ''. \end{array}$$

CASE 2 [$\gamma \geq c \geq \boldsymbol{\beta}$]. Then

$$\begin{array}{lllll} \ell & \succ & r & \Leftrightarrow & \pi(E_2^b)(U(\boldsymbol{\delta}) - U(\gamma)) > \pi(E_3^w)(U(\boldsymbol{\beta}) - U(\alpha)); \\ '' & \sim & '' & \Leftrightarrow & \quad '' \qquad\qquad '' \qquad = \qquad '' \qquad\qquad '', \\ '' & \prec & '' & \Leftrightarrow & \quad '' \qquad\qquad '' \qquad < \qquad '' \qquad\qquad ''. \end{array}$$

CASE 3 [$\alpha \geq c$]. Then

$$\begin{array}{lllll} \ell & \succ & r & \Leftrightarrow & \pi(E_2^b)(U(\boldsymbol{\delta}) - U(\gamma)) > \pi(E_3^{E_2})(U(\boldsymbol{\beta}) - U(\alpha)); \\ '' & \sim & '' & \Leftrightarrow & \quad '' \qquad\qquad '' \qquad = \qquad '' \qquad\qquad '', \\ '' & \prec & '' & \Leftrightarrow & \quad '' \qquad\qquad '' \qquad < \qquad '' \qquad\qquad ''. \end{array}$$

Assume that we take α,$\boldsymbol{\beta}$,γ, and $\boldsymbol{\delta}$ such that indifference results in Case 2; see Figure 10.4.1. It is a useful exercise to figure out by yourself, without reading further, which preferences are implied in Cases 1 and 3 by convexity of the weighting function and which are implied by concavity. Their derivations are analogous to those in §7.4 and are not repeated here, except for likelihood insensitivity in the following exercise.

We have:

CASE 1 [$c \geq \boldsymbol{\delta}$]. Then

$$\begin{array}{llllll} \ell & \succ & r & \Leftrightarrow & \pi(E_2^A) > \pi(E_2^b) & \text{(pessimism);} \\ '' & \sim & '' & \Leftrightarrow & \quad '' \quad = \quad '' & \text{(EU);} \\ '' & \prec & '' & \Leftrightarrow & \quad '' \quad < \quad '' & \text{(optimism and likelihood ins.).} \end{array}$$

CASE 3 [$\alpha \geq c$]. Then

$$\begin{array}{llllll} \ell & \succ & r & \Leftrightarrow & \pi(E_3^{E_2}) < \pi(E_3^W) & \text{(pessimism and likelihood ins.);} \\ '' & \sim & '' & \Leftrightarrow & \quad '' \quad = \quad '' & \text{(EU);} \\ '' & \prec & '' & \Leftrightarrow & \quad '' \quad > \quad '' & \text{(optimism).} \end{array}$$

Exercise 10.4.6.[c] Derive the above predictions of likelihood insensitivity, where you need only predict weak inequalities and not the strict inequalities as claimed above. In doing so, specify for which insensitivity regions your reasoning works. That is, specify the required relation between W_{rb} and E_3 and the required relation between B_{rb} and E_2. □

10.5   What rank-dependent utility shares with expected utility for uncertainty (in the same way as it did for risk)

I hope that the reader will notice how very analogous the following analysis is to the analysis under EU in Chapter 4.

10.5.1   Rank-preference conditions

This subsection explains how, in general, techniques from EU under uncertainty can be used to analyze RDU by restricting attention to prospects with the same ranks, and illustrates this technique through a preference condition. As before, we denote prospects as $E_1x_1\ldots E_nx_n$ with usually $x_1 \geq \cdots \geq x_n$. And, as under risk, we have some flexibility regarding the partition chosen because we allow different x_j's to be identical. This makes it easier to relate different prospects to the same ordered partition, and to use the same ranked events and decision weights when evaluating these prospects. In Appendix 10.11, we will see that for the RDU value of a prospect, it is immaterial which of several possible rankings of events we choose.

Consider a fixed partition $(E_1,\ldots,E_n)$, and the set of prospects $E_1x_1 \cdots E_nx_n$ with $x_1 \geq \cdots \geq x_n$. The ranks of the outcome events E_j agree for all prospects considered, and the same decision weights can be used for all prospects. Define an EU functional with probabilities $P(E_j) = \pi(E_j^{E_{j-1}\cup\cdots\cup E_1}) = \pi_j$ for all j. Then the RDU functional $\sum_{j=1}^n \pi_j U(x_j)$ agrees with that EU functional $\sum_{j=1}^n \pi_j U(x_j)$ for all prospects now considered. The EU functional, and the as-if subjective probabilities π_j, are merely mathematical devices at this stage. The π_j's may deviate from real (subjective or objective) probabilities if the latter exist, and may for instance relate to transformed subjective probabilities rather than to the subjective probabilities themselves.

The sets of prospects just described, and any of their subsets, are called comonotonic (formally defined in §10.12). Within them, all techniques of EU can be used conveniently, which is the basis of most analyses of RDU. The difference between RDU and EU shows up, of course, as soon as we consider prospects with differently ranked outcome events, such as $E_1z_1 \cdots E_nz_n$ with $z_1 < z_2$. For such prospects, RDU and its decision weights will deviate from the EU functional just defined. The following notation, proposed by Mohammed Abdellaoui (personal communication), conveniently expresses ranks.

Notation 10.5.1. $\alpha_{ER}x$ is the prospect resulting from x if all outcomes for event E are replaced by α, as in α_Ex; with R the rank of E in the resulting prospect. □

The following condition imposes the sure-thing principle only under the special circumstances of same ranks and, hence, is less restrictive. The *rank-sure-thing principle* holds if

$$\alpha_{E^R}x \succcurlyeq \alpha_{E^R}y \Leftrightarrow \beta_{E^R}x \succcurlyeq \beta_{E^R}y. \tag{10.5.1}$$

Exercise 10.5.1.[a] Show that Figure 4.12.2 violates the sure-thing principle. We saw before (Exercise 10.4.1), that the preferences in Figure 4.12.2 can be accommodated by RDU. The following observation will demonstrate that RDU implies the rank-sure-thing principle. The figure, consequently, cannot entail a violation of the rank-sure-thing principle. Show the latter directly by verifying that the rank of event L cannot be the same for the four prospects in the figure. □

Observation 10.5.2. RDU implies the rank-sure-thing principle. □

Tail independence imposes Eq. (10.5.1) only if R is best or worst. For risk, Figure 6.5.5 is to be restricted to best or worst r. The condition is strong enough to imply the full rank-sure-thing principle under common assumptions (Chateauneuf & Wakker 1993).

E^R is *nonnull* if $\gamma_{E^R}x \succ \beta_{E^R}x$ for some $\gamma > \beta$ and x, and E^R is *null* otherwise.

Exercise 10.5.2.[b] Assume RDU. Show: E^R is null $\Leftrightarrow \pi(E^R) = 0$. □

The following technical lemma, extending Lemma 6.5.4 from risk to uncertainty and proved in Appendix 10.13, will be used in some proofs.

Lemma 10.5.3. For the two prospects $\alpha_{E^R}x$ and $\beta_{E^R}x$, not only E^R, but all nonempty ranked outcome events can be chosen the same. □

10.5.2 *Measuring utility (and event weighting) under RDU*

As we verified in Observation 6.5.1 and Exercise 6.5.1, the utility measurements of Figures 4.1.1 (TO upwards) and 4.1.2 (2nd TO upwards) – and, likewise, the TO measurements in Figure 4.1.4 – retain their validity under RDU under the extra Assumption 4.10.1 (50–50). We now show that they also retain their validity under RDU for uncertainty, that is, without Assumption 4.10.1. Now no probabilities need to be given.

Exercise 10.5.3.[a] Reconsider the measurement in Figures 4.1.1 and assume RDU, but without Assumption 4.10.1. Assume that the ranked event (cand$_1$ wins)[b] is nonnull. Show that the α^j's are still equally spaced in utility units, so that Figure 4.3.2 still correctly depicts the utility function. □

Crucial in Exercise 10.5.3 is that the outcomes considered have the same rank for all prospects considered. It leads to the following notation, extending the same notation from risk to uncertainty. For outcomes $\alpha, \beta, \gamma, \delta$, we write

$$\alpha \ominus \beta \sim^t_c \gamma \ominus \delta \tag{10.5.2}$$

if

$$\alpha_{E^R} x \sim \beta_{E^R} y \text{ and} \tag{10.5.3}$$

$$\gamma_{E^R} x \sim \delta_{E^R} y \tag{10.5.4}$$

for some prospects x, y and a nonnull ranked event E^R. The subscript c indicates that an event with a <u>C</u>ommon rank was used, so that the measurement is valid under RDU. Because the proof of the following observation is useful for understanding the analysis in this section, it is given in the main text.

Observation 10.5.4. Under RDU,

$$\alpha \ominus \beta \sim_c^t \gamma \ominus \delta \Rightarrow U(\alpha) - U(\beta) = U(\gamma) - U(\delta). \tag{10.5.5}$$

Proof. Consider the equalities that generate the $\sim_c^t$ relationship,

$$RDU(\alpha_{E^R} x) = RDU(\beta_{E^R} y) \text{ and}$$
$$RDU(\gamma_{E^R} x) = RDU(\delta_{E^R} y).$$

By Lemma 10.5.3, all terms off E are the same for the left two prospects, and they are also the same for the right two prospects.[12] Hence, the difference between the left two prospects is $\pi(E^R)(U(\alpha) - U(\gamma))$, and it is $\pi(E^R)(U(\beta) - U(\delta))$ between the right two prospects. By nonnullness, $\pi(E^R) > 0$ can be dropped, and the terms $U(\beta)$ and $U(\gamma)$ can be switched. $\square$

Exercise 10.5.4.[a] Reconsider the measurements in Figures 4.1.1 and 4.1.2 and assume RDU, but without Assumption 4.10.1. Let $g > \beta^4$. Assume that the ranked events (cand$_1$ wins)[b] and (cand$_1$ wins)[w] are nonnull. Show that the β^j's should still be equal to the α^j's, so that the tests of RDU for risk in the left columns of Table 4.11.2 also apply to RDU for uncertainty. $\square$

With utility measured, the weighting function W can be measured straightforwardly and similarly as under risk (§6.5.4). For instance:

$$\text{If } \alpha \sim 1_E 0 \text{ then } W(E) = U(\alpha)/U(1). \tag{10.5.6}$$

In this book, utility measurement precedes event weighting measurement because we assume rich outcome sets (the real numbers, designating money). If rich event spaces are assumed, then the measurement of event weighting can precede utility measurement (Abdellaoui & Wakker 2005; Savage 1954). This will briefly be indicated in §10.9.

---

[12] They may be denoted $\pi_i U(x_i)$, $i = 2, \ldots, m$ for the two left prospects, and $\pi_i' U(y_i)$, $i = 2, \ldots, n$ for the two right prospects. They can be different for the left prospects than for the right prospects.

10.5.3   A behavioral foundation for RDU

As with $\sim^t$, we have natural symmetries for $\sim_c^t$ with the following four relationships equivalent:

$$\alpha \ominus \beta \sim_c^t \gamma \ominus \delta; \quad \gamma \ominus \delta \sim_c^t \alpha \ominus \beta; \quad \beta \ominus \alpha \sim_c^t \delta \ominus \gamma; \quad \delta \ominus \gamma \sim_c^t \beta \ominus \alpha. \qquad (10.5.7)$$

Exercise 10.5.5.[a] Assume RDU. Let $\alpha \ominus \beta \sim_c^t \gamma \ominus \delta$ and $\alpha' \ominus \beta \sim_c^t \gamma \ominus \delta$. Show that $\alpha' = \alpha$. □

Rank-tradeoff consistency holds if the utility measurements using the relation $\sim_c^t$ do not run into contradictions; i.e., we have the following implication:[13]

$$[\alpha \ominus \beta \sim_c^t \gamma \ominus \delta \text{ and } \alpha' \ominus \beta \sim_c^t \gamma \ominus \delta] \Rightarrow \alpha' = \alpha.$$

Because of the symmetry of outcomes in $\sim_c^t$, similar requirements hold for β, γ, and δ.

Definition 10.5.5. Rank-tradeoff consistency holds if improving an outcome in any $\sim_c^t$ relationship breaks that relationship. □

From Exercise 10.5.5 it follows that rank-tradeoff consistency is a necessary condition for RDU. The following theorem shows that, in the presence of some natural conditions, rank-tradeoff consistency is not only necessary, but also sufficient to imply RDU.

Theorem 10.5.6. Under Structural Assumption 1.2.1 (decision under uncertainty), the following two statements are equivalent for the preference relation $\succcurlyeq$ over the prospects.

(i) RDU holds, where utility is continuous and strictly increasing.
(ii) $\succcurlyeq$ satisfies:
  • weak ordering;
  • monotonicity;
  • continuity;
  • rank-tradeoff consistency. □

Observation 10.5.6′ [Uniqueness result for Theorem 10.5.6]. In (i), the weighting function is uniquely determined, and utility is unique up to level and unit. □

Theorem 10.5.6 shows that it is not only necessary, but also sufficient for the validity of RDU that utility elicitations by means of $\sim_c^t$ do not yield contradictions. The experiment described in §4.1, with the comparisons of the α^j's and the β^j's, in fact comprised tests of rank-tradeoff consistency. Example 4.6.1 demonstrated a violation of tradeoff consistency in the data, as we saw before. Because all outcome events there have the same rank, the violation entails also a violation of rank-tradeoff consistency.

Although it is relatively easy to state how the behavioral foundation of EU based on tradeoff consistency (Theorem 4.6.4) can be adapted to RDU, which is what Theorem 10.5.6 does, its proof is considerably more complex than that of Theorem 4.6.4.

---

[13] For general nonmonetary outcomes, $\alpha' \sim \alpha$ would be required.

Exercise 10.5.6.[b] We reconsider Example 6.5.7, but now do not make Assumption 4.10.1. Hence, no probabilities are known. We do assume a symmetry condition between the candidates, being that $100_{cand_1} 0 \sim 100_{cand_2} 0$. Check out which conclusions about utility of Example 6.5.7 and Exercise 6.5.3 remain valid. What is $W(cand_1)$ and what is $W(cand_2)$? □

10.6 Binary rank-dependent utility

As for risk in §7.11, also for uncertainty the domain of *binary* (= two-outcome) *prospects* $\alpha_E \beta$ is of special interest. *Binary rank-dependent utility* holds if RDU holds on the subset of all binary prospects (Luce 2000 Ch. 3). That is:

$$\text{For } \alpha \geq \beta, \alpha_E \beta \text{ is evaluated by } W(E)U(\alpha) + (1 - W(E))U(\beta). \tag{10.6.1}$$

Not only for risk, but also for uncertainty, binary RDU appeared in several works (Fishburn 1986 for the special case of transitivity; Ghirardato & Marinacci 2001a; Luce 1991). A remarkable special case arises if W is *symmetric*; i.e., $W(E^c) = 1 - W(E)$ for all events E. This special case was central to Pfanzagl (1959 pp. 287–288). Then for each fixed event E, on the set of prospects $\alpha_E \beta$ with E and its complement as outcome events, the functional is an EU functional with $P(E) = W(E)$ and $P(E^c) = W(E^c) = 1 - W(E)$. Violations of EU can then be revealed by showing that the function W does not satisfy additivity.

A convenient feature is, again, that binary prospects suffice to completely identify utility U and the weighting function W (Ghirardato & Marinacci 2001a; Gonzalez & Wu 2003; Luce 1991, 2000; Miyamoto 1988; Pfanzagl 1959 p. 287 top and middle; Wakker & Deneffe 1996 p. 1143 and pp. 1144–1145). Ghirardato, Maccheroni, & Marinacci (2005 2nd para of §3 on p. 135), and Luce & Narens (1985 Theorems 7.1 and 6.5.2) demonstrated that RDU is the only model for binary prospects that satisfies some invariance conditions with utility unique up to unit and level.

A useful feature of the restricted domain of binary prospects is that most of the models used in the literature agree with binary RDU on this domain. Such models include the α-Hurwicz criterion (Arrow & Hurwicz 1972), the maxmin expected utility model and the α-maxmin model (introduced in §11.5 with our claim proved in Observation 11.5.1), Gajdos *et al.*'s (2008) contraction expected utility, and prospect theory (Ch. 12) when restricted to gains or to losses. The following exercise shows that binary RDU can be reformulated as a two-dimensional mean-variance model in utility units.

Exercise 10.6.1. Assume that $S = \{s_1, s_2\}$, with the following evaluation function:

$$\alpha_{s_1} \beta \mapsto pU(\alpha) + (1 - p)U(\beta) - \mu|U(\alpha) - U(\beta)| \tag{10.6.2}$$

for a strictly increasing continuous utility function $U, 0 < p < 1$, and $|\mu| < \min\{p, 1-p\}$.

(a)[b] Show that monotonicity holds.
(b)[b] Show that binary RDU holds if and only if Eq. 10.6.2 holds. □

The convenient generality of binary RDU, agreeing with most models considered in the literature, was exploited by Luce (1991) and Miyamoto (1988). It was presented most clearly and convincingly by Ghirardato & Marinacci (2001a). These references presented behavioral foundations for binary RDU. Köbberling & Wakker (2003 Observation 18) demonstrated that a behavioral foundation of binary RDU can also be obtained simply by restricting our behavioral foundation of RDU (Theorem 10.5.6) to binary prospects. Several empirical studies restricted attention to binary prospects for one fixed event E, and then took W(E) in Eq. (10.6.1) as an index of ambiguity aversion. They commonly refer to one model, such as Gul's (1991) disappointment aversion model (Choi *et al.* 2007), or α-maxmin expected utility (Huettel *et al.* 2006). Hsu *et al.* (2005) noted that the model captures both rank-dependent utility and the multiple priors model. Wakai (2008 Eq. 2) used the model for an intertemporal aggregation function, referring to the multiple priors model. It is worthy of note that the aforementioned references are relevant for all models that comprise binary RDU.

10.7 A hybrid case: rank-dependent utility for uncertainty when also objective probabilities are given

As with EU, measurements and behavioral foundations of rank dependence can be greatly simplified for uncertainty if probabilities are given for some events. Such probabilities are commonly assumed in empirical studies of ambiguity attitudes, where they serve as a benchmark. This is the topic of Chapter 11.

As with Chapter 2 and §4.9, the analysis in this section can be applied to general, nonmonetary outcomes without requiring essential changes. It is instructive to compare the analysis in this section to that of §4.9, and to see the analogies between EU and RDU, with ranked probabilities and ranked events here playing the roles of probabilities and events in §4.9.

10.7.1 A general ("single-stage") approach
We make the same structural assumption as in §4.9.1, but with RDU instead of EU.

Structural Assumption 10.7.1 [Uncertainty plus RDU-for-risk]. Structural Assumption 1.2.1 (decision under uncertainty) holds. In addition, for some of the events R, called *probabilized events*, a probability P(R) is given. If, for a prospect $R_1x_1...R_nx_n$, all outcome events are probabilized with $P(R_j) = p_j$, then this prospect generates the probability distribution $p_1x_1...p_nx_n$ over the outcomes, a probability-contingent prospect. Event-contingent prospects that generate the same probability-contingent prospect are equivalent, and are equated with that probability-contingent prospect. The set of generated probability-contingent prospects contains all finite probability distributions over the outcomes (richness).

Preferences over probability-contingent prospects maximize RDU with utility U and with probability weighting function w.[14] □

The weighting function W can be measured as follows, assuming w and U derived for risk as in Chapters 5–7. If $P(R) = p$, then obviously $W(R) = w(P(R)) = w(p)$. For a general event E, the matching probability q was defined in Eq. (4.9.1) by the indifference $1_E 0 \sim 1_q 0$. This number q, if existing, is unique under RDU for probability-contingent prospects. Later assumptions will imply that it does not depend on the particular outcomes (0 and 1) used. The weighting function W can easily be measured for general events once it has been measured for probabilities (where it is the composition of w and probability):

Under RDU, $W(E) = w(q)$ with q the matching probability of E.   (10.7.1)

The result follows from substitution.

10.7.2 A behavioral foundation for the single-stage approach

In the rank-dependent approach, outcome events cannot play the same role they played under EU. In many respects, ranks will now be central. We thus immediately turn to a comprehensive way to measure W, using a partition $E_1,\ldots,E_n$ of the state space, and probabilities $q_1,\ldots,q_n$ summing to 1.

Definition 10.7.2. Ranked matching holds if

$$E_1 x_1 \ldots E_n x_n \sim q_1 x_1 \ldots q_n x_n \qquad (10.7.2)$$

whenever $x_1 \geq \cdots \geq x_n$ and $q_1 + \cdots + q_j$ is the matching probability of $F_1 \cup \cdots \cup E_j$ for each j. □

Elicitations of decision weights from complex prospects as in Eq. (10.7.2) should be consistent with the measurements based on matched probabilities. I give one example of such an elicitation. Under RDU,

$$0_{E_j}(E_1 x_1 \ldots E_n x_n) \sim 0_{q_j}(q_1 x_1 \ldots q_n x_n) \ \&$$

$$1_{E_j}(E_1 x_1 \ldots E_n x_n) \sim 1_{q_j}(q_1 x_1 \ldots q_n x_n) \Rightarrow$$

$$\pi(E_j^{E_{j-1} \cup \cdots \cup E_1}) = \pi(q_j^{q_{j-1} + \cdots + q_1})$$

whenever $x_1 \geq \cdots \geq x_{j-1} \geq 1 > 0 \geq x_{j+1} \geq \cdots \geq x_n$.

This is in fact a special case of Example 7.5.1 with $\beta = 0$ and $\gamma = 1$.

Because the proof of the following theorem is instructive and elementary, we give it here prior to stating the theorem. The derivation is simpler than the one in §4.9.2 because we use ranks instead of outcome events. We assume RDU for risk. For each event E we define W(E) by Eq. (10.7.1), assuming existence of q. Take an arbitrary prospect $E_1 x_1 \cdots E_n x_n$, where we may assume that $x_1 \geq \cdots \geq x_n$ (otherwise reorder

---

[14] This book assumes that U is strictly increasing under RDU. The only implication needed in this section is that U is nonconstant.

the x_j's). Assume that the matching probability p_j for $E_1 \cup \cdots \cup E_j$ exists for each j. Monotonicity of preference implies $p_1 \leq \cdots \leq p_n$, so that we can define $q_1 = p_1$ and $q_j = p_j - p_{j-1}$ for all $j \geq 2$. Ranked matching implies that

$$\text{RDU}(E_1 x_1 \cdots E_n x_n) = \text{RDU}(q_1 x_1 \cdots q_n x_n)$$
$$= \textstyle\sum_{j=1}^{n}(w(q_j + \cdots + q_1) - w(q_{j-1} + \cdots + q_1))U(x_j)$$
$$= \textstyle\sum_{j=1}^{n}(W(E_j \cup \cdots \cup E_1) - W(E_{j-1} \cup \cdots \cup E_1))U(x_j) = \text{RDU}(E_1 x_1 \cdots E_n x_n).$$

This establishes the RDU representation. The reasoning just given shows that the preference conditions are sufficient for an RDU representation. Necessity follows from substitution. We thus obtain the following theorem.

Theorem 10.7.3. Assume that for each event a matching probability exists. Then, under Structural Assumption 10.7.1 (Uncertainty plus RDU-for-Risk), the following two statements are equivalent.

 (i) RDU holds.
(ii) $\succcurlyeq$ satisfies:
   • weak ordering;
   • monotonicity;
   • ranked matching. $\square$

Theorem 10.7.3, especially when combined with EU for risk, provides the simplest behavioral foundation of RDU available in the literature. This result is of special interest to readers who use RDU for normative purposes and who consider EU to be appropriate for given probabilities. Then we can characterize EU by the usual preference conditions (Theorem 2.6.3) and, next, use ranked matching as in Theorem 10.7.3. Sarin & Wakker (1992 Theorem 3.1) considered this special case, although they derived the additive probabilities and EU endogenously from Savage's (1954) preference conditions rather than assuming the probabilities exogenously as we do.

10.7.3 Schmeidler's and Jaffray's two-stage approaches

Under EU for given probabilities (w additive), W in Theorem 10.7.3 need not be additive for events for which no probabilities are given. This special case of our theorem is a modification of Schmeidler (1989) that needs no multistage setup or commitment to dynamic decision-principles such as backward induction. Backward induction is needed for the Anscombe & Aumann (1963) approach that Schmeidler adopted. As mentioned in §4.9.3, such commitments are controversial for nonEU.[15] Figure 10.7.1 illustrates the problem, as explained next.

---

[15] In brief they imply, for each ambiguous elementary event, that the evaluation of probability-contingent prospects conditional on that event be independent of what happens outside the event. Thus the integral under event E in Eq. (10.7.3) below is independent of what happens outside E. Such separability conditions are undesirable under nonexpected utility.

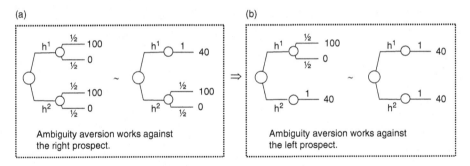

(a)   (b)

Ambiguity aversion works against   Ambiguity aversion works against
the right prospect.   the left prospect.

Figure 10.7.1 An implication of Anscombe & Aumann (1963) that is implausible under ambiguity aversion.

The Anscombe & Aumann model requires the implication in Figure 10.7.1. When we move from Fig. a to Fig. b, however, the left prospect becomes more ambiguous and the right prospect becomes less ambiguous. Hence, it is more plausible under ambiguity aversion that the indifference in Fig. a implies a strict preference for the sure 40 in Fig. b. The figure illustrates the implausible assumption underlying the Anscombe & Aumann model that what happens conditional on horse h^1 not be affected by what happens under horse h^2. Under nonexpected utility such a "separable" treatment of ambiguous events (implied by backward induction) is implausible. The certainty of 40 for sure for the utmost right prospect will generate extra preference value across the two horses.

Our approach allows for, but does not need, a product structure of the state space where the events with given probabilities are causally ("statistically") independent from the other events. We next elaborate on an example that presents Schmeidler's two-stage approach, and that also illustrates the role of the product structure just discussed. It is similar to Example 4.9.8 (binumbered balls), further illustrating that the multistage setup of Anscombe & Aumann (1963) requires a kind of causal independence between the probabilized events of one stage and the nonprobabilized events of the other stage.

Example 10.7.4 [Schmeidler's (1989) approach]. Assume a utility function U. Let E denote the event of some rain tomorrow between noon and 1 p.m., and W(E) = 0.4 = W(E^c), W(∅) = 0, and W(E ∪ E^c) = 1. Let c denote the part of the time between noon and 1 p.m. during which the sun will be covered by clouds. Assume that the probability distribution of c is known and is uniform over [0,1] (assigning to each interval its length). Then, for example, the probability that the sun will be covered for less than 40 minutes is ⅔. For any interval [a,b] ⊂ [0,1] the probability of c being in that interval is the length b−a.

Schmeidler's (1989) approach is as follows. We define S as the product set {E,E^c} × [0,1], where an ordered pair (E,c) designates the event of both E and c.

(E,c) can be equated with the intersection E ∩ c if the latter is taken as (E × [0,1]) ∩ ({E,E^c} × {c}). A prospect f is evaluated by

$$\pi_E \int_0^1 U(f(E, c))dc + (1 - \pi_E) \int_0^1 U(f(E^c, c))dc, \tag{10.7.3}$$

where $\pi_E = W(E)$ if the left integral in Eq. (10.7.3) exceeds the right, and $\pi_E = 1 - W(E^c)$ otherwise. The integral $\int_0^1 U(f(E,c))dc$ can be interpreted as the EU of the "conditional" prospect f(E,·) that results if event E happens. Then for each c in [0,1] the outcome f(E,c) results, with the uniform distribution on [0,1] as probability measure of c occurring. Similarly, $EU(f(E^c, \cdot)) = \int_0^1 U(f(E^c,c))dc$ is the EU of the conditional prospect f(E^c,·) assigning f(E^c,c) to each c in [0,1]. Further, $\pi_E = W(E)$ if $EU(f(E,\cdot)) \geq EU(f(E^c,\cdot))$ and $\pi_E = 1 - W(E^c)$ if $EU(f(E,\cdot)) < EU(f(E^c,\cdot))$.

Some restrictions for this approach, in addition to EU maximization for c-events, are as follows. The approach is reasonable only if E and c are causally independent events, which is most plausible if [0,1] is an artificial auxiliary device unrelated to the uncertainty of interest. Eq. (10.7.3) requires a backward-induction approach with c treated as a separable second-stage event. That is, we substitute certainty equivalents at intermediate nodes in a way that should not depend on what happens at other nodes (cf. Figure 10.7.1). Such separability principles are natural under EU but not under nonEU.

Equation (10.7.3) is an RDU model if we take {E,E^c} as a two-element state space, the conditional prospects f(E,·) and f(E^c,·) as their outcomes, and the EU values of these outcomes as utilities. It is, however, not an RDU model if we take {E,E^c} × [0,1] as state space (Sarin & Wakker 1992 §5). Very briefly explained, it then is not RDU because changes of outcomes may generate a change in the ranking of EU(f(E,·)) and EU(f(E^c,·)) without changing the ranking of any state in {E,E^c} × [0,1], and vice versa.

The aforementioned restrictions of Schmeidler's approach are avoided in Theorem 10.7.3. We need not commit ourselves to any weight of intersections E ∩ [a,b] of event E with subintervals [a,b] of [0,1] pertaining to c, and any causal relation between E and c is allowed. For instance, rain (E) may be impossible if c is below some threshold value. We further need not restrict to EU with respect to c. Thus we can handle any RDU model. In fact, we need not consider any intersections E ∩ c if we allow the set of events not to be an algebra but, for instance, a mosaic as introduced by Kopylov (2007) and used by Abdellaoui & Wakker (2005). □

For a didactical presentation of preference foundations of nonexpected utility models using the Anscombe & Aumann setup, see Ryan (2009). We next present Jaffray's (1989) model of ambiguity in a brief and informal manner.

Example 10.7.5 [Jaffray's (1989) approach]. We use a version of Example 4.9.6 and Fig. 4.9.4a to analyze ambiguity. Jaffray considered informational states where we receive what are called random messages B$_1$,...,B$_n$ (subsets of the state space, i.e., events) with probabilities $p_1, \ldots, p_n$ (as in Dempster 1967). A message B_j means that the true state of nature is contained in B_j. Jaffray used principles of total absence of information (Luce & Raiffa 1957 §13.4; a sophisticated theory is in Cohen & Jaffray 1980) that apply conditional on each message B_j. These principles seek to completely avoid every subjective processing of ambiguity, and imply that the only relevant aspect of a prospect conditional on message B_j is the infimum outcome m_{B_j} and the supremum outcome M_{B_j} of the prospect on B_j. Thus, a prospect can be described as $(p_1 : (m_{B_1}, M_{B_1}), \ldots, p_n : (m_{B_n}, M_{B_n}))$, a probability distribution over ordered pairs. Each pair (m_{B_j}, M_{B_j}) reflects the ambiguous state of information that an outcome between m_{B_j} and M_{B_j} will be received with no other information available. Jaffray assumed EU for the probabilities p_j, justified and discussed by Jaffray (1991a). It avoids the problem of Figure 10.7.1. Backward induction with a separability of the events h^1 and h^2 is, indeed, more convincing if the first-stage events h^1 and h^2 have known probabilities and the second-stage events have unknown probabilities, as in Jaffray's approach, than in the Anscombe & Aumann model as in Figure 10.7.1 and as commonly used in the literature today. Jaffray's approach leads to a representation

$$\sum\nolimits_{j=1}^{n} p_j V(m_{B_j}, M_{B_j}). \tag{10.7.4}$$

Here we can, in principle, apply all the techniques of multiattribute utility.

Cases of $m_{B_j} = M_{B_j}$ for all j concern an absence of ambiguity. There we have EU for risk, and $U(\alpha)$ defined as $V(\alpha, \alpha)$ captures the risk attitude. By monotonicity, $U(m) \leq V(m, M) \leq U(M)$, so that we can define $0 \leq \lambda(m, M) \leq 1$ with

$$V(m, M) = \lambda(m, M)U(M) + (1 - \lambda(m, M))U(m). \tag{10.7.5}$$

$\lambda(m, M)$ captures the ambiguity attitude. Jaffray's model achieves a clear separation of:

- the beliefs about ambiguity, captured by the probabilities over the random messages;
- the risk attitude, captured by $U(\cdot)$;
- the ambiguity attitude, captured by $\lambda(m, M)$.

Jaffray (1989 in the text preceding Eq. 10) explained that $\lambda(m, M)$, denoted λ next, can be elicited from indifferences $(m, M) \sim M_\lambda m$. That is, λ is a matching probability for the ambiguous situation (m, M). This model requires less than N^2 elicitations if there are N outcomes. Thus it is remarkably tractable. □

10.8   Bad-news events or loss-ranks

As with risk, we could equally well have based RDU on loss-ranks as on gain-ranks, by using a *dual* weighting function defined by $Z(E) = 1 - W(E^c)$. Then, for a ranked event E^R, and writing $L = (E \cup R)^c$ for the bad-news event or *loss-rank* L, we have

$$\pi(E^R) = W(E \cup R) - W(R) = (1 - Z(L)) - (1 - Z(E \cup L)) = Z(E \cup L) - Z(L).$$

That is:

Observation 10.8.1. For an event E with (gain-)rank R and loss-rank L, the decision weight can both be obtained as $\pi(E^R)$ (E's marginal W-contribution to its gain-rank R) and also as $\pi(E_L)$ (E's marginal Z-contribution to its loss-rank L). □

We call E_L, with L the loss-rank of E, a *loss-ranked* event. For RDU we can use W which concerns ranked events, or the dual Z which concerns loss-ranked events. For prospect theory, it will be most convenient to work with ranked events for gains and with loss-ranked events for losses.

In §7.6 we cautioned against interpretations of a weighting function that do not reckon with the weighting function describing best-rank decision weights. It is, for example, better to think of convexity of the rank-weighting function than to think of convexity of the weighting function. Similar points hold for uncertainty. Many interpretations of weighting functions for uncertainty have been advanced in the literature that did not pay sufficient attention to ranks of events – or to comonotonicity, a concept not used in our analysis. Many debates in the literature about different ways of updating weighting functions can be explained by different assumptions about ranks (Denneberg 1994; Gilboa & Schmeidler 1993; Halpern 2003 Ch. 3; Jaffray 1992; Sarin & Wakker 1998 §9).

10.9 Further observations regarding rank dependence

Alternative direct measurement of weighting function. The following example adapts the technique of Example 7.5.1 for measuring weighting functions from risk to uncertainty (Abdellaoui & Wakker 2005). It will not be used in this book (because we focus on dual techniques based on outcome-richness).

Example 10.9.1. Figure 10.9.1 is the analog of Figure 7.5.1. The question mark concerns a preference yet to be determined, and we have $\gamma > \beta$. The preference at the question mark will be determined by which decision weight is larger, $\pi(E^R)$ or $\pi(F^{R'})$ (using same ranks by Lemma 10.5.3). The only change regarding the RDU values of the prospects is that the third prospect yields $\pi(E^R)(U(\gamma) - U(\beta))$ more than the first, and the fourth yields $\pi(F^{R'})(U(\gamma) - U(\beta))$ more than the second. The preference between the third and fourth prospect, consequently, agrees with the ordering of $\pi(E^R)$ and $\pi(F^{R'})$, with the left prospect preferred if and only if $\pi(E^R) \geq \pi(F^{R'})$. The configuration of the figure thus gives a direct way to compare decision weights of different ranked events, independently of utility. □

If we find that $\pi(E_j^{E_{j-1} \cup \cdots \cup E_1})$ is the same for all j, for a partition $E_1, \ldots, E_n$, then we can conclude that these decision weights are all $1/n$. Then, for instance, $W(E_1 \cup \cdots \cup E_j) = j/n$ for all j. This entails a quick way to measure W.

Convexity in outcome-mixing. Chateauneuf & Tallon (2002) provided an appealing behavioral foundation of pessimism together with concave utility. $\succcurlyeq$ is *convex in outcome-mixing* if, for all prospects $x = E_1 x_1 \cdots E_n x_n$ and $y = E_1 y_1 \cdots E_n y_n$ (outcomes

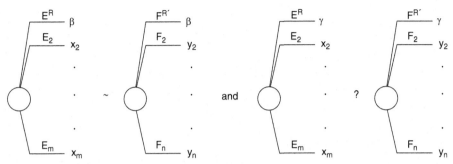

The superscript R indicates the rank of E, and is the same in the
first and third prospect. The superscript R′ indicates the rank of F,
and is the same in the second and fourth prospect.

Figure 10.9.1

not necessarily ranked), and all $0 < \lambda < 1$, $[x \succcurlyeq y \Rightarrow \lambda x + (1-\lambda)y \succcurlyeq y]$ where the
mixing is outcome-wise for each state (or event); i.e., $\lambda x + (1-\lambda)y = (E_1: (\lambda x_1 + (1-\lambda)y_1),\ldots,E_n: (\lambda x_n + (1-\lambda)y_n))$.

Theorem 10.9.2 [Chateauneuf & Tallon]. Under Structural Assumption 1.2.1
(decision under uncertainty), assume that RDU holds with U differentiable.
Then the following two statements are equivalent:

(i) Pessimism holds and U is concave.
(ii) $\succcurlyeq$ satisfies convexity with respect to outcome mixing. □

Solvability. For technical purposes we sometimes use the following property. It is an
analog of continuity for w.[16] W is *solvable* if for all events $A \subset C$ and $W(A) < \mu < W(C)$
there exists an event B with $A \subset B \subset C$ and $W(B) = \mu$. This holds for instance
if $S = [0,1]$ and $W = P$ is the usual (additive) Lebesgue measure. Gilboa (1987) used
the term convex-ranged.[17]

Exercise 10.9.1. Assume RDU with $W(\cdot) = w(P(\cdot))$ for a probability measure P on the
state space S, and w: $[0,1] \to [0,1]$, $w(0) = 0$, $w(1) = 1$, and w strictly increasing.

(a)[b] Show [w convex $\Rightarrow$ W convex] and [w concave $\Rightarrow$ W concave].
(b)[c] Conversely, assume that W satisfies solvability. Show the reverse implications.
        That is, we have [W convex $\Leftrightarrow$ w convex] and [W concave $\Leftrightarrow$ w concave]. □

Exercise 10.9.1 shows that, for the special case of decision under risk with
$W(\cdot) = w(P(\cdot))$, convexity [concavity] of w and W are essentially the same. This

---

[16] More specifically, it is an analog of the intermediate value property for w which, for the increasing w, is
equivalent to continuity.
[17] For specialists in probability theory: A countably additive probability measure P is solvable if and only if it is
atomless.

observation illustrates once more that decision under uncertainty is a natural generalization of decision under risk.

Exercise 10.9.2.^{c} Assume RDU with $W(\cdot) = w(P(\cdot))$. Assume that P satisfies
solvability. Show that w is continuous if and only if W satisfies solvability. □

The following observation underscores that insensitivity for uncertainty is a natural
generalization of the corresponding concept for risk. Rather than reading its proof in
the appendix, you may derive the observation as an exercise.

Observation 10.9.3. Assume that probabilities P(E) are given for all events, and
$W(E) = w(P(E))$ for all E and a weighting function w. Then insensitivity of W on
$[B_{rb}, W_{rb}]$ is implied by insensitivity of w on $[b_{rb}, w_{rb}]$ for $b_{rb} = P(B_{rb})$ and $w_{rb} = P(W_{rb})$.
If W satisfies solvability, then the reverse implication also holds. Then we have:
insensitivity of W on $[B_{rb}, W_{rb}]$ ⟺ insensitivity of w on $[b_{rb}, w_{rb}]$. □

Table 10.9.1 summarizes some results of this section, and shows one more result in
the last column that will be derived in §10.13. This column relates tradeoff consistency for uncertainty to tradeoff consistency for risk.

Table 10.9.1. *Logical relations between properties for W under uncertainty and w under risk*

W	solvable	convex	concave	insensitive on $[B_{rb}, W_{rb}]$	rank-tradeoff consistency
w	continuous	convex	concave	insensitive on $[P(B_{rb}), P(W_{rb})]$	rank-tradeoff consistency
	Exercise 10.9.2	Exercise 10.9.1	Exercise 10.9.1	Observation 10.9.3	Lemma 10.13.1

Note: Assume RDU with $W(\cdot) = w(P(\cdot))$, where P satisfies solvability. Then each property of w
implies the corresponding property of W. Each property of W implies the corresponding property of
w if W satisfies solvability. These claims follow from the lowest rows.

Assignment 10.9.3^c. Assume, in deviation from the rest of this section, Structural
Assumption 2.5.2 (decision under risk and richness), and assume RDU with
U differentiable and w continuous. ≽ is *convex in outcome-mixing* if, for all prospects
$x = p_1x_1 \cdots p_nx_n$ and $y = p_1y_1 \cdots p_ny_n$ and all $0 < \lambda < 1$, [$x \succcurlyeq y \Rightarrow \lambda x + (1-\lambda)y \succcurlyeq y$]
where the mixing is outcome-wise[18]; i.e., $\lambda x + (1-\lambda)y = (p_1: (\lambda x_1 + (1-\lambda)y_1), \ldots,$
$p_n: (\lambda x_n + (1-\lambda)y_n))$. Because now no states of nature are given, it must have been
specified what the probability vector $(p_1, \ldots, p_n)$ is for both prospects. The outcomes
need not be rank-ordered. Outcome mixing is different than the probabilistic mixing
for RDU considered in Exercise 6.6.2. Use Theorem 10.9.2 to show that the following
two statements are equivalent:

(i) w is convex (pessimism) and U is concave.
(ii) ≽ satisfies convexity with respect to outcome mixing. □

---

[18] For mathematical readers: Formally we take prospects here as 2n-tuples, as in the definition of ranks.

Additivity to characterize rank-dependent weights. The following exercise adapts Exercise 6.6.1 from risk to uncertainty.

Exercise 10.9.4 [Additivity of decision weights].

(a)$^{'a}$ Show that $\pi((E_2 \cup E_1)^b) = \pi(E_1^b) + \pi(E_2^{E_1})$. Note that all decision weights concern the evaluation of a prospect $E_1x_1, E_2x_2, \ldots, E_nx_n$ with a complete ranking $x_1 \geq \cdots \geq x_n$.

(b)^b Show that $\pi((E_2 \cup E_1)^R) = \pi(E_1^R) + \pi(E_2^{E_1 \cup R})$. Note that all decision weights concern the evaluation of a prospect $Rx_0, E_1x_1, E_2x_2, \ldots, E_nx_n$ with complete ranking $x_0 \geq x_1 \geq \cdots \geq x_n$.

(c)^b For any disjoint $A_1, \ldots, A_k$ and disjoint $B_1, \ldots, B_m$ with $\cup_{i=1}^k A_i = \cup_{j=1}^m B_j$, we must have
$$\pi(A_1^b) + \pi(A_2^{A_1}) + \cdots + \pi(A_k^{A_{k-1} \cup \cdots \cup A_1}) = \pi(B_1^b) + \pi(B_2^{B_1}) + \cdots + \pi(B_m^{B_{m-1} \cup \cdots \cup B_1}). \square$$

Exercise 10.9.4 derived restrictions on decision weights. Part (a) showed that decision weights cannot depend on ranks in just any way, but must satisfy additivity to agree with RDU. The following exercise shows that this additivity is, essentially, the only requirement.

Exercise 10.9.5^b [General rank dependence + additivity of decision weights = RDU]. Assume that π is a general function, assigning to each pair of disjoint events E,R $\subset$ S the number $\pi(E^R)$, with the notation $\pi(E^b) = \pi(E^{\varnothing})$ and $\pi(E^w) = \pi(E^{E^c})$. Assume the normalization $\pi(S^b) = 1$ and $\pi(\varnothing^b) = 0$, and assume that $0 \leq \pi(E^R)$ for all E,R. Further assume additivity: $\pi((E_2 \cup E_1^b)) = \pi(E_1^b) + \pi(E_2^{E_1})$ for all E_1, E_2. Show that there exists a weighting function W such that $\pi(E^R) = W(E \cup R) - W(R)$. $\square$

Thus, a set of general decision weights can be derived from a weighting function using rank dependence if and only if they satisfy the additivity of the preceding exercises.

Convexity and concavity as local properties. The following exercise is similar to Exercise 7.4.1, showing how convexity and concavity of W can be inspected using small outcome events E with varying ranks R_i. Uncertainty is more complex than risk in the sense that the following exercise will only investigate one nested set of ranks, and there can be many other ranks that remain to be inspected.

Exercise 10.9.6.^{b} Assume RDU. Assume a partition $(B_1, \ldots, B_{98}, E, A)$. We define $R_i = \cup_{j=1}^i B_j$ and $C_i = \cup_{j=i+1}^{98} B_j$ for each i. Assume $9 \geq \alpha_i \geq 4$ such that

$$(R_i : 9, E : \alpha_i, C_i : 2, A : 0) \sim$$
$$(R_i : 9, E : 4, \ C_i : 2, A : 1).$$

Show that:

- If R_i is in a region where W is concave then α_i increases in i. More specifically, if $\pi(E^{R_{i+1}}) = \pi(E^{R_i \cup B_{i+1}}) \leq \pi(E^{R_i})$ then $\alpha_{i+1} \geq \alpha_i$.
- If R_i is in a region where W is convex then α_i decreases in i. More specifically, if $\pi(E^{R_i \cup B_{i+1}}) \geq \pi(E^{R_i})$ then $\alpha_{i+1} \leq \alpha_i$. $\square$

Assignment 10.9.7. Assume the preference

$$E_1 60E_2 50E_3 30E_4 20 \succcurlyeq E_1 60E_2 50E_3 40E_4 10.$$

(a)[a] Show that 2-fold application of the ranked sure-thing principle implies $E_1 80E_2 70E_3 30E_4 20 \succcurlyeq E_1 80E_2 70E_3 40E_4 10$. In this preference, all events have the same rank as in the assumed preference.

(b)[b] Show that 2-fold application of the ranked sure-thing principle implies $E_1 50E_2 60E_3 30E_4 20 \succcurlyeq E_1 50E_2 60E_3 40E_4 10$. This preference involves different ranks for some events than in the assumed preference.

(c)[b] Show that 3-fold application of the ranked sure-thing principle implies $E_1 80E_2 90E_3 30E_4 20 \succcurlyeq E_1 80E_2 90E_3 40E_4 10$. This preference again involves different ranks for some events than in the assumed preference. □

Degenerate special versions. The version of RDU when nondegeneracy does not hold was characterized by Chambers (2007). A special case, where a quantile of a subjective probability distribution is maximized, is in Rostek (2010).

Appendix 10.10   An integral representation

Similarly to the integral definition of RDU in Eq. (6.9.1) for risk, RDU for uncertainty can be calculated as

$$RDU(x) = \int_{\mathbb{R}^+} W\{s \in S : U(x(s)) > t\} dt$$

$$- \int_{\mathbb{R}^-} [1 - W\{s \in S : U(x(s)) > t\}] dt. \tag{10.10.1}$$

Again, this equation can readily be used for infinite state spaces and prospects that take infinitely many values. Such prospects are not considered in this book. The equation can be rewritten as

$$RDU(x) = \int_{\mathbb{R}^+} W(x^{-1}(U^{-1}(t, \infty))) dt - \int_{\mathbb{R}^-} [1 - W(x^{-1}(U^{-1}(t, \infty)))] dt. \tag{10.10.2}$$

In Eq. (10.10.1), we may replace $U(x(s)) > t$ by $U(x(s)) \geq t$ and in Eq. (10.10.2) we may replace $U^{-1}(t, \infty)$ by $U^{-1}[t, \infty)$.[19] The equations show that, to evaluate a prospect x, all we need to know about W is its values at the ranks $x^{-1}(U^{-1}(t, \infty))$.

Exercise 10.10.1.[c] Verify that the integral sum in Eq. (10.10.1) gives the RDU value of the prospect $E_1 x_1 \cdots E_n x_n$. □

---

[19] W must have a positive "jump" at points where the replacement matters, and different jumps cover different rational numbers so that there cannot be more jumps than there are rational numbers, i.e., at most countably many. Countably many points t cannot affect the integral.

Appendix 10.11   Ranking states and collapsing outcomes

It can sometimes be useful to consider prospects $E_1x_1\cdots E_nx_n$ for which the outcomes have not been ranked; i.e., not $x_1 \geq \cdots \geq x_n$. This can happen if we have committed ourselves to the numbering of states in a finite state space $S = \{s_1,\ldots,s_n\}$, and always want x_1 to relate to s_1 regardless of whether or not x_1 is the best outcome. RDU is then defined as $\sum_{j=1}^{n}\pi_j U(x_j)$, with the *decision weights* π_j obtained as follows.

(1) Choose a complete ranking ρ of $E_1,\ldots,E_n$ such that $x_{\rho_1} \geq \cdots \geq x_{\rho_n}$. For each
    event E_{ρ_j}, $R_{\rho_j} = E_{\rho_{j-1}} \cup \cdots \cup E_{\rho_1}$ is the rank ($R_{\rho_1} = \emptyset$).
(2) Take $\pi_{\rho_j} = \pi(E_{\rho_j}{}^{R_{\rho_j}})$ for each j.[20]

Again, π_j is the marginal W contribution of E_j to its rank.

As for decision under risk, identical outcomes can be collapsed. If, for example, $x_1 = x_2$, then we have the liberty to rewrite $E_1x_1,\ldots,E_nx_n$ as $(E_1\cup E_2)x_1,E_3x_3,\ldots,E_nx_n$, and apply the RDU calculations to this $n-1$ fold partition. It yields the same RDU value, as is to be demonstrated in the following exercise. It also follows that the RDU value is not affected if we reverse the ranking of identical outcomes $x_i = x_j$ for $i \neq j$.

Exercise 10.11.1. Consider $E_1x_1\cdots E_nx_n$ with $x_1 \geq \cdots \geq x_n$, and assume that $x_i = x_{i+1}$.

(a)[b] Show that the RDU formula is not affected if we collapse x_i and x_{i+1}; i.e.,
    $\mathrm{RDU}(x) = \sum_{j=1}^{i-1}\pi_j U(x_j) + \pi((E_{i+1}\cup E_i)^{E_{i-1}\cup\cdots\cup E_1})U(x_i) + \sum_{j=i+2}^{n}\pi_j U(x_j)$.
(b)[b] Show that the procedure for calculating RDU(x) yields the same result if we
    reverse the ranking of E_i and E_{i+1}. Consider $E_1x_1,\ldots,E_{i-1}x_{i-1},E_{i+1}x_{i+1},E_ix_i$, $E_{i+2}x_{i+2},\ldots,E_nx_n$, and calculate its RDU as

$$\sum_{j=1}^{i-1}\pi_j U(x_j) + \pi(E_{i+1}{}^{E_{i-1}\cup\cdots\cup E_1})U(x_{i+1}) + \pi(E_i{}^{E_{i+1}\cup E_{i-1}\cup\cdots\cup E_1})U(x_i)$$
$$+ \sum_{j=i+2}^{n}\pi_j U(x_j). \ \square$$

Appendix 10.12   Comonotonicity

The comonotonicity concept, introduced by Schmeidler (1989) for rank dependence, has proved to be important in theoretical analyses in many domains (Dhaene *et al.* 2002). Because of this importance, we briefly consider some elementary properties, even though the rest of this book does not use comonotonicity. A set of prospects is *comonotonic* if the same complete ranking of events (further discussed below) can be used for all prospects. In other words, each outcome event has the same rank for all prospects in the set. An equivalent definition that does not refer to ranks is given later (Eq. (10.12.1)). On comonotonic sets of prospects, RDU agrees with an EU functional with each event having its decision weight given its rank as its probability. This useful observation underlies many results for RDU.

---

[20] As usual, $\{E_{\rho_{j-1}} \cup \cdots \cup E_{\rho_1}\} = \emptyset$ for $j=1$, and, hence, then $W(E_{\rho_{j-1}} \cup \cdots \cup E_{\rho_1})=0$.

A maximal comonotonic sets results if we specify a complete ranking of the entire state space and take the set of all prospects compatible with this ranking. Such a complete ranking of an entire state space is, however, complex to handle, especially for infinite state spaces. The complexity will be even more problematic if measure theory (Appendix H) is imposed on the state space and compatibility of the ranking with the measure structure becomes an issue. We have simplified the analysis in the main text by putting ranks central, avoiding complete rankings of entire state spaces.

For finite state spaces S, it has been customary in the literature to fix a numbering $S = \{s_1,...,s_n\}$ from the beginning. Then the complex notation with permutations ρ (§10.11) cannot be avoided to model rank dependence, and this has hampered the popularity of RDU for uncertainty. The notation with flexible partitions used in this book is more tractable. Sometimes, however, the use of complete rankings can still be convenient. We now turn to this topic. Formally, a *complete ranking* ρ is a weak order that furthermore is antisymmetric; i.e., two different elements cannot be ρ equivalent – no ties allowed. We pronounce

$$s \quad \rho \quad t$$

as "s is ranked better than t (by ρ)" or "s is ρ better than t." When calculating the RDU value of a prospect in the main text we always specified a complete ranking of the outcome events.

It can be seen that a set of prospects is comonotonic if and only if there exists a complete ranking ρ of the entire state space such that, for all prospects x in the set and for all states s,t, $x(s) \geq x(t)$ whenever s is ranked better than t by ρ. The prospects are called *compatible* with ρ, and the set of all prospects compatible with ρ is called a *comoncone*. It is a maximal comonotonic set. Each comoncone contains all constant prospects (Exercise 10.12.1). As we will see in Exercise 10.12.3, a set of prospects of the form $E_1x_1\cdots E_nx_n$, for a fixed partition $\{E_1,...,E_n\}$, is comonotonic if and only if there exists a complete ranking ρ of the events E_j such that $x_{\rho_1} \geq \cdots \geq x_{\rho_n}$ for all prospects x considered, and this holds if and only if we can assign to each outcome event the same rank for all prospects contained in the set.

Comonotonicity has been known for a long time in mathematics (Hardy, Littlewood & Pòlya 1934 No.236, "similarly ordered"), and has been used in decision theory in discussions of hedging (Yaari 1969 p. 328). Its importance for nonadditive measures in decision under uncertainty was first understood by Schmeidler (1986).

Exercise 10.12.1.[b] Show that a constant prospect is comonotonic with every other prospect. □

Exercise 10.12.2. In this exercise we will see that a set of prospects is comonotonic if and only if:

There exist no prospects x and y in that set, and states s and t, such that

$$x(s) > x(t) \text{ but } y(s) < y(t). \tag{10.12.1}$$

(a)[b] Show that a comonotonic set of prospects satisfies Eq. (10.12.1).

(b)[c] In this part you can use Szpilrajn's (1930) lemma, implying that for each weak order $\geq'$ of S there exists a complete ranking ρ that extends $\geq'$; i.e., [s $\geq'$ t $\Rightarrow$ s ρ t] (ρ breaks all ties of $\geq'$). Show that a set of prospects that satisfies Eq. (10.12.1) is comonotonic.

(c)[a] Show that a set of prospects is comonotonic if and only if every pair of prospects in the set is comonotonic. □

Exercise 10.12.3. You can use the result of Exercise 10.12.2 in this exercise.

(a)[b] Use Eq. (10.12.1) to show that, for each partition $(E_1,\ldots,E_n)$, the set of prospects of the form $E_1x_1\cdots E_nx_n$ with $x_1 \geq \cdots \geq x_n$ is comonotonic.

(b)[c] Consider a partition $\{E_1,\ldots,E_n\}$, and a set of prospects of the form $E_1x_1\cdots E_nx_n$, without the requirement of $x_1 \geq \cdots \geq x_n$. Assume that the set of prospects is comonotonic. Show that the events E_j can be renumbered (completely ranked) in such a way that after the renumbering the outcomes are ordered from best to worst. That is, show that there exists a permutation $\rho_1,\ldots,\rho_n$ of $1,\ldots,n$ such that $x_{\rho_1} \geq \cdots \geq x_{\rho_n}$ for all prospects contained in the set. We can "renumber" the events as $E_1' = E_{\rho_1}, \ldots, E_n' = E_{\rho_n}$, so as to have them ranked as in part (a). □

It can also be seen that a set of prospects is comonotonic if and only if any countable subset is an increasing (in the sense of nondecreasing) transform of one underlying prospect. The result holds for the whole comonotonic set of prospects if the state space is finite. Given marginal distributions, comonotonicity maximizes correlation and minimizes the expectation of concave functions (Cheung 2008; Denneberg 1994 Ch. 4; Dhaene *et al.* 2002). We next discuss relations between ranks and comonotonicity, first verbally and then formalized. We also discuss in more detail the construction of a probability measure for a comoncone such that RDU on that comoncone coincides with EU for that probability measure. For a comonotic set of prospects we can, for each prospect contained and outcome event pertaining to that prospect, choose as rank of that event the set of all states that are ranked better than all states in the outcome event. In this way, ranks are the same for all prospects in the set. Conversely, if we can assign ranks to all outcome events the same way for all prospects in a set, then we can define the complete ranking in two steps. First, we set s ρ t if s is contained in all ranks that contain t. This ρ can be seen to be a weak order. Second, ρ can be extended to an antisymmetric weak order by Szpilrajn's (1930) lemma (see Exercise 10.12.2b). Thus RDU reduces to EU by defining as probability of each outcome event the decision weight given its rank. Details are as follows.

Consider a comonotonic set of prospects with a complete ranking ρ of the state space. Define a probability measure P on S as follows. For each state s define P$\{$t $\in$ S: t is ρ better than s$\} = $ W$\{$t $\in$ S: t is ρ better than s$\}$ and P$\{$t $\in$ S: t is ρ better than[21]

---

[21] For infinite-valued prospects we would also consider events E that are ρ-intervals in the sense that: if t∈E and s is ρ better than t, then s∈E.

s or $t = s$} $= W\{t \in S: t$ is ρ better than s or $t = s$}. If not all subsets of S are in the domain of W but, say, only an algebra of subsets is, then define P only for the above sets if they are in the domain of W. P is defined on a nested set of events and can be extended to a probability measure P defined on an algebra on S. It can be seen that EU defined with respect to this P agrees with RDU on the comonotonic set. For example, we can write every prospect x in a maximally collapsed way (its *collapsed form*) as $E_1x_1 \cdots E_nx_n$ with $x_1 > \cdots > x_n$. Then each decision weight $\pi(E_j^{E_{j-1} \cup \cdots \cup E_1})$ agrees with $P(E_j)$ as just defined. Here the outcome events E_j always have the same rank, namely the states of nature ranked ρ-better than those in E_j. Hence, when studying RDU, within comonotonic sets of prospects we can use results from EU. We do not elaborate on this point, and only refer to the experiment in §4.1. The prospects in Figures 4.1.1 (TO upwards) are comonotonic, and so are they in Figures 4.1.2 (2nd TO upwards) and 4.1.4 if $\delta^0 \geq 8$. From this observation we can immediately conclude that the questions in these figures measure utilities under RDU as they do under EU.

An appealing example of a naturally arising comonotonic set is in Halevy (2008). I next describe his model using the concepts of this book. Uncertainty concerns the timepoint a consumer will die. The longer he lives, the more he can consume, always yielding higher utility (consumption is nonnegative and is at least as good as dying). This generates a natural rank-ordering of the states of nature (time of dying). With outcomes being consumption streams truncated at the moment of dying, his model amounts to an RDU model restricted to a comonotonic set. Thus, it can combine empirical features of nonexpected utility with the tractable additive aggregations of classical expected and discounted utility and with, for instance, the sure-thing principle satisfied within this comonotonic set.

Most of the behavioral foundations advanced in the literature have used "comonotonic" versions of traditional conditions, starting with Schmeidler's (1989) comonotonic independence, Gilboa's (1987) comonotonic P2* condition, the comonotonic sure-thing principle (Chew & Wakker, 1996) and comonotonic tradeoff consistency (Köbberling & Wakker 2003; Wakker 1989a, b; Wakker & Tversky 1993). The adjective comonotonic indicates that the preference conditions are imposed only within comoncones. They are thus somewhat weaker than the preference conditions considered in this book. They do not impose restrictions as soon as the relevant outcome event has the same rank for all prospects considered as we did. Rather, they impose restrictions only within comoncones, i.e., if all events for all prospects involved have all ranks identical.

Observation 10.12.1. Preference conditions restricted to comoncones apply only if all events have the same rank for all prospects considered, and are implied by the corresponding rank-preference conditions. □

Comonotonicity preference conditions lead to stronger theorems on behavioral foundations. I find the rank conditions so much more tractable that I have nevertheless decided to use these throughout this book. For completeness, I present a comonotonic generalization. *Comonotonic tradeoff consistency* excludes contradictions between observations $\sim_c^t$ as did rank-tradeoff consistency, only now the observations $\sim_c^t$ are restricted to the case where all four prospects in Eqs. (10.5.3) and (10.5.4) are comonotonic.

Theorem 10.12.2. In Theorem 10.5.6, rank-tradeoff consistency can be weakened to comonotonic tradeoff consistency.

Proof. The proof of Theorem 10.5.6 was based on Köbberling & Wakker (2003) who never used more than the comonotonic condition. Hence, this proof holds with no modification for Theorem 10.12.2. □

Further generalizations can be obtained by replacing comonotonicity by a weaker condition introduced by Anger (1977 Definition 2 and Theorem 3), called maxmin relatedness by Wakker (1990b), and used also by Chateauneuf (1991 A.5). I will not present this condition here.

Exercise 10.12.4. Assume RDU with a finite number $n \geq 2$ of states of nature.

(a)^b Show that strong monotonicity implies that all decision weights of ranked events E^R with $E \neq \emptyset$ are positive.

(b)^c Show that positivity of all decision weights implies strong monotonicity. □

Appendix 10.13 Proofs for Chapter 10

Lemma 10.13.1. Under the assumptions of Table 10.9.1, the two entries in the last column are equivalent.

Proof. Each event-contingent prospect used in an observation $\sim_c^t$ in Eqs. (10.5.2)–(10.5.4) can be replaced by the corresponding probability-contingent prospect, leading to an observation $\sim_c^t$ as in Notation 6.5.2. Here p^r (with $p > 0$) in Notation 6.5.2 corresponds to the nonnull ranked event E^R in Eqs. (10.5.2)–(10.5.4). A violation of rank-tradeoff consistency in the sense of Definition 10.5.5 thus implies a violation in the sense of Definition 6.5.5.

Conversely, because P satisfies solvability, for the probability vectors $(p,p_2,...,p_m)$ and $(p,q_2,...,q_n)$ in Notation 6.5.2 we can construct partitions $(E,E_2,...,E_m)$ and $(E,F_2,...,F_n)$ with $P(E) = p$, $p_i = P(E_i)$ for all i and $q_j = P(F_j)$ for all j. Then an observation $\sim_c^t$ as in Notation 6.5.2 generates an observation $\sim_c^t$ as in Eqs. (10.5.2)–(10.5.4) (with $r = P(R)$). A violation of rank-tradeoff consistency in the sense of Definition 6.5.5, therefore, implies a violation in the sense of Definition 10.5.5. □

Proof of Observation 10.5.2. Compare the inequality
$$RDU(\alpha_{E^R}x) \geq RDU(\alpha_{E^R}y) \text{ with the inequality}$$

$$RDU(\beta_{E^R}x) \geq RDU(\beta_{E^R}y).$$

In the upper inequality, the term $\pi(E^R)U(\alpha)$ appears both left and right and can be dropped. In the lower inequality, the term $\pi(E^R)U(\beta)$ appears both left and right and can similarly be dropped. After dropping the two aforementioned terms, the upper and lower inequalities are the same, because, by Lemma 10.5.3, $\alpha_{E^R}x$ and $\beta_{E^R}x$ have all ranked outcome events and, hence, decision weights the same, and so do $\alpha_{E^R}y$ and $\beta_{E^R}y$. $\square$

Proof of Lemma 10.5.3. Empty outcome events can be suppressed and we may, therefore, assume that all outcome events are nonempty. Because α and β have the same rank R, there can be no x_i strictly between them. If x_i coincides with the worst of α and β, then we rank its outcome event E_i as worse than E. If x_i coincides with the best of α and β, then we rank its outcome event E_i as better than E. In this way, each outcome event E_i for each outcome x_i can be given the same rank and the same decision weight π_i in both prospects. $\square$

Proof of Theorem 10.5.6. See Köbberling & Wakker (2003 Corollary 10) for finite state spaces, with the extension to infinite state spaces in Appendix G, and with comments on comonotonicity in Observation 10.12.1. $\square$

Proof of Theorem 10.9.2. The result is in Chateauneuf & Tallon (2002), amidst many other results. It can be inferred from their Proposition 1 plus the equivalence of (i) and (iv) in their Theorem 1. $\square$

Proof of Observation 10.9.3. Consider the following four equivalent lines

$$\pi(E^b) \geq \pi(E^R);$$

$$W(E) \geq W(E \cup R) - W(R);$$

$$w(P(E)) \geq w(P(E \cup R)) - w(P(R));$$

$$w(p) \geq w(p + r) - w(r) \text{ for } p = P(E) \text{ and } r = P(R);$$

If $w_{rb} = P(W_{rb})$, then the last inequality holding for all $p + r \leq w_{rb}$ implies that the first inequality holds for all $E \cup R \preccurlyeq W_{rb}$. This holds because the latter likelihood ordering is equivalent to $W(E \cup R) \leq W(W_{rb})$. Because w increases strictly, the latter inequality holds if and only if $P(E \cup R) \leq P(W_{rb})$, implying $p + r \leq w_{rb}$. For all E and R we can find p and r to carry out the aforementioned substitution, so that likelihood insensitivity for w always implies the same condition on W.

Conversely, assume solvability. Then for each p,r we can find an event A such that $W(A) = w(p + r)$, so that $P(A) = p + r$. Next, by solvability, we can find a subevent R with $\emptyset \subset R \subset A$ and $W(R) = w(r)$, so that $P(R) = r$. Then for $E = A - R$ we have $P(E) = p$. That is, for each p and r we can find disjoint events E and R with $P(E) = p$ and $P(R) = r$. The four displayed lines then are equivalent, and likelihood insensitivity of W is equivalent to likelihood insensitivity of w. $\square$

Appendix 10.14   Proof of Theorem 6.5.6

Necessity of Statement (ii) is obvious and, hence, we consider sufficiency. That is, we assume Statement (ii) and derive Statement (i). This implication is obtained as a corollary of Theorem 10.5.6. Take the state space $S = [0,1]$ and let event-contingent prospects map S to $\mathbb{R}$. Probability-contingent prospects are generated as in §2.3. The conditions of Statement (ii) of Theorem 10.5.6 readily follow: Monotonicity follows from stochastic dominance. For continuity, and a partition $E_1,\dots,E_n$ with probabilities $P(E_j) = p_j$, $\{(x_1,\dots,x_n): E_1x_1\dots E_nx_n \succcurlyeq E_1y_1\dots E_ny_n\} = \{(x_1,\dots,x_n): p_1x_1\dots p_nx_n \succcurlyeq p_1y_1\dots p_ny_n\}$ is closed by continuity of $\succcurlyeq$ over probability-contingent prospects. Similarly, every revelation $\alpha \ominus \beta \sim_c^t \gamma \ominus \delta$ derived from event-contingent prospects immediately implies the same revelation from probability-contingent prospects (Lemma 10.13.1), so that a violation of tradeoff consistency for event-contingent prospects implies one for probability-contingent prospects too.

By Theorem 10.5.6, an RDU representation results for event-contingent prospects with weighting function W. The rest of this proof is similar to Exercise 10.3.2: Stochastic dominance implies, for two events A and B with the same probability (= Lebesgue measure) $P(A) = P(B)$, the equivalence $1_A0 \sim 1_B0$, and this implies $W(A) = W(B)$. This implies that $W(E)$ is $w(P(E))$ for a function w. By strict stochastic dominance, w increases strictly. $\square$

11 Ambiguity: where uncertainty extends beyond risk

This chapter analyzes phenomena under uncertainty that did not show up under risk. §11.1 discusses how the Ellsberg paradox (Example 10.3.1) reveals the main new phenomenon. There are not many tractable models available in the literature to analyze ambiguity empirically. §11.2 proposes some special cases of RDU that can serve this purpose. Analyses in terms of risk and uncertainty premiums are in §11.3. Before turning to pragmatic ways of measuring ambiguity, §11.4–11.6 present some models alternative to RDU, so that these can also be discussed in the pragmatic analysis (although knowledge of these is not necessary for what follows). Besides source preference, which is related to optimism and elevation of the weighting curve (the motivational component in Figures 7.1.1–7.1.3), likelihood sensitivity is another important component of uncertainty attitudes, also depending on sources (the cognitive component in Figures 7.1.1–7.1.3). Tversky & Fox (1995) and Tversky & Wakker (1995) provided theoretical and empirical analyses of this condition for ambiguity. The pragmatic measurements of ambiguity aversion and likelihood sensitivity are presented in §11.7–11.8. Three appendices follow.

11.1 The Ellsberg paradox and the home bias as within-subject between-source comparisons

Sources of uncertainty will play a central role in this chapter. These are sets of uncertain events generated by the same mechanism. Further details will be provided later. The main new phenomenon that can be inferred from the Ellsberg paradox and that will be the topic of this chapter concerns different attitudes within the same person between different sources of uncertainty. Ellsberg revealed such a difference for the special case where one source of uncertainty (the known urn) concerned risk with known, objective probabilities, and the other source (the unknown urn) concerned unknown probabilities. This case has been the focus in the literature up to today. Ellsberg's technique can, however, be used for all sources of uncertainty regardless of whether or not probabilities are known for some of the sources. It can, for instance, be used to analyze the home bias. Because probabilities are rarely known in practice, general between-source comparisons as in the home bias will be of most interest in applications.

We already saw in Example 10.3.1 that, whereas RDU with probabilistic sophistication cannot accommodate some new phenomena of uncertainty, general RDU easily can. Tversky & Fox (1995) and Tversky & Wakker (1995) formalized the new phenomena as follows. A *source* is a specific set of events. At this stage, we take sources as a new formal primitive, to be determined in the modeling stage. Abdellaoui *et al.* (2009) suggested that uniform sources, defined later, are especially well suited for the study of ambiguity. Further criteria for determining sources are left to future studies. For mathematical purposes, it is convenient at this stage to let a source be an "algebra" of events.[1]

We will first investigate systematic preference for one source over another (source preference). Imagine that we observe a preference for gambling on a Dow Jones increase over a Nikkei increase, i.e. $100_{DJ^+}0 \succ 100_{NK^+}0$ as in Figure 10.1.2. This need not reflect a systematic preference for Nikkei events and may instead simply reflect that DJ^+ is believed to be more likely than NK^+. To analyze source preference, we have to find a way to correct for the belief component. This occurred in the home bias in Figure 10.1.2, with a preference both for gambling on the Dow Jones increase and betting against it. If DJ^+ is believed to be more likely then its complement should be believed to be less likely, so that not both preferences can be due to likelihood beliefs and surely something else is going on. We now turn to formal definitions of this idea.

Let $\mathcal{A}, \mathcal{B}$ denote sources. For A from $\mathcal{A}$ and B from $\mathcal{B}$, an observation

$$[A \succcurlyeq B \quad \text{and} \quad A^c \succ B^c] \tag{11.1.1}$$

suggests a general preference for events from $\mathcal{A}$ to those from $\mathcal{B}$. An observation

$$[B \succcurlyeq A \quad \text{and} \quad B^c \succ A^c] \tag{11.1.2}$$

suggests the opposite.

Definition 11.1.1. Source preference holds for $\mathcal{A}$ over $\mathcal{B}$ if, for all $A \in \mathcal{A}$ and $B \in \mathcal{B}$, Eq. (11.1.1) may hold but Eq. (11.1.2) is precluded. $\square$

The Ellsberg paradox reveals source preference for the known urn over the unknown urn, and the home bias reveals source preference for domestic stocks over foreign stocks.

11.2 Using rank dependence to analyze ambiguity

Despite the generally recognized importance of ambiguity and uncertainty, and the appearance of a number of theoretical models in the literature, there have not been

---

[1] For nonmathematical readers, it suffices to know that for an algebra we can carry out all the usual set-theoretic operations of finite unions, intersections, and complementation within a source; for details see Appendix H.

many tractable and quantitative analyses in the literature up to the present. I am, for example, not aware of a study that fits the popular multiple priors models with the set of priors taken endogenously to data other than through parametric fitting (Hey, Lotito, & Maffioletti 2008). One of the most interesting approaches to analyze ambiguity, by Einhorn & Hogarth (1985, 1986) and Hogarth & Einhorn (1990), did provide tractable quantitative results, but used introspective judgments of probability as an input. It therefore does not fit within the revealed-preference approach used in this book.

In this section I briefly outline some possibilities for future research on ambiguity, based on rank dependence. This material is newer and in an earlier stage of development than the rest of this book.

For large state spaces S there exist many weighting functions.[2] The general RDU model then has too many free parameters to be tractable. This problem showed up, for instance, in Example 10.3.1 when we used RDU to accommodate the Ellsberg paradox, and, just so as to obtain a complete model, had to specify many W-values. Other models than RDU for uncertainty, such as the multiple priors models defined later, similarly become intractable for large state spaces when considered in full generality. The collection of all possible sets of priors is of an even larger cardinality than the set of all weighting functions. Hence, tractable subfamilies should be developed for those models too. Grabisch & Labreuche (2008 §2.7 and §7) described special tractable cases of rank dependence that are popular in multi-criteria optimization and in software applications. Hey, Lotito, & Maffioletti (2008) empirically tested several theories for uncertainty, and found that models with too many parameters do not perform well. We will suggest a number of cases of interest for decision under uncertainty. One example of tractable special cases of weighting functions concerns k-additive functions (§11.11 and Grabisch, Kojadinovic, & Meyer 2008).

Another tractable version of RDU was analyzed by Chateauneuf, Eichberger, & Grant (2007). They considered a probabilistically sophisticated analog of neo-additive probability weighting functions w(p).

Definition 11.2.1. A weighting function W is *neo-additive* if there exists a probability measure P and $0 \leq a$, $0 \leq b$, with $a + b \leq 1$, such that $W(\emptyset) = 0$, $W(S) = 1$, and $W(E) = b + aP(E)$ for all other events E. $\square$

Again, more general values of a and b are conceivable, with for instance b negative and W truncated under strict global pessimism. For simplicity of presentation we will focus on the most common case here. We obtain a representation[3]

$$RDU(x) = b \sup_{s \in S} Ux(s) + aEU(x) + (1 - a - b) \inf_{s \in S} Ux(s). \qquad (11.2.1)$$

---

[2] The dimension of the set of weighting functions ($2^{\|S\|} - 2$) grows exponentially.

[3] For P-null events and their complements the definition slightly deviates from probabilistic sophistication. This formal difference is not important for our purposes and we will not discuss it further.

That is, it is an EU model with the best and worst outcomes overweighted. We adapt Eq. (7.2.6) from risk to uncertainty:

a is an index of likelihood sensitivity;

$(2b + a)/2$ is an index of optimism (or source preference).[4]   (11.2.2)

Chateauneuf, Eichberger, & Grant (2007 p. 544) similarly interpreted parameter a as the degree of confidence in the EU-probabilities.

Another tractable version of RDU, analogous to the α-maxmin model defined later, concerns the case where a set of probability measures is given. For example, assume that two different probability measures P and Q are given, and

$$W(E) = a \times \min\{P(E), Q(E)\} + (1 - a) \times \max\{P(E), Q(E)\}.   (11.2.3)$$

Here, a is an index of pessimism. The definition can be extended to any set of probabilities with an $a/(1-a)$ mix of infima and suprema (Jaffray & Philippe 1997).

Abdellaoui *et al.* (2009) and Chew & Sagi (2008) showed that it is convenient to divide the set of uncertain events into uniform sources. *A uniform source is* a set of events that, intuitively, have the same degree of ambiguity. This amounts to probabilistic sophistication holding "within the source" (Wakker 2008b). That is, it holds for preferences restricted to prospects for which all outcome events are from this source. Probabilistic sophistication, thus, does not designate absence of ambiguity (such an absence was suggested by Epstein, 1999, and Epstein & Zhang, 2001), but only a uniform degree of ambiguity. The subjective probabilities for each uniform source can be revealed from preferences. For each event E we can define $W(E)$ as $w_{So}(P_{So}(E))$ where So is the source that E belongs to, P_{So} is the probability measure generating probabilistic sophistication within So, and w_{So} is the probability weighting function corresponding to the source, called the *source function*. w_{So} reflects the uncertainty attitude of the decision maker with respect to the events in So. To examine ambiguity attitudes (reflecting deviations from risk) we can filter out the risk attitude by considering $w^{-1}w_{So}$ where w is the probability weighting function for risk.

Abdellaoui *et al.* (2009) showed how uncertainty and ambiguity attitudes for uniform sources can be captured conveniently by graphs of the functions w_{So}. In this way, the authors could connect many of the ideas of the psychologists Einhorn and Hogarth with the economic revealed-preference approach.

Uncertainty is obviously more complex than risk. For each source So the subjective probabilities P_{So} have to be determined and also the source function w_{So}. The approach is yet considerably more tractable than general RDU with general weighting functions, in particular because we can display the w_{So} functions in graphs. The concepts introduced before for probability weighting functions in Chapter 7 can now be applied to the functions w_{So} to analyze attitudes towards uncertainty and ambiguity. We

---

[4] High values of the weighting function can be interpreted both as optimism and as source preference.

illustrate the approach just described, called the *source method* by Abdellaoui *et al.* (2009), using a simple example.

Example 11.2.2. Consider the two-color Ellsberg Example 10.1.1. We assume RDU and also the following symmetry:

$$1_{B_a}0 \sim 1_{R_a}0. \tag{11.2.4}$$

Then $W(B_a) = W(R_a)$. We define $P(B_a) = P(R_a) = \frac{1}{2}$ and then define the source function w_a such that $w_a(\frac{1}{2}) = W(B_a) = W(R_a)$. If we restrict attention to the unknown urn then, indeed, RDU with probabilistic sophistication does hold and $W(.) = w_aP(.)$. If we know the risk attitude of the decision maker and the probability transformation w for given probabilities, then we can take $w^{-1}(w_a(\frac{1}{2}))$ to reflect the ambiguity attitude of the decision maker with respect to the unknown urn. $w^{-1}(w_a(\frac{1}{2}))$ is the probability p that is weighted as much as the event R_a; i.e., $w(p) = (w_a(\frac{1}{2})) = W(R_a)$. It thus is the matching probability of Eq. (4.9.1), with $1_p0 \sim 1_{R_a}0$.

The matching probability $w^{-1}(w_a(\frac{1}{2}))$ will depend on the subjective beliefs of the decision maker, which need not be Bayesian and may be below $\frac{1}{2}$ for both colors of the unknown urn. It will also depend on the ambiguity attitude of the decision maker. A topic for future study is how subjective beliefs and ambiguity attitudes can be disentangled. It is remarkable that matching probabilities, originating as a central tool in Bayesian analyses (see end of §4.9.2), play a central role in the study of ambiguity too. The first reference signaling such a role is Jaffray (1989, preceding Eq. 10). □

In Example 11.2.2, the difference $\frac{1}{2} - p$ between a "Bayesian" subjective probability $\frac{1}{2}$ and the matching probability p can be taken as an index of ambiguity aversion (Jaffray 1989 Eq. 10; Kahn & Sarin 1988). Alternatively we can, for instance in the experiment in §4.1, use $CE(1_{\frac{1}{2}}0) - CE(1_{cand_1}0)$ as an ambiguity premium that, together with a risk premium, will comprise an overall uncertainty premium. In empirical studies, the aforementioned measures have been used as an index of ambiguity aversion (Chen, Katuščák, & Ozdenoren 2007; Hsu *et al.* 2005; Huettel *et al.* 2006).

Exercise 11.2.1.[b] Consider Example 11.2.2, with $P(B_a) = P(R_a) = \frac{1}{2}$ as defined there and with also $P(B_k) = P(R_k) = \frac{1}{2}$. Show that the preferences assumed there violate Assumption 2.1.2 (decision under risk) for this P. □

For a simple state space with only two states such as $\{cand_1, cand_2\}$ of §4.1, data fitting can be done relatively easily. Exercise 10.5.6 illustrated this point. The following exercise gives another illustration.

Exercise 11.2.2.[b] Reconsider the preferences of subject 5 in Figures 4.1.1, 4.1.2, and 4.1.4. Use the distance measure of §A.2. Assume RDU with $U(\alpha) = \alpha^\theta$. Determine the parameters $0 < \theta = j/100 < 2$, $0 \leq W(cand_1) = k/100 \leq 1$, and $0 \leq W(cand_2) = \ell/100 \leq 1$, that best fit the data, give the distance, and predict $CE(80_{cand_1}40)$. □

11.3   Elaborated examples for ranks, ambiguity premiums, and hedging in finance

This section presents some examples where we calculate risk and uncertainty premiums to measure uncertainty and ambiguity.

Example 11.3.1. A farmer will sell 500,000 bushels of corn in two months from now that took $1,800,000 to produce. We assume no time discounting. The farmer is uncertain about the price of corn in two months. The price may be high (event H: $4 per bushel) or low (event L: $3.80 per bushel). The profits will be $2,000,000 − $1,800,000 = $200,000 for the high price, and $1,900,000 − $1,800,000 = $100,000 for the low price. With $10,000 as the unit for outcomes, the prospect faced is 20_H10. It is very useful for the farmer to know now what his financial position will be in two months. The farmer can insure with a bank. The bank will guarantee a sure amount in two months but will charge a risk premium. The bank knows the probabilities $P(H) = P(L) = \frac{1}{2}$. The farmer maximizes RDU with $U(\alpha)$ and W to be specified. We consider the minimum amount that the farmer wants to be assured of (the CE), and the maximum profit (the risk premium) for the bank accordingly, for four cases (Figure 11.3.1). Calculations are left to the readers.

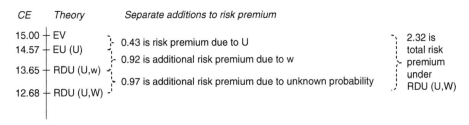

Figure 11.3.1 Various components contributing to risk premium.

CASE A   [EV]. The farmer knows the probabilities too and maximizes EV, so that $W(H) = \frac{1}{2}$. The risk premium is 0.

CASE B   [EU with U]. The farmer knows the probabilities too and maximizes EU, so that $W(H) = \frac{1}{2}$. $U(\alpha) = \alpha^{0.5}$. The risk premium is 0.43.

CASE C   [RDU with U, w]. The farmer knows the probabilities too and maximizes RDU with $w(p) = p^{1.3}$, so that $W(H) = \frac{1}{2}^{1.3} = 0.4061$. $U(\alpha) = \alpha^{0.5}$. The risk premium is 1.35 (= 0.43 + 0.92).

CASE D   [RDU with U,W]. The farmer behaves as in part (c) for known probabilities but, in this case, does not know the probabilities. The farmer is averse to unknown probabilities. For all $\alpha > 0$, $\alpha_H 0 \sim \alpha_L 0 \sim \alpha_{0.4} 0$ (matching probability 0.4). Thus, $W(H) = 0.4^{1.3} = 0.3039$. The risk premium is 2.32 (= 0.43 + 0.92 + 0.97).
□

Example 11.3.2 [Hedging in finance]. This example extends Example 11.3.1. Five chains of restaurants plan on a special monthly dish in two months, for which each needs 100,000 bushels of corn. The profits for each chain depend on the corn price.

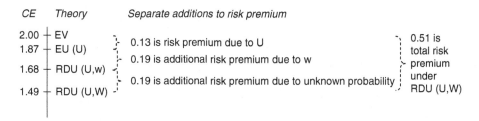

Figure 11.3.2 Various components contributing to risk premium.

Each restaurant faces the prospect 1_H3. Each would like to insure with a bank, willing to pay a risk premium for it. We next consider the same risk attitudes as in Example 11.3.1. Figure 11.3.2 shows the risk premiums.

We now consider an alternative and more efficient way to reduce the risk, involving also the farmer of Example 11.3.1. Assume that there are many farmers who produce corn and there are many restaurant chains that buy corn. They set up an exchange market. Each restaurant chain can take a forward contract for 100,000 bushels of corn where already now, two months ahead of time, it is determined that the corn will be bought from the exchange market in two months for $390,100 per forward contract. Thus the restaurant chain knows already now that its profit in two months will be 1.99 and faces no more uncertainty. Similarly, the farmer can also take five forward contracts for 100,000 bushels of corn where already now, two months ahead of time, it is determined that the price in two months will be $389,900 per forward contract. Thus, the farmer knows already now that his profit in two months will be 14.95. By directly matching producers and consumers of corn, the exchange market can reduce risk in a more efficient manner than the bank can, and the farmer and restaurant chains pay strongly reduced risk premiums. The difference in prices, $1000, goes to the exchange market. It is considerably less than the risk premiums to be paid to insurers or banks. □

A crucial aspect in the reduction of risk in Example 11.3.2 is that the financial positions of the farmer and the five restaurant chains involve different ranks of events. Whereas H has the best rank and L has the worst rank for the farmer, it is the reverse for the restaurant chains. The farmer and the restaurant chains can thus provide hedges to each other, where the risks of one neutralize those of the other. Such hedges constitute the essence of finance (Hull 2005). By matching financial positions that have opposite ranks, risk can be reduced much more efficiently than an insurance company or bank could do. Thus money-flows run smoothly.

Exercise 11.3.1.[a] Consider the case of Example 11.3.1. Assume, however, that the payment in case of L is 15 and not 10, continuing to use $10,000 as unit, so that the prospect faced now is 20_H15. Redo the analysis of Example 11.3.1. □

11.4   The CORE

This section introduces the CORE, an important theoretical concept that prepares for the alternative models presented in the next section. For a given weighting function W, a probability measure P on S is a *CORE element* if $P(E) \geq W(E)$ for all E. The CORE is important in many domains, for instance in cooperative game theory. There the s_j's designate players, any subset of S is a coalition, W indicates the amount of money that any coalition can make on its own, and a probability measure indicates a way to divide total earnings over the group. For a CORE division, no coalition has an incentive to deviate. Applications of the CORE in decision under uncertainty are discussed in §11.5.

Exercise 11.4.1.[a] Assume that $S = \{s_1, s_2\}$, and $W(s_1) = W(s_2) = \frac{1}{3}$. What is the CORE? □

Theorem 11.4.1. If W is convex then its CORE is nonempty and W is the minimum over all of its CORE elements. Further, for any utility function U, $RDU(x) = \min_{P \in CORE} EU_P(x)$ with $EU_P(x)$ the expected utility of x under U and P.

Proof of Theorem 11.4.1. See Anger (1977), Denneberg (1994 Theorem 10.3 applied to $1 - W(E^c)$) or Schmeidler (1989 Proposition on p. 582). These references also show that the conditions in the observation for the RDU functional are necessary and sufficient for W to be convex. □

In the above theorem, not only is W the minimum of CORE probabilities, but also RDU is the minimum of the CORE EUs.

11.5 Multiple priors (Maxmin expected utility and α-maxmin): basic results

This section assumes that a utility function U is given on the outcomes, and defines models for ambiguity other than RDU. We consider two cases and discuss how decision models can be defined for each.

CASE 1 [*Multiple priors*]. A convex set C of *priors* (probability measures P on the state space S) is given.

CASE 2 [*Probability intervals*]. For each event E an interval I_E of probabilities is given, satisfying some natural conditions ($I_\emptyset = \{0\}$, $I_S = \{1\}$, and if $A \supset B$ then the left and right endpoints of I_A weakly exceed those of I_B).

For the case of nonconvex sets C or I_E, it is immaterial for all decision models that we will consider if we replace these sets by their convex hull. Hence we assume convexity from the start. In Case 1 we can obviously specify for each event E the interval

$$I_E = \{P(E) : P \in C\} \tag{11.5.1}$$

of all possible probabilities, and in this sense Case 1 is a special case of Case 2. Case 1 contains more information because in Case 2 it has not been specified how the probabilities for the various events are to be combined into probability measures over the whole state space, if this is at all possible. We saw an example of Case 1 in Theorem 11.4.1, where C was the CORE. C may be exogenous, based on objective data, or it may be endogenous. We will return to this point later.

Models for Case 1 (multiple priors). Bewley (1986) presented a well-known model for Case 1. Prospect x is preferred to prospect y if and only if EU(x) ≥ EU(y) under every P in C. That is, the EU preference must be unanimous. Walley (1991; summarized by Miranda 2008) presented a similar model with upper and lower expectations. One prospect is preferred to another if and only if the lower expectation of the former exceeds the upper expectation of the latter. In the other cases no preference is expressed. In both models, for many pairs of prospects no preference is determined and completeness of preference is violated. We will focus here, as throughout this book, on theories that satisfy completeness.

Rank-dependent decision models can be defined for Case 2 and, consequently, also for Case 1 (with I_E as in Eq. (11.5.1)), by defining W in one of the following three ways.

$$W(E) = \inf(I_E); \tag{11.5.2}$$

$$W(E) = \sup(I_E); \tag{11.5.3}$$

$$\text{There exists a } 0 \leq \alpha \leq 1 \quad \text{with} \quad W(E) = \alpha \times \inf(I_E) + (1-\alpha)\sup(I_E). \tag{11.5.4}$$

It readily follows that these Ws are weighting functions. Given that W specifies weights of ranks ("good-news events"), Eq. (11.5.2) concerns the most pessimistic case. It generates low evaluations and low certainty equivalents of prospects. Equation (11.5.3) concerns the most optimistic case, and Eq. (11.5.4) concerns intermediate cases.

A popular alternative to RDU for Case 1 is the *maxmin expected utility (MEU)* model, also sometimes referred to using the general name multiple priors, with evaluations

$$MEU(x) = \inf_{P \in C} EU_P(x). \tag{11.5.5}$$

In Theorem 11.4.1, where C was the CORE of a convex weighting function, RDU, as in Eq. (11.5.2), was equal to MEU in Eq. (11.5.5). The two models have an important overlap there. In general, however, for other sets C that are not the CORE of a (convex) weighting function, RDU and MEU may be different. Because, for W as in Eq. (11.5.2), we have $W(E) \leq P(E)$ for all $P \in C$, it follows that then RDU ≤ MEU. The inequality can be strict (Exercise 11.9.1). The exercise will also show that there are MEU models that are not rank-dependent models in any sense. Hence, the models are really distinct, and neither is nested in the other.

A dual of MEU, generating optimistic behavior, is

$$x \mapsto \sup_{P \in C} EU_P(x). \tag{11.5.6}$$

A combination of the two forms just proposed gives the *α-maxmin (expected utility) model* (Hurwicz 1951; Luce & Raiffa 1957 §13.5):

$$x \mapsto \alpha \inf_{P \in C} EU_P(x) + (1-\alpha)\sup_{P \in C} EU_P(x) \text{ for some } 0 \leq \alpha \leq 1. \tag{11.5.7}$$

This model is similar to the RDU models in Eqs. (11.2.3) and (11.5.4). Whereas the MEU model reflects an extreme degree of pessimism and, for instance, cannot accommodate likelihood insensitivity, the α-maxmin model does accommodate some optimism similar to likelihood insensitivity.

Wald (1950) introduced the MEU model, Good (1950) discussed it in statistics, and Levi (1980) did so in philosophy. It became popular in decision theory when Gilboa & Schmeidler (1989) proved its soundness by providing a behavioral foundation. They used the Anscombe–Aumann two-stage approach (§4.9.3). In a mathematical sense this approach amounts to the set of outcomes being a convex subset of a linear space and utility being linear. Chateauneuf (1991 Theorem 2) also provided a behavioral foundation of this model. He assumed monetary outcomes and linear utility. Drèze (1961, 1987 Ch. 2) presented a similar model with a similar behavioral foundation. He used Eq. (11.5.6) and interpreted the model as "moral hazard' rather than as unknown probability. That is, the decision maker could choose the probability measure from C, which explains the supremum. Thus Drèze, like the author of this book a strong advocate of expected utility for normative purposes (Drèze 1987 Ch. 1), has been the first person in history to provide a preference foundation for a nonexpected utility model (Drèze 1961). Sup-inf decision models like the ones just discussed are sometimes referred to as models with imprecise probabilities (Walley 1991).

Ghirardato *et al.* (2003) gave necessary and sufficient conditions for the MEU model that do not require linear utility, but they used an endogenous mixture operation that cannot be observed from finitely many observations. Hence, their result is not a behavioral foundation in the sense of this book.[5] The only preference foundation of MEU presently existing that can be considered to be a behavioral foundation in this sense while avoiding the assumption of exogenously given utility (as made by Chateauneuf 1991), or the Anscombe–Aumann (1963) backward induction assumption for nonexpected utility of Gilboa & Schmeidler (1989), is Casadesus-Masanell, Klibanoff, & Ozdenoren (2000). Their constant-independence axiom is complex though. Whereas it does concern finitely many preferences, the number of preferences involved can exceed any finite bound.

The influential Artzner *et al.* (1999 Proposition 4.1) characterized the MEU model with linear utility taking the representing function (their "risk measure" is −1 times the evaluation) rather than binary preference as primitive. They refer to Huber (1981 Ch. 1, Proposition 2.1) for an identical mathematical result. Jaffray (1994 §3.4) provided a behavioral foundation of the α-maxmin model if the set of priors is exogenously given, and Ghirardato, Maccheroni, & Marinacci (2004) did so if it is endogenous; for a discussion of the latter paper see Eichberger *et al.* (2010).

The following observation illustrates further overlap between α-maxmin and rank dependence, in addition to Theorem 11.4.1. The observation follows from substitution.

---

[5] In the terminology of Krantz *et al.* (1971 §10.9.2), Hempel (1952), and Pfanzagl (1968 §1.10), conditions in terms of their mixture operation lead to derived rather than fundamental measurement.

Observation 11.5.1. On the set of binary prospects, the α-maxmin model agrees with binary RDU, with W as in Eq. (11.5.4). In particular, the MEU model agrees there with binary RDU, with W(E) defined as in Eq. (11.5.2). □

Models for Case 2 (probability intervals). Models based on probability intervals include Budescu & Wallsten (1987), Good (1950), Koopman (1940), Kyburg (1983), Manski (2004), Smith (1961), Suppes (1974), and Suppes & Zanotti (1989). Whereas Case 1 is more popular in theoretical studies, Case 2 is more popular in experimental studies for being easier to communicate.

11.6 Approaches in the literature that we will not take

The literature on ambiguity has focused on comparisons of decisions with known probabilities versus decisions with unknown probabilities, often implicitly treating unknown probabilities as one category ("ambiguity"). Most empirical studies have sought to capture ambiguity attitudes in terms of one number that should reflect ambiguity aversion, i.e. a general aversion to unknown probabilities. However, uncertainty is a richer empirical domain than risk, and uncertainties and sources of many kinds exist, which makes a summary in terms of a single number crude. It is instructive to compare ambiguous events to nonmonetary outcomes. Capturing risk aversion for nonmonetary outcomes using one number is just as crude as capturing ambiguity aversion for nonprobabilized events using one number. Both nonmonetary outcomes and ambiguous events constitute rich domains, and it is better not to treat them as one uniform category.

A number of attempts have been made to define ambiguity attitudes without reference to objectively given probabilities, usually attempting to replace those by probabilistic sophistication or by subjective expected utility (Epstein & Zhang 2001; Ghirardato & Marinacci 2002). I believe that objective and extraneously given probabilities provide the best benchmark to define ambiguity attitudes. Subjective probabilities are not easily observable and change from person to person, making them intractable as criteria for ambiguity neutrality as used in the aforementioned references.

In situations where objective probabilities are not available (they are often not even conceivable) such as with the home bias, the exact ambiguity attitudes – deviations from objective probabilities – are not central. As explained before, direct comparisons between different sources with unknown probabilities are then more important. We, for instance, take the performance of the Dow Jones stock index as one source of uncertainty and the performance of the Nikkei stock index as another. We then investigate how American, Japanese, and other investors behave. Probabilities are known for none of the relevant events.

I next turn to an historical accident. The common thinking in the field today is that the Allais paradox reveals violations of EU for risk, the Ellsberg paradox does so for uncertainty, and risk and uncertainty are separate fields. The Allais paradox then suggests probability weighting with the certainty effect, pessimism, and convex[6] probability weighting. The Ellsberg paradox suggests a special aversion to unknown probabilities relative to known probabilities, and names such as uncertainty aversion, ambiguity aversion, or, unfortunately, pessimism have been used in the literature to refer to this phenomenon. The Ellsberg paradox has traditionally been used to justify convex event-weighting functions. Our analysis will lead to different interpretations discussed next.

The Allais paradox reveals violations of EU for risk as much as it does for uncertainty (Figures 4.12.1 and 4.12.2). The violations are modeled by convexity of weighting functions as much under risk as under uncertainty. See the explanation in §6.4.1 on the certainty effect for risk and see Exercise 10.4.1 for the extension to uncertainty. This book has indeed emphasized that risk is not disjoint from uncertainty, but it is a special, limiting, subcase. The Allais paradox is relevant for a single agent and a single source of uncertainty and, in this sense, can be taken as an absolute effect.

The Ellsberg paradox does not reflect an absolute effect, but a relative effect. It does consider a single agent, but compares different sources within this single agent. It reveals that an agent can be more pessimistic for one source of uncertainty than for another and, accordingly, can deviate more from EU for one source than for another. Ellsberg demonstrated this effect when comparing a source with known probabilities to a source with unknown probabilities, but his technique can be used to compare any two sources of uncertainty, also if both have unknown probabilities. If an agent exhibits more pessimism for one source than for another, then from this relative observation we can infer the "absolute" observation that the agent must deviate from EU for at least one of the two sources. This "absolute" conclusion is a by-product of the relative conclusion, and explains how Ellsberg's examples also reveal violations of EU in an absolute sense.[7]

In Schmeidler (1989), EU was assumed for given probabilities. Then a relative conclusion, derived from the Ellsberg paradox, that weighting functions are more convex for unknown probabilities than for known probabilities, happens to coincide with the absolute conclusion that weighting functions for unknown probabilities are convex. This coincidence has led to the historical accident of the unfortunate association of convex weighting functions for uncertainty with the Ellsberg paradox rather than with the Allais paradox.

11.7 Indexes of ambiguity aversion

This and the following section present pragmatic quantifications of ambiguity attitudes. To stay close to the main interests in the current literature, I will consider cases where one source has known probabilities and the other does not. It should be clear

---

[6] We can also use likelihood insensitivity instead of convexity, or nonempty COREs as in Epstein (1999) and Ghirardato & Marinacci (2002). For simplicity, we will focus on convexity and pessimism in this discussion, phenomena that are sometimes taken to be the main deviations from EU.

[7] For an empirical study into the correlations between pessimism and ambiguity, see Pulford (2009).

that the same techniques can be used when all sources have unknown probabilities, and that such cases are more important for applications. This section focuses on an index of ambiguity aversion.

Although we will sometimes refer to binary RDU of §10.6, the hybrid model of §10.7, and the α-maxmin model of §11.5, those sections need not be read for understanding this section. Of §11.2 only the text about neo-additive weighting functions (Definition 11.2.1 and Eqs. (11.2.1)–(11.2.3)) needs to be read.

We only use binary prospects. Throughout this and the following section we assume RDU. In numerical analyses, we always assume power utility. We thus have the following evaluation.

For $\gamma \geq \beta, \mathrm{RDU}(\gamma_E \beta) = \mathrm{W}(\mathrm{E})\gamma^\theta + (1 - \mathrm{W}(\mathrm{E}))\beta^\theta.$ $\hspace{2cm}$ (11.7.1)

(In other words, we consider binary RDU.) For some events E, ("objective") probabilities $\mathrm{P}(\mathrm{E}) = \mathrm{p}$ are known, and for the other events no probabilities are known. We assume that there exists a probability weighting function w such that, whenever event E has known probability p, $\mathrm{W}(\mathrm{E}) = \mathrm{w}(\mathrm{p})$. For such an event:

For $\gamma \geq \beta, \mathrm{RDU}(\gamma_E \beta) = \mathrm{RDU}(\gamma_p \beta) = \mathrm{w}(\mathrm{p})\gamma^\theta + (1 - \mathrm{w}(\mathrm{p}))\beta^\theta.$ $\hspace{1cm}$ (11.7.2)

(Our model amounts to the hybrid model of RDU of §10.7.1.)

In experimental studies where one number is sought to represent a degree of ambiguity aversion, which is the topic of this section, the procedure in the following example is common. Researchers mostly refer to the α-maxmin model for this procedure (§11.5). It is the special case of binary RDU (§10.6) with the assumption added of EU for risk ($\mathrm{w}(\mathrm{p}) = \mathrm{p}$). We first present the procedure in general, and then illustrate it using numerical examples. The numerical examples concern the following assumption.

Assumption 11.7.1. An event with unknown probability is compared to an event with known probability. Each event is as likely (in the sense of willingness to bet) as its complement, so that the event with known probability has probability ½. □

Procedure 11.7.2 [Measuring ambiguity aversion assuming EU for risk (α-maxmin)]. We assume Eqs. (11.7.1) and (11.7.2) with $\mathrm{w}(\mathrm{p}) = \mathrm{p}$. We estimate utility (possibly, for convenience, only from risky choices) and the decision weight(s) of the unknown event(s). Under Assumption 11.7.1, the difference between ½ and the decision weight of the event with unknown probability is taken as an index of ambiguity aversion. □

Example 11.7.2′ [Numerical illustration]. Assume the Ellsberg urns as in Example 10.1.1. That is, urn_k contains 50 red balls and 50 black balls, and urn_a contains 100 red and black balls in an unknown proportion. A subject is asked to choose a color to gamble on and, being indifferent between them, selects black. B_k denotes black drawn from urn_k and B_a denotes black drawn from urn_a. B_k has known probability ½ so that $\mathrm{W}(\mathrm{B}_k) = \mathrm{w}(½) = ½$. B_a's probability is unknown.

CASE 1   [Deterministic analysis]. Assume that we measure

$$\mathrm{CE}(100_{\mathrm{B_k}}0) = 40 \text{ and } \mathrm{CE}(100_{\mathrm{B_a}}0) = 30. \tag{11.7.3}$$

We use the risky CE observation to determine the utility function, and obtain $U(\alpha) = \alpha^{0.76}$. Then, indeed, $100_{0.5}0 \sim 40$ under EU. The weight[8] $W(B_a)$ is $30^{0.76}/100^{0.76} = 0.40$. The difference of $0.10 = 0.50 - 0.40$ is the index of ambiguity aversion. Such indexes have often been used in regressions with between-subject comparisons.
CASE 2   [Data fitting][9]. Assume that we observed more data, namely, the CEs in Table 11.7.1.

Table 11.7.1. *CEs*

prospect	$100_{\mathrm{B_k}}0$	$100_{\mathrm{B_k}}20$	$100_{\mathrm{B_k}}50$	$100_{\mathrm{B_k}}80$	$100_{\mathrm{B_a}}0$	$100_{\mathrm{B_a}}20$	$100_{\mathrm{B_a}}50$	$100_{\mathrm{B_a}}80$
CE	40	52	72	88	30	45	66	86

The first four CEs concern decision under risk. Eqs. (11.7.1) and (11.7.2) (with $w(p) = p$) best fit the data for $\theta = 75$ and $W(B_a) = 0.38$, with distance[10] \$2.25. The index of ambiguity aversion is $0.50 - 0.38 = 0.12$. □

Although the approach in the preceding example is most common in the literature today, I will propose two variations. The first, presented in the remainder of this section, is to relax the assumption of EU for risk. The second variation will be the topic of the next section. The first relaxation is motivated by the many empirical violations of EU. An additional reason is that for the moderate amounts considered in the examples, utility curvature, the tool used in EU, will be weak. Probability weighting will capture more of risk attitude than nonlinear utility (Selten, Sadrieh, & Abbink 1999). Hence, if we want to use only one parameter to capture risk attitude, it may be preferable to use it for probability weighting rather than for utility curvature. The following procedure considers this approach with linear utility assumed. Thus, it uses the same number of free parameters as Procedure 11.7.2.

Procedure 11.7.3 [Measuring ambiguity aversion assuming linear utility]. We assume Eqs. (11.7.1) and (11.7.2) with $U(\alpha) = \alpha$ ($\theta = 1$). We estimate the decision weight(s) of all event(s). Under Assumption 11.7.1, $w(\frac{1}{2})$ (which was $\frac{1}{2}$ in Procedure 11.7.2) minus the decision weight of the unknown event is taken as the index of ambiguity aversion. □

---

[8] The weight $W(B_a)$ is often denoted $1-\alpha$ in the literature on α-maxmin models (with all probabilities assumed possible in the set of priors; otherwise the $\alpha/1-\alpha$ mixture of the highest and lowest conceivable probabilities should be equated with $W(B_a)$). We will maintain the notation of this book, with α designating an outcome. We do so in particular because the α-maxmin model used is binary RDU. The first example presents the simplest way to measure ambiguity aversion. This deterministic approach is typically used if there is little time for carrying out measurements and those are not required to be very accurate at the individual level.

[9] Throughout this and the following section, optimal fits are based on minimized sums of squared distances (§A.2).

[10] The distance is as in §A.2. With the parameter choices mentioned the theoretically predicted CEs are 39.68, 56.25, 73.93, 89.86, 27.52, 46.76, 67.98, and 87.47, respectively, with distance 2.25.

Example 11.7.3' [Numerical illustration]. We reanalyze the cases of Example 11.7.2'. Given that the only objective probability playing a role in our analysis is p = ½, the only parameter of w to be determined is w(½).

CASE 1 [Deterministic analysis]. Assume only the data of Eq. (11.7.3). The first indifference implies w(½) = 40/100 = 0.40 and the second one implies $W(B_a) = 30/100 = 0.30$. The difference 0.40 − 0.30 = 0.10 is the index of ambiguity aversion.

CASE 2 [Data fitting]. Assume the data of Table 11.7.1. The best fit is obtained with w(½) = 0.41 and $W(B_a) = 0.31$, with distance[11] $0.81. It yields 0.41 − 0.31 = 0.10 as an index of ambiguity aversion. □

We saw that probability weighting gives a better fit than utility curvature. Further improvements result if we use both probability weighting and utility curvature.

Procedure 11.7.4 [Measuring ambiguity aversion using probability weighting for risk and utility curvature]. We assume Eqs. (11.7.1) and (11.7.2) and estimate utility and the decision weights. Under Assumption 11.7.1, w(½) minus the decision weight of the unknown event is taken as the index of ambiguity aversion. □

Example 11.7.4' [Numerical illustration].

CASE 1 [Deterministic analysis]. For a deterministic analysis of the data in Eq. (11.7.3) there are too many parameters given the limited data. Had we observed two CEs under risk, then a deterministic derivation of utility curvature and probability weighting would have been possible.

CASE 2 [Data fitting]. We reanalyze the data of Table 11.7.1 with Eqs. (11.7.1) and (11.7.2) in full generality. The best fit is obtained with θ = 0.95, w(½) = 0.42, and $W(B_a) = 0.32$, with distance[12] 0.57. The ambiguity aversion index is 0.42 − 0.32 = 0.10. □

Table 11.7.2. *Optimal Fits of RDU for Data in Table 11.7.1 under Various Restrictions for Eqs. (11.7.1) and (11.7.2)*

Restrictions assumed	θ (for U)	w(0.5)	$W(B^a)$	distance from data	ambiguity aversion
EU for Risk (α-maxmin)	**0.75**	0.50*	**0.38**	$2.25	0.12
RDU for risk with U(α) = α	1*	**0.41**	**0.31**	$0.81	0.10
RDU in general	**0.95**	**0.42**	**0.32**	$0.57	0.10

Note: *: assumed; bold print: fitted.

Table 11.7.2 summarizes the results of data fitting. The distances show that ignoring probability weighting, by assuming EU for risk as done in the α-maxmin model, does not fit the data well. The overly concave utility function then leads to a

---

[11] With these parameter choices the theoretically predicted CEs are 41.00, 52.80, 70.50, 88.20, 31.00, 44.80, 65.50, and 86.20, respectively.

[12] With these parameter choices the theoretically predicted CEs are 40.13, 52.86, 70.79, 86.38, 30.14, 44.91, 65.81, and 86.38, respectively.

large overestimation of $W(B_a)$, and also to an overestimation of ambiguity aversion. This overestimation may be different for different individuals, so that interpersonal comparisons may be distorted. Using the same number of free parameters by allowing for probability weighting and taking utility linear fits the data better. Taking both utility curvature and probability weighting as free parameters leads to some further improvement in fit, which should be weighed against the price of using an extra parameter. The improvement of adding utility curvature to probability weighting can be expected to be bigger when the outcomes are larger than they are in our examples.

11.8   Indexes of ambiguity aversion and sensitivity

This section presents the second modification for ambiguity indexes relative to Procedure 11.7.2 (α-maxmin). We will adapt arguments put forward for risk (§7.10) to the context of ambiguity. The analysis in the preceding section focused on one aspect of uncertainty, namely a single number for a source to reflect ambiguity aversion. We considered only one kind of event, being an event that is equally likely as its complement. It has been found that such measurements of ambiguity aversion, even for events within one source, depend much on the likelihood of the events considered, and are different for events that are more or less likely than their complements. For unlikely events, people are often even ambiguity seeking (§10.4.2). This makes it hard to interpret the indexes obtained as global traits of individuals. The aforementioned dependence can be explained by likelihood insensitivity. Likelihood insensitivity can explain why source preference and ambiguity aversion as analyzed in the preceding section will depend so much on the likelihood of the events. By incorporating likelihood insensitivity, we will also get better estimates of the ambiguity aversion component.

In the same way as ambiguity aversion in the preceding section was a comparative concept, where we first measured optimism for known probabilities using $w(\frac{1}{2})$ and for unknown probabilities using $W(B_a)$, and then took the difference to reflect ambiguity aversion, the ambiguity concepts of this section will also be comparative. We first define source preference (optimism) and source sensitivity for individual sources in an absolute manner and then use their comparisons to reflect ambiguity attitudes.

Abdellaoui et al. (2009) and Craig Fox (1995 personal communication) proposed using neo-additive weighting functions, in the same way as we did for risk in §7.10. Again, we use these functions primarily for the clear interpretation of their parameters rather than for an optimal fit of the data.

Procedure 11.8.1 [Measuring ambiguity aversion and ambiguity sensitivity assuming linear utility]. Assume Eq. (11.7.1) (RDU), with $U(\alpha) = \alpha$ and W neo-additive (Definition 11.2.1) in a source-dependent manner. That is, first, for each source So we take a probability measure P_{So} and nonnegative a_{So} and b_{So} with $a_{So} + b_{So} \leq 1$. Then, for each event E from source So with probability $0 < P_{So}(E) < 1$,

$$W(E) = b_{So} + a_{So}P_{So}(E).$$ (11.8.1)

For simplicity, we treat all P_{So}-null events alike and set $W(E) = 0$ if $P_{So}(E) = 0$ and $W(E) = 1$ if $P_{So}(E) = 1$. We then find the parameters that best fit the data. As in Eq. (11.2.2),

$(2b_{So} + a_{So})/2$ is So's index of optimism (source preference)   (11.8.2)

and

a_{So} is So's index of source sensitivity.   (11.8.3)

Sources are compared by taking differences between their indexes. □

Example 11.8.1' [Numerical illustration]. Assume a known urn_k containing 1000 balls of 10 different colors, with 100 balls of each color, and an ambiguous urn_a also containing 1000 balls of 10 different colors, but it is unknown how many of each color are contained in urn_a. Let D_a denote the event of a ball drawn with one of the five darkest colors from urn_a, with D_k the corresponding event for urn_k. B_a denotes the event of a black ball drawn from urn_a, with black one of the 10 colors. B_k denotes the corresponding event for urn_k.

A subject is indifferent between gambling on D_a or on its complement, with the same holding for D_k. For each urn, the person is indifferent between gambling on any of the 10 colors. We will consider gambles on black. In Eq. (11.8.1), we write a_k and b_k for the parameters of the known urn, and a_a and b_a for the parameters of the unknown urn. In view of symmetry, the subjective probability of each color is 1/10, including $P_k(B_k) = P_a(B_a) = 1/10$.

CASE 1   [Deterministic analysis]. Say we observe

$$CE(100_{B_k}0) = 13; CE(0_{B_k}100) = 77, CE(100_{B_a}0) = 16.5; CE(0_{B_a}100) = 68.5.$$

We assume linear utility, $U(\alpha) = \alpha$. The first two CEs were analyzed in Example 7.10.1, where we found $a_k = 0.80$ and $b_k = 0.05$. For the second two CEs we get

$$(b_a + a_a \times 0.10) \times 100 = 16.5 \quad \text{and} \quad (b_a + a_a \times 0.90) \times 100 = 68.5$$

from which we solve ($a_a \times 0.80 \times 100 = 52$ and then)

$$a_a = 0.65 \text{ and } b_a = 0.10.$$

We have source-preference (or optimism) index $(2b_k + a_k)/2 = 0.45$ for risk and $(2b_a + a_a)/2 = 0.42$ for uncertainty, and source-sensitivity indexes $a_k = 0.80$ and $a_a = 0.65$. It leads to the joint assessment of an ambiguity aversion index $0.45 - 0.42 = 0.03$ and of an ambiguity insensitivity index $0.80 - 0.65 = 0.15$. By filtering out the source sensitivity component, we obtain a more reliable index of ambiguity aversion that can be expected not to vary much across events of different likelihoods.

CASE 2 ,   [Data fitting]. We next consider an example with a richer data set, where we also allow utility curvature. Say we observe the CEs in Tables 11.8.1 and 11.8.2.

Table 11.8.1. *CEs for risky choice*

prospect	$100_{D_k}0$	$100_{D_k}50$	$100_{B_k}0$	$100_{B_k}50$	$100_{B_k^c}0$	$100_{B_k^c}50$
CE	40	70	15	60	68	85

Table 11.8.2. *CEs for ambiguous choice*

prospect	$100_{D_a}0$	$100_{D_a}50$	$100_{B_a}0$	$100_{B_a}50$	$100_{B_a^c}0$	$100_{B_a^c}50$
CE	33	68	16	60	58	80

The best fit[13] is obtained for $\theta = 0.89$, $a_k = 0.65$, $b_k = 0.12$, $a_a = 0.53$, and $b_a = 0.13$, with distance[14] \$1.11. We have more likelihood sensitivity for risk than for ambiguity, with $a_k - a_a = 0.65 - 0.53 = 0.12$ an index of ambiguity insensitivity. There is also more optimism for risk than for ambiguity, with the difference $(2b_k+a_k)/2 - (2b_a + a_a)/2 = 0.45 - 0.40 = 0.05$ an index of ambiguity aversion. □

Example 11.8.1′ illustrates how we can obtain both an index of ambiguity aversion and one of ambiguity insensitivity. Summarizing, we assume a different neo-additive weighting function for known than for unknown probabilities, or in general, for different sources, find the optimal fit with data, and then interpret the parameters (and differences between parameters) of the obtained neo-additive weighting functions according to Eq. (11.2.2).

Abdellaoui *et al.* (2009) provided yet more refined tools for analyzing ambiguity attitudes in their source method. These tools can be used whenever we can divide events into sources such that probabilistic sophistication holds within each source, and we can obtain subjective probabilities for each source. Consider Example 11.8.1′. The events concerning urn_k constitute one source and the events concerning urn_a another. Each source in isolation satisfies probabilistic sophistication, with each color having probability 0.10. Therefore, we can define source functions w_k and w_a such that $W(E) = w_k(P_k(E))$ for all events E concerning urn_k, and $W(E) = w_a(P_a(E))$ for all events E concerning urn_a. Then the utility function U, the probability measures for both sources, and w_k and w_a, together completely capture the decision attitudes in a tractable manner. In particular, the functions w_k and w_a completely capture the deviations from expected utility, and their comparisons provide complete information about ambiguity attitudes. In this manner we can capture all aspects of general

---

[13] This fit, with one θ, was optimized at one blow for the whole data set. It would thus be well conceivable that θ would be somewhat different if only fit to the data of Table 11.8.1, which is in fact what we did in Example 7.10.2. As it so happens, however, the parameters found in Example 7.10.2 are found here too.

[14] The theoretically predicted CEs are given by $100_{D_k}0 \sim 40.26$; $100_{D_k}50 \sim 71.78$; $100_{B_k}0 \sim 15.02$; $100_{B_k}50 \sim 58.95$; $100_{B_k^c}0 \sim 67.52$; $100_{B_k^c}50 \sim 84.87$; $100_{D_a}0 \sim 35.22$; $100_{D_a}50 \sim 69.29$; $100_{B_a}0 \sim 14.84$; $100_{B_a}50 \sim 58.85$; $100_{B_a^c}0 \sim 57.07$; $100_{B_a^c}50 \sim 79.91$.

ambiguity attitudes in a tractable manner. This approach is more refined than when describing ambiguity attitudes by one or two numbers.

A noteworthy point in the analysis in this section is that events with known and unknown probabilities were compared as in the hybrid models introduced before. A multi-stage structure as in Anscombe & Aumann (1963) never played a role. §11.6 argued for a third modification with regard to the present literature: that there will be less focus on comparing known to unknown probabilities, and more on comparing unknown to other unknown probabilities.

Exercise 11.8.1[b] [Deterministic estimation of both ambiguity aversion and likelihood insensitivity assuming linear utility]. Redo the analysis of Case 1 in Example 11.8.1′, with, however, different observations, namely

$$\text{CE}(100_{B_k}0) = 17; \text{CE}(0_{B_k}100) = 75, \text{CE}(100_{B_a}0) = 20; \text{CE}(0_{B_a}100) = 60.$$

Calculate a_k, b_k, a_a, b_a, the indexes of optimism and likelihood sensitivity, and their differences that reflect the ambiguity attitude. □

Exercise 11.8.2[b] [Estimation of ambiguity attitudes]. Assume the same urn and events as in Example 11.8.1′. Say we observe the CEs in Tables 11.8.3 and 11.8.4 instead of those in Tables 11.8.1 and 11.8.2. Provide indexes for optimism and likelihood sensitivity, and compare differences between risk and ambiguity so as to discuss the ambiguity attitude.

Table 11.8.3. *CEs for risky choice*

prospect	$100_{D_k}0$	$100_{D_k}50$	$100_{B_k}0$	$100_{B_k}50$	$100_{B_k^c}0$	$100_{B_k^c}50$
CE	34	69	08	56	63	83

Table 11.8.4. *CEs for ambiguous choice*

prospect	$100_{D_a}0$	$100_{D_a}50$	$100_{B_a}0$	$100_{B_a}50$	$100_{B_a^c}0$	$100_{B_a^c}50$
CE	28	67	13	59	44	75

□

Appendix 11.9   Discussion of multiple priors and other models

The MEU and α-maxmin models are easier to understand than RDU, which contributes to their popularity (Gilboa 2009 §17.2). The way of presenting decision models used in this book, with all subjective parameters directly related to preferences, cannot yet be applied to the MEU and α-maxmin models to the best of my knowledge. That is, I do not know an easy way to directly elicit the set of priors from preferences. Developing such ways is an important topic for future research. Further, even if the set of priors has been determined, then determining the infimum (and supremum) expected utility over this set can be hard ("NP-hard") if the set is not of a tractable form. Another drawback of models with multiple priors is that they cannot yet handle deviations from expected utility for risk.

At first it may be felt as an advantage that one need not exactly specify one prior. When it comes to implementation, however, one will have to exactly specify the set of priors and this is more difficult than exactly specifying one prior (Camerer & Weber 1992 p. 346; Lindley 1996; Tversky & Koehler 1994 p. 563).

In Gilboa & Schmeidler (1989) and all preference axiomatizations mentioned in the preceding section except Jaffray (1994), the set C of Case 1 in §11.5 is endogenous. It is subjective and is to be derived from preference. A different, cognitive, interpretation is most popular in experiments. Then C is exogenously given. There is a true probability measure on the state space that is an element of C, but it is not known which element it is. Here C reflects a state of information rather than a decision attitude. Often probability intervals are given for separate events, as in Case 2, rather than sets of priors (probability measures over the whole state space). Škulj (2006) discussed mathematical differences between models with probability intervals and multiple priors models, and Walley (1991 §6.6) examined the more general question of extendability of lower previsions defined on subdomains. Gajdos *et al.* (2008 and its references) combined endogenous and exogenous aspects in their set C of priors.

As pointed out by Arrow (1951 p. 429) and Klibanoff, Marinacci, & Mukerji (2005 p. 1873), the focusing of MEU and α-maxmin on the infimum and supremum EU over the priors is too crude for refined analyses. If two prospects take the same minimal EU at the same prior, and the same maximal EU at the same other prior, but one prospect dominates the other for all remaining priors, then the models will take the two prospects as equivalent, ignoring all priors except the maximum and minimum. It is natural, however, that the dominating prospect be preferred. The following example illustrates this point. A more sophisticated example is in Appendix 11.10.

Example 11.9.1 [Violations of monotonicity for MEU and α-maxmin]. Let $S = \{s_1, s_2, s_3, s_4, s_5\}$, and $U(\alpha) = \alpha$ for all α; i.e., U is the identity. C contains all probability distributions over S. We suppress states when denoting prospects, and consider $x = (1,1,1,1,0)$ and $y = (1,0,0,0,0)$. The minimal EU of x and y over C is 0 ($P(s_5) = 1$) and the maximal EU is 1 ($P(s_1) = 1$). Hence $x \sim y$ according to both MEU and α-maxmin. Yet $x \succ y$ is natural. □

Maccheroni, Marinacci, & Rustichini (2006) provided an interesting modification of the multiple priors models, capturing the robust control models that are popular in macroeconomics (Hansen & Sargent 2001). They relaxed one of the weakest points of multiple priors models: the crude way in which probability measures are either fully included or fully excluded from the set of priors. One drawback of their model is that it is too general to be measurable, with the extra parameter (their c-function) of high dimensionality. Tractable subcases will have to be developed. Another drawback is that their model can only capture ambiguity aversion and not likelihood insensitivity.

In summary then, the pros of the MEU and α-maxmin models are that they are easy to understand at first, involving transparent calculations. The cons are that the models require the descriptively problematic EU for given probabilities, and that the calculations are too crude to capture the rich spectrum of ambiguity attitudes. If the set C of priors is taken endogenous, no tractable way is known to measure it.

Numerous experimental studies have generated ambiguity by providing subjects with probability intervals. In general, Case 2 in §11.5 is more tractable than Case 1 because probability intervals for some relevant event are easier to specify than probability measures over the whole state space. Models with probability intervals have, however, not yet received a behavioral foundation and have not been widely used in economics.

Probability intervals and sets of priors are often used in human communication to express imprecision. In natural situations, however, uncertainty rarely comes in the form of a precise interval or of a precise set of priors with no other information than the crude in-or-out. The main case that I am aware of concerns incomplete data sets, elaborated later in Example 11.11.4.

Klibanoff, Marinacci, & Mukerji (2005) introduced a smooth model for ambiguity, avoiding the nondifferentiability of RDU (§6.4.2) and the other models discussed in this section. A drawback of their model is that it involves unobservable concepts, such as second-order acts. The authors discussed this point on p. 1856. They used an endogenous two-stage decomposition that gives much richness but is, again, hard to test (Hey, Lotito, & Maffioletti 2008). Another drawback is that attitudes towards uncertainty and ambiguity are to be captured entirely by the utility function, which primarily concerns outcomes. Modeling such attitudes using the weighting function W – which directly concerns uncertainty – is more natural. Finally, their model requires expected utility within each stage, making it vulnerable to violations of expected utility as generated by the Allais and Ellsberg paradoxes when occurring within a stage. The latter two drawbacks also apply to Chew *et al.*'s (2008) source-dependent expected utility. They used a single-stage model, as in §10.7.1, with expected utility for each source and utility source dependent.

Siniscalchi (2009) introduced a new vector model for ambiguity that can handle Ellsberg's three-color paradox in a very appealing manner. One problem with his model is that it is very general, adding any number of signed measures to capture interactions between events. This makes it hard to measure the model, and makes a development of tractable subcases desirable. An empirical problem with his model is that it precludes likelihood insensitivity. When combined with RDU, it implies existence of a probability measure P such that W underweights each event E as much relative to P as the complement E^c ($W(E) - P(E) = W(E^c) - P(E^c)$).

Exercise 11.9.1. Assume three states of nature, s_1, s_2, s_3, with utility being the identity function.

(a)^c Give an example of a set C of priors and a prospect such that RDU with W as in Eq. (11.5.2) is strictly smaller than MEU as in Eq. (11.5.5). This implies that the certainty equivalent under RDU is also strictly smaller than it is under MEU.

(b)^c Give an example where MEU cannot be a rank-dependent model. □

Appendix 11.10   Violations of monotonicity for multiple priors

This appendix shows that the violation of monotonicity for the MEU and the α-maxmin models of Example 11.9.1 cannot easily be avoided. First, the next example displays an equivalence between two prospects with a strict dominance relation.[15]

Example 11.10.1 [Violations of monotonicity for MEU and α-maxmin]. The state space S is the open interval (0,1). Let U be the identity. The "true" probability P on S is a uniform distribution over a subinterval (a,b) of (0,1), but a and b are unknown. The set C of priors thus consists of all uniform distributions over (a,b) with $0 < a < b < 1$. The convex combinations of these distributions can be added to C if desirable without affecting the analysis to follow. Prospects x and y are defined by $x(s) = s$ and $y(s) = s^2$. We have $x(s) > y(s)$ for all s so that $x \succ y$ is natural. Yet, x and y are indifferent under the MEU model and under every α-maxmin model.[16] Hence these models violate monotonicity. □

   In Example 11.9.1, the dominance at states s_2, s_3, s_4 plays no role in the MEU and α-maxmin calculations because these states are null under the priors with minimum and maximum EU. In Example 11.10.1, every event $\{x(s) - y(s) > \epsilon\}$ for $\epsilon > 0$, while nonnull for most priors, becomes null for the infimum and supremum prior calculations. Assumptions are sometimes added to the MEU and α-maxmin models so as to avoid the effects of null events as in those examples. We may require that all priors have the same null events, or add monotonicity as a preference condition. Such a remedy, although avoiding the two previous examples, does not resolve the basic problem of a crude ignoring of all priors outside the infimum and supremum. With this remedy added, examples to illustrate the anomalies generated by the problem become more complex. Basically, the following example replaces statewise dominance of preceding examples by stochastic dominance.

Example 11.10.2. Throughout, U is the identity, and we suppress states when denoting prospects.

(a) [Violations of stochastic dominance for MEU]. Let $S = \{s_1, s_2\}$. Let

$$C = \{P : P(s_1) = 1/2 + \lambda; P(s_2) = 1/2 - \lambda; 0 \leq \lambda \leq 0.4\}. \quad x = (1,0) \text{ and } y = (0.5, 0.5).$$

All priors have the same null events, being only the empty set. Strong monotonicity holds for MEU. For MEU, $x \sim y$. Yet, x has higher EU than y for all priors, where the difference is strict except for $\lambda = 0$. Hence, $x \succ y$ is natural.

(b) [Violations of stochastic dominance for α-maxmin]. Let $S = \{s_1, s_2, s_3\}$. We suppress states and denote prospects as (x_1, x_2, x_3), (y_1, y_2, y_3), and so on. Prospect

---

[15] For readers who know topology: in Example 11.10.1, the set C is not compact (Dugundji 1966). In all other examples it is.

[16] $\text{Inf}_{P \in C} \ EU_P(x) = \text{inf}_{P \in C} EU_P(y) = 0$ (resulting for instance from uniform distributions over (ε, 2ε) for $\epsilon > 0$ tending to 0) and $\text{sup}_{P \in C} \ EU_P(x) = \text{sup}_{P \in C} EU_P(y) = 1$ (resulting for instance from uniform distributions over (1−2ε, 1−ε) for $\epsilon > 0$ tending to 0).

$x = (x_1, x_2, x_3) = (1,1,0)$. Prospect $y = (y_1, y_2, y_3) = (0,1,1)$. For each $0 \leq \lambda \leq 1$, $P_\lambda(s_1) = (1-\lambda)(1+\lambda)/2$, $P_\lambda(s_2) = \lambda$, $P_\lambda(s_3) = (1-\lambda)(1-\lambda)/2$. Thus the state s_2, favorable to both x and y, receives probability mass λ. The remaining probability mass, $1-\lambda$, is first distributed evenly over s_1 and s_3 but then a $(\lambda/2)(1-\lambda)$ part is taken from s_3 and moved to s_1. The latter move is immaterial for $\lambda = 0$ or $\lambda = 1$ but favors prospect x relative to prospect y for all $0 < \lambda < 1$. For both prospects, the value increases in λ, with maximum EU, equal to 1, for $\lambda = 1$ and minimal EU, equal to 0.5, for $\lambda = 0$. We, finally, define P_u by $P_u(s_1) = P_u(s_2) = P_u(s_3) = \frac{1}{3}$ and define C as the convex hull of the 50–50 mixes of P_u and the P_λ's: $C = \{P: P = P_{u_{0.5}} P_\lambda : 0 \leq \lambda \leq 1\}$.

All priors have the same null events, being only the empty set. Strong monotonicity holds for MEU and every α-maxmin model (because of the P_u part in each prior). For MEU and every α-maxmin model, $x \sim y$. Yet, x has higher EU than y for all priors, where the difference is strict except for $\lambda = 0$ and $\lambda = 1$. Hence, $x \succ y$ is natural. $\square$

Appendix 11.11   Möbius transforms and belief functions

Möbius transforms φ provide a useful tool for analyzing weighting functions. I assume a finite state space S throughout this appendix, and first explain how W is related to φ:

$$W(E) = \sum_{D \subset E} \varphi(D) \tag{11.11.1}$$

for all E. Given this equation, φ can be derived from W inductively: $\varphi(\emptyset) = 0$; $\varphi(s_i) = W(s_i)$ for all i; $\varphi(s_i, s_j) = W(s_i, s_j) - W(s_i) - W(s_j)$ for all $i \neq j$; in general, the *Möbius transform* of W is defined by

$$\varphi(E) = \sum_{D \subset E} (-1)^{|E|-|D|} W(D) \tag{11.11.2}$$

(Chateauneuf & Jaffray 1989; Dempster 1967; Denneberg 1994; Grabisch, Marichal, & Roubens 2000; Rota 1964; Shafer 1976; Stanley 1986). Thus, W and φ are uniquely related to each other.

The Möbius transform reflects interactions between states. For example, for an additive probability P, φ is zero except at singletons, and we have

$$P(E) = \sum_{s_i \in E} P(s_i). \tag{11.11.3}$$

Then there are no interactions. In the two-color Ellsberg paradox (Example 10.1.1) with an urn with 100 black (B_a) and red (R_a) colors in an unknown proportion, the values $W(B_a) = W(R_a) = 0.4$ are plausible under ambiguity aversion. The difference $W(B_a, R_a) - W(B_a) - W(R_a) = 1 - 0.4 - 0.4 = 0.2$, which is $\varphi(B_a, R_a)$, reflects a complementary interaction between the two colors. Each color in isolation comprises ambiguity but their combination brings extra value by the elimination of ambiguity. This difference has, hence, been proposed as an index of ambiguity aversion by Schmeidler (1989), Dow & Werlang (1992), and others. In general, $\varphi(E)$ is the weight of E as a whole that is not captured by any of its subsets. A *k-additive* weighting function has $\varphi(E) = 0$ for all events E with more than k elements. Then there are no interactions that involve more than k elements. For low k, such functions provide tractable versions of weighting functions (Grabisch, Kojadinovic, & Meyer 2008).

Example 11.11.1 [2-additivity]. $S = \{s_1, s_2, s_3, s_4\}$ with $\varphi(E) = 0.1$ for all events E with one or two elements, and $\varphi(E) = 0$ for all other events. Then $W(E) = 0.1$ for all singleton events E, $W(E) = 0.3$ for all two-state events E, $W(E) = 0.6$ for all three-state events, and $W(S) = 1$. $\square$

Example 11.11.2 [Variation of Example 11.11.1 with some negative interactions]. $S = \{s_1, s_2, s_3, s_4\}$ with $W(E) = 0.1$ for all singleton events E, $W(E) = 0.3$ for all two-state events E, $W(E) = 0.5$ for all three-state events, and $W(S) = 1$. Then $\varphi(E) = 0.1$ for all one- or two-state events E, $\varphi(E) = -0.1$ for all three-state events, and $\varphi(S) = 0.4$. $\square$

Example 11.11.3 [3-additivity]. Consider an urn that contains 50 balls containing dark-blue (DB), dark-green (DG), and dark-yellow (DY) balls in an unknown proportion, and another 50 balls containing light-blue (LB), light-green (LG), and light-yellow (LY) balls in an unknown proportion. Then, under usual ambiguity aversion, reasonable weighting values are $W(DB) = W(DG) = W(DY) = 2/18$, $W(DB,DG) = W(DB,DY) = W(DG,DY) = 4/18$, $W(DB,DG,DY) = 9/18$, with the weighting function for the light colors the same as for the dark colors, and the weight of any union of dark colors and light colors the sum of the separate weights. Then $\varphi(E) = 2/18$ for all singleton events E, $\varphi(DB,DG,DY) = 3/18 = \varphi(LB,LG,LY)$, and $\varphi(E) = 0$ for all other events E. Again, φ reflects the complementary interactions between the colors. The combination of DG, DB, and DY brings extra weight by the elimination of ambiguity, and so does the combination of the three light colors. W is 3-additive. $\square$

Dempster (1967) and Shafer (1976) introduced *belief functions*, defined as those weighting functions that have nonnegative Möbius transforms. As the authors showed, this requirement is equivalent to

$$W\left(\cup_{j=1}^n E_j\right) \geq \sum\nolimits_{\{I:\emptyset \neq I \subset \{1,\ldots,n\}\}} (-1)^{|I|+1} \, W(\cap_{i \in I} E_i). \qquad (11.11.4)$$

Additive measures P satisfy Eq. (11.11.4) with equality. Convexity is Eq. (11.11.4) restricted to the case $n = 2$. Whereas in Shafer's approach the belief function is an endogenous reflection of subjective beliefs, in Dempster's approach it is exogenous and objective, based on random messages. In Eq. (11.11.1), D is the message that the true state will be contained in D, and this message is received with probability $\varphi(D)$. Then $W(E)$ is a lower bound for the probability of E occurring. Similarly, as $W(E^c)$ is a lower bound for the probability of E^c occurring, $1 - W(E^c)$ is an upper bound. The latter is the value of the dual of W at E. Informational states as described by Dempster can arise in data sets with missing data (Jaffray 1991b):

Example 11.11.4 [Objective belief functions resulting from missing data]. Assume that we have an incomplete data set about a population of patients concerning diseases A and B, displayed in Table 11.11.1.

Table 11.11.1. *An incomplete data set*

	B surely present	B surely absent	B unknown
A surely present	25%	11%	08%
A surely absent	09%	20%	05%
A unknown	02%	05%	15%

The groups of patients with missing information are not representative for the whole patient population so that extrapolations of data are problematic. Assume that we consider a patient known to be a random member of the patient population, with no further information. We can interpret the cells in the table as random messages. Writing W for lower bounds of probabilities, we have:

- W(AB) (*both diseases*) $= 0.25$;
- W((AB)^c) (*at most one disease*) $= 0.11 + 0.09 + 0.20 + 0.05 + 0.05 = 0.50$ (shows that the probability of AB is at most 0.50);
- W(AB^c) (*A but not B*) $= 0.11$;
- W(A) (*disease A*) $= W(AB \cup AB^c) = 0.25 + 0.11 + 0.08 = 0.44 > W(AB) + W(AB^c) = 0.25 + 0.11 = 0.36$. $\square$

Wakker (2000) used the interpretations just described in combination with pessimism-assumptions about complete absence of information to interpret belief functions. Jaffray (1989) did not consider upper or lower probabilities, but mixes of these, in the context of random messages (§10.7.3). The belief function reflects an objective state of information and the mixing weights reflect the attitude towards ambiguity. A mathematical generalization is in Philippe, Debs, & Jaffray (1999). For extensions of belief functions to infinite state spaces, also see Gilboa & Schmeidler (1995) and Marinacci (1996).

For some time belief functions were popular in artificial intelligence for modeling ambiguous beliefs. Because they entail an extreme degree of convexity, updating rules based on them turned out to be too conservative. Hence, they have lost popularity there. Ghirardato (2001) presented an appealing interpretation of belief functions in terms of their Möbius transforms. Equation (11.11.1) suggests an additive property of weighting functions that was central to Gilboa & Schmeidler (1995). Some recent works using belief functions include Petit-Renaud & Denoeux (2004) for statistical classification, Denoeux (2008) for updating, and Hilhorst *et al.* (2008) for multiattribute evaluations in finance. Yager & Liu (2008) give further references.

12 Prospect theory for uncertainty

Tversky & Kahneman (1992) corrected the theoretical problem of probability weighting of Kahneman & Tversky's (1979) original prospect theory. Thus, the theory could be extended to general probability-contingent prospects and this was the topic of Chapter 9. A more important advance of Tversky & Kahneman (1992) was that it extended prospect theory from risk to uncertainty. A common misunderstanding in decision theory today is that prospect theory supposedly concerns only risk, and that other models should be used for ambiguity. This chapter shows that prospect theory is well suited for analyzing uncertainty and ambiguity.

Prospect theory for risk generalizes rank dependence by adding reference dependence, with risk attitudes for losses different from those for gains. Although there have not been many studies into ambiguity with losses, the existing evidence suggests that ambiguity attitudes for losses deviate much from those for gains, with ambiguity seeking rather than ambiguity aversion prevailing for losses (references in §12.7). Hence, for the study of ambiguity, the reference dependence of prospect theory is highly desirable.

All models presented so far were special cases of the model of this chapter, and all preceding chapters have prepared for this chapter. All the ingredients have, accordingly, been developed by now. Hence, all that remains to be done is to put these ingredients together. This chapter on the most important model of this book will accordingly be brief, and will only add some theoretical observations.

12.1 Prospect theory defined

We again take the 0 outcome as the, fixed, reference outcome, with gains and losses as before. The extension of RDU to PT for uncertainty is similar as it was for risk, and we describe it briefly. Utility U again increases strictly, and we set $U(0) = 0$.

There are two weighting functions, W^+ for gains and W^- for losses. As for risk, W^+ relates to gain-ranked events and W^- relates to loss-ranked events, where we expect W^+ and W^- to exhibit similar properties. For example, if future cognitive or neuro studies discover properties of W^+ for gains, such as a particular relation to likelihood beliefs, then we expect similar properties and relations to hold for

W^- (weighing bad-news events), rather than for W^-'s dual (weighing good-news events) as RDU-integrations would have it.

Formally, we consider prospects $E_1x_1 \cdots E_nx_n$ with a complete sign-ranking

$$x_1 \geq \cdots \geq x_k \geq 0 \geq x_{k+1} \geq \cdots \geq x_n. \tag{12.1.1}$$

Under Eq. (12.1.1),

$$PT(x) = \sum_{j=1}^{n} \pi_j U(x_j), \tag{12.1.2}$$

where the decision weights π_j are nonnegative and are defined next, first for general outcomes, then for the prospect x.

Definition 12.1.1. Under PT, an outcome event E with outcome α has the following *decision weight*:

- If $\alpha > 0$, then $\pi = \pi(E^G) = W^+(E \cup G) - W^+(G)$ with G the gain-rank.
- If $\alpha = 0$, then $U(\alpha) = 0$ and the decision weight is irrelevant; we usually take it to be $\pi(E^G)$.
- If $\alpha < 0$, then $\pi = \pi(E_L) = W^-(E \cup L) - W^-(L)$ with L the loss-rank. □

As a convention, it will be understood implicitly in the notation $\pi(E^G)$ that the decision weight is to be derived from W^+, pertaining to gain outcomes, and that for $\pi(E_L)$ the decision weight is to be derived from W^-, pertaining to loss outcomes. Substituting in Eqs. (12.1.1) and (12.1.2), we get

$$\text{for } j \leq k: \pi_j = \pi(E_j^{E_{j-1} \cup \cdots \cup E_1}) = W^+(\{E_j \cup \cdots \cup E_1\}) - W^+(\{E_{j-1} \cup \cdots \cup E_1\}); \tag{12.1.3}$$

$$\text{for } j > k: \pi_j = \pi(E_{jE_{j+1} \cup \cdots \cup E_n}) = W^-(\{E_j \cup \cdots \cup E_n\}) - W^-(\{E_{j+1} \cup \cdots \cup E_n\}). \tag{12.1.4}$$

Definition 12.1.2. Under Structural Assumption 1.2.1 (decision under uncertainty), *prospect theory (PT)* holds if there exist a strictly increasing continuous *utility function* $U : \mathbb{R} \to \mathbb{R}$ with $U(0) = 0$ and two *weighting functions* W^+ and W^-, such that each prospect $E_1x_1 \cdots E_nx_n$ with completely sign-ranked outcomes $x_1 \geq \cdots \geq x_k \geq 0 \geq x_{k+1} \geq \cdots \geq x_n$ for some $0 \leq k \leq n$ is evaluated by

$$\sum_{j=1}^{n} \pi_j U(x_j) = \sum_{i=1}^{k} \pi(E_i^{E_{i-1} \cup \cdots \cup E_1}) U(x_i) + \sum_{j=k+1}^{n} \pi(E_{jE_{j+1} \cup \cdots \cup E_n}) U(x_j)$$

$$= \sum_{i=1}^{k} (W^+(E_i \cup \cdots \cup E_1) - W^+(E_{i-1} \cup \cdots \cup E_1)) U(x_i)$$

$$+ \sum_{j=1}^{k} (W^-(E_j \cup \cdots \cup E_n) - W^+(E_{j+1} \cup \cdots \cup E_n)) U(x_j),$$

the *PT value* of the prospect. □

The utility function U and the weighting functions W^+ and W^- are the subjective parameters that characterize the decision maker. U comprises basic utility u and a loss aversion parameter λ as explained in §8.4. In this theoretical analysis we confine our attention to cases where the reference point has already been determined. We, again, have some liberty regarding the exact choice of the complete sign-ranking of the outcomes, but these choices do not affect the value of the PT evaluation.

The decision weights in PT need not sum to 1, similarly as they need not do so under risk. They can again be considered to sum to 2, by separating the positive and negative part of a prospect. For a prospect x, x^+ replaces all negative outcomes of x by 0 and x^- replaces all positive outcomes of x by 0. Under Eq. (12.1.1), $x^+ = E_1x_1, \ldots, E_kx_k, E_{k+1}0, \ldots, E_n0$ and $x^- = E_10, \ldots, E_k0, E_{k+1}x_{k+1}, \ldots, E_nx_n$.

Exercise 12.1.1.[b] Assume, as throughout this section, that $U(0) = 0$, and assume RDU. Show that

$$RDU(x) = RDU(x^+) + RDU(x^-). \qquad (12.1.5)$$

Does this equality also hold if $U(0) \neq 0$? ☐

Exercise 12.1.2.[b] Show that

$$PT(x) = PT(x^+) + PT(x^-). \qquad (12.1.6)$$
☐

Assignment 12.1.3.[b] Formulate a condition on W^+ and W^- such that the PT functional is an RDU functional. ☐

12.2   Where prospect theory deviates from rank-dependent utility and expected utility

Most deviations of PT for uncertainty from preceding theories combine those of PT for risk with those of RDU under uncertainty. We, therefore, do not discuss them in detail. Probabilistic sophistication with sign-dependent probabilities is left to future studies. The derivation of ambiguity indexes, for which the reference dependence of PT is a desirable generalization relative to RDU, will be presented in §12.7. The next section turns to the properties of EU that are maintained under PT.

12.3   What prospect theory shares with rank-dependent utility and expected utility under uncertainty

12.3.1   Sign-preference conditions
Consider a fixed partition $(E_1, \ldots, E_n)$, and the set of prospects $E_1x_1 \cdots E_nx_n$ with $x_1 \geq \cdots \geq x_k \geq 0 \geq x_{k+1} \geq \cdots \geq x_n$ as in Eq. (12.1.1). Under PT, the ranks and signs of the outcome events E_j agree for all prospects considered, and the same decision weights can be used for all prospects. Hence, PT agrees with an EU functional on such sets of prospects and the techniques of EU can be applied there.[1] For example, tradeoff consistency still holds on such sets.

---

[1] To define the EU functional we can take decision weights as probabilities as we did under RDU. Only now we have to normalize the probabilities to ensure that they sum to 1. If all decision weights are zero so that normalization is not possible, then all prospects of this set are equivalent. The latter case can be excluded by monotonicity conditions.

The notation $\alpha_{E^G}x$, introduced before, specifies that G is the gain-rank of E. It is implicitly understood that $\alpha \geq 0$ in the notation $\alpha_{E^G}x$. If α is a loss, then the ranked event E^G and its decision weight $\pi(E^G)$, derived from W^+, are not relevant, but the loss-ranked event E_L and its decision weight $\pi(E_L)$, derived from W^- are. Hence, for a loss α it is more useful to specify the loss-ranked event $L = (E \cup G)^c$. We do so using the notation $\alpha_{E_L}x$. It is then implicit that $\alpha \leq 0$.[2]

E^G is *nonnull* if $\gamma_{E^G}x \succ \beta_{E^G}x$ for some $\gamma > \beta \geq 0$ and x, and E^G is *null* otherwise. E^G is nonnull if and only if $\pi(E^G) > 0$ (derivation similar to Exercise 10.5.2). E_L is *nonnull* if $\gamma_{E_L}x \succ \beta_{E_L}x$ for some $0 \geq \gamma > \beta$ and x, and E_L is *null* otherwise. E_L is nonnull if and only if $\pi(E_L) > 0$.

12.3.2 *Measuring utility (and event weighting) under prospect theory*

For PT, the utility of gains can be measured as under RDU. For example, the measurements in Figure 4.1.1 (TO upwards) retain their validity under PT as long as not only the ranking requirements of RDU are verified, but furthermore all values elicited from subjects; i.e., $\alpha^1, \ldots, \alpha^4$ are nonnegative. It is not necessary that all other outcomes used are positive, and the "gauge" outcomes 1 and 8 for the lower branches could also have been negative. The outcome event of the upper branch has the same rank and sign of outcomes and, hence, the same decision weight, which is all that is needed. Utility for losses can be measured similarly, with losses instead of gains. For instance, if in Figure 4.1.2 (2nd TO upwards) we do not take $\beta^4 = \alpha^4 \geq 0$ and $\beta^3 = \alpha^3 \geq 0$, but take some $\beta^3 \leq \beta^4 \leq 0$, then β^2, β^1, and β^0 will be negative also and the β^j's are still equally spaced in utility units.

For outcomes $\alpha \succcurlyeq \beta$, $\gamma \succcurlyeq \delta$, we write

$$\alpha \ominus \beta \sim_{cs}^t \gamma \ominus \delta \tag{12.3.1}$$

if

$$\boldsymbol{\alpha}_{E^G}x \sim \boldsymbol{\beta}_{E^G}y \text{ and} \tag{12.3.2}$$

$$\boldsymbol{\gamma}_{E^G}x \sim \boldsymbol{\delta}_{E^G}y \tag{12.3.3}$$

or

$$\boldsymbol{\alpha}_{E_L}x \sim \boldsymbol{\beta}_{E_L}y \text{ and} \tag{12.3.4}$$

$$\boldsymbol{\gamma}_{E_L}x \sim \boldsymbol{\delta}_{E_L}y \tag{12.3.5}$$

for some prospects x, y and a nonnull ranked event E^G or a nonnull ranked event E_L. The relation requires that the outcome event E has the same rank in both indifferences

---

[2] A notational convention: In particular cases it may happen that we want to leave unspecified whether outcomes are gains or losses, and whether ranked or loss-ranked events are relevant. Then we can write $\alpha_{ER}x$ and $\beta_{ER}x$ with the understanding that E has the same rank R, which either reflects a superscript G or a subscript L, and E has the same sign in both prospects. Such cases will not occur in this book.

used and that the nonzero outcomes under event E have the same sign. The subscript s indicates that not only the rank but also the sign was kept constant during the measurement, so that, as we will see, utility measurements can be obtained that are valid under PT.

Because the following exercise clarifies the nature of PT and of utility measurement, we present its elaboration in the main text.

Observation 12.3.1. Under PT,

$$\alpha \ominus \beta \sim^t_{cs} \gamma \ominus \delta \Rightarrow U(\alpha) - U(\beta) = U(\gamma) - U(\delta). \tag{12.3.6}$$

Proof of Observation 12.3.1. First assume that all nonzero outcomes in Eq. (12.3.1) are gains. The equalities

$$PT(\alpha_{E^G}x) = PT(\beta_{E^G}y) \text{ and}$$

$$PT(\gamma_{E^G}x) = PT(\delta_{E^G}y)$$

can be analyzed as they were under RDU (§6.5.1). By Lemma 10.5.3, all events off E can be given the same ranks for the left prospects $\alpha_{E^G}x$ and $\gamma_{E^G}x$ and also for the right prospects $\beta_{E^G}y$ and $\delta_{E^G}y$. In addition they, obviously, have the same sign of outcomes under each event for the left prospects and also for the right prospects.

For losses, the equalities

$$PT(\alpha_{E_L}x) = PT(\beta_{E_L}y) \text{ and}$$

$$PT(\gamma_{E_L}x) = PT(\delta_{E_L}y)$$

can be analyzed similarly. $\square$

Exercise 12.3.1.[a] Assume PT. Let $\alpha \ominus \beta \sim^t_{cs} \gamma \ominus \delta$ and $\alpha' \ominus \beta \sim^t_{cs} \gamma \ominus \delta$. Show that $\alpha' = \alpha$. $\square$

Once utility has been measured for gains and for losses, event weighting can be measured the same way as under RDU as in §10.5.2, done separately for gains and losses. We can use Eq. (10.5.6) for gains and W^+ instead of W. For W^- we have, for a loss $-\alpha$:

$$\text{If } -\alpha \sim (-1)_E 0 \text{ then } W^-(E) = U(-\alpha)/U(-1) = u(-\alpha)/u(-1). \tag{12.3.7}$$

12.3.3   *Measuring loss aversion under prospect theory*

To measure the entire utility function, loss aversion should be measured too. The details of this measurement are not needed for the behavioral foundation presented later. We first consider pragmatic ways to measure loss aversion. If we can find an event E that has probability ½, or that at least is symmetric with its complement both for gains and for losses, then we can use a method as under risk (Example 9.4.2), with E instead of the probability ½. The next example gives a method that works in general, but is more complex in involving two indifferences.

Example 12.3.2 [A pragmatic way to measure loss aversion]. A pragmatic estimate of loss aversion λ can be obtained as follows:

$$\text{If } 2_E1 \sim \mu_E0 \text{ and } 2_E0 \sim \mu_E(-\alpha) \text{ then } \lambda \approx 1/\alpha. \tag{12.3.8}$$

That is, we take an event E, then first find a $\mu > 2$ giving the first indifference, and finally find a loss $-\alpha$ giving the second indifference. To clarify, we substitute PT in the two indifferences:

$$W^+(E)(u(\mu) - u(2)) = (1 - W^+(E))(u(1) - u(0))$$

$$W^+(E)(u(\mu) - u(2)) = W^-(E)\lambda(u(0) - u(-\alpha)).$$

With the pragmatic assumptions that $1-W^+(E) = W^-(E)$ and that u is linear near zero, we get

$$\lambda = \frac{u(1) - u(0)}{u(0) - u(-\alpha)} = 1/\alpha. \ \square$$

A general method works as in Exercise 9.4.3. The following exercise gives details.

Exercise 12.3.2.[b] Scale utility as in Eq. (8.4.2). Take a positive $\alpha > 0$ such that $1 \sim \alpha_E0$, $\beta > 0$ such that $\alpha_E(-\beta) \sim 0$, and $\delta > 0$ such that $-\delta \sim 0_E(-\beta)$. Show that $\lambda = -1/u(-\delta)$. $\square$

12.3.4 A behavioral foundation for prospect theory
Sign-tradeoff consistency holds if the utility measurements of the preceding subsection do not run into contradictions. We then have the following implication:

$$[\alpha \ominus \beta \sim^t_{cs} \gamma \ominus \delta \text{ and } \alpha' \ominus \beta \sim^t_{cs} \gamma \ominus \delta] \Rightarrow \alpha' = \alpha.$$

Definition 12.3.3. Sign-tradeoff consistency holds if improving an outcome in any $\sim^t_{cs}$ relationship breaks that relationship. $\square$

Observation 12.3.4. Assume PT. Consider Figures 4.1.1 (TO upwards), 4.1.2 (2nd TO upwards), and 4.1.4 (TO downwards). Assume that the ranked events $cand_1{}^b$ and $cand_1{}^w$ are nonnull. Then the α's in Figure 4.1.1 are still equally spaced in utility units (cf. Exercise 4.3.1). So are the corresponding β's in Figure 4.1.2 (cf. Exercise 4.3.2) whenever the proper rank conditions hold ($\beta^4 \le g$), so that the β's must still equal the α's. The δ's in Figure 4.1.4 must also equal the α's (cf. Exercise 4.3.4). $\square$

For the behavioral foundation of PT, we use some further assumptions. We first impose a richness condition to ensure that nontrivial tradeoffs exist between gains and losses, so that loss aversion can be determined. $\succcurlyeq$ is *truly mixed* if $\gamma_E0 \succ \gamma_E\beta \succ 0_E\beta$ for some event E and outcomes $\gamma > 0 > \beta$. This requirement reinforces the nondegeneracy assumption. *Gain–loss consistency* holds if $x \sim y$ whenever $x^+ \sim y^+$ and $x^- \sim y^-$. The condition suggests a separable evaluation of gains and losses. The following theorem entails the most general preference foundation in this book, and all other results could have been derived as easy corollaries of the following theorem.[3]

Theorem 12.3.5. Under Structural Assumption 1.2.1 (decision under uncertainty), assume that $\succcurlyeq$ is truly mixed. Then the following two statements are equivalent for the preference relation $\succcurlyeq$ on the set of prospects.

(i) PT holds, where utility is continuous and strictly increasing.
(ii) $\succcurlyeq$ satisfies:
  - weak ordering;
  - monotonicity;
  - continuity;
  - gain–loss consistency;
  - sign-tradeoff consistency. $\square$

Observation 12.3.5' [Uniqueness result for Theorem 12.3.5]. In (i), the weighting functions are uniquely determined, and, given $U(0) = 0$, utility is unique up to a unit. $\square$

Obviously, under PT a rank-sign sure-thing principle will hold, with the following logical equivalences:

$$[\alpha_{E^G}x \succcurlyeq \alpha_{E^G}y \Leftrightarrow \beta_{E^G}x \succcurlyeq \beta_{E^G}y] \text{ for all gains (or zero outcomes) } \alpha \text{ and } \beta,$$

and

$$[\gamma_{E_L}x \succcurlyeq \gamma_{E_L}y \Leftrightarrow \delta_{E_L}x \succcurlyeq \delta_{E_L}y] \text{ for all losses (or zero outcome) } \gamma \text{ and } \delta.$$

It easily follows that the rank-sure-thing principle then holds in full force, and that we also have

$$[\alpha_{E^G}x \succcurlyeq \alpha_{E^G}y \Leftrightarrow \gamma_{E_L}x \succcurlyeq \gamma_{E_L}y] \text{ for all gains } \alpha > 0 \text{ and losses } \beta < 0 \text{ whenever}$$
E has the same gain-rank in all four prospects.

E having the same gain-rank means that $L = (G \cup E)^c$. This follows immediately from equivalence with the preferences $0_{E^G}x \succcurlyeq 0_{E^G}y$ and $0_{E_L}x \succcurlyeq 0_{E_L}y$, where $0_{E^G}x = 0_{E_L}x$ and $0_{E_L}y = 0_{E^G}y$. Hence, we do not define a separate rank-sign sure-thing principle.

This section has demonstrated that a behavioral foundation can be established for PT in the same way as for the other models considered in this book, i.e., by demonstrating how to measure utility and requiring that these measurements do not run into inconsistencies. It implies that, if a subject's attitude towards loss aversion

---

[3] Wakker & Tversky (1993 Observation 8.1) showed that, for a finite number n ≥ 3 of states of nature, gain–loss consistency and true mixedness can be dropped from Statement (ii) if strong monotonicity holds. Bleichrodt & Miyamoto (2003) obtained an extension of Theorem 12.3.5 for health outcomes, generalizing Wakker & Tversky (1993). Wakker & Tversky (1993) and Köbberling & Wakker (2003) showed that sign-tradeoff consistency in Statement (ii) can be replaced by a weaker condition called sign-comonotonic tradeoff consistency, using comonotonicity instead of ranks. Schmidt & Zank (2009) provided a preference foundation for linear utility using a rank- and sign-dependent generalization of the additivity preference condition of Definition 1.5.1.

or probability weighting is inconsistent, then this inconsistency will generate inconsistencies in our measurements of utility too.

Assignment 12.3.3. Assume that all conditions in Theorem 12.3.5 hold for the preference relation ≽, so that we have a PT representation. Define a new and general theory, called PT′, which satisfies all requirements of Definition 12.1.2 except the requirement of U(0) = 0. That is, for PT′ we consider the formulas of PT but allow U(0) to be different from 0. Obviously, the general PT′ theory holds because PT holds, and we can take the special case of PT′ with U(0) = 0.

(a)[a] Give an example of ≽ for which PT′ can hold with U(0) ≠ 0.
(b)[c] Give an example of ≽ for which PT′ can only hold with U(0) = 0. Specify the PT parameters to a sufficient extent that it can be proved that U(0) = 0 must also hold under PT′.
(c)[c] Give a necessary and sufficient condition for the weighting functions W^+ and W^- in the PT model such that PT′ can only hold with U(0) = 0. □

12.4 A hybrid case: prospect theory for uncertainty when also objective probabilities are given

Also for prospect theory, measurements and behavioral foundations can sometimes be simplified if probabilities are given for some events. There is, however, one complication for PT that does not show up under RDU. Under PT, we may not always be able to find "matching" probability-contingent prospects for event-contingent prospects if the total decision weights involved in the evaluation of the latter is too large. We will not elaborate on this issue, but refer to Sarin & Wakker (1994a, §4), who give results.

12.5 Loss aversion versus ambiguity aversion

Roca, Hogarth, & Maule (2006) presented an experiment where two different aspects of prospect theory under uncertainty, loss aversion and ambiguity aversion, are tested against each other. Consider the choice situation in Figs. 12.5.1a, with full details and notation in the Ellsberg Example 10.1.1. Fig. a depicts the majority preference, where most people prefer to gamble on the known urn. Roca *et al.* considered an alternative treatment, depicted in Fig. b. First subjects were endowed with the ambiguous prospect, and told that they were entitled to take it. Then, next, they were offered to either keep their right to play the ambiguous prospect or alternatively to exchange it for the unambiguous prospect and play the unambiguous prospect.

Roca *et al.* (2006) found that the majority in Fig. b did not want the exchange. By any common rational theory, subjects should prefer to end up with the same prospect in Fig. b as in Fig. a because these are the same in terms of final wealth. The data, however, violate this prediction. This violation can be explained if we assume that, after having been endowed with the ambiguous prospect, subjects take this as their

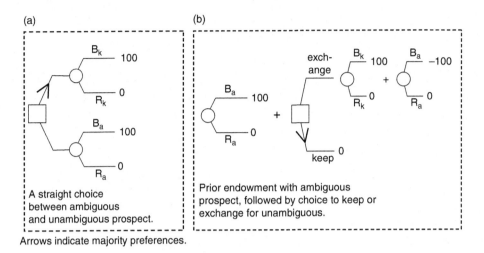

Figure 12.5.1 Ambiguity aversion versus loss aversion.

reference point. A random reference point this is, with wealth level depending on the resolution of uncertainty (Sugden 2003). They then perceive not exchanging as the unambiguous and sure receipt of nothing, whereas exchanging is perceived as a prospect $(B_a\&B_k:0, B_a\&R_k:-100, R_a\&B_k:100, R_a\&R_k:0)$. The latter prospect comprises ambiguity and yields a loss in the case of $B_a\&R_k$, which may explain its aversiveness for the subjects.

The finding in Figure 12.5.1 can be compared to that in §8.1. It illustrates once more how strong and important framing and reference points are, even if it is hard to develop formal theory for these phenomena. In the experiment described, reference dependence and loss aversion have led in Fig. b to what any classical analysis would interpret as ambiguity seeking. In reality, it rather reflects reference dependence.

12.6 Violations of prospect theory and rank dependence

There are many factors underlying human decisions that are as yet unknown to us. Many of these are driven by irrational details of framing and will always be hard to model systematically. Repeated within-subject observations of nontrivial choices, sufficiently separated in time and tasks not to be remembered, typically find inconsistency rates of about 25 percent, suggesting that 50 percent of the data is noise (Harless & Camerer 1994 p. 1263; Hey & Orme 1994). Hence, empirical tests of individual choice contain more noise than found in most other empirical fields, and any decision theory will face many empirical violations. We saw some violations of fundamental aspects of our models in §4.11. Because of the major importance of understanding human decisions and optimizing these, decision theories nevertheless deserve to be studied empirically and they are nevertheless applied widely.

There are many violations of fundamental properties, such as weak ordering and monotonicity. Such violations concern biases and heuristics (Tversky & Kahneman

1974; Gigerenzer 1991), and these can be expected to disappear in well-contemplated choices. They have, therefore, not been central to this book. For example, reference points in Chapter 8 depended so much on volatile factors that we left their determination to the informal modeling stage.

Rank dependence and prospect theory are the best-performing and most-confirmed empirical models for decisions under risk and uncertainty to date. Because of their extensive use, numerous empirical violations have been documented also. It has turned them by now into not only the most confirmed, but also the most falsified, models. For example, the extensive evidence in favor of likelihood insensitivity cited in §7.1, in combination with the empirical violations of likelihood insensitivity cited there, together can be interpreted as evidence against the general model of prospect theory.

Several authors have searched for systematic violations of prospect theory and rank dependence. For example, although the basic concepts and findings in the works by Lola Lopes and co-authors are close in spirit to prospect theory and support it, with even an impressive independent development of rank dependence in Lopes (1984), she often emphasized the violations of prospect theory that she found. A recent reference is Lopes & Oden (1999). Michael Birnbaum developed psychological RAM and TAX models that reckon with several biases and heuristics (Birnbaum 2008a). These models thus fitted many large data sets collected by Birnbaum and co-authors better than prospect theory did. In return, they are less well-suited for developing theory and deriving predictions. They do not have the particularly tractable form of prospect theory, with psychological interpretations for its parameters and with preference foundations to identify its exact empirical content. Ido Erev initiated a stream of studies where aspects of prospects are not conveyed verbally to subjects ("description"), but subjects have to infer them from repeated observations ("experience"), which has also led to violations of prospect theory (Hertwig *et al.* 2003). Other studies reporting violations of rank dependence and prospect theory include Baltussen, Post, & van Vliet (2006), González-Vallejo, Reid, & Schiltz (2003), Neilson & Stowe (2001), Payne (2005), Starmer (1999), and Wu (1994). Barberis, Huang, & Thaler (2006), Quiggin (2003 for linear utility), and Safra & Segal (2008) showed that nonexpected utility theories, including the rank-dependent ones, have difficulties incorporating background risks. Cox *et al.* (2007) presented an analog for probability weighting of Rabin's (2000) paradox for utility (Exercise 7.4.2).

We consider in detail a violation of rank dependence advanced by Machina (2009) because this violation is instructive about an essential component of rank dependence. Baillon, L'Haridon, & Placido (2009) demonstrated that Machina's examples also violate other ambiguity models that are popular today, including the MEU model (Gilboa & Schmeidler 1989), the α-maxmin model, the variational preference model (Maccheroni, Marinacci, & Rustichini 2006), and the smooth model (Klibanoff, Marinacci, & Mukerji 2005). Machina's examples thus pose a general challenge to the study of ambiguity and not just to rank dependence. We will, however, analyze their implications only for RDU.

	50 balls		50 balls	
	E_1	E_2	E_3	E_4
x	4000	8000	4000	0
y	4000	4000	8000	0

Figure 12.6.1 Two prospects x, y.

The key for the rank-dependent models is that likelihoods of ranks are central rather than likelihoods of outcome events (§5.4). The latter likelihoods were central to the theories of probability transformation that preceded rank dependence (Eq. (5.2.1), old weighting). Although Eq. (5.2.1) is not plausible for multi-outcome prospects, it does capture some psychological aspects of decision making for prospects with few outcomes. It can be expected that people are also driven by likelihoods of outcome events to some extent, in addition to likelihoods of ranks. Some recent papers have found support for the descriptive relevance of outcome-event likelihoods (Gonzalez & Wu 2003; Starmer 1999). Machina (2009) provided a particularly clear test, presented next.

Example 12.6.1 [Relevance of likelihood of outcome events]. An urn contains 100 balls, of which 50 are marked 1 or 2 in an unknown proportion, and 50 are marked 3 or 4 in an unknown proportion. One ball is drawn randomly. E_j denotes the event that the ball drawn is marked j.

It is reasonable to assume informational symmetry, meaning that likelihoods are not affected by exchanges of E_1 with E_2, of E_3 with E_4, and of the pair E_1,E_2 with the pair E_3,E_4. Hence, for each of the following four categories of events, gambles on events within a category are indifferent. It implies that events within one category have the same weighting function value W under RDU.

(1) E_1, E_2, E_3, and E_4 (one-number events);
(2) $E_1 \cup E_2$ and $E_3 \cup E_4$;
(3) $E_1 \cup E_3$, $E_1 \cup E_4$, $E_2 \cup E_3$, and $E_2 \cup E_4$.
(4) not-E_1, not-E_2, not-E_3, and not-E_4 (three-number events).

Figure 12.6.1 illustrates prospects $x = (E_1:4000, E_2:8000, E_3:4000, E_4:0)$ and $y = (E_1:4000, E_2:4000, E_3:8000, E_4:0)$.

We have the following ranks for outcomes under x and y:

	$\alpha < 0$	$0 \le \alpha < 4000$	$4000 \le \alpha < 8000$	$8000 \le \alpha$
rank for α under x	universal event	not-E_4	E_2	$\varnothing$
rank for α under y	universal event	not-E_4	E_3	$\varnothing$

	50 balls		50 balls	
	E_1	E_2	E_3	E_4
x	4000	8000	4000	0
y	4000	4000	8000	0
x′	4000	8000	4000	4000
y′	4000	4000	8000	4000
x″	0	8000	4000	4000
y″	0	4000	8000	4000

Figure 12.6.2 Six prospects.

Under RDU, for each outcome α the rank has the same W value under x and y. It readily follows from Eq. (10.2.6) that x and y then have the same RDU value.[4] Under RDU, we must have x $\sim$ y.

For prospect y, one of the three outcome events is unambiguous, namely the outcome event of receiving 4000 ($E_1 \cup E_2$). For prospect x all outcome events are ambiguous. Hence, given that people will not only consider ranks but also outcome events, it is plausible that ambiguity aversion will generate a strict preference for y. This preference was confirmed experimentally by L'Haridon & Placido (2009). It entails a violation of RDU. □

We next present an alternative way to show that RDU implies indifference in the preceding example. This alternative way provides a nice application of the rank-sure-thing principle and was used by Machina.

Example 12.6.2 [Machina's example reanalyzed using the rank-sure-thing principle]. Assume the prospects x and y as in Example 12.6.1. Assume x $\prec$ y, and consider the six prospects in Figure 12.6.2. Under RDU the rank-sure-thing principle (Eq. (10.5.1)) holds. By this principle, applied to events with the worst rank ("ordinal independence" in Machina's terminology) the preference implies x′ $\prec$ y′ and then x″ $\prec$ y″. However, by informational symmetry we obtain y″ from x by interchanging the pair of events E_1, E_2 with the pair of events E_3, E_4, and we obtain x″ from y the same way. Hence, informational symmetry implies y″ $\prec$ x″, contradicting the strict preference derived from the rank-sure-thing principle: RDU is violated. An initial preference x $\succ$ y similarly violates RDU. Machina did not discuss his example in terms of outcome events as we did. Instead, he referred to stakes "riding on" two small ambiguities for x and on one big ambiguity for y. □

---

[4] Sarin & Wakker (1992) provided a behavioral foundation of RDU using this preference condition ("cumulative dominance"), with a betting-on condition to capture same W values in terms of preference.

Besides the example discussed, called reflection example, Machina (2009) also analyzed what he called a 50–51 example, which is more complex and will not be presented here.

12.7   Indexes of ambiguity attitudes under prospect theory

Although ambiguity aversion, while not universal, is prevailing for gains, the case is less clear for losses. There have not been many studies on ambiguity with losses. Some found ambiguity aversion for losses (Keren & Gerritsen 1999), some found mixed evidence (Cohen, Jaffray, & Said 1987; Dobbs 1991; Hogarth & Kunreuther 1989; Mangelsdorff & Weber 1994; Viscusi & Chesson 1999), but the majority found ambiguity seeking (Abdellaoui, Vossman & Webber 2005; Chakravarty & Roy 2009; Davidovich & Yassour 2009; Di Mauro & Maffioletti 1996 Table 6; Di Mauro & Maffioletti 2002; Du & Budescu 2005 p. 1797 2nd column; Einhorn & Hogarth 1986; Ho, Keller, & Keltyka 2002; Kahn & Sarin 1988 p. 270; Kuhn 1997). Given the large difference between ambiguity attitudes for gains and losses (see also Bier & Connell 1994), the reference dependence of prospect theory is highly warranted for the study of ambiguity.

Under PT, we can simply apply the techniques and procedures of §11.7 and 11.8 to gains and losses separately. A numerical example illustrates the case.

Example 12.7.1 [Ambiguity attitudes for losses; Example 11.8.1′ continued]. Assume the same urn and events as in Example 11.8.1′, and assume that we have observed the 12 CEs for gains in Case 2 of that example. In addition, we have observed CEs for losses, depicted in Tables 12.7.1 and 12.7.2. For simplicity, we do not consider mixed prospects in this example so that loss aversion plays no role.

The prospects are the reflections of those in Case 2 in Example 11.8.1′, which means that all outcomes have been multiplied by -1. The CEs observed are close to the reflections of those for gains in Example 11.8.1′, but deviate somewhat, usually in the direction of risk neutrality. Such reflections imply that risk aversion for gains corresponds to risk seeking for losses, and that ambiguity aversion for gains corresponds to ambiguity seeking for losses. These reflections are empirically plausible, as referenced before.

We assume that the model of Procedure 11.8.1 holds for gains, with $W = W^+$ and so on, but with nonlinear utility as in Case 2 of Example 11.8.1′. We similarly assume the following general model for losses.

$$\text{For} -\gamma \le -\beta \le 0 : RDU(-\gamma_E - \beta) = -W^-(E)(\gamma)^{\theta^-} - (1 - W^-(E))(\beta)^{\theta^-}. \quad (12.7.1)$$

Whenever event E has known probability p, $W^-(E) = w^-(p)$ for a probability weighting function w^-. Then for such an event we have

$$\text{For} -\gamma \le -\beta \le 0 : RDU(-\gamma_E - \beta) = RDU(-\gamma_p - \beta) = -w^-(p)(\gamma)^{\theta^-} - (1 - w^-(p))(\beta)^{\theta^-}. \quad (12.7.2)$$

Table 12.7.1. *CEs for risky choices with losses*

prospect	$-100_{D_k}0$	$-100_{D_k}-50$	$-100_{B_k}0$	$-100_{B_k}-50$	$-100_{B_kc}0$	$-100_{B_kc}-50$
CE	-43	-72	-13	-60	-72	-86

Table 12.7.2. *CEs for ambiguous choice with losses*

prospect	$-100_{D_a}0$	$-100_{D_a}-50$	$-100_{B_a}0$	$-100_{B_a}-50$	$-100_{B_ac}0$	$-100_{B_ac}-50$
CE	-36	-70	-14	-62	-59	-81

We again use neo-additive weighting functions, and different ones for the known urn than for the ambiguous urn. We do assume that the probability measure P (no confusion will arise from dropping subscripts), assigning probability $1/10$ to each color, is used in the neo-additive model for losses as it is for gains, but otherwise the model for losses can be different, indicated by superscripts $-$. We assume that $W^-(E) = 0$ for all events with objective or source-dependent probability 0, and $W^-(E) = 1$ for all events with objective or source-dependent probability 1. Further

$$W^-(E) = w^-(p) = b_k^- + a_k^- p \qquad (12.7.3)$$

with $a_k^- + b_k^- \leq 1$ for all events E concerning urn_k with probability $0 < p < 1$ (Definition 11.2.1). We assume for $0 < P(E) < 1$

$$W^-(E) = b_a^- + a_a^- P(E) \qquad (12.7.4)$$

for all events E concerning urn_a, for some nonnegative b_a^- and a_a^- with $b_a^- + a_a^- \leq 1$.

Using these equations, the best fit is obtained for $\theta^- = 0.85$, $a_k^- = 0.71$, $b_k^- = 0.12$, $a_a^- = 0.54$, and $b_a^- = 0.15$, with distance 1.12.[5] Although these numbers are similar to their counterparts for gains, several of them have opposite empirical meanings because of the reflected formulas used by PT. Thus, $\theta^- = 0.85$ now reflects convex and not concave utility. Likelihood sensitivity for losses behaves similarly as it did for gains. As for gains, also for losses risk exhibits more likelihood sensitivity than ambiguity, with $a_k^- - a_a^- = 0.71 - 0.54 = 0.17$ an index of the difference. There now is more optimism for ambiguity than for risk, with the difference $\left(2b_k^- + a_k^-\right)/2 - \left(2b_a^- + a_a^-\right)/2 = 0.47 - 0.42 = 0.05$ now an index of ambiguity seeking. □

In Example 12.7.1, the cognitive component of likelihood sensitivity behaved similarly for losses as it did for gains. For the other, motivational, components, the patterns were different and almost opposite to those found for gains, with ambiguity seeking and utility convex. These phenomena are in agreement with the empirical

---

[5] The theoretically predicted CEs are -41.65, -73.11, -14.26, -59.13, -72.29, -87.50, -36.04, -70.37, -15.41, -59.76, -58.72, and -81.22.

findings in the literature so far. Classical models that do not treat gains and losses differently cannot accommodate the data of Examples 11.8.1′ and 12.7.1 jointly. They would end up with something close to ambiguity neutrality and a poor fit with the data.

Appendix 12.8   Some theoretical issues concerning prospect theory for uncertainty

We first give the integral definition of PT, which can also be used for prospects with infinitely many outcomes.

$$PT(x) = \int_{\mathbb{R}^+} W^+(\{s \in S : U(x(s)) > t\})dt - \int_{\mathbb{R}^-} [W^-(\{s \in S : U(x(s)) < t\})]dt. \quad (12.8.1)$$

The derivation of this formula is identical to that of Eq. (10.10.1) (of RDU) in Exercise 10.10.1, with $W^-(E)$ substituted for $1 - W(E^c)$ for losses. It can be rewritten as

$$PT(x) = \int_{\mathbb{R}^+} W^+(x^{-1}(U^{-1}(t, \infty)))dt - \int_{\mathbb{R}^-} W^-(x^{-1}(U^{-1}(-\infty, t)))dt. \quad (12.8.2)$$

As before, it is immaterial in Eq. (12.8.1) whether we take weak or strict inequalities in the integrands.

We next present notation for prospects $E_1x_1 \cdots E_nx_n$ that are not completely ranked; i.e., $x_i < x_{i+1}$ may hold for some i. Then PT is still defined as in Eq. (12.1.2), where the *decision weights* π_j are however defined differently, which will be explained next. We first take a complete sign-ranking ρ on $\{1, \ldots, n\}$ such that

$$x_{\rho_1} \geq \cdots \geq x_{\rho_k} \geq 0 \geq x_{\rho_{k+1}} \geq \cdots \geq x_{\rho_n}. \quad (12.8.3)$$

We define

$$\text{for } j \leq k: \ \pi_{\rho_j} = W^+(E_{\rho_j} \cup \cdots \cup E_{\rho_1}) - W^+(E_{\rho_{j-1}} \cup \cdots \cup E_{\rho_1}). \quad (12.8.4)$$

$$\text{for } j > k: \ \pi_{\rho_j} = W^-(\{E_{\rho_j} \cup \cdots \cup E_{\rho_n}\}) - W^-(\{E_{\rho_{j+1}} \cup \cdots \cup E_{\rho_n}\}). \quad (12.8.5)$$

To the extent that ρ and k are not uniquely determined, any possible choice yields the same PT value.

Analogously to the comoncones C^ρ of Appendix 10.12, which were maximal comonotonic sets, we define maximal sign-comonotonic sets. Let ρ be a complete ranking of S, and A an event such that every state in A is ρ-better than every state in A^c. We define $\mathcal{F}^{A\rho}$ as the set of prospects that are compatible with ρ and that yield gains or 0 on A and losses or 0 on A^c. Sets $\mathcal{F}^{A\rho}$ of this kind are called *sign-comonotonic*. Within such sets, all outcome events have both the same ranks and the same sign. They, therefore, have the same decision weights and PT is in agreement with EU there.

Exercise 12.8.1.[b] Consider a set of prospects $\{E_1x_1^k \cdots E_nx_n^k\}_{k \in K}$ (for any index set K) with all events nonempty, and such that their outcomes need not be rank-ordered the same way. In particular, $x_1^k \geq \cdots \geq x_n^k$ need not hold. Use Exercise 10.12.2, and show that the prospects are sign-comonotonic if and only if the following two conditions hold:

(i) $x_i > x_j$ and $y_i < y_j$ for no i,j and prospects x,y from the set;
(ii) $x_i > 0$ and $y_i < 0$ for no i and prospects x,y from the set. $\square$

Exercise 12.8.2. Assume PT with a finite number $n \geq 2$ of states of nature. Show that:

(a)[b] Strong monotonicity implies that all decision weights are positive.
(b)[c] If all decision weights are positive, then strong monotonicity holds. $\square$

Appendix 12.9   Proofs for Chapter 12

Proof of Observation 12.3.4. This follows from substitution, or Exercise 12.3.1. $\square$

Proof of Theorem 12.3.5 and Observation 12.3.5′. See Köbberling & Wakker (2003 Theorem 12 and Observation 13) for finite state spaces, with the extension to infinite state spaces in Appendix G, and with comments on comonotonicity in Observation 10.12.1. $\square$

13 Conclusion

This book has presented a number of theories for decision under uncertainty and risk, primarily classical expected utility, rank-dependent utility, and prospect theory. Throughout we have treated risk with given probabilities as a special limiting case of uncertainty. We have strived for homeomorphic models, where the algebraic operations in models resemble psychological processes. To achieve this goal, we developed nonparametric deterministic measurement methods, where model parameters can directly be linked to observable choice, the empirical primitive. Behavioral foundations were derived from consistency requirements for the measurements of the model parameters.

In Part I, on expected utility, there were relatively many exercises and applications because this model is classic and has existed for a long time. The first new concept beyond the classical model was rank dependence, introduced informally in Chapter 5 and developed in the following chapters. Using rank dependence we could define pessimism and optimism which, while formally new, were closely related to the classical risk aversion and risk seeking. We also found a new phenomenon, likelihood insensitivity, the second new concept beyond the classical model. It reflects a lack of understanding of risk and uncertainty rather than an aversion or a preference. No similar phenomenon can be modeled with expected utility. The third new concept was reference dependence, leading to a different treatment of gains than losses, in prospect theory. The fourth new concept was source dependence, with ambiguity referring to differences between sources with unknown probabilities versus chance (known probabilities).

As we moved on, there were fewer exercises and applications because the models became more novel. I hope that in 10 years from now, Parts II and III of this book can have as many applications as Part I does, and that readers of this book will contribute to developing such applications in their fields of expertise.

We ended with prospect theory for uncertainty. This model is most important for descriptive purposes because uncertainty is more important than risk and because prospect theory accommodates the most important empirical phenomena to be incorporated in a quantitative model. I hope that this book has made its models more accessible to a large audience, and that it will encourage applications of these new models in many domains.

Appendix A: Models never hold perfectly: how to handle their deficiencies?

This appendix discusses the case where models do not fit data perfectly well and we nevertheless try to get by as well as we can (Gilboa 2009 §7.1). It is the case almost exclusively met in descriptive applications. We will use a simple least-squares criterion to fit data.

A.1 Nonparametric measurements and parametric fittings for imperfect models: general discussion

This section presents a general discussion with methodological considerations. It can be skipped by readers who only want to use techniques for fitting data. In most descriptive applications, the model we use does not describe the empirical reality perfectly well and the preference conditions of our model are violated to some extent. One reason is that there usually is randomness and noise in the data. Another reason is that there may be systematic deviations. We then nevertheless continue to use our model if no more realistic and tractable model is available. We then try to determine the parameters of our model that best fit the data, for instance by minimizing a distance, such as a sum of squared differences, between the predictions of the model and the actual data. Alternatively, we may add a probabilistic error theory to the deterministic decision model (called the core model) and determine the parameters that maximize the likelihood of the data.

In cases where decision models only approximate observed data, we usually reduce the dimensionality of the parameters considered. We may assume, for instance, that the utility function is a power function, so that only the power of utility has to be found to optimally fit the data. Such approaches are called parametric fittings. They can be applied to all kinds of measurements, also if not devised to optimally reveal the subjective parameters of interest. Measurements that, to the contrary, have been devised for such a purpose, such as the standard-gamble measurement under expected utility[1], will give better results under parametric fittings than unstructured

---

[1] Described in the preface as step 3 in the five-step presentation of decision models.

measurements do. This holds especially if there are several parameters, such as utility and probability weighting in prospect theory, because measurements can be devised to optimally tease the various parameters apart. Unstructured certainty equivalent observations usually will not separate utility and probability weighting well (Zeisberger & Vrecko 2009). The danger of unwarranted interactions between parameters (called multicollinearity in regressions) was pointed out by Gonzalez & Wu (1999 p. 157), Harrison (2006 p. 61), Loomes, Moffat, & Sugden (2002), and Stott (2006 pp. 112, 121). These papers found that conclusions from parametric fittings of general measurements may depend much on the particular parametric families chosen.

Most of this book presents measurements to optimally reveal subjective parameters that can be used not only for parametric fittings, but also for what are called nonparametric measurements. In the latter, the parameter values such as utilities are directly related to the data without interference of numerical computer-fitting procedures, and no reduction of the dimensionality of the parameters needs to be assumed. We saw this in the aforementioned measurement of utility under expected utility using the standard gamble method, where for instance no power utility needed to be assumed. Such direct relations to observable preferences avoid the risk of numerical anomalies in parametric fittings (for the latter see, for example, §9.6). They provide the shortest path from the theoretical model to empirical reality and, thus, the clearest illustration of the empirical content of the model. They also clarify to what extent there are collinearities between the parameters of the model.

Measurements devised for direct nonparametric revelations of subjective parameters can be used in prescriptive decision aiding. With such measurements, the parameters of decision models can directly be related to decisions, which facilitates discussions about them in interactive sessions. For descriptive purposes, nonparametric measurements are desirable if there is uncertainty about the properness of reductions of the dimensionality of the parameters, such as when our best guess is to assume power utility but we are nevertheless uncertain about its appropriateness. An advantage of parametric fitting is that it can smooth noise in the data. If data is very noisy, then we rely more on a priori chosen power utilities, say, than on whatever nonparametric utility function the data generates. In the case of extreme noise at the individual level, a group average may better represent a single individual than the data of that individual alone. Conte, Moffat, & Hey (2008) provided a sophisticated application of this principle in the context of maximum likelihood estimation.

Stimuli suited for nonparametric measurements usually separate the parameters in a model most clearly, both for deterministic analyses and for statistical analyses and regressions, and hence will also serve well for parametric measurements. The following example illustrates the point. Booij & van de Kuilen (2009) used the tradeoff method of §4.1 to measure utility and the method of §9.4.2 to measure loss aversion, all in nonparametric ways, for a large sample representative of the Dutch population. Booij, van de Kuilen, & van Praag (2010) subsequently used this same data set in a parametric fitting, confirming the findings of the nonparametric measurements.

In prescriptive applications, models will also be violated to some extent. Subjects will usually violate the preference conditions in behavioral foundations of the model to a certain degree. It may happen that a decision recommended in a complex real decision situation and derived from simple choice situations deviates from the preference that results from direct intuitive introspection in the real situation. In such a case, at least one of the choices considered should be revised – unless the rational model is abandoned. Paradoxically, such situations with preferences to be revised do not entail a failure of the prescriptive decision model, but on the contrary are where prescriptive decision models are most useful. The revised preferences generate new insights into one's true values. In a way, it is only if such situations arise that the decision models provide new insights. If natural preferences automatically satisfy a prescriptive decision model then the model has little prescription to offer. Raiffa (1961 pp. 690–691) wrote about this point, in relation to Savage's (1954) expected utility: "If most people behaved in a manner roughly consistent with Savage's theory then the theory would gain stature as a descriptive theory but would lose a good deal of its normative importance. We do not have to teach people what comes naturally."

Sometimes prescriptive theories are not used to determine one's own decisions, but rather to convince outside parties of the properness of decisions already taken (von Winterfeldt 2007 p. 537). In such a case, verification of the preference conditions is extra desirable, so that status can be assigned to decisions to be defended. In medicine, decision theory is especially popular in radiotherapy for analyzing palliative treatments (reducing pain), the results of which are difficult to measure. Decision theory then not only serves to find optimal treatments, but also to convince other departments in the hospital that such treatments are useful, justifying the budget allocated to such treatments.

In some applications, especially in economics, we do not even seek to closely approximate reality with our models. We may be satisfied with some global qualitative conclusions about optima, and we only require that our models provide the appropriate conceptual framework to obtain those conclusions.

A.2 Our distance measure for parametric fitting

This section presents the distance measure used to fit data in several exercises. It will be a simple Euclidean distance between the theoretical model and the observed data that is most commonly used for the purpose of data fitting (Gourieroux & Monfort 1995). Based on probabilistic choice theories with errors explicitly incorporated[2], more sophisticated data fitting methods have been used in the literature, mostly based on maximum likelihood fitting.[3] It is not clear at present which error theory is best

---

[2] Becker, de Groot, & Marschak (1963); Falmagne (1985 Ch. 11); Luce, Bush, & Galanter (1965 Chs. 19.5–19.8, pp. 331–402, §19.5.3, §19.7); McFadden (1981); Thurstone (1927).

[3] Blavatskyy (2007); Conte, Hey, & Moffatt (2008); Harless & Camerer (1994); Harrison & Rutström (2008, 2009); Hey & Orme (1994); Loomes, Moffat, & Sugden (2002); Stott (2006); Wang & Fischbeck (2004).

(Blavatskyy & Pogrebna 2009; Choi *et al.* 2007 §IV.E). For normally distributed choice errors, minimization of Euclidean distance as done in this book usually leads to maximum likelihood and minimal variance unbiased estimates. Keller & Strazzera (2002) presented different data-fitting techniques in an accessible manner.

We will only consider data consisting of indifferences here. (Exercise 3.6.3 deals with data fitting for choices.) This section presents the definition and an example, and §A.3 discusses some details. The exercises throughout the book use limited data sets to estimate parameters. In reality, it is wiser to use large data sets. For example, estimating two parameters from only three observations as done in some exercises is statistically unreliable. We nevertheless present such exercises for didactic purposes, using only a few observations so as to minimize the readers' calculation time.

We make the default assumption that outcomes are monetary. For an indifference x ∼ y and a decision model, we determine the extent to which the model is off according to a least-squares criterion, as follows. We first determine the certainty equivalents CE(x) and CE(y) of the prospects x and y according to the model, where we obviously assume that these CEs exist. Next, the absolute value of the CE difference, |CE(x) − CE(y)|, is taken as the distance. It is the square root of the square of CE(x) − CE(y). If we observe several indifferences $x^i \sim y^i$, then the normalized Euclidean distance of the vector $(CE(x^1) − CE(y^1), CE(x^2) − CE(y^2), \ldots)$ to the origin $(0,\ldots,0)$ is taken as distance. That is, we then take the average of the squared differences, and then take the square root. The distance is 0 if the model agrees perfectly well with the data because indifferent prospects $x^j \sim y^j$ then have the same $CE(x^j) = CE(y^j)$. The unit of the distance measure is monetary. We display the definition.

Definition A.1. Assume a data set consisting of a number of observed indifferences $x^i \sim y^i$, i = 1, ..., n between prospects, and a decision model. Then the *distance of the model to the data* is

$$\sqrt{\frac{\sum_{i=1}^{n}(CE(x^i)-CE(y^i))^2}{n}}. \tag{A.1}$$

Here, for each prospect, its CE value is determined according to the model. We also say that the *model is off by this amount of dollars*. □

Grabisch, Kojadinovic, & Meyer (2008) reviewed studies on different distance measures for fitting a weighting function and RDU to data, and presented public-domain software to implement these measures. We end this section with an example. It concerns expected utility defined in Chapter 2 and, therefore, can only be read if you know this theory. Example 1.4.3 provides an alternative illustration.

Example A.2. Assume Structural Assumption 2.5.2 (decision under risk and richness), and EU (Definition 2.5.3) with power utility (§3.5). The following data will exhibit so much risk aversion that only negative powers θ are relevant; i.e., $U(\alpha) = 1 - \alpha^{\theta}$ for $\theta < 0$. Assume the following indifferences:

$$90_{0.5}5 \sim 22.45_{0.9}5,$$
$$80_{0.1}5 \sim 9.34_{0.4}5,$$
$$90_{0.4}5 \sim 13.10_{0.8}5, \quad \text{and}$$
$$80_{0.05}5 \sim 8.89_{0.15}5.$$

The minimal outcome 5 in these prospects can be interpreted as initial wealth. A power $\theta = -0.10$ fits the first two indifferences perfectly well, and a power $\theta = -0.50$ fits the second two indifferences perfectly well. It is natural that the power best fitting the data will be between -0.10 and -0.50. Using the distance measure in Eq. (A.1), the power -0.21 results as optimal (interior) solution, with distance 1.49. That is, the model is off by about \$1.49.

We finally give calculations for $\theta = -0.21$, with small deviations because of rounding in reported intermediate steps:

$$EU(90_{0.5}5) = 0.50 \times U(90) + 0.50 \times U(5) = 0.50 \times 0.61 + 0.50 \times 0.29 = 0.45.$$
$$CE(90_{0.5}5) = U^{-1}(0.45) = (1 - 0.45)^{-1/0.21} = 17.09.$$
$$EU(22.45_{0.9}5) = 0.90 \times U(22.45) + 0.10 \times U(5) = 0.90 \times 0.48 + 0.10 \times 0.29 = 0.46.$$
$$CE(22.45_{0.9}5) = U^{-1}(0.46) = (1 - 0.46)^{-1/0.21} = 18.88.$$

For the first indifference, the model is off by about $|17.09 - 18.88| = \$1.78$ (not 1.79 because of rounding). Similar calculations of CEs for the other prospects, and substitution in the distance formula, give the distance

$$\sqrt{\frac{(17.09 - 18.88)^2 + (6.20 - 6.36)^2 + (13.01 - 10.63)^2 + (5.56 - 5.43)^2}{4}} = 1.49.$$

$\square$

A.3   Discussion of the distance measure

This section can be skipped without loss of continuity. We first discuss boundary solutions for the distance measure just introduced. We then discuss an alternative distance measure using utility units, and boundary solutions for that measure. The examples illustrate particular general problems of distance measures, based on the unavoidable complication that the unit of distance can have different, and not always completely relevant, meanings in different contexts. For example, an insurance company examining the risk preferences of their clients will primarily be interested in distances in monetary units, but the clients may be more interested in distances in utility units. Usually, however, different distance measures give approximately the same results and difficulties as exhibited by these examples are rare.

Observation A.3 [Boundary solution for Example A.2]. In Example A.2, smaller distances than for $\theta = -0.21$ result for very negative powers $\theta < -4.50$. For very extreme powers, such as $\theta < -10$, the distance is less than 1 cent. For such negative powers, risk aversion is so strong that the certainty equivalents of all prospects are compressed within a close neighbourhood of the minimal outcome 5, so that there are no differences between certainty equivalents anymore and our distance measure tends to 0. If such extreme powers, with corresponding concave utility functions, are empirically irrelevant, then our distance measure is not satisfactory. The meaning of a distance of \$1 then depends so much on the wealth level that it cannot serve as a meaningful index. In practice, such extreme degenerate solutions should be excluded on empirical grounds. □

Because our models all use a utility function for money, an alternative measure is available, based on utility differences $U(CE(x^i)) - U(CE(y^i))$ rather than monetary differences as in the measure in Eq. (A.1). Here $U(CE(\cdot))$ is the value of the prospect according to the relevant theory. For example, it is the EU value of the prospect under EU theory, and the PT value of the prospect under prospect theory. The main advantage of the measure in Eq. (A.1) is that its unit is physically meaningful, so that it is easy to convey to laypersons. One drawback is that the unit of a dollar can have different meanings in different circumstances. A dollar difference at \$1 million is not the same as at \$0. A utility correction may be desirable here. Another drawback is that our measure usually is more complex computationally, because we obtain it by taking utility-inverses of values of prospects according to particular theories.[4] Inverses of utility may not always be easy to obtain.

A disadvantage of utility as a distance measure is that its scale is arbitrary, so that we then have to settle on a convention of scaling such as $U(1) - U(0) = 1$. Such a scaling may not be appropriate for interpersonal comparisons. Usually optimal solutions are not very sensitive to the particular distance measure chosen, and in practice the utility distance measure is mostly used because it is computationally more tractable.

Example A.4 [Distance in utility units]. We now reconsider the indifferences in Example A.2, but use a distance measure with utility as unit. It then is necessary to normalize utility. We will consider negative-power utility functions normalized at 4 and 100; i.e.,

$$U(\alpha) = \frac{(1 - \alpha^\theta) - (1 - 4^\theta)}{(1 - 100^\theta) - (1 - 4^\theta)} \text{ for } \theta < 0.$$

The distance measure is

$$\sqrt{\frac{\sum_{i=1}^n (EU(x^i) - EU(y^i))^2}{n}}.$$

---

[4] For readers who know expected utility (Definition 2.5.3), under that theory $CE(x) = U^{-1}(EU(x))$.

For the four indifferences of Example A1, the optimal power now is $\theta = -0.27$, with distance 0.037 according to the distance measure just displayed, as can be calculated by computers.

The problem of boundary solutions arises here similarly as it did in Observation A.3. Again, we obtain better fits for very negative powers, with $\theta < -10$. For extreme powers, the distance again tends to 0. For $\theta < -16$ the distance is below 0.0001. For such negative powers ($\theta < -16$), U, normalized at 4 and 100, already exceeds 0.97 for every $\alpha \geq 5$, so that there is almost no variation in utility for all outcomes relevant in the data set. Then, obviously, any utility distance is small, irrespective of the data. Again, such boundary solutions should be excluded on empirical grounds. $\square$

Another difficulty with the distance measure proposed here can arise when there are some small-stake prospects and also some large-stake prospects. Then the distances pertaining to the large-stake prospects will dominate the results of fitting procedures. Normalizations of prospects would then be desirable. We will not pursue this point.

Appendix B: Choosing from multiple prospects and binary choice: the principles of revealed preference

This appendix uses parts of Wakker (1989a, Ch. 1). Throughout this book we adopt the *revealed-preference paradigm*: A decision maker chooses the most preferred prospect from a set of available prospects. Then, besides the descriptions of the prospects (that can be general choice options here), the only observable primitives are assumed to be those choices. Utilities, subjective probabilities, and other concepts exclusively obtain their empirical meaning from their implications for the choices made.[1]

In most practical situations there are more than two prospects to choose from. Revealed-preference theory examines when such general choice situations can be represented by preferences – binary choices – after all (Chipman *et al.* 1971; Houthakker 1950; Mas-Colell, Whinston, & Green 1995 §1.D).[2] Because all of the main text has assumed that optimal choices are fully specified by preferences, this appendix shows how the preference theories in this book are relevant for general decisions.

This appendix assumes a general choice function, defined formally later, as the empirical primitive, rather than binary preference. Binary preference now is the theoretical construct used to model the empirical primitive. Thus, this appendix gives a behavioral foundation for binary preference, justifying its use throughout the book. The elicitation method now does not derive other parameters from binary preference, as this happened in the main text, but it derives binary preference from the choice function. Hence, the term revealed preference has sometimes been used to designate this particular version of the elicitation method, initiated by Samuelson (1938). The term is more commonly used to refer to the general approach of decision theory, where subjective parameters such as utility and decision weights are derived from choices or preferences.

A number of general assumptions underlying decision theory are best discussed for general decision situations with possibly more than two prospects available. We will

---

[1] In this sense, psychological interpretations of the concepts proposed were only based on our interpretations, and suggestions about homeomorphic models were based only on plausibility and face validity.
[2] Unlike some other authors, I do not distinguish between preference and choice. Preference is nothing other than binary choice. Appendix B shows how preferences can model general choice.

therefore discuss them here. Other general assumptions were discussed in the context of behavioral foundations in the introduction and in §1.8. §B.1 presents a number of simple choice examples to illustrate assumptions of revealed preference. The theoretical §B.2 presents a behavioral foundation of preference. We take general choice as empirical primitive in this appendix and show how preference can be derived from general choice. §B.3 discusses underlying assumptions in detail.

For decision under risk or uncertainty I am only aware of a few empirical studies that considered choices between more than two prospects: Hopfensitz & van Winden (2008), studies of proper scoring rules including Offerman *et al.* (2009) who used prospect theory to analyze their observations, Stewart *et al.* (2003), and Choi *et al.* (2007 and some follow-up papers) who developed an appealing format for multiple-choice experiments.

B.1   Examples

The following example gives a preparatory and simplified illustration of the use of revealed preference. An application is in §3.1.

Example B.1 [Thought experiments of revealed preference bringing new insights]. A decision maker is in a fruit store and has to decide whether to buy a banana (b), a mango (m), or nothing (n). The real choice situation is, therefore, to choose one element from {b,m,n}. The decision maker prefers to buy a banana rather than a mango (choosing b from {b,m}), because bananas are easier to consume than mangos. He will buy a mango in a fruit store that has only mangos (choosing m from {m,n}), because he thinks mangos are interesting. It seems that b is preferred to m, and m to n. Hence buying a banana seems to be the best decision (choosing b from {b,m,n}), and this is the decision that is considered first for the real choice situation. The decision maker, however, feels doubts about this decision.

The decision maker imagines what the choice would be from a fruit store with only bananas, so that the choice is from {b,n}. It would be n. The decision maker would not buy the banana because he does not like bananas enough, and feels sure about this decision. However, it seems to contradict the first considered real decision. An introspection follows, and the conclusion is that the choice of m from {m,n} was not well motivated. On reflection, the decision maker chooses n from {m,n}. That is, n is preferred to m, and n is preferred to b as before. The real decision is that n is chosen from {b,m,n}, and nothing is bought. □

The decision maker in the example used thought experiments with hypothetical choice situations to determine the real choice. An inconsistency after an initially considered real decision led to new insights into preference values and, thus, to a new and better final decision. The following example illustrates limitations of revealed preference, followed by a discussion of some misunderstandings about these limitations.

Example B.2 [Thought experiments of revealed preference bringing no new insights]. Imagine you are applying for an assistant professor position at some universities.

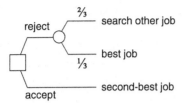

Figure B.1 Decision tree for job offer.

Your second-most preferred university offers you a job and you have to decide today whether or not to accept. Your most preferred university is considering two other candidates and you judge your probability of getting a job there to be ⅓. Because the decision is important and you do not know what to do, you consult a decision analyst. The analyst recommends setting up a decision tree, and the result is Figure B.1.

A scaling U(search other job) = 0 and U(best job) = 1 is chosen. The decision analyst plans to conclude his consultancy with the advice: Now determine your utility for the second-best job and then choose the prospect with maximal expected utility. However, you are not sure what your utility of the second-best job is, and ask for advice. The decision analyst concludes that you are apparently not well versed in decision theory. He explains how to determine your utility, using Figure B.2. In the terminology of the SG Figure 2.5.3, your standard-gamble probability p is to be determined, and this is your utility of the second-best job. The decision analyst concludes his consultancy with the advice to accept the offer whenever p in Figure B.2 exceeds ⅓.

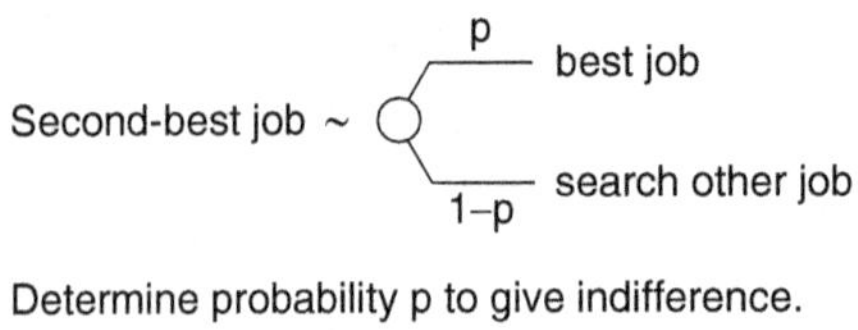

$$
\text{Second-best job} \sim \underset{1-p}{\overset{p}{\diagup\diagdown}} \quad \begin{array}{l} \text{best job} \\ \\ \text{search other job} \end{array}
$$

Determine probability p to give indifference.

Figure B.2 Determining utility of second-best job.

The advice of the decision analyst is of little value. It can be summarized as: "People choose what they want and want what they choose" (Lewin 1996 p. 1303). Some value may be derived from the understanding that the utility of the second job relative to the alternatives is important, and so is the probability that the best job will offer you a position. This value is, however, limited and will not help readers who are already familiar with these concepts. The decision whether or not to accept is equivalent to the decision whether p in Figure B.2 should exceed ⅓. One decision is, however, as difficult for you as the other, and the equivalence of the two questions does not help you much in deciding. Figure B.2 has just brought us back to square 1.

Conclusion: Although expected utility is general enough to *accommodate* your choice in this example, in itself it does not *explain* much about what your choice should be. □

An example of naïve advice of decision analysts of similar limited value as in the example is in Kadane & Larkey (1982). They argued that in game theory a player should "simply" determine the subjective probabilities of moves of opponents, and then maximize expected utility. Their argument may be correct (for complications, see Mandler 2007) but does not help, giving no insights into what those subjective probabilities should be. Game theory can be considered to be the theory of how to choose those subjective probabilities, and this is where all the work is to be done. This criticism was properly put forward by Harsanyi (1982), who called the "SEU-for-game-theory" of Kadane and Larkey a "highly uninformative statement" (p. 122). Unfortunately, Kadane & Larkey (1983) remained unconvinced. Similar overestimations of the value of decision theory underlie overly strict interpretations of what is called the coherence viewpoint (Alchian, 1953 p. 34 ll. 2–3; de Finetti 1931b). This point is properly discussed by Gilboa, Postlewaite, & Schmeidler (2008 p. 180) and Tversky & Kahneman (1981 p. 458). For recent references, see Olsson (2005).[3]

For decision analysis to be useful, there should be other decision situations or other sources of information that give new insights into the parameters such as utilities relevant to your present decision situation. Instructive illustrations of this point are in Kreps (1988 pp. 82–92) and Winkler (1972, Example 5.10). In the early literature on decision analysis, authors were often overly optimistic about the usefulness of decision theory, suggesting that decision theory be used in every decision in every situation in life (Howard & Matheson 1984). Readers of Savage (1954) often misinterpreted his model in this manner. Such misinterpretations and overstatements have led to many counterreactions and discussions (Dijksterhuis *et al.* 2006; Dawes, Faust, & Meehl 1989; Wilson & Schooler 1991).

One of the most fruitful fields of application of decision theory is in the health domain. Still, decision theory has no help to offer for the majority of diseases. It is only in particular cases that the decision techniques are useful. Those cases are frequent enough to make the theory valuable. Keeney (2004 Figures 1 and 2) estimated that somewhere between 50 and 1000 out of 10,000 decisions might potentially benefit from decision analysis.

The following example illustrates the subtle difference between observing a preference system and observing repeated choice.

---

[3] Many authors introducing a new formal principle in a particular theory use naïve and overly broad terms such as rational, coherent, consistent, and so on, for their particular principle to make it appear impressive. Besides de Finetti (1931b), examples include Mas-Colell, Whinston, & Green's (1995) Definition 1.B.1 for weak ordering of preference, and Definitions 8.C.2 (rationalizable strategies) and 9.C.2 (sequential rationality) for dynamic games, and Artzner *et al.* (1999) for coherent risk measures. Sometimes, such authors go to great lengths to argue that their particular principle is not only necessary, but also sufficient, for rationality (de Finetti 1931b). Citation scores show that such naïve terminologies can nevertheless be effective.

Example B.3 [Preference system versus repeated choice]. A researcher ("he") wants to test whether a consumer's ("she") preferences over a banana (b), a mango (m), and nothing (n) satisfy transitivity. We consider three cases.

CASE 1 [Hypothetical choices but no repetitions]. First assume that the researcher uses only hypothetical choice. He thus infers, first, $C\{m,n\} = n$, second, $C\{b,n,\} = b$, and, third and finally, $C\{b,m\} = m$. It seems that transitivity is violated. The consumer adds an explanation. He usually prefers b from $\{b,m\}$. Now, however, he already received b from the second choice situation. Because he likes changes, he now rather chooses m from $\{b,m\}$ in the ensuing third choice situation, so as to avoid receiving two bananas.

What went wrong in the experiment is that the choices were taken jointly (repeated choice), whereas each should have been considered in isolation. When considering $C\{b,m\}$ in the third choice situation, the consumer should assume in this thought experiment that $C\{b,m\}$ is the only choice to be made and that the first and second choices did not really take place. In particular, only one piece of fruit is received and the joint receipt of two or more pieces of fruit never plays a role. The phenomenon that receipt of an outcome in one choice situation can affect preference in subsequent choices is called the *income effect* in experimental economics, and this is what we should avoid here. Holt & Laury (2002) found a way to observe two within-subject choices, both incentivized, yet without any income effect.

CASE 2 [Real incentives but no repetitions]. We now want to use real choices and real incentives. Then observing preference systems and testing transitivity is more complicated. Whereas with hypothetical choice in the second and third choice situation we can ask the consumer to imagine these situations as anew, a real receipt of a banana in the second situation cannot be made undone in the third choice situation. Hence, avoiding the income effect is more difficult.

One commonly used way to avoid the income effect is through the random incentive system. Then the consumer is asked for hypothetical choices in several situations with the understanding that at the end of the experiment one, and only one, of the choice situations will be played for real. Then the receipt of more than one fruit never plays a role. Holt (1986) put forward some restrictive assumptions underlying the random incentive system, related to it inducing a meta lottery. In Starmer & Sugden (1991), these restrictive assumptions were empirically verified ("isolation"). Alternative implementations of real incentives assume that no income effect takes place, e.g., by repeated choices spread out over time with an assumption of unchanged preference, or by considering choices of different people who are all assumed to have identical preferences ("representative agent").

CASE 3 [Repeated choice]. Assume now that the experimenter is genuinely interested in repeated choice, and in consumptions of more than one piece of fruit. Then the experimenter may ask for a real choice in each of the three situations. Then, however, prospects are not elements of the set $\{b,m,n\}$ considered above, but they concern repeated decisions with multiple and not single fruits. Prospects should then be modeled that way (Gilboa 2009 §10.2 2nd para). The interaction between the consumption of different fruits then becomes relevant. We then deal with a different model than the one considered above. □

The following example illustrates an approach outside the revealed-preference paradigm.

Example B.4 [Measuring utility through introspection and without revealed preference]. In the health domain, the visual analog scale (VAS) is often used to measure the utility of health states (Drummond *et al.* 1987; Gold *et al.* 1996; Sox *et al.* 1986; Weinstein *et al.* 1980). A patient is presented with a line. One extreme represents death and the other represents perfect health. The patient is asked to indicate a point on the line to represent the value of the health state. The closer the point indicated is to perfect health, the better the health state is. The point indicated is usually taken as a cardinal index of utility that is used in calculations of group averages, expectations, and discounted sums.

The VAS method is of a fundamentally different nature than revealed-preference measurements. The evaluation by the patient is based on introspection. The patient is not asked in any manner to consider choices between different prospects, neither real nor hypothetical. The difference between hypothetical choice and introspection is discussed by Savage (1954 §3.1). In many applications in health, the pragmatic VAS method is better suited than revealed-preference based methods. The latter can encounter many psychological and practical problems. There often is not enough time to help patients make sophisticated choices, and first-gut choices may be subject to many biases. □

B.2   A behavioral foundation of preference relations derived from choice behavior

For readers with an economic background, it may be instructive to relate the formal setup of this appendix to consumer demand theory in Example B.5 from the start. We now present, briefly, the basic definitions of revealed preference. We will consider situations where from a set D, called *choice situation* or *set of available prospects*, the decision maker chooses one prospect. We will also specify, more generally, a subset C(D) of D consisting of all prospects in D that the decision maker would be willing to choose from D. C(D) is called the *choice set*. This covers the case where several prospects in D tie for being best. The actually chosen prospect is then arbitrarily selected from C(D). We will relate C, the *choice function*, to a preference relation. In Example B.1, for instance, C{b,m} = b. In this appendix, the choice function is taken as the empirical primitive and the preference relation is the derived theoretical construct. We do not need any structure on the set of prospects, and prospects can be general objects.

X denotes the set of all conceivable *prospects*. It contains the union of all choice situations D considered. In Example B.1, $X \supset \{b,m,n\}$. The domain of C contains all choice situations considered. In the theorem presented later we will assume that this domain includes all two- and three-element subsets of X, and no infinite subsets. This assumption was satisfied in Example B.1 for $X = \{b,m,n\}$. To avoid triviality we assume that all Ds considered are nonempty. Each choice set C(D) is nonempty too. The final choice in Example B.1 was the nonempty set $C(D) = \{n\}$. C(D) can contain more than one element, in which case the decision maker is willing to select any element from C(D) as the final choice from D. The decision maker is completely free to choose C(D) from D as he likes. This choice is the influence of the decision maker only, and not of any other person or force. Obviously, the decision maker can be an individual but can also be a firm or an organization or any group of people, or an animal. We next present a well-known example of our setup.

Example B.5 [Consumer demand theory]. A consumer has a fixed positive amount of money, the *income* I, to spend, and can choose from commodity bundles $(x_1, \ldots, x_m) \in \mathbb{R}^m_+$. There is a price vector $(c_1, \ldots, c_m) \in \mathbb{R}^m_+$ and the price of the commodity bundle is $\sum_{j=1}^n c_j x_j$. The *budget set*, the analog of a choice situation, consists of all commodity bundles for which the price does not exceed the income I. Its upper boundary, the *budget frontier*, consists of all commodity bundles with price equal to I. The *demand function* chooses the most preferred commodity bundle from every budget set.

In this example we can set $X = \mathbb{R}^m_+$, and commodity bundles are prospects. The demand function is like the choice function. The set of chosen prospects, i.e., the choice set, is often assumed to be a singleton in consumer demand theory, which under a preference condition called strict quasiconvexity is natural. This example differs from the cases considered in Theorem B.7 because budget sets contain infinitely many prospects. This implies that not all two- and three-element subsets of X are contained in the domain of the choice function. In fact, none is. □

A *preference representation* holds for C if a weak order $\succcurlyeq$ exists on X such that for each D

$$C(D) = \{x \in D : x \succcurlyeq y \text{ for all } y \in D\}. \tag{B.1}$$

That is, C chooses the elements of D that are best in terms of a weak order $\succcurlyeq$. In keeping with the approach taken throughout this book, we first explain how preference can be "revealed," i.e., can be derived from the choice function. The most straightforward way to derive preference from choice is by setting $x \succcurlyeq y$ whenever $x \in C\{x,y\}$, $x \succ y$ if $\{x\} = C\{x,y\}$ (for $x \neq y$), and $x \sim y$ if $\{x,y\} = C\{x,y\}$. More efficient measurements can result from an observation for a set D with more than 2 elements. Then:

$$x \in C(D) \text{ implies } x \succcurlyeq y \text{ for each } y \in D, x \sim y \text{ for each } y \in C(D),$$
$$\text{and } x \succ y \text{ for each } y \in D - C(D). \tag{B.2}$$

If contradictions result from the measurements just described, then preference representability is falsified. For example, assume that for two prospects x and y and two choice situations D, E we have both D and E contain x and y; $x \in C(D), y \notin C(D)$, but $y \in C(E)$.   (B.3)

The first two choice observations imply $x \succ y$, but the last choice observation implies $y \succcurlyeq x$. A contradiction has resulted. Such a case arose in Example B.1 for the firstly considered real decision, with $D = \{b,n\}$, $E = \{b,m,n\}$, $x = n$, and $y = b$. The contradiction then led the decision maker to reconsider the choices and resolve the contradiction.

A necessary condition for preference representability is the requirement that contradictions as in Eq. (B.3) do not arise. This condition is the *weak axiom of revealed preference*, and was introduced by Samuelson (1938). It turns out to be sufficient to require the condition only if D and E are nested, i.e., one is a subset of the other. This condition is known as *independence of irrelevant alternatives*. It was introduced by Arrow (1959) as a generalization of a condition in Nash (1950 Axiom 3).[4] Luce (1959) simultaneously introduced a probabilistic generalization. It turns out that precluding the contradictions described is not only necessary, but also sufficient, for preference representability.

Structural Assumption B.6 [Revealed preference]. X is the set of *prospects*. C is defined on a collection of nonempty subsets of X that includes all two- and three-element subsets of X and no infinite subsets of X, and $\emptyset \neq C(D) \subset D$ for all D. □

Theorem B.7 [Revealed preference]. Under Structural Assumption B.6, the following two statements are equivalent.

 (i) Preference representability holds.
(ii) Independence of irrelevant alternatives holds. □

Proof. That independence of irrelevant alternatives is necessary for preference representability was demonstrated in the main text. We next assume independence of irrelevant alternatives and derive preference representability. We define $x \succcurlyeq y$ if $x \in C\{x,y\}$, with added $x \succcurlyeq x$ for all x so as to ensure reflexivity. Completeness follows from nonemptiness of $C\{x,y\}$ and reflexivity. For transitivity, assume that $x \succcurlyeq y$ and $y \succcurlyeq z$. The implication

$$[z \in C\{x,y,z\} \Rightarrow y \in C\{x,y,z\}]$$

follows from independence of irrelevant alternatives and $y \in C\{y,z\}$.
 Similarly, the implication

$$[y \in C\{x,y,z\} \Rightarrow x \in C\{x,y,z\}]$$

follows from independence of irrelevant alternatives and $x \in C\{x,y\}$.

---

[4] Arrow, however, used another term for this revealed-preference condition. He used the term independence of irrelevant alternatives in another context, social choice, for another condition (Arrow 1951b). The condition for revealed preference that we consider is widely known under the name independence of irrelevant alternatives today, which is why we use this term.

C{x,y,z} must be nonempty. It must contain x.[5] By independence of irrelevant alternatives, x must then also be contained in C{x,z}. It follows that $x \succcurlyeq z$, so that $\succcurlyeq$ is transitive and it is a weak order.

Next, to establish Eq. (B.1), consider a general C(D). If $y \succ x$ for all $x \in D$ then $y \notin$ C(D) would give Eq. (B.3) for any $x \in C(D)$ and $E = \{x,y\}$, violating independence of irrelevant alternatives. Conversely, assume $y \in C(D)$. Then $y \notin C\{x,y\}$ for any x in D would generate Eq. (B.3) by setting D of Eq. (B.3) equal to $\{x,y\}$ and setting E of Eq. (B.3) equal to D. □

B.3   Assumptions underlying revealed preference

Thought experiments. Basically, we assume that the decision maker has to choose one element from one set D once. This concerns the *real choice situation*. Other choice situations in principle concern thought experiments that serve to analyze the real choice situation. The concepts of decision theory, such as preference relations and utility functions, describe relations between the various choice situations considered. Behavioral foundations justify the use of such concepts and thus show what the essential parameters of the real choice situation are. The thought experiments used in revealed-preference theory, and throughout this book, always change the real choice situation by assuming that the set of available prospects has been changed. Savage (1954 §3.1) discussed the difference between such thought experiments that are still part of the revealed-preference paradigm, and introspection ("direct interrogation") which is not.

Other theories consider other thought experiments that we have done. For example, in voting theory the set of available alternatives is usually assumed fixed but the preference relations of a group of individuals is assumed variable (Arrow 1951b; Arrow, Sen, & Suzumura 2007). In case-based decision theory, the set of available alternatives usually is also assumed fixed, and information available from cases in memory is assumed variable (Gilboa & Schmeidler 2001a).

Ceteris Paribus. As is usual in science, ceteris paribus assumptions are made. When changing the set of available prospects, no other relevant aspects are assumed to be changed. In particular, the information regarding the prospects and their quality is not changed. Distributed over various papers, Amartya Sen put forward many examples where the ceteris paribus condition is violated. Some examples are discussed next.

Example B.8 [The very availability of prospects gives information about the value of other prospects; Luce & Raiffa (1957 p. 288, §13.3)]. We reconsider Example B.1.

Now the decision maker assumes that, if a fruit store has only mangos and no bananas, then the fruit store must be specialized in mangos so that they will be of good quality. Hence, C{m,n} = m. If there are also bananas available then the mangos

---

[5] Proof: if C{x,y,z} = {x} then we are done. If C{x,y,z} contains y then it must contain x by the last implication displayed. If C{x,y,z} contains z then it contains y by the next to last implication displayed, and then it contains x by the last implication displayed. Consequently, x is always contained in C{x,y,z}.

probably are not so good. Hence $C\{b,m\} = b$. The latter choice and $C\{b,n\} = n$ lead to the choice $C\{b,m,n\} = n$. These choices are not affected by the choice $C\{m,n\} = m$ because in the latter case the information about the mangos is different. Independence of irrelevant alternatives is violated by the choices $C\{b,m,n\} = n$ and $C\{m,n\} = m$. This violation is explained by the different informational state in the two situations, with m being better in one situation than in the other. Thus, the ceteris paribus assumption underlying revealed preference fails. □

Example B.9 [Condorcet paradox; Arrow, Sen, & Suzumura, 2007]. We reconsider Example B.1. Now, however, the decision maker knows nothing about fruits and must entirely go by three advisors. Advisor 1 has preferences $b \succ_1 m \succ_1 n$, advisor 2 has preferences $n \succ_2 b \succ_2 m$, and advisor 3 has preferences $m \succ_3 n \succ_3 b$. A caveat is that the decision maker, when in a store, is only informed about the preferences of the advisors regarding the prospects available. It is then reasonable to go by the majority rule. Thus, $C\{b,m\} = b$, $C\{b,n\} = n$, and $C\{m,n\} = m$. However, $C\{b,m,n\} = \{b,m,n\}$ because in the latter case the preferences exhibit a symmetry. The latter choice violates independence of irrelevant alternatives relative to any two-prospect choice situation.

The violation of independence of irrelevant alternatives is explained by informational differences. In $C\{b,m\}$, it is reasonable to prefer b because two of the three advisors, 1 and 2, recommend b and no other information is available. In $C\{b,m,n\}$ more information is available. It is now known that advisors 1 and 2 probably have relatively weak preferences, with m next in ranking to b, whereas the preference of advisor 3 is probably stronger, with b ranked way lower than m. Hence, b may be considered to be better than m in the choice situation $\{b,m\}$, but not in the choice situation $\{b,m,n\}$. The ceteris paribus assumption of revealed preference is violated again. □

Example B.10 [Holistic considerations; Sen 1993]. Consider Example B.1 for a decision maker with preferences $m \succ b \succ n$ if choice were not observed by others. The choice is, however, observed by others. The decision maker thinks that it is impolite to choose the most preferred prospect and that doing so will harm his reputation, so that he always chooses the second best. He reveals the choices $C\{m,b,n\} = b$ and $C\{b,n\} = n$, implying a violation of independence of irrelevant alternatives. Here the value of the prospects is not determined in isolation, but depends on which other prospects are available in view of the impact on reputation. Hence, the ceteris paribus assumption of revealed preference is violated. □

It can be seen that completeness of preference is not essential for the equivalence of independence of irrelevant alternatives and preference representability in Theorem B.7, whereas transitivity is. Transitivity of preference has sometimes been interpreted as a unary valuation of prospects (Burks 1977; Cubitt & Sugden 1998). That is, each prospect available has its own value independent of the other prospects available, and there is no interaction between the values of the prospects available. This intuition is captured by independence of irrelevant alternatives.

Real implementation of choices. In revealed-preference theory, the variations in available prospects need not always merely concern thought experiments, but they may concern actually occurring choice situations. These may concern other people and/or other times. Then the relevant ceteris paribus conditions must obviously be satisfied. As stressed in Example B.3, the choice situations are to be taken as isolated choices, and repeated choice plays no explicit role. Case 2 in that example explained that, in experiments, the random incentive system is commonly used to observe several choices and yet each is taken as isolated.

Expected value and repeated choice. The difference between thought experiments and repeated choice, illustrated in Example B.3, played a role in the analysis of expected value maximization in Chapter 1. It did so in particular in §1.10 for our interpretation of de Finetti's bookmaking argument. An argument often advanced to justify expected value maximization, other than the behavioral foundation in Chapter 1, involves the law of large numbers. The law of large numbers entails that independent repetitions of a prospect yield a total average gain that is approximately equal to the expected value of the prospect if the number of repetitions is large. Thus, if we choose between independent repetitions of prospects, we may want to maximize expected value. I did not use the argument of the law of large numbers for four reasons.

1. The argument concerns repeated choice situations, which is not the topic considered here (Example B.3). There have been many misunderstandings about this aspect of decision theory, especially concerning the subjective probabilities derived in Chapter 1. These probabilities have sometimes been confused with objective probabilities, the latter being defined as relative frequencies in repetitions. Several authors have been confused in thinking that probabilities are not relevant for single decisions (Baumann 2008; Gigerenzer 1991 Examples 1 and 2; Lopes 1981; Shackle 1949a p. 71). In the health domain, it has often been argued that every patient is unique, so that statistics is not useful for individual treatment decisions (d'Amador 1837 p. 33).[6] Such confusion usually arises from inappropriately restricting attention to the frequentist interpretation of probability (defined by von Mises 1957 p. 11) and unawareness of de Finetti's ideas in Chapter 1.

2. The independent repetitions of events necessary for the law of large numbers are often inconceivable. For example, the weather conditions may never have been as they will be tomorrow. Decision theory is also relevant for one-shot decisions.

---

[6] "Your problem precludes the investigation of individual applications: because the problem of the numerists is not to cure this or that patient, but to cure the largest possible on a predetermined total. Hence, this problem essentially is anti-medical." Original French text: "Votre principe vous interdit cette recherche des applications individuelles: car le problème de numéristes n'est pas de guérir tel ou tel malade, mais d'en guérir le plus possible sur un totale déterminé. Or ce problème est essentiellement anti-médicale." See also d'Amador (1837 p. 14): "medicine will no more be an art, but a lottery – it is scepticism embracing empiricism." Original French text: "la médicine ne serait plus un art, mais une loterie – c'est le scepticisme embrassant l'empirisme." Murphy (1981) describes the historical context of the citation.

3. The law of large numbers requires that only the final sum of the payments matters. In many situations this requirement is not reasonable. If during the first 35 months you receive no salary so that you die from starvation, and in month 36 more than a 36-fold months' salary is awaiting you that you cannot consume because you have died, then you will like this arrangement less than when you receive your regular salary each month.

4. The law of large numbers typically involves large total payments, for which expected value with linear utility is questionable. You will prefer receiving $10 million for sure as the final sum total after many repeated decisions rather than receiving a 50–50 gamble yielding $25 million or $0 then.

For these four reasons I did not use the law of large numbers to justify expected-value maximization in Chapter 1. In many situations, considered in later chapters, risk aversion and concave utility are appropriate. Then it is immediately obvious that the law of large numbers and expected value do not provide appropriate decision criteria.

The preliminary-choice problem. For theoretical analyses it is convenient to allow for indifference between different prospects. Indifference, however, poses a problem for revealed preference given that the decision maker ultimately only chooses one prospect. Strictly speaking, it can never be demonstrated by revealed-preference data that a decision maker was not indifferent between all prospects and chose randomly in all situations (Davidson & Suppes 1956). To avoid this problem in theory, we assume that C(D) contains all the best prospects contained in D. In practice we may be able to find out what the whole set C(D) is if we can observe choices from D many times – possibly implemented by the random incentive system to exclude repeated choice – or by communication with the decision maker. We can call C(D) the *preliminary choice* from D, where the prospect finally chosen from D is a random selection from C(D).

The problem of indifference just explained is called the *preliminary choice problem*. It is not very serious for normative applications because it does not matter which element from C(D) is chosen. It is more problematic for descriptive purposes because it is hard to distinguish between indifference and strict preference.

Things we do not consider. Probabilistic choice theories assume that the choice from a set D is not deterministic but probabilistic. We only consider deterministic choice, where C(D) is deterministically known.

Under bounded rationality, a decision maker may not choose most preferred prospects because determining those is too complex. Then calculation costs play a role. We do not consider the difficulty and calculation costs of decision making. In other words, we assume unbounded rationality.

There is much evidence that first-gut preferences, determined quickly and intuitively without much deliberation, can be affected by framing, by irrelevant details in the way they are presented. For example, subjects may treat a prospect for decision under uncertainty differently when presented as $(A{:}\alpha, B{:}\alpha, C{:}\beta)$ than when presented as $(A \cup B{:}\alpha, C{:}\beta)$ in an experiment (event splitting; Starmer & Sugden 1993). Again, after some learning and training such framing effects will disappear and this is what we will assume throughout. In our approach, prospects are indeed defined formally as functions from the state space S to the outcomes, and then (A:α,B:α,C:β) and (A ∪ B:α,C:β) are identical by definition because they concern the same function.

Theories that consider framing effects as relevant for first-gut preferences have been developed by Luce (1990, 2000). Then (A:α,B:α,C:β) is not defined formally as a function from S to the outcomes, but interpreted as a general sextuple, so that (A:α, B:α,C:β) can be formally distinguished from (A ∪ B:α,C:β). Framing effects are also central to many studies by Birnbaum (2008a). In original prospect theory (Kahneman & Tversky 1979), framing effects were incorporated under the name of editing. Editing had been added only in the last version of the paper and was not present in an earlier working paper version (Kahneman & Tversky 1975). It had been added to deal with the violations of monotonicity generated by original prospect theory.

First-gut preferences that are subject to elementary irrationalities have been examined primarily by psychologists. Experimental economists have usually focused on more sophisticated preferences, so that transitivity, monotonicity, and framing invariance may be assumed. The new version of prospect theory (Tversky & Kahneman 1992) no longer incorporated framing effects[7], focusing on sophisticated preferences that are also the topic of this book. In this respect we follow Pareto (1906 Ch. 3, §1), who wrote:

A man who buys a certain food for the first time may buy more of it than is necessary to satisfy his tastes, price taken into account. But in a second purchase he will correct his error, in part at least, and thus, little by little, will end up by procuring exactly what he needs. *We will examine this action at the time when he has reached this state.* Similarly, if at first he makes a mistake in his reasoning about what he desires, he will rectify it in repeating the reasoning and will end up by making it completely logical. [Italics added here.]

B.4   The history of revealed preference

Before 1900, economists would freely use introspective ("choiceless") inputs, in agreement with Bentham's (1789) profound writings on utility. Fisher (1892 §II. IV.8, p. 89) and Pareto (1906 paragraph 36b) pointed out that a number of economic questions, such as what a market equilibrium will be, can be answered using only revealed-preference data. Many economists subsequently argued for restricting attention to revealed-preference ("choice-based") data, and this became widely accepted as the definition of the economic field (Robbins 1932; Hicks & Allen 1934). In a mathematical sense this point often implies that utility is only "ordinal," which is why this development is known as the ordinal revolution in economics (Blaug 1962).

In the 1930s, logical positivism had similar implications in psychology, which also tended to restrict attention to directly observable behavior under the name of behaviorism (Skinner 1971; Watson 1913). This parallel development in the two fields was

---

[7] The term does not refer to reference dependence here. Reference dependence, discussed in Chapter 8, is a crucial component of prospect theory.

pointed out by Edwards (1954 p. 385) and discussed by Lewin (1996). In the 1960s behaviorism lost popularity in psychology because it does not generate sufficiently rich data, and psychologists became interested in cognitive data (Chomsky 1959; Gardner, 1985; Luce 2000 p. 26). Similarly, there have always been economists who argued that introspective data are also useful for questions central to economics (Suppes & Winet 1955 p. 261; van Praag 1968). Recently, the interest in introspective data has increased in economics because of the growing number of empirical difficulties for revealed preference, with the preference reversal as the most influential finding (Grether & Plott 1979; Lichtenstein & Slovic 1971; Lindman 1971). Frey (2008 §15.1) wrote: "Utility must be measured when it is known or suspected that revealed preferences do not faithfully reflect individuals' utility." The health domain, when considering the allocation of scarce resources as in economics, has always taken a pragmatic position. Measuring utility and quality of life using revealed preference is often too complex practically, and then introspective data works better and leads to better economic decisions; see Example B.4 and the references there.

Kahneman argued that especially in intertemporal evaluations the biases in revealed preference are often so big that it is better to then resort to introspective evaluations (Kahneman 1994; Kahneman, Wakker, & Sarin 1997). It is desirable to restrict these introspective evaluations, if possible, to outcomes when they are actually experienced (Kahneman *et al.* 2004). Many other authors have recently argued that broader interpretations of utility than purely ordinal are useful for questions central to economics (Broome 1991; Gilboa & Schmeidler 2001b; Kapteyn 1994; Loomes & Sugden 1982; Rabin 2000 footnote 3; Robson 2001 §III.D; Tinbergen 1991). Under the name of happiness, introspective measurements of utility, studied extensively in the psychological literature, have recently attracted interest in economics (Clark, Frijters, & Shields 2008; Diener & Biswas-Diener 2008; Frey 2008; van Praag & Ferrer-i-Carbonell 2004).

Abdellaoui, Barrios, & Wakker (2007) argued for the use of introspective data in economics under the restriction that evidence be provided that this data can serve to predict decisions. We then do not go back to Bentham but maintain the valuable clarifications and rigor that the ordinal revolution brought to economics. This view adheres to Savage's (1954 §3.1) requirement that data should in the end manifest itself in decisions, but broadens the scope.

Appendix C: Dynamic decisions

This appendix briefly considers the implementation of nonexpected utility models in dynamic decisions. It describes a fundamental problem of such implementations, a problem that is one of the greatest challenges to nonexpected utility in general. Consider the choice situation in Figure C.1. The square designates a choice node where you can choose to go down, receiving 40 for sure, or to go up. If you go up you arrive at the circle 2, designating a chance node. With probability 0.3 you go down, receiving 49 for sure. With probability 0.7 you go up, arriving at the circle 3, another chance node. Then with probability[1] 0.8 you receive 100, and with probability 0.2 you receive nil.

First assume that the decision maker maximizes EU for static decisions with $U(\alpha) = \sqrt{\alpha}$. One way of evaluating the move up in node 1 is by what is sometimes called forward induction: The move up results in outcome 100 with probability $0.7 \times 0.8 = 0.56$, in outcome 0 with probability $0.7 \times 0.2 = 0.14$, and in outcome 49 with probability 0.3. In forward induction the move up is evaluated as the static probability distribution (0.56: 100, 0.14: 0, 0.3: 49). Its EU is 7.60, and its certainty equivalent is 59.29. This exceeds the payment 40 of the down move, so that the move up is chosen.

A second way of evaluating the move up in node 1 is by *backward induction*, also called folding back. At node 3 we face the prospect $100_{0.8}0$, which has EU 8 and certainty equivalent 64. Under backward induction, we replace the chance node 3 by this certainty equivalent. Then chance node 2 yields the prospect $64_{0.7}49$. Its EU is 7.70, with certainty equivalent 59.29. This is taken as the evaluation of the move up, again implying a choice up.

In the calculations, forward and backward induction yield the same evaluation with certainty equivalent 59.29 for the move up and the same choice of moving up. It can be proved in general for EU that forward and backward inductions always agree and lead to the same decisions. According to many authors, including myself, both methods of evaluation are normatively appropriate, so that the obtained consistency is a normative requirement.

---

[1] Formally, this is a conditional probability, with arrival at node 3 as the conditioning event.

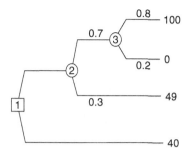

Figure C.1 A dynamic decision tree.

One of the major difficulties of nonexpected utility is that it does not satisfy the consistency that we just observed for EU, as we will see. Forward and backward induction can yield different evaluations and decisions. We illustrate this claim by reconsidering Figure C.1, now assuming RDU with $U(\alpha) = \sqrt{\alpha}$ and $w(p) = p^2$. Forward induction yields RDU(0.56: 100, 0.14: 0, 0.3: 49) = 6.12, with certainty equivalent 37.43. This RDU model exhibits considerably more risk aversion than the EU model, and the decision maker now prefers the move down yielding 40 for sure.

For backward induction, RDU($100_{0.8}0$) = 6.40, with certainty equivalent 40.96. Then chance node 2 yields the prospect $40.96_{0.7}49$. Its RDU is 6.45, with certainty equivalent 41.65. It deviates from the forward induction and now exceeds 40, so that a different decision results, of moving up.

We considered a consistency requirement only for a simply dynamic situation, with only one choice to be made at the beginning. In complex decision trees there can be many stages of sequential decisions with intermediate chance nodes. Then many different dynamic decision principles can be considered for different ways in which chance nodes follow decision nodes, chance nodes follow other chance nodes, and so on.

It turns out that a number of normatively desirable consistency conditions for the implementation of a static model in dynamic decisions, similar to the one discussed above but not specified in detail here, have a surprising implication for the static model: they can be satisfied only if static preferences satisfy the independence preference condition for decision under risk (§2.7) and the sure-thing principle for decision under uncertainty (§4.8.1) (Burks 1977 Ch. 5; Cubitt 1996; Ghirardato 2002; Gollier 2001a, §1.5.2; Hammond 1988; Wakker 1999). This provides a strong normative argument against nonexpected utility. Authors who consider nonexpected utility to be rational faced a difficult question when this point became known: which of the conditions considered normatively desirable above should be abandoned? For each condition there have been authors arguing that this

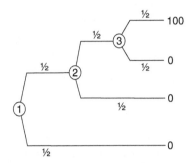

Figure C.2 A multistage prospect.

is the condition to be abandoned (Epstein 1992; Machina 1989; Karni & Safra 1990; Segal 1990).

Descriptively, nonexpected utility will be applied in dynamic decisions in many different ways (Cubitt, Starmer, & Sugden 1998; Tversky & Kahneman 1981 Problems 5 and 6). The way it is done will depend on the particular dynamic decision problem, and its perception. In most complex dynamic decisions, backward induction is easier to implement and it can therefore be expected to be the most common evaluation method. It has for instance been used in analyses of the "Deal or No Deal" TV game show using prospect theory (Post *et al.* 2008). Sometimes, however, forward induction is more plausible. Figure C.2 presents an example. It is plausible that subjects perceive the multistage chance node 1 simply as a ⅛ probability of receiving 100, and nothing otherwise.

Whereas the updating of preferences and of probability is well established under expected utility, their generalization to nonexpected utility is problematic, having to deal with the fundamental problems of dynamic decision making under nonexpected utility. For example, should such updatings reckon with foregone decisions and uncertainties from the past? Should actual updatings at time t agree with the preferences at time 0 about the updatings at time t? Many normatively oriented debates in the field, initiated 20 years ago (Machina 1989) have not led to any clear conclusions. Related to the question of updating, there is no clear definition of independence for nonadditive measures (Halpern 2003 §4.3). I do not consider nonexpected utility to be normative and think that no normatively satisfactory method for updating or implementation in dynamic decisions will be found. This may explain why the belief functions of Dempster (1967) and Shafer (1976) have lost their popularity in artificial intelligence. Bayesian networks, based on classical probabilities, are used almost exclusively today. Which method of updating is most appropriate for descriptive applications is an interesting topic for empirical research (Busemeyer *et al.* 2000; Cubitt, Starmer, & Sugden 1998).

Exercise C.1.[b] Consider the decision tree in Figure C.3.

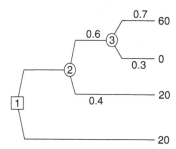

Figure C.3 A dynamic decision tree.

(a) Assume EU with $U(\alpha) = \alpha^{0.88}$. Evaluate the certainty equivalent of the choice up both with forward and with backward induction. Which decision is taken in the decision node 1?

(b) Assume RDU with $U(\alpha) = \alpha^{0.88}$ and $w(p) = p^2$. Evaluate the certainty equivalent of the choice up both with forward and with backward induction. Which decision is taken in each case? ☐

Appendix D: Applications other than decision under uncertainty

The main text has considered decision under uncertainty and decision under risk. The results in this book can be reinterpreted for other contexts such as welfare evaluations, intertemporal choice, multiattribute utility, and numerous other applications. In some contexts a quantitative function V on the prospects, rather than a preference relation $\succcurlyeq$, is taken as a primitive. These can often be related to each other, where $\succcurlyeq$ is the preference relation represented by V and V is for instance the certainty equivalent function generated by the preference relation. Many conditions for preferences can readily be restated in terms of the certainty equivalent function. For simplicity, we assume that S is finite in this appendix. Extensions to general sets S are straightforward.

Structural Assumption D.1 Structural Assumption 1.2.1 (decision under uncertainty) holds with $S = \{s_1,\ldots,s_n\}$. We write $(x_1,\ldots,x_n)$ for $(s_1{:}x_1,\ldots,s_n{:}x_n)$. $\square$

Interpretation D.2 [Welfare]. Assume Structural Assumption D1. States now designate persons. A prospect $(x_1\ldots x_n)$ is a welfare allocation assigning x_j to each person s_j. An evaluation $\sum_{j=1}^n p_j U(x_j)$ gives a utilitarian welfare evaluation where p_j measures the importance of person s_j. $\square$

The evaluation $(x_1\ldots,x_n)\mapsto \min\{x_j\}$, which is a rank-dependent form, is the famous Rawlsian evaluation that assigns maximal importance to the person worse off in society. Rank dependence has often been used in welfare evaluations. People are not only sensitive to their absolute level of wealth but also to their rank in society, i.e., which percentage of the population is richer (Moyes 2007). Weymark (1981 Theorem 3) may have been the first to define a rank-dependent form, together with Quiggin (1981). Weymark's Theorem 3 is, in fact, the same as Yaari's (1987) main result but it is formulated for welfare instead of risk. A recent example using rank-tradeoff consistency (in a comonotonic version) is Ebert (2004). Bleichrodt & van Doorslaer (2006) used rank dependence to analyze measures of inequality in the health domain.

Interpretation D.3 [Intertemporal choice]. Assume Structural Assumption D1. States $s_j \in \mathbb{R}$ now designate time points. A prospect $(x_1,\ldots, x_n)$ is a consumption profile assigning consumption x_j to time point s_j. An evaluation $\sum_{j=1}^n p_j U(x_j)$ with $p_j = e^{-\theta s_j}$ gives discounted utility with θ the discount factor. $\square$

Williams & Nassar (1966 Theorem II) obtained a close analog of Theorem 1.6.1.iii for intertemporal choice, with their Axiom III the same as our additivity condition. Abdellaoui, Attema, & Bleichrodt (2009) used the tradeoff method of §4.1 to measure intertemporal utility. In the same way as for decision under risk unknown probabilities or decision weights drop from the equations when measuring utilities using the tradeoff method, for intertemporal choice the unknown discount weights drop from the equations. Gilboa (1989a) proposed a rank-dependent approach. Epper, Fehr-Duda, & Bruhin (2009) and Halevy (2008) demonstrated that probability weighting may underlie discounting.

Interpretation D.4 [Multiattribute utility]. Assume Structural Assumption D1. Prospects now designate objects to be chosen, such as cars, and states s_j describe attributes of the object, such as the color of a car, its maximum speed, or its price. In situations where from little data we want to derive multiattribute representations, an efficient statistical technique called conjoint analysis, originating from marketing, has been widely used (Cattin & Wittink 1989; Green & Srinivasan 1978; Gustafsson, Herrmann, & Huber 2007; Louviere, Hensher, & Swait 2000). It assumes additive representations $\sum_{j=1}^{n} V_j(x_j)$. The sawtooth method used there is similar to the standard sequences that we have elicited using tradeoff techniques (cf. Fishburn 1967 p. 450). §3.7 considered the case of probability distributions over multiattribute objects. Interestingly, Yager (1988) introduced a rank-dependent multiattribute evaluation independently of the other discoveries of rank dependence. Recent applications of rank dependence in this context include Galand, Perny & Spanjaard (2010) and Grabisch, Kojadinovic, & Meyer (2008). □

Interpretation D.5 [Consumer theory]. Assume Structural Assumption D1. States $s_j \in \mathbb{R}$ now designate commodities. A prospect $(x_1, \ldots, x_n)$ is a commodity bundle yielding x_j units of commodity s_j. An evaluation $\sum_{j=1}^{n} p_j x_j^{\theta}$ designates utility with constant elasticity of substitution (CES). □

Interpretation D.6 [Production theory]. Assume Structural Assumption D1. States $s_j \in \mathbb{R}$ now designate inputs in a production process, such as capital, labor, and materials. A prospect $(x_1, \ldots, x_n)$ is a production process with x_j units of input s_j. In this context often a quantitative production function, rather than a preference relation $\succcurlyeq$ is taken as a primitive. □

Interpretation D.7 [Price index theory]. Assume Structural Assumption D1. States $s_j \in \mathbb{R}$ now designate a representative set of commodities available in a particular country. A prospect $(x_1, \ldots, x_n)$ is a price vector with x_j the price per unit of the commodity s_j in the country in a particular year. In this context often not a preference relation $\succcurlyeq$, but a quantitative production function giving the overall price level, is taken as primitive. □

To illustrate that the list of possible interpretations is unbounded, I give one more. Related topics in multicriteria optimization are in Bouyssou *et al.* (2006).

Interpretation D.8 [Radiotherapy]. Assume Structural Assumption D1 with n = 6. Prospects now designate radiotherapy treatments with radiation for two organs and three consecutive days. $(x_1,\ldots,x_6)$ denotes a treatment with intensity of radiation, in units of Gy, of x_1,x_2,x_3 for organ 1 on days 1,2,3, and x_4,x_5,x_6 for organ 2 on days 1,2,3. Prospects are ordered according to whether they better cure the disease, whether they have fewer side effects, and tradeoffs between these two. □

Appendix E: Bisymmetry-based preference conditions

Expected utility, rank-dependent utility, and prospect theory all use generalized weighted averages of utilities for evaluating prospects. We have used tradeoff consistency conditions to provide measurements and behavioral foundations for such models. Alternative conditions, based on a bisymmetry condition, have been used in the literature to obtain behavioral foundations. These conditions use certainty equivalents of prospects, so that a richness assumption must be added that certainty equivalents always exist. To avoid details concerning null events, we will assume that S is finite and that all states are nonnull. The latter is implied by strong monotonicity in the following assumption.

Structural Assumption E.1. Structural Assumption 1.2.1 (decision under uncertainty) holds with S finite. Further, $\succcurlyeq$ is a monotonic and strongly monotonic weak order, and for each prospect a certainty equivalent exists. $\square$

Although the following multisymmetry condition is a static preference condition, it is best explained by thought experiments using multistage uncertainty. Consider Figure E.1, where we use backward induction (Appendix C) to evaluate the prospects. The indifference sign $\sim$ indicates that backward induction generates the same certainty equivalent for both two-multistage prospects. This condition amounts to a static preference condition: *multisymmetry* holds if

$$CE((E_1\!:x_1,\ldots,E_n\!:x_n)_A CE(E_1\!:y_1,\ldots,E_n\!:y_n)) \sim$$

$$(E_1\!:CE(x_{1_A}y_1),\ldots,E_n\!:CE(x_{n_A}y_n))$$

for all events A, partitions $\{E_1,\ldots,E_n\}$, and outcomes $x_1,\ldots,y_n$.

The indifference implies that the certainty equivalents in Figure E.1 are identical. For the left prospect in Figure E.1, the uncertainty regarding A is resolved first, and the uncertainty regarding E_j next, and for the right prospect the order of resolution is reversed. An alternative illustration is in Table E.1, which illustrates the payments in Figure E.1 resulting from the two prospects. Backward induction in the left prospect in Figure E.1 amounts to first replacing the two rows in the table by their certainty equivalents, and next taking a certainty equivalent as in

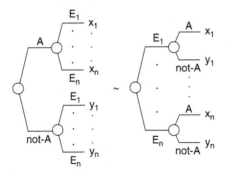

Figure E.1 A dynamic illustration of multisymmetry.

Table E.1

	$E_1 \ldots E_n$
A	$x_1 \ldots x_n$
not-A	$y_1 \ldots y_n$

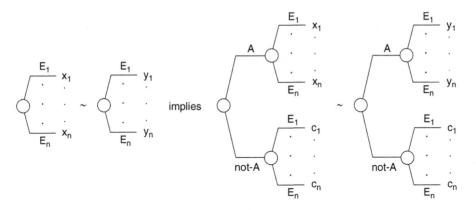

Figure E.2 A dynamic illustration of act-independence.

the left chance node in the left prospect. Backward induction in the right prospect in Figure E.1 amounts to first replacing the n columns in the table by their certainty equivalents, and next a certainty equivalent as in the left chance node in the right prospect.

An appealing version of multisymmetry is the act-independence condition introduced by Gul (1992). Again, it is a static preference condition, but is best illustrated using backward induction (Figure E.2).

Act independence holds if

$$(E_1:x_1,\ldots,E_n:x_n) \sim$$

$$(E_1:y_1,\ldots,E_n:y_n)$$

$$\Rightarrow$$

$$CE(E_1:x_1,\ldots,E_n:x_n)_A CE(E_1:c_1,\ldots,E_n:c_n) \sim$$

$$CE(E_1:y_1,\ldots,E_n:y_n)_A CE(E_1:c_1,\ldots,E_n:c_n).$$

The condition is appealing because it can be interpreted as a generalization of the independence condition for expected utility under risk. More specifically, it is a generalization of the substitution condition defined in §2.7, with event A playing the role of the mixing probability λ.

Exercise E.1.[c] Show that EU implies multisymmetry and act independence. □

Köbberling & Wakker (2003 §7) demonstrated that, under Assumption E.1, act independence and multisymmetry are equivalent, and these conditions imply tradeoff consistency in an elementary manner. It thus follows as a corollary of Theorem 4.6.4 (uncertainty-EU) that these conditions can provide alternative behavioral foundations of EU.

Köbberling & Wakker (2003 §7) also demonstrated that the conditions of this appendix can be used for behavioral foundations of rank-dependent utility, by imposing proper ranking restrictions. Again, these conditions imply rank-tradeoff consistency (or comonotonic tradeoff consistency) so that the behavioral foundations stated in terms of these conditions can be obtained as corollaries of the results in the main text of this book. In this way Köbberling & Wakker (2003 §7) demonstrated that the rank-dependent and rank-independent results in the following references can be obtained as corollaries of Theorems 4.6.4 and 10.5.6: Chew (1989), Chew & Karni (1994), Gul (1992), Ghirardato *et al.* (2003), Krantz *et al.* (1971 §6.9), Münnich, Maksa, & Mokken (2000), Nakamura (1990, 1992), and Quiggin (1982). Similarly, the following results derived on the domain of binary prospects follow as corollaries from our §10.6 (through Köbberling & Wakker 2003 Observation 18): Ghirardato & Marinacci (2001a), Luce (2000 Theorem 3.7.5), Pfanzagl (1959 Theorem 2), and Nakamura (1990 Theorem 1).

Unlike tradeoff consistency, bisymmetry conditions cannot be extended to prospect theory because sign constraints cannot be combined with the certainty equivalents used in these conditions. Hence, preliminary notes by Chew & Tversky (1990) were never completed.

Despite the appealing interpretations in Figures E.1 and E.2, I have preferred to use tradeoff conditions in behavioral foundations rather than bisymmetry conditions, for the following reasons:

- Tradeoff consistency is less restrictive so that more general theorems result;
- tradeoff consistency can be applied to prospect theory;

- tradeoffs play a natural role in decision making (end of Appendix 4.14);
- tradeoff consistency can be related to empirical utility measurements;
- the subjective independence of repeated events underlying Figures E.1 and E.2 is hard to imagine for events with unknown probabilities;
- bisymmetry conditions involve many certainty equivalents, which complicates empirical measurements.

For a criticism of tradeoff consistency, see Luce (2000 §3.7.3 and 5.3.1.1).

Appendix F: Nonmonotonic rank-dependent models and the Fehr–Schmidt model of welfare evaluation

This appendix considers the generalization of rank-dependent utility to nonmonotonic and possibly negative weighting functions. It then shows that the welfare model by Fehr & Schmidt (1999), one of the most influential models on welfare evaluations, is a rank-dependent form. This was pointed out by Rohde (2010).

We consider general set functions W. We make Structural Assumption 1.2.1 (decision under uncertainty) and assume that W is a general set function defined on S. For a ranked event E^R, we still define the *decision weight* $\pi(E^R)$ as $W(E \cup R) - W(R)$. It can now take any real value and, for instance, be negative. *Generalized rank-dependent utility (RDU)* holds if there exist a strictly increasing continuous *utility function* U: $\mathbb{R} \to \mathbb{R}$ and a general set function W such that each prospect $E_1 x_1 \cdots E_n x_n$ with completely ranked outcomes $x_1 \geq \cdots \geq x_n$ is evaluated by

$$\sum_{j=1}^{n} \pi_j U(x_j) = \sum_{j=1}^{n} \pi(E_j^{E_{j-1} \cup \cdots \cup E_1}) U(x_j)$$

$$= \sum_{j=1}^{n} (W(E_j \cup \cdots \cup E_1) - W(E_{j-1} \cup \cdots \cup E_1)) U(x_j).$$

$W(\emptyset)$ need not be 0, so that $W(E_{j-1} \cup \cdots \cup E_1)$ is not 0 for $j = 1$. Schmeidler (1986 Propositions 1, 2, and 3) considered the generalization of the Choquet integral to general set functions, and De Waegenaere & Wakker (2001) provided behavioral foundations. It is surprising how much of the characteristics of rank-dependent utility are maintained under the generalization now considered, especially regarding convexity and concavity.

Fehr & Schmidt (1999) introduced one of the most influential models for welfare evaluations. To explain their model, we adopt Interpretation D.2 [Welfare] of Appendix D. Preferences are assumed to be of person s_1, who receives x_1. This person dislikes inequity of the welfare allocation, and evaluates $(x_1, \ldots, x_n)$ by

$$x_1 - \sum_{j=2}^{n} a \times \max(x_j - x_1, 0) - \sum_{j=2}^{n} b \times \min(x_j - x_1, 0) \text{ with } a > 0 \text{ and } b > 0.$$

That is, each x_j different from x_1 reduces the welfare evaluation of person s_1. The Fehr–Schmidt form is a generalized rank-dependent utility form with U the identity and with W defined by W(E) =:

−ma if $s_1 \in E$

$1 - (n - m - 1)b$ if $s_1 \in E$.

where m is $\|E\|$.

This result is proved by Rohde (2010).

Appendix G: Extensions of finite-dimensional results to infinite-dimensional results: a meta-theorem

The general extension of finite-dimensional behavioral foundations to infinite-dimensional ones is discussed in detail by Wakker (1993a). This book does consider infinite state spaces, but confines its attention to prospects with finitely many outcomes. Then the extension of results from finite state spaces to infinite state spaces is not difficult. The procedure will now be explained. We give an explanation for the special case of Theorem 4.6.4 (uncertainty-EU), and an explanation in general for all theorems of this book. For Theorem 4.6.4, explanations between square brackets should be read. For the other results, these explanations should be skipped, or adapted to more general models.

Assume that we have established preference conditions that are necessary and sufficient for the existence of a representation [EU] for finite state spaces S, with a utility function U that is unique up to unit and level. Assume that the behavioral foundation also involves one or more set functions [only one, namely P] defined on the subsets of S – or, for mathematicians, on an algebra of events – and that these set functions are uniquely determined. Besides the probability P in EU such as in Theorem 4.6.4, we deal with a nonadditive measure in rank-dependent utility and with two nonadditive measures in prospect theory. Then this behavioral foundation [of EU] also holds under Structural Assumption 1.2.1 (decision under uncertainty) if S is infinite. The proof is as follows.

We normalize all utility functions U to be constructed the same way. That is, we choose two outcomes $\gamma \succ \beta$ (say, $\gamma = 1$ and $\beta = 0$ if these are contained in the domain) and throughout set

$$U(\gamma) = 1 \text{ and } U(\beta) = 0. \tag{G.1}$$

STEP 1. We take a finite partition $(E_1,\ldots,E_n)$ that is rich enough [satisfying nondegeneracy as imposed by Assumption 1.2.1 (decision under uncertainty), implying that at least two of its members are nonnull] to have the finite-dimensional theorem satisfied for all prospects with these E's as their outcome events. For these prospects we establish the representation [EU] with U satisfying Eq. (G.1) so that it is uniquely determined.

STEP 2. Next, for each other partition of S we take the *extended partition*, defined as the common refinement of that other partition with $(E_1, \ldots, E_n)$, which consists of all intersections of events of the two partitions. The extended partition, and prospects generated by these outcome events, is sufficiently rich so that the finite-dimensional theorem [Theorem 4.6.4] can still be applied for all theorems considered in this book. On the extended partition we obtain a new [EU] representation, where U still satisfies Eq. (G.1).

STEP 3. Consider the [EU] representations of two different partitions and their extensions in Step 2, and consider the prospects covered by both representations. These are the prospects with outcome events that are a union of elements of the first extended partition and also of the second extended partition; i.e., these events are in the common "coarsening" of the two extended partitions. They include all prospects with the E_j's as their outcome events. Here we have two [EU] representations that, because of uniqueness – which includes Eq. (G.1) for U – are in agreement. In other words, every pair of [EU] representations obtained in Step 2 are in agreement for the prospects in the intersection of their domain.

STEP 4. We now give the definition of the [EU] functional that will represent preference. This step only gives the definition. The next step will show that the functional does indeed represent preference. For each prospect we define the [EU] functional as follows. Take any extended partition such that the outcome events of the prospect are a union of events of that partition. Take the [EU] functional value of the prospect for that extended partition. By Step 3, the resulting [EU] functional is independent of the particular extended partition chosen, so that it is well defined.

STEP 5. We show that the functional defined in Step 4 represents preference. For each preference between two prospects, we can take an extended partition such that both prospects have outcome events generated by this extended partition. The [EU] representation within that extended partition ensures that the prospects are ordered properly by the functional defined in Step 4. So it is indeed representing.

In this way we have established the desired behavioral foundation. The usual uniqueness results follow from considering any values $U(\gamma) > U(\beta)$ in Eq. (G.1) in the above reasoning.

Theorem 4.8.3 is different in nature than the functionals considered in the above reasoning in that there is no separation of utility and weighting functions. Debreu (1960) provided the result only for finite state spaces. For the extension to infinite S, we normalize each V_E to be 0 at 0, and let $V_S(1)$ be 1. Then we follow the same five steps as before and the result follows.

Appendix H: Measure theory

In this appendix we assume Structural Assumption 1.2.1 [decision under uncertainty]. By repeated application, additivity of a probability measure P on S implies *finite additivity*: for every array of disjoint events $E_1, \ldots, E_n$, $P(E_1 \cup \cdots \cup E_n) = P(E_1) + \cdots + P(E_n)$. For many purposes it is desirable to extend this property to *countable additivity*: for every countable sequence of disjoint events $E_1, E_2, \ldots$, $P(E_1 \cup E_2 \cup \cdots) = P(E_1) + P(E_2) + \cdots$. Finite additivity does not imply countable additivity, as examples can show. Instead of countable additivity, the term σ-additivity is sometimes used in the literature.

It turned out that for the best-known measure, the regular Lebesgue measure (that assigns to each interval in the reals its length) there exists no countably additive extension to all subsets of the reals (Banach & Kuratowski 1929; Ulam 1930). Hence, mathematicians nowadays often use measure theory. In measure theory, the domain of definition of measures is restricted to algebras or sigma-algebras of subsets. A textbook on measure theory is Halmos (1950).

An *algebra* on a set S is a collection of subsets of S that contains $\varnothing$ and S, and is closed under union (if the algebra contains two sets A and B then it also contains their union $A \cup B$) and complementation (if the algebra contains a set E then it also contains its complement $E^c = S - E$). It can be demonstrated that algebras are closed under finite unions and finite intersections. Obviously, the collection of all subsets of S is an algebra. Hence, the approach used in this book is a special case. A *sigma-algebra* is an algebra that is closed under countable unions (if it contains $A_1, A_2, \ldots$ then it also contains $\cup_{j=1}^{\infty} A_j$). As can be seen, it then is also closed under countable intersections.

In measure theory, we endow the state space S with an algebra of subsets, possibly a sigma-algebra, denoted $\mathcal{A}$. Only the elements of $\mathcal{A}$ are called *events*. The set of prospects is restricted to the set $E_1 x_1 \ldots E_n x_n$ whose outcome events E_j are contained in $\mathcal{A}$; only such prospects are in the domain of preference. We summarize the case.

Structural Assumption H.1 [Decision under uncertainty with measure theory]. S is a, finite or infinite, state space endowed with an algebra $\mathcal{A}$. The term *event* is used only for subsets of S that are contained in $\mathcal{A}$. $\mathbb{R}$ is the outcome set. Prospects map states to outcomes, taking only finitely many values, with all outcome events contained in $\mathcal{A}$.

The set of prospects is the set of all such maps. $\succcurlyeq$ is a preference relation on the set of prospects. Nondegeneracy holds. □

The measure-theoretic structure does not affect any result in this book.

Observation H.2. In all results in this book, Structural Assumption 1.2.1 (decision under uncertainty) can be replaced by Structural Assumption H.1 (decision under uncertainty with measure theory). □

It can be seen that a finitely additive P is countably additive if and only if it satisfies *set-continuity* (Wakker 1993a, §4): $P(A_j) \downarrow 0$ whenever $A_j \downarrow 0$, where the latter means that $A_{j+1} \subset A_j$ for all j and $\cap_{j=1}^{\infty} A_j$ is empty. The following preference condition is necessary and sufficient for countable additivity of probability measures: $\succcurlyeq$ satisfies *set-continuity* if for all events $A_j \downarrow \emptyset$, outcomes $\gamma \succ \beta$, and prospects x with $x \succ \beta$, we have $x \succ \gamma_{A_j}\beta$ for all j sufficiently large[1]. Although countable additivity can be defined and given a behavioral foundation on general algebras of events, its properties are most useful on sigma-algebras. We, hence, consider only the latter for countable additivity. Because the following observation readily follows from substitution, no proof is given.

Observation H.3. In all behavioral foundations in this book that concern probability measures (de Finetti's Theorem 1.6.1 and the uncertainty-EU Theorem 4.6.4), under Structural Assumption H.1 (decision under uncertainty with measure theory) with $\mathcal{A}$ a sigma-algebra, P is countably additive if and only if the preference relation satisfies set-continuity. □

Set-continuity can similarly be defined for weighting functions, and behavioral foundations can similarly be obtained straightforwardly. However, for weighting functions it is interesting to develop more advanced concepts of set continuity referring to ranks and decision weights. Such definitions will include set continuity of the duals of weighting functions. We will not pursue this topic here.

Extensions of the theoretical results of this book to nonsimple (*simple* means finite-valued) prospects can be obtained as in Wakker (1993a). We do not pursue this point. For decision theory, the assumption of algebras of events is undesirably restrictive for many purposes (Krantz *et al.* 1971 p. 373; Luce 2000 §1.1.6.1). Mosaic structures, introduced by Kopylov (2007) and used by Abdellaoui & Wakker (2005), are promising generalizations.

---

[1] "Sufficiently large" means that there exists a J such that $\gamma_{A_j}\beta \prec x$ for all $j > J$.

Appendix I: Related textbooks and surveys

The topic of the first part of this book, expected utility, has been covered by many textbooks and surveys. The focus on measurement and behavioral foundations, as in this book, is primarily found in books from decision analysis (risk theory applied to management science). These include Bunn (1984), Clemen (1991; the first part has much material on modeling actual decision situations and there are many case studies), von Winterfeldt & Edwards (1986), Keeney & Raiffa (1976; Chs. 1–4, with Chs. 5 and 6 focusing on questions of aggregation as in our §3.7; read Raiffa 1968 first), and Raiffa (1968 Chs. 1, 2 ,4, 5, 6). Although Luce & Raiffa (1957) is mostly on game theory, its presentation of uncertainty and risk in Chs. 2 and 13 is outstanding. Economic works include the well-written Drèze (1987 first two chapters), Gollier (2001a), Kreps (1988), Machina (1987), and Mas-Colell, Whinston, & Green (1995 Chs. 1, 6). Mathematical works include the valuable and efficient collection of material in Fishburn (1970, 1981), the deep and rich Krantz *et al.* (1971), and the impressive and mature Pfanzagl (1968). Fishburn (1972) gives a convenient introduction to the mathematics of decision theory. Medical works close to the topic of this book include the accessible Sox *et al.* (1986) and the deeper and more technical Weinstein *et al.* (1980), with a broader exposition on cost-effectiveness analyses in Drummond *et al.* (1987) and Gold *et al.* (1996). Philosophical works include the impressive Broome (1991). Statistically oriented textbooks are Pratt, Raiffa, & Schlaifer (1965) and Winkler (1972).

There have not been as many books and surveys that incorporate nonexpected utility theories. Economic works include Camerer (1995), Camerer & Weber (1992), and Starmer (2000). Halpern (2003) concerns non Bayesian measures of belief and the different ways to update these as relevant to artificial intelligence, and Sugden (2004) is philosophically oriented. Psychological works include Baron (2008), the impressive Edwards (1954) containing many modern ideas, Luce (2000; with an accessible introduction in Luce 1990), and Yates (1990) with an emphasis on probability measurement. Mathematical topics are the primary focus in Karni &

Schmeidler (1991), Schmidt (2004), and Wakker (1989a). For rank-dependent utility, the only book known to me is Quiggin (1993), a rich source of research ideas. I am not aware of a textbook on prospect theory. Close to this book is Gilboa (2009). It presents various theories of decision under uncertainty and behavioral foundations, focusing on philosophical and methodological aspects.

Appendix J: Elaborations of exercises

If you do not know how to solve an exercise, then it is not yet time to inspect the elaborations provided here. It is better then to restudy the preceding theory so as to find out what is missing in your knowledge. Such searches for lacks in knowledge comprise the most fruitful part of learning new ideas.

Exercise 1.1.1.

(a) A: {Bil}; B: {Bill, no-one}; C: {Bill, Jane, Kate}; D: {Jane, Kate}; E: {Jane, Kate}. Note that D = E.

(b) x: (Bill: n, Jane: α, Kate: α, no-one: α); y: (Bill: n, Jane: n, Kate: α, no-one: n); z: (Bill: α, Jane: n, Kate: n, no-one: n).

(c) $2^4 = 16$, being the number of ways to assign either an apple or nothing to each element of S.

(d) Two exist, being α and n. It is allowed to denote constant prospects just by their outcome, as we did. We can also write them as (Bill: α, Jane: α, Kate: α, no-one: α) and (Bill: n, Jane: n, Kate: n, no-one: n). □

Exercise 1.1.2. The anwer is no. Because only one state of nature is true, s_1 and s_2 cannot both happen, and $s_1 \cap s_2 = \varnothing$. Indeed, it is not possible that both horses win. $P(s_1 \cap s_2) = 0 \neq 1/8 = P(s_1) \times P(s_2)$. Stochastic independence is typically interesting for repeated observations. Decision theory as in this book focuses on single decisions, where a true state of nature obtains only one time. The horse race takes place only once. Hence stochastic independence plays no role in this book. □

Exercise 1.2.1. To verify transitivity, assume $x \succcurlyeq y$ and $y \succcurlyeq z$. $V(x) \geq V(y)$ and $V(y) \geq V(z)$ imply $V(x) \geq V(z)$. Now $x \succcurlyeq z$ follows.

To verify completeness, consider x,y. We have $V(x) \geq V(y)$ or $V(y) \geq V(x)$ (possibly both) and, hence, $x \succcurlyeq y$ or $y \succcurlyeq x$ (possibly both). □

Exercise 1.2.2.

(a) If V represents $\geqslant$, then $\geqslant$ is a weak order. Then, for all prospects x,y, we have equivalence of the following four statements:

$$[V(x) > V(y)]; \; [V(x) \geq V(y) \text{ and not } V(y) \geq V(x)];$$
$$[x \geqslant y \text{ and not } y \geqslant x]; [x \succ y],$$

the second and third statement being equivalent because V is representing. Equivalence of the first and fourth statement is what was to be proved. A reverse implication can be proved in the sense that the claim in (a) of the exercise implies that V represents $\geqslant$.

(b) If V represents $\geqslant$, then $\geqslant$ is a weak order. Then we have equivalence of the following four statements

$$[x \sim y]; [x \geqslant y \text{ and } y \geqslant x]; [V(x) \geq V(y) \text{ and } V(y) \geq V(x)]; [V(x) = V(y)].$$

Equivalence of the first and fourth statement is what was to be proved. □

Exercise 1.2.3.

(a) Completeness means that, for all prospects x,y, we have $x \geqslant y$ or $y \geqslant x$. Because this holds for all x,y, it also holds for x,y with $y = x$. That is, $x \geqslant x$ or $x \geqslant x$ must hold. This means, of course, that $x \geqslant x$ must hold for all x: $\geqslant$ is reflexive. $x \geqslant x$ implies $[x \geqslant x \text{ and } x \leqslant x]$, that is, $x \sim x$. This implies that $\sim$ is reflexive.

(b) Assume that $x \succ y$ and $y \succ z$. This implies $x \geqslant y$ and $y \geqslant z$. By transitivity, $x \geqslant z$. To prove that $x \succ z$ we must prove that, furthermore, not $z \geqslant x$. Well, $z \geqslant x$ leads to contradiction because $z \geqslant x$, $x \geqslant y$, and transitivity imply $z \geqslant y$, which, however, contradicts the assumed $y \succ z$.

(c) $x \succ y$ implies $x \geqslant y$. $y \succ x$, however, implies $[\text{not } x \geqslant y]$. This contradicts the preceding sentence and, hence $[x \succ y \text{ and } y \succ x]$ cannot hold.

(d) $y \succ x$ implies $[\text{not } x \geqslant y]$, contradicting $x \geqslant y$. Hence, $[y \succ x \text{ and } x \geqslant y]$ cannot hold.

(e) $x \geqslant y$ and $y \geqslant z$ (the latter implied by the assumed $y \succ z$) imply $x \geqslant z$. For contradiction, assume $z \geqslant x$. This and $x \geqslant y$ imply $z \geqslant y$, contradicting the assumed $y \succ z$. Hence, $z \geqslant x$ cannot hold. We have shown that $x \geqslant z$ and not $z \geqslant x$, so that $x \succ z$.

(f) $x \succ y$ implies $x \geqslant y$. This, $y \geqslant z$, and transitivity imply $x \geqslant z$. To get $x \succ z$ we must show that not $z \geqslant x$. Well, $z \geqslant x$, $y \geqslant z$, and transitivity imply $y \geqslant x$ which contradicts the assumed $x \succ y$.

(g) $x \geqslant y$, $y \geqslant f$, and transitivity imply $x \geqslant f$. This, $f \geqslant g$, and transitivity imply $x \geqslant g$.

(h) Reflexivity was proved in (a). For transitivity, assume $x \sim y$ and $y \sim z$. We show that $x \sim z$. $[x \sim y \text{ and } y \sim z]$ implies $x \geqslant y$ and $y \geqslant z$, so that, by transitivity, $x \geqslant z$. Also $[x \sim y \text{ and } y \sim z]$ implies $z \geqslant y$ and $y \geqslant x$. By transitivity, $z \geqslant x$. We have derived both $x \geqslant z$ and $z \geqslant x$, implying $x \sim z$.

(i) Assume $y \sim x$. Then $y \succcurlyeq x$ and $x \succcurlyeq y$.

$x \succcurlyeq f$ and $y \succcurlyeq x$ imply $y \succcurlyeq f$.

$y \succcurlyeq f$ and $x \succcurlyeq y$ imply $x \succcurlyeq f$.

So, $x \succcurlyeq f$ is equivalent to $y \succcurlyeq f$. A similar reasoning, with everywhere $\preccurlyeq$ instead of $\succcurlyeq$, shows that $x \preccurlyeq f$ is equivalent to $y \preccurlyeq f$.

$x \succ f, y \succcurlyeq x$, and part (e) (write $y \succcurlyeq x$ and $x \succ f$) imply $y \succ f$.

$y \succ f, x \succcurlyeq y$, and part (e) (write $x \succcurlyeq y$ and $y \succ f$) imply $x \succ f$.

So, $x \succ f$ is equivalent to $y \succ f$.

$x \prec f, y \preccurlyeq x$, and part (f) (write $f \succ x$ and $x \succcurlyeq y$) imply $f \succ y$.

$y \prec f, x \preccurlyeq y$, and part (f) (write $f \succ y$ and $y \succcurlyeq x$) imply $f \succ x$.

So, $x \prec f$ is equivalent to $y \prec f$.

$x \sim f, y \sim x$ and transitivity of $\sim$ (part (h)) imply $y \sim f$.

$y \sim f, x \sim y$ and transitivity of $\sim$ (part (h)) imply $x \sim f$.

So, $x \sim f$ is equivalent to $y \sim f$.

(j) By definition, $x \succ y$ implies [not $y \succcurlyeq x$].

If [not $y \succcurlyeq x$] then, by completeness, $x \succcurlyeq y$. This and [not $y \succcurlyeq x$] imply $x \succ y$. $\square$

Exercise 1.2.4.

(a) Define the E_m's as intersections $A_i \cap B_j$. In formal notation,

$$E_1 = A_1 \cap B_1, E_{\ell+1} = A_2 \cap B_1, \dots, E_{(k-1)\ell+1} = A_k \cap B_1$$
$$E_2 = A_1 \cap B_2, E_{\ell+2} = A_2 \cap B_2, \dots, E_{(k-1)\ell+2} = A_k \cap B_2$$
$$\vdots$$
$$E_\ell = A_1 \cap B_\ell, E_{2\ell} = A_2 \cap B_\ell, \dots, E_{k\ell} = A_k \cap B_\ell,$$

with $n = k\ell$. There is no restriction on these events being dependent or independent in any sense, and some intersections may be empty for instance. To obtain $E_1 x_1 \cdots E_n x_n = A_1 a_1 \cdots A_k a_k$, we "remember" for each E_m which A_i was involved in $E_m = A_i \cap B_j$ and then set $x_m = a_i$, so that $x_1 = \cdots = x_\ell = a_1, x_{\ell+1} = \cdots = x_{2\ell} = a_2$, $x_{(k-1)\ell+1} = \cdots = x_{k\ell} = a_k$. To obtain $E_1 y_1 \cdots E_n y_n = B_1 b_1 \cdots B_\ell b_\ell$ we, similarly, define $y_1 = b_1, \dots, y_\ell = b_\ell, y_{\ell+1} = b_1, \dots, y_{2\ell} = b_\ell, \dots, y_{k\ell} = b_\ell$.

(b) This follows from repeated application of (a). It can also be seen immediately: For each way to specify an outcome event for each prospect there is an event E_j. Each prospect assigns to E_j the outcome of its corresponding outcome event. If there are m prospects in total, having $k_1, \dots, k_m$ outcomes in total, respectively, then there are $k_1 \times \cdots \times k_m = n$ events E_j, of which some may be empty. $\square$

Exercise 1.2.5.

(a) Because of monotonicity, with α,β to the left designating real numbers and α,β
to the right designating constant prospects, we have:

if $α > β$ then $α \succ β$;
if $α = β$ then $α \sim β$;
if $α < β$ then $α \prec β$.

In all three cases, preferences agree with the natural ordering of real numbers.
Because of completeness, there are no cases other than these three. Hence, $[α \geq β$
$\Leftrightarrow (α,\ldots,α) \succcurlyeq (β,\ldots,β)]$ always holds.

(b) $x \sim (CE(x),\ldots,CE(x))$ and $y \sim (CE(y),\ldots,CE(y))$ imply
$[x \succcurlyeq y \Leftrightarrow (CE(x),\ldots,CE(x)) \succcurlyeq (CE(y),\ldots,CE(y))]$. By part (a), this holds if and
only if $CE(x) \geq CE(y)$. That is, CE represents $\succcurlyeq$. □

Exercise 1.3.2. $EV(x) = 150$ and $EV(y) = 125$. Hence, $x \succ y$. □

Exercise 1.3.3. The preference implies $P(s_1) \times 400 > P(s_3) \times 400$. Cancel 400. □

Exercise 1.3.5. $P(s_1)100 + (1-P(s_1))0 = 50$, which implies $P(s_1) = ½$. Similarly,
$P(s_2) = ¼$. $P(s_3) = 1 - ½ - ¼ = ¼$. CE $(100_{s_3}0) = ¼ \times 100 = 25$. $100_{s_2}0 \sim 100_{s_3}0$. □

Exercise 1.4.2.

(a) The first indifference implies $p_1 = ¼$, and the second $p_1 + p_2 = ½$ so that $p_2 = ¼$.
It follows that $p_3 = 1 - ¼ - ¼ = ½$. These findings are consistent with the
last indifference, which implies $p_2 + p_3 + ⅔$.

(b) $CE(6, 6, 12) = ⁶⁄₄ + ⁶⁄₄ + ¹²⁄₂ = 9$. $CE(32, 0, 0) = ³²⁄₄ = 8$. The resulting
preference is $(6,6,12) \succ (32,0,0)$. □

Exercise 1.4.3.

(a) The first two indifferences imply $p_1 = 0.25$, $p_2 = 0.25$, and $p_3 = 0.50$, as we
saw in Exercise 1.4.2. Then the third prospect should, however, have a CE value
3 and not 2 as it does now.

(b) (0.28, 0.22, 0.50) fits the data best (see table).

(c) The best-fitting probability vector is (0.30, 0.20, 0.50); see the table. Then
$CE(8,0,8) = 6.40$, $CE(24,0,0) = 7.20$, and (24,0,0) is preferred.

Table. *CEs for probability vectors (rows), prospects (columns)*

	(8,0,0)	(8,8,0)	(0,4,4)	distance
(0.25, 0.25, 0.50)	2.00	4.00	3.00	0.58
(0.28, 0.22, 0.50)	2.24	4.00	2.88	0.53
(0.24, 0.24, 0.52)	1.92	3.84	3.04	0.61
(0.30, 0.20, 0.50)	2.40	4.00	2.80	0.52

□

Exercise 1.5.1.

(a) $x^i \succcurlyeq y^i$ and additivity immediately imply $x^i + \sum_{j \neq i} y^j \succcurlyeq y^i + \sum_{j \neq i} y^j$.

(b) This follows, simply, from repeated application of part (a): $y^1 + \cdots + y^m \preccurlyeq x^1 + y^2$
$+ \cdots + y^m \preccurlyeq x^1 + x^2 + y^3 + \cdots + y^m \preccurlyeq \cdots x^1 + \cdots + x^{m-1} + y^m \preccurlyeq x^1 + \cdots + + x^m$
and transitivity imply the claim. $\square$

Exercise 1.5.2. Assume a Dutch book. By transitivity, additivity, and Exercise 1.5.1b, the assumed preferences imply the preference $\sum_{j=1}^m x^j \succcurlyeq \sum_{j=1}^m y^j$. This preference, however, violates monotonicity. $\square$

Exercise 1.5.3.

(a) Assume, for contradiction, $x(s) < y(s)$ for all s but not $x \prec y$; i.e., $x \succcurlyeq y$.
We derive a Dutch book. Defining $m = 1$, $x^1 = x$, $y^1 = y$ immediately gives a Dutch book.

(b) Assume, for contradiction, $x(s) \geq y(s)$ for all s but $x \prec y$, so that $CE(x) < CE(y)$.
We derive a Dutch book. We have

$$CE(x) \sim x$$

$$y \sim CE(y)$$

$$CE(x) + y(s) < x(s) + CE(y) \text{ for all } s$$

constituting a Dutch book.

(c) To derive additivity of preference, we first prove that CE is *additive*; i.e.,
$CE(x + y) = CE(x) + CE(y)$.
Consider

$$x \sim CE(x)$$

$$y \sim CE(y)$$

$$CE(x + y) \sim x + y.$$

If $CE(x + y) < CE(x) + CE(y)$, then a Dutch book is obtained by replacing all equivalences by $\succcurlyeq$ and adding left-hand sides of the preferences and right-hand sides. If $CE(x + y) > CE(x) + CE(y)$, then a Dutch book similarly is obtained by replacing all equivalences by $\preccurlyeq$. Hence, CE must be additive.

Now assume $x \succcurlyeq y$. Then $CE(x) \geq CE(y)$, $CE(x) + CE(z) \geq CE(y) + CE(z)$, by additivity of CE we get $CE(x + z) \geq CE(y + z)$, and $x + z \succcurlyeq y + z$ follows. This proves additivity. $\square$

Exercise 1.6.1. Example 1.6.2 also provides a Dutch book here. $(1,1,1) \succcurlyeq (3,3,0)$, $(1,1,1) \succcurlyeq (0,0,3)$ provides another, with $(2,2,2)$ dominated by $(3,3,3)$. $\square$

Exercise 1.6.2.

	no rain	some rain	all rain			no rain	some rain	all rain
x^1	301	0	0	$\succcurlyeq$	y^1	300	300	300
x^2	0	301	0	$\succcurlyeq$	y^2	300	300	300
x^3	0	0	301	$\succcurlyeq$	y^3	300	300	300
$x^1 + x^2 + x^3$	301	301	301		$y^1 + y^2 + y^3$	900	900	900

□

Exercise 1.6.3.

	no rain	some rain	all rain			no rain	some rain	all rain
x^1	−1	1	1	$\succcurlyeq$	y^1	100	−1	−1
x^2	1	−1	1	$\succcurlyeq$	y^2	−1	100	−1
x^3	1	1	−1	$\succcurlyeq$	y^3	−1	−1	100
$x^1 + x^2 + x^3$	1	1	1		$y^1 + y^2 + y^3$	98	98	98

□

Exercise 1.6.4. Weak ordering has been derived in Exercise 1.2.1 and the certainty equivalent CE(x) of a prospect x is its expected value. We first derive the most difficult implication, of (ii). Assume a Dutch book. By Exercise 1.2.4 (partition flexibility), we may assume that the prospects involved relate to the same partition $E_1,\ldots,E_n$ of events, that we suppress. The Dutch book consists of preferences as in Figure 1.5.1. Consider the two matrices

$$
\begin{array}{ccc}
P(E_1)x_1^1 \cdots P(E_n)x_n^1 & & P(E_1)y_1^1 \cdots P(E_n)y_n^1 \\
\vdots \qquad \vdots & \text{and} & \vdots \qquad \vdots \\
P(E_1)x_1^m \cdots P(E_n)x_n^m & & P(E_1)y_1^m \cdots P(E_n)y_n^m
\end{array}
$$

In the following proof we will compare the sum of all elements of the left matrix with the sum of all elements of the right matrix, first summing column-wise and then summing row-wise. Each jth x-column sums to strictly less than the corresponding y-column whenever $P(E_j) > 0$, and to the same whenever $P(E_j) = 0$. Therefore, the sum of the left columns does not exceed the sum of the right columns. Because at least one $P(E_j) > 0$, at least one left column is strictly less than the corresponding right column and, therefore:

total sum of the elements in the left matrix

<

total sum of the elements in the right matrix.

The preferences imply, however, that the element-sum of each row of the left matrix weakly exceeds the element-sum of the corresponding row of the right column, by Statement (i). It follows that total sum of the elements in the left matrix

$\geq$

total sum of the elements in the right matrix.

A contradiction has resulted. No Dutch book can exist, and Part (ii) holds. Part (ii) can also be derived from Part (iii) (which is easier to prove) plus Exercise 1.5.2.

[(i) $\Rightarrow$ (iii)] follows from [(i) $\Rightarrow$ (ii)] and the (difficult) Exercise 1.5.3. A direct proof of [(i) $\Rightarrow$ (iii)] is simpler: Monotonicity is immediate and additivity of preference easily follows from additivity of the representing certainty-equivalent function CE (i.e. $CE(x + y) = CE(x) + CE(y)$), CE being expected value. $\square$

Exercise 1.6.5.

(a) The expected value is $P(E)(1-(1-r)^2) + (1-P(E))(1-r^2)$. The first-order optimality condition for r yields $2P(E)(1-r) - 2r(1-P(E)) = 0$, $P(E)(1-r) = r(1-P(E))$, and cancelling the term $-rP(E)$ gives $P(E) = r$.
(b) The expected value is $P(E)ln(r) + (1-P(E))ln(1-r)$. The first-order optimality condition for r yields $P(E)/r - (1-P(E))/(1-r) = 0$,

$$\frac{P(E)(1-r) - r(1-P(E))}{r(1-r)} = 0, P(E)(1-r) = r(1-P(E)),$$

and cancelling the term $-rP(E)$ gives $P(E) = r$.

Comment. This exercise demonstrates a particularly simple, and highly appealing, method for eliciting probabilities, known as proper scoring rules. One observed choice of r immediately gives a subjective probability $P(E) = r$. This can also be inferred from an indifference $1_E 0 \sim p$, but indifferences are hard to observe empirically. Proper scoring rules were discovered independently by Brier (1950), de Finetti (1962; see also Savage 1971), Good (1952 p. 112), and others. A recent work is Prelec (2004). Yates (1990) provides a well-written explanation of proper scoring rules. $\square$

Exercise 1.6.6.

(a) We have, with the first preference even holding with indifference and the second following from symmetry:

$$CE_H CE \geqslant \gamma_H \beta$$
$$CE_H CE \geqslant \beta_H \gamma$$
$$\overline{2CE_H 2CE \quad (\gamma+\beta)_H(\gamma+\beta)} +$$

which entails a Dutch book because $2CE < \gamma + \beta$.
(b) As (a), with preferences and inequality reversed. $\square$

Exercise 1.7.1. In this case, the decision maker can partly influence the truth of events. The analyses of this book are valid, however, only if the decision maker cannot influence the truth of the events. In particular, monotonicity is normatively compelling only under this restriction. □

Exercise 2.1.1. Assumption 2.1.2 does not hold. $1_{E_1}0$ and $1_{E_2}0$ both generate the probability-contingent prospect $1_{1/6}0$ but they are not equivalent because $1_{E_1}0 \succ 1_{E_2}0$. □

Exercise 2.1.2.

(a) x generates ($\frac{1}{3}$:8, $\frac{1}{3}$:3, $\frac{1}{3}$:2).
   y generates ($\frac{1}{3}$:5, $\frac{1}{3}$:4, $\frac{1}{3}$:3).
   f generates the same probability-contingent prospect as x, and g as y.
   By Assumption 2.1.2, f $\sim$ x and g $\sim$ y, and y $\succcurlyeq$ x implies g $\succcurlyeq$ f.
(b) $[0,\frac{1}{4})8[\frac{1}{4},1)2$ and $[0,\frac{3}{4})2[\frac{3}{4},1)8$ are two examples. $[0,\frac{3}{8})2[\frac{3}{8},\frac{5}{8})8[\frac{5}{8},1)2$ is yet another example. □

Exercise 2.3.1. Each event-contingent prospect $100_{E_j}0$ generates the same probability-contingent prospect $100_{1/6}0$, where the probabilities refer to the objective probability measure P. By Assumption 2.1.2 (decision under risk), these prospects are all equivalent. By strict stochastic dominance for Q, this can only be if $Q(E_j)$ is the same for all j. Because the six $Q(E_j)$'s sum to 1, each is $\frac{1}{6}$. □

Exercise 2.5.2. $EU(49_{0.9}16) = 0.9 \times \sqrt{49} + 0.1 \times \sqrt{16} = 6.3 + 0.4 = 6.7$.
$EU(81_{0.7}16) = 0.7 \times \sqrt{81} + 0.3 \times \sqrt{16} = 6.3 + 1.2 = 7.5$. Hence, $49_{0.9}16 \prec 81_{0.7}16$. □

Exercise 2.5.4. $U(60) = 0.70$ and indifference results with $EU = 0.49$. □

Exercise 2.6.1. $U(\alpha) = pU(M) + (1-p)U(m)$ so that $U(\alpha) - U(m) = p(U(M) - U(m))$. This implies $p = (U(\alpha) - U(m))/(U(M) - U(m))$. □

Exercise 2.6.2. We consider $M > m$. The outcomes are associated with riskless prospects and the EU of M is U(M) and of m it is U(m). Because U is strictly increasing, $U(M) > U(m)$. This implies, for $p > q$, that $pU(M) + (1-p)U(m) > qU(M) + (1-q)U(m)$; i.e., it implies the preference depicted for SG dominance. □

Exercise 2.6.3.

(a) By SG dominance, for any two different probabilities $q \neq r$, the prospects M_qm and M_rm are not equivalent. Hence, $\alpha \sim M_pm$ for no more than one p.
(b) If $p = 0$ then the prospect is the riskless prospect yielding m for sure. By assumption, we have identified this riskless prospect with the outcome m and, hence, the prospect is equivalent to m. We can choose $p = 0$ in Figure 2.5.3 and by (a) we have to do so.
(c) This is similar to (b).
(d) $p = 0$ would imply $\alpha \sim m$ and, hence, is excluded; $p = 1$ would imply $\alpha \sim M$ and, hence, is also excluded. □

Exercise 2.6.4. Replacing U by σU simply means that all expected utilities of prospects are also multiplied by σ. Because σ is positive, this multiplication does not change the EU ordering of prospects. Adding τ to the utility function means that all expected utilities of prospects are increased by τ which, again, does not change the EU ordering of prospects. In all these operations, the utility function continues to be strictly increasing, as is required under EU. $\square$

Exercise 2.6.5. First assume that U is continuous. Then for each prospect x, EU(x) is between the utility of the best and the worst outcomes of x. By continuity of U, there is an outcome between these best and worst outcomes with utility equal to EU(x). This is the certainty equivalent. Conversely, suppose that a certainty equivalent exists for each prospect. Take some outcomes $m < M$, and consider the prospects $M_p m$. For each p there exists a certainty equivalent, so that all values between U(m) and U(M) are contained in the range of U. The strictly increasing U cannot make jumps, and must be continuous. Whereas SG solvability implies that the probability scale is at least as refined as the outcome scale, continuity implies the opposite. $\square$

Exercise 2.6.6. For mathematicians: This result reflects the well-known property of integrals of being linear in probability. The result can be verified algebraically by substituting the formula and regrouping terms. To see this point, let x be the prospect $p_1 x_1 \cdots p_n x_n$ and y the prospect $q_1 y_1 \cdots q_m y_m$. Their mixture is

$$\lambda p_1 x_1 \cdots \lambda p_n x_n (1 - \lambda) q_1 y_1 \cdots (1 - \lambda) q_m y_m.$$

The EU value of the mixture is

$$\lambda p_1 U(x_1) + \cdots + \lambda p_n U(x_n) + (1 - \lambda) q_1 U(y_1) + \cdots + (1 - \lambda) q_m U(y_m)$$
$$= \lambda(p_1 U(x_1) + \cdots + p_n U(x_n)) + (1 - \lambda)(q_1 U(y_1) + \cdots + q_m U(y_m))$$
$$= \lambda EU(x) + (1 - \lambda) EU(y). \square$$

Exercise 2.7.1. Assume that a probability mass p is shifted from an outcome β to a better outcome γ in a prospect, so that the probability of β is decreased by p and the probability of γ is increased by p. (A special case occurs if the probability of outcome γ was 0 and the probability of outcome β was p originally, and it is changed to a probability p of γ and probability 0 of β. In this case, outcome β has been improved into outcome γ.) Then the EU of the prospect increases by $p(U(\gamma) - U(\beta))$, which is nonnegative. Repeated shifts of probability mass as just described generate repeated improvements of the EU of a prospect. $\square$

Exercise 2.7.2.
For $0 < \lambda < 1$, the ordering of

$$EU(x_\lambda C) = \lambda EU(x) + (1 - \lambda) EU(C) \text{ and}$$
$$EU(y_\lambda C) = \lambda EU(y) + (1 - \lambda) EU(C)$$

is the same as that of EU(x) and EU(y). Because EU represents preference, the independence condition for preference follows. $\square$

Exercise 2.7.3. The first preference in Figure 2.7.1 implies $pU(\beta)+$ $\sum_{j=2}^{n} p_{j}U(x_{j}) \geq pU(\beta) + \sum_{i=2}^{m} q_{i}U(y_{i})$, which implies $\sum_{j=2}^{n} p_{j}U(x_{j}) \geq \sum_{i=2}^{m} q_{i}U(y_{i})$, and $pU(\gamma) + \sum_{j=2}^{n} p_{j}U(x_{j}) \geq pU(\gamma) + \sum_{i=2}^{m} q_{i}U(y_{i})$. This implies the second preference. □

Exercise 3.1.1. The switching utility, denoted β, must be such that the EU of radiotherapy, $0.6 \times 1 + 0.4 \times 0.4 \times \beta + 0.4 \times 0.6 \times 0$, which is $0.6 + 0.16 \times \beta$, is equal to the EU of surgery, $0.7 \times \beta + 0.3 \times 0.3 \times \beta + 0.3 \times 0.7 \times 0$, which is $0.79 \times \beta$. Hence, $0.6 = 0.63 \times \beta$ and, therefore, $\beta = 0.6/0.63 = 20/21 = 0.9524$. □

Exercise 3.2.1. We only treat the case of concavity and risk aversion, the other cases being similar.

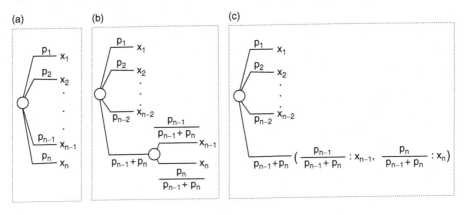

(a) Risk aversion means that for any prospect $p_{1}x_{1} \cdots p_{n}x_{n}$, the utility of its expectation is at least as large as its EU; i.e., $U\left(\sum_{j=1}^{n} p_{j}x_{j}\right) \geq \sum_{j=1}^{n} p_{j}U(x_{j})$. Concavity of utility means that for every pair of outcomes x_{1}, x_{2}, and every pair of numbers p_{1}, p_{2} that are nonnegative and sum to 1, we have $U\left(\sum_{j=1}^{2} p_{j}x_{j}\right) \geq \sum_{j=1}^{2} p_{j}U(x_{j})$. This shows that concavity of utility is equivalent to risk aversion when restricted to two-outcome prospects $(n = 2)$.

(b) We only consider concavity, convexity and linearity being similar. We demonstrate that risk aversion, when restricted to two-outcome prospects, implies risk aversion for all prospects. That is, we show that concavity of U implies that always $U\left(\sum_{j=1}^{n} p_{j}x_{j}\right) \geq \sum_{j=1}^{n} p_{j}U(x_{j})$. The reasoning is depicted in the figure. The idea is to isolate the last two outcomes x_{n-1} and x_{n} of the general prospect in Fig. a into a conditional two-outcome prospect (compare Fig. b) and then to apply risk aversion to that two-outcome prospect.

The EU of the prospect in Fig. a is

$$\sum_{j=1}^{n} p_{j}U(x_{j}) = \sum_{j=1}^{n-2} p_{j}U(x_{j}) + (p_{n-1} + p_{n})(p_{n-1}/(p_{n-1} + p_{n})$$
$$\times U(x_{n-1}) + p_{n}/(p_{n-1} + p_{n}) \times U(x_{n})).$$

The last big bracket describes the EU of the two-outcome prospect $(p_{n-1}/(p_{n-1}+p_n)$: $x_{n-1}, p_n/(p_{n-1}+p_n)$: $x_n)$ in the second stage at the bottom of Fig. b. Applying risk aversion to this prospect implies that the preceding EU is less than

$$\sum_{j=1}^{n-2} p_j U(x_j) + (p_{n-1}+p_n)U(p_{n-1}/(p_{n-1}+p_n) \times x_{n-1} + p_n/(p_{n-1}+p_n) \times x_n),$$

which is the EU of the prospect in Fig. c.

We have demonstrated that replacing two outcomes in a prospect by their average increases the EU of the prospect. It is readily verified that the replacement does not affect the expected value of the prospect. We can continue this process for the $n-1$ outcome prospect in Fig. c, again replace the last two outcomes by their average, thus increasing the EU while maintaining the expected value. After performing this operation $n-1$ times, a one-outcome prospect has resulted with higher EU than the prospect in Fig. a but with the same expected value. Obviously, the one-outcome prospect yields the expected value of the prospect in Fig. a with probability 1, and the utility of this expected value exceeds the EU of the prospect in Fig. a. That is, we have established risk aversion for the general prospect.

We could similarly use a proof by induction: We isolate the first $n-1$ outcomes of an n-outcome prospect. Conditional upon the occurrence of these $n-1$ outcomes we apply an induction hypothesis. It allows us to replace these $n-1$ outcomes by a fixed amount that is equivalent to them and that is smaller than their conditional expectation. Then we use part (a) for the remaining two-outcome prospect.

Remark. The reverse move from Fig. c to Fig. a – splitting out one outcome into two outcomes while preserving the same expected value – is an elementary mean-preserving spread (defined later in §3.3). The first derivation of part (b) in fact demonstrated that concavity of utility implies aversion to elementary mean-preserving spreads. Hence, under EU this is equivalent to risk aversion. □

Exercise 3.2.2. CE abbreviates certainty equivalent. The EU is ½U(80) + ½U(−20) = 0.1123. CE = $U^{-1}(0.1123) = \frac{-ln(1-0.1123)}{\theta} = 23.81$. The risk premium = 30.00 − 23.81 = 6.19. □

Exercise 3.2.3.

(a) Start in the figure at the small *. Draw a horizontal line leftwards. Stop when this line intersects the utility curve. From there, draw a vertical line down. Stop when it hits the x-axis. This point, between α and $p\alpha + (1-p)\beta$, is the certainty equivalent of the prospect; it has utility equal to the EU of the prospect. The distance from this point to the expected value $p\alpha + (1-p)\beta$ is the risk premium.
(b) The risk premium is nonnegative if and only if the expected value exceeds the certainty equivalent, which holds, because utility increases strictly, if and only if the expected value is preferred to the certainty equivalent, which holds if and only if the expected value is preferred to the prospect. □

Exercise 3.3.1. You will not insure your bike. Even though you do not know the probability of theft, you do know that the insurance company makes money. Hence your expected value of insuring must be negative. Hence you, expected value maximizer, prefer not to insure. □

Exercise 3.3.2. The Dutch book is as follows, where E_1: suitcase no. 13 contains $\$2.5 \times 10^6$ and E2: suitcase no. 13 contains \$0.05 are suppressed.

$$(10^6 \, , \, 10^6) \quad \succ \quad (2.5 \times 10^6 \, , \quad 0.05)$$
$$\underline{(10^6 \, , \, 10^6) \quad \succ \quad (0.05 \, , \quad 2.5 \times 10^6)}$$
$$(2 \times 10^6, \, 2 \times 10^6) \qquad \begin{pmatrix} 2.5 \times 10^6 & 25 \times 10^6 \\ + & , & + \\ 0.05 & 0.05 \end{pmatrix}$$

EU can accommodate the preferences with $P(E_1) = P(E_2) = \frac{1}{2}$, $U(0) = 0$, and $U(2.5 \times 10^6) + U(0.05) < 2U(10^6)$.

Although there is more total money to the right of the displayed preferences than to the left, this money to the right is arranged in an unfavorable manner. The money is located in places with much other money present, so that it is worth relatively little. The utility function formalizes these points. □

Exercise 3.3.3.

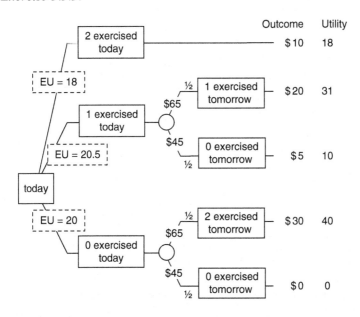

When drawing decision trees one wants to incorporate everything relevant, but also keep the tree simple and tractable. Thus, for the second day, we only depicted the optimal action chosen in each case, because it is all too obvious that the other actions are inferior and will not be chosen anyhow. For example, if no option is exercised today and the price tomorrow turns out to be $65, then it is obvious that exercising both options tomorrow brings more money than exercising only one or none tomorrow. Hence we only depicted the action there of exercising both options.

The optimal strategy, yielding the highest EU, is to exercise one option immediately. The second option is kept until tomorrow, and then it is decided whether the second option will be exercised depending on the price tomorrow. This strategy results in an EU of 20.5, which is the maximal EU available. Apparently, the most risky approach of exercising no option today is too risky given the degree of risk aversion, and the safest approach of exercising both options today is too prudent. The optimum is the intermediate strategy with some safety resulting from one option exercised today and some risk resulting from one option not exercised today. □

Exercise 3.4.1. We use the following notation:

Notation [Function composition]. We use the symbol $\circ$ to denote function composition, which means for instance that $\varphi \circ U_1(\alpha) = \varphi(U_1(\alpha))$. Thus, $\varphi \circ U_1$ means that we first apply U_1, and then φ.

Because utility increases strictly, we have $U_2(\cdot) = \varphi \circ U_1$ for a strictly increasing φ (i.e. $\varphi = U_2 \circ U_1^{-1}$). Because U_1' is positive and continuous, φ is also twice continuously differentiable. We have:

$$U_2' = (\varphi' \circ U_1)U_1' \text{ and } U_2'' = (\varphi'' \circ U_1)(U_1')^2 + (\varphi' \circ U_1)U_1'';$$
$$U_2''/U_2' = ((\varphi'' \circ U_1)(U_1')^2 + (\varphi' \circ U_1)U_1'')/((\varphi' \circ U_1)U_1')$$
$$= ((\varphi'' \circ U_1)/(\varphi' \circ U_1)) \times U_1' + U_1''/U_1'.$$

Given positivity of first derivatives ($U_2' > 0$ implies, by the chain rule for derivatives, $\varphi' > 0$), the ordering of the two Pratt–Arrow indexes is determined by the sign of φ'', and $-U_2''/U_2' \geq -U_1''/U_1'$ everywhere if and only if $\varphi'' \leq 0$ everywhere, which means that φ is concave. □

Exercise 3.5.1. First assume that $\theta \neq 0$. Then multiplying all outcomes of two prospects by a factor $\lambda > 0$ means that all their utilities are multiplied by λ^θ and, hence, so is the EU of the two prospects. This does not affect the ordering of these expected utilities and, hence, it does not affect the preference between them either.

Next consider $\theta = 0$. Then multiplying all outcomes of two prospects by a factor $\lambda > 0$ means that all their utilities are increased by a term $ln(\lambda)$ and, hence, so is the EU of the two prospects. This does not affect the ordering of these expected utilities and, hence, it does not affect the preference between them either. □

Exercise 3.5.2. For $\theta = 0$ we have $U' = 1$ and $U'' = 0$ and the result follows. For $\theta > 0$, $U'(x) = \theta e^{-\theta x}$, $U''(x) = -\theta^2 e^{-\theta x}$, and $-U''/U' = \theta$. For $\theta < 0$, $U'(x) = -\theta e^{-\theta x}$, $U''(x) = \theta^2 e^{-\theta x}$, and $-U''/U' = \theta$. □

Exercise 3.5.3. First assume that $\theta \neq 0$. For $\theta > 0$ we may take $U(\alpha) = -e^{-\theta\alpha}$, dropping the term 1, because U is unique up to level (and unit). For $\theta < 0$ we may take $U(\alpha) = e^{-\theta\alpha}$, dropping the term -1. Then increasing outcomes of two prospects by a term μ means that all their utilities are multiplied by $e^{-\theta\mu}$ and, hence, so is the EU of the two prospects. This does not affect the ordering of these expected utilities and, hence, does not affect the preference between them either.

For $\theta = 0$, utility is linear and adding a term μ to the outcomes means adding the same term to all expected utilities, which, again, does not affect expected utilities. □

Exercise 3.5.4.

(a) Indifference between S and R implies the following equalities: $30^\theta = \frac{1}{2} \times 100^\theta + \frac{1}{2} \times 0^\theta$; $\theta ln(30) = ln(\frac{1}{2}) + \theta ln(100)$; $\theta ln(30) - \theta ln(100) = ln(\frac{1}{2})$ giving the analytic expression $\theta = \frac{ln(\frac{1}{2})}{ln(30) - ln(100)}$. It follows that $\theta \approx 0.576$. S is preferred for all smaller θ, and R for all larger θ.

For CE_1 we have $[CE_1^\theta = \frac{1}{2} \times 200^\theta \Rightarrow CE_1 = (\frac{1}{2} \times 200^\theta)^{1/\theta}]$. For $\theta = 0.576$ this yields $CE_1 = 60.03$. This is close to twice 30, which should come as no surprise in view of Eq. (3.5.3).

For CE_2 we have $[CE_2^\theta = \frac{1}{2} \times 200^\theta + \frac{1}{2} \times 100^\theta \Rightarrow CE_2 = (\frac{1}{2} \times 200^\theta + \frac{1}{2} \times 200^\theta)^{1/\theta}]$. For $\theta = 0.576$ this yields $CE_2 = 146.366$, which exceeds $30 + 100$ considerably.

(b) Indifference between S and R implies the following equalities:

$$1 - e^{-\theta 30} = \frac{1}{2} \times (1 - e^{-\theta 100}) + \frac{1}{2} \times 0 = \frac{1}{2} - \frac{1}{2}e^{-\theta 100};$$

$1 = 2e^{-\theta 30} - e^{-\theta 100}$. I do not know an analytic solution for θ to this equation. Numerical trial and error yields $\theta = 0.018$. Larger θ generate more risk aversion and preference for S, and smaller θ bring preference for R.

For CE_1 we have $1 - e^{-\theta CE_1} = \frac{1}{2} \times (1 - e^{-\theta 200}) + \frac{1}{2} \times 0$, which implies $1 - \frac{1}{2} \times (1 - e^{-\theta 200}) = e^{-\theta CE_1}$, $ln(1 - \frac{1}{2} \times (1 - e^{-\theta 200})) = - CE_1\theta$, and $CE_1 = - \frac{ln(1 - \frac{1}{2} \times (1 - e^{-\theta 200}))}{\theta}$. For $\theta = 0.018$ this implies $CE_1 = 37.011$. Note how far this is below twice 30.

For CE_2 we have $1 - e^{-\theta CE_2} = \frac{1}{2} \times (1 - e^{-\theta 200}) + \frac{1}{2} \times (1 - e^{-\theta 100})$, which implies

$$1 - \frac{1}{2} \times (1 - e^{-\theta 200}) - \frac{1}{2} \times (1 - e^{-\theta 100}) = e^{-\theta CE_2},$$

$$ln\left(1 - \frac{1}{2} \times (1 - e^{-\theta 200}) - \frac{1}{2} \times (1 - e^{-\theta 100})\right) = -\theta CE_2,$$

$$CE_2 = - \frac{ln(1 - \frac{1}{2} \times (1 - e^{-\theta 200}) - \frac{1}{2} \times (1 - e^{-\theta 100}))}{\theta},$$

which, for $\theta = 0.018$, implies $CE_2 = 130.009$. This is close to $30 + 100$, which should come as no surprise in view of Eq. (3.5.6). □

Exercise 3.5.5.

(a) The EU is $\frac{1}{2} - \frac{1}{2}e^{-\theta\beta} + \frac{1}{2} - \frac{1}{2}e^{\theta\beta/2}$. To maximize it, we set the derivative w.r.t. β zero.

$1/2\theta e^{-\theta\beta} - 1/4\theta e^{\theta\beta/2} = 0; 1/2\theta e^{-\theta\beta} = 1/4\theta e^{\theta\beta/2}; 2 = e^{3\theta\beta/2}; ln(2) = 3\theta\beta/2; \beta = 2ln(2)/3\theta.$

So, $\beta \approx 0.46/\theta$. For the second-order condition, the second derivative is $-0.5\theta^2 e^{-\theta\beta} - 0.125\theta^2 e^{\theta\beta/2} < 0$ (because all quantities except the minus signs are positive), so that an optimum is indeed obtained at $\beta \approx 0.46/\theta$.

(b) The result can be calculated simply by substitution: $EU = (1 - e^{-0.96} + 1 - e^{0.48})/2 \approx 0$. I next show how the value of β can be obtained if it had not been given beforehand.

The prospect is indifferent to not gambling if $(1 - e^{-\theta\beta} + 1 - e^{\theta\beta/2})/2 = 1 - e^{-\theta 0} = 0$; i.e., $(-e^{-\theta\beta} - e^{\theta\beta/2})/2 = -e^{-\theta 0}$, and $e^{-\theta\beta} + e^{\theta\beta/2} = 2$. Writing μ for $e^{\theta\beta/2}$ gives $1/\mu^2 + \mu = 2, 1 + \mu^3 = 2\mu^2$, and $\mu^3 - 2\mu^2 + 1 = 0$. We have to solve a third-power polynomial. It can be simplified here because we already know a solution, namely $\beta = 0$ (and $\mu = e^{\theta\beta/2} = 1$). Hence, we can divide the third-power polynomial by $(\mu - 1)$. We get $(\mu - 1)(\mu^2 - \mu - 1) = 0$. $\mu^2 - \mu - 1 = 0$ gives $\mu = 0.5 \pm \sqrt{5/4}$. μ must be positive, so that $\mu = 0.5 + \sqrt{5/4} = 1.62$. $e^{\theta\beta/2} = 1.62$ implies $\theta\beta/2 = ln(1.62)$, $\beta = (2ln(1.62))/\theta \approx 0.96/\theta$. □

Exercise 3.6.1.

(a) Eq. (1.3.2) implies $U(0.01) = 0.10$, $U(0.36) = 0.60$, and $U(0.81) = 0.90$.

(b) $EU(0.81_{2/3}0) = 2/3 \times 0.90 = 0.60$. This is also the utility of 0.36. Hence, $CE(0.81_{2/3}0) = 0.36$.

(c) $\theta = 0.5$. $CE(1_{0.80}0) = U^{-1}(EU(1_{0.80}0)) = 0.80^2 = 0.64$.
$CE(0.80_{0.70}0.25) = U^{-1}(EU(0.80_{0.70}0.25)) = (0.70 \times \sqrt{0.80} + 0.30 \times \sqrt{0.25})^2 = 0.602$.
Hence, $1_{0.80}0$ has the higher CE and is preferred. □

Exercise 3.6.2. The optimal fit is obtained for $\theta = 0.52$, with optimal distance 0.016. The calculation of the distance is as follows, with $U(\alpha) = \alpha^{0.52}$.

$$CE(0.01) = 0.01; CE(1_{0.10}0) = U^{-1}(0.10 \times 1^{0.52} + 0.90 \times 0^{0.52}) = U^{-1}(0.10) = 0.012.$$

$$CE(0.36) = 0.36; CE(1_{0.60}0) = U^{-1}(0.60) = 0.374.$$

$$CE(0.81) = 0.81; CE(1_{0.90}0) = U^{-1}(0.90) = 0.817.$$

$$CE(0.40) = 0.40; CE(0.81_{0.67}0) = U^{-1}(0.67 \times U(0.81)) = 0.371.$$

The distance is

$$\sqrt{\frac{(0.012 - 0.01)^2 + (0.374 - 0.36)^2 + (0.817 - 0.81)^2 + (0.371 - 0.40)^2}{4}} = 0.016.$$

You can carry out similar calculations with some powers other than $\theta = 0.52$ to verify that the distance then is always bigger. For example, $\theta = 0.50$ gives a distance of 0.020.

$CE(1_{2/3}0) = 0.46$, $CE(0.81_{2/3}0.20) = 0.56$, and $0.81_{2/3}0.20$ is preferred. □

Exercise 3.6.3.

(a) We calculate the EU differences of the seven indifference pairs

$$dEU1 = 20^\theta - 0.50 \times 300^\theta; dEU2 = 100^\theta - 0.50 \times 200^\theta;$$

$$dEU3 = 10^\theta - 0.01 \times 200^\theta; dEU4 = 14^\theta - 0.05 \times 100^\theta;$$

$$dEU5 = 39^\theta - 0.50 \times 96^\theta; dEU6 = 55^\theta - 0.95 \times 72^\theta;$$

$$dEU7 = 78^\theta - 0.95 \times 100^\theta,$$

for various θ. A positive difference dEUj implies a safe jth choice.

θ	dEU1	dEU2	dEU3	dEU4	dEU5	dEU6	dEU7
1	−130	0	8	9	−9	−13.4	−17
0.50	−4.19	2.93	3.02	3.24	1.35	−0.64	−0.67
0.75	−26.6	5.03	5.09	5.66	0.27	−3.29	−3.80
0.85	−51.0	4.95	6.18	6.92	−1.69	−5.86	−7.04
0.80	−37.0	5.15	5.61	6.27	−0.52	−4.40	−5.19
0.77	−30.4	5.11	5.30	5.90	−0.0077	−3.70	−4.30
0.76	−28.4	5.07	5.19	5.78	0.14	−3.49	−4.04

$\theta = 1$ has only 2 safe choices and 1 indifference and, hence, is boundary. All $\theta > 1$ are more risk seeking and generate fewer safe choices and, hence, do not work. Some $\theta < 1$ will work, and we find the smallest such.

$\theta = 0.50$ has 4 safe choices and, hence is too risk averse and too small. After some trial and error we find that $\theta = 0.77$ just works, but $\theta = 0.76$ generates too much risk aversion and is too small. There are exactly three positive differences, indicating three safe choices, for $0.77 \leq \theta < 1$. These three safe choices occur for x^2, x^3, and x^4. The index of relative risk aversion is between 0 and 0.23.

(b) For positive θ, calculate the seven EU differences

$$dEU1 = (1 - \exp(-20\theta)) - 0.50 \times (1 - \exp(-300\theta)),$$

$$dEU2 = (1 - \exp(-100\theta)) - 0.50 \times (1 - \exp(-200\theta)),$$

$$dEU3 = (1 - \exp(-10\theta)) - 0.01 \times (1 - \exp(-200\theta)),$$

$$dEU4 = (1 - \exp(-14\theta)) - 0.05 \times (1 - \exp(-100\theta)),$$

$$dEU5 = (1 - \exp(-39\theta)) - 0.50 \times (1 - \exp(-96\theta)),$$

$$dEU6 = (1 - \exp(-55\theta)) - 0.95 \times (1 - \exp(-72\theta)),$$

$$dEU7 = (1 - \exp(-78\theta)) - 0.95 \times (1 - \exp(-100\theta)).$$

A positive difference indicates a safe choice of s, a negative difference indicates a risky choice of r. For negative θ, the seven differences are the EU difference multiplied by −1. The table gives some results for some values of θ.

θ	dEU1	dEU2	dEU3	dEU4	dEU5	dEU6	dEU7
−0.00001	0.0013	0.0000005	−0.00008	−0.00009	0.00009	0.0001	0.0002
0	−130	0	8	9	−9	−13.4	−17
0.1	0.36	0.50	0.62	0.70	0.48	0.047	0.050
0.01	−0.29	0.20	0.087	0.099	0.014	−0.065	−0.059
0.001	−0.11	0.0045	0.0081	0.0091	−0.0075	−0.012	−0.015
0.005	−0.29	0.077	0.042	0.047	−0.013	−0.047	−0.05
0.008	−0.31	0.15	0.069	0.078	−0.000012	−0.060	−0.059
0.009	−0.30	0.18	0.078	0.089	0.0068	−0.063	−0.059

For $\theta = 0$ we have expected value, with indifference for x^2 and safe choices for x^3 and x^4. For $\theta < 0$ the dEUj formulas are EU times -1. Then even for θ close to 0 such as $\theta = -0.00001$, we have too few safe choices, only x^3 and x^4 and maybe fewer if θ is more negative (generating more risk seeking). Trying positive θ's, we see that $\theta = 0.1$ and $\theta = 0.01$ have too many positive EU differences, implying too many safe choices and too much risk aversion. θ will have to be smaller. $\theta = 0.001$ is as desired, with three safe choices. So are $\theta = 0.005$ and $\theta = 0.008$. $\theta = 0.009$ is too large with four safe choices. We conclude that there are exactly three positive differences, indicating three safe choices, for $0 < \theta \leq 0.0080$. These three safe choices then occur for x^2, x^3, and x^4. The Pratt–Arrow index of risk aversion is between 0 and 0.0080. The risk tolerance is $1/0.008 = \$125$ or more. □

Exercise 3.6.4.

(a) The footnote at the exercise with the hint gives the first part of the elaboration. For large θ, such as $\theta = 1$ for my computer, the numbers in the calculations become too large and the computer was not able to calculate results. These θ's give bad fits anyway and are of no interest. For smaller θ, such as $\theta \leq 0.1$ as considered in this exercise, we can calculate distances and find the θ giving the smallest distance. Inspecting all those θ shows that $\theta = 0.006$ performs best, with the smallest distance, 26.78. Table * gives calculations.

Table * *Theoretical CEs for exponential utility with $\theta = 0.006$*

$300_{0.5}0$	$200_{0.5}0$	$200_{0.01}0$	$100_{0.05}0$	$96_{0.5}0$	$72_{0.95}0$	$100_{0.95}0$
90.03	71.64	1.17	3.80	41.18	67.56	93.29

Table ** give some distance for different values of θ. The distance become larger as θ is farther remote from 0.006.

Table **

θ	0.001	0.004	0.005	**0.006**	0.007	0.008	0.01	0.1
distance	32.66	27.45	26.88	**26.78**	27.06	27.59	29.04	43.23

$\mathrm{CE}(300_{2/3}250) = 281.62$ and $\mathrm{CE}(285_{2/3}276) = 281.95$, so that the safer $(286_{2/3}275)$ is just preferred.

(b) Calculating the distance for all $\theta = j/100$ shows that $\theta = 0.59$ fits the data best, with distance 23.88. Table *** gives some calculations.

Table *** *Theoretical CEs for power utility with* $\theta = 0.59$.

$300_{0.5}0$	$200_{0.5}0$	$200_{0.01}0$	$100_{0.05}0$	$96_{0.5}0$	$72_{0.95}0$	$100_{0.95}0$
92.66	61.77	0.08	0.62	29.65	66.00	91.67

Table ****gives some distance.

Table ****

θ	0.01	0.07	0.10	0.50	0.57	0.58	**0.59**	0.60	0.61	1
distance	51.13	46.60	46.93	25.35	23.97	23.91	**23.880**	23.882	23.91	35.46

Under $\theta = 0.59$, EU predicts $\mathrm{CE}(300_{2/3}250) = 282.92$ and $\mathrm{CE}(285_{2/3}276) = 281.99$, predicting preference for the riskier $(300_{2/3}250)$.

As the table shows, there is a local optimum near $\theta = 0.07$ that is not a global optimum. Some programs may erroneously give $\theta = 0.07$ as the optimal result.

(c) The power family, when optimally fitting, has a smaller distance than the exponential family, because $23.88 < 26.78$. Hence, the power family seems to be preferable. I would recommend taking the prospect $300_{2/3}250$ as recommended by power utility. Besides power fitting better, a second reason is that, under exponential utility, the preference is close to indifference so that a wrong choice there would not entail a big mistake anyhow. One could inspect more closely how the data fit is on the outcome domain relevant for the choice now considered, with all outcomes between 250 and 300, but we will not elaborate on this point. □

Exercise 3.6.5. $\theta = 0.0076$, with risk tolerance 131.58, and distance 9.12. $\mathrm{CE}(-100_{0.05}(-200)) = -196.45$.

Table * *Theoretical CEs for* $\theta = 0.0076$

$-100_{0.05}-200$	$150_{0.05}50$	$100_{0.5}0$	$100_{0.95}0$	$0_{0.75}-100$	$0_{0.50}-50$	$0_{0.05}-100$	$101_{0.50}-50$	$50_{0.50}-20$	$112_{0.50}-50$
-196.45	53.54	40.72	92.72	-32.95	-27.36	-96.45	4.93	10.40	7.50

□

Exercise 3.6.5'. It is off by $-196.45 - (-179) = -17.45$. The actual observation is considerably more risk seeking. □

Exercise 3.7.1. The implication (ii) $\Rightarrow$ (i) follows from substitution. We next assume Statement (ii) and derive Statement (i). Fix one health state H. We scale

$U(H,0) = 0$. By the null condition, $U(Q,0) = 0$ for all Q. We define $W(\cdot) = U(H,\cdot)$. Then $W(0) = 0$. Consider another health state Q. Let $M > 0$ (if such an M does not exist the theorem trivially follows). Define $V(Q) = U(Q,M)/U(H,M)$. Substitution of SG consistency implies $U(Q,T) = V(Q)W(T)$, first for all $T < M$, next for all $T > M$ by interchanging T and M in Figure 3.7.1. $\square$

Exercise 4.2.2.

$$EU(x) = \tfrac{1}{2} \times 1 + \tfrac{1}{3} \times \tfrac{1}{2} + \tfrac{1}{6} \times (-2) = \tfrac{1}{3};$$

$$EU(y) = \tfrac{1}{2} \times (-2) + \tfrac{1}{3} \times \tfrac{1}{2} + \tfrac{1}{6} \times 1 = -\tfrac{2}{3};$$

$$EU(0) = 0;$$

$$EU(x+y) = \tfrac{1}{3} \times 0.7 = 7/30 < \tfrac{1}{3}.$$

Hence x has the highest EU and is chosen. $\square$

Exercise 4.2.4. The first indifference implies, after dropping U(25), $P(E_1 \cup E_2) = P(E_3)$. Because these probabilities sum to 1 they are ½ each. The second indifference implies, after dropping U(25), $P(E_1) = P(E_2)$. Their sum being ½, each is ¼. $U(15) = P(E_1)U(100) = \tfrac{1}{4}$. $\square$

Exercise 4.2.5.

(a) $f(s) \geq g(s)$ for all s implies $x_j \geq y_j$ for all j. Hence $U(x_j) \geq U(y_j)$ for all j, and $\sum_{j=1}^n P(E_j)U(x_j) \geq \sum_{j=1}^n P(E_j)U(y_j)$ follows, implying $f \succcurlyeq g$.

   An alternative solution is as follows, with P the probability on S. Write $EU(f) = \int_S U(f(s))dP(s)$, $EU(g) = \int_S U(g(s))dP(s)$. Note that $U(f(s)) \geq U(g(s))$ for all s ($U(f(s))$ pointwise dominates $U(g(s))$). Use the general rule for integrals that a function ($U(f(s))$ here) that pointwise dominates another ($U(g(s))$ here) gives an integral at least as large. It follows that $EU(f) \geq EU(g)$, so that $f \succcurlyeq g$.

(b) If $f(s) > g(s)$ for all s then $U(x_j) > U(y_j)$ for all j. We have $P(E_j)U(x_j) \geq P(E_j)U(y_j)$ for all j, with strict inequality for a j with $P(E_j) > 0$. $\sum_{j=1}^n P(E_j)U(x_j) > \sum_{j=1}^n P(E_j)U(y_j)$ follows, implying $f \succ g$.

Additional comment for mathematicians: The result of part (a) also holds for prospects that take infinitely many values. The result of part (b) essentially required that prospects take only finitely many values. For general prospects, the result holds if probability measures are countably additive, but need not hold if probability measures are only finitely additive (Wakker 1993b). $\square$

Exercise 4.2.6. Obviously, if $P(E) = 0$ then a change in outcome under event E does not affect the EU value of a prospect and, hence, does not affect the preference class of the prospect either, so that E is null. If $P(E) > 0$ then increasing an outcome under E strictly increases its utility and, hence, the EU of the prospect, so that the prospect becomes strictly better. Hence, event E cannot be null. $\square$

Exercise 4.2.7. Derived the same way as Exercise 2.6.4. $\square$

Exercise 4.3.1. The indifference in Fig. 4.1.1a implies, after applying EU,

$$p_1(U(\alpha^1) - U(\alpha^0)) = p_2(U(8) - U(1)).$$

The other indifferences in Figure 4.1.1 similarly imply

$$p_1(U(\alpha^2) - U(\alpha^1)) = p_2(U(8) - U(1)).$$
$$p_1(U(\alpha^3) - U(\alpha^2)) = p_2(U(8) - U(1)).$$
$$p_1(U(\alpha^4) - U(\alpha^3)) = p_2(U(8) - U(1)).$$

The right-hand side of these equations is always the same. Hence, so is the left-hand side. After dropping the common positive factor p_1, the equalities between utility differences as in the exercise follow.

The derivation shows in algebraic terms why we need not know p_1. Whatever p_1 is, it drops from the equations. This simple algebraic point will have considerable empirical and psychological implications. It will be the key in later extensions to nonEU. □

Exercise 4.3.2.

(a) The reasoning is similar to Exercise 4.3.1, with the β's instead of the α's and G and g instead of 8 and 1, and is not repeated here.

(b) $\beta^0 = \alpha^0$ and $\beta^1 = \alpha^1$ hold by definition. Hence, $U(\beta^2) - U(\beta^1) = U(\beta^1) - U(\beta^0) = U(\alpha^1) - U(\alpha^0) = U(\alpha^2) - U(\alpha^1)$. Because U increases strictly, $\beta^2 = \alpha^2$. Similarly, the equations

$$U(\beta^4) - U(\beta^3) = U(\beta^3) - U(\beta^2) = U(\beta^2) - U(\beta^1) = U(\beta^1) - U(\beta^0)$$

$$=$$

$$U(\alpha^1) - U(\alpha^0) = U(\alpha^2) - U(\alpha^1) = U(\alpha^3) - U(\alpha^2) = U(\alpha^4) - U(\alpha^3)$$

imply $\beta^j = \alpha^j$ for all j.

An alternative reasoning is as follows. Substituting α^2 in Fig. 4.1.2b and calculating EU shows that α^2 gives indifference in Fig. 4.1.2b. Hence, α^2 can be chosen for β^2. Because U increases strictly, β^2 is unique and, hence, it must be α^2. Similarly $\beta^3 = \alpha^3$ and $\beta^4 = \alpha^4$. □

Exercise 4.3.3. Under EU, $U(\gamma^2)$ is the midpoint between $U(\alpha^4)$ and $U(\alpha^0)$. The equalities of Exercise 4.3.1 imply that $U(\alpha^2)$ is also the midpoint between $U(\alpha^4)$ and $U(\alpha^0)$. Therefore, α^2 is a possible choice for γ^2. Because U increases strictly, α^2 is the only possible choice for γ^2.

Given $\gamma^2 = \alpha^2$, we see that $U(\gamma^1)$ is the midpoint between $U(\alpha^2)$ and $U(\alpha^0)$ and $U(\gamma^3)$ is the midpoint between $U(\alpha^4)$ and $U(\alpha^2)$. Because of the equalities of Exercise 4.3.1, and because U increases strictly, $\gamma^1 = \alpha^1$ and $\gamma^3 = \alpha^3$. □

Exercise 4.3.4. The left-hand prospect in Fig. 4.1.1d (with α^4 substituted on the dotted line) is the same as the right-hand prospect in Fig. 4.1.4a. Thus Fig. 4.1.1d shows that indifference is obtained in Fig. 4.1.4a if α^3 is substituted on the dotted line. By strong monotonicity, α^3 is the only value that gives indifference there. Hence, $\delta^3 = \alpha^3$ necessarily follows. Given this equality, Fig. 4.1.1c implies $\delta^2 = \alpha^2$ in Fig. 4.1.4b, next Fig. 4.1.1b implies $\delta^1 = \alpha^1$ in Fig. 4.1.4c, and, finally, Fig. 4.1.1a implies $\delta^0 = \alpha^0$ in Fig. 4.1.4d. □

Exercise 4.3.5. The SG Eq. (2.5.1) shows that $U(\alpha^j) = PE^j$ in Figure 4.1.5. Exercise 4.3.1 (with the normalization chosen here) shows that $U(\alpha^j) = j/4$ for all j in Figure 4.1.1. Thus, EU can hold only if $PE^j = j/4$. □

Exercise 4.5.2. Assume that $\alpha \ominus \beta \sim^t \gamma \ominus \delta$; i.e., $\alpha_E x \sim \beta_E y$ and $\gamma_E x \sim \delta_E y$ for a nonnull event E and prospects x,y. Then, obviously, $\gamma_E x \sim \delta_E y$ and $\alpha_E x \sim \beta_E y$, implying $\gamma \ominus \delta \sim^t \alpha \ominus \beta$. By the definition of $\sim$, we have $\beta_E y \sim \alpha_E x$ and $\delta_E y \sim \gamma_E x$, so that $\beta \ominus \alpha \sim^t \delta \ominus \gamma$. $\delta \ominus \gamma \sim^t \beta \ominus \alpha$ follows by applying the two results found. We have demonstrated that the first $\sim^t$ relation implies the other three. Similarly, each one of the other three implies all others. □

Exercise 4.5.3. Assume $\alpha \ominus \beta \sim^t \gamma \ominus \delta$. Then $\alpha_E x \sim \beta_E y$ and $\gamma_E x \sim \delta_E y$ for some x,y, and nonnull E. Assume $x = A_1 x_1 \cdots A_n x_n$ and $y = B_1 y_1 \cdots B_m y_m$. (By the partition flexibility Exercise 1.2.4 we could assume identical outcome events for x and y.) Applying EU to the first indifference gives

$$P(E)U(\alpha) + \sum\nolimits_{j=1}^{n} P(A_j - E)U(x_j) = P(E)U(\beta) + \sum\nolimits_{i=1}^{m} P(B_i - E)U(y_i) \text{ so that}$$

$$P(E)(U(\alpha) - U(\beta)) = \sum\nolimits_{i=1}^{m} P(B_i - E)U(y_i) - \sum\nolimits_{j=1}^{n} P(A_j - E)U(x_j). \text{ Similarly,}$$

$$P(E)(U(\gamma) - U(\delta)) = \sum\nolimits_{i=1}^{m} P(B_i - E)U(y_i) - \sum\nolimits_{j=1}^{n} P(A_j - E)U(x_j).$$

As the right-hand sides are identical, so must the left-hand sides be. By nonnullness of E, $P(E) > 0$. Hence, we can drop $P(E)$ from the equation, implying $U(\alpha) - U(\beta) = U(\gamma) - U(\delta)$. □

Exercise 4.7.1. The left indifference implies $p(U(\alpha) - U(\beta)) = \sum_{j=2}^{n} q_j U(y_j) - \sum_{i=2}^{m} p_i U(x_i)$. The right indifference implies $p(U(\gamma) - U(\delta)) = \sum_{j=2}^{n} q_j U(y_j) - \sum_{i=2}^{m} p_i U(x_i)$. Noting same right-hand sides and dropping $p > 0$, we get $U(\alpha) - U(\beta) = U(\gamma) - U(\delta)$. □

Exercise 4.8.1. Apply EU and drop the common term corresponding to the event with the common outcome. □

Exercise 4.8.2. The forward implication has been derived in Exercise 4.5.3. Hence, we only derive the backward implication, assuming $U(\alpha) - U(\beta) = U(\gamma) - U(\delta)$. Many students will take the indifference in Eq. (4.5.1), i.e., $\alpha_j x \sim \beta_j y$, as point of departure, then find the exercise easy, and maybe (hopefully) feel amazed that they did not need continuity. What is wrong with this approach is that the assumption $U(\alpha) - U(\beta) = U(\gamma) - U(\delta)$ in general need not ensure that x,y, and j exist such that

$\alpha_j x \sim \beta_j y$. They do always exist, but ensuring this existence is the major part of the work to be done, and needs continuity. Here it comes.

If $\alpha = \beta$ then $U(\alpha) = U(\beta)$ so that $U(\gamma) = U(\delta)$ and $\gamma = \delta$. $\alpha \ominus \alpha \sim^t \gamma \ominus \gamma$ was demonstrated following Eq. (4.5.5), and everything follows. Assume henceforth that $\alpha > \beta$, implying $U(\alpha) > U(\beta)$, $U(\gamma) > U(\delta)$ and, hence, $\gamma > \delta$ (the case $\alpha < \beta$ is similar). By nondegeneracy, there exists a partition $\{E_1, E_2\}$ with both events nonnull and, hence, with positive probabilities. We suppress the events. We may assume that $P(E_1) \leq P(E_2)$ (otherwise interchange the events). Then $P(E_1)(U(\alpha) - U(\beta)) \leq P(E_2)(U(\alpha) - U(\beta))$, and by continuity we can find μ between α and β with $P(E_1)(U(\alpha) - U(\beta)) = P(E_2)(U(\mu) - U(\beta))$. It implies

$$(\alpha, \beta) \sim (\beta, \mu).$$

This is an indifference of the form $\alpha_j x \sim \beta_j y$, and the rest of the exercise is easy. It is as follows.

$U(\alpha) - U(\beta) = U(\gamma) - U(\delta)$ and $(\alpha, \beta) \sim (\beta, \mu)$ imply
$(\gamma, \beta) \sim (\delta, \mu)$. This and $(\alpha, \beta) \sim (\beta, \mu)$ imply $\alpha \ominus \beta \sim^t \gamma \ominus \delta$.

It can be seen that with bounded utility and with $P(E_1) > \frac{1}{2}$ (contrary to what we assumed) it may be impossible to find x_2, y_2 with $(\alpha, x_2) \sim (\beta, y_2)$, if α has utility close to the maximum and β close to the minimum. Then, no matter how much y_2 dominates x_2, this domination is not enough to obtain an indifference $(\alpha, x_2) \sim (\beta, y_2)$, and always $(\alpha, x_2) \succ (\beta, y_2)$. This is why we assumed $P(E_1) \leq P(E_2)$ in the above analysis. $\square$

Exercise 4.8.3. If U is concave, then (with U' decreasing) U is steeper on the interval $[\alpha^{j-1}, \alpha^j]$ than on the interval $[\alpha^j, \alpha^{j+1}]$. Hence, to generate a U increase of $\frac{1}{4}$, the latter interval has to be larger than the former. If U is convex, then the converse holds. These two findings together imply the result for linear utility. For the latter, it can also be seen immediately that being equally spaced in utility must imply being equally spaced in monetary units. $\square$

Exercise 4.8.4. The condition is less useful because the probabilities $p_1, \ldots, p_n$ are not given a priori in decision under uncertainty, so that $\sum_{j=1}^n p_j f_j$ cannot be calculated.[1] In general, theoretical constructs such as the subjective probabilities $p_1, \ldots, p_n$ (Budescu & Wallsten 1987 p. 68) and utilities should not be used in preference conditions that are meant to be directly observable (c.f. footnote 5 in §11.5). Equation (4.8.2) has been stated in terms of t-indifference, and can be reformulated directly in terms of the empirical primitive $\succcurlyeq$. In the experiments of §4.1 we can verify the condition, which requires that $\alpha_{j+1} - \alpha_j$ increases in j. The condition is, therefore, empirically meaningful and is well suited for experimental testing. $\square$

---

[1] To calculate this value after all we usually first have to carry out an elicitation task to elicit the probabilities, and only then it can be calculated.

Exercise 4.8.5. By Exercise 1.2.4 (partition flexibility), we may fix a partition $\{E_1,\ldots,E_n\}$ containing the outcome-events for both x and y, and with E a union of events in the partition. Throughout this elaboration we restrict attention to prospects with outcome-events in this partition, and we suppress the partition.

Part 1. Assume $\alpha_E x \succ y$ and $\gamma_E x \prec y$. The set $\{\delta: \delta_E x \succ y\}$ is nonempty, containing α. It is open because for a sequence of outcomes δ^i converging to an outcome δ, $\delta^i_E x \preccurlyeq y$ for all i implies $\delta_E x \preccurlyeq y$ by continuity of preference, so that the complement of the set $\{\delta: \delta_E x \succ y\}$ is closed and the set is, indeed, open. Similarly, the set $\{\delta: \delta_E x \prec y\}$ is nonempty and open. By connectedness of the reals, there must be an outcome β contained in neither set. $\beta_E x \sim y$ follows.

Part 2. Assume $\alpha_E x \sim \alpha_E y$ and $\beta_E x \prec \beta_E y$. Obviously, $\alpha \neq \beta$. We derive a contradiction for the two remaining cases.

First assume $\alpha > \beta$. By monotonicity we have $\beta_E x \prec \beta_E y \preccurlyeq \alpha_E y \sim \alpha_E x$. By restricted solvability, $\gamma_E x \sim \beta_E y$ for an outcome γ between β and α (take $\gamma = \alpha$ if $\beta_E y \sim \alpha_E y$). $\alpha_E x \sim \alpha_E y$ and $\gamma_E x \sim \beta_E y$ imply $\alpha \ominus \alpha \sim^t \gamma \ominus \beta$. However, the trivial $\alpha_E x \sim \alpha_E x$ and $\beta_E x \sim \beta_E x$ imply the natural $\alpha \ominus \alpha \sim^t \beta \ominus \beta$. Since $\gamma \neq \beta$, this violates tradeoff consistency. Part (2) in the exercise cannot hold with $\alpha > \beta$.

Next assume $\alpha < \beta$. By monotonicity we have $\beta_E y \succ \beta_E x \succcurlyeq \alpha_E x \sim \alpha_E y$. By restricted solvability, $\gamma_E y \sim \beta_E x$ for an outcome γ between β and α (take $\gamma = \alpha$ if $\beta_E x \sim \alpha_E x$). $\alpha_E y \sim \alpha_E x$ and $\gamma_E y \sim \beta_E x$ imply $\alpha \ominus \alpha \sim^t \gamma \ominus \beta$. However, the trivial $\alpha_E x \sim \alpha_E x$ and $\beta_E x \sim \beta_E x$ imply the natural $\alpha \ominus \alpha \sim^t \beta \ominus \beta$. Since $\gamma \neq \beta$, this violates tradeoff consistency. Part (2) cannot hold with $\alpha < \beta$. Part (2) always leads to a contradiction, and cannot arise.

Part 3. Assume $\alpha_E x \succ \alpha_E y$ and $\beta_E x \prec \beta_E y$. We again derive a contradiction.

Consider the set $\{\gamma: \gamma_E x \succ \gamma_E y\}$. It is nonempty because it contains α. We next derive openness. Let γ be an element of the set. Because of continuity of preference, there exists a small $\varepsilon > 0$ such that $\delta_E x \succ \gamma_E y$ for all δ between $\gamma - \varepsilon$ and γ. Because of monotonicity, $\delta_E x \succ \delta_E y$ for all such δ. Similarly, because of continuity of preference, there exists a small $\varepsilon' > 0$ such that $\gamma_E x \succ \delta_E y$ for all δ between γ and $\gamma + \varepsilon'$. Because of monotonicity, $\delta_E x \succ \delta_E y$ for all such δ. The set $\{\gamma: \gamma_E x \succ \gamma_E y\}$ contains an interval $(\gamma - \varepsilon, \gamma + \varepsilon')$ around each of its elements γ, and is indeed open.

The set $\{\gamma: \gamma_E x \prec \gamma_E y\}$ is similarly nonempty and open. By connectedness of the reals, there must be an outcome δ contained neither in $\{\gamma: \gamma_E x \succ \gamma_E y\}$ nor in $\{\gamma: \gamma_E x \prec \gamma_E y\}$, so that $\delta_E x \sim \delta_E y$. We have $\delta_E x \sim \delta_E y$ and $\beta_E x \prec \beta_E y$ which amounts to Case (2). We already saw that Case (2) cannot be. Hence, Case (3) cannot arise either.

For $\alpha_E x$ and $\alpha_E y$ versus $\beta_E x$ and $\beta_E y$, there cannot be indifference between one pair and strict preference between another, and no contradictory strict preferences either. The only possibility remaining is that both pairs are indifferent or both pairs have the same strict preference, so that, in particular, the preference between the two pairs is always the same. This establishes the sure-thing principle. □

Exercise 4.9.1. (a) and (b): ¼. (c): EU is violated. The subjective probabilities of the three events are ¼, ¼, and ⅓ but they have to sum to 1 which they don't. □

Exercise 4.10.1. Under EU with utility U, α^i should satisfy

$$\tfrac{1}{2} \times U(\alpha^i) + \tfrac{1}{2} \times U(1) = \tfrac{1}{2} \times U(\alpha^{i-1}) + \tfrac{1}{2} \times U(8)$$

so that

$U(\alpha^i) = U^{-1}(2(\tfrac{1}{2} \times U(\alpha^{i-1}) + \tfrac{1}{2} \times U(8) - \tfrac{1}{2} \times U(1)))$. Previous exercises have shown that the β's, γ's, and δ's are equal to the α's, and that the PE^j's are $j/4$. Hence, we only calculate the α's.

(a) $\alpha^0 = 10$; we obtain $\alpha^1 = 24.91$, $\alpha^2 = 46.50$, $\alpha^3 = 74.78$, and $\alpha^4 = 109.75$.
(b) $\alpha^0 = 10$; we obtain $\alpha^1 = 19.51$, $\alpha^2 = 32.86$, $\alpha^3 = 55.47$, and $\alpha^4 = 173.15$.

Note that U in (a) is more concave and, under EU, more risk averse, than U in (b) for low outcomes, but less so for high outcomes. □

Exercise 4.10.2.

(a) $\theta = 0.56$. We calculate the distance in Eq. (4.10.2) under EU with $U(\alpha) = \alpha^{0.56}$. Equation (4.10.1) gives $\alpha^{1*} = 19.63$, $\alpha^{2*} = 30.36$, and $\alpha^{3*} = 46.14$. The distance is

$$\sqrt{\frac{(19.63 - 17)^2 + (30.36 - 32)^2 + (46.14 - 47)^2}{3}} = 1.86.$$

All other powers θ give greater distances as calculations can show. CE(80$_{1/2}$40) = 58.49.
(b) $\theta = 0.51$. The distance is

$$\sqrt{\frac{(17.69-17)^2 + (27.72-27.5)^2 + (40.09-41)^2}{3}} = 0.67. \ CE(80_{1/2}40) = 58.31.$$

(c) $\theta = 0.54$. The distance is

$$\sqrt{\frac{(22.77-22)^2 + (33.42-35)^2 + (47.84-47)^2}{3}} = 1.12. \ CE(80_{1/2}40) = 58.42. \ \square$$

Exercise 4.10.3. $\theta = -0.72$, with distance 1.12. CE(62.5$_{0.5}$10) = 18.85, CE(20$_{0.5}$10) = 13.55, CE(62.5$_{0.5}$20) = 31.55. Further, CE(80$_{1/2}$40) = 54.20. □

Exercise 4.10.4. $\theta = -0.52$, with distance 1.91. Then CE(62.5$_{0.25}$10) = 13.78, CE(62.5$_{0.75}$10) = 32.80, CE(62.5$_{0.9}$10) = 47.03. CE(80$_{1/2}$40) = 54.84. □

Exercise 4.10.5.

(a) $\theta = 0.68$, with distance 0.91. CE(80$_{cand_1}$40) = 58.90.
(b) $\theta = 0.51$, with distance 0.62. CE(80$_{cand_1}$40) = 58.32.
(c) $\theta = 0.73$, with distance 0.52. CE(80$_{cand_1}$40) = 59.08.
(d) $\theta = 0.65$, with distance 1.34. CE(80$_{cand_1}$40) = 58.80.

The tables give theoretical CEs for prospects in various parts.

	$17_{0.5}1$	$10_{0.5}8$	$32_{0.5}1$	$17_{0.5}8$	$47_{0.5}1$	$32_{0.5}8$	$62.5_{0.5}1$	$47_{0.5}8$
part (a)	7.49	8.98	13.19	12.23	18.81	18.73	24.57	24.94
part (d)	7.34	8.98	12.85	12.21	18.26	18.61	23.81	24.70

	$17_{0.5}100$	$10_{0.5}122$	$27.5_{0.5}100$	$17_{0.5}122$	$41_{0.5}100$	$27.5_{0.5}122$	$55_{0.5}100$	$41_{0.5}122$
part (b)	50.04	50.79	58.21	57.77	67.33	66.51	75.86	76.22
part (d)	52.53	55.36	59.82	61.24	68.24	68.91	76.33	77.75

	$22_{0.5}1$	$13_{0.5}8$	$35_{0.5}1$	$22_{0.5}8$	$47_{0.5}1$	$35_{0.5}8$	$62.50_{0.5}1$	$47_{0.5}8$
part (c)	9.76	10.42	14.95	14.54	19.70	20.23	25.82	25.35
part (d)	9.19	10.39	13.94	14.40	18.26	19.85	23.81	24.70

□

Exercise 4.10.6.

(a) $p = 0.541$, with distance 0.83, and $CE(80_{cand_1}, 40) = 60.41$.
(b) $p = 0.541$, $\theta = 0.63$, with distance 0.80, and $CE(80_{cand_1}, 40) = 60.34$.

The tables give theoretical CEs for prospects in the two parts. c1 denotes $cand_1$.

	$17_{c1}1$	$10_{c1}8$	$32_{c1}1$	$17_{c1}8$	$47_{c1}1$	$32_{c1}8$	$62.5_{c1}1$	$47_{c1}8$
part (a)	8.01	9.06	14.15	12.57	20.20	19.59	26.41	26.29
part (b)	7.90	9.06	13.91	12.55	19.83	19.51	25.89	26.13

	$17_{c1}100$	$10_{c1}122$	$27.5_{c1}100$	$17_{c1}122$	$41_{c1}100$	$27.5_{c1}122$	$55_{c1}100$	$41_{c1}122$
part (a)	49.21	50.86	56.92	57.03	65.89	65.13	74.54	74.51
part (b)	48.86	50.22	56.70	56.54	65.76	64.80	74.47	74.30

	$22_{c1}1$	$13_{c1}8$	$35_{c1}1$	$22_{c1}8$	$47_{c1}1$	$35_{c1}8$	$62.5_{c1}1$	$47_{c1}8$
part (a)	10.07	10.60	15.37	14.96	20.20	20.95	26.41	26.29
part (b)	9.92	10.59	15.11	14.93	19.83	20.85	25.89	26.13

□

Exercise 4.10.7.

(a) $\theta = 0.47$ with distance 5.22. $CE(80_{cand_1}40) = 58.18$.

(b) $P(cand_1) = 0.57$ and $\theta = 0.45$ with distance 5.07. Although the subjective probability of 0.57 improves the data fit relative to probability 0.50, the improvement is not big. $CE(80_{cand_1}40) = 60.95$.

A drawback of incorporating the PE data is that, because of the inconsistent answers PE^2 and PE^3, all models will have large deviations here and, in view of the quadratic distance criterion, this part of the data will primarily determine the optimally fitting data.

The tables give theoretical CEs for prospects in the two parts. c1 denotes $cand_1$.

	$17_{c1}1$	$10_{c1}8$	$32_{c1}1$	$17_{c1}8$	$47_{c1}1$	$32_{c1}8$	$62.5_{c1}1$	$47_{c1}8$
part (a)	6.40	8.97	10.72	12.06	14.85	17.88	19.01	23.19
part (b)	7.46	9.11	12.73	12.68	17.80	19.51	22.93	25.83

	$17_{c1}100$	$10_{c1}122$	$27.5_{c1}100$	$17_{c1}122$	$41_{c1}100$	$27.5_{c1}122$	$55_{c1}100$	$41_{c1}122$
part (a)	49.33	49.48	57.75	56.77	67.07	65.82	75.73	75.79
part (b)	43.39	41.41	52.59	49.24	62.89	59.07	72.55	70.03

	$22_{c1}1$	$13_{c1}8$	$35_{c1}1$	$22_{c1}8$	$47_{c1}1$	$35_{c1}8$	$62.5_{c1}1$	$47_{c1}8$
part (a)	7.87	10.34	11.56	14.08	14.85	18.97	19.01	23.19
part (b)	9.25	10.69	13.75	15.04	17.80	20.81	22.93	25.83

	$62.5_{0.50}10$	$20_{0.50}10$	$62.5_{0.50}20$	$62.5_{0.25}10$	$62.5_{0.75}10$	$62.5_{0.9}10$
part (a)	30.28	14.54	38.12	18.69	44.86	55.07
part (b)	30.04	14.53	38.00	18.54	44.65	54.97

□

Exercise 4.10.8.

(a) For $\theta = 0.56$, the sure outcome has higher expected utility and is preferred. For smaller θ utility is only the more concave and the sure amount is only preferred extra.

(b) For $\theta = 0.63$, the risky prospect has higher expected utility and is preferred.

(c) The result in Exercise 4.10.6b uses more data. Yet I think that these data bring more distortion than improvement and I would prefer to give the sure outcome, as in part (a), to subject 5. Theoretical arguments will be developed later showing that the results of Exercise 4.106b are distorted by violations of EU and those of Exercise 4.10.2 are not, supporting the preferability of the latter. □

Exercise 4.12.1.

(a) Set $U(0) = 0$. Consider, with (in)equalities or preferences to be substituted for the question marks, and 10^6 the unit of payment:

$$0.8 \times U(50) \; ? \; U(10) \qquad 0.04 \times U(50) \; ? \; 0.05 \times U(10)$$
$$50_{.8}0 \; ? \; 10 \qquad\qquad 50_{.04}0 \; ? \; 10_{.05}0.$$

The second (in)equality results from the first by division by 20 and, hence, the first and second question marks must be the same inequality sign. By EU, the first preference (Fig. 2.4.1e) corresponds with the first inequality sign, and the second preference (Fig. 2.4.1f) corresponds with the second inequality sign. Hence, the two preferences must be the same too.

Figs. 2.4.1e and f provide a test of the independence condition. To see this point, let x be the upper prospect in Fig. 2.4.1e; i.e., $x = (50 \times 10^6)_{0.8}0$ (in the notation of Figure 2.6.5, $M = 50 \times 10^6$, $m = 0$, $p = 0.8$), α is the lower prospect of Fig. 2.4.1e ($\alpha = 10 \times 10^6$), $C = 0$ (the riskless prospect yielding 0 for sure), and $\lambda = 0.05$. Then $x_\lambda C$ is the upper prospect in Fig. 2.4.1f and the utmost right prospect in Figure 2.6.5, and $\alpha_\lambda C$ is the lower prospect in Fig. 2.4.1f, and the left prospect to the right of "implies" in Figure 2.6.5.

For those interested, a subtle point concerns which condition of Theorem 2.6.3 (EU for risk), Statement (ii), is violated by the majority choice in Figs. 2.4.1e and f. No single one is clearly violated in isolation. For example, SG consistency is not directly violated because SG consistency concerns only indifferences and in this exercise there are strict preferences. Obviously, the four conditions in Statement (ii) cannot hold together because EU is violated, but it takes an advanced reasoning to show this directly and to show that at least one must be violated. This exercise thus demonstrates that for the purpose of falsifying a theory empirically strong preference conditions (such as independence) can be more useful than weak preference conditions (such as SG consistency).

(b) Applying EU shows that the preferences in Figs. g and h must be the same (cancel a common term $0.89 \times U(10 \times 10^6)$ and 0.89×0, respectively).

(c) The following figure illustrates that the majority preferences in Figs. 2.4.1g and h violate Figure 2.7.1, with $p = 0.89$, $\beta = 0$, $\gamma = 10 \times 10^6$, and so on.

Figs. 2.4.1g and h violate the owe-thing principle for risk.

□

Exercise 5.1.1.

(a) Under EU with $U(0) = 0$, $U(100) = 1$, the indifference $\alpha \sim 100_p0$ implies $U(\alpha) = p$. We have to express p in terms of α. Here $p = \sqrt{\alpha/100}$, so that $U(\alpha) = \sqrt{\alpha/100}$.

(b) Under RDU with linear utility, $\alpha = w(p)100$; i.e., $w(p) = \alpha/100$. We have to express α in terms of p. Here $\alpha = 100p^2$. Then $w(p) = \alpha/100 = p^2$. Obviously, this result holds under RDU with linear utility and fails under RDU with general utility.

   An alternative mathematical reasoning is as follows. Because $x \sim 100_p0$ and $x = w(p)100$, Fig. 5.1.2b shows a nonnormalized graph of w. The figure has resulted from Fig. a by interchanging axes, so that the function is the inverse of the function in Fig. a. Because Fig. a shows a nonnormalized square root function, Fig. b must show a nonnormalized square function. w is normalized at 0 and 1 so that it must be the square function. □

Exercise 5.4.1.

(a) Consider a prospect y and assume that probability mass $\varepsilon > 0$ is shifted from an outcome β to a better outcome γ, yielding prospect x. Then the ranks at any δ for $\delta < \beta$ and $\delta \geq \gamma$ remain unaffected. For $\beta \leq \delta < \gamma$, they are all increased by ε. The new prospect x does indeed dominate the original prospect y stochastically. Of course, further shifts of probability mass from worse to better outcomes lead to new prospects that still dominate the original one in all ranks.

(b) Consider two prospects $r_1y_1 \ldots r_{n'}y_{jn'}$ and $s_1z_1 \ldots s_{n''}z_{jn''}$. It is convenient to use the same set of outcomes for both prospects. Hence, we define $x_1, \ldots, x_n$ to be the union of the y_j's and z_j's, with $x_1 > \cdots > x_n$. We can write the former prospect as $p_1x_1 \ldots p_nx_n$ and the latter as $q_1x_1 \ldots q_nx_n$. In this part we have the following inequalities between ranks: $p_j + \cdots + p_1 \geq q_j + \cdots + q_1$ for all j. We prove that the p-prospect stochastically dominates the q-prospect. We transform the q-prospect into the p-prospect step by step, in each step improving the one constructed before in the sense of stochastic dominance.

   We first rewrite the inequalities as

$$p_j + \cdots + p_n \leq q_j + \cdots + q_n \text{ for all j.} \tag{$*$}$$

Let k be the largest integer such that $p_k + \cdots + p_n < q_k + \cdots + q_n$. Then $p_j = q_j$ for all $j > k$ and $p_k < q_k$. If there is no such k then we are done because then the two prospects are identical. If there is such a k, then it exceeds 1 because probabilities sum to 1. We move probability mass $\varepsilon = q_k - p_k$ from x_k to x_{k-1}, obtaining a new prospect $q_1x_1, \ldots, (q_{k-1} + \varepsilon)x_{k-1}, (q_k-\varepsilon)x_k, \ldots, q_nx_n$. The new prospect stochastically dominates the original q-prospect, and has one more probability agreeing with the p-prospect than the original q-prospect did (because $q_k-\varepsilon = p_k$). We can continue to transform the q-prospect just constructed, each time getting a new prospect that stochastically dominates the one constructed before and that has more probabilities agreeing with the p-prospect than the q-prospect constructed before. This process must stop after n (and even n−1) steps, after which the finally constructed q-prospect agrees with the p-prospect. This shows that the p-prospect stochastically dominates the q-prospect. □

Exercise 5.6.1.

(a) It is convenient to reorder the outcomes:

The ranks are, besides 0 (probability of more than 64), $\frac{1}{3}$ (probability of more than 49), and $\frac{1}{6} + \frac{1}{3} = \frac{1}{2}$ (probability of more than 9). $w(\frac{1}{3}) = \frac{1}{9}, w(\frac{1}{2}) = \frac{1}{4}$. The RDU value of the prospect is $w(\frac{1}{3})U(64) + (w(\frac{1}{2}) - w(\frac{1}{3}))U(49) + (1 - w(\frac{1}{2}))U(9) = \frac{1}{9} \times 80 + (\frac{1}{4} - \frac{1}{9}) \times 70 + (1 - \frac{1}{4}) \times 30 = \frac{320 + 350 + 810}{36} = 41.111$.

(b) The ranks are, besides 0 (probability of more than 80), $\frac{1}{12}$ (probability of more than 60), $\frac{1}{3}$ (probability of more than 40), and $\frac{1}{2}$ (probability of more than 20). $w(\frac{1}{12}) = 1/144, w(\frac{1}{3}) = \frac{1}{9}, w(\frac{1}{2}) = \frac{1}{4}$. The RDU value of the prospect is $w(\frac{1}{12})U(80) + (w(\frac{1}{3}) - w(\frac{1}{12}))U(60) + (w(\frac{1}{2}) - w(\frac{1}{3}))U(40) + (1 - w(\frac{1}{2}))U(20) = \frac{1}{144} \times U(80) + (\frac{1}{9} - \frac{1}{144}) \times U(60) + (\frac{1}{4} - \frac{1}{9}) \times U(40) + (1 - \frac{1}{4}) \times U(20) = 0.007 \times 89.4 + 0.104 \times 77.5 + 0.139 \times 63.2 + 0.75 \times 44.7 = 0.62 + 8.07 + 8.78 + 33.54 = 51.01.$ □

Exercise 5.6.2.
$w(\frac{1}{6}) = \frac{1}{36}, w(\frac{2}{3}) = \frac{4}{9}$.
    The RDU value of the prospect is

$$\frac{1}{36} \times 80 + (\frac{4}{9} - \frac{1}{36}) \times 30 + (1 - \frac{4}{9}) \times 20$$
$$= \frac{80 + 450 + 400}{36} = \frac{930}{36} = \frac{155}{6} = 25.83.$$

Because U is the identity, the certainty equivalent is $U^{-1}(25.83) = 25.83$. □

Exercise 6.3.1. The certainty equivalent is 52.92. The expected value of 60 is preferred to the prospect, consistent with risk aversion. □

Exercise 6.4.1.

(a) Take utility linear. We take w(0.8) very small (say 0.01), so that the risky prospect in Figure 2.2.1e is evaluated much lower than the riskless prospect there (20 times lower). If w(0.04) and w(0.05) are similar (say you take w linear between 0 and 0.8), then the bigger prize will decide and the upper prospect in Figure 2.2.1g will have a much higher value than the lower one (four times higher). Then the commonly found preferences are accommodated.

(b) The preferences can be obtained by greatly overweighting the 0 outcome of the upper prospect in Fig. g, which can be obtained by letting w be very steep on [0.99, 1] and very shallow on [0, 0.99]. For example, let $w(0.99) = 0.01$, and let w be linear on [0, 0.99] (so that $w(p) = p/99$ there) and also linear on [0.99, 1]. Let U be linear. Then the RDU value of the upper prospect in Fig. g is $w(0.10) \times 50 \times 10^6 + (w(0.99) - w(0.10)) \times 10 \times 10^6 + (1 - w(0.99)) \times 0 < w(0.10) \times 50 \times 10^6 + (w(0.99) - w(0.10)) \times 50 \times 10^6 = w(0.99) \times 50 \times 10^6 < 10 \times 10^6$, which is the RDU value of the lower prospect. Consequently, the lower prospect is preferred in Fig. g.

In Fig. h, all RDU values are the expected values divided by 99. That is, the RDU value of the upper prospect is $w(0.10) \times 50 \times 10^6 = 0.10 \times 50 \times 10^6/99$, and the RDU value of the lower prospect is $w(0.11) \times 10 \times 10^6 = 0.11 \times 10 \times 10^6/99$, which is lower. Hence, the upper prospect is preferred there. In this choice, the great overweighting of the 0.01 probability mass assigned to the worst outcome reduces the RDU value of both prospects equally much. □

Exercise 6.4.2. Any $\pi(\frac{1}{2}^b) \neq \frac{1}{2}$ implies that the γ^j's differ from the α^j's. For example, if $\pi(\frac{1}{2}^b) < \frac{1}{2}$ then $U(\gamma^2) < \frac{U(\alpha^4) + U(\alpha^0)}{2} = U(\alpha^2)$ so that $\gamma^2 < \alpha^2$. Similarly, $U(\gamma^1) < \frac{U(\gamma^2) + U(\alpha^0)}{2} < \frac{U(\alpha^2) + U(\alpha^0)}{2} = U(\alpha^1)$ so that $\gamma^1 < \alpha^1$, and $U(\gamma^3) > \frac{U(\alpha^4) + U(\gamma^2)}{2} < \frac{U(\alpha^4) + U(\alpha^2)}{2} = U(\alpha^3)$ so that $\gamma^3 < \alpha^3$.
If $\pi(\frac{1}{2}^h) > \frac{1}{2}$ then $U(\gamma^2) > \frac{U(\alpha^4) + U(\alpha^0)}{2} = U(\alpha^2)$ so that $\gamma^2 > \alpha^2$. Similarly, $\gamma^1 > \alpha^1$ and $\gamma^3 > \alpha^3$ can then be proved. The γ^j's are identical to the α^j's only if $\pi(\frac{1}{2}^b) = \frac{1}{2}$. The empirical finding of the γ's smaller than the α's suggests $w(\frac{1}{2}) < \frac{1}{2}$. □

Exercise 6.4.3. In (a), write CE for your certainty equivalent.

(b) Under EU, $U(CE) = 10^{-6}U(10^6)$. This can be explained by EU with a linear utility function if and only if $CE = 1$. If $CE < 1$, then EU with a concave utility function can explain it. Your choice exhibits strict risk seeking if $CE > 1$, which is found for the majority of people. Then, by Theorem 3.2.1a, EU with concave utility is falsified.

(c) Let $w(10^{-6}) = CE/10^6$. The empirical finding $CE > 1$ implies $w(10^{-6}) > 10^{-6}$; i.e., the small probability is overestimated. As an aside, if utility is not linear but is concave, so that with $U(0) = 0$, $U(10^6) < 10^6 U(1)$, then the overweighting $w(10^{-6}) > 10^{-6}$ must be even stronger.

(d) Take any strictly concave utility function, and set $w(10^{-6}) > U(1)/U(10^6)$. For example, $U(\alpha) = \sqrt{\alpha}$, and $w(10^{-6}) > 10^{-3}$. □

Exercise 6.4.4. Take $U(\alpha) = \alpha$, $w(p) = 0$ for $p < 0.99$, and $w(p) = 1$ for $p \geq 0.99$. Then $\pi(p^r) = 1$ if $r < 0.99$ and $p + r \geq 0.99$, which happens exactly for the VaR. In particular, $1_{0.99}0$ has value 1.

Additional comment: If we change w by setting $w(0.99) = 0$, then $1_{0.99}0$ has RDU value 0. Then the value of a prospect is the supremum over all outcomes with rank strictly exceeding 0.99. □

Exercise 6.5.1. Applying RDU gives $\frac{\pi(1/2^b)}{\pi(1/2^w)}(U(G) - U(g)) = U(\beta^{j+1}) - U(\beta^j)$ for all j, from which it follows that $U(\beta^{j+1}) - U(\beta^j)$ is the same for all j. The derivation that the β^j's coincide with the α^j's is similar to the elaboration of Exercise 4.3.2b, again using that U increases strictly.

An alternative reasoning can be used, as in Exercise 4.3.2. Substituting α^2 in Fig. 4.1.2b and calculating RDU shows that α^2 gives indifference in Fig. 4.1.2b. Hence, α^2 can be chosen for β^2. Because U increases strictly, β^2 is unique and, hence, it must be α^2. Similarly $\beta^3 = \alpha^3$ and $\beta^4 = \alpha^4$. This alternative reasoning shows that under RDU we must have $\beta^4 = \alpha^4 \leq g$, so that the latter need not be assumed a priori but follows. □

Exercise 6.5.2. We first consider the comparisons of the α^j's to the γ^j's, and of the PE^j's to j/4. EU predicts equalities, but the γ^j's are significantly lower and the PE^j's are significantly higher. We thus reject the null hypothesis of EU. RDU does not predict equalities, but, given that mostly $w(p) < p$ for moderate and high probabilities, it predicts that $\gamma^j < \alpha^j$ for all j and $PE^j > j/4$, in agreement with what we found.

We next consider the comparisons of the α^j's with the β^j's. EU predicts equality of these values, and so does RDU whenever $\beta^4 \leq g$. The statistical claims remain valid if the subjects with $\beta^4 > g$ are not incorporated in the analysis. Indeed, for these comparisons equality was not rejected, and the null hypothesis of EU and RDU is accepted here.

The first two comparisons (α^j with γ^j and α^j with β^j) seem to be favorable for RDU. These findings do not prove, however, that RDU is preferable to EU for descriptive purposes. RDU is a more general theory with more parameters and, therefore, it is trivial that it can better accommodate data. Its fit should be so much better that it makes the extra complication of extra parameters (probability weighting) worthwhile. Besides such statistical arguments, another requirement for RDU is that the new parameters of the theory, probability transformation in this case, should have an intuitive meaning and should be well suited for connections to concepts from other domains. They should not just be parameters to fit the data.

We next discuss the comparisons of the α^j's with the δ^j's. These comparisons do not test sophisticated implications of RDU or EU, but they test elementary conditions, such as transitivity, and rejections of equality are problematic for RDU as much as they are for EU. From this perspective, it is unfortunate that the α^j's are significantly different from the δ^j's. The difference is probably caused by a framing effect, because the δ^j-questions concern reductions of outcomes, and the α^j-questions concern increases of outcomes ("how much more do you want"). This finding should provide a warning against overly optimistic expectations about risk theories. As time proceeds, the field has come to recognize more and more that most violations of theories concern basic conditions. This fact seriously complicates any empirical study of decision under risk. We need to investigate how the elementary conditions are violated, and how we can avoid or correct for such violations. Several empirical violations of RDU and prospect theory have indeed been found in the literature, and are still awaiting explanations. Given the importance of decision under risk and utility theory, and given that it is not easy to develop better theories than RDU and prospect theory (introduced later), we continue to use these theories despite their obvious limitations.

Arguments can be advanced that the utilities derived from the tradeoff measurement are not distorted by loss aversion, or by another well-known bias, called scale compatibility (Bleichrode 2002). Even if these biases are effective in the measurements of the δ^j's, they do not affect the correctness of the equalities $U(\alpha^4) - U(\delta^3) = \cdots = U(\delta^1) - U(\delta^0)$. When we fitted power utility to the data of subject 5 in Exercise 4.10.2, we did indeed find that the curvature of utility implied by the measurements of the α^j's, β^j's, and δ^j's was very similar. $\square$

Exercise 6.5.3. We normalize $U(\alpha^0) = 0$ and $U(\alpha^4) = 1$. Under RDU, $U(\alpha^j) = j/4$ for all j. Fig. 6.5.3a implies $\pi(\frac{1}{2}^w)(U(\alpha^1) - U(\alpha^0)) = \pi(\frac{1}{2}^b)(U(\alpha^4) - U(\alpha^2))$, so that $\pi(\frac{1}{2}^w) = 2\pi(\frac{1}{2}^b)$. We substitute $w(\frac{1}{2})$, implying $1 - w(\frac{1}{2}) = 2w(\frac{1}{2})$, so that $w(\frac{1}{2}) = \frac{1}{3}$, and $\pi(\frac{1}{2}^w) = \frac{2}{3}$, $\pi(\frac{1}{2}^b) = \frac{1}{3}$. The indifferences in Figs. b and c are accommodated by RDU this way. Fig. d implies $\frac{1}{3}(U(\beta^4) - U(\beta^3)) = \frac{2}{3}(U(\alpha^4) - U(\alpha^2))$ or $(U(\beta^4) - 1)) = 2 \times 0.5$. Thus, $U(\beta^4) = 2$. All utility values are accommodated by a renormalized $U(\alpha) = \sqrt{\alpha}$. $\square$

Exercise 6.5.4. Because $\alpha^0 > 1$ and all other α's are larger, the outcome probability $\frac{1}{2}$ of the α's always has the same rank, being best. By RDU, all α's are equally spaced in utility units. From $\alpha^1{}_{1/2}\alpha^1 \sim \alpha^0{}_{1/2}\alpha^4$ we infer that $\pi(\frac{1}{2}^b)(U(\alpha^4) - U(\alpha^1)) = \pi(\frac{1}{2}^w)$ $(U(\alpha^1) - U(\alpha^0))$, $3\pi(\frac{1}{2}^b) = \pi(\frac{1}{2}^w)$, so that $3w(\frac{1}{2}) = 1 - w(\frac{1}{2})$. $w(\frac{1}{2}) = \frac{1}{4}$ follows. The indifference $\beta^2{}_{2/3}g \sim \beta^1{}_{2/3}G$ is trivially satisfied because the two prospects are identical. For β^3, we have $\beta^3{}_{1/3}\alpha^1 \sim \alpha^4{}_{1/3}\alpha^4$ so that $\frac{1}{4}(U(\beta^3) - U(\alpha^4)) = \frac{3}{4}(U(\alpha^4) - U(\alpha^1))$ and β^3 must be α^{13}. Similarly, $\frac{1}{4}(U(\beta^4) - U(\alpha^{13})) = \frac{3}{4}(U(\alpha^4) - U(\alpha^1))$ implies $\beta^4 = \alpha^{22}$. $\square$

Exercise 6.5.6. $j/4 = U(\alpha^j) = w(PE^j)U(\alpha^4) + (1 - w(PE^j))U(\alpha^0) = w(PE^j)1 + (1 - w(PE^j))0 = w(PE^j)$. $\square$

Exercise 6.5.7. The elaboration is similar to EU as in Exercise 2.7.3 if we may assume that the same decision weights can be used in left and right choices. This follows from Lemma 6.5.4. Now the left preference implies $\pi(p^r)U(\beta) + \sum_{j=2}^{m} \pi_j U(x_j) \geq \pi(p^r)U(\beta) + \sum_{i=2}^{n} \pi'_i U(y_i)$, which implies $\sum_{j=2}^{m} \pi_j U(x_j) \geq \sum_{i=2}^{n} \pi'_i U(y_i)$, and $\pi(p^r)U(\gamma) + \sum_{j=2}^{m} \pi_j U(x_j) \geq \pi(p^r)U(\gamma) + \sum_{i=2}^{n} \pi'_i U(y_i)$. This implies the second preference. $\square$

Exercise 6.5.8. In the upper prospect in Fig. g, the rank of probability 0.89 (p in the notation of Figure 6.5.5) must be 0.10. In the lower prospect in Fig. h, the rank of probability 0.89 must be the worst (0.11). Hence, the rank of the common-outcome probability cannot be the same in both choice situations, and the rank-sure-thing principle is not being tested here. □

Exercise 6.5.9.

(a) Under EU with probabilities ½, $\alpha^1 \text{cand}_1 \alpha^4 \sim \alpha^0 \text{cand}_1 \alpha^5$ because $\frac{1}{2}U(\alpha^1) + \frac{1}{2}U(\alpha^4) = \frac{1}{2}U(\alpha^0) + \frac{1}{2}U(\alpha^5)$. If we further have $\beta^2 \text{cand}_1 \alpha^4 \sim \alpha^1 \text{cand}_1 \alpha^5$ then, reasoning as before, $U(\beta^2) - U(\alpha^1) = U(\alpha^1) - U(\alpha^0) = U(\beta^3) - U(\beta^2) = U(\beta^4) - U(\beta^3)$. This implies that all β's are equal to the corresponding αs, that is, $\beta^2 = 36$, $\beta^3 = 49$, $\beta^4 = 62$. This is what the experimenter expects.

(b) Consider $\beta^2 \text{cand}_1 \alpha^4 \sim \alpha^1 \text{cand}_1 \alpha^5$. Under RDU this implies $\frac{7}{20}(\alpha^5 - \alpha^4) = \frac{13}{20}(\beta^2 - \alpha^1)$. That is, $\beta^2 - \alpha^1 = \frac{7}{13}13 = 7$, and $\beta^2 = 23 + 7 = 30$. Similarly, $\beta^3 = 37$ and $\beta^4 = 44$.

(c) Under EU, the β's should be equal to the α's, but they are not. The cross check has revealed an inconsistency in utility measurement under EU. Formally, we have $\alpha^2 \ominus \alpha^1 \sim^t \alpha^1 \ominus \alpha^0$ but also, from $\alpha^1 \text{cand}_1 \alpha^4 \sim \alpha^0 \text{cand}_1 \alpha^5$ (as erroneously assumed) and $\beta^2 \text{cand}_1 \alpha^4 \sim \alpha^1 \text{cand}_1 \alpha^5$ (as observed) we have $\beta^2 \ominus \alpha^1 \sim^t \alpha^1 \ominus \alpha^0$. Because $\beta^2 \neq \alpha^2$, tradeoff consistency is violated.

This signals to the experimenter that his assumption of EU is not correct and, consequently, some of his inferences about utility are not correct. He will have to reanalyze the data using a different model, such as RDU. He can then find out that utility need not be concave around 10 but, instead, is linear. □

Exercise 6.6.1.

(a) $\pi((p_1+p_2)^b) = w(p_1+p_2) = w(p_1) + (w(p_2+p_1) - w(p_1)) = \pi(p_1{}^b) + \pi(p_2{}^{p_1})$.

(b) $\pi((p_1+p_2)^r) = w(p_1+p_2+r) - w(r) = w(p_1+r) - w(r) + (w(p_2+p_1+r) - w(p_1+r)) = \pi(p_1{}^r) + \pi(p_2{}^{p_1+r})$. □

Exercise 6.6.2a. [(2) ⇒ (3)] and [(3) ⇒ (4)] are obvious. We, finally, assume (1), and derive (2). RDU(z) is the expectation of the random variable with distribution function $1 - w(P(U(z) \geq t))$. For $z = x_\lambda y$, we have $P(U(z) \geq t) = P(z \geq U^{-1}(t)) = $ (see figure) $\lambda P(x \geq U^{-1}(t)) + (1-\lambda)P(y \geq U^{-1}(t)) = \lambda P(U(x) \geq t) + (1-\lambda)P(U(y) \geq t)$. Hence, $w(P(U(z) \geq t)) = w(\lambda P(U(x) \geq t) + (1-\lambda)P(U(y) \geq t)) \leq$ (because w is convex) $\lambda w(P(U(x) \geq t)) + (1-\lambda)w(P(U(y) \geq t))$. Hence,

$$1 - w(P(U(z) \geq t)) \geq \lambda(1 - w(P(U(x) \geq t))) + (1 - \lambda)(1 - w(P(U(y) \geq t))).$$

We can take the latter as a distribution function. It stochastically dominates the one corresponding to $1 - w(P(U(z) \geq t))$, and has expectation $\lambda RDU(x) + (1-\lambda)RDU(y)$. The latter, by stochastic dominance, must exceed the expectation of the former, which is RDU(z), and the desired result follows.

A similar reasoning to derive (2) from (1) can be based on Eq. (6.9.1):

$$RDU(z) = \int_{\mathbb{R}^+} w(G_{z,U}(t))dt - \int_{\mathbb{R}^-} [1 - w(G_{z,U}(t))]dt.$$

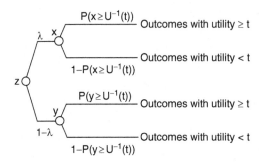

Mathematicians may see immediately that, because of linearity of Eq. (6.9.1) in w for gains and its dual for losses, convexity of w generates convexity of the functional. The algebraic derivation is as follows. For $z = x_\lambda y$, we have $G_{z,U}(t) = P(U(z) \geq t) = P(z \geq U^{-1}(t)) = \lambda P(x \geq U^{-1}(t)) + (1-\lambda)P(y \geq U^{-1}(t)) = \lambda P(U(x) \geq t) + (1-\lambda) P(U(y) \geq t) = \lambda G_{x,U}(t) + (1-\lambda)G_{y,U}(t)$. Hence, $w(G_{z,U}(t)) = w(\lambda G_{x,U}(t) + (1-\lambda)G_{y,U}(t)) \leq$ (by convexity of w) $\lambda w(G_{x,U}(t)) + (1-\lambda)w(G_{y,U}(t))$. Substituting this in the formula displayed for RDU(z) and using linearity of integration with respect to the integrand gives the desired result. □

Exercise 6.6.3.

(a) If a citizen pays a τ-part of total (or "final") wealth I, then the utility loss is $U(I) \quad U((1-\tau)I) = ln(I) - ln((1-\tau)I) = ln(I) - ln(I) - ln(1-\tau) = -ln(1-\tau)$. It is the same for all citizens if τ is the same for all of them because income I drops from the formula for utility loss. The total wealth in the country is \$2 million, so that ¼ should be paid as tax to yield \$500,000. Hence, $\tau = ¼$, and the rich person pays \$250,000, and the poor pay \$250 each.

(b) Table * gives CEs. The order of parameters chosen in tables in this exercise results from centering in on the optimal parameter.
   For $\theta = 1$, $\theta = 0$, and $\theta = -0.1$ they are too large, and these θ's do not generate sufficient risk aversion. For $\theta = -1$, $\theta = -2$, and $\theta = -0.5$ the CEs are too small, and these θ's generate too much risk aversion. $\theta = -0.188$ is about right.

Table *

θ	1	0	−1	−2	−0.1	−0.5	−0.188
CE	15465	5282	1804	1315	4546	2690	3997

(c) Table** gives utility differences, namely $U(1000) - U(1000 - t)$ for the poor and $U(1000000) - U(500000 + 1000t)$ for the rich. The taxes 250, 200, 150, and 125 are too large for the poor, and the others are too small. $t = 125$ is about right, and this tax will be imposed on the poor. The rich person pays tax 375000.

Table **

t	250	200	100	150	125	120
U-loss rich	0.004	0.005	0.0075	0.0063	0.00688	0.0070
U-loss poor	0.015	0.012	0.0055	0.0085	0.00694	0.0066
difference	−0.011	−0.007	0.002	−0.0022	−0.00006	0.0004

(d) Table *** gives CEs. For $\theta = 1$ the CE is too large, and this θ does not generate sufficient risk aversion. For negative θ the CEs are too small, and these θ generate too much risk aversion. $\theta = 0$ is about right.

Table ***

θ	1	0	−1	−2	−0.1	−0.5	−0.188
CE	13139	4000.47	1568	1221	3465	2175	3076

(e) $250,000 on the rich citizen, and $2500 on each poor citizen (see part (a)).

(f) Under EU the rich person pays $375,000 tax (parts b and c), and under RDU the rich person pays $250,000 (parts d and e). If the rich person is selfish then he will lobby for RDU, because under RDU he pays less tax, saving him $125,000. □

Exercise 6.7.1. We may use normalized utility $\frac{U(\cdot)-U(0)}{U(1)-U(0)}$, that is, we may assume that $U(1) = 1$ and $U(0) = 0$. Define $w(p) = V(1_p0) = \pi_1^2(p, 1 - p)$. $w(0) = V(1:0) = \pi_1^1 \times U(0) = 0$. $w(1) = V(1:1) = \pi_1^1 \times U(1) = 1$. That w increases strictly will be proved later.

By collapsing outcomes, $V(p_1 1 \cdots p_j 1 p_{j+1} 0 \cdots p_n 0) = V((p_1 + \cdots + p_j)1, 0)$, that is,

$$\pi_1^n(p_1, \ldots, p_n) + \cdots + \pi_j^n(p_1, \ldots, p_n) = w(p_1 + \cdots + p_j).$$

Similarly,

$$\pi_1^n(p_1, \ldots, p_n) + \cdots + \pi_{j-1}^n(p_1, \ldots, p_n) = w(p_1 + \cdots + p_{j-1}).$$

Subtracting these gives

$$\pi_j^n(p_1, \ldots, p_n) = w(p_1 + \cdots + p_j) - w(p_1 + \cdots + p_{j-1}).$$

Because this difference is positive whenever p_j is, w increases strictly and it is a weighting function. It implies that decision weights are as in RDU with weighting function w. □

Exercise 6.9.1. The integral in Eq. (6.9.1) means, in terms of Figure 6.9.2, that we take the areas of all layers and sum these. Definition 6.1.1 calculates RDU by first taking the areas of all columns in Figure 6.9.2 and then summing these. Hence, writing all terms of the integral in Eq. (6.9.1) and then rearranging terms will lead to Definition 6.1.1. For general integrals such reversals of orderings of integration – this is what the difference between summing areas of layers versus summing areas of columns amounts to – are based on Fubini's theorem (Halmos 1950). We do not use this theorem, but give an alternative algebraic derivation.

(a) For all $t < 0$, $G_{x,U}(t) = 1$; i.e., the probability of receiving utility U equal to t or more is 1. Then so is its w value, and the integrand in this part is 0 on all of $\mathbb{R}^-$, so that the integral is also 0.

(b) The right integral in Eq. (6.9.1) is 0, as we just saw, so that we can focus on the left integral. The result is most easily inferred from Figure 5.5.3.

   On the interval $[0,U(x_n)]$, we have $G_{x,U}(t) = 1 = w(G_{x,U}(t))$, so that

   - $\int_0^{U(x_n)} w(G_{x,U}(t))dt = U(x_n)$.

   For $j = n-1,\ldots,1$, on the interval $[U(x_{j+1}),U(x_j)]$, the function $G_{x,U}(t)$ is $p_j + \cdots + p_1$, so that

   - $\int_{U(x_{j+1})}^{U(x_j)} w(G_{x,U}(t))dt = w(p_j + \cdots + p_1)(U(x_j) - U(x_{j+1}))$.

   On the interval $[U(x_1),\infty)$, we have $G_{x,U}(t) = 0 = w(G_{x,U}(t))$, so that

   - $\int_{U(x_n)}^{\infty} w(G_{x,U}(t))dt = 0$.

   The integral in part (b) is the sum of all terms described, which is $\sum_{j=1}^{n-1} w(p_j + \cdots + p_1)(U(x_j) - U(x_{j+1})) + U(x_n)$. This is $\sum_{j=1}^{n-1} w(p_j + \cdots + p_1)U(x_j) - \sum_{j=1}^{n-1} w(p_j + \cdots + p_1)U(x_{j+1}) + w(p_n + \cdots + p_1)U(x_n) =$ [writing j + 1 for j in the second summation, and moving the last term to the first summation]

   $$\sum_{j=1}^n w(p_j + \cdots + p_1)U(x_j) - \sum_{j=2}^n w(p_{j-1} + \cdots + p_1)U(x_j)$$

   $$= [w(p_{j-1} + \cdots + p_1) = 0 \text{ for } j = 1] \sum_{j=1}^n w(p_j + \cdots + p_1)U(x_j) -$$

   $$\sum_{j=1}^n w(p_{j-1} + \cdots + p_1)U(x_j) = \sum_{j=1}^n (w(p_j + \cdots + p_1) - w(p_{j-1} + \cdots + p_1))U(x_j).$$

   This is, indeed, RDU.

(c) The RDU of negative utilities can be obtained by calculating $U(x_n) + \sum_{j=1}^n \pi_j(U(x_j) - U(x_n))$, where the latter sum concerns only positive terms and can be treated as in (b). We, nevertheless, gave the general formula for negative terms in the main text and present its elaboration here. The derivation is most easily inferred from Figure 6.9.2.

   On the interval $[-\infty,U(x_n)]$, we have $G_{x,U}(t) = 1$, so that the integrand is 0, and

   - $\int_{-\infty}^{U(x_n)} (1 - w(G_{x,U}(t)))dt = 0$.

   For $j = n-1, \cdots, k+1$, on the interval $[U(x_{j+1}),U(x_j)]$, the function $G_{x,U}(t)$ is $p_j + \cdots + p_1$, so that

   - $-\int_{U(x_{j+1})}^{U(x_j)} (1 - w(G_{x,U}(t)))dt = -(1 - w(p_j + \cdots + p_1))(U(x_j) - U(x_{j+1}))$

   $= (w(p_j + \cdots + p_1) - 1)(U(x_j) - U(x_{j+1}))$

   On the interval $[U(x_{k+1}),0]$, we have $(1-w(G_{x,U}(t))) = (1-w(p_k + \cdots + p_1))$, so that

   - $-\int_{U(x_{k+1})}^0 (1 - w(G_{x,U}(t)))dt = (1 - w(p_k + \cdots + p_1))U(x_{k+1})$.

Summing these negative terms yields:

$$(1 - w(p_k + \cdots + p_1))U(x_{k+1}) + \sum_{j=k+1}^{n-1}(w(p_j + \cdots + p_1) - 1)(U(x_j) - U(x_{j+1}))$$

$$= (1 - w(p_k + \cdots + p_1))U(x_{k+1}) + \sum_{j=k+1}^{n-1}(w(p_j + \cdots + p_1) - 1)U(x_j)$$

$$- \sum_{j=k+1}^{n-1}(w(p_j + \cdots + p_1) - 1)U(x_{j+1})$$

$$= (1 - w(p_k + \cdots + p_1))U(x_{k+1}) + \sum_{j=k+1}^{n}(w(p_j + \cdots + p_1) - 1)U(x_j)$$

$$- \sum_{j=k+2}^{n}(w(p_{j-1} + \cdots + p_1) - 1)U(x_j)$$

$$= \sum_{j=k+1}^{n}(w(p_j + \cdots + p_1) - 1)U(x_j) - \sum_{j=k+1}^{n}(w(p_{j-1} + \cdots + p_1) - 1)U(x_j)$$

$$= \sum_{j=k+1}^{n}(w(p_j + \cdots + p_1) - w(p_{j-1} + \cdots + p_1))U(x_j).$$

This is, indeed, what the negative utilities should contribute to RDU.

The integral over the positive utility-domain yields $\sum_{j=1}^{k}(w(p_j + \cdots + p_1) - w(p_{j-1} + \cdots + p_1))U(x_j)$ by a reasoning similar to part (b), starting with the interval $[0, U(x_k)]$ that yields $w(p_k + \cdots + p_1)U(x_k)$ (instead of the first term $w(p_n + \cdots + p_1)U(x_n)$ in part (b)). The sum is, indeed, what the positive utilities should contribute to RDU. Hence, both the positive and negative utility terms are as required for RDU, and the integral is, indeed, in agreement with RDU. $\square$

Exercise 7.2.1.

(b) $\sqrt{1/5} = 0.447$, $\sqrt{4/5} = 0.894$. $w(1/5) = 0.447/(0.447 + 0.894)^2 = 0.447/1.798 = 0.248$.
 $w(4/5) = 0.894/(0.894 + 0.447)^2 = 0.894/1.798 = 0.497$.
(c) Outcome 70 has decision weight $w(1/5) = 0.248$.
 Outcome 50 has decision weight $w(1/5 + 3/5) - w(1/5) = 0.497 - 0.248 = 0.249$.
 Outcome 30 has decision weight $w(1) - w(4/5) = 1 - 0.497 = 0.503$.
(d) The RDU value of the prospect is $0.248 \times 70/100 + 0.249 \times 50/100 + 0.503 \times 30/100 = 0.449$. Hence, the certainty equivalent is 44.9. $\square$

Exercise 7.2.2.

the 1/3 probability mass allocated to the lowest outcomes receives this decision weight.

the 1/3 probability mass allocated to the middle outcomes receives this decision weight.

the 1/3 probability mass allocated to the highest outcomes receives this decision weight.

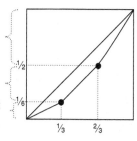

the ¼ probability mass allocated to the lowest outcomes receives this decision weight.

the ¼ probability mass allocated to the highest outcomes receives this decision weight.

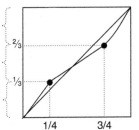

□

Exercise 7.2.3. EU was calculated in Exercise 3.2.2. We next consider RDU with U linear, as in the fourth row of Table 7.2.1. The expected value is 30. CE abbreviates certainty equivalent. $\text{RDU} = 0.421 \times U(80) + 0.579 \times U(-20) = 22.0639$. $\text{CE} = U^{\text{inv}}(22.06) = 22.06$. The risk premium is $30.00 - 22.06 = 7.94$.

We, finally, consider RDU with nonlinear U and w, as in the last row of Table 7.2.1. $\text{RDU} = 0.421 \times U(80) + 0.579 \times U(-20) = 0.0777$. $\text{CE} = U^{-1}(0.08) = 16.19$. The risk premium is $30.00 - 16.19 = 13.81$. □

Exercise 7.3.1. $\theta = 0.0053$ (risk tolerance \$188.68), $c = 0.75$, distance 8.29.

Table. *Theoretical CEs*

$-100_{0.05}-200$	$150_{0.05}50$	$100_{0.50}0$	$100_{0.95}0$	$0_{0.75}-100$	$0_{0.50}-50$	$0_{0.05}-100$	$101_{0.50}-50$	$50_{0.50}-20$	$112_{0.50}-50$
-192.33	57.67	40.73	84.98	-40.05	-28.04	-92.32	6.798	9.84	9.88

□

Exercise 7.3.1'. It is off by $-192.33 - (-179) = -13.33$. In Exercise 3.6.5, $\text{CE}(-100_{0.05}(-200)) = -196.45$ was predicted, which was off by more, namely -17.45. □

Exercise 7.3.2. $\theta = 0.0099$ (risk tolerance \$101.01), $a = 0.76$, $b = 0.17$, with distance 6.41. This distance is smaller than the distance in Exercise 7.3.1, which should be no surprise given that our family has one more free parameter to fit the data.

Table. *Theoretical CEs*

$-100_{0.05}-200$	$150_{0.05}50$	$100_{0.50}0$	$100_{0.95}0$	$0_{0.75}-100$	$0_{0.50}-50$	$0_{0.05}-100$	$101_{0.50}-50$	$50_{0.50}-20$	$112_{0.50}-50$
-185.85	64.15	42.84	83.05	-36.81	-25.58	-85.85	6.19	12.48	8.46

□

Exercise 7.3.2'. It is off by $-185.85 - (-179) = -6.85$. In Exercise 7.3.1', $\text{CE}(-100_{0.05}(-200)) = -192.33$ was predicted, which was off by more. Again, the better result here may simply be due to the use of more parameters. □

Exercise 7.3.3. Under RDU with utility U, α^i should satisfy

$$w(^1/_2) \times U(\alpha^i) + (1 - w(^1/_2)) \times U(1) = w(^1/_2) \times U(\alpha^{i-1}) + (1 - w(^1/_2)) \times U(8)$$

so that

$$\alpha^i = U^{-1}((w(^1/_2) \times U(\alpha^{i-1}) + (1 - w(^1/_2)) \times (U(8) - U(1))/w(^1/_2)).$$

Substituting the assumptions about U and w gives

$$\alpha^1 = 21.36, \alpha^2 = 33.54, \alpha^3 = 46.28, \text{ and } \alpha^4 = 59.46.$$

Exercise 6.5.1 showed that the β's are the same as the α's, and Exercise 4.3.4 showed that the δ's are also the same. The γ's will be different.

$$\gamma^2 = U^{-1}(w(^1/_2)U(\alpha^4) + (1 - w(^1/_2))U(10)) = 29.60$$

$$\gamma^1 = U^{-1}(w(^1/_2)U(\gamma^2) + (1 - w(^1/_2))U(10)) = 17.94$$

$$\gamma^3 = U^{-1}(w(^1/_2)U(\alpha^4) + (1 - w(^1/_2))U(\gamma^2)) = 41.86.$$

By Observation 6.5.8, $PE^j = w^{-1}(j/4)$ for all j. Trial and error using my computer gave:

$$PE^1 = 0.18; PE^2 = 0.65; PE^3 = 0.93. \ \square$$

Exercise 7.3.4. $\theta = 0.14$ and $c = 0.49$ ($w(^1/_2) = 0.35$), with distance 0.44. Theoretical CEs: $CE(62.5_{,5}10) = 19.91$, $CE(20_{,5}10) = 12.81$, $CE(62.5_{,5}20) = 30.29$.). Further, $CE(80_{1/_2}40) = 51.24$. $\square$

Exercise 7.3.5. $\theta = -0.20$, $c = 0.84$, with distance 1.46. Theoretical CEs: CE $(62.5_{.25}10) = 15.65$, $CE(62.5_{.75}10 = 33.70$, $CE(62.5_{.9}10 = 45.71)$. Further, CE $(80_{1/_2}40) = 55.49$. $\square$

Exercise 7.3.6. In parts (a)–(c), the special case of EU turns out to give the best fit.

(a) $\theta = 0.68$ and $c = 1.00$ ($w(^1/_2) = ^1/_2$), with distance 0.91. $CE(80_{1/_2}40) = 58.90$.
(b) $\theta = 0.510$ and $c = 1.00$ ($w(^1/_2) = ^1/_2$) with distance 0.62. $CE(80_{1/_2}40) = 58.32$.
    (Calculations with 3 digits shows that $c = 0.998$ gives a slightly better fit.)
(c) $\theta = 0.73$ and $c = 1.00$ ($w(^1/_2) = ^1/_2$), with distance 0.52. $CE(80_{1/_2}40) = 59.08$.
    (Calculations with 3 digits shows that $c = 0.999$ gives a slightly better fit.)
(d) $\theta = 0.80$ and $c = 0.62$ ($w(^1/_2) = 0.43$) with distance 1.16. $CE(80_{1/_2}40) = 56.34$.

The theoretical CEs for parts (a)–(c) are as in Exercise 4.10.5. The table gives theoretical CEs for part (d).

	$17_{0.5}1$	$10_{0.5}8$	$32_{0.5}1$	$17_{0.5}8$	$47_{0.5}1$	$32_{0.5}8$	$62.5_{0.5}1$	$47_{0.5}8$
part (d)	6.88	8.84	12.17	11.66	17.41	17.43	22.81	23.01

	$17_{0.5}100$	$10_{0.5}122$	$27.5_{0.5}100$	$17_{0.5}122$	$41_{0.5}100$	$27.5_{0.5}122$	$55_{0.5}100$	$41_{0.5}122$
part (d)	48.95	51.70	56.13	57.02	64.83	64.41	73.49	73.35

	$22_{0.5}1$	$13_{0.5}8$	$35_{0.5}1$	$22_{0.5}8$	$47_{0.5}1$	$35_{0.5}8$	$62.5_{0.5}1$	$47_{0.5}8$
part (d)	8.65	10.07	13.22	13.62	17.41	18.55	22.81	23.01

□

Exercise 7.3.7.

(a) $\theta = 0.64$, $c = 0.85$ (w(0.541) = 0.53), with distance 0.90. CE($80_{0.541}40$) = 59.78.
(b) $\theta = 0.62$, $c = 0.94$ (w(0.459) = 0.45), with distance 0.83. CE($80_{0.541}40$) = 60.19.
(c) $\theta = 0.66$, $c = 1.00$ (w(0.541) = 0.54), with distance 0.48. CE($80_{0.541}40$) = 60.49.
(d) $\theta = 0.63$, $c = 1.01$, with distance 0.8032. CE($80_{0.541}40$) = 60.40.

The tables give theoretical CEs for prospects in various parts. c1 denotes $cand_1$ (p = 0.541).

	$17_{c1}1$	$10_{c1}8$	$32_{c1}1$	$17_{c1}8$	$47_{c1}1$	$32_{c1}8$	$62.5_{c1}1$	$47_{c1}8$
part (a)	7.71	9.03	13.55	12.43	19.29	19.18	25.18	25.61
part (d)	7.93	9.06	13.96	12.57	19.90	19.54	25.98	26.18

	$17_{c1}100$	$10_{c1}122$	$27.5_{c1}100$	$17_{c1}122$	$41_{c1}100$	$27.5_{c1}122$	$55_{c1}100$	$41_{c1}122$
part (b)	48.70	49.93	56.60	56.32	65.71	64.65	74.45	74.21
part (d)	48.74	50.06	56.59	56.39	65.68	64.66	74.41	74.18

	$22_{c1}1$	$13_{c1}8$	$35_{c1}1$	$22_{c1}8$	$47_{c1}1$	$35_{c1}8$	$62.5_{c1}1$	$47_{c1}8$
part (c)	10.16	10.60	15.53	14.99	20.44	21.02	26.74	26.41
part (d)	9.96	10.60	15.16	14.95	19.90	20.89	25.98	26.18

□

Exercise 7.3.8. $\theta = 0.82$, $c = 0.53$ (w(½) = 0.37), with distance 3.19.
CE($80_{½}40$) = 54.40.
The tables give theoretical CEs for prospects in the two parts. c1 denotes $cand_1$.

$17_{c1}1$	$10_{c1}8$	$32_{c1}1$	$17_{c1}8$	$47_{c1}1$	$32_{c1}8$	$62.5_{c1}1$	$47_{c1}8$
6.17	8.74	10.82	11.23	15.43	16.30	20.17	21.22

$17_{c1}100$	$10_{c1}122$	$27.5_{c1}100$	$17_{c1}122$	$41_{c1}100$	$27.5_{c1}122$	$55_{c1}100$	$41_{c1}122$
45.13	46.69	52.71	52.24	61.99	60.01	71.28	69.49

$22_{c1}1$	$13_{c1}8$	$35_{c1}1$	$22_{c1}8$	$47_{c1}1$	$35_{c1}8$	$62.5_{c1}1$	$47_{c1}8$
7.73	9.82	11.74	12.95	15.43	17.30	20.17	21.22

$62.5_{0.5}10$	$20_{0.5}10$	$62.5_{0.5}20$	$62.5_{0.25}10$	$62.5_{0.75}10$	$62.5_{0.9}10$
27.74	13.60	34.91	22.82	34.05	41.29

□

Exercise 7.3.9. In all formulas of RDU in this exercise, the outcome-probability $\sqrt{1/2}$ has the best rank, and its decision weight is always $w\left(\sqrt{1/2}\right) = 1/2$. Hence, the whole exercise can be done in the same way as Exercise 3.5.4 and all answers are the same. □

Exercise 7.4.1. We have $\pi(0.01^{r_i})(U(\alpha_i) - U(4)) = \pi(0.01^w)(U(1) - U(0))$ for each i. If w is concave on $[r_i, r_i + 0.02]$ then $\pi(0.01^{r_{i+1}}) \le \pi(0.01^{r_i})$ so that $\alpha_{i+1} \ge \alpha_i$. The case of convexity is similar. □

Exercise 7.4.2. For each i, $\pi(0.01^{i/100})(U(6)-U(2)) < \pi(0.01^{(i+1)/100})U(2)$ so that $w((i+1)/100) - w((i)/100)) < 1.1^{-1}(w((i+2)/100) - w((i+1)/100)))$. This implies, in particular, for each $0 \le i \le 49$ that $w((i+1)/100) - w(i/100)) < 1.1^{-50}(w((i+51)/100) - w((i+50)/100))) < 0.01(w((i+51)/100) - w((i+50)/100)))$. Summing over $i = 0, \ldots, 49$ implies $w(0.5) - w(0) < 0.01(w(1) - w(0.5))$. This implies $w(0.5) < 0.01$. □

Exercise 7.7.1. We want to use Eq. (7.7.1) to obtain $\pi(p_2^b) \ge \pi(p_2^q)$, which gives the weakened implication of Case 1. Equation (7.7.1) can only be used if $p_2 + q \le w_{rb}$, i.e. $p_3 \ge 1 - w_{rb}$. We similarly want to use Eq. (7.7.2) to obtain $\pi(p_3^w) \ge \pi(p_3^{p_2})$, which gives the weakened implication of Case 3. Equation (7.7.2) can only be used if $p_2 \ge b_{rb}$. □

Exercise 7.8.2. In words: the larger the insensitivity region, the more weights $\pi(p^r)$ have to satisfy the required inequalities, and the more restrictive the preference conditions become. In inequalities: $\pi(p^b) \ge \pi(p^r)$ on $[0, w_{rb}]$ immediately implies

$\pi(p^b) \geq \pi(p^r)$ on $[0,a_{rw}]$ because $[0,a_{rw}] \subset [0,w_{rb}]$. $\pi(p^w) \geq \pi(p^r)$ on $[b_{rb},1]$ immediately implies $\pi(p^w) \geq \pi(p^r)$ on $[a_{rb},1]$ because $[a_{rb},1] \subset [b_{rb},1]$. $\square$

Exercise 7.8.3. $\pi(p^b) = b + ap \geq ap = \pi(p^r)$ for all $p > 0$ and $r > 0$ with $p + r < 1$. $\pi(p^w) = (1-a-b) + ap \geq ap = \pi(p^r)$ for all $p > 0$ and $r > 0$ with $p + r < 1$. $\square$

Exercise 7.10.1. $a = 0.72$ and $b = 0.10$. We have optimism index $(2b + a)/2 = 0.46$ and likelihood sensitivity index $a = 0.725$. $\square$

Exercise 7.10.2. The optimal fit results for $\theta = 0.86$, $a = 0.69$, and $b = 0.05$, with distance 0.23. We have optimism index $(2b + a)/2 = 0.40$ and likelihood sensitivity index $a = 0.69$. The theoretically predicted CEs are given by $100_{\frac{1}{2}}0 \sim 33.96$, $100_{\frac{1}{2}}50 \sim 69.17$, $100_{0.1}0 \sim 8.42$; $100_{0.1}50 \sim 55.68$; $100_{0.9}0 \sim 66.88$; $100_{0.9}50 \sim 83.04$. $\square$

Exercise 8.6.1. $w(\frac{1}{2})11 < (1-w(\frac{1}{2})10; 21w(\frac{1}{2}) < 10; w(\frac{1}{2}) < 10/21$. The preference with general m immediately follows. $\square$

Exercise 8.8.1. The new u in the exercise results from the u in Example 8.8.2 by a multiplication by $\frac{1}{1-\exp(-0.0032\mu)}$ for gains, and by a multiplation by $\frac{1}{1-\exp(-0.0061\mu)}$ for losses. The λ of 0.94 has to be multiplied by the ratio of the former fraction to the latter one, leading to Eq. (8.8.2). For $\mu = 0.01$ we get $\lambda = 1.792$, and for $\mu = 2$ we get $\lambda = 1.787$.

We next consider Eq. (3.5.5). For gains we multiply the u on top of Exercise 8.8.1 by $\frac{1}{0.0032}$, and for losses we multiply that u by $\frac{1}{0.0061}$. The λ of 0.94 has to be multiplied by the ratio of the former fraction to the latter one, leading to $\lambda = 1.792$. $\square$

Exercise 9.3.1. The outcomes, denoted $x_1, \ldots, x_n$, in x, x^+, and x^- are ranked the same way. Therefore, we can use the same decision weights π_j for the RDU calculation of each prospect. The positive terms in $\sum_{j=1}^n \pi_j U(x_j)$ yield $RDU(x^+)$, and the negative terms yield $RDU(x^-)$. We conclude that $RDU(x) = RDU(x^+) + RDU(x^-)$.

In general, assume that $U(0)$ need not be 0, and that $x_1 \geq \cdots \geq x_k \geq 0 \geq x_{k+1} \geq \cdots \geq x_n$. Then $RDU(x^+) = \sum_{j=1}^k \pi_j U(x_j) + \sum_{j=k+1}^n \pi_j U(0)$ and $RDU(x^-) = \sum_{j=1}^k \pi_j U(0) + \sum_{j=k+1}^n \pi_j U(x_j)$. Their sum is $\sum_{j=1}^n \pi_j U(x_j) + \sum_{j=1}^n \pi_j U(0) = RDU(x) + U(0)$. Then, $RDU(x) = RDU(x^+) + RDU(x^-) - U(0)$. So, Eq. (9.3.1) does not hold if $U(0) \neq 0$. $\square$

Exercise 9.3.2. This elaboration is analogous to that of Exercise 9.3.1, with everywhere PT instead of RDU. $\square$

Exercise 9.3.3. Take $x = 10_{\frac{1}{2}} - 10$, and let $w^+(\frac{1}{2}) = w^-(\frac{1}{2}) = 0.4$. Then both outcomes have decision weight 0.4, summing to 0.8 and not to 1. With $w^+(\frac{1}{2}) = w^-(\frac{1}{2}) = 0.6$ the decision weights sum to $1.2 > 1$. $\square$

Exercise 9.3.4.

(a) The decision weight of outcome 9 is $w^+(0.1) = 0.01$.

   The decision weight of outcome 4 is

$$w^+(0.4 + 0.1) - w^+(0.1) = w+(0.5) - w^+(0.1) = 0.25 - 0.01 = 0.24.$$

   The decision weight of outcome -9 is $w^-(0.1) = 0.1$. (I prefer going from lowest to highest for negative outcomes and, hence, I start with -9.)

   The decision weight of outcome -4 is

$$w^-(0.4 + 0.1) - w^-(0.1) = w^-(0.5) - w^-(0.1) = 0.5 - 0.1 = 0.4.$$

   The PT value is -1.69. The certainty equivalent is -0.71. (Hope you did not forget the loss aversion parameter!)

(b) The decision weight of outcome 36 is $w^+(0.1) = 0.01$.

   The decision weight of outcome 25 is $w^+(0.2 + 0.1) - w^+(0.1) = w^+(0.3) - w^+(0.1) = 0.09 - 0.01 = 0.08$.

   The decision weight of outcome -16 is $w^-(0.4) = 0.4$.

   The decision weight of outcome -9 is $w^-(0.3 + 0.4) - w^-(0.4) = w^-(0.7) - w^-(0.4) = 0.7 - 0.4 = 0.3$.

   The PT value of the prospect is -4.54. The certainty equivalent is -5.15. $\square$

Exercise 9.3.6. The expected value is 30. CE abbreviates certainty equivalent. The calculation for EU was done in Exercise 3.2.2, and the calculations for RDU were done in Exercise 7.2.3.

   For the sixth row, $PT(\lambda)$ which is PT with linear u and w, we have:
$PT = 0.50U(80) + 0.50U(-20) = 0.50 \times 80 + 2.25 \times 0.50 \times (-20) = 17.50$.
$CE = U^{-1}(17.50) = 17.50$. The risk premium is $30.00 - 17.50 = 12.50$.

   For the seventh row, PT with linear w, we have: $PT = 0.50U(80) + 0.50U(-20) = 0.0465$. $CE = U^{-1}(0.05) = 9.53$. The risk premium $= 30.00 - 9.53 = 20.47$.

   For the eighth row, PT with linear U, we have $PT = 0.421U(80) + 0.421U(-20) = 14.7224$. $CE = U^{-1}(14.72) = 14.72$. The risk premium $= 30.00 - 14.72 = 15.28$.

   For the last row, general PT, we have $PT = 0.421U(80) + 0.421U(-20) = 0.0391$. $CE = U^{-1}(0.04) = 7.99$. The risk premium is $30.00 - 7.99 = 22.01$. $\square$

Exercise 9.3.7. The expected value is 23.60. Certainty equivalents are given without elaboration.

(a) The risk premium is $23.60 - 3.25 = 20.35$. The decision weights are $\pi(x_1) = 0.055$, $\pi(x_2) = 0.294$, $\pi(x_3) = 0.191$, and $\pi(x_4) = 0.321$.

(b) The risk premium is $23.60 - 20.91 = 2.69$. The decision weights are the probabilities; i.e., $\pi(x_1) = 0.01$, $\pi(x_2) = 0.35$, $\pi(x_3) = 0.35$, and $\pi(x_4) = 0.29$.

(c) The risk premium is $23.60 - 14.02 = 9.58$. The decision weights are $\pi(x_1) = 0.055$, $\pi(x_2) = 0.294$, $\pi(x_3) = 0.191$, and $\pi(x_4) = 0.460$.

(d) The risk premium is $23.60 - 18.42 = 5.18$. The decision weights are
$\pi(x_1) = 0.055$, $\pi(x_2) = 0.294$, $\pi(x_3) = 0.191$, and $\pi(x_4) = 0.313$.

(e) The risk premium is $23.60 - 12.72 = 10.88$. The decision weights are the
probabilities, $\pi(x_1) = 0.01$, $\pi(x_2) = 0.35$, $\pi(x_3) = 0.35$, and $\pi(x_4) = 0.29$. □

Exercise 9.3.8. At first, it may seem that the pure loss prospect is entirely affected
by loss aversion whereas the mixed prospect is only partly affected by loss aversion.
Hence, at first hunch it may seem that the pure loss prospect y would be affected more
negatively by an increase in loss aversion than the mixed prospect, so that the pure
loss prospect would be preferred less by $\succcurlyeq_2$. However, this is not so. The mixed
prospect has a more extreme negative part and, hence, loses more value by an increase
in loss aversion than the pure loss prospect does. Hence, the pure loss prospect is
preferred by $\succcurlyeq_2$. An algebraic derivation is given next.

Because $PT_1(x^+) > 0$, we have $PT_1(x^-) < PT_1(y^-) < 0$. Hence, the mixed
prospect has a more extreme loss part. Now consider a loss-neutral decision maker $\succcurlyeq$
with the same probability weighting and basic utility as $\succcurlyeq_1$ and $\succcurlyeq_2$, but with loss
aversion $\lambda = 1 < \lambda_1 < \lambda_2$, and with a prospect theory evaluation functional PT.
Because of the increased loss aversion, for $\succcurlyeq_1$ the prospect x loses $(\lambda_1 - 1)PT(x^-)$ in
prospect theory value, and the prospect y loses $(\lambda_1 - 1)PT(y^-)$ $(= (\lambda_1 - 1)PT(y))$,
relative to PT. Because of the extra loss aversion, for $\succcurlyeq_2$, x loses $(\lambda_2 - \lambda_1)PT(x^-)$
extra, and y loses $(\lambda_2 - \lambda_1)PT(y^-)$ *extra*. The former is more negative. This and
$PT_1(x) = PT_1(y)$ imply $PT_2(x) < PT_2(y)$ and $x \prec_2 y$. (Similarly, $x \succ y$ follows for the
loss-neutral $\succcurlyeq$.)

An implication of this exercise is that, whereas the certainty equivalent of the
pure loss prospect is not affected by an increase in loss aversion, the certainty
equivalent of the mixed prospect becomes lower, also if this certainty equivalent is
a loss itself. □

Exercise 9.4.1. Consider Figure 6.5.5, and first assume that β and γ are of the
same sign, where one may be 0. By Lemma 6.5.4, all outcomes can be given the
same rank. They can also be given the same sign with, in particular, β and γ of
the same sign. The required result can now be proved the same way as in the
elaboration of Exercise 6.5.7.

Next assume that β and γ are of different sign. The preference with β implies the
same preference with 0 instead of β, as we already saw, and the preference with 0
instead of β implies the preference with γ instead of β, as we already saw. □

Exercise 9.4.2. Because of stochastic dominance, the α outcomes must all exceed
α^0 and all be positive, and so must the β outcomes be. Hence PT is the same as
RDU here, and the exercise follows from the corresponding results under RDU. □

Exercise 9.4.3. PT implies $U(1) = 1 = \pi(\frac{1}{2}^b)U(\alpha)$. It also implies $\pi(\frac{1}{2}^b)U(\alpha) + \pi(\frac{1}{2}_w)$
$U(-\beta) = U(0) = 0$, so that $\pi(\frac{1}{2}^b)U(\alpha) = -\pi(\frac{1}{2}_w)U(-\beta)$. Then $\pi(\frac{1}{2}_w)U(-\beta) = -1$.
The indifference $-\delta \sim 0_{\frac{1}{2}}(-\beta)$ then implies $U(-\delta) = -1$. Because $U(-\delta) = \lambda u(-\delta)$,
$\lambda = -1/u(-\delta)$ follows. □

Exercise 9.5.1. The table should be filled out as follows.

	x_1	p_1	π_1	x_2	p_2	π_2	x_3	p_3	π_3	x_4	p_4	π_4	PT	CE	choice
$F_{1,I}$	−3000	.50	.45	4500	.50	.42	0	0	0	0	0	0	−482.63	−446.01	71%
$G_{1,I}$	−6000	.25	.29	3000	.75	.57	0	0	0	0	0	0	−742.80	−728.02	27%
F_2	−1600	.25	.29	−200	.25	.16	1200	.25	.13	1600	.25	.29	−215.70	−178.60	38%
G_2	−1000	.25	.29	−800	.25	.16	800	.25	.13	2000	.25	.29	−137.63	−107.19	62%
$F_{3,III}$	−1500	.50	.45	4500	.50	.42	0	0	0	0	0	0	52.75	90.59	76%
$G_{3,III}$	−3000	.25	.29	3000	.75	.57	0	0	0	0	0	0	−105.77	−79.47	23%

For each pair F,G, the choice predicted by prospect theory is the majority choice. □

Exercise 9.5.2.

(a) $\theta = 0.0058$ (risk tolerance is \$172.41); $c = 0.62$; λ plays no role. Distance is 5.48.

Table. *Theoretical CEs*

$-100_{0.05}-200$	$150_{0.05}50$	$100_{0.50}0$	$100_{0.95}0$	$0_{0.75}-100$	$0_{0.50}-50$	$0_{0.05}-100$	$101_{0.50}-50$	$50_{0.50}-20$	$112_{0.50}-50$
−184.23	60.09	35.75	74.98	−35.58	−23.06	−84.23	8.03	9.71	10.69

(b) $\theta = 0.0012$ (with risk tolerance \$833.33); $c = 0.61$; $\lambda = 1.83$; Distance is 3.25. $CE(-100_{0.05}(-200)) = -180.28$.

Table. *Theoretical CEs*

$-100_{0.05}-200$	$150_{0.05}50$	$100_{0.50}0$	$100_{0.95}0$	$0_{0.75}-100$	$0_{0.50}-50$	$0_{0.05}-100$	$101_{0.50}-50$	$50_{0.50}-20$	$112_{0.50}-50$
−180.28	62.49	40.61	78.31	−30.33	−21.40	−80.28	0.34	4.85	4.43

(c) $\theta = 0.0045$ (risk tolerance \$222.22); $\theta' = -0.0045$; $c = 0.66$; $\lambda = 1.78$. Distance is 2.54.

Table. *Theoretical CEs*

$-100_{0.05}-200$	$150_{0.05}50$	$100_{0.50}0$	$100_{0.95}0$	$0_{0.75}-100$	$0_{0.50}-50$	$0_{0.05}-100$	$101_{0.50}-50$	$50_{0.50}-20$	$112_{0.50}-50$
−179.60	59.79	38.87	79.60	−24.99	−20.77	−79.60	0.649	4.80	3.70

(d) $\theta = 0.0055$ (risk tolerance \$181.82); $\theta' = -0.0033$; $c = 0.66$; $\lambda = 1.63$. Distance is 2.4244. (I give more digits to distinguish from a local optimum at $\theta = 0.0060$, $\beta = -0.0038$, $\gamma = 0.67$, and $\lambda = 1.61$, with distance 2.4252.) $CE(-100_{1/2}(-200)) = -140$.

Table. *Theoretical CEs*

$-100_{0.05}-200$	$150_{0.05}50$	$100_{0.5}0$	$100_{0.95}0$	$0_{0.75}-100$	$0_{0.50}-50$	$0_{0.05}-100$	$101_{0.50}-50$	$50_{0.50}-20$	$112_{0.50}-50$
-140.28	59.39	37.72	78.74	-26.10	-21.13	-80.59	1.05	5.47	3.80

□

Exercise 9.5.2′.

(a) It is off by $-184.23 - (-179) = -5.23$.
(b) It is off by $-180.28 - (-179) = -1.28$.
(c) It is off by $-179.60 - (-179) = -0.60$. □

Exercise 9.6.1. Equation (9.6.7) implies $\lambda^* = 0.39$. □

Exercise 10.2.1.

1. We rank outcomes from best to worst, and define $E_1 = s_3$, $E_2 = s_1$, $E_3 = s_2$. The prospect then is $E_1 9 E_2 1 E_3 0$.
2. Outcome 9: rank is $\varnothing$ (i.e. best); outcome 1: rank is E_1 (i.e. s_3); outcome 0: rank is $E_1 \cup E_2$ (i.e. $\{s_3, s_1\}$).
3. The W values of the ranks are $W(\varnothing) = 0$, $W(E_1) = W(s_3) = 0.4$, and $W(E_1 \cup E_2) = W(s_3, s_1) = 0.6$.
4. For outcome 9, the marginal W contribution of its outcome event to its rank is $W(E_1) - W(\varnothing) = W(E_1) = 0.4$.

   For outcome 1, the marginal W contribution of its outcome event to its rank is $W(E_2 \cup E_1) - W(E_1) = W(s_1, s_3) - W(s_3) = 0.6 - 0.4 = 0.2$.

   For outcome 0, the marginal W contribution of its outcome event to its rank is $W(E_3 \cup E_2 \cup E_1\} - W(E_2 \cup E_1) = W(s_2, s_1, s_3) - W(s_1, s_3) = 1 - 0.6 = 0.4$.
5. $U(9\} = 3$, $U(1\} = 1$, $U(0) = 0$.
6. The RDU value is $0.4 \times 3 + 0.2 \times 1 + 0.4 \times 0 = 1.4$.

The CE is $U^{-1}(1.4) = 1.4^2 = 1.96$. □

Exercise 10.2.2. The RDU value is $W(s_3) \times 5 + (W(s_2, s_3) - W(s_3)) \times 3 + (1 - W(s_2, s_3)) \times 0 = 0.4 \times 5 + (0.7 - 0.4) \times 3 + (1 - 0.7) \times 0 = 2 + 0.9 + 0 = 2.9$. The CE is $U^{-1}(2.9) = 2.9$. □

Exercise 10.2.3. For part

(a) see the main text following Eq. (10.2.7).
(b) An indifference $(x_1, x_2, x_3) \sim (y_1, y_2, y_3)$ with $x_1 \geq x_2 \geq x_3$ and $y_1 \geq y_2 \geq y_3$ gives an equality $\pi(G^b)x_1 + \pi(E^G)x_2 + \pi(L^w)x_3 = \pi(G^b)y_1 + \pi(E^G)y_2 + \pi(L^w)y_3$ with two unknowns $\pi(G^b)$ and $\pi(E^G)$ ($\pi(L^w)$ is 1 minus these two weights). Hence, if we observe two such indifferences then, unless there are some degenerate cases, we can resolve these two unknowns, and we then know $\pi(E^G)$.

An easy way is to observe $1_{G \cup E}0 \sim \varepsilon$ and $1_G 0 \sim \delta$, implying $W(G \cup E) = \varepsilon$
and $W(G) = \delta$. Then $\pi(E^G) = \varepsilon - \delta$.

(c) An indifference $(x_1, x_2 + 1, x_3) \sim (x_1 + \varepsilon, x_2 + \varepsilon, x_3 + \varepsilon)$ with $x_1 \geq x_2 + 1 \geq x_2 \geq x_3$
implies $\pi(G^b)x_1 + \pi(E^G)(x_2 + 1) + \pi(L^w)x_3 = \pi(G^b)(x_1 + \varepsilon) + \pi(E^G)(x_2 + \varepsilon) +$
$\pi(L^w)(x_3 + \varepsilon)$, i.e., $\pi(E^G) = \varepsilon$. $\square$

Exercise 10.2.4. We have $\pi_j = W(E_j \cup \cdots \cup E_1) - W(E_{j-1} \cup \cdots \cup E_1) \geq 0$
as a consequence of monotonicity with respect to set inclusion. We have
$\pi_n + \pi_{n-1} + \cdots + \pi_2 + \pi_1 = [W(E_n \cup \cdots \cup E_1) - W(E_{n-1} \cup \cdots \cup E_1)] +$
$[W(E_{n-1} \cup \cdots \cup E_1) - W(E_{n-2} \cup \cdots \cup E_1)] + \cdots + [W(E_3 \cup E_2 \cup E_1) - W(E_2 \cup$
$E_1)] + [W(E_2 \cup E_1) - W(E_1)] + W(E_1) = W(E_n \cup \cdots \cup E_1) = 1$. $\square$

Exercise 10.3.1. Exercise 10.2.1 has what are sometimes called exchangeable states
of nature, displaying symmetry. Because $W(s_1) = W(s_2) = W(s_3)$, P will have to
satisfy $P(s_1) = P(s_2) = P(s_3)$. Summing to 1, these must all be ⅓. Then $W(s_1) = 0.4$
implies $w(\tfrac{1}{3}) = 0.4$. $W(s_1, s_2) = 0.6$ implies $w(\tfrac{2}{3}) = 0.6$. With these choices,
$W(E) = w(P(E))$ for all events E.

In Exercise 10.2.2, again, because $W(s_1) = W(s_2) = W(s_3)$, P, if existing, will
have to satisfy $P(s_1) = P(s_2) = P(s_3)$. Summing to 1, these must all be ⅓. Also,
$W(s_1) = 0.4$ implies that $w(\tfrac{1}{3}) = 0.4$ must be. $W(s_1, s_2) = 0.6$ implies that $w(\tfrac{2}{3}) = 0.6$
must be. However, then $w(P(s_2, s_3)) = w(\tfrac{2}{3}) = 0.6$ would follow, contradicting the
assumed $W(s_2, s_3) = 0.7$. Hence there cannot exist P, w as described. $\square$

Exercise 10.3.2. Assume that $P(A) = P(B)$. Then, by stochastic dominance,
$1_A 0 \sim 1_B 0$. Applying RDU shows that $W(A) = W(B)$. It is well known that, if
$[P(A) = P(B) \Rightarrow W(A) = W(B)]$, then a function w exists such that $W(\cdot) = w(P(\cdot))$.[2]
By strict stochastic dominance, $P(A) > P(B)$ implies $1_A 0 \succ 1_B 0$ and, hence,
$W(A) > W(B)$. This implies that w increases strictly. $\square$

Exercise 10.4.1. The choices can be accommodated by a linear utility function
with a decision weight of M^w, which is relevant for the right choice situation,
considerably larger than that of M^H, which is relevant for the left choice situation.
This can be achieved by letting W-values all be low, so that most decision weight
goes to the event ranked worst. For example, $W(H \cup M) = \tfrac{2}{6}$ and $W(H) = \tfrac{1}{6}$
imply decision weight $\tfrac{2}{6} - \tfrac{1}{6} = \tfrac{1}{6}$ for M^H as in the left choice situation, and
accommodates the left preference. $W(L \cup H) = \tfrac{2}{6}$ implies decision weight $1 - \tfrac{2}{6} = \tfrac{4}{6}$
for M^w in the right choice situation, and accommodates the right preference.

Alternatively, we can: (a) Take a mathematical probability P, without necessarily
an empirical meaning, defined as $P(H) = 0.06$, $P(M) = 0.07$, and $P(L) = 0.87$;
(b) take a probability weighting function w piecewise linear with $w(0.93) = 0.093$;
(c) define $W(E) = w(P(E))$ for all events E. $\square$

---

[2] For each value p in the range of P, take an arbitrary event A with $P(A) = p$, and define $w(p) = W(A)$. By the
implication between brackets, for all events B with $P(B) = p$ then $w(P(B))$ is the proper value $W(B)$.

Exercise 10.4.2.
We can rewrite pessimism in the following ways:

$$\pi(E^{C \cup R}) \geq \pi(E^R)$$

$$W(E \cup C \cup R) - W(C \cup R) \geq W(E \cup R) - W(R)$$

$$W(E \cup C \cup R) \geq W(E \cup R) + W(C \cup R) - W(R)$$

and then, substituting $A = E \cup R$, $B = C \cup R$, the inequalities are equivalent to Eq. (10.4.3). □

Exercise 10.4.3. Event E_1 generates the same RDU difference $\pi(E^b)(U(12) - U(11))$ in favor of the right prospect under both common outcomes. Event E_3 generates the same RDU difference $\pi(E_3^{E_1 \cup E_2})(U(6) - U(6)) = 0 = \pi(E_3^{E_1})(U(10) - U(10))$ under both common outcomes. Event E_4 generates the same RDU difference $\pi(E_4^w)(U(1) - U(1)) = 0$ under both common outcomes. Only for event E_2 something changes. It generates RDU difference $\pi(E_2^{E_1})(U(9) - U(8))$ in favor of the left prospect if the common outcome is 6, and $\pi(E_2^{E_1 \cup E_3})(U(9) - U(8))$ if the common outcome is 10. Because of pessimism, $\pi(E_2^{E_1 \cup E_3}) \geq \pi(E_2^{E_1})$, and the difference in favor of the left prospect is larger for common outcome 10 than for common outcome 6. □

Exercise 10.4.4. Take any $\gamma \succ \beta$. Because $U(\gamma) > U(\beta)$, the following statements are equivalent: $\gamma_C \beta \succcurlyeq \gamma_D \beta$; $W(C)U(\gamma) + (1 - W(C))U(\beta) \geq W(D)U(\gamma) + (1 - W(D))U(\beta)$; $W(C) \geq W(D)$. □

Exercise 10.4.5. In words: the larger the insensitivity region, the more weights $\pi(E^R)$ have to satisfy the required inequalities, and the more restrictive the preference conditions become. In inequalities: $\pi(E^b) \geq \pi(E^R)$ on $[\emptyset, W_{rb}]$ immediately implies $\pi(E^b) \geq \pi(E^R)$ on $[\emptyset, A_{rw}]$ because $[\emptyset, A_{rw}] \subset [\emptyset, W_{rb}]$. $\pi(E^w) \geq \pi(E^R)$ on $[B_{rb}, S]$ immediately implies $\pi(E^w) \geq \pi(E^R)$ on $[A_{rb}, S]$ because $[A_{rb}, S] \subset [B_{rb}, S]$. □

Exercise 10.4.6. We want to use Eq. (10.4.5) to obtain $\pi(E_2^b) \geq \pi(E_2^A)$, which gives the weakened implication of Case 1. Equation (10.4.5) can only be used if $E_2 \cup A \preccurlyeq W_{rb}$. We similarly want to use Eq. (10.4.6) to obtain $\pi(E_3^w) \geq \pi(E_3 E2)$, which gives the weakened implication of Case 3. Equation (10.4.6) can only be used if $E_2 \succcurlyeq B_{rb}$. □

Exercise 10.5.1. The only change between the two choices is the common outcome under event L, changing from 0 to 25K. Hence, the change of preference constitutes a violation of the sure-thing principle. It does not constitute a violation of the rank-sure-thing principle because the event L cannot be given the same rank for all prospects. With common outcome 0, L must have the worst rank for the left safe prospect s in the left choice situation. With common outcome 25K, L cannot have the worst rank for the right risky prospect in the right choice situation but its rank must be H. □

Exercise 10.5.2. By Lemma 10.5.3, all events have the same rank for $\gamma_{E^R}x$ and $\beta_{E^R}x$. Hence, the RDU difference between these prospects is $\pi(E^R)(U(\gamma)-U(\beta))$. If $\pi(E^R)=0$ then the RDU difference between the two prospects is always 0 and E^R must be null.

Next suppose that $\pi(E^R)>0$. We derive nonnullness. Take some $\gamma>\beta$; say, $\gamma=1$ and $\beta=0$. Let x take values at least as large as γ on R, and at most as large as β on $(E \cup R)^c$. In both $\gamma_E x$ and $\beta_E x$, the rank of E can be taken R, so that we can write $\gamma_{E^R}x$ and $\beta_{E^R}x$ for these prospects. The RDU difference between these two prospects is $\pi(E^R)(U(\gamma)-U(\beta))>0$ because both the weight and the utility difference are strictly positive. $\gamma_{E^R}x \succ \beta_{E^R}x$ follows and E^R is nonnull. $\square$

Exercise 10.5.3. We can copy the reasoning preceding Observation 6.5.1, with $\pi(\frac{1}{2}^b)$ replaced by $\pi((\text{cand}_1 \text{ wins})^b)$ and $\pi(\frac{1}{2}^w)$ replaced by $\pi((\text{cand}_2 \text{ wins})^w)$ in the analysis of Figure 4.1.1. $\square$

Exercise 10.5.4. We use the result of Exercise 10.5.3. We further copy the reasoning preceding Observation 6.5.1 for the analysis of Figure 4.1.2 but now with $\pi(\frac{1}{2}^w)$ replaced by $\pi((\text{cand}_1 \text{ wins})^w)$ and $\pi(\frac{1}{2}^b)$ replaced by $\pi((\text{cand}_2 \text{ wins})^b)$, obtaining equalities $\frac{\pi((\text{candidate2 wins})^b)}{\pi((\text{candidate1 wins})^w)}(U(G) - U(g)) = U(\beta^{j+1}) - U(\beta^j)$. The reasoning now proceeds as in the elaboration of Exercise 6.5.1. $\square$

Exercise 10.5.5. Under RDU, $\alpha \ominus \beta \sim^t_c \gamma \ominus \delta$ implies $U(\alpha) - U(\beta) = U(\gamma) - U(\delta)$. $\alpha' \ominus \beta \sim^t_c \gamma \ominus \delta$ implies $U(\alpha') - U(\beta) = U(\gamma) - U(\delta)$. Because U increases strictly, $\alpha' = \alpha$ follows. $\square$

Exercise 10.5.6. We still have $\alpha^i \ominus \alpha^{i-1} \sim^t \alpha^1 \ominus \alpha^0$ for all i, and $\alpha^i \ominus \alpha^{i-1} \sim^t_c \alpha^1 \ominus \alpha^0$ for all i. By Exercise 4.3.2, EU is still falsified, and $\mathbf{199.74} \ominus 109.75 \sim^t$ $109.75 \ominus 46.50$ joint with $\mathbf{316.47} \ominus 109.75 \sim^t 109.75 \ominus 46.50$ still exhibit a violation of tradeoff consistency. RDU is not violated with $\pi(\text{cand}_1{}^b) \neq \pi(\text{cand}_1{}^w)$.

Fig. 6.5.3a implies $\pi(\text{cand}_1{}^w)(U(\alpha^1) - U(\alpha^0)) = \pi(\text{cand}_2{}^b)(U(\alpha^4) - U(\alpha^2))$, so that $\pi(\text{cand}_1{}^w) = 2\pi(\text{cand}_2{}^b)$. Thus, $1 - W(\text{cand}_1) = 2W(\text{cand}_2)$. The indifference $100_{\text{cand}_1}0 \sim 100_{\text{cand}_2}0$ implies $W(\text{cand}_1) = W(\text{cand}_2)$. $1-W(\text{cand}_1) = 2W(\text{cand}_1)$ implies $W(\text{cand}_1) = \frac{1}{3}$, which is also $W(\text{cand}_2)$. $\pi(\text{cand}_1{}^w)=\pi(\text{cand}_2{}^w)=2/3$, $\pi(\text{cand}_1{}^b)=\pi(\text{cand}_2{}^b)=1/3$. We again get $U(\beta^4) = 2$. Thus, all indifferences in Figures 6.5.2 and 6.5.3 are accommodated. $\square$

Exercise 10.6.1.

(a) Assume that α is increased to $\alpha + \varepsilon$ for $\varepsilon > 0$. If $\alpha + \varepsilon \leq \beta$ then the evaluation increases by $(p+\mu)(U(\alpha + \varepsilon) - U(\alpha))$. If $\beta \leq \alpha < \alpha + \varepsilon$ then the evaluation increases by $(p-\mu)(U(\alpha + \varepsilon) - U(\alpha))$. Thus, the evaluation is increasing in α. It similarly is increasing in β. If both α and β are increased then there is a $\delta > 0$ such that the utilities of both outcomes increases by at least δ, generating an increase of the functional of at least δ.

(b) Equation (10.6.2) is a case of binary RDU with $W(s_1) = p-\mu$ and $W(s_2) = 1 - p - \mu$. Binary RDU is a case of Eq. (10.6.2) with $\mu = (1 - W(s_1) - W(s_2))/2$ (proposed as a measure of ambiguity aversion by Dow & Werlang, 1992, and Schmeidler, 1989 pp. 571–572), $p = W(s_1) + \mu$. $\square$

Exercise 10.9.1.
The following four question marks refer to the same inequality:

$$W(E \cup R') - W(R') \ ? \ W(E \cup R) - W(R)$$

$$w(P(E \cup R')) - w(P(R')) \ ? \ w(P(E \cup R)) - w(P(R))$$

$$w(P(E) + P(R')) - w(P(R')) \ ? \ w(P(E) + P(R)) - w(P(R))$$

Substituting e for $P(E)$, r' for $P(R')$, and r for $P(R)$, we get

$$w(e + r') - w(r') \ ? \ w(e + r) - w(r).$$

If $R' \supset R$, then always $r' \geq r$. Therefore, convexity of w (Eq. (6.3.3)) always implies convexity of W (Eq. (10.4.4)), and concavity of w (Eq. (6.3.4)) always implies concavity of W. This is the answer to part (a).

For part (b), take some e, r, r' from [0,1] with $e + r' \leq 1$ and $r \leq r'$. By solvability, we can find the following events:

- An event A with $\emptyset \subset A \subset S$ and $W(A) = w(e + r')$, implying $P(A) = e + r'$.
- An event R' with $\emptyset \subset R' \subset A$ and $W(R') = w(r')$; define $E = A - R'$. We have $P(R') = r'$ so that, by additivity of P, $P(E) = e + r' - r' = e$.
- An event R with $\emptyset \subset R \subset R'$ and $W(R) = w(r)$.

Convexity of W now implies that the first question mark is the $\geq$ sign, from which it then follows that the last question mark is also the $\geq$ sign, and w must be convex too. The $\leq$ sign for the question mark shows that concavity of W similarly implies concavity of w. $\square$

Exercise 10.9.2. If W satisfies solvability, then for all values μ between 0 and 1 there must be an event with W value μ. It implies that the increasing w cannot make jumps. Hence, it must be continuous. Conversely, assume that w is continuous, and let $W(A) < \mu < W(C)$ for $A \subset C$. There exists a p with $P(A) < p < P(C)$ and $w(p) = \mu$. By solvability of P, we can take B with $P(B) = p$ and $A \subset B \subset C$. $\square$

Exercise 10.9.4.

(a) $\pi((E_2 \cup E_1)^b) = w(E_2 \cup E_1) = W(E_1) + (W(E_2 \cup E_1) - W(E_1)) = \pi(E_1{}^b) + \pi(E_2{}^{E_1})$.
(b) $\pi((E_2 \cup E_1)^R) = W(E_2 \cup E_1 \cup R) - W(R) = W(E_1 \cup R) - W(R) + (W(E_2 \cup E_1 \cup R) - W(E_1 \cup R)) = \pi(E_1{}^R) + \pi(E_2{}^{E_1 \cup R})$.
(c) Both summations equal the W-value of the union of the events. $\square$

Exercise 10.9.5. Define $W(E) = \pi(E^b)$ for all events E. Then $W(\emptyset) = 0$ and $W(S) = 1$. If $A \supset B$ then write $B = E_1$, $A - B = E_2$. By additivity,

$W(A) = \pi((E_1 \cup E_2)^b) = \pi(E_1^b) + \pi(E_2^{E_1}) = W(B) + \pi(E_2^{E_1})$. By nonnegativity of π, this implies $W(A) \geq W(B)$ and monotonicity holds. Now consider a general $\pi(E^R)$. Additivity implies $\pi((E \cup R)^b) = \pi(R^b) + \pi(E^R)$; i.e., $\pi(E^R) = W(E \cup R) - W(R)$, as required. This result also shows that parts (b) and (c) of Exercise 10.9.4, although seemingly stronger than part (a), are implied by part (a) after all. It can also be seen that besides the collapsing of outcomes it was mainly additivity that drove the derivation in Exercise 6.7.1. $\square$

Exercise 10.9.6. We have $\pi(E^{R_i})(U(\alpha_i) - U(4)) = \pi(A^w)(U(1) - U(0))$ for each i, so that in particular $\pi(E^{R_i})(U(\alpha_i) - U(4)) = \pi(E^{R_{i+1}})(U(\alpha_{i+1}) - U(4))$. If W is concave in the sense specified in the exercise then $U(\alpha_{i+1}) - U(4) \geq U(\alpha_i) - U(4)$ so that $\alpha_{i+1} \geq \alpha_i$. The case of convexity is similar. $\square$

Exercise 10.10.1. This exercise is analogous to Exercise 6.9.1. Probabilities $p_j + \cdots + p_1$ are replaced by events $E_j \cup \cdots \cup E_1$ (both being ranks), the rank $P_x(U > \tau)$ is replaced by the rank $T_\tau = \{s \in S: U(x(s)) > \tau\}$, and $w(G(\tau))$ is replaced by $W(T_\tau)$. $\square$

Exercise 10.11.1. This exercise is similar to Assignment 6.7.2.

(a) $(W(E_{\rho_{i+1}} \cup \cdots \cup E_{\rho_1}) - W(E_{\rho_i} \cup \cdots \cup E_{\rho_1}))U(x_{\rho_{i+1}}) + (W(E_{\rho_i} \cup \cdots \cup E_{\rho_1}) - W(E_{\rho_{i-1}} \cup \cdots \cup E_{\rho_1}))U(x_{\rho_i}) = (W(E_{\rho_{i+1}} \cup \cdots \cup E_{\rho_1}) - W(E_{\rho_{i-1}} \cup \cdots \cup E_{\rho_1}))U(x_{\rho_i})$.

(b) The right-hand side of the preceding equation is equal to

$$(W(E_{\rho_{i+1}} \cup \cdots \cup E_{\rho_1}) - W(E_{\rho_{i+1}} \cup E_{\rho_{i-1}} \cup \cdots \cup E_{\rho_1}))U(x_{\rho_i}) +$$

$$(W(E_{\rho_{i+1}} \cup E_{\rho_{i-1}} \cup \cdots \cup E_{\rho_1}) - W(E_{\rho_{i-1}} \cup \cdots \cup E_{\rho_1}))U(x_{\rho_i}),$$

which is equal to (with $E_{\rho'_{i+1}} = E_{\rho_i}$, $E_{\rho'_i} = E_{\rho_{i+1}}$) $(W(E_{\rho'_{i+1}} \cup \cdots \cup E_{\rho'_1}) - W(E_{\rho'_i} \cup \cdots \cup E_{\rho'_1}))$ $U(x_{\rho'_{i+1}}) + (W(E_{\rho'_i} \cup \cdots \cup E_{\rho'_1}) - W(E_{\rho'_{i-1}} \cup \cdots \cup E_{\rho'_1}))U(x_{\rho'_i})$ (note that $x_{\rho'_i} = x_{\rho'_{i+1}} = x_{\rho_i} = x_{\rho_{i+1}}$). Hence, the left-hand side of (i), i.e., the ith and (i+1)th terms of the RDU formula under complete ranking ρ, contribute the same total as the ith and (i+1)th terms of the RDU formula under complete ranking ρ'. The other terms for both calculations of RDU are identical and, hence, the two complete ranks yield the same total RDU value. $\square$

Exercise 10.12.1. Left to the readers. $\square$

Exercise 10.12.2. Let F denote the set of prospects considered.

(a) If $x(s) > x(t)$ for some $x \in F$, then the complete ranking must rank the outcome event containing s as better than the one containing t. Then for all $y \in F$ we must have $y(s) \geq y(t)$; i.e., not $y(s) < y(t)$.

(b) We define a weak order $\geq'$ on S as follows:
   - If $x(s) > x(t)$ for some x, then $s >' t$. By the assumption made, then $y(s) \geq y(t)$ for all $y \in F$.
   - If $x(s) < x(t)$ for some x, then $s <' t$. By the assumption made, then $y(s) \leq y(t)$ for all $y \in F$.
   - If $x(s) = x(t)$ for all x, then $s \sim' t$.

It elementarily follows that $\sim'$ is an equivalence relation (symmetric, transitive, reflexive) and that $\geq'$ is a weak order. Let ρ be any complete ranking of S such that ρ agrees with $\geq'$ in the sense that $s \geq' t$ implies that ρ ranks s as better than t. It means that ρ respects all strict $>'$ relations, and arbitrarily orders ties $\sim'$. ρ is an order refining the weak order $\geq'$. Such refinements exist for all weak orders (Szpilrajn 1930). It follows that all $x \in F$ are in the comoncone C^ρ generated by ρ.

(c) This immediately follows from Eq. (10.12.1), because it defines comonotonicity as a condition to apply to all pairs of prospects.

The result of the exercise can be extended to nonsimple prospects. This book, however, only considers simple prospects. □

Exercise 10.12.3.

(a) If, for some prospect x from the set, $x(s) > x(t)$ for some states s, t, then $s \in E_i$ and $t \in E_j$ for some $i < j$. Then $y(s) = y_i \geq y_j = y(t)$ for all prospects y from the set. Eq. (10.12.1) holds and the set is comonotonic.

(b) By Exercise 10.12.2, Eq. (10.12.1) holds. We can now replicate the elaboration of Exercise 10.12.2b with $E_1, \ldots, E_n$ playing the role of a finite state space S.

As an aside, the order ρ of $E_1, \ldots, E_n$ generates a weak order ρ' on S defined by $s\ \rho'\ t$ if, for $s \in E_i$ and $t \in E_j$, $i \leq j$. This can be extended to an order on S by Szpilrajn's (1930) lemma, and then the set of prospects is contained in the comoncone C^ρ.

As another aside, the results of this exercise can be extended to nonsimple prospects. This book only considers simple prospects. □

Exercise 10.12.4.

(a) For $E \neq \varnothing$, strong monotonicity implies $1_{E \cup R}0 \succ 1_R 0$, which implies $\pi(E^R) > 0$.

(b) Conversely, assume that all decision weights are positive. Let $\alpha > \beta$ and consider $\alpha_E x$ and $\beta_E x$ with E nonempty. Then it can be shown that the RDU difference between the two prospects is at least $\lambda(U(\alpha) - U(\beta))$, where $\lambda > 0$ is the minimum decision weight of nonempty events. For instance, one can keep all outcomes constant except β, increase β slowly towards α, and consider the derivative of RDU with respect to $U(\beta)$. This derivative always exceeds the minimum decision weight except at a finite number of points at which the derivative is not defined because then the rank changes and RDU is kinked. The point will not be elaborated further. □

Exercise 11.2.1. $1_{B_a}0$ and $1_{B_k}0$ generate the same probability-contingent prospect $1_{\frac{1}{2}}0$, so that they should be indifferent according to Assumption 2.1.2. This is violated by the strict preference $1_{B_a}0 \prec 1_{B_k}0$. □

Exercise 11.2.2. The best fit is obtained with $\theta = 0.55$; $W(cand_1) = 0.59$, and $W(cand_2) = 0.49$; with distance 0.7734. Some calculations for the distance:

$$CE(17_{cand_1}1) = U^{-1}(W(cand_1)U(17) + (1 - W(cand_1))U(1)) = 8.35$$
$$CE(10_{cand_1}8) = U^{-1}(W(cand_1)U(10) + (1 - W(cand_1))U(8)) = 9.16$$

The other CEs are calculated similarly, generating distance
$\sqrt{(((8.3487 - 9.1558)^2 + (14.6603 - 12.9461)^2 + (20.8388 - 20.4289)^2 +}$
$(27.1497 - 27.5084)^2 + (49.9241 - 50.9823)^2 + (57.9450 - 57.7108)^2 +$
$(67.0020 - 66.2504)^2 + (75.5488 - 75.8478)^2 + (10.4750 - 10.8187)^2 +$
$(15.9036 - 15.5083)^2 + (20.8388 - 21.8681)^2 + (27.1497 - 27.5084)^2)/12) = 0.7734.$
$CE(80_{cand1}40) = U^{-1}(W(cand_1)U(80) + (1 - W(cand_1))U(40)) = (0.59 \times 80^{0.55} +$
$0.41 \times 40^{0.55})^{1/0.55} = 62.10.$ □

Exercise 11.3.1.

(a) [EV]. The risk premium is 0.
(b) [EU with U]. The risk premium is 0.09.
(c) [RDU with U, w]. The risk premium is 0.56.
(d) [RDU with U,W]. The risk premium is 1.06.

Various components contributing to risk premium

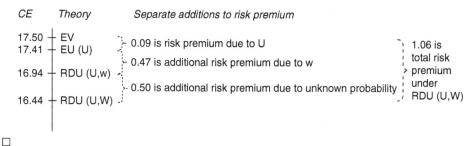

□

Exercise 11.4.1. For P in the CORE, we must have $P(s_1) \geq W(s_1) = \frac{1}{3}$ and $P(s_2) \geq W(s_2) = \frac{1}{3}$. The latter inequality is equivalent to $P(s_1) \leq \frac{2}{3}$. Hence the CORE is $\{P: \frac{1}{3} \leq P(s_1) \leq \frac{2}{3}\}$ □

Exercise 11.8.1. We find $a_k = 0.72$ and $b_k = 0.10$, as in Exercise 7.10.1, and $a_a = 0.60$, and $b_a = 0.10$. We have optimism index $(2b_k + a_k)/2 = 0.46$ and likelihood sensitivity index $a_k = 0.72$ for risk, and optimism index $(2b_a + a_a)/2 = 0.40$ and likelihood sensitivity index $a_a = 0.60$ for ambiguity. We can take $0.46 - 0.40 = 0.06$ as the index of ambiguity aversion and $0.72 - 0.60 = 0.12$ as the index of the likelihood insensitivity that is due to ambiguity. □

Exercise 11.8.2. The best fit is obtained for $\theta = 0.83$, $a_k = 0.69$, $b_k = 0.06$, $a_a = 0.40$, and $b_a = 0.15$, with distance[3] \$0.35. The data from Table 11.8.3 for risk were

[3] The theoretically predicted CEs are given by $100_{D_k}0 \sim 33.66$; $100_{D_k}50 \sim 69.54$; $100_{B_k}0 \sim 08.48$; $100_{B_k}50 \sim 56.10$; $100_{B_kc}0 \sim 62.95$; $100_{B_kc}50 \sim 83.44$; $100_{D_a}0 \sim 28.23$; $100_{D_a}50 \sim 66.82$; $100_{B_a}0 \sim 13.52$; $100_{B_a}50 \sim 59.03$; $100_{B_ac}0 \sim 44.43$; $100_{B_ac}50 \sim 74.78$.

analyzed in Exercise 7.10.2, where we found the same optimal a and b but a slightly different optimal power θ (= 0.86) for utility. The reason is that in the present exercise utility is also used for fitting the ambiguous-choice data. The difference is, however, small.

We have more likelihood sensitivity for risk than for ambiguity, with $a_k - a_a = 0.69 - 0.40 = 0.29$ an index of ambiguity insensitivity. There is also more optimism for risk than for ambiguity, with the difference $(2a_k + b_k)/2 - (2a_a + b_a)/2 = 0.72 - 0.47 = 0.25$ an index of ambiguity aversion. $\square$

Exercise 11.9.1. In both parts we assume that C contains all convex combinations of P^1 and P^2 with

$$P^1(s_1) = 0.1, P^1(s_2) = 0.9, P^1(s_3) = 0 \text{ and}$$
$$P^2(s_1) = 0.2, P^2(s_2) = 0, P^2(s_3) = 0.8.$$

We suppress states in the notation of prospects. Prospect x is $(2,1,0)$.

Using Eq. (11.5.2), $W(\emptyset) = 0$, $W(s_1) = 0.1$, $W(s_1,s_2) = 0.2$, and $W(s_1,s_2,s_3) = 1$. (Further $W(s_2) = 0 = W(s_3)$, $W(s_1,s_3) = 0.1$, and $W(s_2,s_3) = 0.8$.)

(a) We get $RDU(x) = 0.1 \times 2 + (0.2 - 0.1) \times 1 = 0.3$ so that 0.3 is the certainty equivalent of x under RDU. Under MEU (Eq. (11.5.5)) we get $MEU(x) = EU_{P_2}(x) = 0.4$ which now is the certainty equivalent. $MEU(x) > RDU(x)$ and MEU implies less pessimism.

As an aside, Eq. (11.5.4) yields an RDU value $\alpha \times 0.3 + (1-\alpha) \times 1.2$, and α-maxmin yields a value $\alpha \times 0.4 + (1-\alpha) \times 1.1$. Hence, RDU spans a larger region of possible attitudes.

(b) Assume that MEU is an RDU functional. We first show that U must be linear for positive outcomes, as in part (a). We may set $U(0) = 0$ and $U(1) = 1$. Equivalences $(j \times \varepsilon, -\varepsilon/9, 0) \sim ((j-1)\varepsilon, 0, 0)$ imply $(j+1)\varepsilon \ominus j\varepsilon \sim_c^t j\varepsilon \ominus (j-1)\varepsilon$ for all natural numbers j and $\varepsilon > 0$. This implies that U is linear so that it is the identity function for positive outcomes (Observation 10.5.4).

$MEU(1,0,0) = 0.1$ implies that $W(s_1)$ must be 0.1. $MEU(1,1,0) = 0.2$ implies that $W(s_1,s_2)$ must be 0.2. That is, under RDU these W values agree with Eq. (11.5.2) as considered in part (a). It implies that the evaluations of $(2,1,0)$ must be the same as in part (a): $RDU(2,1,0) = 0.3$ so that 0.3 must be the certainty equivalent of $(2,1,0)$ under RDU. However, under MEU we have $MEU(2,1,0) = 0.4$ and this is the certainty equivalent under MEU. Thus, MEU cannot be an RDU form even if we are allowed to choose W and U as we like. $\square$

Exercise 12.1.1. It is readily verified that all outcome events for x, x^+, and x^- can be given the same rank. Therefore, we can use the same decision weights π_j for the RDU calculation of each prospect. The positive terms in $\sum_{j=1}^n \pi_j U(x_j)$ yield $RDU(x^+)$, and the negative terms yield $RDU(x^-)$. Hence, (Eq. 12.1.5) follows.

Using Eqs. (12.1.1)–(12.1.4), $RDU(x^+) = \sum_{j=1}^k \pi_j U(x_j) + \sum_{j=k+1}^n \pi_j U(0)$ and $RDU(x^-) = \sum_{j=1}^k \pi_j U(0) + \sum_{j=k+1}^n \pi_j U(x_j)$. Hence, then their sum is

$\sum_{j=1}^{n} \pi_j U(x_j) + \sum_{j=1}^{n} \pi_j U(0) = RDU(x) + U(0)$. Hence, $RDU(x) = RDU(x^+) + RDU(x^-) - U(0)$ and Eq. (12.5.1) does not hold for $U(0) \neq 0$. $\square$

Exercise 12.1.2. This exercise is similar to Exercise 12.1.1 (and 9.3.2), with everywhere PT instead of RDU. $\square$

Exercise 12.3.1. Assume PT. By Observation 12.3.1, $\alpha \ominus \beta \sim_{sc}^t \gamma \ominus \delta$ implies $U(\alpha) - U(\beta) = U(\gamma) - U(\delta)$ and $\alpha' \ominus \beta \sim_{sc}^t \gamma \ominus \delta$ implies $U(\alpha') - U(\beta) = U(\gamma) - U(\delta)$. Because U increases strictly, $\alpha' = \alpha$ follows. $\square$

Exercise 12.3.2. PT implies $U(1) = 1 = \pi(E^b)U(\alpha)$. It also implies $\pi(E^b)U(\alpha) + \pi(E^c_w) U(-\beta) = U(0) = 0$, so that $\pi(E^b)U(\alpha) = -\pi(E^c_w)U(-\beta)$. Then $\pi(E^c_w)U(-\beta) = -1$. The indifference $-\delta \sim 0_E(-\beta)$ then implies $U(-\delta) = -1$. Because $U(-\delta) = \lambda u(-\delta)$, $\lambda = -1/u(-\delta)$ follows. $\square$

Exercise 12.8.1. Condition (i) holds if and only if the set is comonotonic (Exercise 10.12.2). It suffices, therefore, to show that Condition (ii) implies, and is implied by, the further restriction of sign-comonotonicity. It is obvious that sign-comonotonicity implies condition (ii), because, with A as defined above the exercise, the inequalities imply $E_i \cap A = \emptyset$ and $E_i \cap A^c = \emptyset$, but this cannot be if E_i is nonempty. Next assume condition (ii). We define the event A, distinguishing three cases. Consider an i.

(a) There exists an x such that $x_i > 0$. Then $y_i \geq 0$ must hold for all y. Take $E_i \subset A$.
(b) There exists an x such that $x_i < 0$. Then $y_i \leq 0$ must hold for all y. Take $E_i \subset A^c$.
(c) $x_i = 0$ for all x. Then we can take $E_i \subset A$ or $E_i \subset A^c$ as we please.

With the event A defined in this way, we see that the set of prospects is sign-comonotonic. $\square$

Exercise 12.8.2. The following elaboration is similar to the elaboration of Exercise 10.12.4.

(a) Assume strong monotonicity. Assume, for contradiction, that a decision weight π_j is 0 on a set $\mathcal{F}^{Ap}$. One can construct $\alpha_j x$ and $\beta_j x$ in $\mathcal{F}^{Ap}$ such that $\alpha > \beta$; this construction is left to the readers. Applying PT and substituting $\pi_j = 0$ implies $\alpha_j x \sim \beta_j x$, contradicting strong monotonicity. Hence, strong monotonicity implies that all decision weights are positive.
(b) Conversely, assume that all decision weights are positive. Let $\alpha > \beta$ and consider $\alpha_j x$ and $\beta_j x$. Then it can be shown that the PT difference between the two prospects is at least $\lambda(U(\alpha) - U(\beta))$, where λ is the minimum decision weight and is positive. The latter point is similar to Exercise 10.12.4b and will not be elaborated on. $\square$

Exercise C.1.

(a) First consider forward induction: The move up generates the static probability distribution (0.42:60, 0.18:0, 0.4:20), with EU = 21.00, and its certainty equivalent is 31.81. This exceeds the payment 20 of the down move, so that the move up is chosen.

Next consider backward induction. At node 3 we face the prospect $60_{0.7}0$, which has EU 25.70 and certainty equivalent 40.01. We replace the chance node 3 by this certainty equivalent. Then chance node 2 yields the prospect $40.01_{0.6}20$. Its EU is 21.00, with certainty equivalent 31.81, as for forward induction and again the move up is chosen.

(b) First consider forward induction: Then the move up is evaluated as the static probability distribution $(0.42{:}60, 0.18{:}0, 0.4{:}20)$. Its PT is 13.40, and its certainty equivalent is 19.09. This is less than the payment 20 of the down move, so that the move down is chosen.

Next consider backward induction. At node 3 we face the prospect $60_{0.7}0$, which has PT value 17.99 and certainty equivalent 26.67. We replace the chance node 3 by this certainty equivalent. Then chance node 2 yields the prospect $26.67_{0.6}20$. Its PT value is 15.41, with certainty equivalent 22.38. It now exceeds the sure 20, so that now the move up is chosen.

Forward and backward induction yield a different evaluation and a different decision in part (b). $\square$

Exercise E.1. Multisymmetry follows because the certainty equivalent of both prospects in Figure E.1 is the utility inverse of

$$P(A) \sum_{j=1}^n P(E_j)U(x_j) + (1 - P(A)) \sum_{j=1}^n P(E_j)U(y_j)$$

$$= \sum_{j=1}^n P(E_j)(P(A)U(x_j) + (1 - P(A))U(y_j)).$$

Act independence follows because

$$\sum_{j=1}^n P(E_j)U(x_j) = \sum_{j=1}^n P(E_j)U(y_j) \text{ implies}$$

$$P(A) \sum_{j=1}^n P(E_j)U(x_j) + (1 - P(A)) \sum_{j=1}^n P(E_j)U(c_j)$$

$$= P(A) \sum_{j=1}^n P(E_j)U(y_j) + (1 - P(A)) \sum_{j=1}^n P(E_j)U(c_j). \quad \square$$

Appendix K: Skipping parts and interdependencies between sections

This appendix presents figures depicting the relations between the sections in this book. An arrow from one section to another section indicates that, for reading the latter section, the former section should be read first. For example, the figure for Chapter 12 shows that, to read §12.1 with the definition of PT (prospect theory) for unknown probabilities, first §10.2 with the definition of RDU (rank-dependent utility) for unknown probabilities has to be read, along with §9.2 with the definition of PT for risk. The figure for Chapter 10 then shows that, before reading §10.2, first §10.1 has to be read, and the figure for Chapter 9 shows that §8.4 and §7.6 have to be read before §9.2 can be read; and so on. Starting with the section of interest, one first encircles this section, and then all preceding sections needed to read it. One then moves back section by section, for each encircled section along the way encircling the required preceding ones. All encircled sections then have to be read.

Figure K.1 depicts all sections that have to be read this way before §12.1 can be read. In the figures, a dashed "double" arrow ⇓ from a first section – always printed in bold and underlined – to a set of sections contained within a dashed square or polytope indicates that the first section should be read before any of the other sections can be read.

Some obvious relations, which can be handled using the subject index, or which will not cause problems because interested readers will read the required prior parts anyway, have not been indicated so as to optimize transparency of the figures. For example, §3.5 refers to indexes from §3.4 that need no entire reading of §3.4. Some exercises in §4.12, and tests in §10.4.3, concern the sure-thing principle that can be inferred from §4.8.1, which does not require further reading of that section. No arrow from §4.8 to §4.12 has been added. Similarly, some data-fitting exercises in §7.3 use data from §4.1. Appendices G and H concern every behavioral foundation in the book and require a study of some of them, but this will be understood by any potential reader. Further, some appendices have not been included, again to optimize transparency.

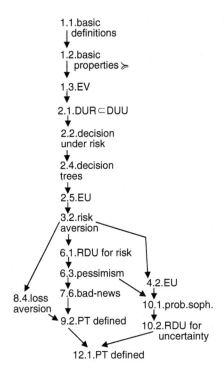

Figure K.1 The reading required to understand the definition of PT for uncertainty in §12.1.

The figures of this appendix will help readers interested in particular topics who want to skip unrelated topics. For example, if you are interested only in decision under risk and want to read the definition of PT in §9.2, then you will have to read §§8.4, 7.6, 6.3, 6.1, 3.2, 2.5, 2.4, 2.2, 2.1, 1.3, 1.2, and 1.1 as preparation. This way, nothing has to be read about decision under uncertainty.

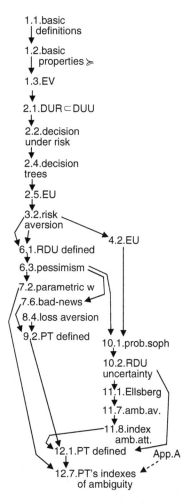

Figure K.2 The reading required to understand the pragmatic indexes of ambiguity attitudes based on prospect theory.

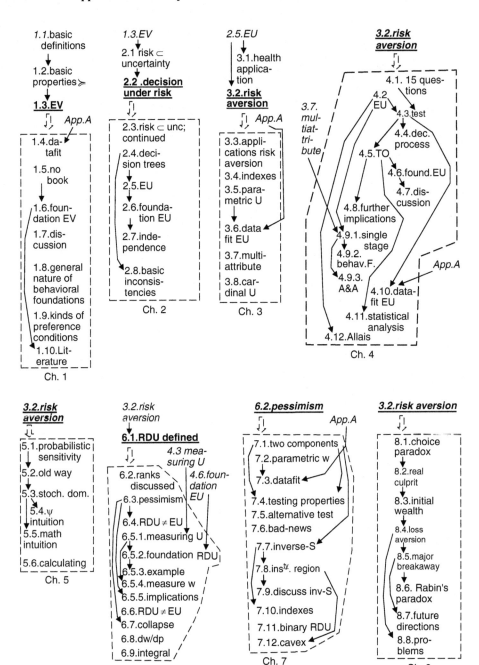

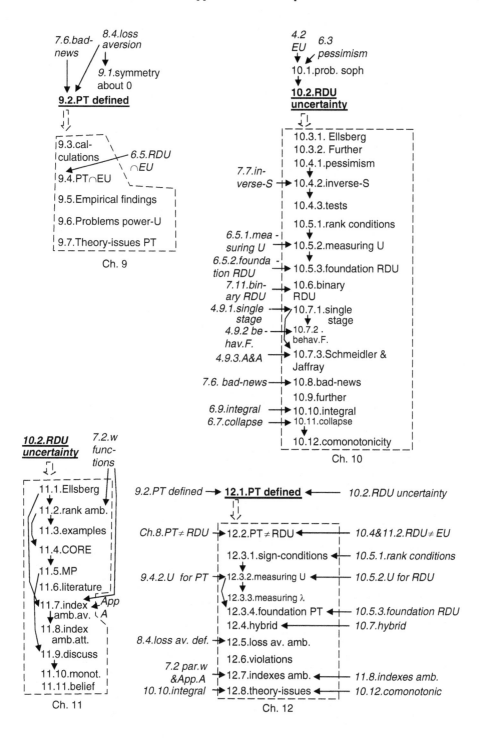

1.1.basic ———▶ App.A distance measure
definitions
1.2.basic ——▶ App.B revealed pref.
properties
6.1.RDU ——▶ App.C dynamic
defined
                 ↘ App.D other fields
    4.2.EU ＜
                 ↘ App.E bisymmetry

10.2.RDU ——▶ App.F nonmonotonic RDU
uncertainty
4.6.founda- ─▶ App.G Infinite dimensions
tion EU   ↓
                 App.H measure theory
                 App.I other books
APPENDICES

References

Abdellaoui, Mohammed (2000) "Parameter-Free Elicitation of Utilities and Probability Weighting Functions," *Management Science* 46, 1497–1512.

Abdellaoui, Mohammed (2002) "A Genuine Rank-Dependent Generalization of the von Neumann-Morgenstern Expected Utility Theorem," *Econometrica* 70, 717–736.

Abdellaoui, Mohammed, Arthur E. Attema, & Han Bleichrodt (2009) "Intertemporal Tradeoffs for Gains and Losses: An Experimental Measurement of Discounted Utility," *Economic Journal*, forthcoming.

Abdellaoui, Mohammed, Aurélien Baillon, Laetitia Placido, & Peter P. Wakker (2009) "The Rich Domain of Uncertainty: Source Functions and their Experimental Implementation" *American Economic Review*, forthcoming.

Abdellaoui, Mohammed, Carolina Barrios, & Peter P. Wakker (2007) "Reconciling Introspective Utility with Revealed Preference: Experimental Arguments Based on Prospect Theory," *Journal of Econometrics* 138, 336–378.

Abdellaoui, Mohammed & Han Bleichrodt (2007) "Eliciting Gul's Theory of Disappointment Aversion by the Tradeoff Method," *Journal of Economic Psychology* 28, 631–645.

Abdellaoui, Mohammed, Han Bleichrodt, & Olivier L'Haridon (2008) "A Tractable Method to Measure Utility and Loss Aversion under Prospect Theory," *Journal of Risk and Uncertainty* 36, 245–266.

Abdellaoui, Mohammed, Han Bleichrodt, & Corina Paraschiv (2007) "Loss Aversion under Prospect Theory: A Parameter-Free Measurement," *Management Science* 53, 1659–1674.

Abdellaoui, Mohammed, Frank Vossmann, & Martin Weber (2005) "Choice-Based Elicitation and Decomposition of Decision Weights for Gains and Losses under Uncertainty," *Management Science* 51, 1384–1399.

Abdellaoui, Mohammed & Peter P. Wakker (2005) "The Likelihood Method for Decision under Uncertainty," *Theory and Decision* 58, 3–76.

Aczél, János, (1966) *Lectures on Functional Equations and Their Applications*. Academic Press, New York.

Ahn, David S. (2008) "Ambiguity Without a State Space," *Review of Economic Studies* 75, 3–28.

Ainslie, George W. (2001) *Breakdown of Will*. Cambridge University Press, Cambridge.

Alchian, Armen A. (1953) "The Meaning of Utility Measurement," *American Economic Review* 43, 26–50.

Ali, Mukhtar M. (1977) "Probability and Utility Estimates for Racetrack Betting," *Journal of Political Economy* 85, 803–815.

Allais, Maurice (1953a) "Le Comportement de l'Homme Rationnel devant le Risque: Critique des Postulats et Axiomes de l'Ecole Américaine," *Econometrica* 21, 503–546.

462   **References**

Allais, Maurice (1953b) "Fondements d'une Théorie Positive des Choix Comportant un Risque et Critique des Postulats et Axiomes de l'Ecole Américaine," *Colloques Internationaux du Centre National de la Recherche Scientifique (Econométrie)* 40, 257–332. Paris: Centre National de la Recherche Scientifique. Translated into English, with additions, as "The Foundations of a Positive Theory of Choice Involving Risk and a Criticism of the Postulates and Axioms of the American School." In Maurice Allais & Ole Hagen (1979, eds.) *Expected Utility Hypotheses and the Allais Paradox*, 27–145, Reidel, Dordrecht.

Allais, Maurice (1988) "The General Theory of Random Choices in Relation to the Invariant Cardinal Utility Function and the Specific Probability Function." In Bertrand R. Munier (ed.) *Risk, Decision and Rationality*, 233–289, Reidel, Dordrecht.

Allen, Franklin (1987) "Discovering Personal Probabilities when Utility Functions are Unknown," *Management Science* 33, 542–544.

Andersen, Steffen, Glenn W. Harrison, Morten I. Lau, & E. Elisabet Rutström (2006) "Elicitation Using Multiple Price List Formats," *Experimental Economics* 9, 383–405.

André, Francisco J. (2009) "Indirect Elicitation of Non-Linear Multi-Attribute Utility Functions. A Dual Procedure Combined with DEA," *Omega* 37, 883–895.

Anger, Bernd (1977) "Representations of Capacities," *Mathematische Annalen* 229, 245–258.

Anscombe, Frank J. & Robert J. Aumann (1963) "A Definition of Subjective Probability," *Annals of Mathematical Statistics* 34, 199–205.

Apesteguia, Jose & Miguel A. Ballester (2009) "A Theory of Reference-Dependent Behavior," *Economic Theory* 40, 427–455.

Arkes, Hal R. (1991) "Costs and Benefits of Judgments Errors: Implications for Debiasing," *Psychological Bulletin* 110, 486–498.

Arrow, Kenneth J. (1951a) "Alternative Approaches to the Theory of Choice in Risk-Taking Situations," *Econometrica* 19, 404–437.

Arrow, Kenneth J. (1951b) *Social Choice and Individual Values.* Wiley, New York. (9th edn. 1972, Yale University Press, New Haven.)

Arrow, Kenneth J. (1959) "Rational Choice Functions and Ordering," *Economica, N. S.,* 26, 121–127.

Arrow, Kenneth J. (1971) *Essays in the Theory of Risk Bearing.* North-Holland, Amsterdam.

Arrow, Kenneth J. & Leonid Hurwicz (1972) "An Optimality Criterion for Decision Making under Ignorance." In Charles F. Carter & James L. Ford (1972) *Uncertainty and Expectations in Economics: Essays in Honour of G. L. S. Shackle*, 1–11, Basil Blackwell, Oxford.

Arrow, Kenneth J. & Robert C. Lind (1970) "Uncertainty and the Evaluation of Public Investment Decisions," *American Economic Review* 60, 364–378.

Arrow, Kenneth J., Amartya K. Sen, & Kotaro Suzumura (2007) *Handbook of Social Choice and Welfare, Vol. 2* Elsevier, Amsterdam.

Artzner, Philippe, Freddy Delbaen, Jean-Marc Eber, & David Heath (1999) "Coherent Measures of Risk," *Mathematical Finance* 9, 203–228.

Attneave, Fred (1959) "A Priori Probabilities in Gambling," *Nature* 183, 842–843.

Aujard, Henry (2001) "The 'Allais Effect' Is Real," *21st Century Science and Technology* 14, 70–75.

Baillon, Aurélien, Bram Driesen, & Peter P. Wakker (2009) "Relative Concave Utility, and Risk and Ambiguity," Erasmus University, Rotterdam.

Baillon, Aurélien, Olivier L'Haridon, & Laetitia Placido (2009) *"Ambiguity Models and the Machina Paradoxes,"* American Economic Review, forthcoming.

Baltussen, Guido, Thierry Post, & Pim van Vliet (2006) "Violations of CPT in Mixed Gambles," *Management Science* 52, 1288–1290.

Banach, Stefan & Kazimierz Kuratowski (1929) "Sur une Généralisation du Problème de la Mesure," *Fundamentà Mathematicae* 14, 127–131.

Barberis, Nicholas, Ming Huang, & Tano Santos (2001) "Prospect Theory and Asset Prices," *Quarterly Journal of Economics* 116, 1–53.

Barberis, Nicholas, Ming Huang, & Richard H. Thaler (2006) "Individual Preferences, Monetary Gambles, and Stock Market Participation: A Case for Narrow Framing," *American Economic Review* 96, 1069–1090.

Bardsley, Nick (2000) "Control without Deception: Individual Behavior in Free-Riding Experiments Revisited," *Experimental Economics* 3, 215–240.

Bardsley, Nick, Robin Cubitt, Graham Loomes, Peter Moffat, Chris Starmer, & Robert Sugden (2010) *Experimental Economics; Rethinking the Rules.* Princeton University Press, Princeton, NJ.

Baron, Jonathan (1997) "Confusion of Relative and Absolute Risk in Valuation," *Journal of Risk and Uncertainty* 14, 301–309.

Baron, Jonathan (2008) *Thinking and Deciding.* Cambridge University Press, Cambridge (4th edn.).

Barron, Greg & Ido Erev (2003) "Small Feedback-Based Decisions and Their Limited Correspondence to Description-Based Decisions," *Journal of Behavioral Decision Making* 16, 215–233.

Barsky, Robert B., F. Thomas Juster, Miles S. Kimball, & Matthew D. Shapiro (1997) "Preference Parameters and Behavioral Heterogeneity: An Experimental Approach in the Health and Retirement Study," *Quarterly Journal of Economics* 112, 537–579.

Baucells, Manel & Franz H. Heukamp (2006) "Stochastic Dominance and Cumulative Prospect Theory," *Management Science* 52, 1409–1423.

Baucells, Manel & Lloyd S. Shapley (2008) "Multiperson Utility," *Games and Economic Behavior* 62, 329–347.

Baumann, Peter (2008) "Single-Case Probabilities and the Case of Monty Hall: Levy's View," *Synthese* 162, 265–273.

Bawa, Vijay S. (1982) "Stochastic Dominance: A Research Bibliography," *Management Science* 28, 698–712.

Beach, Lee R. & Lawrence D. Phillips (1967) "Subjective Probabilities Inferred from Estimates and Bets," *Journal of Experimental Psychology* 75, 354–359.

Bearden, J. Neil, Thomas S. Wallsten, & Craig R. Fox (2007) "Contrasting Stochastic and Support Theory Accounts of Subadditivity," *Journal of Mathematical Psychology* 51, 229–241.

Becker, Gordon M., Morris H. de Groot, & Jacob Marschak (1963) "Stochastic Models of Choice Behavior," *Behavioral Science* 8, 41–55.

Becker, Gordon M., Morris H. de Groot, & Jacob Marschak (1964) "Measuring Utility by a Single-Response Sequential Method," *Behavioral Science* 9, 226–232.

Bell, David E. (1982) "Regret in Decision Making under Uncertainty," *Operations Research* 30, 961–981.

Bell, David E. (1985) "Disappointment in Decision Making under Uncertainty," *Operations Research* 33, 1–27.

Benartzi, Shlomo & Richard H. Thaler (1995) "Myopic Loss Aversion and the Equity Premium Puzzle," *Quarterly Journal of Economics* 110, 73–92.

Bentham, Jeremy (1789) *The Principles of Morals and Legislation.* At the Clarendon Press, Oxford.

Bentham, Jeremy (1828–1843) [1782–1787], "The Rationale of Reward." John Bowring (ed.), *The Works of Jeremy Bentham*, part VII, 297–364.

Berg, Joyce E., Lane A. Daley, John W. Dickhaut, & John R. O'Brien (1986) "Controlling Preferences for Lotteries on Units of Experimental Exchange," *Quarterly Journal of Economics* 101, 281–306.

Bernasconi, Michele (1994) "Nonlinear Preference and Two-Stage Lotteries: Theories and Evidence," *Economic Journal* 104, 54–70.

Bernouli, Daniel (1738) "Specimen Theoriae Novae de Mensura Sortis," *Commentarii Academiae Scientiarum Imperialis Petropolitanae*, 5, 175–192. Translated into English by Louise Sommer (1954) "Exposition of a New Theory on the Measurement of Risk," *Econometrica*, 22, 23–36.

Berns, Gregory S., C. Monica Capra, Jonathan Chappelow, Sara Moore, & Charles Noussair (2008) "Neurobiological Regret and Rejoice Functions for Aversive Outcomes," *Neuroimage* 39, 2047–2057.

Bewley, Truman F. (1986) "Knightian Decision Theory Part I," Cowles Foundation Discussion Paper No. 807. Reprinted in *Decisions in Economics and Finance* 25 (2002) 79–110.

Bier, Vicky M. & Brad. L. Connell (1994) "Ambiguity Seeking in Multi-Attribute Decisions: Effects of Optimism and Message Framing," *Journal of Behavioral Decision Making* 7, 169–182.

Bierman, H. Scott & Luis Fernandez (1995) *Game Theory with Economic Applications.* Addison-Wesley, Reading, MA (2nd edn. 1998)

Binswanger, Hans P. (1981) "Attitudes towards Risk: Theoretical Implications of an Experiment in Rural India," *Economic Journal* 91, 867–890.

Birnbaum, Michael H. (1972) "Morality Judgments: Tests of an Averaging Model," *Journal of Experimental Psychology* 93, 35–42.

Birnbaum, Michael H. (1973) "Morality Judgment: Test of an Averaging Model with Differential Weights," *Journal of Experimental Psychology* 99, 395–399.

Birnbaum, Michael H. (1974) "The Nonadditivity of Personality Impressions," *Journal of Experimental Psychology* 102, 543–561.

Birnbaum, Michael H. (2008a) "New Paradoxes of Risky Decision Making," *Psychological Review* 115, 463–501.

Birnbaum, Michael H. (2008b) "Evaluation of the Priority Heuristic as a Descriptive Model of Risky Decision Making: Comment on Brandstätter, Gigerenzer, and Hertwig (2006)" *Psychological Review* 115, 253–260.

Birnbaum, Michael H., Gregory Coffey, Barbara A. Mellers, & Robin Weiss (1992) "Utility Measurement: Configural-Weight Theory and the Judge's Point of View," *Journal of Experimental Psychology: Human Perception and Performance* 18, 331–346.

Birnbaum, Michael H., Allen Parducci, & Robert K. Gifford (1971) "Contextual Effects in Information Integration," *Journal of Experimental Psychology* 88, 158–170.

Birnbaum, Michael H. & Steven E. Stegner (1981) "Measuring the Importance of Cues in Judgment for Individuals: Subjective Theories of IQ as a Function of Heredity and Environment," *Journal of Experimental Social Psychology* 17, 159–182.

Blackburn, McKinley, Glenn W. Harrison, & E. Elisabet Rutström (1994) "Statistical Bias Functions and Informative Hypothetical Surveys," *American Journal of Agricultural Economics* 76, 1084–1088.

Blake, David (1996) "Efficiency, Risk Aversion and Portfolio Insurance: An Analysis of Financial Asset Portfolios Held by Investors in the United Kingdom," *Economic Journal* 106, 1175–1192.

Blaug, Mark (1962) *Economic Theory in Retrospect.* Cambridge University Press, Cambridge. (5th edn. 1997).

Blavatskyy, Pavlo R. (2007) "Stochastic Expected Utility Theory," *Journal of Risk and Uncertainty* 34, 259–286.

Blavatskyy, Pavlo & Ganna Pogrebna (2009) "Models of Stochastic Choice and Decision Theory: Why Both Are Important for Analyzing Decisions," *Journal of Applied Econometrics*, forthcoming.

Bleichrodt, Han (2001) "Probability Weighting in Choice under Risk: An Empirical Test," *Journal of Risk and Uncertainty* 23, 185–198.

Bleichrodt, Han (2002) "A New Explanation for the Difference between SG and TTO Utilities," *Health Economics* 11, 447–456.

Bleichrodt, Han (2007) "Reference-Dependent Utility with Shifting Reference Points and Incomplete Preferences," *Journal of Mathematical Psychology* 51, 266–276.

Bleichrodt, Han (2009) "Reference-Dependent Expected Utility with Incomplete Preferences," *Journal of Mathematical Psychology* 53, 287–293.

Bleichrodt, Han, Jasan Doctor, & Elly Stolk (2005) "A Nonparametric Elicitation of the Equity-Efficiency Tradeoff in Cost-Utility," *Journal of Health Econonomics* 24, 655–678.

Bleichrodt, Han & John Miyamoto (2003) "A Characterization of Quality-Adjusted Life-Years under Cumulative Prospect Theory," *Mathematics of Operations Research* 28, 181–193.

Bleichrodt, Han & José Luis Pinto (2000) "A Parameter-Free Elicitation of the Probability Weighting Function in Medical Decision Analysis," *Management Science* 46, 1485–1496.

Bleichrodt, Han & José Luis Pinto (2005) "The Validity of QALYs under NonExpected Utility," *Economic Journal* 115, 533–550.

Bleichrodt, Han, José Luis Pinto, & Peter P. Wakker (2001) "Making Descriptive Use of Prospect Theory to Improve the Prescriptive Use of Expected Utility," *Management Science* 47, 1498–1514.

Bleichrodt, Han, Ulrich Schmidt, & Horst Zank (2009) "Additive Utility in Prospect Theory," *Management Science* 55, 863–873.

Bleichrodt, Han & Eddy van Doorslaer (2006) "A Welfare Economics Foundation for Health Inequality Measurement," *Journal of Health Economics* 25, 945–957.

Bleichrodt, Han, Jaco van Rijn, & Magnus Johannesson (1999) "Probability Weighting and Utility Curvature in QALY-Based Decision Making," *Journal of Mathematical Psychology* 43, 238–260.

Bliss, Robert R. & Nikolaos Panigirtzoglou (2004) "Option-Implied Risk Aversion Estimates," *Journal of Finance* 59, 407–446.

Blumenschein, Karen, Glenn C. Blomquist, Magnus Johannesson, Nancy Horn, & Patricia Freeman (2008) "Eliciting Willingness to Pay Without Bias: Evidence from a Field Experiment," *Economic Journal* 118, 114–137.

Booij, Adam. S. & Gijs van de Kuilen (2009) "A Parameter-Free Analysis of the Utility of Money for the General Population under Prospect Theory," *Journal of Economic Psychology* 30, 651–666.

Booij, Adam S., Bernard M. S. Van Praag, & Gijs van de Kuilen (2010) "A Parametric Analysis of Prospect Theory's Functionals," *Theory and Decision* 68, 115–148.

Bouyssou, Denis, Thierry Marchant, Marc Pirlot, Alexis Tsoukias, & Philippe Vincke (2006) *Evaluation and Decision Models with Multiple Criteria.* Springer, Berlin.

Bouyssou, Denis & Marc Pirlot (2003) "Nontransitive Decomposable Conjoint Measurement," *Journal of Mathematical Psychology* 46, 677–703.

Bouyssou, Denis & Marc Pirlot (2004) "A Note on Wakker's Cardinal Coordinate Independence," *Mathematical Social Sciences* 48, 11–22.

Brandstätter, Eduard, Gerd Gigerenzer, & Ralph Hertwig (2006) "The Priority Heuristic: Making Choices without Trade-offs," *Psychological Review* 113, 409–432.

Brandstätter, Eduard, Anton Kühberger, & Friedrich Schneider (2002) "A Cognitive-Emotional Account of the Shape of the Probability Weighting Function," *Journal of Behavioral Decision Making* 15, 79–100.

Brenner, Lyle (2000) "Should Observed Overconfidence Be Dismissed as a Statistical Artifact? Critique of Erev, Wallsten, and Budescu (1994)," *Psychological Review* 107, 943–946.

Brier, Glenn W. (1950) "Verification of Forecasts Expressed in Terms of Probability," *Monthly Weather Review* 78, 1–3.

Broome, John R. (1991) *Weighing Goods.* Basil Blackwell, Oxford.

Brown, Gordon D. A., Jonathan Gardner, Andrew J. Oswald, & Jing Qian (2008) "Does Wage Rank Affect Employees' Well-Being?," *Industrial Relations* 47, 355–389.

Bruhin, Adrian, Helga Fehr-Duda, & Thomas Epper (2010) Risk and Rationality: Uncovering Heterogeneity in Probability Distortion. *Econometrica*, forthcoming.

Bruine de Bruin, Wändi, Baruch Fischhoff, Susau G. Millstein, & Bannie L. Halpern-Felsher (2000) "Verbal and Numerical Expressions of Probability: 'It's a Fifty-Fifty Chance'," *Organizational Behavior and Human Decision Processes* 81, 115–131.

Brunnermeier, Markus K. & Stefan Nagel (2008) "Do Wealth Fluctuations Generate Time-Varying Risk Aversion? Micro-Evidence on Individuals' Asset Allocation," *American Economic Review* 98, 713–736.

Brunnermeier, Markus K. & Jonathan A. Parker (2005) "Optimal Expectations," *American Economic Review* 95, 1092–1118.

Budescu, David V. & Thomas S. Wallsten (1987) "Subjective Estimation of Precise and Vague Uncertainties." In George Wright & Peter Ayton (eds.) *Judgmental Forecasting*, 63–82. Wiley, New York.

Budescu, David V., Shalva Weinberg, & Thomas S. Wallsten (1988) "Decisions Based on Numerically and Verbally Expressed Uncertainties," *Journal of Experimental Psychology, Human Perception and Performance* 14, 281–294.

Bunn, Derek W. (1984) *Applied Decision Analysis.* McGraw-Hill Book Company, New York.

Burks, Arthur W. (1977) *Chance, Cause, Reason (An Inquiry into the Nature of Scientific Evidence).* The University of Chicago Press, Chicago.

Burks, Stephen V., Jeffrey P. Carpenter, Loreuz Goette, & Aldo Rustichini (2009) "Cognitive Skills Affect Economic Preferences, Strategic Behavior, and Job Attachment," *Proceedings of the National Academy of Sciences* 106, 7745–7750.

Busemeyer, Jerome R. & Adele Diederich, (2002) "Survey of Decision Field Theory," *Mathematical Social Sciences* 43, 345–370.

Busemeyer, Jerome R., Ethan Weg, Rachel Barkan, Xuyang Li, & Zhengping Ma (2000) "Dynamic and Consequential Consistency of Choices between Paths of Decision Trees," *Journal of Experimental Psychology: General* 129, 530–545.

Camerer, Colin F. (1992) "Recent Tests of Generalizations of Expected Utility Theory." In Ward Edwards (ed.) *Utility Theories: Measurement and Applications*, 207–251, Kluwer Academic Publishers, Dordrecht.

Camerer, Colin F. (1995) "Individual Decision Making." In John H. Kagel & Alvin E. Roth (eds.) *Handbook of Experimental Economics*, 587–703, Princeton University Press, Princeton, NJ.

Camerer, Colin F. (2007) "Neuroeconomics: Using Neuroscience to Make Economic Predictions," *Economic Journal* 117, C26–C42.

Camerer, Colin F. & Teck-Hua Ho (1994) "Violations of the Betweenness Axiom and Nonlinearity in Probability," *Journal of Risk and Uncertainty* 8, 167–196.

Camerer, Colin F. & Robin M. Hogarth (1999) "The Effects of Financial Incentives in Experiments: A Review and Capital-Labor-Production Framework," *Journal of Risk and Uncertainty* 19, 7–42.

Camerer, Colin F. & Martin Weber (1992) "Recent Developments in Modeling Preferences: Uncertainty and Ambiguity," *Journal of Risk and Uncertainty* 5, 325–370.

Campbell, John Y. (1996) "Understanding Risk and Return," *Journal of Political Economy* 104, 298–345.

Carthy, Trevor, Susan Chilton, Judith Covey, Lorraine Hopkins, Michael Jones-Lee, Graham Loomes, Nick Pidgeon, & Anne Spencer (1999) "On the Contingent Valuation of Safety and the Safety of Contingent Valuation: Part 2—The CV/SG 'Chained' Approach," *Journal of Risk and Uncertainty* 17, 187–213.

Casadesus-Masanell, Ramon, Peter Klibanoff, & Emre Ozdenoren (2000) "Maxmin Expected Utility over Savage Acts with a Set of Priors," *Journal of Economic Theory* 92, 35–65.

Castagnoli, Erio & Marco Li Calzi (2005) "Benchmarking Real-Valued Acts," *Games and Economic Behavior* 57, 236–253.

Cattin, Philippe & Dick R. Wittink (1989) "Commercial Use of Conjoint Analysis: An Update," *Journal of Marketing* 53, 91–96.

Chakravarty, Sujoy & Jaideep Roy (2009) "Recursive Expected Utility and the Separation of Attitudes towards Risk and Ambiguity: An Experimental Study," *Theory and Decision* 66, 199–228.

Chambers, Christopher (2007) "Ordinal Aggregation and Quantiles," *Journal of Economic Theory* 137, 416–431.

Chateauneuf, Alain (1985) "On the Existence of a Probability Measure Compatible with a Total Preorder on a Boolean Algebra," *Journal of Mathematical Economics* 14, 43–52.

Chateauneuf, Alain (1991) "On the Use of Capacities in Modeling Uncertainty Aversion and Risk Aversion," *Journal of Mathematical Economics* 20, 343–369.

Chateauneuf, Alain (1996) "Decomposable Capacities, Distorted Probabilities and Concave Capacities," *Mathematical Social Sciences* 31, 19–37.

Chateauneuf, Alain (1999) "Comonotonicity Axioms and Rank-Dependent Expected Utility Theory for Arbitrary Consequences," *Journal of Mathematical Economics* 32, 21–45.

Chateauneuf, Alain & Michèle Cohen (1994) "Risk Seeking with Diminishing Marginal Utility in a Non-Expected Utility Model," *Journal of Risk and Uncertainty* 9, 77–91.

Chateauneuf, Alain, Jürgen Eichberger, & Simon Grant (2007) "Choice under Uncertainty with the Best and Worst in Mind: NEO-Additive Capacities," *Journal of Economic Theory* 137, 538–567.

Chateauneuf, Alain & Jean-Yves Jaffray (1989) "Some Characterizations of Lower Probabilities and Other Monotone Capacities through the Use of Möbius Inversion," *Mathematical Social Sciences* 17, 263–283.

Chateauneuf, Alain & Jean-Marc Tallon (2002) "Diversification, Convex Preferences and Non-Empty Core," *Economic Theory* 19, 509–523.

Chateauneuf, Alain & Peter P. Wakker (1993) "From Local to Global Additive Representation," *Journal of Mathematical Economics* 22, 523–545.

Chateauneuf, Alain & Peter P. Wakker (1999) "An Axiomatization of Cumulative Prospect Theory for Decision under Risk," *Journal of Risk and Uncertainty* 18, 137–145.

Chen, Yan, Peter Katuščák, & Emre Ozdenoren (2007) "Sealed Bid Auctions with Ambiguity: Theory and Experiments," *Journal of Economic Theory* 136, 513–535.

Cheung, Ka Chun (2008) "Characterization of Comonotonicity Using Convex Order," *Insurance: Mathematics and Economics* 43, 403–406.

Chew, Soo Hong (1989) "The Rank-Dependent Quasilinear Mean," Unpublished manuscript, Department of Economics, University of California, Irvine.

Chew, Soo Hong & Edi Karni (1994) "Choquet Expected Utility with a Finite State Space: Commutativity and Act-Independence," *Journal of Economic Theory* 62, 469–479.

Chew, Soo Hong, Edi Karni, & Zvi Safra (1987) "Risk Aversion in the Theory of Expected Utility with Rank Dependent Probabilities," *Journal of Economic Theory* 42, 370–381.

Chew, Soo Hong, King King Li, Robin Chark, & Songfa Zhong (2008) "Source Preference and Ambiguity Aversion: Models and Evidence from Behavioral and Neuroimaging Experiments," *Advances in Health Economics and Health Services Research* 20, 179–201.

Chew, Soo Hong & Kenneth R. MacCrimmon (1979) "Alpha-Nu Choice Theory: An Axiomatization of Expected Utility," University of British Columbia Faculty of Commerce working paper 669.

Chew, Soo Hong & Jacob Sagi (2006) "Event Exchangeability: Small Worlds Probabilistic Sophistication without Continuity or Monotonicity," *Econometrica* 74, 771–786.

Chew, Soo Hong & Amos Tversky (1990) "Cumulative Prospect Theory: Reference-Dependent Axiomatization of Decision under Uncertainty." *In preparation (never completed) Stanford University*; presented by Tversky at the 5th Foundations of Utility and Risk (FUR) conference, Duke University, Durham NC, 1990.

Chew, Soo Hong & Peter P. Wakker (1996) "The Comonotonic Sure-Thing Principle," *Journal of Risk and Uncertainty* 12, 5–27.

Chew, Soo Hong & William S. Waller (1986) "Empirical Tests of Weighted Utility Theory," *Journal of Mathematical Psychology* 30, 55–72.

Chipman, John S. (1960) "Stochastic Choice and Subjective Probability." In Dorothy Willner (ed.) *Decisions, Values and Groups vol. 1*, 70–95, Pergamon Press, New York.

Chipman, John S., Leonid Hurwicz, Marcel K. Richter, & Hugo F. Sonnenschein (1971, eds.) *Preferences, Utility, and Demand*. Hartcourt, New York.

Choi, Syngjoo, Raymond Fisman, Douglas Gale, & Shachar Kariv (2007) "Consistency and Heterogeneity of Individual Behavior under Uncertainty," *American Economic Review* 97, 1921–1938.

Chomsky, Noam (1959) "A Review of B. F. Skinner's Verbal Behavior," *Language* 35, 26–58.

Choquet, Gustave (1953–1954) "Theory of Capacities," *Annales de l'Institut Fourier* 5 (Grenoble) 131–295.

Clark, Andrew E., Paul Frijters, & Michael A. Shields (2008) "Relative Income, Happiness, and Utility: An Explanation for the Easterlin Paradox and Other Puzzles," *Journal of Economic Literature* 46, 95–144.

Clemen, Robert T. (1991) *Making Hard Decisions: An Introduction to Decision Analysis*. PWS-Kent, Boston, MA.

Cohen, Alma & Liran Einav (2007) "Estimating Risk Preferences from Deductible Choice," *American Economic Review* 97, 745–788.

Cohen, Michèle (1992) "Security Level, Potential Level, Expected Utility: A Three-Criteria Decision Model under Risk," *Theory and Decision* 33, 101–134.

Cohen, Michèle & Jean-Yves Jaffray (1980) "Rational Behavior under Complete Ignorance," *Econometrica* 48, 1281–1299.

Cohen, Michèle & Jean-Yves Jaffray (1988) "Certainty Effect versus Probability Distortion: An Experimental Analysis of Decision Making under Risk," *Journal of Experimental Psychology: Human Perception and Performance* 14, 554–560.

Cohen, Michèle, Jean-Yves Jaffray, & Tanios Said (1987) "Experimental Comparisons of Individual Behavior under Risk and under Uncertainty for Gains and for Losses," *Organizational Behavior and Human Decision Processes* 39, 1–22.

Cohn, Richard A., Wilbur G. Lewellen, Ronald C. Lease, & Gary G. Schlarbaum (1975) "Individual Investor Risk Aversion and Investment Portfolio Composition," *Journal of Finance* 30, 605–620.

Constantinides, George M. (1990) "Habit Formation: A Resolution of the Equity Premium Puzzle," *Journal of Political Economy* 98, 519–543.

Conte, Anna, John D. Hey, & Peter G. Moffatt (2008) "Mixture Models of Choice Under Risk," *Journal of Econometrics*, forthcoming.

Cox, James C. & Vjollca Sadiraj (2006) "Small- and Large-Stakes Risk Aversion: Implications of Concavity Calibration for Decision Theory," *Games and Economic Behavior* 56, 45–60.

Cox, James C., Vjollca Sadiraj, Bodo Vogt, & Utteeyo Dasgupta (2007) "Is there a Plausible Theory for Risky Decisions?", paper presented at ESA meeting, Tucson, AZ, October 2007.

Cubitt, Robin P. (1996) "Rational Dynamic Choice and Expected Utility Theory," *Oxford Economic Papers* 48, 1–19.

Cubitt, Robin P., Chris Starmer, & Robert Sugden (1998) "Dynamic Choice and the Common Ratio Effect: An Experimental Investigation," *Economic Journal* 108, 1362–1380.

Cubitt, Robin P. & Robert Sugden (1998) "The Selection of Preferences through Imitation," *Review of Economic Studies* 65, 761–771.

Cubitt, Robin P. & Robert Sugden (2001) "On Money Pumps," *Games and Economic Behavior* 37, 121–160.

Curley, Shawn. P. & J. Frank Yates (1989) "An Empirical Evaluation of Descriptive Models of Ambiguity Reactions in Choice Situations," *Journal of Mathematical Psychology* 33, 397–427.

d'Amador, Risueño (1837) "Memoire sur Le Calcul des Probabilités Appliqué à la Médicine, Lu à l'Académie Royale de Médicine dans Sa Scéance du 25 Avril 1837." Baillière-J. B., Librairie de l'Académie Royale de Médicine, Paris.

Davidovich, Liema & Yossi Yassour (2009) "Ambiguity Preference," Ruppin Academic Center, Emek Hefer, Israel.

Davidson, Donald & Patrick Suppes (1956) "A Finitistic Axiomatization of Utility and Subjective Probability," *Econometrica* 24, 264–275.

Davidson, Donald, Patrick Suppes, & Sidney Siegel (1957) *Decision Making: An Experimental Approach.* Stanford University Press, Stanford, CA; Ch. 2 has been reprinted in Ward Edwards & Amos Tversky (1967, eds.) *Decision Making*, 170–207, Penguin, Harmondsworth.

Dawes, Robyn M., David Faust, & Paul E. Meehl (1989) "Clinical versus Actuarial Judgment," *Science* 243, 1668–1673.

de Finetti, Bruno (1931a) "Sul Significato Soggettivo della Probabilità," Fundamenta Mathematicae 17, 298–329. Translated into English as "On the Subjective Meaning of Probability," *in* Paola Monari & Daniela Cocchi (1993, eds.) *"Probabilità e Induzione,"* 291–321, Clueb, Bologna.

de Finetti, Bruno (1931b) "Probabilism," *Logos* 14, 163–219. Translated into English by Maria Concetta Di Maio, Maria Carla Galavotti, & Richard C. Jeffrey as: de Finetti, Bruno (1989) "Probabilism," *Erkenntnis* 31, 169–223.

de Finetti, Bruno (1932) "Sulla Preferibilità," *Giornale degli Economisti e Annali di Economia* 11, 685–709.

de Finetti, Bruno (1962) "Does It Make Sense to Speak of 'Good Probability Appraisers'?". In Isidore J. Good (ed.) *The Scientist Speculates: An Anthology of Partly-Baked Ideas*, William Heinemann Ltd., London. Reprinted as Ch. 3 in Bruno de Finetti (1972) *Probability, Induction and Statistics*. Wiley, New York.

de Finetti, Bruno (1972) *Probability, Induction and Statistics*. Wiley, New York.

de Finetti, Bruno (1974) *Theory of Probability*. Vol. I. Wiley, New York.

de Giorgi, Enrico & Thorsten Hens (2006) "Making Prospect Theory Fit for Finance", *Financial Markets and Portfolio Management* 20, 339–360.

De Waegenaere, Anja & Peter P. Wakker (2001) "Nonmonotonic Choquet Integrals," *Journal of Mathematical Economics* 36, 45–60.

Debreu, Gérard (1960) "Topological Methods in Cardinal Utility Theory." In Kenneth J. Arrow, Samuel Karlin, & Patrick Suppes (eds.) *Mathematical Methods in the Social Sciences*, 16–26, Stanford University Press, Stanford, CA.

DeGroot, Morris H. (1970) *Optimal Statistical Decisions*. McGraw-Hill, New York.

DeKay, Michael L., Dalia Patiño-Echeverri, & Paul S. Fischbeck (2009) Distortion of Probability and Outcome Information in Risky Decisions," *Organizational Behavior and Human Decision Processes* 109, 79–92.

Dempster, Arthur P. (1967) "Upper and Lower Probabilities Induced by a Multivalued Mapping," *Annals of Mathematical Statistics* 38, 325–339.

Denneberg, Dieter (1994) *Non-Additive Measure and Integral*. Kluwer Academic Publishers, Dordrecht.

Denoeux, Thierry (2008) "Conjunctive and Disjunctive Combination of Belief Functions Induced by Non Distinct Bodies of Evidence," *Artificial Intelligence* 172, 234–264.

Denuit, Michel, Jan Dhaene, Marc Goovaerts, Rob Kaas, & Roger Laeven (2006) "Risk Measurement with Equivalent Utility Principles," *Statistics and Decisions* 24, 1–26.

Dhaene, Jan, Michel Denuit, Marc J. Goovaerts, Rob Kaas, & David Vyncke (2002) "The Concept of Comonotonicity in Actuarial Science and Finance: Theory," *Insurance: Mathematics and Economics* 31, 3–33.

Di Mauro, Camela & Anna Maffioletti (1996) "An Experimental Investigation of the Impact of Ambiguity on the Valuation of Self-Insurance and Self-Protection," *Journal of Risk and Uncertainty* 13, 53–71.

Di Mauro, Camela & Anna Maffioletti (2002) "The Valuation of Insurance under Uncertainty: Does Information Matter?," *Geneva Papers on Risk and Insurance Theory* 26, 195–224.

Diecidue, Enrico, Ulrich Schmidt, & Horst Zank (2009) "Parametric Weighting Functions," *Journal of Economic Theory* 144, 1102–1118.

Diecidue, Enrico & Peter P. Wakker (2001) "On the Intuition of Rank-Dependent Utility," *Journal of Risk and Uncertainty* 23, 281–298.

Diecidue, Enrico & Peter P. Wakker (2002) "Dutch Books: Avoiding Strategic and Dynamic Complications, and a Comonotonic Extension," *Mathematical Social Sciences* 43, 135–149.

Diecidue, Enrico, Peter P. Wakker, & Marcel Zeelenberg (2007) "Eliciting Decision Weights by Adapting de Finetti's Betting-Odds Method to Prospect Theory," *Journal of Risk and Uncertainty* 34, 179–199.

Diener, Ed, & Robert Biswas-Diener (2008) *Rethinking Happiness: The Science of Psychological Wealth.* Blackwell Publishing, Malden, MA.

Dijksterhuis, Ap, Maarten W. Bos, Loran F. Nordgren, & Rick B. van Baaren (2006) "On Making the Right Choice: The Deliberation-without-Attention Effect," *Science* 311, 1005–1007.

Dobbs, Ian M. (1991) "A Bayesian Approach to Decision-Making under Ambiguity," *Economica* 58, 417–440.

Dolan, Paul & Martin Jones (2004) "Explaining Attitudes towards Ambiguity: An Experimental Test of the Comparative Ignorance Hypothesis," *Scottish Journal of Political Economy* 51, 281–301.

Dow, James & Sérgio R. C. Werlang (1992) "Uncertainty Aversion, Risk Aversion and the Optimal Choice of Portfolio," *Econometrica* 60, 197–204.

Drèze, Jacques H. (1961) "Les Fondements Logiques de l'Utilité Cardinale et de la Probabilité Subjective," *La Décision*, 73–83, Paris, CNRS.

Drèze, Jacques H. (1987) *Essays on Economic Decision under Uncertainty.* Cambridge University Press, Cambridge.

Drummond, Michael F., Gregg L. Stoddart, & George W. Torrance (1987) *"Methods for the Economic Evaluation of Health Care Programmes."* Oxford University Press, Oxford; 2nd edn. 1997.

Du, Ning & David Budescu (2005) "The Effects of Imprecise Probabilities and Outcomes in Evaluating Investment Options," *Management Science* 51, 1791–1803.

Dubra, Juan, Fabio Maccheroni, & Efe A. Ok (2004) "Expected Utility without the Completeness Axiom," *Journal of Economic Theory* 115, 118–133.

Dugundji, James (1966) *Topology.* Allyn and Bacon, Boston.

Easterling, Richard A. (1995) "Will Raising the Incomes of All Increase the Happiness of All?," *Journal of Economic Behavior and Organization* 27, 35–48.

Ebert, Jane E. J. & Drazen Prelec (2007) "The Fragility of Time: Time-Insensitivity and Valuation of the Near and Far Future," *Management Science* 53, 1423–1438.

Ebert, Udo (1988) "Rawls and Bentham Reconciled," *Theory and Decision* 24, 215–223.

Ebert, Udo (2004) "Social Welfare, Inequality, and Poverty when Needs Differ," *Social Choice and Welfare* 23, 415–448.

Edwards, Ward (1954) "The Theory of Decision Making," *Psychological Bulletin* 51, 380–417.

Edwards, Ward (1962) "Subjective Probabilities Inferred from Decisions," *Psychological Review* 69, 109–135.

Eichberger, Jürgen, Simon Grant, David Kelsey, & Gleb A. Koshevoy (2010) "The Alpha-Meu Model; A Comment."

Einhorn, Hillel J. & Robin M. Hogarth (1985) "Ambiguity and Uncertainty in Probabilistic Inference," *Psychological Review* 92, 433–461.

Einhorn, Hillel J. & Robin M. Hogarth (1986) "Decision Making under Ambiguity," *Journal of Business* 59, S225–S250.

Eliaz, Kfir & Efe A. Ok (2006) "Indifference or Indecisiveness? Choice-Theoretic Foundations of Incomplete Preferences," *Games and Economic Behavior* 56, 61–86.

Ellsberg, Daniel (1961) "Risk, Ambiguity and the Savage Axioms," *Quarterly Journal of Economics* 75, 643–669.

Ellsberg, Daniel (2001) *Risk, Ambiguity and Decision.* Garland Publishers, New York. Original Ph.D. dissertation: Ellsberg, Daniel (1962) *"Risk, Ambiguity and Decision."* Harvard University, Cambridge, MA.

Epper, Thomas, Helga Fehr-Duda, & Adrian Bruhin (2009) "Uncertainty Breeds Decreasing Impatience: The Role of Risk Preferences in Time Discounting," mimeo.

Epstein, Larry G. (1992) "Behavior under Risk: Recent Developments in Theory and Applications." In Jean-Jacques Laffont (ed.) *Advances in Economic Theory II* , 1–63, Cambridge University Press, Cambridge.

Epstein, Larry G. (1999) "A Definition of Uncertainty Aversion," *Review of Economic Studies* 66, 579–608.

Epstein, Larry G. (2008) "Living with Risk," *Review of Economic Studies* 75, 1121–1141.

Epstein, Larry G. & Michel Le Breton (1993) "Dynamically Consistent Beliefs Must Be Bayesian," *Journal of Economic Theory* 61, 1–22.

Epstein, Larry G. & Jiangkang Zhang (2001) "Subjective Probabilities on Subjectively Unambiguous Events," *Econometrica* 69, 265–306.

Erev, Ido, Thomas S. Wallsten, & David V. Budescu (1994) "Simultaneous Over- and Under-confidence: The Role of Error in Judgment Processes," *Psychological Review* 101, 519–527.

Ert, Eyal & Ido Erev (2008) "The Rejection of Attractive Gambles, Loss Aversion, and the Lemon Avoidance Heuristic," *Journal of Economic Psychology* 29, 715–723.

Etchart, Nathalie (2004) "Is Probability Weighting Sensitive to the Magnitude of Consequences? An Experimental Investigation on Losses," *Journal of Risk and Uncertainty* 28, 217–235.

Falmagne, Jean-Claude (1985) *Elements of Psychophysical Theory.* Oxford University Press, New York.

Farquhar, Peter H. (1984) "Utility Assessment Methods," *Management Science* 30, 1283–1300.

Fatas, Enrique, Tibor Neugebauer, & Pilar Tamborero (2007) "How Politicians Make Decisions: A Political Choice Experiment," *Journal of Economics* 92, 167–196.

Fetherstonhaugh, David, Paul Slovic, Stephen M. Johnson, & James Friedrich (1997) "Insensitivity to the Value of Human Life: A Study of Psychophysical Numbing," *Journal of Risk and Uncertainty* 14, 283–300.

Fehr, Ernst & Klaus Schmidt (1999) "A Theory of Fairness, Competition and Cooperation," *Quarterly Journal of Economics* 114, 817–868.

Fehr-Duda, Helga, Manuele de Gennaro, & Renate Schubert (2006) "Gender, Financial Risk, and Probability Weights," *Theory and Decision* 60, 283–313.

Fellner, William (1961) "Distortion of Subjective Probabilities as a Reaction to Uncertainty," *Quarterly Journal of Economics* 75, 670–689.

Fishburn, Peter C. (1965) "Independence in Utility Theory with Whole Product Sets," *Operations Research* 13, 28–45.

Fishburn, Peter C. (1967) "Methods of Estimating Additive Utilities," *Management Science* 13, 435–453.

Fishburn, Peter C. (1970) *Utility Theory for Decision Making.* Wiley, New York.

Fishburn, Peter C. (1972) *Mathematics of Decision Theory.* Mouton, The Hague.

Fishburn, Peter C. (1978) "On Handa's 'New Theory of Cardinal Utility' and the Maximization of Expected Return," *Journal of Political Economy* 86, 321–324.

Fishburn, Peter C. (1981) "Subjective Expected Utility: A Review of Normative Theories," *Theory and Decision* 13, 139–199.

Fishburn, Peter C. (1982) *The Foundations of Expected Utility.* Reidel, Dordrecht.

Fishburn, Peter C. (1986) "The Axioms of Subjective Probability," *Statistical Science* 1, 335–358.

Fishburn, Peter C. (1988) "Expected Utility: An Anniversary and a New Era," *Journal of Risk and Uncertainty* 1, 267–283.

Fisher, Irving (1892) "Mathematical Investigations in the Theory of Values and Prices," *Transactions of Connecticut Academy of Arts and Sciences* 9, 1–124. Reprinted as book in 1965 (1st edn. 1925), Yale University Press, New Haven.

Fleming, J. Marcus (1952) "A Cardinal Concept of Welfare," *Quarterly Journal of Economics* 66, 366–384.

Fox, Craig R., Brett A. Rogers, & Amos Tversky (1996) "Options Traders Exhibit Subadditive Decision Weights," *Journal of Risk and Uncertainty* 13, 5–17.

Fox, Craig R. & Amos Tversky (1995) "Ambiguity Aversion and Comparative Ignorance," *Quarterly Journal of Economics* 110, 585–603.

Fox, Craig R. & Amos Tversky (1998) "A Belief-Based Account of Decision under Uncertainty," *Management Science* 44, 879–895.

Frank, Robert H. (1989) "Frames of Reference and the Quality of Life," *American Economic Review* 79, 80–85.

French, Kenneth R. & James M. Poterba (1991) "Investor Diversification and International Equity Markets," *American Economic Review* 81, 222–226.

Frey, Bruno S. (2008) *Happiness. A Revolution in Economics.* The MIT Press, Cambridge, MA.

Friedman, Milton (1953) *Methodology of Positive Economics.* University of Chicago Press, Chicago.

Friend, Irwin & Marshall E. Blume (1975) "The Demand for Risky Assets," *American Economic Review* 65, 900–922.

Furlong William J., David H. Feeny, George W. Torrance, & Ronald D. Barr (2001) "The Health Utilities Index (HUI) System for Assessing Health-Related Quality of Life in Clinical Studies," *Annals of Medicine* 33, 375–384.

Gächter, Simon, Andreas Herrmann, & Eric J. Johnson (2007) "Individual-Level Loss Aversion in Riskless and Risky Choice." Working Paper, University of Nottingham.

Gajdos, Thibault, Takashi Hayashi, Jean-Marc Tallon, & Jean-Christophe Vergnaud (2008) "Attitude towards Imprecise Information," *Journal of Economic Theory* 140, 27–65.

Galand, Lucie, Patrice Perny & Olivier Spanjaard (2010) "Choquet-Based Optimisation in Multiobjective Shortest Path and Spanning Tree Problems," *European Journal of Operational Research* 204, 303–315.

Gandjour, Afschin (2008) "Incorporating Feelings Related to the Uncertainty about Future Health in Utility Measurement," *Health Economics* 17, 1207–1213.

Gärdenfors, Peter & Nils-Eric Sahlin (1982) "Unreliable Probabilities, Risk Taking, and Decision Making," *Synthese* 53, 361–386.

Gardner, Howard (1985) *The Mind's New Science: A History of the Cognitive Revolution.* Basic Books, New York.

Gayer, Gabi (2010) "Perception of Probabilities in Situations of Risk; A Case Based Approach," *Games and Economic Behavior* 68, 130–143.

Ghirardato, Paolo (2001) "Coping with Ignorance: Unforeseen Contingencies and Non-Additive Uncertainty," *Economic Theory* 17, 247–276.

Ghirardato, Paolo (2002) "Revisiting Savage in a Conditional World," *Economic Theory* 20, 83–92.

Ghirardato, Paolo, Fabio Maccheroni, & Massimo Marinacci (2004) "Differentiating Ambiguity and Ambiguity Attitude," *Journal of Economic Theory* 118, 133–173.

Ghirardato, Paolo, Fabio Maccheroni, & Massimo Marinacci (2005) "Certainty Independence and the Separation of Utility and Beliefs," *Journal of Economic Theory* 120, 129–136.

Ghirardato, Paolo, Fabio Maccheroni, Massimo Marinacci, & Marciano Siniscalchi (2003) "A Subjective Spin on Roulette Wheels," *Econometrica* 71, 1897–1908.

Ghirardato, Paolo & Massimo Marinacci (2001a) "Risk, Ambiguity, and the Separation of Utility and Beliefs," *Mathematics of Operations Research* 26, 864–890.

Ghirardato, Paolo & Massimo Marinacci (2001b) "Range Convexity and Ambiguity Averse Preferences," *Economic Theory* 17, 599–617.

Ghirardato, Paolo & Massimo Marinacci (2002) "Ambiguity Made Precise: A Comparative Foundation," *Journal of Economic Theory* 102, 251–289.

Gigerenzer, Gerd (1991) "From Tools to Theories: A Heuristic of Discovery in Cognitive Psychology," *Psychological Review* 98, 254–267.

Gigerenzer, Gerd (2008) *Rationality for Mortals: Risk and Rules of Thumb.* Oxford University Press, New York.

Gilboa, Itzhak (1985) "Subjective Distortions of Probabilities and Non-Additive Probabilities," Working paper 18–85, Foerder Institute for Economic Research, Tel-Aviv University, Ramat Aviv, Israel.

Gilboa, Itzhak (1987) "Expected Utility with Purely Subjective Non-Additive Probabilities," *Journal of Mathematical Economics* 16, 65–88.

Gilboa, Itzhak (1988) "A Combination of Expected Utility Theory and Maxmin Decision Criteria," *Journal of Mathematical Psychology* 32, 405–420.

Gilboa, Itzhak (1989a) "Expectation and Variation in Multi-Period Decisions," *Econometrica* 57, 1153–1169.

Gilboa, Itzhak (1989b) "Duality in Non-Additive Expected Utility Theory," *Annals of Operations Research* 19, 405–414.

Gilboa, Itzhak (2009) *Theory of Decision under Uncertainty.* Cambridge University Press, Cambridge.

Gilboa, Itzhak, Andrew W. Postlewaite, & David Schmeidler (2008) "Probability and Uncertainty in Economic Modeling," *Journal of Economic Perspectives* 22, 173–188.

Gilboa, Itzhak & David Schmeidler (1989) "Maxmin Expected Utility with a Non-Unique Prior," *Journal of Mathematical Economics* 18, 141–153.

Gilboa, Itzhak & David Schmeidler (1993) "Updating Ambiguous Beliefs," *Journal of Economic Theory* 59, 33–49.

Gilboa, Itzhak & David Schmeidler (1995) "Canonical Representation of Set Functions," *Mathematics of Operations Research* 20, 197–212.

Gilboa, Itzhak & David Schmeidler (2001a) *A Theory of Case-Based Decisions.* Cambridge University Press, Cambridge.

Gilboa, Itzhak & David Schmeidler (2001b) "A Cognitive Model of Individual Well-Being," *Social Choice and Welfare* 18, 269–288.

Gintis, Herbert (2009) *The Bounds of Reason; Game Theory and the Unification of the Behavioral Sciences.* Princeton University Press, Princeton NJ.

Glöckner, Andreas & Tilmann Betsch (2008) "Do People Make Decisions under Risk Based on Ignorance? An Empirical Test of the Priority Heuristic against Cumulative Prospect Theory," *Organizational Behavior and Human Decision Processes* 107, 75–95.

Goeree, Jacob K., Charles A. Holt, & Thomas R. Palfrey (2002) "Quantal Response Equilibrium and Overbidding in Private-Value Auctions," *Journal of Economic Theory* 104, 247–272.

Goeree, Jacob K., Charles A. Holt, & Thomas R. Palfrey (2003) "Risk Averse Behavior in Generalized Matching Pennies Games," *Games and Economic Behavior* 45, 97–113.

Gold, Marthe R., Joanna E. Siegel, Louise B. Russell, & Milton C. Weinstein (1996) *Cost-Effectiveness in Health and Medicine.* Oxford University Press, New York.

Goldstein, William M. & Hillel J. Einhorn (1987) "Expression Theory and the Preference Reversal Phenomena," *Psychological Review* 94, 236–254.

Gollier, Christian (2001a) *The Economics of Risk and Time*. The MIT Press, Cambridge MA.

Gollier, Christian (2001b) "Wealth Inequality and Asset Pricing," *Review of Economic Studies* 68, 181–203.

González-Vallejo, Claudia C., Aaron A. Reid, & Joel Schiltz (2003) "Context Effects: The Proportional Difference Model and the Reflection of Preference," *Journal of Experimental Psychology: Learning, Memory, and Cognition* 29, 942–953.

Gonzalez, Cleotilde, Jason Dana, Hideya Koshino, & Marcel A. Just (2005) "The Framing Effect and Risky Decisions: Examining Cognitive Functions with fMRI," *Journal of Economic Psychology* 26, 1–20.

Gonzalez, Richard & George Wu (1999) "On the Shape of the Probability Weighting Function," *Cognitive Psychology* 38, 129–166.

Gonzalez, Richard & George Wu (2003) "Composition Rules in Original and Cumulative Prospect Theory," mimeo.

Good, Isidore J. (1950) *Probability and the Weighing of Evidence*. Hafners, New York.

Good, Isidore J. (1952) "Rational Decisions," *Journal of the Royal Statistical Society Series B* 14, 107–114.

Gourieroux, Christian & Alain Monfort (1995) *Statistics and Econometrics Models*. Cambridge University Press, Cambridge.

Grabisch, Michel, Ivan Kojadinovic, & Patrick Meyer (2008) "A Review of Methods for Capacity Identification in Choquet Integral Based Multi-Attribute Utility Theory; Applications of the Kappalab R Package," *European Journal of Operational Research* 186, 766–785.

Grabisch, Michel & Christophe Labreuche (2008) "A Decade of Application of the Choquet and Sugeno Integrals in Multi-Criteria Decision Aid," *4OR* 6, 1–44.

Grabisch, Michel, Jean-Luc Marichal, & Marc Roubens (2000) "Equivalent Representations of Set Functions," *Mathematics of Operations Research* 25, 157–178.

Grant, Simon & Edi Karni (2005) "Why Does It Matter that Beliefs and Valuations Be Correctly Represented?", *International Economic Review* 46, 917–934.

Green, Edward J. & Kent Osband (1991) "A Revealed Preference Theory for Expected Utility," *Review of Economic Studies* 58, 677–696.

Green, Paul E. & V. Srinivasan (1978) "Conjoint Analysis in Consumer Research: Issues and Outlook," *Journal of Consumer Research* 5, 103–123.

Greenspan, Alan (2004) "Innovations and Issues in Monetary Policy: The Last Fifteen Years," *American Economic Review, Papers and Proceedings* 94, 33–40.

Gregory, Robin, Sarah Lichtenstein, & Paul Slovic (1993) "Valuing Environmental Resources: A Constructive Approach," *Journal of Risk and Uncertainty* 7, 177–197.

Grether, David M. & Charles R. Plott (1979) "Economic Theory of Choice and the Preference Reversal Phenomenon," *American Economic Review* 69, 623–638.

Griffith, Richard M. (1949) "Odds Adjustments by American Horse Race Bettors," *American Journal of Psychology* 62, 290–294.

Guerrero, Ana M. & Carmen Herrero (2005) "A Semi-Separable Utility Function for Health Profiles," *Journal of Health Economics* 24, 33–54.

Gul, Faruk (1991) "A Theory of Disappointment Aversion," *Econometrica* 59, 667–686.

Gul, Faruk (1992) "Savage's Theorem with a Finite Number of States," *Journal of Economic Theory* 57, 99–110. ("Erratum," 1993, *Journal of Economic Theory* 61, 184.)

Guppy, Andrew (1992) "Subjective Probability of Accident and Apprehension in Relation to Self-Other Bias, Age, and Reported Behavior," *Accident Analysis and Prevention* 25, 375–382.

Gurevich, Gregory, Doron Kliger, & Ori Levy (2009) "Decision-Making under Uncertainty – A Field Study of Cumulative Prospect Theory," *Journal of Banking & Finance*, forthcoming.

Gustafsson, Anders, Andreas Herrmann, & Frank Huber (2007) *Conjoint Measurement: Methods and Applications* (2nd edn.). Springer, Berlin.

Halevy, Yoram (2007) "Ellsberg Revisited: An Experimental Study," *Econometrica* 75, 503–536.

Halevy, Yoram (2008) "Strotz Meets Allais: Diminishing Impatience and the Certainty Effect," *American Economic Review* 98, 1145–1162.

Halmos, Paul R. (1950) *Measure Theory.* Van Nostrand, New York.

Halpern, Joseph Y. (2003) *Reasoning about Uncertainty.* The MIT Press, Cambridge, MA.

Hammond, Kenneth R. (2006) *Beyond Rationality.* Oxford University Press, New York.

Hammond, Peter J. (1988) "Consequentialist Foundations for Expected Utility," *Theory and Decision* 25, 25–78.

Handa, Jagdish (1977) "Risk, Probabilities, and a New Theory of Cardinal Utility," *Journal of Political Economy* 85, 97–122.

Hansen, Lars P. & Thomas J. Sargent (2001) "Robust Control and Model Uncertainty," *American Economic Review, Papers and Proceedings* 91, 60–66.

Hardisty, David J. & Elke U. Weber (2009) "Discounting Future Green: Money versus the Environment," *Journal of Experimental Psychology* 138, 329–340.

Hardy, Godfrey H., John E. Littlewood, & George Pòlya (1934) *Inequalities.* Cambridge University Press, Cambridge, UK. (2nd edn. 1952, reprinted 1978.)

L'Haridon, Olivier & Laetitia Placido (2009) "Betting on Machina's Reflection Example: An Experiment on Ambiguity," *Theory and Decision,* forthcoming.

Harless, David W. & Colin F. Camerer (1994) "The Predictive Utility of Generalized Expected Utility Theories," *Econometrica* 62, 1251–1289.

Harré, Rom (1970) *The Principles of Scientific Thinking.* Macmillan, London.

Harrison, Glenn W. (1986) "An Experimental Test for Risk Aversion," *Economic Letters* 21, 7–11.

Harrison, Glenn W. (2006) "Hypothetical Bias over Uncertain Outcomes." In John A. List (ed.), *Using Experimental Methods in Environmental and Resource Economics,* 41–69, Elgar, Northampton, MA.

Harrison, Glenn W., Morten I. Lau, & E. Elisabet Rutström (2007) "Estimating Risk Attitudes in Denmark: A Field Experiment," *Scandinavian Journal of Economics* 109, 341–368.

Harrison, Glenn W. & E. Elisabet Rutström (2008) "Risk Aversion in the Laboratory." In Jim C. Cox & Glenn W. Harrison (eds.), *Risk Aversion in Experiments,* Research in Experimental Economics Vol. 12, Bingley.

Harrison, Glenn W. & E. Elisabet Rutström (2009) "Expected Utility Theory and Prospect Theory: One Wedding and a Decent Funeral," *Experimental Economics* 12, 133–158.

Harsanyi, John C. (1955) "Cardinal Welfare, Individualistic Ethics, and Interpersonal Comparisons of Utility," *Journal of Political Economy* 63, 309–321.

Harsanyi, John C. (1982) "Subjective Probability and the Theory of Games: Comments on Kadane and Larkey's Paper," *Management Science* 28, 120–125.

Heath, Chip, Steven Huddart, & Mark Lang (1999) "Psychological Factors and Stock Option Exercise," *Quarterly Journal of Economics* 114, 601–627.

Hempel, Carl G. (1952) *Fundamentals of Concept Formation in Empirical Science.* University of Chicago Press, Chicago.

Henrich, Joseph & Richard Mcelreat (2002) "Are Peasants Risk-Averse Decision Makers?," *Current Anthropology* 43, 172–181.

Hershey, John C. & Paul J. H. Schoemaker (1985) "Probability versus Certainty Equivalence Methods in Utility Measurement: Are They Equivalent?," *Management Science* 31, 1213–1231.

Hertwig, Ralf, Greg Barron, Elke U. Weber, & Ido Erev (2003) "Decisions from Experience and the Effect of Rare Events in Risky Choice," *Psychological Science* 15, 534–539.

Hertwig, Ralf & Andreas Ortmann (2001) "Experimental Practices in Economics: A Challenge for Psychologists?," *Behavioral and Brain Sciences* 24, 383–403.

Hevell, Steven K. & Frederick A. A. Kingdom (2008) "Color in Complex Scenes," *Annual Review of Psychology* 59, 143–166.

Hey, John D., Gianna Lotito, & Anna Maffioletti (2008) "The Descriptive and Predictive Adequacy of Theories of Decision Making under Uncertainty/Ambiguity," Dept. of Economics, University of York, Discussion paper no. 2008/04.

Hey, John D. & Chris Orme (1994) "Investigating Generalizations of Expected Utility Theory Using Experimental Data," *Econometrica* 62, 1291–1326.

Hicks, John R. & Roy G. D. Allen (1934) "A Reconsideration of the Theory of Value: I; II," *Economica* 1, 52–75; 196–219.

Hilhorst, Cokky, Piet Ribbers, Eric van Heck, & Martin Smits (2008) "Using Dempster–Shafer Theory and Real Options Theory to Assess Competing Strategies for Implementing IT Infrastructures: A Case Study," *Decision Support Systems* 46, 344–355.

Ho, Joanna L. Y., L. Robin Keller, & Pamela Keltyka (2002) "Effects of Outcome and Probabilistic Ambiguity on Managerial Choices," *Journal of Risk and Uncertainty* 24, 47–74.

Hoelzl, Erik & Aldo Rustichini (2005) "Overconfident: Do You Put Your Money on It," *Economic Journal* 115, 305–318.

Hogarth, Robin M. & Hillel J. Einhorn (1990) "Venture Theory: A Model of Decision Weights," *Management Science* 36, 780–803.

Hogarth Robin M. & Howard C. Kunreuther (1985) "Ambiguity and Insurance Decisions," *American Economic Review, Papers and Proceedings* 75, 386–390.

Hogarth, Robin M. & Howard C. Kunreuther (1989) "Risk, Ambiguity, and Insurance," *Journal of Risk and Uncertainty* 2, 5–35.

Holt, Charles A. (1986) "Preference Reversals and the Independence Axiom," *American Economic Review* 76, 508–513.

Holt, Charles A. & Susan K. Laury (2002) "Risk Aversion and Incentive Effects," *American Economic Review* 92, 1644–1655.

Hopfensitz, Astrid & Frans Winden (2008) "Dynamic Choice, Independence and Emotions," *Theory and Decision* 64, 249–300.

Houthakker, Hendrik S. (1950) "Revealed Preference and the Utility Function," *Economica*, N. S. 17, 159–174.

Howard, Ronald A. & James E. Matheson (1984, eds.) *The Principles and Applications of Decision Analysis.* (Two volumes) Strategic Decisions Group, Palo Alto, CA.

Hsee, Christopher K. & Robert P. Abelson (1991) "Velocity Relation: Satisfaction as a Function of the First Derivative of Outcome over Time," *Journal of Personality and Social Psychology* 60, 341–347.

Hsu, Ming, Meghana Bhatt, Ralph Adolphs, Daniel Tranel, & Colin Camerer (2005) "Neural Systems Responding to Degrees of Uncertainty in Human Decision Making," *Science* 310, 9 Dec., 1680–1683.

Huber, Joel, Dan Ariely, & Gregory Fischer (2001) "Expressing Preference in a Principal-Agent Task: A Comparison of Choice, Rating, and Matching," *Organizational Behavior and Human Decision Processes* 87, 66–90.

Huber, Peter J. (1981) *Robust Statistics.* Wiley, New York.

Huettel, Scott A., C. Jill Stowe, Evan M. Gordon, Brent T. Warner, & Michael L. Platt (2006) "Neural Signatures of Economic Preferences for Risk and Ambiguity," *Neuron* 49, 765–775.

Hull, John C. (2005) *Options, Futures, and Other Derivatives.* Prentice-Hall, Englewood Cliffs, NJ (6th edn.).

Humphrey, Stephen J. & Arjan Verschoor (2004) "The Probability Weighting Function: Experimental Evidence from Uganda, India and Ethiopia," *Economics Letters* 84, 419–425.

Hurvich, Leo M. & Dorothea Jameson (1951) "Psychophysical Study of White. I. Neutral Adaptation," *Journal of the Optical Society of America* 41, 521–527.

Hurwicz, Leonid (1951) "Some Specification Problems and Applications to Econometric Models" (Abstract), *Econometrica* 19, 343–344.

Hurwicz, Leonid (1972) "On Informationally Decentralized Systems." In C. Bartlett McGuire & Roy Radner (eds.) *Decision and Organization*, 297–336, North-Holland, Amsterdam.

Jaffray, Jean-Yves (1989) "Linear Utility Theory for Belief Functions," *Operations Research Letters* 8, 107–112.

Jaffray, Jean-Yves (1991a) "Linear Utility Theory and Belief Functions: A Discussion." In Atilla Chikan (ed.), *Progress in Decision, Utility and Risk Theory*. Kluwer Academic Publishers, Dordrecht.

Jaffray, Jean-Yves (1991b) "Belief Functions, Convex Capacities, and Decision Making." In Jean-Paul Doignon & Jean-Claude Falmagne (eds.) *Mathematical Psychology: Current Developments*, 127–134, Springer, Berlin.

Jaffray, Jean-Yves (1992) "Bayesian Updating and Belief Functions," *IEEE Transactions on Systems, Man, and Cybernetics* 22, 1144–1152.

Jaffray, Jean-Yves (1994) "Dynamic Decision Making with Belief Functions." In Ronald R. Yager, Mario Fedrizzi, & Janus Kacprzyk (eds.), *Advances in the Dempster-Shafer Theory of Evidence*, 331–352, Wiley, New York.

Jaffray, Jean-Yves & Fabrice Philippe (1997) "On the Existence of Subjective Upper and Lower Probabilities," *Mathematics of Operations Research* 22, 165–185.

James, William (1884) "What is an Emotion?," *Mind* 9, 188–205.

Jeffrey, Richard C. (1965) *The Logic of Decision*. McGraw-Hill, New York. (2nd edn. 1983, University of Chicago Press, Chicago.)

Jevons, W. Stanley (1871) *The Theory of Political Economy*. (5th edn. 1957, Kelley and MacMillan, New York; other edn. Penguin, 1970.)

Johansson-Stenman, Olof (2010) "Risk Behavior and Expected Utility of Consumption over Time," *Games and Economic Behavior* 68, 208–219.

Johnson, Cathleen (2008) in preparation.

Johnson, Eric J. & David A. Schkade (1989) "Bias in Utility Assessments: Further Evidence and Explanations," *Management Science* 35, 406–424.

Jullien, Bruno & Bernard Salanié (2000) "Estimating Preferences under Risk: The Case of Racetrack Bettors," *Journal of Political Economy* 108, 503–530.

Just, David R. & Hikaru Hanawa Peterson (2003) "Diminishing Marginal Utility of Wealth and Calibration of Risk in Agriculture," *American Journal of Agricultural Economics* 85, 1234–1241.

Kachelmeier, Steven J. & Mohamed Shehata (1992) "Examining Risk Preferences under High Monetary Incentives: Experimental Evidence from the People's Republic of China," *American Economic Review* 82, 1120–1141; for comment see Steven J. Kachelmeier & Mohammed Shehata (1994) *American Economic Review* 84, 1104–1106.

Kadane, Joseph B. & Patrick D. Larkey (1982) "Subjective Probability and the Theory of Games," *Management Science* 28, 113–120.

Kadane, Joseph B. & Patrick D. Larkey (1983) "The Conflict of Is and Ought in Game Theoretic Contexts," *Management Science* 29, 1365–1379.

Kadane, Joseph B. & Robert L. Winkler (1988) "Separating Probability Elicitation from Utilities," *Journal of the American Statistical Association* 83, 357–363.

Kahn, Barbara E. & Rakesh K. Sarin (1988) "Modeling Ambiguity in Decisions under Uncertainty," *Journal of Consumer Research* 15, 265–272.

Kahneman, Daniel (1994) "New Challenges to the Rationality Assumption," *Journal of Institutional and Theoretical Economics* 150, 18–36.

Kahneman, Daniel (2003) "Maps of Bounded Rationality: Psychology for Behavioral Economics," *American Economic Review* 93, 1449–1475.

Kahneman, Daniel & Alan B. Krueger (2006) "Developments in the Measurement of Subjective Well-Being," *Journal of Economic Perspectives* 20, 3–24.

Kahneman, Daniel, Alan B. Krueger, David A. Schkade, Norbert Schwarz, & Arthur A. Stone (2004) "A Survey Method for Characterizing Daily Life Experience: The Day Reconstruction Method," *Science* 306, 1776–1780.

Kahneman, Daniel & Dan Lovallo (1993) "Timid Choices and Bold Forecasts: A Cognitive Perspective on Risk Taking," *Management Science* 39, 17–31.

Kahneman, Daniel & Amos Tversky (1975) "Value Theory: An Analysis of Choices under Risk," paper presented at a conference on Public Economics, Jerusalem, 1975.

Kahneman, Daniel & Amos Tversky (1979) "Prospect Theory: An Analysis of Decision under Risk," *Econometrica* 47, 263–291.

Kahneman, Daniel, Peter P. Wakker, & Rakesh K. Sarin (1997) "Back to Bentham? Explorations of Experienced Utility," *Quarterly Journal of Economics* 112, 375–405.

Kapteyn, Arie (1994) "The Measurement of Household Cost Functions: Revealed Preference versus Subjective Measures," *Journal of Population Economics* 7, 333–350.

Karmarkar, Uday S. (1978) "Subjectively Weighted Utility: A Descriptive Extension of the Expected Utility Model," *Organizational Behavior and Human Performance* 21, 61–72.

Karni, Edi (1993) "A Definition of Subjective Probabilities with State-Dependent Preferences," *Econometrica* 61, 187–198.

Karni, Edi (1996) "Probabilities and Beliefs," *Journal of Risk and Uncertainty* 13, 249–262.

Karni, Edi (2006) "Subjective Expected Utility Theory without States of the World," *Journal of Mathematical Economics* 42, 325–342.

Karni, Edi & Zvi Safra (1990) "Behaviorally Consistent Optimal Stopping Rules," *Journal of Economic Theory* 51, 391–402.

Karni, Edi & David Schmeidler (1991) "Utility Theory with Uncertainty." In Werner Hildenbrand & Hugo F. Sonnenschein (eds.) *Handbook of Mathematical Economics* 4, Ch. 33, 1763–1831, North-Holland, Amsterdam.

Keeney, Ralph L. (2004) "Making Better Decision Makers," *Decision Analysis* 1, 193–204.

Keeney, Ralph L. & Howard Raiffa (1976) *Decisions with Multiple Objectives.* Wiley, New York (2nd edn. 1993, Cambridge University Press, Cambridge).

Keller, L. Robin & Elisabetta Strazzera (2002) "Examining Predictive Accuracy among Discounting Models," *Journal of Risk and Uncertainty* 24, 143–160.

Keren, Gideon B. & Léonie E. M. Gerritsen (1999) "On the Robustness and Possible Accounts of Ambiguity Aversion," *Acta Psychologica* 103, 149–172.

Keynes, John Maynard (1921) *A Treatise on Probability.* Macmillan, London. 2nd edn. 1948.

Kilka, Michael & Martin Weber (2001) "What Determines the Shape of the Probability Weighting Function under Uncertainty," *Management Science* 47, 1712–1726.

Kirkpatrick, Lee A. & Seymour Epstein (1992) "Cognitive-Experiential Self-Theory and Subjective Probability: Further Evidence for Two Conceptual Systems," *Journal of Personality and Social Psychology* 63, 534–544.

Klibanoff, Peter, Massimo Marinacci, & Sujoy Mukerji (2005) "A Smooth Model of Decision Making under Ambiguity," *Econometrica* 73, 1849–1892.

Knight, Frank H. (1921) *Risk, Uncertainty, and Profit.* Houghton Mifflin, New York.

Köbberling, Veronika & Hans J. M. Peters (2003) "The Effect of Decision Weights in Bargaining Problems," *Journal of Economic Theory* 110, 154–175.

Köbberling, Veronika, Christiane Schwieren, & Peter P. Wakker (2007) "Prospect-Theory's Diminishing Sensitivity versus Economics' Intrinsic Utility of Money: How the Introduction of the Euro Can Be Used to Disentangle the Two Empirically," *Theory and Decision* 63, 205–231.

Köbberling, Veronika & Peter P. Wakker (2003) "Preference Foundations for Nonexpected Utility: A Generalized and Simplified Technique," *Mathematics of Operations Research* 28, 395–423.

Köbberling, Veronika & Peter P. Wakker (2004) "A Simple Tool for Qualitatively Testing, Quantitatively Measuring, and Normatively Justifying Savage's Subjective Expected Utility," *Journal of Risk and Uncertainty* 28, 135–145.

Köbberling, Veronika & Peter P. Wakker (2005) "An Index of Loss Aversion," *Journal of Economic Theory* 122, 119–131.

Koopman, Bernard O. (1940) "The Bases of Probability," *Bulletin of the American Mathematical Society* 46, 763–774.

Kopylov, Igor (2007) "Subjective Probabilities on "Small" Domains," *Journal of Economic Theory* 133, 236–265.

Köszegi, Botond & Matthew Rabin (2006) "A Model of Reference-Dependent Preferences," *Quarterly Journal of Economics* 121, 1133–1165.

Krantz, David H., R. Duncan Luce, Patrick Suppes, & Amos Tversky (1971) *Foundations of Measurement, Vol. I (Additive and Polynomial Representations)*. Academic Press, New York. (2nd edn. 2007, Dover Publications, New York.)

Kreps, David M. (1988) *Notes on the Theory of Choice*. Westview Press, Boulder, CO.

Krzysztofowicz, Roman (1994) "Generic Utility Theory: Explanatory Model, Behavioral Hypotheses, Empirical Evidence." In Maurice Allais & Ole Hagen (eds.) *"Cardinalism; A Fundamental Approach,"* 249–288, Kluwer Academic Publishers, Dordrecht.

Kühberger, Anton, Michael Schulte-Mecklenbeck, & Josef Perner (1999) "The Effects of Framing, Reflection, Probability, and Payoff on Risk Preference in Choice Tasks," *Organizational Behavior and Human Decision Processes* 78, 204–231.

Kuhn, Kristine M. (1997) "Communicating Uncertainty: Framing Effects on Responses to Vague Probabilities," *Organizational Behavior and Human Decision Processes* 71, 55–83.

Kunreuther, Howard C., Nathan Novemsky, & Daniel Kahneman (2001) "Making Low Probabilities Useful," *Journal of Risk and Uncertainty* 23, 103–120.

Kunreuther, Howard C. & Mark Pauly (2003) "Neglecting Disaster: Why Don't People Insure against Large Losses," *Journal of Risk and Uncertainty* 28, 5–21.

Kusuoka, Shigeo (2001) "On Law Invariant Coherent Risk Measures," *Advances in Mathematical Economics* 3, 83–95.

Kyburg, Henry E. Jr. (1983) *Epistemology and Inference*. University of Minnesota Press, Minneapolis, MN.

Lancaster, Kelvin J. (1966) "A New Approach to Consumer Theory," *Journal of Political Economy* 74, 132–157.

Lapidus, André & Nathalie Sigot (2000) "Individual Utility in a Context of Asymmetric Sensitivity to Pleasure and Pain: An Interpretation of Bentham's Felicific Calculus," *European Journal of the History of Economic Thought* 7, 45–78.

Lattimore, Pamela M., Joanna R. Baker, & Ann D. Witte (1992) "The Influence of Probability on Risky Choice," *Journal of Economic Behavior and Organization* 17, 377–400.

Laughhunn, Dan J., John W. Payne, & Roy L. Crum (1980) "Managerial Risk Preferences for Below-Target Returns," *Management Science* 26, 1238–1249.

Laury, Susan K. & Charles A. Holt (2008) "Further Reflections on Prospect Theory." In Cox, James C. & Glenn Harrison (eds.) *Risk Aversion in Experiments* (Experimental Economics, Volume 12) JAI Press, Greenwich, CT.

LaValle, Irving H. (1978) *Fundamentals of Decision Analysis*. Holt, Rinehart, Winston, New York.

Lee, Jinkwon (2008) "The Effect of the Background Risk in a Simple Chance Improving Decision Model," *Journal of Risk and Uncertainty* 36, 19–41.

LeRoy, Stephen F. (2003) "Expected Utility: A Defense," *Economics Bulletin* 7, 1–3.

Levi, Isaac (1980) *The Enterprise of Knowledge*. MIT Press, Cambridge, MA.

Levy, Haim (1992) "Stochastic Dominance and Expected Utility: Survey and Analysis," *Management Science* 38, 555–593.

Levy, Moshe & Haim Levy (2002) "Prospect Theory: Much Ado about Nothing," *Management Science* 48, 1334–1349.

Lewin, Shira (1996) "Economics and Psychology: Lessons for Our Own Day from the Early Twentieth Century," *Journal of Economic Literature* 34, 1293–1323.

Lewis, David (1987) "Causal Decision Theory." In Peter Gärdenfors & Nils-Eric Sahlin (eds.), *Decision, Probability, and Utility*, 377–405, Cambridge University Press, Cambridge.

Libby, Robert & Peter C. Fishburn (1977) "Behavioral Models of Risk Taking in Business Decisions: A Survey and Evaluation," *Journal of Accounting Research* 15, 272–292.

Lichtenstein, Sarah & Paul Slovic (1971) "Reversals of Preference between Bids and Choices in Gambling Decisions," *Journal of Experimental Psychology* 89, 46–55.

Lindley, Dennis L. (1996) "Discussion of Walley (1996)," *Journal of the Royal Statistical Society B* 58, 47–48.

Lindman, Harold R. (1971) "Inconsistent Preferences among Gambles," *Journal of Experimental Psychology* 89, 390–397.

Loehman, Edna (1998) "Testing Risk Aversion and Nonexpected Utility Theories," *Journal of Economic Behavior and Organization* 33, 285–302.

Loewenstein, George F. & Drazen Prelec (1991) "Negative Time Preference," *American Economic Review, Papers and Proceedings* 81, 347–352.

Loewenstein, George F. & Nachum Sicherman (1991) "Do Workers Prefer Increasing Wage Profiles?," *Journal of Labor Economics* 9, 67–84.

Loewenstein, George F., Elke U. Weber, Christopher K. Hsee, & Edward S. Welch (2001) "Risk as Feelings," *Psychological Bulletin* 127, 267–286.

Loomes, Graham (1991) "Evidence of a new Violation of the Independence Axiom," *Journal of Risk and Uncertainty* 4, 92–109.

Loomes, Graham, Peter G. Moffat, & Robert Sugden (2002) "A Microeconometric Test of Alternative Stochastic Theories of Risky Choice," *Journal of Risk and Uncertainty* 24, 103–130.

Loomes, Graham & Robert Sugden (1982) "Regret Theory: An Alternative Theory of Rational Choice under Uncertainty," *Economic Journal* 92, 805–824.

Lopes, Lola L. (1981) "Decision Making in the Short Run," *Journal of Experimental Psychology, Human Learning and Memory* 7, 377–385.

Lopes, Lola L. (1984) "Risk and Distributional Inequality," *Journal of Experimental Psychology: Human Perception and Performance* 10, 465–485.

Lopes, Lola L. (1987) "Between Hope and Fear: The Psychology of Risk," *Advances in Experimental Psychology* 20, 255–295.

Lopes, Lola L. (1995) "Algebra and Process in the Modeling of Risky Choice," *Psychology of Learning and Motivation* 32, 177–220.

Lopes, Lola L. & Gregg C. Oden (1999) "The Role of Aspiration Level in Risky Choice: A Comparison of Cumulative Prospect Theory and SP/A Theory," *Journal of Mathematical Psychology* 43, 286–313.

Louviere, Jordan J., David A. Hensher, & Joffre D. Swait (2000) *Stated Choice Methods, Analysis and Applications*. Cambridge University Press, New York.

Luce, R. Duncan (1959) *Individual Choice Behavior*. Wiley, New York.

Luce, R. Duncan (1990) "Rational versus Plausible Accounting Equivalences in Preference Judgments," *Psychological Science* 1, 225–234.

Luce, R. Duncan (1991) "Rank- and Sign- Dependent Linear Utility Models for Binary Gambles," *Journal of Economic Theory* 53, 75–100.

Luce, R. Duncan (1996) "When Four Distinct Ways to Measure Utility Are the Same," *Journal of Mathematical Psychology* 40, 297–317.

Luce, R. Duncan (2000) *"Utility of Gains and Losses: Measurement-Theoretical and Experimental Approaches."* Lawrence Erlbaum Publishers, London.

Luce, R. Duncan, Robert R. Bush, & Eugene Galanter (1965, eds.) *Handbook of Mathematical Psychology* Vol. III. Wiley, New York.

Luce, R. Duncan & Peter C. Fishburn (1991) "Rank- and Sign-Dependent Linear Utility Models for Finite First-Order Gambles," *Journal of Risk and Uncertainty* 4, 29–59.

Luce, R. Duncan & David H. Krantz (1971) "Conditional Expected Utility," *Econometrica* 39, 253–271.

Luce, R. Duncan, David H. Krantz, Patrick Suppes, & Amos Tversky (1990) *Foundations of Measurement, Vol. III. (Representation, Axiomatization, and Invariance).* Academic Press, New York.

Luce, R. Duncan & Louis Narens (1985) "Classification of Concatenation Measurement Structures According to Scale Type," *Journal of Mathematical Psychology* 29, 1–72.

Luce, R. Duncan & Howard Raiffa (1957) *Games and Decisions.* Wiley, New York.

Luce, R. Duncan & Patrick Suppes, (1965) "Preference, Utility, and Subjective Probability." In R. Duncan Luce, Robert R. Bush, & Eugene Galanter (eds.) *Handbook of Mathematical Psychology*, Vol. III, 249–410, Wiley, New York.

Maccheroni, Fabio, Massimo Marinacci, & Aldo Rustichini (2006) "Ambiguity Aversion, Robustness, and the Variational Representation of Preferences," *Econometrica* 74, 1447–1498.

MacCrimmon, Kenneth R. & Stig Larsson (1979) "Utility Theory: Axioms versus 'Paradoxes'." In Maurice Allais & Ole Hagen (eds.) *Expected Utility Hypotheses and the Allais Paradox*, 333–409, Reidel, Dordrecht.

Machina, Mark J. (1982) "'Expected Utility' Analysis without the Independence Axiom," *Econometrica* 50, 277–323.

Machina, Mark J. (1987) "Choice under Uncertainty: Problems Solved and Unsolved," *Journal of Economic Perspectives* 1 no. 1, 121–154.

Machina, Mark J. (1989) "Dynamic Consistency and Non-Expected Utility Models of Choice under Uncertainty," *Journal of Economic Literature* 27, 1622–1688.

Machina, Mark J. (2004) "Almost-Objective Uncertainty," *Economic Theory* 24, 1–54.

Machina, Mark J. (2009) "Risk, Ambiguity, and the Rank-Dependence Axioms," *American Economic Review* 99, 385–392.

Machina, Mark J. & David Schmeidler (1992) "A More Robust Definition of Subjective Probability," *Econometrica* 60, 745–780.

Mandler, Michael (2005) "Incomplete Preferences and Rational Intransitivity of Choice," *Games and Economic Behavior* 50, 255–277.

Mandler, Michael (2007) "Strategies as States," *Journal of Economic Theory* 135, 105–130.

Mangelsdorff, Lukas & Martin Weber (1994) "Testing Choquet Expected Utility," *Journal of Economic Behavior and Organization* 25, 437–457.

Manski, Charles F. (2004) "Measuring Expectations," *Econometrica* 72, 1329–1376.

Marinacci, Massimo (1996) "Decomposition and Representation of Coalitional Games," *Mathematics of Operations Research* 21, 1000–1015.

Mark, Tami L. & Joffre Swait (2004) "Using Stated Preference and Revealed Preference Modeling to Evaluate Prescribing Decisions," *Health Economics* 13, 563–573.

Markowitz, Harry M. (1952) "The Utility of Wealth," *Journal of Political Economy* 60, 151–158.

Marshall, Alfred (1890) *Principles of Economics.* 8th edn. 1920 (9th edn. 1961) Macmillan, New York.

Mas-Colell, Andreu, Michael D. Whinston, & Jerry R. Green (1995) *Microeconomic Theory.* Oxford University Press, New York.

McCord, Mark R. & Richard de Neufville (1986) "'Lottery Equivalents': Reduction of the Certainty Effect Problem in Utility Assessment," *Management Science* 32, 56–60.

McFadden, Daniel L. (1981) "Econometric Models of Probabilistic Choice." In Charles F. Manski & Daniel L. McFadden (eds.) *Structural Analysis of Discrete Data and Econometric Applications*, 198–272, The MIT Press, Cambridge, MA.

McGlothlin, William H. (1956) "Stability of Choices among Uncertain Alternatives," *American Journal of Psychology* 69, 604–615.

McNeil, Barbara J., Ralph Weichselbaum, & Stephen G. Pauker (1978) "Fallacy of the Five-Year Survival in Lung Cancer," *New England Journal of Medicine* 299, 1397–1401.

McNeil, Barbara J., Ralph Weichselbaum, & Stephen G. Pauker (1981) "Speech and Survival: Tradeoffs between Quality and Quantity of Life in Laryngeal Cancer," *New England Journal of Medicine* 305, 982–987.

Menger, Karl (1871) *Principles of Economics.* Translated into English by James Dingwall & Bert F. Hoselitz, Free Press of Glencoe, New York, 1950.

Meyer, Donald J. & Jack Meyer (2005) "Relative Risk Aversion: What Do We Know?," *Journal of Risk and Uncertainty* 31, 243–262.

Miranda, Enrique (2008) "A Survey of the Theory of Coherent Lower Previsions," *International Journal of Approximate Reasoning* 48, 628–658.

Miyamoto, John M. (1983) "An Axiomatization of the Ratio/Difference Representation," *Journal of Mathematical Psychology* 27, 439–455.

Miyamoto, John M. (1988) "Generic Utility Theory: Measurement Foundations and Applications in Multiattribute Utility Theory," *Journal of Mathematical Psychology* 32, 357–404.

Miyamoto, John M., Peter P. Wakker, Han Bleichrodt, & Hans J. M. Peters (1998) "The Zero-Condition: A Simplifying Assumption in QALY Measurement and Multiattribute Utility," *Management Science* 44, 839–849.

Mongin, Philippe (1998) "The Paradox of the Bayesian Experts and State-Dependent Utility Theory," *Journal of Mathematical Economics* 29, 331–361.

Mosteller, Frederick & Philip Nogee (1951) "An Experimental Measurement of Utility," *Journal of Political Economy* 59, 371–404.

Moyes, Patrick (2007) "An Extended Gini Approach to Inequality Measurement," *Journal of Economic Inequality* 5, 279–303.

Münnich, & Àkos, Gyula Maksa, & Robert J. Mokken (2000) "n-Variable Bisection," *Journal of Mathematical Psychology* 44, 569–581.

Murphy, Terence D. (1981) "Medical Knowledge and Statistical Methods in Early Nineteenth Century France," *Medical History* 25, 301–319.

Myagkov, Mikhail G. & Charles R. Plott (1997) "Exchange Economies and Loss Exposure: Experiments Exploring Prospect Theory and Competitive Equilibria in Market Environments," *American Economic Review* 87, 801–828.

Nakamura, Yutaka (1990) "Subjective Expected Utility with Non-Additive Probabilities on Finite State Spaces," *Journal of Economic Theory* 51, 346–366.

Nakamura, Yutaka (1992) "Multi-Symmetric Structures and Non-Expected Utility," *Journal of Mathematical Psychology* 36, 375–395.

Narens, Louis (2002) *Theories of Meaningfulness.* Lawrence Erlbaum, Mahwah, NJ.

Nash, John F. (1950) "Rational Nonlinear Utility." In Shubik, Martin (1982) *Game Theory in the Social Sciences*, Appendix A2, The MIT Press, Cambridge, MA.

Nau, Robert F. (1995) "Coherent Decision Analysis with Inseparable Probabilities and Utilities," *Journal of Risk and Uncertainty* 10, 71–91.

Nau, Robert F. (2001) "De Finetti Was Right: Probability Does not Exist," *Theory and Decision* 51, 89–124.

Nau, Robert F. (2003) "A Generalization of Pratt-Arrow Measure to Non-Expected-Utility Preferences and Inseparable Probability and Utility," *Management Science* 49, 1089–1104.

Nehring, Klaus D. O. (1994) "On the Interpretation of Sarin and Wakker's "A Simple Axiomatization of Nonadditive Expected Utility," *Econometrica* 62, 935–938.

Neilson, William S. (2001) "Calibration Results for Rank-Dependent Expected Utility," *Economics Bulletin* 4, 1–5.

Neilson, William S. & C. Jill Stowe (2001) "A Further Examination of Cumulative Prospect Theory Parameterizations," *Journal of Risk and Uncertainty* 24, 31–46.

Netzer, Nick (2009) "Evolution of Time Preferences and Attitudes toward Risk," *American Economic Review* 99, 937–955.

Nichol, Michael B. & Joshua D. Epstein (2008) "Separating Gains and Losses in Health when Calculating the Minimum Important Difference for Mapped Utility," *Quality of Life Research* 17, 955–961.

Nowlis, Vincent & Helen. H. Nowlis (1956) "The Description and Analysis of Mood," *Annals of the New York Academy of Science* 65, 345–355.

Offerman, Theo, Joep Sonnemans, Gijs van de Kuilen, & Peter P. Wakker (2009) "A Truth-Serum for Non-Bayesians: Correcting Proper Scoring Rules for Risk Attitudes," *Review of Economic Studies* 76, 1461–1489.

Officer, Robert R. & Alfred N. Halter (1968) "Utility Analysis in a Practical Setting," *American Journal of Agricultural Economics* 50, 257–277.

Ogaki, Masao & Qiang Zhang (2001) "Decreasing Relative Risk Aversion and Tests of Risk Sharing," *Econometrica* 69, 515–526.

Olsson, Erik (2005) *Against Coherence. Truth, Probability and Justification.* Oxford University Press, Oxford.

Onay, Selçuk & Aysc Öncüler (2007) "Intertemporal Choice under Timing Risk: An Experimental Approach," *Journal of Risk and Uncertainty* 34, 99–121.

Ostaszewski, Pawel, Leonard Green & Joel Myerson (1998) "Effects of Inflation on the Subjective Value of Delayed and Probabilistic Rewards," *Psychonomic Bulletin & Review* 5, 324–333.

Palacios-Huerta, Ignacio & Roberto Serrano (2006) "Rejecting Small Gambles under Expected Utility," *Economic Letters* 91, 250–259.

Pälsson, Anne-Marie (1996) "Does the Degree of Relative Risk Aversion Vary with Household Characteristics?," *Journal of Economic Psychology* 17, 771–787.

Parducci, Allen (1965) "Category Judgment: A Range-Frequency Model," *Psychological Review* 72, 407–418.

Parducci, Allen (1995) *Happiness, Pleasure, and Judgment: The Contextual Theory and its Applications.* Lawrence Erlbaum Associates, Hillsdale, NJ.

Pareto, Vilfredo (1906) *Manuele di Economia Politica.* Piccolo Biblioteca Scientifica, Milan. Translated into English by Ann S. Schwier (1971) *Manual of Political Economy,* Macmillan, London.

Payne, John W. (2005) "It is Whether You Win or Lose: The Importance of the Overall Probabilities of Winning or Losing in Risky Choice," *Journal of Risk and Uncertainty* 30, 5–19.

Payne, John W., Dan J. Laughhunn, & Roy L. Crum (1984) "An Experimental Study of Multiattribute Risky Choice," *Management Science* 30, 1350–1361.

Peeters, Guido & Janusz Czapinski (1990) "Positive-Negative Asymmetry in Evaluations: The Distinction between Affective and Informational Negative Effects." In Wolfgang Stroebe & Miles Hewstone (eds.), *European Review of Social Psychology* 1, 33–60.

Peters, Hans J.M. & Peter P. Wakker (1987) "Convex Functions on Non-Convex Domains," *Economics Letters* 22, 251–255.

Petit-Renaud, Simon & Thierry Denoeux (2004) "Nonparametric Regression Analysis of Uncertain and Imprecise Data Using Belief Functions," *International Journal of Approximate Reasoning* 35, 1–28.

Pfanzagl, Johann (1959) "A General Theory of Measurement – Applications to Utility," *Naval Research Logistics Quarterly* 6, 283–294.

Pfanzagl, Johann (1968) *Theory of Measurement.* Physica-Verlag, Vienna.

Philippe, Fabrice, Gabriel Debs, & Jean-Yves Jaffray (1999) "Decision Making with Monotone Lower Probabilities of Infinite Order," *Mathematics of Operations Research* 24, 767–784.

Piaget, Jean & Bärbel Inhelder (1951) *La Genèse de l'Idée de Hasard chez l'Enfant*. Presses Universitaires de France, Paris. Translated into English by Lowell Leake, Jr., Paul Burrell, & Harold D. Fishbein:

Piaget, Jean & Bärbel Inhelder (1975) *The Origin of the Idea of Chance in Children*. Norton, New York.

Pietras, Cynthia J., Gabriel D. Searcy, Brad E. Huitema, & Andrew E. Brandt (2008) "Effects of Monetary Reserves and Rate of Gain on Human Risky Choice under Budget Constraints," *Behavioural Processes* 78, 358–373.

Pliskin, Joseph S., Donald S. Shepard, & Milton C. Weinstein (1980) "Utility Functions for Life Years and Health Status," *Operations Research* 28, 206–224.

Plott, Charles R. & Kathryn Zeiler (2005) "The Willingness to Pay-Willingness to Accept Gap, the 'Endowment Effect,' Subject Misconceptions, and Experimental Procedures for Eliciting Valuations," *American Economic Review* 95, 530–545.

Post, Thierry, Martijn van den Assem, Guido Baltussen, & Richard Thaler (2008) "Deal or No Deal? Decision Making under Risk in a Large-Payoff Game Show," *American Economic Review* 98, 38–71.

Pratt, John W., Howard Raiffa, & Robert O. Schlaifer (1965) *Introduction to Statistical Decision Theory*. McGraw-Hill, New York.

Prelec, Drazen (1998) "The Probability Weighting Function," *Econometrica* 66, 497–527.

Prelec, Drazen (2004) "A Bayesian Truth Serum for Subjective Data," *Science* 306, October 2004, 462–466.

Preston, Malcolm G. & Philip Baratta (1948) "An Experimental Study of the Auction Value of an Uncertain Outcome," *American Journal of Psychology* 61, 183–193.

Pulford, Briony D. (2009) "Is Luck on My Side? Optimism, Pessimism, and Ambiguity Aversion," *Quarterly Journal of Experimental Psychology* 62, 1079–1087.

Quiggin, John (1981) "Risk Perception and Risk Aversion among Australian Farmers," *Australian Journal of Agricultural Economics* 25, 160–169.

Quiggin, John (1982) "A Theory of Anticipated Utility," *Journal of Economic Behaviour and Organization* 3, 323–343.

Quiggin, John (1993) *Generalized Expected Utility Theory – The Rank-Dependent Model*. Kluwer Academic Publishers, Dordrecht.

Quiggin, John (2003) "Background Risk in Generalized Expected Utility Theory," *Economic Theory* 22, 607–611.

Rabin, Matthew (2000) "Risk Aversion and Expected-utility Theory: A Calibration Theorem," *Econometrica* 68, 1281–1292.

Raiffa, Howard (1961) "Risk, Uncertainty and the Savage Axioms: Comment," *Quarterly Journal of Economics* 75, 690–694.

Raiffa, Howard (1968) *Decision Analysis*. Addison-Wesley, London.

Ramsey, Frank P. (1931) "Truth and Probability." In *The Foundations of Mathematics and other Logical Essays*, 156–198, Routledge and Kegan Paul, London. Reprinted in Henry E. Kyburg Jr. & Howard E. Smokler (1964, eds.), *Studies in Subjective Probability*, 61–92, Wiley, New York. (2nd edn. 1980, Krieger, New York.)

Rapoport, Anatol (1984) "Effects of Wealth on Portfolios under Various Investment Conditions," *Acta Psychologica* 55, 31–51.

Read, Daniel, George Loewenstein, & Matthew Rabin (1999) "Choice Bracketing," *Journal of Risk and Uncertainty* 19, 171–197.

Reyna, Valerie F. & Charles J. Brainerd (1995) "Fuzzy-Trace Theory: An Interim Synthesis," *Learning and Individual Differences* 7, 1–75.

Richard, S. F. (1975) "Multivariate Risk Aversion, Utility Independence, and Separable Utility Functions," *Management Science* 22, 12–21.

Rieger, Marc Oliver & Mei Wang (2008) "Prospect Theory for Continuous Distributions," *Journal of Risk and Uncertainty* 36, 83–102.

Robbins, Lionel (1932) *An Essay on the Nature and Significance of Economic Science*. Macmillan, London.

Robertson, Dennis H. (1915) *A Study of Industrial Fluctuation; An Enquiry into the Character and Causes of the So-Called Cyclical Movement of Trade*. P. S. King & Son Ltd., London.

Robinson, Angela, Graham Loomes, & Michael Jones-Lee (2001) "Visual Analog Scales, Standard Gambles, and Relative Risk Aversion," *Medical Decision Making* 21, 17–21.

Robson, Arthur J. (2001) "Why Would Nature Give Individuals Utility Functions?," *Journal of Political Economy* 109, 900–914.

Roca, Mercè, Robin M. Hogarth, & A. John Maule (2006) "Ambiguity Seeking as a Result of the Status Quo Bias," *Journal of Risk and Uncertainty* 32, 175–194.

Rode, Catrin, Leda Cosmides, Wolfgang Hell, John Tooby (1999) "When and why Do People Avoid Unknown Probabilities in Decisions under Uncertainty? Testing some Predictions from Optimal Foraging Theory," *Cognition* 72, 269–304.

Rohde, Kirsten I. M. (2010) "A Preference Foundation for Fehr and Schmidt's Model of Inequity Aversion," *Social Choice and Welfare* 34, 537–547.

Rosenblatt-Wisch, Rina (2008) "Loss Aversion in Aggregate Macroeconomic Time Series," *European Economic Review* 52, 1140–1159.

Rosett, Richard N. (1965) "Gambling and Rationality," *Journal of Political Economy* 73, 595–607.

Rosett, Richard N. (1971) "Weak Experimental Verification of the Expected Utility Hypothesis," *Review of Economic Studies* 38, 481–492.

Rostek, Marzena J. (2010) "Quantile Maximization in Decision Theory," *Review of Economic Studies* 77, 339–371.

Rota, G. C. (1964) "On the Foundations of Combinatorial Theory I. Theory of Möbius Functions," *Zeitschrift für Warscheinlichkeitstheorie und Verwandte Gebiete* 2, 340–368.

Roth, Alvin E. & Michael W. Malouf (1979) "Game-Theoretic Models and the Role of Information in Bargaining," *Psychological Review* 86, 574–594.

Roy, Andrew D. (1952) "Safety First and the Holding of Assets," *Econometrica* 20, 431–449.

Rubin, Herman (1987) "A Weak System of Axioms for "Rational" Behavior and the Nonseparability of Utility from Prior," *Statistics and Decision* 5, 47–58.

Rubinstein, Ariel (2006) "Dilemmas of an Economic Theorist," *Econometrica* 74, 865–883.

Russell, James A. & James M. Carroll (1999) "On the Bipolarity of Positive and Negative Affect," *Psychological Bulletin* 125, 3–30.

Ryan, Matthew J. (2006) "Risk Aversion in RDEU," *Journal of Mathematical Economics* 42, 675–697.

Ryan, Matthew J. (2009) "Generalizations of SEU: A Geometric Tour of Some Non-Standard Models," *Oxford Economic Papers* 61, 327–354.

Saaty, Thomas L. (1980) *The Analytic Hierarchy Process*. McGraw-Hill, New York.

Safra, Zvi & Uzi Segal (2008) "Calibration Results for Non-Expected Utility Theories," *Econometrica* 76, 1143–1166.

Samuelson, Larry (2005) "Economic Theory and Experimental Economics," *Journal of Economic Literature* 63, 65–107.

Samuelson, Paul A. (1938) "A Note on the Pure Theory of Consumer's Behaviour," *Economica*, N.S. 5, 61–71, 353–354.

Sarin, Rakesh K. & Peter P. Wakker (1992) "A Simple Axiomatization of Nonadditive Expected Utility," *Econometrica* 60, 1255–1272.

Sarin, Rakesh K. & Peter P. Wakker (1994a) "Gains and Losses in Nonadditive Expected Utility." In Mark J. Machina & Bertrand R. Munier (eds.) *Models and Experiments on Risk and Rationality*, 157–172, Kluwer Academic Publishers, Dordrecht.

Sarin, Rakesh K. & Peter P. Wakker (1994b) "A General Result for Quantifying Beliefs," *Econometrica* 62, 683–685.

Sarin, Rakesh K. & Peter P. Wakker (1997) "A Single-Stage Approach to Anscombe and Aumann's Expected Utility," *Review of Economic Studies* 64, 399–409.

Sarin, Rakesh K. & Peter P. Wakker (1998) "Revealed Likelihood and Knightian Uncertainty," *Journal of Risk and Uncertainty* 16, 223–250.

Sarin, Rakesh K. & Peter P. Wakker (2000) "Cumulative Dominance and Probabilistic Sophistication," *Mathematical Social Sciences* 40, 191–196.

Sarin, Rakesh K. & Martin Weber (1993) "Effects of Ambiguity in Market Experiments," *Management Science* 39, 602–615.

Savage, Leonard J. (1953) "Une Axiomatisation du Comportement Raisonnable Face à l'Incertitude." *Colloques Internationaux du Centre National de la Recherche Scientifique (Econométrie)* 40, 29–40.

Savage, Leonard J. (1954) *The Foundations of Statistics.* Wiley, New York. (2nd edn. 1972, Dover Publications, New York.)

Savage, Leonard J. (1971) "Elicitation of Personal Probabilities and Expectations," *Journal of the American Statistical Association* 66, 783–801.

Schervish, Mark J., Teddy Seidenfeld, & Joseph B. Kadane (1990) "State-Dependent Utilities," *Journal of the American Statistical Association* 85, 840–847.

Schimmack, Ulrich (2001) "Pleasure, Displeasure, and Mixed Feelings: Are Semantic Opposites Mutually Exclusive?," *Cognition and Emotion* 15, 81–97.

Schmeidler, David (1971) "A Condition for the Completeness of Partial Preference Relations," *Econometrica* 39, 403–404.

Schmeidler, David (1986) "Integral Representation without Additivity," *Proceedings of the American Mathematical Society* 97, 255–261.

Schmeidler, David (1989) "Subjective Probability and Expected Utility without Additivity," *Econometrica* 57, 571–587.

Schmidt, Ulrich (2003) "Reference Dependence in Cumulative Prospect Theory," *Journal of Mathematical Psychology* 47, 122–131.

Schmidt, Ulrich (2004) "Alternatives to Expected Utility: Some Formal Theories." In Salvador Barberà, Peter J. Hammond, & Christian Seidl, *Handbook of Utility Theory II*, Ch. 15, 757–838, Kluwer Academic Publishers, Dordrecht.

Schmidt, Ulrich & Stefan Traub (2002) "An Experimental Test of Loss Aversion," *Journal of Risk and Uncertainty* 25, 233–249.

Schmidt, Ulrich & Horst Zank (2007) "Linear Cumulative Prospect Theory with Applications to Portfolio Selection and Insurance Demand," *Decisions in Economics and Finance* 30, 1–18.

Schmidt, Ulrich & Horst Zank (2008) "Risk Aversion in Cumulative Prospect Theory," *Management Science* 54, 208–216.

Schmidt, Ulrich & Horst Zank (2009) "A Simple Model of Cumulative Prospect Theory," *Journal of Mathematical Economics* 45, 308–319.

Schmidt, Ulrich & Alexander Zimper (2007) "Security and Potential Level Preferences with Thresholds," *Journal of Mathematical Psychology* 51, 279–289.

Segal, Uzi (1990) "Two-Stage Lotteries without the Reduction Axiom," *Econometrica* 58, 349–377.

Segal, Uzi & Avia Spivak (1990) "First-Order versus Second-Order Risk-Aversion," *Journal of Economic Theory* 51, 111–125.

Seidl, Christian & Stefan Traub (1999) "Biases in the Assessment of von Neumann-Morgenstern Utility Functions," *Journal of Economics* Suppl. 8, 203–239.

Selten, Reinhard, Abdolkarim Sadrieh, & Klaus Abbink (1999) "Money Does not Induce Risk Neutral Behavior, but Binary Lotteries Do even Worse," *Theory and Decision* 46, 211–249.

Sen, Amartya K. (1993) "The Internal Consistency of Choice," *Econometrica* 61, 495–521.

Seo, Kyoungwon (2009) "Ambiguity and Second-Order Beliefs," *Econometrica* 77, 1575–1605.

Shafer, Glenn (1976) *A Mathematical Theory of Evidence*. Princeton University Press, Princeton, NJ.

Shapiro, Leonard (1979) "Necessary and Sufficient Conditions for Expected Utility Maximizations: The Finite Case, with a Partial Order," *Annals of Statistics* 7, 1288–1302.

Shackle, George L. S. (1949a) "A Non-Additive Measure of Uncertainty," *Review of Economic Studies* 17, 70–74.

Shackle, George L. S. (1949b) *Expectation in Economics*. Cambridge University Press, Cambridge.

Sherrick, Bruce J., Steven T. Sonka, Peter J. Lamb, & Michael A. Mazzocco (2000) "Decision-Maker Expectations and the Value of Climate Prediction Information: Conceptual Considerations and Preliminary Evidence," *Meteorological Applications* 7, 377–386.

Showers, Carolin (1992) "The Motivational and Emotional Consequences of Considering Positive and Negative Possibilities for an Upcoming Event," *Journal of Personality and Social Psychology* 63, 474–484.

Siniscalchi, Marciano (2009) "Vector Expected Utility and Attitudes toward Variation," *Econometrica* 77, 801–855.

Šipoš, Ján (1979) "Integral with Respect to a Pre-Measure," *Mathematica Slovaca* 29, 141–155.

Skiadas, Costis (1997) "Conditioning and Aggregation of Preferences," *Econometrica* 65, 347–367.

Skiadas, Costis (1998) "Recursive Utility and Preferences for Information," *Economic Theory* 12, 293–312.

Skinner, Burrhus F. (1971) *Beyond Freedom and Dignity*. Knopf, New York.

Škulj, Damjan (2006) "Jeffrey's Conditioning Rule in Neighbourhood Models," *International Journal of Approximate Reasoning* 42, 192–211.

Slovic, Paul (1995) "The Construction of Preference," *American Psychologist* 50, 364–371.

Smith, Cedric A. B. (1961) "Consistency in Statistical Inference and Decision," *Journal of the Royal Statistical Society B* 23, 1–25.

Smith, James E. & Detlof von Winterfeldt (2004) "Decision Analysis in Management Science," *Management Science* 50, 561–574.

Smith, Vernon L. (1982) "Microeconomic Systems as an Experimental Science," *American Economic Review* 72, 923–955.

Sox, Harold C., Marshall A. Blatt, Michael C. Higgins, & Keith I. Marton (1986) *Medical Decision Making*. Butterworths, Boston.

Sprowls, R. Clay (1953) "Psychological-Mathematical Probability in Relationships of Lottery Gambles," *American Journal of Psychology* 66, 126–130.

Stalmeier, Peep F. M. & Thom G. G. Bezembinder (1999) "The Discrepancy between Risky and Riskless Utilities: A Matter of Framing?," *Medical Decision Making*, 19, 435–447.

Stanley, Richard P. (1986) *Enumerative Combinatorics*. Vol. I. Wadsworth & Brooks/Cole, Monterey, CA.

Starmer, Chris (1999) "Cycling with Rules of Thumb: An Experimental Test for a New Form of Non-Transitive Behavior," *Theory and Decision* 46, 141–158.

Starmer, Chris (2000) "Developments in Non-Expected Utility Theory: The Hunt for a Descriptive Theory of Choice under Risk," *Journal of Economic Literature* 38, 332–382.

Starmer, Chris & Robert Sugden (1989) "Violations of the Independence Axiom in Common Ratio Problems: An Experimental Test of Some Competing Hypotheses," *Annals of Operations Research* 19, 79–102.

Starmer, Chris & Robert Sugden (1991) "Does the Random-Lottery Incentive System Elicit True Preferences? An Experimental Investigation," *American Economic Review* 81, 971–978.

Starmer, Chris & Robert Sugden (1993) "Testing for Juxtaposition and Event-Splitting Effects," *Journal of Risk and Uncertainty* 6, 235–254.

Stevens, Stanley S. & Hallowell Davis (1938) *Hearing: Its Psychology and Physiology*. Wiley, New York.

Stewart, Neil, Nick Chater, Henry P. Stott, & Stian Reimers (2003) "Prospect Relativity: How Choice Options Influence Decision under Risk," *Journal of Experimental Psychology: General* 132, 23–46.

Stigler, George J. (1950) "The Development of Utility Theory: I; II," *Journal of Political Economy* 58, 307–327; 373–396.

Stigler, George J. (1971) "Introduction." In Frank H. Knight, *Risk, Uncertainty, and Profit*, Chicago University Press, Chicago.

Stott, Henry P. (2006) "Cumulative Prospect Theory's Functional Menagerie," *Journal of Risk and Uncertainty* 32, 101–130.

Sugden, Robert (2003) "Reference-Dependent Subjective Expected Utility," *Journal of Economic Theory* 111, 172–191.

Sugden, Robert (2004) "Alternatives to Expected Utility." In Salvador Barberà, Peter J. Hammond, & Christian Seidl (eds.) *Handbook of Utility Theory, Vol. II*, 685–755, Kluwer Academic Publishers, Dordrecht.

Suppes, Patrick (1974) "The Measurement of Belief," *Journal of the Royal Statistical Society* 36, 160–191.

Suppes, Patrick & Muriel Winet (1955) "An Axiomatization of Utility Based on the Notion of Utility Differences," *Management Science* 1, 259–270.

Suppes, Patrick & Mario Zanotti (1989) "Conditions on Upper and Lower Probabilities to Imply Probabilities," *Erkenntnis* 31, 323–345.

Swait, Joffre (2001) "A Non-Compensatory Choice Model Incorporating Attribute Cutoffs," *Transportation Research Part B* 35, 903–928.

Szpilrajn, Edward (1930) "Sur l'Extension de l'Ordre Partiel, *Fundamenta Mathematicae* 16, 386–389.

Szpiro, George G. (1986) "Measuring Risk Aversion: An Alternative Approach," *Review of Economics and Statistics* 68, 156–159.

Tanaka, Tomomi, Colin F. Camerer, & Quang Nguyen (2010) "Risk and Time Preferences: Linking Experimental and Household Survey Data from Vietnam," *American Economic Review* 100, 557–571.

Teitelbaum, Joshua C. (2007) "A Unilateral Accident Model under Ambiguity," *Journal of Legal Studies* 36, 431–477.

Thaler, Richard H. (1985) "Mental Accounting and Consumer Choice," *Marketing Science* 4, 199–214.

Thaler, Richard H. & William T. Ziemba (1988) "Parimutual Betting Markets: Racetracks and Lotteries," *Journal of Economic Perspectives* 2 no. 2, 161–174.

Thurstone, Louis L. (1927) "A Law of Comparative Judgment," *Psychological Review* 34, 273–286.

Tinbergen, Jan (1991) "On the Measurement of Welfare," *Journal of Econometrics* 50, 7–13.

Tom, Sabrina M., Craig R. Fox, Christopher Trepel, & Russell A. Poldrack (2007) "The Neural Basis of Loss Aversion in Decision Making under Risk," *Science* 315, 515–518.

Torrance, George W., William J. Furlong, David H. Feeny, & Michael H. Boyle (1995) "Multi-Attribute Preference Functions. Health Utilities Index," *PharmacoEconomics* 7, 490–502.

Tsanakas, H (2008) "Risk Measurement in the Presence of Background Risk," *Insurance: Mathematics and Economics* 42, 520–528.

Tsukahara, Hideatsu (2009) "One-Parameter Families of Distortion Risk Measures," *Mathematical Finance* 19, 691–705.

Tversky, Amos (1969) "Intransitivity of Preferences," *Psychological Review* 76, 31–48.

Tversky, Amos & Craig R. Fox (1995) "Weighing Risk and Uncertainty," *Psychological Review* 102, 269–283.

Tversky, Amos & Daniel Kahneman (1974) "Judgment under Uncertainty: Heuristics and Biases," *Science* 185, 1124–1131.

Tversky, Amos & Daniel Kahneman (1981) "The Framing of Decisions and the Psychology of Choice," *Science* 211, 453–458.

Tversky, Amos & Daniel Kahneman (1986) "Rational Choice and the Framing of Decisions," *Journal of Business* 59, S251–S278.

Tversky, Amos & Daniel Kahneman (1992) "Advances in Prospect Theory: Cumulative Representation of Uncertainty," *Journal of Risk and Uncertainty* 5, 297–323.

Tversky, Amos & Derek J. Koehler (1994) "Support Theory: A Nonextensional Representation of Subjective Probability," *Psychological Review* 101, 547–567.

Tversky, Amos & Peter P. Wakker (1995) "Risk Attitudes and Decision Weights," *Econometrica* 63, 1255–1280.

Ulam, Stanislaw (1930) "Zur Masstheorie in der Allgemeinen Mengenlehre," *Fundamentà Mathematicae* 16, 140–150.

van de Kuilen, Gijs (2009) "Subjective Probability Weighting and the Discovered Preference Hypothesis," *Theory and Decision* 67, 1–22.

van de Kuilen, Gijs & Peter P. Wakker (2009) *"The Midweight Method to Measure Attitudes towards Risk and Ambiguity,"* Econometric Institute, Erasmus University, Rotterdam, the Netherlands.

van den Steen, Eric (2004) "Rational Overoptimism (and Other Biases)" *American Economic Review* 94, 1141–1151.

van Osch, Sylvie M. C. & Anne M. Stiggelbout (2008) "The Construction of Standard Gamble Utilities," *Health Economics* 17, 31–40.

van Praag, Bernard M. S. (1968) *Individual Welfare Functions and Consumer Behavior.* North-Holland, Amsterdam, 1968.

van Praag, Bernard M. S. & Ada Ferrer-i-Carbonell (2004) *Happiness Quantified.* Oxford University Press, Oxford.

Vendrik, Maarten & Geert Woltjer (2007) "Happiness and Loss Aversion: Is Utility Concave or Convex in Relative Income?," *Journal of Public Economics* 91, 1423–1448.

Viscusi, W. Kip (1989) "Prospective Reference Theory: Toward an Explanantion of the Paradoxes," *Journal of Risk and Uncertainty* 2, 235–264.

Viscusi, W. Kip & Harrell Chesson (1999) "Hopes and Fears: The Conflicting Effects of Risk Ambiguity," *Theory and Decision* 47, 153–178.

Viscusi, W. Kip & William N. Evans (2006) "Behavioral Probabilities," *Journal of Risk and Uncertainty* 32, 5–15.

von Mises, Richard (1957) *Probability, Statistics, and Truth.* Allen & Unwin, London.

von Neumann, John & Oskar Morgenstern (1944, 1947, 1953) *Theory of Games and Economic Behavior.* Princeton University Press, Princeton NJ.

von Winterfeldt, Detlof (2007) "Choosing a Tritium Supply for Nuclear Weapons: A Decision Analysis Caught in Controversy." In Ward Edwards, Ralph F. Miles, & Detlof von Winterfeldt (eds.), *Advances in Decision Analysis: From Foundations to Applications*, 514–538, Cambridge University Press, Cambridge.

von Winterfeldt, Detlof & Ward Edwards (1986) *Decision Analysis and Behavioral Research.* Cambridge University Press, Cambridge.

Wakai, Katsutoshi (2008) "A Model of Utility Smoothing," *Econometrica* 76, 137–153.

Wakker, Peter P. (1984) "Cardinal Coordinate Independence for Expected Utility," *Journal of Mathematical Psychology* 28, 110–117.

Wakker, Peter P. (1988) "The Algebraic versus the Topological Approach to Additive Representations," *Journal of Mathematical Psychology* 32, 421–435.

Wakker, Peter P. (1989a) *Additive Representations of Preferences, A New Foundation of Decision Analysis.* Kluwer Academic Publishers, Dordrecht.

Wakker, Peter P. (1989b) "Continuous Subjective Expected Utility with Nonadditive Probabilities," *Journal of Mathematical Economics* 18, 1–27.

Wakker, Peter P. (1990a) "Under Stochastic Dominance Choquet-Expected Utility and Anticipated Utility are Identical," *Theory and Decision* 29, 119–132.

Wakker, Peter P. (1990b) "A Behavioral Foundation for Fuzzy Measures," *Fuzzy Sets and Systems* 37, 327–350.

Wakker, Peter P. (1993a) "Unbounded Utility for Savage's "Foundations of Statistics," and other Models," *Mathematics of Operations Research* 18, 446–485.

Wakker, Peter P. (1993b) "Savage's Axioms Usually Imply Violation of Strict Stochastic Dominance," *Review of Economic Studies* 60, 487–493.

Wakker, Peter P. (1994) "Separating Marginal Utility and Probabilistic Risk Aversion," *Theory and Decision* 36, 1–44.

Wakker, Peter P. (1999) "Justifying Bayesianism by Dynamic Decision Principles," Medical Decision Making Unit, Leiden University Medical Center, the Netherlands.

Wakker, Peter P. (2000) "Dempster Belief Functions Are Based on the Principle of Complete Ignorance," *International Journal of Uncertainty, Fuzziness and Knowledge-Based Systems* 8, 271–284.

Wakker, Peter P. (2001) "Testing and Characterizing Properties of Nonadditive Measures through Violations of the Sure-Thing Principle," *Econometrica* 69, 1039–1059.

Wakker, Peter P. (2003) "The Data of Levy and Levy (2002) 'Prospect Theory: Much Ado about Nothing?' Actually Support Prospect Theory," *Management Science* 49, 979–981.

Wakker, Peter P. (2004) "On the Composition of Risk Preference and Belief," *Psychological Review* 111, 236–241.

Wakker, Peter P. (2008a) "Explaining the Characteristics of the Power (CRRA) Utility Family," *Health Economics* 17, 1329–1344.

Wakker, Peter P. (2008b) "Uncertainty." In Lawrence Blume & Steven N. Durlauf (eds.), *The New Palgrave: A Dictionary of Economics*, 6780–6791, The Macmillan Press, London.

Wakker, Peter P. & Daniel Deneffe (1996) "Eliciting von Neumann-Morgenstern Utilities when Probabilities Are Distorted or Unknown," *Management Science* 42, 1131–1150.

Wakker, Peter P., Sylvia J. T. Jansen, & Anne M. Stiggelbout (2004) "Anchor Levels as a New Tool for the Theory and Measurement of Multiattribute Utility," *Decision Analysis* 1, 217–234.

Wakker, Peter P. & Amos Tversky (1993) "An Axiomatization of Cumulative Prospect Theory," *Journal of Risk and Uncertainty* 7, 147–176.

Wald, Abraham (1950) *Statistical Decision Functions.* Wiley, New York.

Walley, Peter (1991) *Statistical Reasoning with Imprecise Probabilities.* Chapman and Hall, London.

Walras, M. E. Léon (1874) *Elements of Pure Economics.* Translated by W. Jaffe, Irwin, Homewood IL, 1954.

Walras, M. E. Léon (1896, 3rd edn.) *Eléments d'Économie Politique Pure.* F. Rouge, Lausanne.

Wang, Mei & Paul S. Fischbeck (2004) "Incorporating Framing into Prospect Theory Modeling: A Mixture-Model Approach," *Journal of Risk and Uncertainty* 29, 181–197.

Watson, John B. (1913) "Psychology as the Behaviorist Views It," *Psychological Review* 20, 158–177.

Watt, Richard (2002) "Defending Expected Utility Theory," *Journal of Economic Perspectives* 16, 227–228.

Weber, Elke U. (1994) "From Subjective Probabilities to Decision Weights: The Effects of Asymmetric Loss Functions on the Evaluation of Uncertain Outcomes and Events," *Psychological Bulletin* 115, 228–242.

Weinstein, Milton C., Harvey V. Fineberg, Arthur S. Elstein, Howard S. Frazier, Duncan Neuhauser, R. R. Neutra, & Barbara J. McNeil (1980). *Clinical Decision Analysis.* Saunders, Philadelphia.

Weller, Joshua A., Irwin P. Levin, Baba Shiv, & Antoine Bechara (2007) "Neural Correlates of Adaptive Decision-Making in Risky Gains and Losses," *Psychological Science* 18, 958–964.

Wenglert, Leif & Anne-Sofie Rosen (2000) "Measuring Optimism-Pessimism from Beliefs about Future Events," *Personality & Individual Differences* 28, 717–728.

Weymark, John A. (1981) "Generalized Gini Inequality Indices," *Mathematical Social Sciences* 1, 409–430.

Williams, C. Arthur Jr. & J. I. Nassar (1966) "Financial Measurement of Capital Investments," *Management Science* 12, 851–864.

Wilson, Timothy D. & Jonathan W. Schooler (1991) "Thinking too Much: Introspection Can Reduce the Quality of Preferences and Decisions," *Journal of Personality and Social Psychology* 60, 181–192.

Winkler, Robert L. (1971) "Probabilistic Prediction: Some Experimental Results," *Journal of the American Statistical Association* 86, 675–685.

Winkler, Robert L. (1972) *An Introduction to Bayesian Inference and Decision Theory.* Holt, Rinehart and Winston, New York.

Winkler, Robert L. (1991) "Ambiguity, Probability, and Decision Analysis," *Journal of Risk and Uncertainty* 4, 285–297.

Winter, Laraine & Barbara Parker (2007) "Current Health and Preferences for Life-Prolonging Treatments: An Application of Prospect Theory to End-of-Life Decision Making," *Social Science & Medicine* 65, 1696–1707.

Wu, George (1994) "An Empirical Test of Ordinal Independence," *Journal of Risk and Uncertainty* 9, 39–60.

Wu, George (1999) "Anxiety and Decision Making with Delayed Resolution of Uncertainty," *Theory and Decision* 46, 159–198.

Wu, George & Richard Gonzalez (1996) "Curvature of the Probability Weighting Function," *Management Science* 42, 1676–1690.

Wu, George & Richard Gonzalez (1998) "Common Consequence Conditions in Decision Making under Risk," *Journal of Risk and Uncertainty* 16, 115–139.

Wu, George & Richard Gonzalez (1999) "Nonlinear Decision Weights in Choice under Uncertainty," *Management Science* 45, 74–85.

Wu, George, Jiao Zhang, & Mohammed Abdellaoui (2005) "Testing Prospect Theories Using Tradeoff Consistency," *Journal of Risk and Uncertainty* 30, 107–131.

Yaari, Menahem E. (1965) "Convexity in the Theory of Choice under Risk," *Quarterly Journal of Economics* 79, 278–290.

Yaari, Menahem E. (1969) "Some Remarks on Measures of Risk Aversion and on Their Uses," *Journal of Economic Theory* 1, 315–329.

Yaari, Menahem E. (1987) "The Dual Theory of Choice under Risk," *Econometrica* 55, 95–115.

Yager, Ronald R. (1988) "On Ordered Weighted Averaging Aggregation Operators in Multicriteria Decisionmaking," *IEEE Transactions on Systems, Man, and Cybernetics* 18, 183–190.

Yager, Ronald R. & Liping Liu (2008) *Classic Works of the Dempster-Shafer Theory of Belief Functions.* Springer, Berlin.

Yang, I-Tung (2008) "Utility-Based Decision Support System for Schedule Optimization," *Decision Support Systems* 44, 580–594.

Yates, J. Frank (1990) *Judgment and Decision Making.* Prentice Hall, London.

Yesuf, Mahmud & Randall A. Bluffstone (2009) "Poverty, Risk Aversion, and Path Dependence in Low-Income Countries: Experimental Evidence from Ethiopia," *American Journal of Agricultural Economics* 91, 1022–1037.

Young, H. Peyton (1990) "Progressive Taxation and Equal Sacrifice," *American Economic Review* 80, 253–266.

Zauberman, Gal, James R. Bettman, & Selin Malkoc (2005) "Time Horizon Neglect: Prospective Duration Insensitivity in Intertemporal Choice," University of North Carolina.

Zeisberger, Stefan & Dennis Vrecko (2009) "Are Prospect Theory Preferences Stable over Time?," mimeo.

Author index

Subject index

First, italicized, page numbers refer to definitions.

Printed in the United States
By Bookmasters